PUBLICATIONS OF THE
FOUNDATION FOR FINNISH ASSYRIOLOGICAL RESEARCH
NO. 27

STATE ARCHIVES OF ASSYRIA STUDIES
VOLUME XXXII

STATE ARCHIVES OF ASSYRIA STUDIES

Published by the Neo-Assyrian Text Corpus Project, Helsinki
in association with the
Foundation for Finnish Assyriological Research

Project Director
Simo Parpola

VOLUME XXXII

Zack Cherry

ARAMAIC LOANWORDS IN NEO-ASSYRIAN 911–612 B.C.

THE NEO-ASSYRIAN TEXT CORPUS PROJECT

State Archives of Assyria Studies is a series of monographic studies relating to and supplementing the text editions published in the SAA series. Manuscripts are accepted in English, French and German. The responsibility for the contents of the volumes rests entirely with the authors.

Published with the support of the

Foundation for

Finnish Assyriological Research

FAR

Set in Times
The Assyrian Royal Seal emblem drawn by Dominique Collon from original Seventh Century B.C. impressions (BM 84672 and 84677) in the British Museum
Cover: Aramean and Assyrian scribes listing booty (BM 124596)

Typesetting by Zack Cherry
Cover typography by Mikko Heikkinen

Printed in the USA
Distributed by Eisenbrauns,
an imprint of Penn State University Press

ISBN 978-952-10-9504-7 (Volume 32)
ISSN 1235-1032 (SAAS)
ISSN 1798-7431 (PFFAR)

ARAMAIC LOANWORDS IN NEO-ASSYRIAN 911–612 B.C.

By

Zack Cherry

THE NEO-ASSYRIAN TEXT CORPUS PROJECT

2023

Dedicated to
Esagila Ramat & Sharrat Ninua

ACKNOWLEDGMENTS

This publication was originally my PhD dissertation published and presented to the Department of Linguistics and Philology of Uppsala University in candidacy for the degree of Doctor of Philosophy in Assyriology in 2017. Its subject was inspired by Prof. Wolfram von Soden's articles titled *Aramäische Wörter in neuassyrischen und neu- und spätbabylonischen Texten. Ein Vorbericht*, I–III, the last of which was published in 1977. This revised version of my dissertation is not drastically different from the original work. I have revised some of the suggested loanwords, treated a couple new words, fixed some errors, and added the indices.

I remain very much indebted for all the people who helped me during my PhD work. Foremost I would like to express my sincere gratitude to my supervisor Prof. Olof Pedersén for his support of my work and research, and for sharing his vast knowledge with me. His guidance helped me to accomplish this work. I also express my warmest gratitude to my associate supervisor Prof. Mats Eskhult for providing me with valuable feedback and for all the support and encouragement he gave me.

I would particularly like to express my special appreciation and thanks to my associate supervisor Prof. Simo Parpola of the University of Helsinki for his insightful comments, excellent guidance and support. I am grateful to Prof. Parpola for suggesting and sharing many loanwords with me and for granting me permission to access the State Archives of Assyria Project's electronic database, *The Corpus of Neo-Assyrian Texts* (CNA), which I utilized effectively for examining and enlarging the data used in this work. I am also grateful to him for accepting this volume to be published in SAAS.

My warmest thanks are due to the reviewers of my thesis, Prof. Mario Fales of the University of Udine and Prof. Michael P. Streck of the Altorientalisches Institut, Universität Leipzig for providing me with feedbacks filled with insightful comments and suggestions from which I have greatly benefited

It is also my pleasure to thank Prof. Eleanor Coghill and Prof. Beáta Megyesi of the Department of Linguistics and Philology, Uppsala University for facilitating my research. Many thanks to my Assyriological colleagues Dr. Jakob Andersson and Dr. Mattias Karlsson for some technical help. My sincere thanks are due to my friend Dr. Robert Karoukian for his encouragement. Finally, I would like to express my deep and sincere gratitude to my family for your unvarying and unparalleled love and for all the sacrifices that you have made on my behalf. Any errors or misjudgments that remain in this study are mine alone.

Stockholm, September 2022 Zack Cherry

CONTENTS

ACKNOWLEDGMENTS vii

LIST OF FIGURES xi

ABBREVIATIONS xii
A. Bibliographical abbreviations xii
B. Other abbreviations and symbols xxii

1. INTRODUCTION 1
1.1 What is a loanword? 2
1.2 Definitions of other key terms 3
1.3 Previous research on Aramaic loanwords in Akkadian 4
1.4 The purpose and scope of the present study 6
1.5 Material of the study 8
1.6 The methods used in identifying Aramaic loanwords 10
1.6.1 Phonological criteria 11
1.6.2 Morphological criterion 15
1.6.3 Semantic criterion 16
1.6.4 Source words 16
1.6.5 Chronology 17
1.6.6 Distribution of the words 18
1.6.7 Criteria used in rejecting some previous proposals 18
1.6.8 Utilizing later forms of Aramaic in this study 19
1.7 A short account of the developmental phases of Akkadian 20
1.8 A short account of the developmental phases of Aramaic 31
1.9 Evidence of the use of Aramaic in Assyria proper 35
1.9.1 Textual evidence 37
1.9.2 Visual evidence 51
1.10 The scheme for presentation of data 57

2. ANALYSIS OF LOAN HYPOTHESES 61
2.1 Analysis of the proposed Aramaic loanwords in Neo-Assyrian 61
2.2 Rejected proposals of Aramaic loanwords in Neo-Assyrian 256

3. SUMMARY AND CONCLUSIONS 301
3.1 Summary 301
3.2 Conclusions 304
3.2.1 The proposed Aramaic loanwords in Neo-Assyrian 304
3.2.2 The provenance, origin, genre and date of Neo-Assyrian texts with confirmed Aramaic loanwords 309

3.2.3 Semantic distribution of the confirmed Aramaic loanwords in Neo-Assyrian 312
3.2.4 Distribution of the confirmed Aramaic loanwords in Neo-Assyrian according to part of speech 314
3.2.5 Phonological analysis of the certain Aramaic loanwords in Neo-Assyrian 316
3.2.6 Morphological analysis of the certain Aramaic loanwords in Neo-Assyrian 319
3.2.7 Frequency of the certain Aramaic loanwords in Neo-Assyrian texts 321
3.3 Avenues for further research 330

BIBLIOGRAPHY 331

INDICES 367

LIST OF FIGURES

Fig. 1: A map of the excavation sites with Neo-Assyrian texts 30
Fig. 2: A Neo-Assyrian conveyance document from Nineveh bearing an Aramaic caption 41
Fig. 3: A corn loan docket from Assur written entirely in Aramaic 42
Fig. 4: A bilingual Neo-Assyrian legal document 43
Fig. 5: Bronze lion-weight from Calah/Nimrud inscribed in Aramaic 44
Fig. 6: Part of a set of bronze lion-weights from the palace at Nimrud 44
Fig. 7: The Assur Ostracon 47
Fig. 8: The convex side of the Aramaic ostracon from Calah/Nimrud 48
Fig. 9: A clay bulla from Dūr-Šarrukēn representing a stamp seal 49
Fig. 10: A fresco from Til-Barsip representing Assyrian scribes 53
Fig. 11: A stone relief from Calah/Nimrud depicting an Assyrian official and two scribes recoding booty 54
Fig. 12: A stone relief from the reign of Assurbanipal or later depicting Assyrian scribes recording booty 54

ABBREVIATIONS

A. Bibliographical abbreviations

The bibliographical abbreviations generally follow the conventions of the *Reallexikon der Assyriologie* and *The Prosopography of the Neo-Assyrian Empire* 3/II (B–31ff.), with a number of additions.

3 R	H.C. Rawlinson & G. Smith, *The Cuneiform Inscriptions of Western Asia*, III: *A Selection from the Miscellaneous Inscriptions of Assyria* (London 1870)
AbB	F.R. Kraus (ed.), *Altbabylonische Briefe in Umschrift und Übersetzung* (Leiden 1964)
ABL	R.F. Harper, *Assyrian and Babylonian Letters* (London & Chicago 1892–1914)
Abraham & Sokoloff, *Reassessment*	K. Abraham & M. Sokoloff, "Aramaic Loanwords in Akkadian – A Reassessment of the Proposals," *AfO* 52 (2011): 22–76
ABRT	J.A. Craig, *Assyrian and Babylonian Religious Texts*, I/II (Leipzig 1895/1897)
ABZ	R. Borger, *Assyrisch-babylonische Zeichenliste* (Kevelaer 1978)
AcAn	Acta Antiqua Academiae Scientiarum Hungaricae (Budapest 1951–)
ADD	C.H.W. Johns, *Assyrian Deeds and Documents* (Cambridge 1898–1923)
AEAD	S. Parpola et al. (eds.), *Assyrian-English-Assyrian Dictionary* (Helsinki 2007)
AECT	F.M. Fales, *Aramaic Epigraphs on Clay Tablets of the Neo-Assyrian Period* (Rome 1986)
AF	H. Zimmern, *Akkadische Fremdwörter als Beweis für babylonischen Kultureinfluß* (Leipzig 1917)
AfO	Archiv für Orientforschung (Berlin, Graz, Horn 1923–)
AfO 32	K. Deller & A.R. Millard "Zwei Rechtsurkunden aus Aššur im British Museum," *AfO* 32 (1985): 38–52
AHw.	W. von Soden, *Akkadisches Handwörterbuch* (Wiesbaden 1965–1981)
AIA	S.A. Kaufman, *The Akkadian Influences on Aramaic* (Chicago & London 1974)
AION	Annali dell'Istituto Universitario Orientale di Napoli. Sezione linguistica (Napoli 1959–)
AJSL	American Journal of Semitic Languages and Literatures (Chicago 1895–1941)
AKA	E.A.W. Budge & L.W. King, *The Annals of the Kings of Assyria*, I (London 1902)

ALA	O. Pedersén, *Archives and Libraries in the City of Assur: A Survey of the Material from the German Excavations*, vols. I (Uppsala 1985) and II (Uppsala 1986)
ALBH	P.V. Mankowski, *Akkadian Loanwords in Biblical Hebrew* (Winona Lake 2000)
Al-munğidu	*Al-munğidu fīl-luġati wal'e'lāmi* (Beirut 1984)
AMT	R.C. Thompson, *Assyrian Medical Texts from the Originals in the British Museum* (London 1923)
AnOr	Analecta Orientalia (Rome 1931–)
AnSt	Anatolian Studies. Journal of the British Institute of Archaeology at Ankara (London 1951–)
AO	Siglum of texts in the Département des Antiquités Orientales, Musée du Louvre
AOAT	Alter Orient und Altes Testament (Neukirchen-Vluyn 1969–)
AOAT 2	H. Hunger, *Babylonische und assyrische Kolophone* (Kevelaer 1968) (= BAK)
AoF	Altorientalische Forschungen. Schriften zur Geschichte und Kultur des alten Orients (Berlin 1971–)
AR	J. Kohler & A. Ungnad, *Assyrische Rechtsurkunden* (Leipzig 1913)
ARM	Archives royales de Mari (= TCL 22–31)
As	Assur excavation number (Münchner Grabungen 1990)
AS	Assyriological Studies (Chicago 1931–)
Asb.	Assurbanipal (A = Prisma A nach VAB 7, 2ff.)
Asb IIT	A. Fuchs, "Kapitel VII: Die Inschrift vom Ištar-Tempel," in R. Borger, *Beiträge zum Inschriftenwerk Assurbanipals* (Wiesbaden 1996), pp. 259–296
Ashitha	O.M.G. Ashitha, *Hilqa de Leshana* (Baghdad 1997)
Asn.	Ashurnasirpal II. E.A.W. Budge & L.W. King, *The Annals of the Kings of Assyria* I (London 1902) (= AKA 254)
Ass	Siglum of texts excavated at the German excavations in Assur (Berlin/Istanbul)
ASSF	Acta Societatis Scientiarum Fennicae (Helsinki 1842–)
Audo	T. Audo, *Sīmṯā də-lišānā sūryāyā* (Ann Arbor 1978)
AuOr	Aula Orientalis (Barcelona 1983–)
BabMBK	Babylonian Magic Bowl Koine Aramaic
BAK	H. Hunger, *Babylonische und assyrische Kolophone* (Kevelaer 1968)
BaM	Baghdader Mitteilungen (Berlin/Mainz 1960–)
BASOR	Bulletin of the American Schools of Oriental Research (New Haven etc. 1921–)
BATSH	Berichte der Ausgrabungen Tall Šēḫ Ḥamad/Dūr-Katlimmu (Berlin/Wiesbaden 1991–)
BATSH 6/2	K. Radner, *Die Neuassyrischen Texte aus Tall Šēḫ Ḥamad* (Berlin 2002)

BBVO	Berliner Beiträge zum Vorderen Orient (Berlin 1982–)
BiAr	The Biblical Archaeologist (New Haven 1938–)
Billa	J.J. Finkelstein, "Cuneiform Texts from Tell Billa," *JCS* 7 (1953): 109–176
BiOr	Bibliotheca Orientalis (Leiden 1943/44–)
BM	Siglum of tablets in the collections of the British Museum (London)
BN	Biblische Notizen. Beiträge zur exegetischen Diskussion (Bamberg 1976–)
Borger Esarh.	R. Borger, *Die Inschriften Asarhaddons, Königs von Assyrien* (Graz 1956)
Brauner	R.A. Brauner, *A Comparative Lexicon of Old Aramaic* (Ann Arbor 1974)
BSOAS	Bulletin of the School of Oriental and African Studies (London 1917–)
BZ	Biblische Zeitschrift (Paderborn 1903–)
CA	G. van Driel, *The Cult of Aššur* (Assen 1969)
CAD	A.L. Oppenheim et al. (eds.), *The Assyrian Dictionary of the Oriental Institute of the University of Chicago* (Chicago 1956–2011)
CAL	S.A. Kaufman et al. (eds.), *The Comprehensive Aramaic Lexicon*. Online 15/09/2022: https://cal.huc.edu/
CCENA	F.M. Fales, *Censimenti e catasti di epoca neo-assira* (Rome 1973)
CDA	J. Black et al. (eds.), *A Concise Dictionary of Akkadian* (Wiesbaden 2000)
CLNA	F.M. Fales, *Cento lettere neo-assire* (Venice 1983)
CNA	State Archives of Assyria Project's electronic database, Corpus of Neo-Assyrian Texts (CNA), presently located at: http://oracc.museum.upenn.edu.
CRRA	Compte rendu de la …^{e} Rencontre Assyriologique Internationale (1951–)
CT	Cuneiform Texts from Babylonian Tablets in the British Museum (London 1896–)
CTDS	Siglum of texts excavated in the Chicago excavations at Khorsabad (Dūr-Šarrukēn)
CTN	Cuneiform Texts from Nimrud (London 1972–)
CTN I	J.V. Kinnier-Wilson, *The Nimrud Wine Lists* (London 1972)
CTN II	J.N. Postgate, *The Governor's Palace Archive* (London 1973)
CTN III	S. Dalley & J.N. Postgate, *The Tablets from Fort Shalmaneser* (Oxford 1984)
CTN V	H.W.F. Saggs, *The Nimrud Letters, 1952* (London 2001)
CTSHM	V. Donbaz, *Cuneiform Texts in the Sadberk Hanim Museum* (Istanbul 1999)
Cyr.	J.N. Strassmaier, *Inschriften von Cyrus, König von Babylon* (Leipzig 1890)

Dalman	G.H. Dalman (ed.), *Aramäisch-Neuhebräisches Wörterbuch zu Targum, Talmud und Midrasch* (Frankfurt a. M. 1901)
DCPA	M. Sokoloff, *A Dictionary of Christian Palestinian Aramaic* (Leuven 2014)
DJA	M. Sokoloff, *A Dictionary of Judean Aramaic* (Ramat-Gan 2003)
DJBA	M. Sokoloff, *A Dictionary of Jewish Babylonian Aramaic of the Talmudic and Geonic Periods* (Ramat-Gan 2002)
DJPA	M. Sokoloff, *A Dictionary of Jewish Palestinian Aramaic of the Byzantine Period* (Ramat-Gan 2002)
DNWSI	J. Hoftijzer & K. Jongeling, *Dictionary of the North-West Semitic Inscriptions*, 2 Vols. (Leiden 1995)
DSA	A. Tal, *A Dictionary of Samaritan Aramaic*, 2 Vols. (Leiden 2000)
DUL	G. del Olmo Lete & J. Sanmartin, *A Dictionary of the Ugaritic Language in the Alphabetic Tradition*, 2 Vols. (Leiden 2004)
EI	Eretz-Israel: Archaeological, Historical and Geographical studies (Jerusalem 1951–)
Elias & Elias	A.E. Elias & Ed.E. Elias (eds.), *Elias' Modern Dictionary: Arabic-English* (Cairo 1982)
FNALD	J.N. Postgate, *Fifty Neo-Assyrian Legal Documents* (Warminster 1976)
Fraenkel	S. Fraenkel, *Die Aramäischen Fremdwörter im Arabischen* (Hildesheim & New York 1982)
GAG	W. von Soden, *Grundriss der akkadischen Grammatik.* AnOr 33 (Rome 1952). 3rd revised edition (Rome 1995)
HAF	Heidelberger Assur-Forschungen (= S.M. Maul & N.P. Heeβel, *Assur-Forschungen: Arbeiten aus der Forschungsstelle "Edition literarischer Keilschrifttexte aus Assur" der Heidelberger Akademie der Wissenschaften* (Wiesbaden 2010))
HALOT	L. Koehler & W. Baumgartner, *The Hebrew and Aramaic Lexicon of the Old Testament*, 5 Vols. (Leiden, New York & Köln 1994–2000)
HSAO	Heidelberger Studien zum Alten Orient (Wiesbaden, Heidelberg 1967–)
IEJ	Israel Exploration Journal (Jerusalem 1950–)
IOS	Israel Oriental Studies (Tel Aviv 1971–)
Iraq	Iraq. A Journal of the British School of Archaeology in Iraq (London 1934–)
Isimu	Isimu. Revista sobre Oriente Próximo y Egipto en la antigüedad (Madrid 1998–) (also: ISIMU)
JAAS	Journal of the Assyrian Academic Society (Chicago 1986–)
JANES	Journal of the Ancient Near Eastern Society of Columbia University (New York 1968/69–)
JAOS	Journal of the American Oriental Society (New Haven etc. 1843/49–)

Jastrow	M. Jastrow (ed.), *A Dictionary of the Targumim, the Talmud Babli and Yerushalmi, and the Midrashic Literature* (New York 1989)
JBL	Journal of Biblical Literature (Philadelphia/Atlanta 1890–)
JCS	Journal of Cuneiform Studies (New Haven/Bosten 1947–)
JEOL	Jaarbericht van het Vooraziatisch-Egyptisch Genootschap "Ex Oriente Lux" (Leiden 1933/37–)
JNES	Journal of Near Eastern Studies (Chicago 1942–)
JQR	Jewish Quarterly Review (London/New York 1888/89–, NS = Nova Series Philadelphia 1910–)
JRAS	Journal of the Royal Asiatic Society of Great Britain and Ireland (London 1834–)
JSOTS 325	W. Röllig, "Aramaica Haburensia V: Limu-Datierungen in Aramäischen Urkunden des 7. Jh. v. Chr," in P.M. Michèle Daviau, J.W. Wevers & M. Weigl (eds.), *The World of the Aramaeans II* (Sheffield 2001), pp. 45–56. Journal for the Study of the Old Testament Supplement Series 325 (Sheffield 2001)
JSS	Journal of Semitic Studies ([Manchester/]Oxford 1956–)
K	Siglum of the texts in the Kouyunjik Collection of the British Museum
KADP	F. Köcher, *Keilschrifttexte zur assyrisch-babylonischen Drogen- und Pflanzenkunde* (Berlin 1955)
KAI	H. Donner & W. Röllig, *Kanaanäische und aramäische Inschriften*, vol. I, *Texte* (Wiesbaden 2002)
KAJ	E. Ebeling, *Keilschrifttexte aus Assur juristischen Inhalts* (Leipzig 1927)
KAR	E. Ebeling, *Keilschrifttexte aus Assur religiösen Inhalts* (Leipzig 1920)
Kaufman, AIA	S.A. Kaufman, *The Akkadian Influences on Aramaic* (Chicago & London 1974)
KAV	O. Schroeder, *Keilschrifttexte aus Assur verschiedenen Inhalts* (Leipzig 1920)
LAS I	S. Parpola, *Letters from Assyrian Scholars to the Kings Esarhaddon and Assurbanipal, Part* I*: Texts* (Winona Lake 2007)
LAS II	S. Parpola, *Letters from Assyrian Scholars to the Kings Esarhaddon and Assurbanipal, Part* II: *Commentary and Appendices* (Winona Lake 2007)
Leš.	Lešonénu, Academy of the Hebrew Language (Jerusalem 1928–)
Lipiński, *Semitic Languages*	E. Lipiński, *Semitic Languages: Outline of a Comparative Grammar* (Leuven 1997)
LS	C. Brockelmann, *Lexicon Syriacum* (Hildesheim 1995)
LSp.	F. Schulthess, *Lexicon Syropalaestinum* (Berlin 1903)
LSS	Leipziger semitistische Studien (Leipzig 1903–1920; 1931–1932)
LTBA	W. von Soden, *Die lexikalischen Tafelserien der Babylonier und Assyrer in den Berliner Museen*, vol. 2, *Die akkadischen Synonymenlisten* (Berlin 1933)

Maclean	A.J. Maclean, *A Dictionary of the Dialects of Vernacular Syriac* (Oxford 1901)
MAD	I.J. Gelb, *Materials for the Assyrian Dictionary*, 5 Vols. (Chicago 1952–1970)
MAGr.	B. Meissner, *Kurzgefaßte assyrische Grammatik* (Leipzig 1907)
MAH	Museum siglum of the Musée d'Art et d'Histoire, Geneva
Mankowski, ALBH	P.V. Mankowski, *Akkadian Loanwords in Biblical Hebrew* (Winona Lake 2000)
Manna	J.E. Manna, *leksīqōn kaldāyā-'arbāyā* (Syriac-Arabic Dictionary) (Beirut 1975)
MCS	Manchester Cuneiform Studies (Manchester 1951–1964)
MD	E.S. Drower & R. Macuch, *A Mandaic Dictionary* (Oxford 1963)
MSL	B. Landsberger et al. (eds.), *Materialien zum sumerischen Lexikon/Materials fort the Sumerian Lexikon* (Rome 1937–)
MSL XII	M. Civil et al. (eds.), *The Series lú =* ša *and Related Texts* (Rome 1969)
MVAeG	Mitteilungen der Vorderasiatisch (-Ägyptisch)en Gesellschaft (Berlin/Leipzig 1896–)
MVAeG 41	K.F. Müller, *Das assyrische Ritual*, I: *Texte zum assyrischen Königsritual* (Leipzig 1937)
NABU	Nouvelles assyriologiques brèves et utilitaires (Paris/Rouen 1987–)
NALDK	T. Kwasman, *Neo-Assyrian Legal Documents in the Kouyunjik Collection of the British Museum* (Rome 1988)
Nbk.	J.N. Strassmaier, *Inschriften von Nabuchodonosor, König von Babylon* (Leipzig 1889)
ND	Siglum of texts excavated in the British excavations at Nimrud (Calah)
Nili	I. Nili, *Hapax Legomena in the Akkadian Language*. Unpublished Ph.D. thesis (Ramat-Gan 2004) [in Hebrew]
NL	H.W.F. Saggs, "The Nimrud Letters," parts I–VIII, published originally in *Iraq* 17–18, 20–21, 25, 27–28 and 36 (1955–1974), republished in CTN V
O	Siglum of texts in the Royal Museum of Art and History, Brussels
OIP	Oriental Institute Publications (Chicago 1924–)
OLA	Orientalia Lovaniensia Analecta (Leuven 1974/75–)
OLP	Orientalia Lovaniensia Periodica (Leuven 1970–)
OLZ	Orientalistische Literaturzeitung. Monatsschrift für die Wissenschaft vom ganzen Orient und seine(n) Beziehungen zu den angrenzenden Kulturkreisen (Berlin/Leipzig 1898–)
Or.	Orientalia, Nova Series (Rome 1932–)
Oraham	A.J. Oraham, *Oraham's Dictionary of the Stabilized and Enriched Assyrian Language and English* (Chicago 1943)
OrAnt	Oriens antiquus: rivista del Centro per la antichità e la storia dell'arte del Vicino Oriente (Rome 1962–1990)

Orient	Orient. Report of the Society for Near Eastern Studies in Japan (Tokyo 1960–)
OrS	Orientalia Suecana (Uppsala/Stockholm 1952–)
PEF(QS)	Palestine Exploration Fund, Quarterly Statement (London 1869/70–1936)
PKTA	E. Ebeling, *Parfümrezepte und kultische Texte aus Assur.* Sonderdruck aus Orientalia 17–19 (Rome 1950)
PNA	*The Prosopography of the Neo-Assyrian Empire* (Helsinki 1998–)
PNA 1/I–II	K. Radner (ed.), *The Prosopography of the Neo-Assyrian Empire* ([Helsinki] 1998–1999)
PNA 2/I–II, 3/I–II	H.D. Baker (ed.), *The Prosopography of the Neo-Assyrian Empire* ([Helsinki] 2000–2011)
PRT	E.G. Klauber, *Politisch-religiöse Texte aus der Sargonidenzeit* (Leipzig 1913)
PSBA	Proceedings of the Society of Biblical Archaeology (London 1878/79–1918)
PSm.	J. Payne Smith (ed.), *A Compendious Syriac Dictionary* (Oxford 1903)
PVA	B. Landsberger & O.R. Gurney, "Practical Vocabulary of Assur," *AfO* 18 (1957–58): 328–341
QGS	Quaderni di geografia storica (Rome 1979–)
QuadSem.	Quaderni di Semitistica (Florens 1971–)
RA	Revue d'Assyriologie et d'Archéologie Orientale (Paris 1884/85–)
RCAE	L. Waterman, *Royal Correspondence of the Assyrian Empire,* Parts I, II & III (New York & London 1972)
REJ	Revue des études juives (Paris 1880–)
Rfdn 17	A.Y. Ahmad, "The Archive of Aššur-mātu-taqqin Found in the New Town of Aššur and Dated Mainly by Post-Canonical Eponyms," *Al-Rāfidān* 17 (1996): 207–288
RlA	*Reallexikon der Assyriologie* (*und Vorderasiatischen Archäologie*) (Berlin/Leipzig 1928/32–)
RIMA	The Royal Inscriptions of Mesopotamia, Assyrian Periods (Toronto 1987–)
Rm	Siglum for tablets in the Kuyunjik Collection of the British Museum (Rassam)
RSO	Rivista degli studi orientali (Rome 1907–)
RT	Recueil des travaux relatifs à la philologie et à l'archéologie égyptiennes et assyriennes (Paris 1870–1923)
SAA	State Archives of Assyria (Helsinki 1987–)
SAA I	S. Parpola (ed.), *The Correspondence of Sargon II, Part* I: *Letters from Assyria and the West* (Helsinki 1987)
SAA II	S. Parpola & K. Watanabe (eds.), *Neo-Assyrian Treaties and Loyalty Oaths* (Helsinki 1988)
SAA III	A. Livingstone (ed.), *Court Poetry and Literary Miscellanea* (Helsinki 1989)

SAA IV	I. Starr (ed.), *Queries to the Sungod: Divination and Politics in Sargonid Assyria* (Helsinki 1990)
SAA V	G.B. Lanfranchi & S. Parpola (eds.), *The Correspondence of Sargon II, Part* II: *Letters from the Northern and Northeastern Provinces* (Helsinki 1990)
SAA VI	T. Kwasman & S. Parpola (eds.), *Legal Transactions of the Royal Court of Nineveh, Part* I: *Tiglath-Pileser III through Esarhaddon* (Helsinki 1991)
SAA VII	F.M. Fales & J.N. Postgate (eds.), *Imperial Administrative Records*, Part I: *Palace and Temple Administration* (Helsinki 1992)
SAA VIII	H. Hunger (ed.), *Astrological Reports to Assyrian Kings* (Helsinki 1992)
SAA IX	S. Parpola (ed.), *Assyrian Prophecies* (Helsinki 1997)
SAA X	S. Parpola (ed.), *Letters from Assyrian and Babylonian Scholars* (Helsinki 1993)
SAA XI	F.M. Fales & J.N. Postgate (eds.), *Imperial Administrative Records, Part* II: *Provincial and Military Administration* (Helsinki 1995)
SAA XII	L. Kataja & R. Whiting (eds.), *Grants, Decrees and Gifts of the Neo-Assyrian Period* (Helsinki 1995)
SAA XIII	S.W. Cole & P. Machinist (eds.), *Letters from Priests to the Kings Esarhaddon and Assurbanipal* (Helsinki 1998)
SAA XIV	R. Mattila (ed.), *Legal Transactions of the Royal Court of Nineveh*, Part II: *Assurbanipal through Sin-šarru-iškun* (Helsinki 2002)
SAA XV	A. Fuchs & S. Parpola (eds.), *The Correspondence of Sargon II*, Part III: *Letters from Babylonia and the Eastern Provinces* (Helsinki 2001)
SAA XVI	M. Luukko & G. Van Buylaere (eds.), *The Political Correspondence of Esarhaddon* (Helsinki 2002)
SAA XVII	M. Dietrich (ed.), *The Babylonian Correspondence of Sargon and Sennacherib* (Helsinki 2003)
SAA XVIII	F. Reynolds (ed.), *The Babylonian Correspondence of Esarhaddon* (Helsinki 2003)
SAA XIX	M. Luukko (ed.), *The Correspondence of Tiglath-pileser III and Sargon II from Calah/Nimrud* (Winona Lake 2012)
SAA XX	S. Parpola (ed.), *Assyrian Royal Rituals and Cultic Texts* (Winona Lake 2017)
SAA XXI	S. Parpola (ed.), *The Correspondence of Assurbanipal, Part 1: Letters from Assyria, Babylonia, and Vassal States* (Winona Lake 2018)
SAAB	State Archives of Assyria, Bulletin (Padova 1987–)
SAAB 5	F.M. Fales & L. Jakob-Rost, "Neo-Assyrian Texts from Assur: Private Archives in the Vorderasiatisches Museum of Berlin, Part 1," *SAAB* 5 (1991): 3–157

SAAB 9	K. Deller et al. (eds.), "Neo-Assyrian Texts from Assur: Private Archives in the Vorderasiatisches Museum of Berlin, Part II," *SAAB* 9 (1995, printed 1997): 3–137
SAACT	State Archives of Assyria, Cuneiform Texts (Winona Lake 1997–)
SAAS	State Archives of Assyria Studies (Helsinki 1992–)
SAAS II	A. Millard with a Contribution by R. Whiting, *The Eponyms of the Assyrian Empire 910–612 B C* ([Helsinki] 1994)
SAAS VI	K. Radner, *Die neuassyrischen Privatrechtsurkunden als Quelle für Mensch und Umwelt* (Helsinki 1997)
SAAS VII	M. Nissinen, *References to Prophecy in Neo-Assyrian Sources* ([Helsinki] 1998)
SAAS XIII	J. Hämeen-Anttila, *A Sketch of Neo-Assyrian Grammar* (Helsinki 2000)
SAAS XVI	M. Luukko, *Grammatical Variation in Neo-Assyrian* ([Helsinki] 2004)
Sabar	Y. Sabar, *A Jewish Neo-Aramaic Dictionary* (Wiesbaden 2002)
Semitica	Semitica. Cahiers publiés par l'Institut d'études sémitiques de l'Université de Paris (Paris 1948–)
SL	M. Sokoloff, *A Syriac Lexicon* (Winona Lake & Piscataway 2009)
StAT	Studien zu den Assur-Texten (Saarbrücken etc. 1999–)
StAT 1	K. Radner, *Ein Neuassyrisches Privatarchiv der Tempelgoldschmiede von Assur* (Saarbrücken 1999)
StAT 2	V. Donbaz & S. Parpola (eds.), *Neo-Assyrian Legal Texts in Istanbul* (Saarbrücken 2001)
StAT 3	B. Faist, *Alltagstexte aus neuassyrischen Archiven und Bibliotheken der Stadt Assur* (Wiesbaden 2007)
StEL	Studi Epigrafici e Linguistici sul Vicino Oriente Antico (Verona 1984–)
StOr.	Studia Orientalia (Helsinki 1925–)
Streck Asb.	M. Streck, *Assurbanipal und die letzten assyrischen Könige bis zum Untergange Nineveh's*, I–III. (Vorderasiatisches Bibliothek 7, Leipzig 1916). (Prism A = VAB 7)
SVAT	E. Ebeling, *Stiftungen und Vorschriften für assyrische Tempel* (Berlin 1954)
T	Siglum of texts excavated at Tell Tayinat. Texts in the Hatay Arkeoloji Müzesi, Turkey
TAVO	Tübinger Atlas des Vorderen Orients (Wiesbaden), Beih. = Beihefte, Reihe A: Naturwissenschaften (1977–); Reihe B: Geisteswissenschaften (1972–)
TCAE	J.N. Postgate, *Taxation and Conscription in the Assyrian Empire* (Rome 1974)
TCL	Textes cunéiformes. Musée du Louvre, Département des Antiquités Orientales (Paris 1910–)

TCL III	F. Thureau-Dangin, *Une relation de la huitième Campagne de Sargon*. Textes cunéiformes du Louvre III (Paris 1912)
Tigl. III.	P. Rost, *Die Keilschrifttexte Tiglat-Pilesers III., nach den Papierabklatschen und Originalen des Britischen Museums*, II: *Autographierte Texte* (Leipzig 1893)
TH	Siglum of the Tell Halaf Aramaic/Assyrian texts (= J. Friedrich et al. (eds.), *Die Inschriften vom Tell Halaf: Keilschrifttexte und aramäische Urkunden aus einer assyrischen Provinzhauptstadt*, reprint of the edition published in 1940 (Osnabrük 1967)) (= AfO, Beiheft 6)
TIM	Texts in the Iraq Museum (Baghdad/Wiesbaden 1964–)
TI	S. Langdon, *Tammuz and Ishtar* (Oxford 1914)
TuL	E. Ebeling, *Tod und Leben nach den Vorstellungen der Babylonier* (Berlin/Leipzig 1931)
UF	Ugarit-Forschungen. Internationales Jahrbuch für die Altertumskunde Syrien-Palästinas (Neukirchen-Vluyn 1969–)
VA	Museum siglum of the Vorderasiatisches Museum, Berlin (Vorderasiatische Abteilung)
VAB	Vorderasiatische Bibliothek (Leipzig 1907–)
VAT	Museum siglum of the Vorderasiatisches Museum, Berlin (Vorderasiatische Abteilung Tontafeln)
VIO	Veröffentlichungen des Instituts für Orientforschung (Berlin)
VS	Vorderasiatische Schriftdenkmäler der Königlichen Museen zu Berlin (Leipzig 1907–1917)
VS NF	Vorderasiatische Schriftdenkmäler der Staatlichen Museen zu Berlin (Berlin 1971–)
VT	Vetus Testamentum (Leiden etc. 1951–)
VTE	D.J. Wiseman, "The Vassal-Treaties of Esarhaddon," *Iraq* 20 (1958): 1–99
Wehr-Cowan	J.M. Cowan (ed.), *The Hans Wehr Dictionary of Modern Written Arabic* (Arabic-English Dictionary), 3rd edition (New York 1976)
WO	Die Welt des Orients. Wissenschaftliche Beiträge zur Kunde des Morgenlandes (Wuppertal/Göttingen 1947/52–)
WVDOG	Wissenschaftliche Veröffentlichungen der Deutschen Orient-Gesellschaft (Leipzig/Berlin etc. 1900–)
WZKM	Wiener Zeitschrift für die Kunde des Morgenlandes (Wien 1887–)
YOS	Yale Oriental Series. Babylonian Texts (New Haven/London/Oxford 1915–)
YOS VII	A. Tremayne, *Records from Erech: Time of Cyrus and Cambyses (538–521 B.C.)* (New Haven 1925)
ZA	Zeitschrift für Assyriologie und Vorderasiatische Archäologie (Berlin 1939–)
ZAR	Zeitschrift für Altorientalische und Biblische Rechtsgeschichte (Wiesbaden 1995–)

ZDMG	Zeitschrift der Deutschen Morgenländischen Gesellschaft (Wiesbaden etc. 1847–)
ZTT I	Siglum of the texts nos. 1–28 from Ziyaret Tepe (Tušḫan); see S. Parpola, "Cuneiform Texts from Ziyaret Tepe (Tušḫan), 2002–2003 (Plates I–XXV)," *SAAB* 17 (2008): 1–113

B. Other abbreviations and symbols

adj.	adjective
adv.	adverb, adverbially
Af.	Af'el
Akk.	Akkadian
Ar.	Arabic
Aram.	Aramaic
Asb.	Letters that are either part of Assurbanipal's correspondence or possibly date to his reign
Asn.	Ashurnasirpal II
BA	Biblical Aramaic
BabMBK	Babylonian Magic Bowl Koine Aramaic
cf.	compare
cp.	compound
CPA	Christian Palestinian Aramaic
col.	column
coll.	collective, collated
Com.	Common Aramaic
CW	Culture Word
dem.	demonstrative
e.	edge
emph.	emphatic
Eth.	Ethiopic
Etpa.	Etpa''al
Etpe.	Etpe'el
f.	feminine; and following
fig.	figure
figs.	figures
frg.	fragment
Fw.	foreign word (Fremdwort)
Gal.	Galilean Aramaic (constitutes part of JPA)
gen.	genitive
Haf.	Haf'el
Heb.	Hebrew
int.	interjection
JA	Judean Aramaic
JBA	Jewish Babylonian Aramaic
JLA	Jewish Literary Aramaic of the early trargumim (Onkelos and Jonathan to the Prophets)

JPA	Jewish Palestinian Aramaic
l.	line; left
LB	Late-Babylonian
lex.	Lexical (texts)
LJLA	Late Jewish Literary Aramaic
Lw.	loanword
m.	masculine
Ma.	Mandaic
MA	Middle Assyrian
MB	Middle Babylonian
mng.	meaning
n.	note; noun
NA	Neo-Assyrian
Nab.	Nabatean
NB	Neo-Babylonian
NENA	North-Eastern Neo-Aramaic (a.k.a. Sūret)
no.	number
nos.	numbers
OA	Old Assyrian
OAkk.	Old Akkadian
OAram.	Old Aramaic
OB	Old Babylonian
obv.	obverse
OffAr.	Official Aramaic
p.	person
Pa.	Paʿʿel
Palm.	Palmyrene
Pe.	Peʿal
Phoen.	Phoenician
pl.	plural; plate
pl. tant.	only in plural form (Latin, *plurale tantum*)
PN	Personal name
prep.	preposition
pron.	pronoun, pronominal
PS	Proto-Semitic
PTA	Palestinian Targumic Aramaic
Pun.	Punic
QA	Qumran Aramaic
r.	reverse
RL	Royal letter
s.	substantive; (left) side
Sam.	Samaritan Aramaic
SB	Standard Babylonian
sg.	singular

st. abs.	absolute state (status absolutus)
st. constr.	construct state (status constructus)
st. det.	definite state (status determinatus)
stat.	stative
Sūret	a.k.a. North-Eastern Neo-Aramaic (NENA)
s.v.	under the word (Latin, *sub voce*)
Syr.	Syriac
Ug.	Ugaritic
unkn.	unknown
v.	verb; see (Latin, *vide*)
var.	variant
vol./vols.	volume(s)
vs.	versus
W.Sem.	West-Semitic
?	uncertain reading; uncertain meaning
[?]	to indicate a possible but questionable loan hypothesis
: :.	cuneiform division marks
!	collation (made by the editor(s) of the text in question)
!!	emendation (made by the editor(s) of the text in question)
+	joined to
~	approximately
( )	parentheses enclose supplied word or sign; enclose a definition of a headword
⌜ ⌝	partial break
[ ]	brackets enclose restorations
[...]	minor break (one or two missing words)
[......]	major break
[[ ]]	erasure
*	graphic variants; a hypothetical or reconstructed form; a reconstructed post-canonical date
...	untranslatable word
ə	the neutral vowel "shwa *or* schwa," in phonetic notation
<	comes from; develops from
>	goes to; develops into
< >	angle brackets signify a grapheme
/	line break
//	end of the obverse or edge
/ /	signifies a phoneme
⇒	to indicate a loan direction
// //	to mark a previous loan hypothesis that is now considered false
=▷	to indicate semantic loan; Lehnbildung (formation of a Neo-Assyrian word after the pattern of an Aramaic word)
;	to indicate independent co-receptors of a loan

Uncertain and conjectural translations are indicated by italics

1. INTRODUCTION

Contact between languages is a very old phenomenon which for instance can be traced back historically to the societies of ancient Mesopotamia. A letter (SAA XVIII 192) sent to Assurbanipal, king of Assyria, by Illil-bāni, the governor (*šandabakku*) of Nippur in southern Mesopotamia, between 664 and 661 B.C., and reporting on circumstances in the city, exemplifies this phenomenon. A passage on the reverse side of the letter (SAA XVIII 192 r.5′–8′), reads as follows:

> *ardu u bēl maṣṣarti ša šarri bēlīya akanna anāku / u lišānāti ma'dāti ina Nippur ina ṣilli šarri bēlīya / [[ši]]pirti šarri ušallam u ittīšunu / adabbub.*
>
> I am the king my lord's servant and watchman here. There are many foreign language speakers in Nippur under the aegis of the king, my lord. I implement the king's order and speak to them.[1]

From this passage, we can with certainty infer that language contact and some degree of bilingualism must have existed in the ancient city of Nippur as a result of interaction between speakers of different languages.[2] The same phenomenon also existed, undoubtedly, in many other major or minor cities in ancient Mesopotamia and other parts of the ancient world, just as it is found in many large or small societies of our time as well.[3]

Language contact is simplest explained as "the use of more than one language in the same place at the same time."[4] The most frequent outcome of extended language contact is change in the languages as a result of the influence that they exercise on each other. The most familiar type of such influence is the borrowing of words.[5] In our case, the borrowing of words represents the most explicit influence that was exerted on Neo-Assyrian, a dialect of the Akkadian language, by a cognate language, namely Aramaic, and Aramaic loanwords in Neo-Assyrian constitute the core theme of this study.

---

[1] Here *lišānāti* is not rendered "informants," see CAD (L, p. 214a s.v. *lišānu* mng. no. 4c).
[2] For studies dealing with multilingualism in the Ancient Near East, see S.L. Sanders (ed.), *Margins of Writing, Origins of Cultures* (Chicago 2006).
[3] For studies dealing with bilingualism in ancient societies, see J.N. Adams et al. (eds.), *Bilingualism in Ancient Society: Language Contact and the Written Text* (Oxford 2002).
[4] See S.G. Thomason, *Language Contact: An Introduction* (Edinburgh 2001), p. 1.
[5] Ibid., p. 10. For definition of the term *borrowing*, see Section 1.1 below.

1.1 What is a loanword?

The term *loanword* refers to a *lexical item* (a *word* or a *lexeme* which is the smallest distinctive unit in the lexicon of a language) which was not originally part of the vocabulary of the language, but at some point in the history of that language was added both in form and meaning to the lexical inventory of the language by means of linguistic *borrowing* or *copying* from another language as a result of language contact. Thus, while a loanword points to the importation into a language of lexical material from another *source* language, it also points to historical contact between two languages whose speakers have at least some knowledge of both languages at a certain stage. Loanwords are described as the milestones of philology because they very often assist us in determining the dates of linguistic changes as well as shedding some light on the origins and the wandering paths of inventions and institutions.[6] Usually, loanwords undergo adaptation to fit the phonological system and morphological structure of the *borrowing* language, but sometimes they are adapted gradually or only in part.[7]

As for the term *borrowing*,[8] it is a general expression used in comparative and historical linguistics to refer to the process by which lexical items (or less commonly, some other linguistic features such as sounds, phonological rules, morphemes, syntactic patterns or semantic associations) that exist in a language or a dialect are *copied* or *transferred*[9] into another language or dialect[10] and become part of the vocabulary of the latter language or dialect. Despite the fact that any of the parts of speech may be borrowed, nouns constitute the most frequent loans. The broad sense of the definition of borrowing given above is used in this study.

In discussing the direction of borrowing, the designation *source* or *donor* language refers to the language from which a loanword was borrowed, whereas the designation *borrowing* or *recipient* language refers to the language into which the loanword was borrowed.

The motivation for borrowing words is either *need* or *prestige*.[11] A new term can be needed to express a new item or concept acquired from abroad, or can be used for prestige purposes when the foreign term is highly esteemed because it expresses a higher social status.

---

[6] See O. Jespersen, *Growth and Structure of the English Language* (Oxford 1948), p. 27.

[7] See D. Crystal, *A Dictionary of Linguistics & Phonetics* (Malden 2003), p. 275 s.v. loan; P.H. Matthews, *The Concise Oxford Dictionary of Linguistics* (Oxford 1997), p. 211 s.v. loan word; R.L. Trask, *A Dictionary of Phonetics and Phonology* (London 1996), p. 210 s.v. loan word.

[8] For lexical borrowing and the mechanisms of lexical interference, see D. Winford, *An Introduction to Contact Linguistics* (Malden 2003), pp. 29–60; U. Weinreich, *Languages in Contac: Findings and Problems* (The Hague 1970), pp. 47–62. For concepts and issues in lexical borrowing, see M. Haspelmath, "Lexical Borrowing: Concepts and Issues," in M. Haspelmath & U. Tadmor (eds.), *Loanwords in the World's Languages: A Comparative Handbook* (Berlin 2009), pp. 35–54.

[9] For the term *transfer* or *transference*, see M. Clyne, *Dynamics of Language Contact* (Cambridge 2003), esp. p. 74, for earlier reference.

[10] See Trask, ibid., p. 55 s.v. borrowing; Crystal, ibid., p. 56 s.v. borrowing; Matthews, ibid., p. 41 s.v. borrowing; D. Crystal, *The Penguin Dictionary of Language* (London 1999), p. 40 s.v. borrowing. Cf. S.G. Thomason & T. Kaufman, *Language Contact, Creolization, and Genetic Linguistics* (Berkeley 1988), p. 21.

[11] See U. Weinreich, *Languages in Contact* (The Hague 1970), § 2.43.

There are other borrowing phenomena that are, to some extent, related to loanwords. Borrowing, as a phenomenon, is classified into two distinct categories: *material borrowing* and *structural borrowing*.[12] The former includes, for instance, the borrowing of sound-meaning pairs, i.e., loanwords. The latter includes the borrowing of syntactical and morphological patterns such as word order patterns and case-marking patterns, as well as loan translations (calques), i.e., the translation of the morphemes of the borrowed word item by item into equivalent morphemes in the recipient language. Another type of structural borrowing is loan meaning extension (semantic loan), where a meaning is copied from the donor language into the recipient language. Loan translation and loan meaning extension are sometimes classed together as loan shifts.[13]

This study is restricted to loanwords. However, also included in this study are semantic loans, which here refer to Neo-Assyrian words that share a common root with Aramaic, but have undergone an extension or change of meaning that can be attributed to the influence of Aramaic.

1.2 Definitions of other key terms

Cognate: The term cognate refers here to any one of two or more words that are similar in sound and meaning, i.e., similar phonologically and semantically, have developed from the same source, and are found in two or more dialects of a single language or in two or more genetically related languages as descendants of a common ancestor.[14] As two Semitic languages,[15] Neo-Assyrian and Aramaic are also cognates. This means that historically they are sibling-descendants of a postulated common ancestor, Proto-Semitic (PS).

Culture word (CW): Culture words almost always consist of nouns that belong to specific categories, such as plants and vegetable products, utensils, minerals, metals and wild animals, which are borrowed among many languages and designate a cross-cultural concept. According to Mankowski, "The term 'culture word' (*Kulturwort*), refers to a class of words marked by a high degree of mobility (thus recognizable at the same period in more than one language family

---

[12] See Y. Matras & J. Sakel, *Grammatical Borrowing in Cross-Linguistic Perspective* (Berlin 2007).

[13] See E. Haugen, "The Analysis of Linguistic Borrowing," *Language* 26 (1950), p. 219.

[14] Cf. D. Crystal, *A Dictionary of Linguistics & Phonetics* (Malden 2003), p. 79; R.L. Trask, *A Dictionary of Phonetics and Phonology* (London 1996), p. 78; P.H. Matthews, *The Concise Oxford Dictionary of Linguistics* (Oxford 1997), p. 58.

[15] The term "Semitic" languages was coined in 1781 by A.L. Schlözer, in J.G. Eichhorn's *Repertorium für biblische und morgenländische Literatur* (vol. VIII, p. 161), in reference to the languages spoken by peoples included in Gen. 10:21–31; 11:10–26, among the sons of Shem (Sem). For a current definition of the term Semitic languages, and for the classification of the Semitic languages, see, among others, E. Ullendorff, "What is a Semitic Language?" *Or* 27 (1958), pp. 66–75; S. Moscati, *An Introduction to the Comparative Grammar of the Semitic Languages: Phonology and Morphology* (Wiesbaden 1964), pp. 3–21; E. Lipiński, *Semitic Languages: Outline of a Comparative Grammar* (Leuven 1997), pp. 23–94 (henceforth: Lipiński, *Semitic Languages*); J. Huehnergard, "Comparative Semitic Linguistics," *IOS* 20 (2002), pp. 119–150; idem, "Semitic Languages," in J.M. Sasson et al. (eds.), *Civilizations of the Ancient Near East* (Massachusetts 2006), pp. 2117–2134.

and in disparate geographical regions) for which no ultimate linguistic provenance can be assigned."[16]

Foreign word (Fremdwort): A word or an expression which was taken over from a foreign language and, in contrast to a loanword, remains unintegrated in the sound system, spelling or inflection of the borrowing language and continues designating a foreign entity or object.[17]

Ghost word (cf. *Vox nihili*): A word or word form that in reality did not exist in the original language, but rather originated as a result of an error during the copying, analyzing or learning of the language, such as an editorial misreading, a printing error, or perhaps it was due to an ancient scribal mistake.[18] Accordingly, when we consider a certain Neo-Assyrian word to be a "ghost word," this means that the word in question originated by error; therefore, it does not exist in the extant Neo-Assyrian textual corpus.

Semantic loan: The meaning that a word takes under the influence of another language, whereby a reinterpretation of the original meaning and/or a meaning extension takes place.[19] In this study, semantic loans concern cognate words that may have undergone semantic change or extension of meaning by developing a new sense of the Neo-Assyrian lexical units under the influence of Aramaic.

1.3 Previous research on Aramaic loanwords in Akkadian

Several monographs have been dedicated to researching the Akkadian influences on other languages, primarily loanwords. The earliest is the work by Zimmern, who a century ago studied the Akkadian loanwords in different languages in a book titled, *Akkadische Fremdwörter als Beweis für babylonischen Kultureinfluß*.[20] Much later, two doctoral dissertations on the subject were published, one by Kaufman, *The Akkadian Influences on Aramaic*, which mainly consists of Akkadian loanwords in Aramaic,[21] and the other by Mankowski, *Akkadian Loanwords in Biblical Hebrew*.[22]

Regrettably, no such comprehensive study has been dedicated to Aramaic loanwords in Akkadian, whether in general or in its Neo-Assyrian, Neo- or Late-Babylonian dialects in particular. The major impediment to undertaking such a

[16] See Mankowski, ALBH, p. 7.

[17] See H. Bußmann, *Lexikon der Sprachwissenschaft* (Stuttgart 2002), pp. 226f s.v. Fremdwort.

[18] For the term "ghost word," see M.A. Pei & F. Gaynor (eds.), *A Dictionary of Linguistics* (London 1960), p. 83 s.v. *ghost-word.* Cf. the term "ghost form," in D. Crystal (ed.), *An Encyclopedic Dictionary of Language and Languages* (Cambridge 1992), p. 156; idem, *The Penguin Dictionary of Language* (London 1999), p. 135 s.v. *ghost form.*

[19] Cf. P. Durkin, *The Oxford Guide to Etymology* (Oxford 2009), pp. 136f; Bußmann, ibid., p. 398a s.v. *Lehnbedeutung.*

[20] See H. Zimmern, *Akkadische Fremdwörter als Beweis für babylonischen Kultureinfluß* (Leipzig 1917), (henceforth: Zimmern, AF).

[21] S.A. Kaufman, *The Akkadian Influences on Aramaic* (Chicago 1974), (henceforth: Kaufman, AIA). For additional Akkadian loanwords in Aramaic, see M. Sokoloff, "New Akkadian Loanwords in Jewish Babylonian Aramaic," in Y. Sefati et al. (eds.), *"An Experienced Scribe Who Neglects Nothing": Ancient Near Eastern Studies in Honor of Jacob Klein* (Bethesda 2005), pp. 575–586.

[22] See Mankowski, ALBH.

study has been attributed to our limited knowledge about the Aramaic language during the period of language contact between Akkadian and Aramaic, i.e., the 1st millennium B.C.[23]

However, a preliminary study in this regard was carried out by von Soden, who took the first steps towards studying Aramaic loanwords in Neo-Assyrian and Neo- and Late-Babylonian in his three articles titled *Aramäische Wörter in neuassyrischen und neu- und spätbabylonischen Texten. Ein Vorbericht*, I–III.[24] Von Soden calls attention to the fact that a large number of the words treated in his own study were already included in Zimmern's book mentioned above.[25] He registered in his articles 240 possible Aramaic loanwords, of which 81 were considered to be borrowed into Neo-Assyrian.[26] Some of these 81 words were also considered to be loans in one or both of the other two dialects, i.e., Neo- and Late-Babylonian.

Nevertheless, von Soden's study has been criticized by Kutscher, who commented that "von Soden sometimes tends to view as A[ramaic] an Ak[kadian] lexeme without attempting to prove that it is indeed an A[ramaic] loan in Ak[kadian], and not vice versa."[27] Abraham and Sokoloff published a review of von Soden's list of Aramaic loanwords, in which they reduced the number of the proposed loanwords to slightly more than 40 certain and about the same number of possible loans.[28] They criticize von Soden's work on Aramaic loanwords saying that he frequently adduces Aramaic words without providing any reference to his sources, and that in many cases, especially concerning the Jewish Aramaic dialects, the words appear to either be non-existent or to have a different meaning.[29] They add that von Soden's suggested loanwords from Aramaic remain fraught with difficulties.[30] However, Abraham and Sokoloff's review has been described as being too pessimistic.[31] It is imperative to emphasize that Abraham and Sokoloff's review mentioned above is solely dedicated to treating the proposed Aramaic loanwords that are included in von Soden's articles. More recently, von Soden's research in this regard, for instance his attribution of many

---

[23] See P.-A. Beaulieu, "Aspects of Aramaic and Babylonian Linguistic Interaction in First Millennium BC Iraq," *Journal of Language Contact* 6 (2013), p. 360.

[24] See W. von Soden, "Aramäische Wörter in neuassyrischen und neu- und spätbabylonischen Texten. Ein Vorbericht, I–III," *Or* 35 (1966), pp. 1–20; *Or* 37 (1968), pp. 261–271; *Or* 46 (1977), pp. 183–197, (henceforth: von Soden, *Or* 35 (1966); idem, *Or* 37 (1968); idem, *Or* 46 (1977)).

[25] See von Soden, *Or* 35 (1966), p. 5. Cf. the critique by Abraham & Sokoloff, *Reassessment*, p. 24, n. 30.

[26] The words are: *akku, anēnu, anīna, aqqabu, aṣūdu, buḫḫušu, durā'u, Eber nāri, egertu, gadiu, galû, garīṣtu, gazālu, gubbu, gumāru, ḫalābu, ḫālu, ḫanāpu, ḫangaru, ḫannīu, ḫarurtu, ḫašābu, ḫilpu, ḫulūṭu, ianūqu, im-magāni, izqātu, kanāšu, katāru, kirku, kuspu, la, lapān*(*i*), *laqā'u, madbar,* (*magāṭātu*) *magazzutu, maḫītu, maqartu, marāsu, muāšu, nakālu, napāṣu, nasīku, nibzu, niklu, niqittu, paḫāzu, palû, pušku, qadduru, qallīlu, qapīru, qarābu, qarḫu, qarsu, qarūḫu, qi''u, radāpu, ra'su, saḫaru, salītu, samādiru, samāku, sapāqu, saqālu, ṣaḫūrānūtu, ṣallu, ṣāpītu, ṣappuḫu, ṣibtātu, ṣipirtu, ṣippirrāte, šalṭu, šapānu, šapīnutu, šārītu, šullāmu, šūqāqu, ṭullumâ, urbānu, ziqqu.*

[27] See E.Y. Kutscher, "Aramaic," in T.A. Sebeok (ed.), *Current Trends in Linguistics*, 6. *Linguistics in South West Asia and North Africa* (The Hague 1970), p. 357.

[28] See Abraham & Sokoloff, *Reassessment*, pp. 22–76.

[29] Ibid., p. 22, n. 13.

[30] Ibid., p. 23.

[31] See M.P. Streck, "Akkadian and Aramaic Language Contact," in S. Weninger (ed.), *The Semitic Languages: An International Handbook* (Berlin 2011), p. 419 § 2.2.1.

innovations in Neo-Babylonian to Aramaic influence, has been criticized by Beaulieu for being "often without critical examination of the evidence or much consideration of historical linguistic methodology."[32]

In any case, von Soden's study, although important as a starting point for further research on Aramaic loanwords in Neo-Assyrian and Neo- and Late-Babylonian, requires revision and updating with existing Akkadian and Aramaic lexical tools, which have increased in number and improved.[33] Moreover, a large number of cuneiform texts have been edited and published since the late 1970s, some of which include lexicographical analyses that need to be incorporated into any up-to-date study of Aramaic loanwords in Neo-Assyrian and Neo- and Late-Babylonian. For the Neo-Assyrian texts, the situation has improved significantly with the series of new text editions issued by the *State Archives of Assyria* project (SAA), which not only contain many new Neo-Assyrian texts and improved editions of many old ones but also valuable Neo-Assyrian glossaries. Hence, not only is the corpus of the Neo-Assyrian texts available today larger than before, many of the previously edited texts have also been more accurately re-edited and commented upon by various scholars. In addition, the study of Neo-Assyrian grammar has recently been advanced by the publication of two valuable works, namely *A Sketch of Neo-Assyrian Grammar* by J. Hämeen-Anttila,[34] and *Grammatical Variation in Neo-Assyrian* by M. Luukko.[35]

Thanks to the advancements in lexicography and the increased Neo-Assyrian textual material at hand, it is now possible to interpret and evaluate some of the previous contributions to the study of Aramaic loanwords in Neo-Assyrian differently. Some of the proposed Aramaic loanwords can be rejected[36] and others will be corroborated on a much broader basis. It is also possible to identify additional Aramaic loanwords in Neo-Assyrian that have not yet been recognized.

1.4 The purpose and scope of the present study

This study has the following objectives:

1. To collect and analyze all words that have been previously proposed as Aramaic loanwords in Neo-Assyrian and are accepted as such in recent dictionaries, glossaries, and lexical studies, as well as in current Assyriological literature. Many of these are included in von Soden's groundbreaking study,[37] but

[32] See P.-A. Beaulieu, "Aspects of Aramaic and Babylonian Linguistic Interaction in First Millennium BC Iraq," *Journal of Language Contact* 6 (2013), p. 361.
[33] See below, Section 1.5.
[34] See J. Hämeen-Anttila, *A Sketch of Neo-Assyrian Grammar* (Helsinki 2000), (henceforth: Hämeen-Anttila, SAAS XIII).
[35] See M. Luukko, *Grammatical Variation in Neo-Assyrian* (Helsinki 2004), (henceforth: Luukko, SAAS XVI).
[36] Cf. preliminary Z. Cherry, "Aramaic Loanwords in Neo-Assyrian: Rejecting some Proposals," in M. Luukko et al. (eds.), *Of God(s), Trees, Kings, and Scholars: Neo-Assyrian and Related Studies in Honour of Simo Parpola* (Helsinki 2009), pp. 19–25, (henceforth: Z. Cherry, *Aramaic Loanwords in NA: Rejecting some Proposals*).
[37] See n. 24 above. Cf. Abraham & Sokoloff, *Reassessment*.

additional proposals made in more recent times remain scattered across a wide range of Assyriological publications. This study also intends to carry out further etymological investigation to identify additional Aramaic loanwords in Neo-Assyrian that may not have been recognized yet.[38]

2. To verify the validity of the previously proposed Aramaic loanwords in Neo-Assyrian by systematically scrutinizing the evidence (whether phonological, morphological, semantic or cultural/historical) upon which the items concerned were identified as loanwords, and based on this analysis, to make explicit whether this or that loanword hypothesis is acceptable or should be rejected.

3. To also investigate another type of borrowing that involves semantic loan,[39] i.e., a change in the meaning of an established native word to accommodate a new meaning acquired from a word in another language. As mentioned before, in the present study this applies to Neo-Assyrian words that may have undergone semantic change or extension of meaning by developing a new sense under the influence of their Aramaic cognates.

4. To present information, whenever possible, on the provenance, origin, genre and date of the Neo-Assyrian texts containing Aramaic loanwords, and to examine whether there are any patterns within the groups of the texts and the loanwords studied.

5. To shed light on the frequency of the Aramaic loanwords in the Neo-Assyrian texts. This includes words that are *hapax legomenon*, *dis legomenon* or *tris legomenon*. Also, to identify the Neo-Assyrian texts which include two or more different Aramaic loanwords.

6. To provide information on the semantic categories of the Aramaic loanwords in Neo-Assyrian.

7. To provide a phonological analysis of the Aramaic loanwords in Neo-Assyrian.

The present study does not investigate Neo-Assyrian loan-translations (calques) of Aramaic words and expressions, for example, the occasional use of the Neo-Assyrian preposition *ana* "to, for" as a *nota accusativi* on the model of the Aramaic proclitic -ל.[40] Nor does the study investigate personal names, divine names, phraseology, or details of Neo-Assyrian syntax which might have been borrowed from Aramaic or influenced by it. These types of investigations

---

[38] For instance, S. Parpola proposes additional 28 possible Aramaic loanwords in NA (personal communication). The words are: *akê*, *bašā'u*, *būṣīnu*, *gazāru*, *gerdu*, *gidlu*, *gulē/īnu*, *ḫalīdu*, *ḫarbutu/ḫarbūtu*, *ḫurbu*, *kakkišu*, *kandu*, *kurḫu*, *leḫmu*, *makaḫālutu*, *maqaṭṭu*(*tu*), *parāḫu*, *purṣīnu*, *puṭuru*, *qamāru*, *qumbutu*, *sarābu*, *sarḫu*, *sādiu*, *šernu*, *tukku*, *tūbāqu*, *ziblu*. I am thankful to Prof. Parpola for sharing these words with me and for giving me the opportunity to analyze and discuss them in this study.

[39] Cf. P. Durkin, *The Oxford Guide to Etymology* (Oxford 2009), pp. 136f; H. Bußmann, *Lexikon der Sprachwissenschaft* (Stuttgart 2002), p. 398a s.v. Lehnbedeutung.

[40] See, for instance, the preposition *ana* in SAA XIX 41:8′. See also von Soden, *Or* 35 (1966), p. 13:73; idem, *Or* 46 (1977), p. 189:73; idem, GAG § 114e and 144c; Hämeen-Anttila, SAAS XIII, § 3.9.1; Luukko, SAAS XVI, § 6.6; M.J. Geller, Review of "A Sketch of Neo-Assyrian Grammar," by J. Hämeen-Anttila, *BSOAS* 65 (2002), p. 563; Abraham & Sokoloff, *Reassessment*, p. 24, n. 25 and p. 38:114; Hackl, J., "Language Death and Dying Reconsidered: The Rôle of Late Babylonian as a Vernacular Language," July 2011, p. 13, n. 58. Online 15/09/2022: https://www.academia.edu

deserve their own study. Nevertheless, Neo-Assyrian personal names are occasionally taken into consideration when they contribute to the discussion of the loanword.

Of course, Aramaic loanwords also occur in Neo- and Late-Babylonian dialects of Akkadian, but the study of this group of loanwords lies outside the scope of the present research; they are taken into account only when relevant to the discussion of Aramaic loanwords in Neo-Assyrian. Also, the Aramaic loanwords that are found in Standard Babylonian (SB) and Neo-Babylonian (NB) texts composed in Assyria are not treated in this study.[41] Words with Neo-Assyrian form, which occasionally occur in SB texts composed in Assyria, are not included in the vocabulary analyzed in this study.

No further collation of the Neo-Assyrian texts was undertaken for this study. Thus, all collations cited here were made by the editor(s) of the text(s) concerned and are considered reliable in so far as they are entered into the State Archives of Assyria Project's electronic database, Corpus of Neo-Assyrian Texts (CNA).

1.5 Material of the study

All known Neo-Assyrian texts,[42] with the exception of a few published only recently, have been entered into the electronic database of the State Archives of Assyria Project, Corpus of Neo-Assyrian Texts (CNA), which has the task of collecting all published and unpublished Neo-Assyrian texts in its electronic database.[43] Based on the present corpus, the Neo-Assyrian textual material consists of 9057 unique texts.[44] All the Neo-Assyrian textual material available in the Corpus of Neo-Assyrian Texts (CNA) has been utilized in this study for the purpose of identifying Aramaic loanwords in Neo-Assyrian.

The Akkadian lexical material consulted includes *The Assyrian Dictionary of the Oriental Institute of the University of Chicago* (CAD), which provides rich attestations for its entries and occasionally offers etymological commentaries,[45] and the other dictionary *Akkadisches Handwörterbuch* (AHw.), which provides

[41] I intend to treat the Aramaic loanwords in SB and NB texts that were composed in Assyria elsewhere.

[42] For details on the Neo-Assyrian texts, see below pp. 25ff. s.v. Neo-Assyrian.

[43] See the State Archives of Assyria Project's electronic database, Corpus of Neo-Assyrian Texts (CNA), presently on server, 15–09–2022: oracc.museum.upenn.edu. I am grateful to Prof. Simo Parpola of the University of Helsinki for granting me permission to access at a distance the State Archives of Assyria Project's electronic database, Corpus of Neo-Assyrian Texts (CNA), which I utilized for examining and enlarging the data used in this study.

[44] This information is based on the Corpus of Neo-Assyrian Texts (CNA). I am thankful to Dr. Robert Whiting for calling my attention to the fact that some of the Neo-Assyrian texts have been entered twice in the corpus, sometimes under the museum number and again under the publication reference, and also that there are texts in the corpus entered twice as a result of having been joined to other pieces (personal communication). Caution has been taken to ensure that no Neo-Assyrian textual attestation is cited more than once in the textual citation section under each headword discussed in this study.

[45] *The Assyrian Dictionary of the Oriental Institute of the University of Chicago*, 21 vols., (Chicago 1956–2011), (henceforth: CAD).

comparative etymological information.[46] In addition, *A Concise Dictionary of Akkadian* (CDA),[47] which is in essence based on AHw., is consulted because it includes additions and occasional corrections to AHw., as well as incorporating the reviews of both CAD and AHw., harvested from Assyriological literature.[48] Also important is the *Assyrian-English-Assyrian Dictionary* (AEAD)[49] which focuses, among other things, on the vocabulary of the Neo-Assyrian dialect and seeks to present it as completely and accurately as possible. The dictionary contains about 13,000 Assyrian entries, of which the Neo-Assyrian words and phrases constitute ca. 50%, i.e., approximately 6,500 words.[50] All the updates on the Akkadian words treated in Assyriological literature, which are published in the word lists of the Register Assyriologie of the *Archiv für Orientforschung*, are taken account of, with an emphasis on the Neo-Assyrian material.

Advances in the field of lexicography also apply to Aramaic. In reference to Old and Official Aramaic, the *Dictionary of the North-West Semitic Inscriptions* (DNWSI) is consulted.[51] Also consulted is the *Comprehensive Aramaic Lexicon* (CAL), a new dictionary comprising a major scholarly reference work of the Aramaic language which is currently in preparation by an international team of scholars and is available online.[52] CAL covers almost all dialects and periods of Aramaic and takes account of all modern scholarly discussion of the Aramaic language. In addition, other essential Aramaic dictionaries of different dialects and periods are consulted to collect the Aramaic words relevant to the discussion and analysis of the proposed Aramaic loanwords.[53]

---

46 See AHw.

47 J. Black, A. George & N. Postgate (eds.), *A Concise Dictionary of Akkadian* (Wiesbaden 2000), (henceforth: CDA).

48 Ibid., pp. vii, ix. For a bibliography of the reviews of CAD and AHw., until 2004, see Nili, pp. 301–304.

49 See S. Parpola et al. (eds.), *Assyrian-English-Assyrian Dictionary* (Helsinki 2007).

50 Ibid., p. xiii.

51 J. Hoftijzer & K. Jongeling, *Dictionary of the North-West Semitic Inscriptions,* 2 vols., (Leiden 1995). It is important to note that many Aramaic words in DNWSI are considered loanwords in Akkadian based on von Soden's study mentioned above in n. 24.

52 See CAL.

53 The other Aramaic dictionaries utilized in this study are: G.H. Dalman, *Aramäisch-neuhebräisches Wörterbuch zu Targum, Talmud und Midrasch* (Frankfurt a. M 1901); A.J. Maclean, *A Dictionary of the Dialects of Vernacular Syriac: As Spoken by the Eastern Syrians of Kurdistan, Northwest Persia and the Plain of Mosul* (Oxford 1901); F. Schulthess, *Lexicon Syropalaestinum* (Berlin 1903); J. Payne Smith, *A Compendious Syriac Dictionary* (Oxford 1903); E.S. Drower & R. Macuch, *A Mandaic Dictionary* (Oxford 1963); R.A. Brauner, *A Comparative Lexicon of Old Aramaic* (Ann Arbor 1974); J.E. Manna, *Leksīqōn kaldāyā-ʾarbāyā* (Beirut 1975); T. Audo, *Sīmṯā də-lišānā sūryāyā*, I–II (Ann Arbor 1978); M. Jastrow, *A Dictionary of the Targumim, the Talmud Babli and Yerushalmi, and the Midraschic Literature* (New York 1989); C. Brockelmann, *Lexicon Syriacum* (Hildesheim 1995); A. Tal, *A Dictionary of Samaritan Aramaic* (Leiden 2000); M. Sokoloff, *A Dictionary of Jewish Palestinian Aramaic of the Byzantine Period* (Ramat-Gan 2002); idem, *A Dictionary of Jewish Babylonian Aramaic of the Talmudic and Geonic Periods* (Ramat-Gan 2002); idem, *A Dictionary of Judean Aramaic* (Ramat-Gan 2003); idem, *A Syriac Lexicon* (Winona Lake 2009); idem, *A Dictionary of Christian Palestinian Aramaic* (Leuven 2014).

1.6 The methods used in identifying Aramaic loanwords

Identifying loanwords is a comparative process by which the lexicon of the recipient language and that of any possible candidate donor are examined and compared with each other to identify possible loans and the direction of borrowing.[54] When analyzing a potential loan from Aramaic into Neo-Assyrian, it is imperative to examine and compare not only the lexical data of Neo-Assyrian as the recipient language, and Aramaic as the possible donor language, but also the lexical data of other languages that were in contact with Neo-Assyrian.[55]

The task of identifying Aramaic loanwords in Neo-Assyrian (as also in Neo- and Late-Babylonian) is complicated because the two languages are cognates. Consequently, Neo-Assyrian and Aramaic share with the other Semitic languages some common features as regards their phonological, morphological and semantic systems, as well as a common basic vocabulary, which makes it often very difficult to reliably establish the origin of a possible inter-Semitic loanword.[56] In addition, for some few words that can be considered certain borrowings into Neo-Assyrian, there are several West-Semitic languages which can be possible donors, but at the same time we lack conclusive evidence as to whether the loanwords were borrowed specifically from Aramaic or from some other West-Semitic language. In this study such loanwords will be defined as either Aramaic or other West-Semitic in origin. However, the historical background indicates that the contact between speakers of other West-Semitic languages and Neo-Assyrian occurred mostly in the periphery of the Assyrian empire, and less often in Assyria proper, and it was much less intensive than the contact between Neo-Assyrian and Aramaic.

The designation West-Semitic languages refers basically to all Semitic languages other than Akkadian and Eblaite, which are classified as East Semitic languages. In this study, the designation West-Semitic languages is mainly used to refer to Northwest Semitic languages, of which Ugaritic, Hebrew, Phoenician and Aramaic constitute the major languages. The Northwest Semitic languages are classified by some scholars as a subgroup of the Central Semitic branch of the West-Semitic languages.[57]

The evidence required for the identification of loanwords may consist of one or several different elements of phonology, morphology and semantics, or the

---

[54] See Mankowski, ALBH, p. 4.

[55] For an overview of the languages contemporary with Neo-Assyrian in the ancient Near East, see G. Rubio, "The Languages of the Ancient Near East," in D.C. Snell (ed.), *A Companion to the Ancient Near East* (Malden 2005), pp. 79–94. For the lexica of the Semitic languages, see B. Podolsky, "A Selected List of Dictionaries of Semitic Languages," in S. Izre'el (ed.), *Semitic Linguistics: The State of the Art at the Turn of the Twenty-First Century* (Winona Lake 2002), pp. 213–221.

[56] Cf. M.P. O'Connor, "The Arabic Loanwords in Nabatean Aramaic," *JNES* 45 (1986), p. 215; Mankowski, ALBH, p. 5, n. 20.

[57] For more details, see Section 1.8 below. Cf. J. Huehnergard, "Semitic Languages," in J.M. Sasson et al. (eds.), *Civilizations of the Ancient Near East* (Massachusetts 2006), pp. 2117–2134; idem, "Features of Central Semitic," in A. Gianto (ed.), *Biblical and Oriental Essays in Memory of William L. Moran* (Rome 2005), pp. 155–203.

existence of a cultural-historical claim attested with a given word studied. Together these constitute the most important factors that ought to be taken into consideration as much as possible in the process of identifying loanwords.

Hence, a word is identified as a loanword if its *phonetic shape*, *form* and *meaning* are similar to those of a word in another language from which it might have been borrowed through some kind of language contact, provided that there are no other reasonable alternative explanations for these similarities, for example that the word is a cognate.

In some cases the reasons behind the borrowing of a certain word can be helpful to understanding why the borrowing of that word occurred. These include, for instance, the need to designate something entirely new to the recipient language or to resolve a clash of homonyms in it, or the need for synonyms to increase the expressive capacity of the recipient language.[58]

It is important to point out that it is sometimes still difficult to recognize Aramaic loanwords in Neo-Assyrian because there are no phonological or morphological divergences that are characteristic of a candidate for a loan. In other words, the loanword has undergone adaptation, i.e., has been remodeled to fit the phonological and morphological structure of the words in Neo-Assyrian.[59] In such cases other criteria might be helpful in the process of identifying the loanwords. In the following, an account is provided for the methods used in this study to identify Aramaic loanwords in Neo-Assyrian.

1.6.1 Phonological criterion

Phonological criteria provide the strongest evidence for identifying loanwords and the direction of borrowing. If a word found in a language is incompatible with the phonological patterns of that language, for example if it has a sound which is not normally expected in the native words of that language, then we have an indication that the word in question is borrowed.[60]

1.6.1.1 Comparative method applied to Semitic roots concerning their phonological correspondences

The information obtained from the phonological history of the languages belonging to the same family, in our case the Semitic language family, concerning the sound changes that they have undergone, provides evidence that is crucial for identifying intra-Semitic loanwords and the donor language.[61] In this study, we

[58] Cf. U. Weinreich, *Languages in Contact* (The Hague 1970), pp. 47–60; C. Myers-Scotton, *Contact Linguistics: Bilingual Encounters and Grammatical Outcomes* (New York 2000), pp. 234–242.
[59] Cf. von Soden, *Or* 35 (1966), p. 2.
[60] See L. Campbell, *Historical Linguistics: An Introduction* (Edinburgh 2004), p. 69.
[61] Cf. ibid., p. 70.

apply the comparative method[62] to Semitic roots with regard to the sound changes they have undergone leading to some of the Proto-Semitic (PS) consonantal phonemes being represented by different phonetic shapes, which also vary sometimes in different periods, in the individual Semitic languages. In view of that, if at least one of the root phonemes of a certain Semitic word is expected to develop differently in Neo-Assyrian than in Aramaic and the word exists in both Neo-Assyrian and Aramaic, but the Neo-Assyrian word has the Aramaic form, then we have a strong indication that the word was borrowed from Aramaic into Neo-Assyrian.[63] Table 1 below signifies the relevant consonantal phonemes.

Furthermore, a sound change in Akkadian, known as *e*-coloring, is caused by the influence of certain consonants on the neighboring vowel *a*, resulting in the development *a* > *e*. This happens in syllables where *a* is adjacent to a glottal stop ʾ (hamza) that has developed from a PS **ḫ*, or * ʿ, and sometimes even from a PS **ġ*, when this ʾ occurs at the beginning or at the end of a syllable before itself being completely dropped.[64] This *e*-coloring can also be helpful in identifying loanwords. If a Neo-Assyrian word does not undergo an expected *e*-coloring, then there is a good chance that the word is a borrowing.

For example, the NA word *adê* n. "(vassal) treaty," is considered to be a borrowing from Aramaic *ʿdyʾ* n. "pact, treaty, treaty-stipulations." The Aramaic word appears to be derived from the root ʿDY. On the other hand, there is no indication whatsoever of the preservation of *ʿayin* in first-millennium Akkadian, and no solid proof of any Northwest Semitic borrowing from an Akkadian word with an initial vowel being represented by / ʿ/.[65] Also, when NA words with initial vowel are borrowed into Aramaic, they are written with an initial aleph. Hence, the word is not a borrowing from Akkadian into Aramaic. In addition, the original Semitic voiced pharyngeal fricative / ʿ/ was already reduced in Akkadian and appears from about 2000 B.C. as a glottal stop ʾ (hamza). The latter, then, as a result of the reduction of / ʿ/, disappears totally, causing an *e*-coloring of the neighboring **a*, i.e., an umlaut of *a* > *e*. In our case, the lack of *e*-coloring in the word *adê* also points to a borrowing into NA.

[62] For the comparative method (CM) as an instrumental tool for interpreting data in historical linguistics, see W.P. Lehmann, *Historical Linguistics: An Introduction* (London 1994), p. 9 and pp. 141ff. See also ibid., p. 142, for the linguists' interpretation and use of the comparative method.

[63] See Kaufman, AIA, pp. 19f, for the opposite situation between Aramaic and Akkadian.

[64] See GAG § 9a, § 23c; S. Moscati, *An Introduction to the Comparative Grammar of the Semitic Languages: Phonology and Morphology* (Wiesbaden 1964) § 8.54; J. Huehnergard, *A Grammar of Akkadian* (Atlanta 1997), p. 587; O. Rössler, "Zur Frage der Vertretung der gemeinsemitischen Laryngale im Akkadischen (ʿ = ġ)" in H. Franke (ed.), *Akten des vierundzwanzigsten internationalen Orientalisten-Kongresses München 28. August bis 4. September 1957*, (Wiesbaden 1959), pp. 129–132; L. Kogan, "*ġ in Akkadian," *UF* 33 (2001), pp. 263–298; B. Kouwenberg, "The Reflexes of the Proto-Semitic Gutturals in Assyrian," in G. Deutscher & N.J.C. Kouwenberg (eds.), *The Akkadian Language in its Semitic Context: Studies in the Akkadian of the Third and Second Millennium BC* (Leiden 2006), pp. 150–176.

[65] See Kaufman, AIA, p. 142.

Table 1: The relevant consonantal phonemes[66]

PS	Akk.	NA	OAram. (spelling)[67]	Aram. ca. 500 B.C.[68]	Ug.	Heb.	Ar.	Eth. (Geʿez)
*ʾ	ʾ/ø	ʾ/ø	ʾ	ʾ	ʾ	ʾ	ʾ	ʾ
*ʿ	ʾ/ø	ʾ/ø	ʿ	ʿ	ʿ	ʿ	ʿ	ʿ
*ḏ	*z*	*z*[69]	*z*	*d*	*d*/*ḏ*	*z*	*ḏ*	*z*
*ġ	ʾ/ø	ʾ/ø	ʿ	ʿ	*ġ*	ʿ	*ġ*	ʿ
*h	ʾ/ø	ʾ/ø	*h*	*h*	*h*	*h*	*h*	*h*
*ḥ	ʾ/ø	ʾ/ø[70]	*ḥ*	*ḥ*	*ḥ*	*ḥ*	*ḥ*	*ḥ*
*ḫ	*ḫ*	*ḫ*	*ḥ*	*ḥ*	*ḫ*	*ḥ*	*ḫ*	*ḫ*
*s	*s*	*š*[71]	*s*	*s*	*s*	*s*	*s*	*s*
*ś	*š*	*š*[72]	*š*	*s*	*š*	*ś*	*š*	*š*
*š	*š*	*s*[73]	*š*	*š*	*š*	*š*	*s*	*s*
*ṣ́[74]	*ṣ*	*ṣ*[75]	*q*	ʿ	*ṣ*	*ṣ*	*ḍ*	*ḍ*
*ṯ	*š*	*š*[76]	*š*	*t*	*ṯ*	*š*	*ṯ*	*s*
*ṭ	*ṣ*	*ṣ*	*ṣ*	*ṭ*	*ṭ*	*ṣ*	*ẓ*	*ṣ*

---

[66] Cf. S. Moscati, *An Introduction to the Comparative Grammar of the Semitic Languages: Phonology and Morphology* (Wiesbaden 1964), § 8.59; J. Huehnergard, *A Grammar of Akkadian* (Atlanta 1997), p. 590; Kaufman, AIA, p. 19; Lipiński, *Semitic Languages*, p. 150.

[67] See Moscati, ibid., § 8.18.

[68] Ibid.

[69] Cf. Table 3 below.

[70] Ibid.

[71] Ibid. The Neo-Assyrian <*s*> is used to write West-Semitic <*š*> and vice versa. It has been observed by scholars, through the evidence of alphabetic transcriptions, that in Neo-Assyrian a written sibilant *s* must have been pronounced as /*š*/ and a written sibilant *š* must have been pronounced as /*s*/. In other words, this means that the Neo-Assyrian <*s*> = /*š*/ and <*š*> = /*s*/. Haupt points out that this fact was recognized by Hincks as early as 1857; see P. Haupt, "Some Assyrian Etymologies," *AJSL* 26 (1909), p. 9. See also S. Ylvisaker, *Zur babylonischen und assyrischen Grammatik* (Leipzig 1912), § 5; I.J. Gelb, "Notes on von Soden's Grammar of Akkadian," *BiOr* 12 (1955), p. 103, § 29e; S. Moscati, ibid., § 8.32; A.R. Millard, "[f]*ša ekalli* – *šgl* – [d]*sagale*," *UF* 4 (1972), p. 162; idem, "Assyrian Royal Names in Biblical Hebrew," *JSS* 21 (1976), pp. 1–14; S. Parpola, "The Alleged Middle/Neo-Assyrian Irregular Verb **naṣṣ* and the Assyrian Sound Change *š* > *s*," *Assur* 1/1 (1974), p. 4, n. 13; Kaufman, AIA, pp. 140f; E. Lipiński, "La correspondance des sibilantes dans les textes araméens et les textes cunéiformes néo-assyriens," in P. Fronzaroli (ed.), *Atti del secondo congresso internazionale di linguistica camito-semitica* (Firenze 1978), pp. 201–210; F.M. Fales, AECT, pp. 61ff.; Hämeen-Anttila, SAAS XIII, § 2.1.1; Luukko, SAAS XVI, § 4.1.3. See the guidelines of the transcription system by S. Parpola, in K. Radner, *The Prosopography of the Neo-Assyrian Empire*, Vol. 1/I (Helsinki 1998), pp. xxii–xxv, esp. p. xxiv. In this study the *š* ⋛ *s* interchange between alphabetic and NA cuneiform renderings has been left unmarked in transliterations and transcriptions to avoid confusion.

[72] Cf. Table 3 below.

[73] S. Parpola (personal communication). Cf. Table 3 below.

[74] This interdental is in some scholarly literature transcribed with the symbol *ḍ*.

[75] Cf. Table 3 below.

[76] Ibid.

1.6.1.2 Other phonological criteria

In certain cases the loanwords are not completely integrated into the phonological patterns of the recipient language, and therefore can be identified by their unusual shape, which violates the distinctive phonotactics of the recipient language. Hence, in etymological investigations, use can also be made of phonemic changes that occur in different Semitic languages due to the incompatibility of specific root consonants in certain position. An example is the phenomenon known as "Geers' law,"[77] according to which triconsonantal roots originally containing two different emphatic radicals (*ṭ*, *ṣ*, or *q*) are not tolerated in Akkadian, but instead one of the emphatics dissimilates to its non-emphatic voiceless counterpart in accordance with the following gradation: *ṣ*, *q*, *ṭ*.[78] Thus, *ṭ* becomes *t* in forms that also contain *q* or *ṣ*; in forms that contain both *q* and *ṣ*, the emphatic consonant that comes first dissimilates, i.e., *q* to *k* and *ṣ* to *s*. So, while two emphatic consonants in the same root can be tolerated in other Semitic languages, any word in Akkadian and its dialects that does not adhere to the said law must be a borrowing. The following changes in the emphatic quality of the Akkadian root take place:

Table 2: Changes in the emphatic quality of the Akkadian root

PS root		Akk. root
**q – ṣ*	>	*k – ṣ*
**ṭ – q/ṣ*	>	*t – q/ṣ*
**q – ṭ*	>	*q – t*[79]
**ṣ – q*	>	*s – q*[80]
**q – q*	>	*k – q*[81]

For instance, the NA word **garīṣtu/*girīṣtu* n. f. "round flat loaf of bread," which is attested only in f. pl. form as *garīṣāte/girīṣāte*, is considered to be a borrowing from Aramaic *gərīṣtā* n. f. "loaf of bread or cake." The origin of the Aramaic word is considered to be the Semitic root *QRṢ. If the NA *garīṣāte* is derived from the root QRṢ, the form of the word, according to Geers' law, is expected to appear as *krṣ* not as *grṣ*. Hence, the evidence points to a borrowing from Aramaic into NA.

Also helpful are the graphic renderings of non-Assyrian phonemes in Neo-Assyrian transcriptions of West-Semitic names, which can be used to corroborate the phonological conclusions drawn from other data. The following correlations

[77] See F.W. Geers, "The Treatment of Emphatics in Akkadian," *JNES* 4 (1945), pp. 65–67; GAG § 51e. See also J.H. Greenberg, "The patterning of Root Morphemes in Semitic," *Word* 6 (1950), pp. 162–181.
[78] Cf. GAG § 51e, where *ṣ* before *q* becomes *s* in *sīqum* "narrow, tight" (cf. Ar. ضَيِّق).
[79] See A. Ungnad, *Akkadian Grammar* (Atlanta 1992), § 21a.
[80] See GAG, ibid.
[81] In Neo-Assyrian the dissimilation of two similar emphatics *q* may occur in some nouns, i.e., (*q*...*q* > *k*...*q*), e.g., *kaqquru* "ground." See Hämeen-Anttila, SAAS XIII, § 2.2 and § 2.3, d).

educed by Parpola from *The Prosopography of the Neo-Assyrian Empire* (PNA), are important:[82]

Table 3: Graphic renderings of non-Assyrian phonemes in Neo-Assyrian transcriptions of West-Semitic names:[83]

W.Sem.	NA	W.Sem.	NA
/e/	<*a*> or <*e/i*>	*/ḏ/*	<*d*> or <*z*>
/o/	<*u*>	*/ṣ́/*[84]	<*q*>
		/h/	<*Ø*> or <*ḫ*>
/w/	<*u*> or <*m*>	*/ḥ/*	<*ḫ*>
/y/	<*i*>	*/ʿ/*	<*Ø*>, <'>, <*q*> or <*ḫ*>
		/ġ/	<*q*> or <*ḫ*>
		/s/	<*š*>
		/ś/	<*s*> or <*lt*>
		/š/	<*s*>
		/ṯ/	<*t*> or <*š*>

1.6.2 Morphological criterion

The morphological criterion is also useful in identifying loanwords. As units, loanwords are usually not analyzable in the borrowing language, whereas their corresponding source words in the donor languages may sometimes be a complex or a phrase whose internal structure is lost after entering the recipient language.[85] For instance, the Akkadian word *malāḫu(m)* "boatman, sailor," is considered to be a loan from the Sumerian word $^{(\text{lú})}$MÁ.LAḪ$_{4/5}$ "sailor," which consists of two words, namely MÁ "boat," and LAḪ$_{4/5}$ "to drive along." Hence, the Sumerian word is a compound consisting of two morphemes, but its compound nature was no longer recognized when the word entered the Akkadian language as a monomorphemic word, i.e., *malāḫu(m)*, and consequently it was no longer analyzable by the native speakers of Akkadian. It stands to reason that if a word is attested in two languages and is phonologically and semantically similar, but as a unit is only analyzable as a morphological complex in one of the languages, then we have a good indication that the word was borrowed by the language where it is morphologically not analyzable as a complex unit, and where its

[82] See S. Parpola, "Guidelines of the Transcription System," in K. Radner, *The Prosopography of the Neo-Assyrian Empire, Vol. 1/I* (Helsinki 1998), pp. xxii–xxvii, esp. p. xxiv. Cf. F.M. Fales, "On Aramaic Onomastics in the Neo-Assyrian Period," *OrAnt* 16 (1977): 41–68; idem, AECT, pp. 47–74.

[83] M.P. Streck points out that this Table conceals another important phonological criterion for the establishment of Aramaic loans in NA: the preservation of */'/* (in certain environments), */h/*, */ḥ/*, */ʿ/* and */ġ/*, phonemes lost in Akkadian (personal communication).

[84] Note that S. Parpola used */ḍ/* which here is referred to by */ṣ́/*.

[85] See M. Haspelmath, "Lexical Borrowing: Concepts and Issues," in M. Haspelmath & U. Tadmor (eds.), *Loanwords in the World's Languages: A Comparative Handbook* (Berlin 2009), p. 37.

internal structure instead was lost after the borrowing and it is conceived by the native speakers as a monomorphemic unit.[86]

In our case, a good example is the NA word *akê* "so," which is borrowed from Aramaic הכי "so." The Aramaic word consists of the following compound: הא כן > הכן > הכ, i.e., the interjection הָא "behold!" and the adverb כֵּן "so, thus," with elision of the final *n*. Here, the most explicit feature which points to a borrowing from Aramaic into NA is that the Aramaic source word is an analyzable complex, but as a single unit its internal structure was lost after entering NA. In other words, the Aramaic source word is a compound consisting of two morphemes, but its compound nature was no longer recognizable when the word entered NA as a monomorphemic word, i.e., *akê*.

Another Akkadian sound change which in turn affects the nominal pattern and is expected to provide evidence of borrowing, is the dissimilation of the initial *m* of the nominal preformative *m*^{a}*/e-* (except for *mu-*) to *n* and its becoming *n*^{a}*/e-* when prefixed to roots containing a labial radical according to the so-called "Barth's law,"[87] giving rise to the following development: *maPRaS* > *naPRaS*, e.g., **markabtu(m)* > *narkabtu(m)* "chariot"; **mapḫaru(m)* > *napḫaru(m)* "total." Hence, any noun in NA that has the pattern *maPRaS* instead of the expected *naPRaS* must be a borrowing into NA. A good example is the NA word *madbar* "desert," which most likely is borrowed from Aramaic.

1.6.3 Semantic criterion

As for the semantic criterion, the meaning of the words and their cultural, geographical and ecological associations often provide clues helpful to identifying loanwords and revealing their origin and the donor language. In our study, as explained above, this concerns the Neo-Assyrian words that have cognates in Aramaic and may have obtained an extension or change of meaning by developing a new sense of the Neo-Assyrian lexical units under the influence of their Aramaic cognates. In other words, it involves the extension or change in the meaning of an established Neo-Assyrian word to accommodate a new meaning acquired from its Aramaic cognate. This is designated here as semantic loan.

1.6.4 Source words

An important reason for suspecting a word to be a loan is when the word lacks an etymology, i.e., has no source word or etymon in the language.[88] If a word has no

---

[86] See L. Campbell, *Historical Linguistics: An Introduction* (Edinburgh 2004), § 3.5.2.

[87] See J. Barth, "Das Nominalpräfix *na* im Assyrischen," *ZA* 2 (1887), pp. 111ff; W.C. Delsman, "Das Barth'sche Gesetz und Lehnwörter," *UF* 11 (1979), pp. 187f; GAG § 31b and § 56b; Kaufman, AIA, p. 20.

[88] See M. Haspelmath, "Lexical Borrowing: Concepts and Issues," in M. Haspelmath & U. Tadmor (eds.), *Loanwords in the World's Languages: A Comparative Handbook* (Berlin 2009), p. 44; D. Crystal (ed.), *An Encyclopedic Dictionary of Language and Languages* (Cambridge 1992), p. 128 s.v. etymology.

reasonable etymology within Akkadian, but does have one in Aramaic, then there is a good chance that the word is borrowed from the latter. Hence, if a word is derived from a root attested in Aramaic but the same root is unattested in Akkadian, then we have a good indication that the word was borrowed from Aramaic into Neo-Assyrian. However, if the same root also exists in other West-Semitic languages, and there is no specific reason to attribute the source word to a specific West-Semitic language, then it is more likely that the word was borrowed from Aramaic, because the language contact between Neo-Assyrian and Aramaic was more intensive.

1.6.5 Chronology

As regards chronology, unlike native words, loanwords cannot be traced back to the earliest stages of the history of a recipient language. Of course, our judgment in this regard always depends on how much we know about the history of the recipient language. For the purpose of our study, it is important to know when the earliest Aramaic loanwords are expected to appear in the Akkadian cuneiform texts. Words that are already attested in Middle Assyrian or Middle Babylonian, i.e., prior to 1000 B.C., can hardly be of Aramaic origin because we do not have historical records that attest to language contact between the aforementioned dialects of Akkadian and Aramaic.[89] When there is attestation of a word in the Akkadian textual sources from the period before the first millennium B.C., it means that we have a *precedent* attested in Akkadian from the period prior to language contact between the Neo and Late dialects of Akkadian and Aramaic. As a matter of fact, the earliest record that we have for Aramaic comes from ca. 925 B.C.[90] Words, however, which are attested only in Neo-Assyrian and Neo- and Late-Babylonian texts, and are well known as Aramaic words, prove often to be Aramaic loanwords.

Nevertheless, inferences derived from this method are more useful when coupled with other information. Caution must be taken since many previously unattested words in older dialects of Akkadian that emerge first in Neo-Assyrian and/or in Neo- and Late-Babylonian texts could, in fact, be genuine Akkadian words that were known in the earlier dialects of the language but happened to have vanished from those older dialects and were only preserved in Neo-Assyrian and/or in Neo- and Late-Babylonian, or are only accidentally unknown to us so far. However, these new words could simply be new innovations, as new lexical items, produced by the Neo-Assyrian and Neo- and Late-Babylonian speakers/scribes and borrowed into other languages including Aramaic.[91]

Also, morpheme chronology, as an indicator of loanwords, is important in many etymological inquiries. According to the reconstruction of historical grammar, the more difficult reading of a word in a text is the stronger. That is to say, the word with the more unusual form in a text is expected to be the original.

---

[89] See von Soden, *Or* 35 (1966), pp. 3f.
[90] See under *Old Aramaic* in Section 1.8 below and the references provided there.
[91] See von Soden, *Or* 35 (1966), p. 2.

For example, the independent first person plural nominative pronoun *nēnu* "we," in Old Assyrian and *nīnu* "we," in Old Babylonian is also attested as *anēnu* in Neo-Assyrian and as *anīnu* in Neo- and Late-Babylonian. In Aramaic the corresponding word is *ʾnḥn*. Accordingly, the expected reconstruction of the PS word would be **ʾnḥn*. Since the forms *nēnu/nīnu* are to be considered to be younger than *anēnu/anīnu* on the basis of morphemic development, the fact that *anēnu/anīnu* appears later from the point of chronological attestation can only be accounted for if they are considered to be a borrowing from Aramaic or from another Semitic language, if possible.[92]

1.6.6 Distribution of the words

The distribution of the suspected loanword is an important indicator in deciding the direction of borrowing.[93] When a word existing in Neo-Assyrian and Aramaic is suspected of being a loan, but the word is common in Aramaic, or is attested in most of its major dialects, but is not attested in the other dialects of Akkadian other than Neo-Assyrian, then the evidence points strongly to a borrowing from Aramaic.

If the word is only attested in one dialect of Aramaic, but has cognates with regular sound correspondences across the other West-Semitic languages, and at the same time is not attested in the other dialects of Akkadian other than Neo-Assyrian, then there is a good chance that the word is borrowed from Aramaic into Neo-Assyrian.

On the other hand, if the word is only found in Neo-Assyrian and a single dialect of Aramaic, the borrowing could be in either direction.

1.6.7 Criteria used in rejecting some previous proposals

A previous Aramaic loanword proposal can be rejected for one specific reason or a combination of different reasons. The criteria used in this study for rejecting some of the previously proposed Aramaic loanwords in Neo-Assyrian are as follows:

a) If there is attestation of the word in the Akkadian sources from the period before the first millennium B.C. This means that we have a precedent attested in the Akkadian textual sources from the periods prior to language contact between Akkadian and Aramaic i.e., in OAkk, OA, OB, MA and MB.[94]

b) If an Akkadian etymology is available, a loanword proposal is rejected, because then we have an Akkadian etymon as a source word.[95]

---

[92] See the discussion below s.v. *anēnu*; I.J. Gelb, "Notes on von Soden's Grammar of Akkadian," *BiOr* 11 (1955), p. 100, § 14a.

[93] Kaufman, AIA, p. 21.

[94] See von Soden, *Or* 35 (1966), p. 4.

[95] See Section 1.6.4. above.

c) When the Neo-Assyrian word in question is a "ghost word." This means that the word originated in error during the copying, analyzing or learning of the language, and does not actually exist in Neo-Assyrian.[96]

d) When the Aramaic word in question is a "ghost word." Likewise, this means that the word originated in error during the copying, analyzing or learning of the language, and it does not actually exist in Aramaic.

1.6.8 Utilizing later forms of Aramaic in this study

In order to identify Aramaic loanwords in Neo-Assyrian, we have to compare the lexicons of these two Semitic languages. In the first place, we have to compare the lexicons of Neo-Assyrian with that of Old and Official Aramaic, because these two stages of Aramaic were contemporaneous with Neo-Assyrian during the period of Neo-Assyrian and Aramaic language contact. In other words, we are expected to analyze and establish the relations between single Neo-Assyrian lexical items and similar Aramaic lexical items that occurred in the documentation of the same age.

Unfortunately, the textual material of Old and Official Aramaic is relatively small and its lexicon is far from extensive.[97] In fact many later languages/dialects of Aramaic are textually better attested and lexically richer than Old or Official Aramaic. Classical Syriac, for instance, is considered to be the best attested and richest as regards lexical inventory. Therefore, scholars take into consideration lexical data of the later Aramaic languages/dialects in their efforts to identify Aramaic loanwords in Neo-Assyrian and Neo- and Late-Babylonian. Von Soden, for instance, made use of later languages/dialects of Aramaic in his effort to identify Aramaic loanwords in Neo-Assyrian and Neo- and Late-Babylonian.[98] Abraham and Sokoloff state that they give only limited weight to the fact that the Aramaic language in the period under consideration is only poorly documented.[99]

Nevertheless, objections based on chronological considerations are expected to be voiced against utilizing Aramaic languages/dialects later than Old and Official Aramaic to identify loanwords in Neo- and Late-dialects of Akkadian. An example is Oppenheim's belief that the words *zakakātu* and *zukû* "glass or frit," are West-Semitic in origin and were borrowed into Akkadian, seeing that these words are "well known" in later Aramaic. On this, Mankowski writes: "The fact that the word was common in later Aramaic is of little weight in establishing the direction of the lexical borrowing."[100] Another example is Kutscher's criticism of von Soden's suggestion that the form of the NA word *ḫannīu*, "this," with the initial *ḫ*, is due to the influence of Aramaic *hānā* "this."[101] Kutscher points out

[96] For the term "ghost word," see n. 18 above.
[97] See von Soden, *Or* 35 (1966), pp. 1, 3.
[98] See von Soden, *Or* 35 (1966), pp. 1–20; idem, *Or* 37 (1968), pp. 261–271; idem, *Or* 46 (1977), pp. 183–197.
[99] See Abraham & Sokoloff, *Reassessment*, p. 23.
[100] Mankowski, ALBH, p. 53.
[101] See E.Y. Kutscher, "Aramaic," in T.A. Sebeok (ed.), *Current Trends in Linguistics*, 6. *Linguistics in South West Asia and North Africa* (The Hague 1970), p. 357.

that *hānā* "this," is not attested in Aramaic, but only in Syriac, and adds: "Therefore it is at least problematic whether the Neo-Assyrian (before 600 B.C.) *ḫanniu* owes its existence to the S[yriac] *hānā* (several hundred years later)."[102]

The fact is, however, that our knowledge of the vocabulary of Old and Official Aramaic is incomplete, and we only know a small fraction of all the words that existed in Old and Official Aramaic. This means that we will not be able, based on the lexical inventory of the Old and Official Aramaic available to us at the present time, to identify some Neo-Assyrian words that might have been borrowed from Aramaic. In an effort to overcome this obstacle, our study therefore also makes use of lexical data from the later forms of Aramaic, i.e., those languages/dialects that are subsequent to Old and Official Aramaic. This approach finds support in the internal reconstruction (IR)[103] method applied to the lexicon and semantic system of a (modern) language with no written records or known cognates. According to the internal reconstruction method, the characteristics of a language provide information about its past. The method involves the comparison of different forms found in the language under the assumption that they originated from a single regular form.

In our case, we assume that if a certain word is not attested in the extant textual material of Old and Official Aramaic, but it is widely distributed and attested in different Aramaic languages/dialects later than the Old and Official Aramaic, then it is very likely that the word in question existed in the period prior to that in which it is attested.[104] However, the lexical material obtained from the later languages/dialects of Aramaic should be treated with caution when identifying Aramaic loanwords in Neo-Assyrian. We must, for instance, take into consideration the possibility of innovation and development, such as neologism or semantic development, which might have occurred in the later dialects of Aramaic.

1.7 A short account of the developmental phases of Akkadian

Akkadian is the oldest attested member of Semitic languages known to us. It branched away from an assumed Proto-Semitic (PS) language earlier than its known sister languages. It is the language of the Akkadians, Assyrians and Babylonians of ancient Mesopotamia, which roughly corresponds to the territory of modern Iraq. The designation "Akkadian," which in cuneiform sources occurs as *akkadattu/akkadītu* in reference to the language, is derived from Akkade, the capital of king Sargon and his dynasty (ca. 2334–2150 B.C.) in southern Mesopotamia. The language has occasionally also been called *aššūrītu* "Assyrian," in both ancient and modern times. However, scholars now generally

[102] Ibid. See also Abraham & Sokoloff, *Reassessment*, p. 34:79. Cf. the discussion on the word *ḫannīu*, pp. 132ff below.

[103] Cf. L. Campbell, *Historical Linguistics: An Introduction* (Edinburgh 2004), pp. 122–183; W.P. Lehmann, *Historical Linguistics: An Introduction* (London 1994), pp. 162–174.

[104] Cf. Kaufman, AIA, p. 21.

use the term Akkadian to designate all forms of the Akkadian language, and restrict the other two terms to indicating its two main branches. It is not possible here to cover every aspect of the Akkadian language; rather the purpose is to give a short account of the history and stages of development of the language.[105]

During the third millennium B.C., in Mesopotamia, the speakers of Akkadian lived alongside the Sumerians. The latter spoke Sumerian, a language attested in texts from about 3000 B.C. The Sumerian language is not related to Semitic languages, and it has not been identified as genetically related to any other known language family. The Sumerian language and culture left an indelible imprint on the Akkadian language and culture. For instance, the cuneiform writing system invented by the Sumerians was borrowed by the speakers of Akkadian, being slightly modified and adapted to write Akkadian. Many of the cuneiform signs were originally pictographs. In addition, the cuneiform signs often have multiple sound values and the value of each sign used is determined by the context. The writing system consisted partly of syllabic signs such as *a*, *ab*, *bab*, *baba*, etc., and partly of word signs or logograms which bear certain meanings such as "king" or "old." The number of the cuneiform signs was reduced by ca. 2000 B.C. to about 600 signs.

A large number of all kinds of documents written in different dialects of Akkadian have been discovered. They include lexical lists in Akkadian and Sumerian; synonym lists; political, legal, economic and administrative documents; official and private letters; building inscriptions; royal and private dedicatory inscriptions; monumental texts both royal and private, such as funerary and votive inscriptions; edicts; memoranda; omen-texts; literary compositions in the form of magic spells and incantations; proverbs; love poetry and mythological poetry; wisdom literature; laments; hymns; and prayers.[106]

---

[105] For a historical development of Akkadian, see R.I. Caplice, "Languages (Akkadian)," in D.N. Freedman et al. (eds.), *The Anchor Bible Dictionary: Volume 4, K–N* (New York 1992), pp. 170–173; G. Rubio, "Falling Trees and Forking Tongues: On the place of Akkadian and Eblaite within Semitic," in L. Kogan (ed.), *Orientalia: Papers of the Oriental Institute, 3* (Moscow 2003), pp. 152–189; A. George, "Babylonian and Assyrian: A History of Akkadian," in J.N. Postgate (ed.), *Languages of Iraq, Ancient and Modern* ([London] 2007), pp. 31–71; R. Hasselbach, "The Affiliation of Sargonic Akkadian with Babylonian and Assyrian: New Insights Concerning the Internal Sub-Grouping of Akkadian," *JSS* 52 (2007): 21–43; B. Kouwenberg, "Akkadian in General," in S. Weninger (ed.), *The Semitic Languages: An International Handbook* (Berlin 2011), pp. 330–340. For linguistic characteristics of Akkadian, see G. Bergstässer, *Introduction to the Semitic Languages: Text Specimens and Grammatical Sketches* (Winona Lake 1983), pp. 25–35; G. Buccellati, "Akkadian," in R. Hetzron (ed.), *The Semitic Languages* (London 1997), pp. 69–99; M.P. Streck, "Babylonian and Assyrian," in S. Weninger (ed.), *The Semitic Languages: An International Handbook* (Berlin 2011), pp. 359–396; idem, "Akkadisch," in M.P. Streck (ed.), *Sprachen des Alten Orients* (Darmstadt 2021), pp. 65–102; J. Huehnergard & C. Woods, "Akkadian and Eblaite," in R.D. Woodard (ed.), *The Ancient Languages of Mesopotamia, Egypt, and Aksum* (Cambridge 2008), pp. 83–152. J.-P. Vita (ed.), *History of the Akkadian Language. Vol. 1: Linguistic Background and Early Periods. Vol 2: The Second and First Millennia BCE. Afterlife.* Handbook of Oriental Studies, Vol. 152/2. Leiden-Boston: Brill, 2021.

[106] For a full survey of Akkadian texts and discussions of texts, see R. Borger, *Handbuch der Keilschriftliteratur*, 3 vols., (Berlin 1967–1975), which includes the bibliography of all Akkadian and Sumerian texts published in journals and monographs through the end of 1973. Further texts and discussions of texts published since 1973 appear in the "Register Assyriologie" of the periodical *Archiv für Orientforschung* (*AfO*), as well as in the annual "Keilschriftbibliographie" in the journal *Orientalia* (*Or*).

These records were mostly written on clay tablets which withstood destruction, unlike documents written on perishable material such as papyrus and parchment. For this reason and because of its abundance, the textual documentation written in Akkadian is considered to be the most extensive among any ancient Semitic language. The significance of the Akkadian language for comparative Semitic studies and for the knowledge of languages in general has been amply recognized in recent years.

Akkadian is closely related to Eblaite, the language of the ancient Syrian city of Ebla, which, according to some scholars, might be classified as an early dialect or sub-branch of Akkadian.[107] Both are usually classified as East Semitic. They are contrasted to all the other members of the family, which together form the West-Semitic group. The latter is divided in turn into two main subgroups, namely South Semitic, which consists of South Arabian and Ethiopian (Ge'ez and Amharic), and Central Semitic, which in turn is divided into two subgroups, namely North Arabian and Northwest Semitic. The latter includes Ugaritic, Canaanite (Hebrew and Phoenician), and Aramaic.[108] The most salient feature of the Semitic languages, in comparison with other inflected languages, is that the meanings of words are bound up with a "root," usually consisting of three, though less often two or four, consonantal phonemes or "radicals." Each root, on the other hand, has either a short or a long root vowel. The most conspicuous feature of Akkadian vis-à-vis other Semitic languages is its reduced phonemic inventory, which is probably due to Sumerian influence. In addition, Akkadian displays subject–object–verb (SOV) word order, again probably due to Sumerian substratum influence, whereas the usual Semitic word order is either verb–subject–object (VSO) or subject–verb–object (SVO).

Texts written entirely in Akkadian are attested from ca. 2350 B.C. The latest known datable Akkadian text comes from around 75 A.D., and consists of an astronomical almanac.[109] During its long history of attestation, it was natural for the Akkadian language to undergo changes and evolve. Accordingly, modern scholars generally divide the Akkadian language in its homeland into two major branches, Assyrian and Babylonian.[110] The two major branches and their different

---

[107] See M. Krebernik, "The Linguistic Classification of Eblaite: Methods, Problems, and Results," in J.S. Cooper & G.M. Schwartz (eds.), *The Study of the Ancient Near East in the Twenty-First Century: The William Foxwell Albright Centennial Conference* (Winona Lake 1996), pp. 233–249; J. Huehnergard & C. Woods, "Akkadian and Eblaite," in R.D. Woodard (ed.), *The Ancient Languages of Mesopotamia, Egypt, and Aksum* (Cambridge 2008), pp. 83–152. Cf. J. Tropper, "Eblaitisch und die Klassifikation der semitischen Sprachen," in G.J. Selz (ed.), *Festschrift für Burkhart Kienast zu seinem 70. Geburtstage dargebracht von Freunden, Schülern und Kollegen* (Münster 2003), pp. 647–657. For a description of the Eblaite and Sargonic Akkadian within the history of the Akkadian language, see M.P. Streck, "Eblaite and Old Akkadian," in S. Weninger (ed.), *The Semitic Languages: An International Handbook* (Berlin 2011), pp. 340–359.

[108] Based on the evidence available on Semitic languages, scholars have been led to different classifications of the Semitic languages. See J. Huehnergard, "Semitic Languages," in J.M. Sasson et al. (eds.), *Civilizations of the Ancient Near Easet* (Massachusetts 2006), pp. 2117–2134; idem, "Features of Central Semitic," in A. Gianto (ed.), *Biblical and Oriental Essays in Memory of William L. Moran* (Rome 2005), pp. 155–203.

[109] See M.J. Geller, "The last Wedge," *ZA* 87 (1997), p. 45.

[110] For the understanding that neither the Babylonian nor the Assyrian dialect is a direct, lineal descendant of Old Akkadian, see W. Sommerfeld, "Bemerkungen zur Dialektgliederung

stages distinguish themselves linguistically from each other and from Old Akkadian by a number of phonological, morphological and lexical differences.[111] Scholars distinguish different stages of the development of Akkadian as follows:

Old Akkadian (OAkk.) ca. 2400–2000 B.C.: The oldest stage of the Akkadian language is attested in personal names occurring in Old Sumerian texts of the Fara period, ca. 2600 B.C.[112] Texts written entirely in OAkk are only available from the time of the dynasty of Akkad (ca. 2350–2150 B.C.).[113] The writing system in this period was not yet able to express the Akkadian phonemes, as it would be modified to do later. For instance, distinguishing graphically between initially occurring homorganic voiced and voiceless stops, such as in the syllables *da*, *ta* and *ṭa*, was not yet possible because the same sign was used to express these syllables. Neither consonant doubling nor vowel length was normally expressed, and the aleph sign that later was used to represent the glottal stop in combination with a vowel was not yet developed. The importance of the Old Akkadian texts for historical linguistics as well as for comparative Semitic studies lies in the fact that they reflect early phonological and morphological distinctions of Akkadian that were lost in later periods; for example, the case endings generally include a final *-m* denoting the so-called "mimation." The original Semitic diphthong *ai* was monophthongized and became *ē*, i.e., **baitum* > *bētum* "house," and *au* became *ū*, i.e., **mautum* > *mūtum* "death." Further distinctive features of Old Akkadian that later would no longer be productive are the use of the dual declension and the still uncontracted vowels, which would later undergo the process of contraction.[114] However, because of the relatively small size of the Old Akkadian corpus, many grammatical forms remain so far unattested.

Old Babylonian (OB) ca. 2000–1500 B.C.: This dialect is well attested, especially for the language of the laws of Hammurabi (1792–1750 B.C.). During the period of Hammurabi, and immediately before and after, a careful chancery style of writing Akkadian was established which left a lasting impression on the writing of royal and private inscriptions. Some Old Babylonian literary texts

Altakkadisch, Assyrisch und Babylonisch," in G.J. Selz, (ed.), *Festschrift für Burkhart Kienast: zu seinem 70. Geburtstage dargebracht von Freunden, Schülern und Kollegen* (Münster 2003), pp. 569–586; idem, *Untersuchungen zum Altakkadischen* (unpublished Habilitation, Münster 1987).

[111] See GAG § 188–196, for the different characteristics of the main dialects of Akkadian.

[112] For an opinion on the place of Ur III Akkadian and its relationship with Old Akkadian, see A. George, "Babylonian and Assyrian: A History of Akkadian," in J.N. Postgate (ed.), *Languages of Iraq, Ancient and Modern* ([London] 2007), p. 42. For the understanding that Ur III Akkadian belongs to and represents an early level of the linguistic development of the Babylonian dialect of Akkadian, cf. M. Hilgert, *Akkadisch in der Ur III–Zeit* (Münster 2002); idem, "New Perspectives in the Study of Third Millennium Akkadian," *Cuneiform Digital Library Journal* 4 (2003). Online 15/09/2022:
https://cdli.ucla.edu/file/publications/cdlj2003_004.pdf

[113] See R.I. Caplice, "Languages (Akkadian)," in D.N. Freedman et al. (eds.), *The Anchor Bible Dictionary: Volume 4, K–N* (New York 1992), p. 171.

[114] For the grammar of Old Akkadian, see I. Gelb, *Old Akkadian Writing and Grammar* (Chicago 1961); R. Hasselbach, *Sargonic Akkadian: A Historical and Comparative Study of the Syllabic Texts* (Wiesbaden 2005).

were composed in the so-called "hymn-epic dialect,"[115] which was to remain in use as the literary standard. Old Babylonian is generally considered the classical state of the Akkadian language. Three sub-dialects can be distinguished within Old Babylonian, namely the dialects of North and South Babylonian and the dialect of Mari.

The most salient features of Old Babylonian include the general preference for syllabic writing over logographic writing, and the fact that many signs that were in active use in Old Akkadian were no longer used. Double consonants were usually written out and new means were developed to represent the consonant aleph. The case endings generally include a final *-m*, as in Old Akkadian, denoting the so-called "mimation," which in fact was nonfunctional and was dropped after the Old Babylonian period. The original Semitic diphthong *ai* was monophthongized as *ī*, i.e., **baitum* > *bītum* "house," and *au* became *ū*, i.e., **mautum* > *mūtum* "death."

Old Assyrian (OA) ca. 2000–1500 B.C.: Apart from a few royal inscriptions we know this dialect of Akkadian mainly from business documents, letters, and legal and economic documents which concern the business activities of Assyrian merchant colonies in eastern part of Anatolia, particularly from the site of Kanesh, modern Kültepe. Notably, the Old Assyrian dialect exhibits closer ties to Old Akkadian than does the Old Babylonian. Its writing system has a more limited inventory of signs than that of Old Babylonian and is more archaic in its external form. As in Old Akkadian, the initial homorganic voiced and voiceless stops are still represented by the same sign. A distinctive characteristic of the Assyrian dialect in all periods is the so-called Assyrian vowel harmony, whereby a short *a* in an open unstressed syllable is assimilated to the vowel of the following syllable. For example, the Babylonian word *iṣbatū* "they seized," is written in Assyrian *iṣbutū*.[116] The original Semitic diphthong *ai* was monophthongized as *ē*, i.e., **baitum* > *bētum* "house," and *au* became *ū*, i.e., **mautum* > *mūtum* "death."

Middle Babylonian (MB) ca. 1500–1000 B.C.: Middle Babylonian is the dialect of Akkadian of the Kassite dominated Babylonia. It is somewhat sparsely attested compared with its predecessor and successors. It is for instance attested in inscribed boundary stones known as *kudurru*, which recorded the land granted by the king to his vassals. A salient feature of this dialect is its consonantal shifts; for instance, *š* before a dental becomes *l*, as in *ištēn* > *iltēn* "one"; in addition, the mimation was lost.[117]

In this period, Akkadian, particularly in its Babylonian form, was employed in international communications as a *lingua franca*. Texts written in Akkadian have been found in peripheral areas outside Mesopotamia in many sites such as Alalakh (Tell Açana); Hattusas, the capital of the Hittite empire (modern

[115] See W. von Soden, "Der hymnisch-epische Dialekt des Akkadischen," *ZA* 40 and 41 (1931–1933), pp. 163–227 and 90–183; B.R.M. Groneberg, *Untersuchungen zum hymnisch-epischen Dialekt der altbabylonischen literarischen Texte* (Münster 1971).

[116] A thorough description of Old Assyrian is provided by K. Hecker, *Grammatik der Kültepe-Texte* (Rome 1968).

[117] For a detailed study of Middle Babylonian, see J. Aro, *Studien zur mittelbabylonischen Grammatik* (Helsinki 1955).

Boghazköy) in Turkey; Ugarit (Ras Shamra), Emar (Tell Meskeneh) and Qatna (Tell al-Mishrifeh) in modern Syria; the Egyptian royal archives of El-Amarna (ancient Akhetaten); the Elamite capital Susa; and the Hurrian center Nuzi near modern Kirkuk. All these texts betray the influences of the scribes' native languages.[118]

Middle Assyrian (MA) ca. 1500–1000 B.C.: This dialect is attested in a variety of genres, which include a set of harem decrees, tablets containing a Middle Assyrian law code, unique palace edicts that regulated conduct at the Assyrian court, and the Assyrian coronation ritual, all unearthed in the city of Assur. Distinctive characteristics of this dialect include consonantal shifts paralleling those of Middle Babylonian (for instance, *š* before a dental becomes *l*, as in *ištēn* > *iltēn* "one") and loss of mimation. In contrast to Middle Babylonian, Middle Assyrian reflects the so-called Assyrian vowel harmony, and the initial *wa-* becomes *u-*. Many vowels are still uncontracted; in addition *qt* becomes *qṭ*.[119]

Neo-Babylonian (NB) ca. 1000–600 B.C.: This was the vernacular form of the southern dialect of Akkadian. It occurs mainly in letters, contracts, and economic, business and legal documents.[120] Monumental and literary texts were written in Standard Babylonian (SB). After the expansion of Assyrian hegemony over Babylonia and the destruction of Babylon by Sennacherib in 689 B.C., the Neo-Babylonian dialect was also employed at the imperial Assyrian court.[121] As in Assyria, during this period Aramaic started to gain a foothold in Babylonia and began replacing Akkadian as the vernacular language. Characteristic of NB is the confusion of the short-vowel endings, probably due to the influence of Aramaic.[122] Some changes in spelling conventions of NB are ascribed to the influence of Aramaic writing practices.[123]

Neo-Assyrian (NA) ca. 900–600 B.C.:[124] Around 900 B.C., the Assyrian branch of Akkadian reached the stage that is now designated as Neo-Assyrian.

---

[118] For further reading, see W.H. van Soldt, "Akkadian as a Diplomatic Language," in S. Weninger (ed.), *The Semitic Languages: An International Handbook* (Berlin 2011), pp. 405–415; D. Sivan, *Grammatical Analysis and Glossary of the Northwest Semitic Vocables in Akkadian Texts of the 15th–13th C.B.C. from Canaan and Syria* (Kevelaer 1984); J. Huehnergard, Review of "Northwest Semitic Vocabulary in Akkadian Texts," by D. Sivan, *JAOS* 107 (1987), pp. 713–725. For references to works on different dialects of peripheral Akkadian, see A. George, "Babylonian and Assyrian: A History of Akkadian," in J.N. Postgate (ed.), *Languages of Iraq, Ancient and Modern* ([London] 2007), pp. 51–54.

[119] For a detailed study of Middle Assyrian grammar, see W. Mayer, *Untersuchungen zur Grammatik des Mittelassyrischen* (Neukirchen-Vluyn 1971).

[120] For a study on an individual aspect of Neo-Babylonian, see M. Dietrich, "Untersuchungen zur Grammatik des Neubabylonischen. I. Die neubabylonischen Subjunktionen," in W. Röllig & M. Dietrich (eds.), *Lišān mitḫurti: Festschrift Wolfram Freiherr von Soden zum 19.4.1968 gewidmet von Schülern und Mitarbeitern* (Neukirchen-Vluyn 1969), pp. 65–99.

[121] The language of the Neo-Babylonian letters from Nineveh has been studied in N.R. Woodington, *A Grammar of the Neo-Babylonian Letters of the Kuyunjik Collection* (Ann Arbor 1985); J.M.C.T. Vaan, de *"Ich bin ein Schwertklinge des Königs," die Sprache des Bēl-ibni* (Kevelaer 1995).

[122] See GAG § 192.

[123] See M.P. Streck, "Keilschrift und Alphabet," in D. Borchers et al. (eds.), *Hieroglyphen – Alphabete – Schriftreformen. Studien zu Multiliteralismus, Schriftwechsel und Orthographieneuregelungen* (Göttingen 2001), pp. 77–97.

[124] For a bibliography of scholarly literature on Neo-Assyrian philology including monographs, articles and reviews dealing with Neo-Assyrian language and texts, see J. Hämeen-Anttila, "Bibliography of Neo-Assyrian (Post-War Period)," *SAAB* 1 (1987), pp. 73–92; K. Deller,

However, evidence from Assyrian provincial centers shows that the development of Middle Assyrian into Neo-Assyrian had already begun in the 11th century B.C.[125] Linguistic features anticipating Neo-Assyrian grammar and spelling are found in heavily Assyrianized Babylonian inscriptions belonging to Ashur-ketti-leshir, who was king of Mari and a vassal of Tiglath-pileser I (1115–1077 B.C.).[126] From the same period a small archive of legal documents was unearthed at Giricano (ancient Dunnu-ša-Uzibi), located on the upper Tigris in south-eastern Turkey, and the language of the extant documents reveals a transitional dialect, part of which is already in Neo-Assyrian.[127]

The Neo-Assyrian texts come primarily from public archives and libraries excavated in Assyrian palaces, temples and private houses, and belong to the Neo-Assyrian period extending from ca. 900 B.C. to the end of the Assyrian Empire, ca. 600 B.C. However, texts written in this language stem overwhelmingly from the archives of the great institutions of state in the royal capitals Nineveh and Calah/Nimrud. The language is attested largely in letters; imperial, legal and administrative records; royal grants and decrees; officials' reports, particularly from astrologers and diviners; and oracular queries concerning state affairs. It was also used in treaties and loyalty oaths, and occasionally in literary compositions such as court poetry. Texts written in Neo-Assyrian are preserved in especially great numbers from the Sargonid era, particularly the period 721 to 645 B.C. Contemporary literary texts were composed in Standard Babylonian (SB). Even the Assyrian royal inscriptions of this period were written in Standard Babylonian except for a very few of Ashurnasirpal II (883–859 B.C.), from whose time stems the earliest known text written in the Neo-Assyrian language and script.[128] This is an edict in which Ashurnasirpal II appoints Nergal-āpil-kūmū'a to supervise the transfer of the Assyrian capital from Assur to Calah.[129] The latest material written in Neo-Assyrian comes shortly after the fall of Nineveh and the demise of the imperial Assyrian power. It consists of some deeds of sale dated to the 2nd and 5th years

---

"Bibliography of Neo-Assyrian – 1988 and Updates," *SAAB* 2 (1988), pp. 129–135; R. Mattila & K. Radner, "A Bibliography of Neo-Assyrian Studies (1988–1997)," *SAAB* 11 (1997), pp. 115–137; M. Luukko & S. Gaspa, "A Bibliography of Neo-Assyrian Studies (1998–2006)," *SAAB* 17 (2008), pp. 189–257; S. Gaspa, "A Bibliography of Neo-Assyrian Studies (2007–2012)," *SAAB* 19 (2011–2012), pp. 279–328. F.M. Fales, "Neo-Assyrian," in J.-P. Vita (ed.), *History of the Akkadian Language, Vol. 2, The Second and First Millennia BCE Afterlife* (Leiden 2021), pp. 1347–1395. For archaeological details on the majority of the excavation sites and the locations where the Neo-Assyrian archives and libraries were unearthed, and references to archaeological literature, see below, n. 137.

[125] For a study of the evolution of Middle Assyrian to Neo-Assyrian, see J.N. Postgate, "Middle Assyrian to Neo-Assyrian: The Nature of the Shift," in H. Waetzoldt & H. Hauptmann (eds.), *Assyrien im Wandel der Zeiten* (Heidelberg 1997), pp. 159–168.

[126] See A. George, "Babylonian and Assyrian: A History of Akkadian," in J.N. Postgate (ed.), *Languages of Iraq, Ancient and Modern* ([London] 2007), pp. 54f.

[127] See K. Radner, *Das mittelassyrische Tontafelarchiv von Giricano Dunnu-ša-Uzibi* (Turnhout 2004).

[128] See K. Rander, PNA 1/I, p. xii, n. 1. See also L. Kataja & R. Whiting, SAA XII 82 and 83. For a previous edition of SAA XII 82 and 83, see K. Deller & A.R. Millard, "Die Bestallungsurkunde des Nergal-āpil-kūmūja von Kalḫu," *BaM* 24 (1993): 217–242.

[129] The document was first published by Deller & Millard, ibid. For a re-edition of the document, see SAA XII 82, 83–84.

of the reign of the Neo-Babylonian king Nebuchadnezzar II (604–562 B.C.), which stem from the provincial capital Dur-Katlimmu (modern Tell Šēḫ Ḥamad), on the river Ḫābūr in northeast Syria,[130] as well as small group of documents related to the recording and distribution of provisions, which was found in the remains of an administrative archive from Nebuchadnezzar's South Palace in Babylon and is dated to the years 3–9 (or 3–6?) of the reign of Nebuchadnezzar.[131] Some of the linguistic features that characterize Neo-Assyrian are as follows. Different vowels next to each other are now often contracted, but *ia*, *iu* and *ua* are still very often uncontracted. The consonantal combination *lt* (whether primarily or developed secondarily from *št*) becomes *ss*, for instance *aštapar* > *altapar* > *assapar* "I have sent."[132] In addition, *mt* becomes *nt* or *tt*. Probably under the influence of Aramaic, the preposition *ana* is often used as *nota accusativi*.[133]

Until now Neo-Assyrian texts have been unearthed at 28 different sites (see fig. 1 below). The majority of the texts were excavated in the Assyrian heartland, the northern part of today's Iraq, in the ancient cities and towns of Aššūr (Qalʿat Sherqat), Nīnua (Kuyunjik and Nabi Yunus), Kalḫu (Calah/Nimrud), Dūr-Šarrukēn (Khorsabad), Imgur-Ellil (Balawat), Šibanība (Tell Billa), Tarbīṣu (Sharif Khan), Bēt-Adad-erība (Tell Baqāq 2), and Zamaḫâ (Tell al-Rimaḥ). Other Neo-Assyrian texts were unearthed in the western provinces of the Neo-Assyrian Empire in the sites of Ḫuzīrīna (Sultantepe), Gargamīs (Carchemish), Sam'al (Zinçirli), Tarzi (Tarsus), Gaziantep, Tušḫan (Ziyāret Tepe), Eğriköy (in the vicinity of Yeşil Hisar near Kayseri),[134] the surroundings of Mardin (Şariza, Erzen and Nabula, i.e., modern Girnavaz), Kullanīa (Tell Tayinat), and Kazane Höyük in the vicinity of Urfa, all situated in Turkey, as well as at sites located in Syria such as Dūr-Katlimmu (Tall Šēḫ Ḥamad), Gūzāna (Tell Ḥalaf), Til-Barsip/Tarbusībi (Tell Aḥmar), Burmar'īna (Tell Shiukh Fawqāni), Kār-Aššūrnāṣirapli (Tell Masaikh), Rasm et-Tanjara (Syrian Tell in the Ghāb), and Ma'allanāte.[135] From the State of Israel, Neo-Assyrian texts have been found in Gazru (Gezer, Gazara), Sāmirīna (Samaria), and Tel Hadid.[136]

---

[130] These documents are now published jointly by J.A. Brinkman, F.M. Fales, H. Kühne, J.N. Postgate & W. Röllig, in *SAAB* 7 (1993), pp. 75–150.

[131] See O. Pedersén, "Neo-Assyrian Texts from Nebuchadnezzar's Babylon: A Preliminary Report," in M. Luukko et al. (eds.), *Of God(s), Trees, Kings, and Scholars: Neo-Assyrian and Related Studies in Honour of Simo Parpola* (Helsinki 2009), pp. 193–199.

[132] For grammatical studies of Neo-Assyrian, see S. Ylvisaker, *Zur babylonischen und assyrischen Grammatik, eine Untersuchung auf Grund der Briefe aus der Sargonidenzeit* (Leipzig 1912); K. Deller, *Lautlehre des Neuassyrischen* (Unpublished Ph.D. dissertation, Wien 1959); J. Hämeen-Anttila, *A Sketch of Neo-Assyrian Grammar* (Helsinki 2000); M. Luukko, *Grammatical Variation in Neo-Assyrian* (Helsinki 2004). For some characteristics of Neo-Assyrian, see GAG § 196.

[133] See above, p. 7 and n. 40.

[134] This is a Neo-Assyrian document of sale of fields found at Eğriköy near Yeşil Hisar, Kayseri, cited in V. Donbaz, "Some Neo-Assyrian Contracts from Girnavaz and Vicinity," *SAAB* 2 (1988), p. 6.

[135] The site of Ma'allanāte (Aramaic *m'lnh*), has not yet been identified, but the name of this city comes from an archive of clay tablets which was bought at the antiquities market, and according to the texts the archive originates from Ma'allanāte. The approximate location of the city is between Harran (Ḥarrānu) and Gozan (Gūzāna), probably in the Balikh region. See O. Pedersén, *Archives and Libraries in the Ancient Near East 1500–300 B.C.* (Bethesda 1998), p. 181; K. Radner, *Die neuassyrischen Privatrechtsurkunden als Quelle für Mensch und Umwelt* (Helsinki 1997), pp. 14f;

Almost all of the extant texts are written on clay tablets in cuneiform script and many are dated according to the eponym dating system, specifically the *limmu*-system, which makes it possible for modern scholars to assign a rather reliable dating to the texts. At present, the large majority of the Neo-Assyrian texts are published both in copy and reliable text editions.[137]

Standard Babylonian (SB) ca. 1500–600 B.C.: After the downfall of the Hammurabi dynasty (ca. 1995 B.C.), and during the Kassite period, Old Babylonian was considered to be the classical form of the Akkadian language, and Babylonian and Assyrian scribes began to compose texts in a new, standardized literary dialect, the so-called Standard Babylonian (in German *jungbabylonisch* (jB)), which was modeled on the Old Babylonian literary language. In contrast with Old Babylonian, Standard Babylonian exhibits the loss of mimation in noun and pronoun. The contraction of the vowel sequences *ia*, *ea* is normal, for example *qibiam* > *qibâ* "say (m. sg.) to me"; *išmeā* > *išmâ* "they (f. pl.) heard." As for *š* it usually appears as *l* before the dentals *d*, *t* and *ṭ*. The initial *w* is lost, i.e., OB *wardum* > SB *ardu* "male slave."[138] Standard Babylonian continued to be the language of almost all literary works and royal inscriptions until the end of the Akkadian literary production. The literature of the Neo-Babylonian and Late-Babylonian periods, as well as a great majority of the Assyrian royal inscriptions, are written in Standard Babylonian. Other compositions in Standard Babylonian include hymns and poetic prayers, wisdom literature, omens, and exorcistic texts. The texts written in Standard Babylonian

---

F.M. Fales, "The Use and Function of Aramaic Tablets," in G. Bunnens (ed.), *Essays on Syria in the Iron Age* (Louvain 2000), p. 111.

[136] For an Atlas of the Near East in the Neo-Assyrian period with a gazetteer and Overview Maps (1:2,000,000 scale) and Detail Maps (1:1,000,000 scale), see S. Parpola & M. Porter, *The Helsinki Atlas of the Near East in the Neo-Assyrian Period* (Helsinki 2001). The *Tübinger Atlas des Vorderen Orients* contains two maps of the Neo-Assyrian Empire: K. Kessler, "Assyria until 800 B.C." *TAVO* B IV 10 (1987) at a scale of 1:2,000,000 as well as K. Kessler, "The Neoassyrian Empire (720–612 B.C.) and the Neobabylonian Empire (612–539 B.C.)" *TAVO* B IV 13 (1991) at a scale of 1:4,000,000.

[137] For archaeological details on the majority of the excavation sites and the locations where the Neo-Assyrian archives and libraries were unearthed, and references to archaeological literature, see O. Pedersén, *Archives and Libraries in the Ancient Near East 1500–300 B.C.* (Bethesda 1998), pp. 130–181. See also K. Radner, "Schreiberkonventionen im assyrischen Reich: Sprachen und Schriftsysteme," in J. Renger (ed.), *Assur – Gott, Stadt und Land: 5. Internationales Colloquium der Deutschen Orient-Gesellschaft 18. – 21. Februar 2004 in Berlin* (Wiesbaden 2011), p. 394 n. 32 and p. 395, map (Abb. 4); idem, "An Assyrian View on the Medes," in G.B. Lanfranchi et al. (eds.), *Continuity of Empire (?): Assyria, Media, Persia* (Padova 2003), p. 53, n. 43. Note that the excavation site number 29 in Radner's map (Abb. 4) refers to *Choga Gavaneh*, the ancient tell of Islamabad near Kermanshah in Iran, but should be discarded and not considered among the find-spot of Neo-Assyrian texts because the tablets and fragments from that site are Old Babylonian in date. See G. Beckman, Review of "*Assur – Gott, Stadt und Land: 5. Internationales Colloquium der Deutschen Orient-Gesellschaft 18.–21. Februar 2004 in Berlin* (Wiesbaden 2011), by J. Renger, *JAOS* 132 (2012), p. 168. For the number of excavation sites of the Neo-Assyrian legal texts and references to the edited Neo-Assyrian texts for each site, see K. Radner, *Die neuassyrischen Privatrechtsurkunden als Quelle für Mensch und Umwelt* (Helsinki 1997), pp. 4–18. For a bibliography of scholarly literature on Neo-Assyrian philology including monographs, articles and reviews dealing with Neo-Assyrian language and texts, see above, n. 124.

[138] For grammatical features of Standard Babylonian, see GAG § 191; J. Huehnergard, *A Grammar of Akkadian* (Atlanta 1997), pp. 595–598. The standard treatment of Standard Babylonian is by E. Reiner, *A Linguistic Analysis of Akkadian* (The Hague 1966).

increase markedly in number in the 8th and 7th centuries B.C. Assurbanipal library at Nineveh is a rich source of literature written in Standard Babylonian in particular from about 625 B.C. Important literary works such as the creation epic *Enūma eliš* and the longer and later version of Gilgamesh epic are written in Standard Babylonian, as are other narrative poems such as Anzû, Atram-hasis, and Etana. Although this dialect is quite distinct from the other contemporary dialects, i.e., Neo-Assyrian, Neo-Babylonian and Late-Babylonian, language patterns of these dialects frequently intruded and influenced Standard Babylonian.

Late-Babylonian (LB) ca. 600 B.C.–A.D. 70:[139] There is no consensus among scholars concerning when this stage of Babylonian distinguished itself from Neo-Babylonian. However, the Babylonian language written during the period of Alexander the Great and his successors, as well as during the reign of the Seleucid kings and the Parthian dynasty of Iran, differs from the 7th-century language, for which reason it is designated by scholars as Late-Babylonian.[140] It is preserved largely in administrative records from Babylon which continued to be in use as late as the early 1st century B.C. From the Hellenistic period, the majority of the extant texts have astronomical content.

---

[139] See a sketch of historical development of Akkadian, in G. Buccellati, *A Structural Grammar of Babylonian* (Wiesbaden 1996), pp. 1f. For a study of this dialect, see M.P. Streck, *Zahl und Zeit: Grammatik der Numeralia und des Verbalsystems im Spätbabylonischen* (Groningen 1995).

[140] See A. George, "Babylonian and Assyrian: A History of Akkadian," in J.N. Postgate (ed.), *Languages of Iraq, Ancient and Modern* ([London] 2007), p. 61.

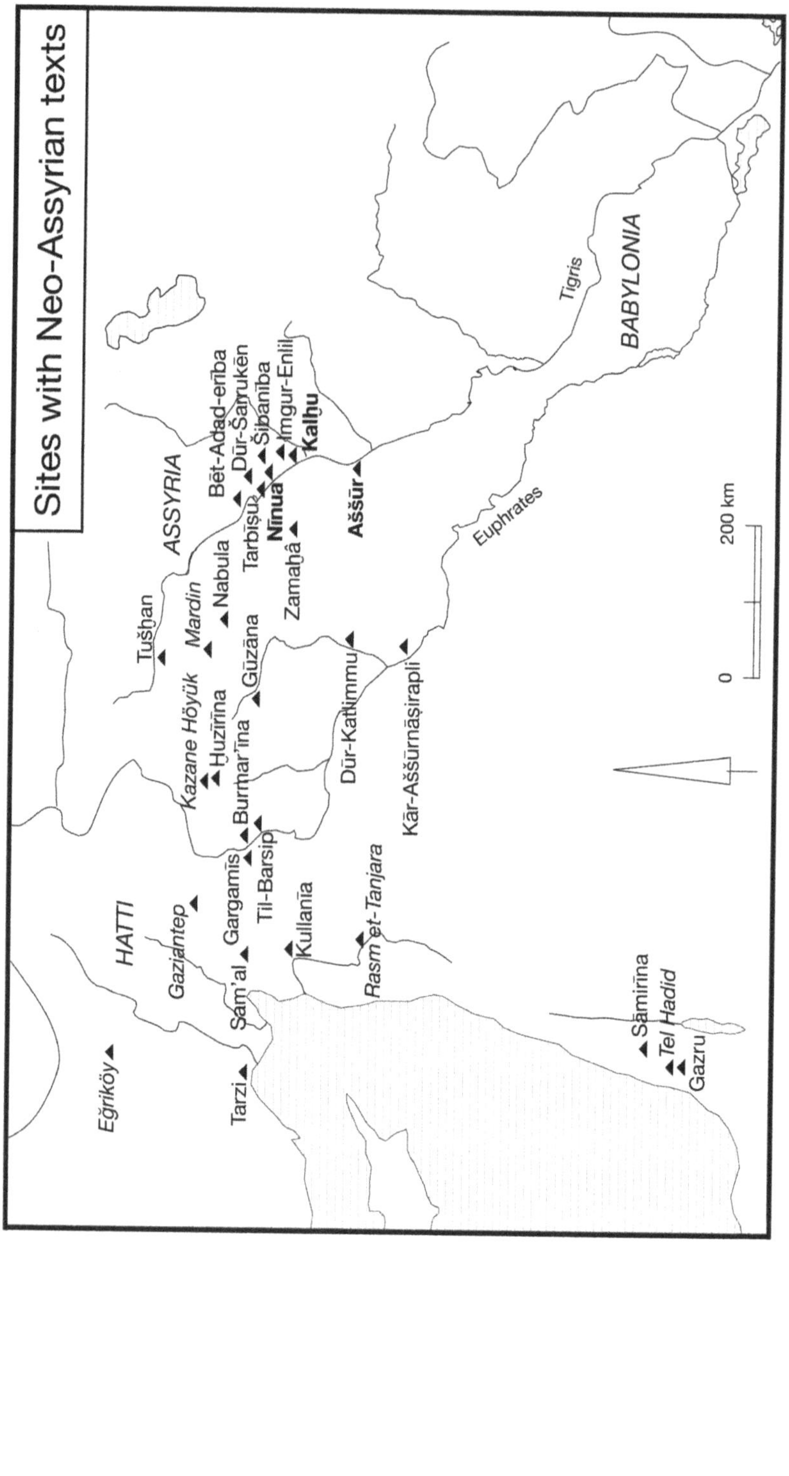

Figure 1. A map of the excavation sites with Neo-Assyrian texts.

1.8 A short account of the developmental phases of Aramaic

Aramaic belongs to what is usually called the Northwest Semitic subfamily. Besides Aramaic, this includes Hebrew, Ugaritic, Phoenician, Moabite, Ammonite and Edomite. Since the mid 1970s, however, following Hetzron's classification, [141] which was subsequently modified by other scholars, the Northwest Semitic languages have been considered to be a subgroup of Central Semitic, which also includes Arabic.[142] Central Semitic, in turn, is regarded as a branch of West-Semitic.[143] Aramaic is the best- and longest-attested member of the Northwest Semitic subfamily. It developed separately from its cognate languages and is first attested in the old Aramaic inscriptions from the early 9th century B.C., which mostly come from the independent Aramean city-states in Syria. The inscriptions were written in the Phoenician alphabet script, which the Arameans borrowed and slightly improved to suit their own language.

The extant Aramaic textual material is written on stone, leather, papyrus, ostracon, or is incised or written in ink on clay tablets. The textual material consists of commemorative and dedicatory inscriptions, treaties, letters, contracts, official documents, seals, bills and legends written on weights.

However, from ca. 800 B.C. Aramaic became alongside Akkadian, the language of administration of the Neo-Assyrian empire. Later, it became the language of administration of the Neo-Babylonian empire as well. During the Achaemenid Persian empire, after Cyrus II conquered Babylon in 539 B.C., Aramaic became the main vehicle of communication in the empire.

The history of the developmental phases of Aramaic is somewhat problematic, because there is no generally accepted division of the different stages of the language. Nevertheless, the phases presented below are, for the most part, based on Kaufman's classification which better suits the purpose of our discussion, especially because it is adopted by the Comprehensive Aramaic Lexicon (CAL),[144] which is frequently cited below for extracting and verifying Aramaic lexical data. The different Aramaic dialects are divided into several periods and groups based on both chronology and geography as follows: [145]

---

[141] See R. Hetzron, "Two Principles of Genetic Reconstruction," *Lingua* 38 (1976), pp. 89–108.

[142] See J. Huehnergard, "Features of Central Semitic," in A. Gianto (ed.), *Biblical and Oriental Essays in Memory of William L. Moran* (Rome 2005), pp. 155–203.

[143] See Huehnergard, ibid., p. 162, fig. 3.

[144] See S.A. Kaufman, "Aramaic," in D.N. Freedman et al. (eds.), *The Anchor Bible Dictionary,* vol. 4, K–N (New York 1992), pp. 173–178; idem, "Aramaic," in R. Hetzron (ed.), *The Semitic Languages* (London 1997), pp. 114–130; idem, "The Comprehensive Aramaic Lexicon Project and Twenty-First Century Aramaic Lexicography: Status and Prospects," in H. Gzella & M.L. Folmer (eds.), *Aramaic in its Historical and Linguistic Setting* (Wiesbaden 2008), pp. 353–371. See also CAL.

[145] For further scholarly literature on history of the development of Aramaic, see J.C. Greenfield, "The Dialects of Early Aramaic," *JNES* 37 (1978), pp. 93–99; idem, "Aramaic and Its Dialects," in H.H. Paper (ed.), *Jewish Languages: Theme and Variations, Proceedings of Regional Conferences of the Association for Jewish Studies Held at The University of Michigan and New York University in March–April 1975* (Cambridge 1978), pp. 29–43; J.A. Fitzmyer, "The Phases of the Aramaic Language," in J.A. Fitzmyer (ed.), *A Wandering Aramean: Collected Aramaic Essays* (Chico 1979), pp. 57–84; K. Beyer, *The Aramaic Language: Its Distribution and Subdivisions* (Göttingen 1986); J. Huehnergard, "What is Aramaic," *ARAM* 7 (1995), pp. 261–282; M.L. Folmer, *The Aramaic*

Old Aramaic (OAram.), ca. 900–600 B.C.: The first extant Aramaic texts come from the early first millennium B.C. They consist mainly of royal inscriptions connected to different Aramean city-states. The textual corpus of this period preserves the earliest known forms of the language and reveals minor dialectal differences corresponding roughly to geographic regions. The material evidence of this phase comes from Syria, southern Turkey, northern Palestine and Mesopotamia, and consists of Bir Hadad inscriptions, the Zakkūr inscription, the Sefire inscriptions, Nērab inscriptions, eight Bar-Rakkāb inscriptions, the Tell Halaf inscription, the so-called Assur Ostracon, the Tell Fekherye Assyrian-Aramaic bilingual inscription on a statue, and the Deir ʿAlla fragmentary text from Jordan, as well as brief economic and legal texts and endorsements incised on clay tablets from Mesopotamia. However, during this phase the Aramaic-speaking people were scattered from Egypt to Lower Mesopotamia as a result of the deportation policies implemented by the rulers of the Neo-Assyrian empire.[146] Also during this period, from ca. 800 B.C. onward, Aramaic was utilized alongside Akkadian as the language of administration in the Neo-Assyrian

---

Language in the Achaemenid Period: A Study in Linguistic Variation (Leuven 1995); Lipiński, *Semitic Languages*, pp. 61–70; J. Tropper, "Dialektvielfalt und Sprachwandel im frühen Aramäischen, Soziolinguistische Überlegungen," in P.M. Michèle Daviau et al. (eds.), *The World of the Aramaeans III: Studies in Language and Literature in Honour of Paul-Eugène Dion* (Sheffield 2001), pp. 213–222; G. Khan, "Aramaic and the Impact of Languages in Contact with it through the Ages," in P.B. de la Peña et al. (eds.), *Lenguas en contacto: el testimonio escrito* (Madrid 2004), pp. 87–108; A. Millard, "Early Aramaic," in J.N. Postgate (ed.), *Languages of Iraq, Ancient and Modern* ([London] 2007), pp. 85–94; A. Lemaire, "Remarks on the Aramaic of Upper Mesopotamia in the Seventh Century B.C.," in H. Gzella & M.L. Folmer (eds.), *Aramaic in its Historical and Linguistic Setting* (Wiesbaden 2008), pp. 77–92; H. Gzella, "Aramaic in the Parthian Period: The Arsacid Inscriptions," in H. Gzella & M.L. Folmer (eds.), *Aramaic in its Historical and Linguistic Setting* (Wiesbaden 2008), pp. 107–130; O. Jastrow, "Old Aramaic and Neo-Aramaic: Some Reflections on Language History," in H. Gzella & M.L. Folmer (eds.), *Aramaic in its Historical and Linguistic Setting* (Wiesbaden 2008), pp. 1–10; S. Creason, "Aramaic," in R.D. Woodard (ed.), *The Ancient Languages of Syria-Palestine and Arabia* (Cambridge 2008), pp. 108–144; F.M. Fales, "Old Aramaic," in S. Weninger (ed.), *The Semitic Languages: An International Handbook* (Berlin 2011), pp. 555–573; H. Gzella, "Imperial Aramaic," in S. Weninger (ed.), *The Semitic Languages: An International Handbook* (Berlin 2011), pp. 574–586; idem, "Late Imperial Aramaic," in S. Weninger (ed.), *The Semitic Languages: An International Handbook* (Berlin 2011), pp. 598–609; M. Folmer, "Imperial Aramaic as an Administrative Language of the Achaemenid Period," in S. Weninger (ed.), *The Semitic Languages: An International Handbook* (Berlin 2011), pp. 587–598; idem, "Old and Imperial Aramaic," in H. Gzella (ed.), *Languages from the World of the Bible* (Boston 2011), pp. 128–159; Gzella, H., *A Cultural History of Aramaic: From the Beginnings to the Advent of Islam* (Leiden 2015). For an account of the research on Aramaic, see F. Rosenthal, *Die aramaistische Forschung seit Th. Nöldeke's Veröffentlichungen* (Leiden 1939); E.Y. Kutscher, "Aramaic," in T.A. Sebeok (ed.), *Current Trends in Linguistics*, 6. *Linguistics in South West Asia and North Africa* (The Hague 1970), pp. 347–412; J.A. Fitzmyer & S.A. Kaufman, *An Aramaic Bibliography, Part I: Old, Official, and Biblical Aramaic* (Baltimore 1992); F.M. Fales, "Most Ancient Aramaic Texts and Linguistics: A Review of Recent Studies," *Incontri Linguistici* 19 (1996), pp. 33–57.

146 See S.A. Kaufman, "Aramaic," in D.N. Freedman et al. (eds.), *The Anchor Bible Dictionary*, vol. 4, K–N (New York 1992), p. 173; idem, "Aramaic," in R. Hetzron (ed.), *The Semitic Languages* (London 1997), p. 114.

empire,[147] and was also used, at least in the West, as an international language of diplomacy in the final epoch of the empire.[148]

Official Aramaic (OffAr.), ca. 600–200 B.C.: During this period Aramaic spread throughout the territories conquered by the Neo-Babylonian empire, and under the rule of the Persian empire Aramaic spread from Upper Egypt to Asia Minor and eastward to the Indian subcontinent. Regrettably, only a small textual corpus is extant from this period because the vast majority of the administrative documents, records and letters pertaining to these empires were written on perishable material. Most of the Aramaic texts from this period come from Egypt, because the dry climate there helped preserve them from deterioration. The extant material consists of the correspondence of the Persian satrap of Egypt as well as the papyrus archives of the Jewish military garrison at Elephantine, which contain deeds of sale, marriage contracts and fragments of literary materials. The most characteristic feature of the language in this period is the emergence of a literary standard form of both the language and its orthography, which is usually designated by scholars as "Standard Aramaic."

This phase of the language is also designated by some scholars as "Reichsaramäisch." The label "Reichsaramäisch," which is sometimes translated into English as "Imperial Aramaic," was first coined in 1927 by Josef Markwart, a scholar of Iranian studies, especially for the sort of "chancery" Aramaic of the 7th century onward which was widely used in the Persian Empire.[149] Other scholars, however, have a different understanding of the term "Reichsaramäisch." Fitzmyer, for instance, criticizes Markwart's classification, saying: "But it seemed to suggest that the use of this sort of Aramaic began in the Persian period, whereas it was obviously in use already in the time of the Neo-Assyrian empire."[150] Fales remarks: "In point of fact, the very concept of Imperial Aramaic as coinciding with the Aramaic of the Achaemenid empire is nowadays somewhat under fire, since it may be reasonably held that such a label should be already applied to the language during the late Assyrian period."[151] Greenfield goes further by saying: "The Aramaic speaking peoples were in close contact with the

---

[147] For the evidence on the use of Aramaic in Assyria proper, see Section 1.9 below. For the term Assyria proper, see n. 160 below.

[148] See Kaufman, ibid; M.L. Folmer, *The Aramaic Language in the Achaemenid Period: A Study in Linguistic Variation* (Leuven 1995), p. 3, n. 16. A frequently quoted incident, supporting the view that Aramaic was most likely the customary language of diplomatic negotiations in the Neo-Assyrian empire in the West, is the appeal of the Judean nobles (2 Kings 18:26–28), to *rab-šāqê,* the envoy of Sennacherib, to address them in Aramaic. See H. Tadmor, "The Aramaization of Assyria: Aspects of Western Impact," in H.-J. Nissen & J. Renger (eds.), *Mesopotamien und Seine Nachbarn: Politische und kulturelle Wechselbeziehungen im Alten Vorderasien vom 4. bis 1. Jahrtausend v. Chr, 2* (Berlin 1982), pp. 451f, (henceforth: Tadmor, *Aramaization*); idem, "On the Role of Aramaic in the Assyrian Empire," in M. Mori (ed.), *Near Eastern Studies Dedicated to H.I.H. Prince Takahito Mikasa on the Occasion of His Seventy-Fifth Birthday* (Wiesbaden 1991), p. 422.

[149] See J.A. Fitzmyer, "The Phases of the Aramaic Language," in J.A. Fitzmyer (ed.), *A Wandering Aramean: Collected Aramaic Essays* (Chico 1979), p. 59.

[150] Ibid. See also *Encyclopaedia Judaica*, vol. 3 ANH–AZ (Jerusalem 1971), p. 266b s.v. Official Aramaic.

[151] See F.M. Fales, "Multilingualism on Multiple Media in the Neo-Assyrian Period: A Review of the Evidence," *SAAB* 16 (2007), p. 100 and n. 18.

Assyrians, and eventually came under their rule; it was in the Neo-Assyrian empire that Aramaic became the *lingua franca*."[152] A similar opinion is expressed by Folmer, who discusses Aramaic texts prior to the Achaemenid period, saying: "In the course of the 8th century B.C.E., a particular variety of Aramaic became the administrative language and *lingua franca* of the Neo-Assyrian empire."[153]

It is of interest to mention here that in classifying Old and Official Aramaic, some scholars utilize additional labels such as "Assyrian Aramaic,"[154] for an Assyrian dialectal variety within Old Aramaic and the term "Mesopotamian Aramaic," for the remnant of Aramaic from Neo-Assyrian and Neo-Babylonian Mesopotamia.[155]

Middle Aramaic, ca. 200 B.C.–200 A.D.: In this phase and during the Hellenistic and Roman periods, Aramaic lost its position to Greek and ceased to be the administrative language of the Near East. This phase also reveals the emergence of local dialects of Aramaic. These dialects can be divided into two groups *Epigraphic* and *Canonical*. The epigraphic group includes Palmyrene inscriptions (Palm.), from Palmyra/Tadmor, Nabatean texts (Nab.), a group of inscriptions from Hatra, a smaller group of inscriptions from Assur. The canonical group includes the Aramaic portions of the biblical books of Daniel and Ezra (BA), Jewish Literary Aramaic (JLA), which includes the Qumran texts (QA), Palestinian Targumic Aramaic (PTA), and Legal Formulas of the rabbinic literature, as well as the Aramaic material written in the demotic script on papyrus Amherst 63, which includes, among other things, the lengthy story of the conflict between the Assyrian king Assurbanipal and his brother Shamashshumukin (Šamaš-šumu-ukīn).

Late Aramaic, ca. 200 A.D.–1200 A.D.: Under the second half of this period, Arabic replaced Aramaic as the spoken language of the vast majority of the Aramaic speaking people. The extant Aramaic textual material consists of an enormous literature and some sporadic inscriptions. This phase can be divided into three geographical groups: *Palestinian*, *Syrian* and *Babylonian*. The Palestinian group consists of Jewish Palestinian Aramaic (JPA), which includes Galilean Aramaic (Gal.), the dialect of the so-called Talmud Yerushalimi, as well as early midrashim of Palestinian origin; a small group of inscriptions of Christian Palestinian Aramaic (CPA); Samaritan Aramaic (Sam.), which includes two different translations of the Torah, and some literary/exegetical works. The Syrian group includes Syriac (Syr.), the liturgical language of Eastern Christianity (with Eastern and Western dialects), and is undoubtedly the best documented of

[152] See J.C. Greenfield, "The Aramaic Legal Texts of the Achaemenian Period," *Transeuphratène* 3 (1990), p. 87.

[153] See M.L. Folmer, *The Aramaic Language in the Achaemenid Period: A Study in Linguistic Variation* (Leuven 1995), p. 3. See also S. Parpola, "The Neo-Assyrian Ruling Class," in T.R. Kämmerer (ed.), *Studien zu Ritual und Sozialgeschichte im Alten Orient / Studies on Ritual and Society in the Ancient Near East: Tartuer Symposien 1998–2004* (Berlin 2007), pp. 261f.; H. Gzella, "Imperial Aramaic," in S. Weninger (ed.), *The Semitic Languages: An International Handbook* (Berlin 2011), p. 574.

[154] See Fales, ibid; idem, "Most Ancient Aramaic Texts and Linguistics: A Review of Recent Studies," *Incontri Linguistici* 19 (1996), p. 53; idem, AECT, pp. 36f; R.A. Bowman, "Arameans, Aramaic, and the Bible," *JNES* 7 (1948), p. 75.

[155] See Kaufman, AIA, pp. 8f.

all Aramaic dialects; Late Jewish Literary Aramaic (LJLA), which was utilized for the composition of Aramaic parabiblical and liturgical texts. The Babylonian group consists of Jewish Babylonian Aramaic (JBA), used for Babylonian Talmud; and Mandaic (Ma.), the language of the Mandaeans.

Modern Aramaic (at the present time):[156] The richest textual corpus of "modern Aramaic" is that of the dialects of Aramaic, usually referred to collectively as Sūret.[157] It is the language of the indigenous Assyrians in Iraq, and parts of Iran, Syria, Lebanon and the Assyrian Diaspora. During the last century, a common literary dialect has emerged from different dialects of Sūret in Iran and Iraq. The Assyrians call it *lišāna aššūrāya/aṯūrāya ḥāta*, i.e., the modern Assyrian language.[158] Scholars usually designate the dialects of the Nineveh plain in Iraq and Urmia in Iran, as well as the dialects formerly spoken by the Assyrians in the Hakkari area in south-eastern Turkey, by terms such as Urmia, Eastern Neo-Syriac (ENS), Eastern Neo-Aramaic (ENA), or North-Eastern Neo-Aramaic (NENA). The other major dialects of modern Aramaic are those of the Ṭūr ʿAbdīn area in south-eastern Turkey, which are designated by terms such as Sūrayt/Ṭūrōyo, Western Neo-Syriac (WNS), or Western Neo-Aramaic (WNA).[159] The other dialects of modern Aramaic are the Aramaic that is still spoken in the town of Maʿlula in Syria, which is heavily influenced by Arabic, and Mandaic, which at least until recently has been preserved in southern Iraq and neighboring areas in Iran.

1.9 Evidence of the use of Aramaic in Assyria proper

Among the earliest excavated evidence for the use of alphabetic script in Assyria proper[160] are some bilingual clay tablets unearthed by Layard in Nineveh. These

---

[156] See G. Khan, "Aramaic in the Medieval and Modern Periods," in J.N. Postgate (ed.), *Languages of Iraq, Ancient and Modern* ([London] 2007), pp. 95–113.

[157] The designation itself i.e., "Sūret" must be very old. Most likely it developed very early from the ancient Assyrian/Akkadian term *aššūrītu* f. "Assyrian (language)," which most probably was pronounced as **assūrītu* in the Neo-Assyrian period. We know that in later periods the Aramaic script was also called "Assyrian writing." See the discussion on pp. 54ff. below. See also S. Parpola, "National and Ethnic Identity in the Neo-Assyrian Empire and Assyrian Identity in Post-Empire Times," *Journal of Assyrian Academic Studies* 18/2 (2004), pp. 5–22; R. Rollinger, "The Terms 'Assyria' and 'Syria' Again," *JNES* 65 (2006), pp. 283–287.

[158] Cf. G. Khan, "The Language of the Modern Assyrians: The North-Eastern Neo-Aramaic Dialect Group," in Ö.A. Cetrez et al. (eds.), *The Assyrian Heritage — Threads of Continuity and Influence* (Uppsala 2012), pp. 173–199; idem, "Remarks on the Historical Background of the Modern Assyrian Language," *The Journal of Assyrian Academic Studies* 21/2 (2007), pp. 4–11; Lipiński, *Semitic Languages*, p. 70; E.Y. Odisho, *The Sound System of Modern Assyrian (Neo-Aramaic)* (Wiesbaden 1988), pp. 3–22; K. Tsereteli, *Grammatik der modernen assyrischen Sprache (Neuostaramäisch)* (Leipzig 1978). Cf. R.C. Steiner, "Why the Aramaic Script Was Called 'Assyrian' in Hebrew, Greek, and Demotic," *Or* 62 (1993): 80–82.

[159] See, for instance, O. Jastrow, "The Neo-Aramaic Languages," in R. Hetzron (ed.), *The Semitic Languages* (London 1997), pp. 334–377; idem, "Neo-Aramaic Dialectology: The State of the Art," in S. Izre'el (ed.), *Semitic Linguistics: The State of the Art at the Turn of the Twenty-First Century* (Winona Lake 2002), pp. 365–377.

[160] Assyria proper, or the Assyrian heartland, covers the territory bounded on the east and north by the foothills of the Zagros Mountains, to the west by the steppes west of the river Tigris and to the

consist of deeds written in Neo-Assyrian, but also bearing alphabetic texts. In the early stages of Assyriology, Rawlinson used the Neo-Assyrian deeds bearing alphabetic annotations as a proof of the accurate decipherment of cuneiform.[161] Initially, the alphabetic annotations were identified by Rawlinson as "Phoenician," but later they were classified by Nöldeke as Aramaic.[162]

The coexistence of the Neo-Assyrian and Aramaic texts has increasingly drawn the attention of scholars because they significantly illuminate these two Semitic languages and provide important information about the language contact that occurred between the two languages and about the people who spoke them.[163] The accumulated evidence for the use of Aramaic in the Assyrian Empire has been in focus in recent years. The evidence has gradually increased due to advances in the research and the progress made within the framework of excavations and archeology.

In comparison with the Assyrians, the Arameans are latecomers in the history of the ancient Near East. They are first mentioned in the inscriptions of the Assyrian king Tiglath-pileser I (1115–1077 B.C.).[164] However, after examining the evidence at hand, modern scholarship has revealed the existence of a distinctive socio-cultural relationship between the Assyrians and the Arameans in the Neo-Assyrian Empire, i.e., during the period extending from the 9th century B.C., to the end of the Assyrian Empire around 612 B.C.[165] Today, scholars define different aspects of this relationship in terms such as, a "symbiosis of Aramaic and Assyrian writing systems,"[166] "Assyrian-Aramaic cultural symbiosis,"[167] "Aramaeo-Assyrian fusion,"[168] and "Assyro-Aramaean amalgam."[169]

---

south by the Lesser Zab. Here lie the major Assyrian cities, Aššūr, Nīnua, Kalḫu, Dūr-Šarrukēn and Arbail (Erbil), the strategic centers of economic and political power. See K. Radner, "The Assur-Nineveh-Arbela Triangle: Central Assyria in the Neo-Assyrian Period," in P.A. Miglus and S. Mühl (eds.), *Between the Cultures: The Central Tigris Region from the 3rd to the 1st Millennium BC; Conference at Heidelberg, January 22nd–24th, 2009* (Heidelberg, 2011), pp. 321–329.

[161] See A.R. Millard, "Some Aramaic Epigraphs," *Iraq* 34 (1972), p. 131, n. 1.

[162] For references, see F.M. Fales, "The Use and Function of Aramaic Tables," in G. Bunnens (ed.), *Essays on Syria in the Iron Age* (Louvain 2000), p. 92, n. 12.

[163] For language contact in general, see M.P. Streck, "Akkadian and Aramaic Language Contact," in S. Weninger (ed.), *The Semitic Languages: An International Handbook* (Berlin 2011), pp. 416–424.

[164] See E. Lipiński, *The Aramaeans: Their Ancient History, Culture, Religion* (Leuven 2000), p. 35.

[165] See F.M. Fales, "Assyrian-Aramaic Cultural Interrelation: Older and Newer Results," in L. Bachelot & F.M. Fales (eds.), *Tell Shiukh Fawqani 1994–1998, II* (Padova 2005), pp. 596–616. Cf. W. Röllig, "Aramäer und Assyrer: die Schriftzeugnisse bis zum Ende des Assyrerreiches," in G. Bunnens (ed.), *Essays on Syria in the Iron Age* (Louvain 2000), pp. 177–186.

[166] See A.R. Millard, "Assyrians and Arameans," *Iraq* 45 (1983), p. 101; Postgate, FNALD, p. 11, § 1.7. For the term "symbiosis of Aramaic and Akkadian," see H. Tadmor, "On the Role of Aramaic in the Assyrian Empire," in M. Mori (ed.), *Near Eastern Studies Dedicated to H.I.H. Prince Takahito Mikasa on the Occasion of His Seventy-Fifth Birthday* (Wiesbaden 1991), p. 419; J.C. Greenfield, "*ana urdūti kabāsu* = כבש לעבד," *StOr* 55:11 (1984), p. 261.

[167] See H. Tadmor, "Towards the Early History of *Qatālu*," *JQR* 76 (1985), p. 45; P. Garelli, "Importance et rôle des araméens dans l'administration de l'empire assyrien," in H.-J. Nissen & J. Renger (eds.), *Mesopotamien und seine Nachbarn* (Berlin 1982), p. 444; A.R. Millard, "Assyria, Aramaeans and Aramaic," in G. Gershon et al. (eds.), *Homeland and Exile: Biblical and Ancient Near Eastern Studies in Honour of Bustenay Oded* (Leiden 2009), p. 212.

[168] See Tadmor, *Aramaization*, p. 458. For the term "Aramaic-Assyrian symbiosis," see Y. Muffs, *Studies in the Aramaic Legal Papyri from Elephantine* (Leiden 1969), p. 189; S.A. Kaufman, "An Assyro-Aramaic *egirtu ša šulmu*," in M. de Jong Ellis, (ed.), *Essays on the Ancient Near East in Memory of J.J. Finkelstein* (Hamden 1977), pp. 119, 127. For the term "Aramaic-Assyrian *koiné*,"

The evidence for the use of Aramaic in Assyria proper can be classified under two main categories, namely textual evidence and visual evidence. The examples for each category given below are not necessarily presented in chronological order, and are intended to be representative rather than comprehensive.

1.9.1 Textual evidence

Evidence for the earliest use of the West-Semitic alphabet in Assyria consists of individual letters in the form of graffiti in black ink or paint found on a number of bricks belonging to a glazed panel in the palace of Shalmaneser III (858–824 B.C.) at Calah/Nimrud. The letters were written by the masons in charge of decorating the palace, and were meant to aid in laying the bricks in a specific sequence. However, it is not possible, based on the letters' features, to conclude with certainty whether the letters were written according to the Aramaic or the Phoenician tradition.[170]

In most cases, the textual evidence consists either of Neo-Assyrian documents written in cuneiform, with a brief Aramaic text in their margins, or Neo-Assyrian tablets bearing a bilingual text, with the Assyrian written on one face of the tablet and the Aramaic on the other. The textual evidence also includes monolingual tablets written entirely in Aramaic.[171]

---

see H. Tadmor, "Assyria and the West: The Ninth Century and its Aftermath," in H. Goedicke & J.J.M. Roberts (eds.), *Unity and Diversity. Essays in the History, Literature, and Religion of the Ancient Near East* (Baltimore 1975), p. 43. For the term "Assyro-Aramaic symbiosis," see F.M. Fales, "Multilingualism on Multiple Media in the Neo-Assyrian Period: A Review of the Evidence," *SAAB* 16 (2007), p. 111.

[169] See A. Kuhrt, *The Ancient Near East, II* (London 1995), p. 493.

[170] See A.R. Millard, "The Graffiti on the Glazed Bricks from Nimrud," appendix in J. Curtis et al., "British Museum Excavations at Nimrud and Balawat in 1989," *Iraq* 55 (1993), pp. 35f; idem, "Aramaic Documents of the Assyrian and Achaemenid Periods," in M. Brosius, (ed.), *Ancient Archives and Archival Traditions: Concepts of Record-Keeping in the Ancient World* (Oxford 2003), p. 231; F.M. Fales, "Assyrian-Aramaic Cultural Interrelation: Older and Newer Results," in L. Bachelot & F.M. Fales (eds.), *Tell Shiukh Fawqani 1994–1998, II* (Padova 2005), p. 603.

[171] The entire corpus of Aramaic epigraphs on clay tablets from Assyria (known until 1986) was re-edited in a monograph by F.M. Fales, *Aramaic Epigraphs on Clay Tablets of the Neo-Assyrian Period* (Rome 1986). See also idem, "Aramaic Epigraphy from Assyria: New Data and Old Issues," in A.M. Maeir et al. (eds.), *Neo Perspectives on Aramaic Epigraphy in Mesopotamia, Qumran, Egypt and Idumea*, pp. 5–16. Tübingen: Mohr Siebeck, 2021. However, Fales calls attention to the fact that the information provided in his monograph is rapidly becoming obsolete due to the considerable addition of texts of the same type which have been excavated since 1986. See F.M. Fales, "Multilingualism on Multiple Media in the Neo-Assyrian Period: A Review of the Evidence," *SAAB* 16 (2007), p. 99. Cf. the review of Fales' monograph by S.A. Kaufman, "Assyro-Aramaica," *JAOS* 109 (1989), pp. 97–102. See also A. Lemaire, *Nouvelles tablettes araméennes* (Geneva 2001). Cf. the review of Lemaire's monograph by E. Lipiński, "New Aramaic Clay Tablets," *BiOr* 59 (2002), cols., 245–259. For Aramaic epigraphs on clay tablets from Babylonia, see L. Delaporte, *Épigraphes araméens* (Paris 1912). For more details on this group of evidence, see F.M. Fales, "The Use and Function of Aramaic Tables," in G. Bunnens (ed.), *Essays on Syria in the Iron Age* (Louvain 2000), p. 92. See also W. Röllig, "Keilschrift versus Alphabetschrift: Überlegungen zu den *Epigraphs* auf Keilschrifttafeln," in P. Bienkowski, C. Mee & E. Slater (eds.), *Writing and Ancient Near Eastern Society: Papers in Honour of Alan R. Millard* (New York & London 2005), pp. 119–126.

Interestingly, the Neo-Assyrian records repeatedly contrast Assyrian scribes with their Aramean counterparts.[172] We find the terms *ṭupšarru aššūrāya*, "Assyrian scribe," and *ṭupšarru armāya*, "Aramean scribe," occurring in a variety of documents referring to officials in the imperial service. The two categories of scribes are, for instance, mentioned in a lexical text of the lú = ša series, i.e., the *Kuyunjik List* as, LÚ.A.BA KUR.*aš-šur-a-a* and LÚ.A.BA KUR.*ár-ma-a-a*.[173]

Although the logogram LÚ.A.BA is read *ṭupšarru*, literally meaning "tablet writer," it has been suggested that in Neo-Assyrian it most likely initially meant *a–ba*-man, namely "ABC-man; writer of the alphabet," where *a* and *ba* represent the first two letters of the West-Semitic alphabet.[174] In quoting Parpola, Tadmor writes: "[T]he logogram LÚ.A.BA, scribe, should be interpreted as "ABC-man" and that it seems to have a western background, since it already occurs in Ugarit (J. Nougayrol, *Ugaritica* 5, 252, colophon to RS. 2o. 196 A, 1.2.)."[175] However, Deller points out that the Ugaritic syllabic alphabet begins with the syllables *a* and *be*, not with *a* and *ba*.[176]

Indeed, Aramean scribes were employed alongside Assyrian scribes in the Assyrian administration. They are occasionally referred to in administrative and economic documents as employees of the royal court. For example, the Aramean scribes are mentioned among other recipients of wine rations in the so-called "Nimrud Wine Lists" from the beginning of the 8th century B.C., as, LÚ.A.BA.MEŠ KUR.*ára-ma-a-a* "Aramean scribes," (CTN I 21 r.8′ = ND 10054 r.8′).[177] Aramean scribes are also mentioned among Assyrian and Egyptian scribes[178] as recipients of wine rations, i.e., LÚ.A.BA.MEŠ KUR.*áš-šur-a-a* "Assyrian scribes," LÚ.A.BA.MEŠ KUR.*mu-ṣu-ra-a-a* "Egyptian scribes," and LÚ.A.BA.MEŠ KUR.*ara-ma-a-a* "Aramean scribes," (CTN I 9 r.18–20 = ND 11048 r.18–20).

---

[172] See P.-A. Beaulieu, "Official and Vernacular Languages: The Shifting Sands of Imperial and Cultural Identities in First-Millennium B.C. Mesopotamia," in S.L. Sanders (ed.), *Margins of Writing, Origins of Cultures* (Chicago 2006), p. 188, n. 6.

[173] See M. Civil, et al. (eds.), *The Series lú =* ša *and Related Texts* (Rome 1969), p. 239, col. v 5–6. According to Wiseman, these two terms are functional rather than ethnic, see D.J. Wiseman, "Assyrian Writing-Boards," *Iraq* 17 (1955), p. 13. Johns had earlier expressed a similar view, see C.H.W. Johns, *Assyrian Deeds and Documents*, Vol., II (Cambridge: Deighton Bell, 1901), p. 109. See also R.P. Dougherty, "Writing upon Parchment and Papyrus among the Babylonians and Assyrians," *JAOS* 48 (1928), p. 129, n. 127. See also F.M. Fales, "Old Aramaic," in S. Weninger (ed.), *The Semitic Languages: An International Handbook* (Berlin 2011), p. 557.

[174] See K. Deller, "Das Siegel des Schreibers Aššur-šumī-aṣbat, Sohn des Rībāte," *BaM* 13 (1982), p. 151. See also M.P. Streck, "Akkadian and Aramaic Language Contact," in S. Weninger (ed.), *The Semitic Languages: An International Handbook* (Berlin 2011), p. 417, § 1.3. For a discussion of the reading and original meaning of the logogram LÚ.A.BA, see K. Radner, SAAS VI, pp. 80ff, with n. 426 and n. 427.

[175] See Tadmor, *Aramaization*, p. 459 (Postscript 3).

[176] Deller, ibid, p. 152.

[177] See J.V. Kinnier Wilson, *The Nimrud Wine Lists* (London 1972), p. 149.

[178] Three Egyptian scribes are mentioned in a list of court personnel from Nineveh (SAA VII 1 r. ii 3–6). Another Egyptian scribe bearing an Assyrian name, Ṣilli-Aššūr, is attested in a document from Nineveh (SAA VI 142:11–e.12, ca. 692 B.C.). See K. Radner, "Schreiberkonventionen im assyrischen Reich: Sprachen und Schriftsysteme," in J. Renger (ed.), *Assur – Gott, Stadt und Land: 5. Internationales Colloquium der Deutschen Orient-Gesellschaft 18.–21. Februar 2004 in Berlin* (Wiesbaden 2011), p. 386, n. 2.

In addition, there exists evidence of Aramean scribes serving as royal officials at the royal court of Nineveh. For instance, an Aramean scribe of the crown prince (7th century B.C.), IGI ^{m}ZALÁG–*e-a* LÚ*.A.BA KUR.*ár-ma-a-a šá* ⸢A$^{!}$⸣–MAN "Witness Nūr-Aia (*or* Nūrāia), Aramean scribe of the crown prince," (SAA XIV 205 r.13), acting as a witness for Nabû-šāpik-zēri who is acquiring some land in the town of Ša-Ṣillaia.[179]

Aramean scribes are also mentioned on other occasions, for example, when performing a legal transaction. We are aware, for instance, of an Aramean scribe from Nineveh (reign of Assurbanipal): ^{m}SUḪUŠ-*i* LÚ.A.BA *ár-ma-*[*a-a*] "Urbî, the Aramean scribe," (SAA XIV 75:3), who, according to a witnessed memorandum, gave twenty sheep and fifty shekels of silver, (as) accounts.[180] Furthermore, an Aramean scribe from Nineveh (reign of Sennacherib), IGI ^{m}⸢*a-ba*$^{?}$⸣*-gu-ú* LÚ*.A.BA / KUR.LÚ*.*ar-ma-a-a*, "Witness Abā-gû, Aramean scribe," (SAA VI 127 r.3′–4′), acts as a witness for the "third man," Atueḫu.[181]

An extant royal order of Sargon II (SAA XIX 154), from Calah/Nimrud (about 710 B.C.) addressed to a high ranking Assyrian official by the name of Aššūr-bēlu-taqqin, asking him to assemble all the Assyrian and Aramean scribes residing in the provinces, and provide them with armed escort so that they should proceed to record the tax contributions.[182] SAA (XIX 154:1–r.3) reads as follows:

> [*a-bat* LUGA]L / [*a-na*] ⸢^{m}*aš-šur*⸣–EN–LÁ[L$^{?}$] / LÚ*.*um-ma-nu ša* É.GAL / *lu-u* LÚ*.*aš-*⸢*šur-a*⸣*-a* / *lu-u* ⸢LÚ*.*ar-ma*⸣*-a-a* / *ša a-na* KUR TI.LA / *a-na* KUR-*ka il-li-ku-ni-ni* / LÚ*.A–KIN.MEŠ-*ni-ka* / *ina na-gi-u ga*[*b*]*-bu* / *ši-tap-par bé-et šá-nu-u-ni* / *gab-bi-šú-nu* [*p*]*aḫ-ḫi-ra* / *ina* UGU-*ḫi-iá še-bi-la-áš-šú-nu* / [B]AD-ḪAL-*lum* LÚ*.*i-tú.ʾu* / ⸢*i*⸣*-si-šú-nu pi-qid* / [*š*]*a* ⸢URU.BÀD⸣–^{m}EN–DINGIR-*a-a* / [*ú*]*-še-ta-qu-ni-šá-nu-u-ni* / [*a*]*t-*[*t*]*a* ⸢*tu*⸣*-u-da-*⸢*a*⸣ / [UD.MEŠ] *ša* [É]Š.QAR *e-ma-du* / ⸢*e*⸣*-tar*$^{!}$*-ba-a-ni*

> [The kin]g's [word to] Aššūr-bēlu-*taqq*[*in*]: (As for any) scribes of the palace, whether Assyrian or Aramean, who have come to your land to revive it – send your messengers to the whole district, gather them all wherever they are and send them to me! Entrust them to [c]avalry and the Itu'u, who will make them pass through

[179] See also PNA 2/II (p. 968b s.v. Nūrāia, no. 10).

[180] See also PNA 3/II (p. 1358a s.v. Ubrî, no. 2).

[181] Note that in SAA VI 127 r.3′–4′, Kwasman and Parpola render LÚ*.A.BA / KUR.LÚ*.*ar-ma-a-a* as "Aramean palaca scribe." Cf. Luukkoo, who interprets LÚ*.A.BA / KUR.LÚ*.*ar-ma-a-a*, differently, as "Aramaean scribe." See M. Luukkoo, "The Administrative Roles of the 'Chief Scribe' and the 'Palace Scribe' in the Neo-Assyrian Period," *SAAB* 16 (2007), p. 232, n. 23. See also PNA 1/I (p. 1a s.v. Abā-gû). For additional references to Aramean scribes, see: IGI ^{m}*am-ma-a* A.BA *ár-ma-a* "Witness Ammâ, Aramean scribe," SAA XIV 29 r.6; ^{m}SUḪUŠ-*i* LÚ.A.BA *ár-ma-*[*a-a*] "Ubrî, the Aramean scribe," SAA XIV 75:3; [IGI ^{m}*sa*$^{?}$]*-i-lu* LÚ.A.BA URU.*ar-ma-a-a* "[Witness Saʾ]īlu, Aramean scribe," SAA XIV 153 r.8′; ^{m}PAB-*bu-u* LÚ.A.BA$^{!!}$ KUR$^{!}$.*ár*$^{!}$*-ma*$^{!}$*-*⸢*a*$^{!}$⸣*-*[*a*] "Aḫabû, Aram[ean] scribe," SAA XI 124 r. ii 4′; ^{m}PAB–AŠ LÚ.A.⸢BA$^{!}$⸣ *ar*$^{!}$*-*[*ma-a-a x x x x*] "Aḫu-iddina, Ar[a-mean] scribe […]" SAA XII 63:19′; LÚ.A.BA.MEŠ KUR.*ara-*[*ma-a-a*] "Aramean scribes," CTN I 13:12 (= ND 10027 + 10028).

[182] See F.M. Fales, "Multilingualism on Multiple Media in the Neo-Assyrian Period: A Review of the Evidence," *SAAB* 16 (2007), p. 109.

Dūr-Bēl-ila'ī to me. Do [y]ou know that [*the days*] for imposing the [*i*]*škāru* dues have [a]rrived?[183]

As for the term *sepīru*, which is rendered "scribe writing alphabetic script (mostly on skin)"[184] or "interpreter-scribe (of Aramaic),"[185] it appears only in Neo-Babylonian and Late-Babylonian texts to indicate a scribe writing in the Aramaic alphabet. The word is considered to be a loanword from Aramaic in NB and LB.[186] In contrast, *sepīru* is not attested in Neo-Assyrian texts,[187] but its corresponding Aramaic term *spr'*, "scribe," is attested in a corn loan docket from Assur dated 659 B.C. (reign of Assurbanipal), and written entirely in Aramaic, in which a reference is given to an individual from Assur, namely *knny spr'*, "Kanūnāyu the scribe," who acts as a witness for Ilu-iqbi.[188]

The use of Aramaic notations or captions had become relatively common in Assyria during the course of the 7th century B.C., serving as labels to identify documents.[189] A good number of Neo-Assyrian legal documents have captions in Aramaic script incised on their edges giving a summary of the contents of the text of the legal documents, for example: *dnt 'rblsr*, "Deed of Arbail-šarrat," SAA XIV 29 s.1, or *'grt ksp' zy 'l zbn*, "Contract of the silver which is at the disposal of Zabinu," SAA XIV 94 r.9–10, or [*l*]*q*$^?$*h ḥ*$^?$ *mn mt'hdd br nn*[*y*] / [*x*]*x h*$^?$ *x* "[*Bou*]*ght* from Matī'-Adda, son of Nan[î ...]" SAA XIV 398 s.2–3 (see fig. 2 below).[190] It has been stated that these captions were used as memoranda for the sake of identifying the tablets quickly, or were intended for those who possessed

[183] Note that SAA XIX 154:3 (= ND 2356), renders the word LÚ*.*um-ma-nu* "the specialists." Cf. the previous editions of the same text, CTN V, p. 239; Postgate, TCAE, p. 370; Fales, ibid. (translation).

[184] See CAD (S, p. 225a s.v. *sepīru*).

[185] See AHw. (p. 1036b s.v. *sepīru*); CDA (p. 320b s.v. *sepīru*).

[186] See CAD, ibid; AHw., ibid. See also M.P. Streck, "Keilschrift und Alphabet," in D. Borchers et al. (eds.), *Hieroglyphen – Alphabete – Schriftreformen. Studien zu Multiliteralismus, Schriftwechsel und Orthographieneuregelungen* (Göttingen 2001), pp. 77, 90 n. 4; idem, "Akkadian and Aramaic Language Contact," in S. Weninger (ed.), *The Semitic Languages: An International Handbook* (Berlin 2011), p. 417 § 1.3; R.P. Dougherty, "Writing upon Parchment and Papyrus among the Babylonians and Assyrians," *JAOS* 48 (1928), pp. 109–135. Cf. H. Tawil, *An Akkadian Lexical Companion for Biblical Hebrew* (Jersey City 2009), p. 266b s.v. סֹפֵר.

[187] See M.P. Streck, "Keilschrift und Alphabet," in D. Borchers et al. (eds.), *Hieroglyphen – Alphabete – Schriftreformen. Studien zu Multiliteralismus, Schriftwechsel und Orthographieneuregelungen* (Göttingen 2001), p. 77. Cf. L.E. Pearce, "*sepīru* and ^{LU}A.BA: Scribes of the Late First Millennium," in K. van Lerberghe & G. Voet (eds.), *Languages and Cultures in Contact at the Crossroads of Civilizations in the Syro-Mesopotamian Realm* (Leuven 1999), p. 356.

[188] See PNA 2/I (p. 603a s.v. Kanūnāiu, no. 33); V. Hug, *Altaramäische Grammatik der Texte des 7. und 6. Jh.s v.Chr.* (Heidelberg 1993), p. 23, no. AssU 4 r.6; M. Lidzbarski, *Altaramäische Urkunden aus Assur* (Leipzig 1921), p. 17, no. 4:13. Cf. M. Blasberg, *Keilschrift in aramäischer Umwelt: Untersuchungen zur spätbabylonischen Orthographie* (Köln 1997), § 3.4.2.1.

[189] See F.M. Fales, AECT; J.H. Stevenson, *Assyrian and Babylonian Contracts with Aramaic Reference Notes* (New York 1902). Mention should be made of the attestation of other writing media in Assyria proper, such as Hieroglyphic Luwian, which is demonstrated by the seven lead strips, found in a house in Assur, bearing private letters in hieroglyphic Luwian. See O. Pedersén, ALA II, pp. 98f; F.M. Fales, "The Use and Function of Aramaic Tablets," in G. Bunnens (ed.), *Essays on Syria in the Iron Age* (Louvain 2000), p. 124, n. 184.

[190] Cf. Fales, ibid., p. 214, no. 38.

little or no knowledge about reading cuneiform.[191] Some of the scribes were probably bilingual.

Figure 2. A Neo-Assyrian conveyance document from Nineveh (BM 123369 = SAA XIV 398 s.2–3), 7th century B.C., bearing an Aramaic caption on its left edge reading: [*l*]*q*?*h ḥ*? *mn mt'hdd br nn*[*y*] / [*x*]*x h*? *x* "[*Bou*]*ght* from Matī'-Adda, son of Nan[î ...]." From: J.N. Postgate (ed.), *Languages of Iraq: Ancient and Modern* ([London], 2007), p. 90.

From private archives, evidence for the use of Aramaic in Assyria proper in the 7th century B.C. is furnished by Neo-Assyrian legal documents in the shape of triangular lumps of clay formed around a knotted string and sometimes inscribed solely in Aramaic. These triangular-shaped tablets are usually referred to in English as "dockets." They almost always bear text about a loan of corn, but may also concern a loan of silver, and are sealed with the seal of the debtor. Most likely, the dockets were once fastened by a string to a document made of perishable material, such as an Aramaic scroll of papyrus or a leather roll.[192] A different interpretation of the purpose of the dockets is provided by Fales, who suggests that the loan dockets were either hung around a debtor's neck, as a sign of his obligation, or were attached to containers.[193]

An example from a private archive is a triangular corn loan docket (VA 7497) from the mid-7th century B.C., unearthed in Assur and written entirely in Aramaic (see fig. 3 below). It belongs to the archive of Aššūr-šallim-aḫḫē and records a loan of barley to Šēp-Aššūr.[194] The Aramaic text of the docket (VA 7497:1–r.4) reads as follows:[195]

---

[191] See S.J. Lieberman, "The Aramaic Argillary Script in the Seventh Century," *BASOR* 192 (1968), p. 27; Postgate, FNALD, § 1.7; Fales, ibid., p. 117.

[192] For more details, and for the purpose of the corn loan dockets, see Postgate, FNALD, p. 5. See also K. Radner, *Die neuassyrischen Privatrechtsurkunden als Quelle für Mensch und Umwelt* (Helsinki 1997), pp. 26–30.

[193] See F.M. Fales, AECT, pp. 18–24. Fales bases his interpretation on a NA letter (SAA XVI 63:12–20 = CT 53 46) sent to Esarhaddon concerning crimes in Gūzāna. Some other scholars do not share Fales's interpretation. See Radner, ibid., p. 29; J.N. Postgate, "Middle Assyrian to Neo-Assyrian: The Nature of the Shift," in H. Waetzoldt & H. Hauptmann (eds.), *Assyrien im Wandel der Zeiten* (Heidelberg 1997), p. 161, n. 8.

[194] See PNA 1/I (p. 217a s.v. Aššūr-šallim-aḫḫē, no. 11); PNA 1/II (p. 329b s.v. Bēl-šarru-uṣur, no. 15); PNA 2/II (p. 654a s.v. Lā-qēpu, no. 27); PNA 3/I (p. 1014a s.v. Qibīt-Issār, no. 13); PNA 3/II (p. 1258a s.v. Šēp-Aššūr, no. 24).

[195] See V. Hug, *Altaramäische Grammatik der Texte des 7. und 6. Jh.s v.Chr.* (Heidelberg 1993), p. 23, no. AssU 3. Cf. Fales, ibid., p. 228, no. 48.

ś'rn zi / 'srslmḥ / 'l sb'sr / 4 (homers) 8 (seah) */ b'drn // yntn śhdn / blsr'ṣr / qby'š / lqp*

Barley belonging to Aššūr-šallim-aḫḫē, is at (the disposal of) Šēp-Aššūr. 4 (homers and) 8 (seah). He will give (back) at the threshing-floor. Witnesses: Bēl-šarru-uṣur, Qibīt-Is(sār) (and) Lā-qēpu.

Figure 3. A triangular corn loan docket (VA 7497), from Assur, mid-7th century B.C., from the archive of Aššūr-šallim-aḫḫē (*'srslmḥ*), written entirely in Aramaic. It records a loan of barley to Šēp-Aššūr (*sb'sr*). From: B. Faist, "Sprachen und Schriften in Assur," in J. Marzahn & B. Salje (eds.), *Wiedererstehendes Assur: 100 Jahre deutsche Ausgrabungen in Assyrien* (Mainz am Rhein, 2003), p. 153.

In fact, there exists a Neo-Assyrian legal transaction from the royal court of Nineveh (SAA XIV 98 = ADD 129). This is a document bearing a text written in NA on its obverse, but whose reverse side bears a text written in Aramaic consisting of an almost complete translation of the NA text (see fig. 4 below). The document concerns a loan of barley belonging to the crown prince and was written in ca. 644* B.C. The Assyrian text (SAA XIV 98:1–9) reads as follows:

5 ANŠE ŠE.PAD.MEŠ / *ša* DUMU–MAN ŠU.2 / ^{m}*ta-qu-u-ni* LÚ*.2-*u* / *ina* IGI ^{m}*ḫa-ma-ṭu-ṭu* / *ša* URU.*ḫa-an-du-a-te* / ŠE.PAD.MEŠ *a-na* 1 ANŠE 5 BÁN-*šá* / *tar*-GAL-*bi* ITI.DUL / *lim-mu* ^{md}PA–MAN–PAB / 5 LÚ*.ŠE.KIN.KUD.MEŠ

Five homers of barley belonging to the crown prince under the control of Taquni, deputy, at the disposal of Ḫamaṭuṭu from the city of Ḫanduate. The barley shall increase 5 seahs per homer. Month Tishri (VII), eponym year of Nabû-šarru-uṣur. 5 harvesters.

On the reverse of the same legal document (SAA XIV 98 r.1–7), the Aramaic caption reads as follows:

ś'rn s$^{!}$*nh zy / br mlk' 'l / ḥmṭṭ mn ḥdwh /* 5 *b* 7 *w / ḥṣdn* 5 */ l'm rbsrs / nbsrṣr*

Deputy's barley which belongs to the crown prince is at the disposal of Ḫamaṭuṭu from Ḫadduwah. 5 according to 7 and 5 harvesters. Eponym year of the chief eunuch Nabû- šarru-uṣur.[196]

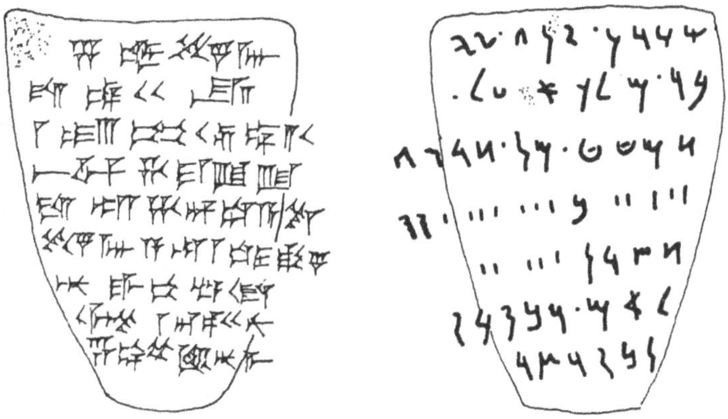

Figure 4. A bilingual Neo-Assyrian legal document (SAA XIV 98 = ADD 129), with two texts of almost identical content. From: F.M. Fales, AECT, pp. 135ff., no. 3 and pl. I, fig. 3.

The first excavated evidence attesting to the coexistence of Neo-Assyrian and Aramaic is a set of bronze lion-weights of Shalmaneser V (726–722 B.C.), unearthed by Layard at Nimrud in the middle of the 19th century of our era, and bearing denominations of weights incised in Assyrian and Aramaic (see figs. 5 and 6 below).[197] The inscriptions on the lion-weights are either bilingual or exclusively Aramaic. Another inscribed weight, in form of a duck bearing the well-known Aramaic notation *zy ʾrqʾ* "(weight-standard) of the land," has been unearthed in a recent excavation at Nimrud.[198]

[196] The translation is slightly different than that provided in SAA XIV 98.

[197] See Tadmor, *Aramaization*, p. 449. For the most recent re-edition of the bronze lion-weights, see F.M. Fales, "Assyro-Aramaica: The Assyrian Lion-Weights," in K. van Lerberghe & A. Schoors (eds.), *Immigration and Emigration within the Ancient Near East: Festschrift E. Lipiński* (Leuven 1995), pp. 33–55. See also C. Zaccagnini, "The Assyrian Lion Weights from Nimrud and the 'mina of the land'," in Y. Avishur & R. Deutsch (eds.), *Michael: Historical, Epigraphical and Biblical Studies in Honor of Prof. Michael Heltzer* (Tel Aviv 1999), pp. 259–265.

[198] See F.M. Fales, "Assyrian-Aramaic Cultural Interrelation: Older and Newer Results," in L. Bachelot & F.M. Fales (eds.), *Tell Shiukh Fawqani 1994–1998, II* (Padova 2005), p. 599, n. 15. See ibid., for weights in the shape of a duck, which are attested in the western provinces of the Assyrian empire.

Figure 5. A bronze lion-weight (BM 91230, 665.7 g), from Calah/Nimrud inscribed in Aramaic "2/3 of a royal mina." Frontispiece of: T. Kwasman & S. Parpola, SAA VI.

Figure 6. Part of a set of bronze lion-weights (BM 91220–35), from the palace at Calah/Nimrud, ca. 730–720 B.C., mostly inscribed in Assyrian and/or Aramaic with a weight and a royal name. From: T. Kwasman & S. Parpola, SAA VI, p. xxiv.

Textual evidence indicates indirectly that correspondence between officials, as well as with the Assyrian king, was occasionally carried out in Aramaic. Several instances from the Assyrian royal correspondence bear witness to the use of Aramaic in communications alongside Akkadian. One case in point is the extant Neo-Assyrian letter (SAA XIX 23), from between 735 and 732 B.C., which was excavated in Calah/Nimrud and now is considered to be an introductory letter. In this letter, Qurdi-Aššūr-lāmur reports to the Assyrian king Tiglath-pileser III (744–727 B.C.) that he is forwarding to the palace the *kanīku annītu armētu*, "this sealed Aramaic document," which was sent by Nabû-šēzib from Tyre. The Aramaic document, which has perished, was most likely providing a fuller account in Aramaic of local events from inside Tyre.[199]

In an often-quoted Neo-Assyrian epistolary passage, from the Assyrian royal correspondence, found in the undated letter SAA XVI (99:10′), probably from

[199] See CTN V, p. 154, ND 2686 (= NL 13 = Iraq 17, 130); PNA 2/II (p. 879 s.v. Nabû-šēzib, no. 1). See the comments on this text by Tadmor, *Aramaization*, p. 452; H.W.F. Saggs, "The Nimrud Letters, 1952 – Part II: Relations with the West," *Iraq* 17 (1955), p. 131.

time of Šamši-Adad V (823–811 B.C.),[200] a reference is made to *egirtu armētu*, "the Aramaic letter."[201] The sender of the Neo-Assyrian letter mentions that the scribe Kabtî,[202] a servant of Aššūr-da''in-aplu son of Shalmaneser (III) gave him "the Aramaic letter," and that he in turn gave it to the king.

In a NA letter (SAA I 34 r.19′) from the reign of Sargon II (721–705 B.C.), concerning the distribution of tribute and audience gifts, we learn that the palace scribe received two scrolls of papyrus: 2 *ki-ir-ki ni-a-ri* LÚ*.A.BA–KUR "2 scrolls of papyrus: the Scribe of the Palace." These were undoubtedly used for writing in the alphabetic script, i.e., Aramaic.[203] The term *kirku* in the sense of "scroll, roll" is actually an Aramaic loanword in NA and LB.[204]

Evidence for the use of scrolls, probably of leather, also comes from a report from Assur (SAA XIII 28) sent to the Assyrian king concerning gold and silver work for the temple of Sîn. The report mentions a *migli*, "scroll," bearing the seal of Sîn-na'id. As a matter of fact, the word *miglu*, "scroll," is itself an Aramaic loanword in NA.[205] SAA XIII 28 r.3–5, reads as follows:

> *ù* 1 GÚ.UN KUG.UD *ina* KALAG-*te* / *mi-ig-li* NA_4.KIŠIB *ša* [md]30–I GAL–SIMUG.KUG.GI / *ina* UGU-*ḫi*
>
> Furthermore, there is one talent of silver by the heavy standard (= 60 kg) with a scroll (bearing) the seal of Sîn-na'id, chief goldsmith, attached to it.

In a frequently quoted passage from a royal letter written in Neo-Babylonian by the Assyrian king Sargon II (SAA XVII 2 = CT 54 10),[206] probably dating to ca. 710 B.C., and addressed to Sîn-iddina, an official from Ur,[207] we find that the

---

[200] See n. ad SAA XVI 99:8f, and the Introduction on p. XLV.

[201] Note that the passage *egirtu armētu* in CAD (E, p. 46a), is quoted from ABL 872:10, and is rendered "a letter in an envelope" (i.e., *armētu* is taken to be from *arāmu* "to cover a tablet in a case"). However, the same passage is not quoted under *arāmu* or *armu* in CAD (A/II, pp. 230, 292). On the other hand, the same passage is quoted in AHw., p. 69b, and is rendered "aramäisches Brief." SAA XVI 99 is in congruence with AHw., in this matter. Cf. Tadmor, *Aramaization*, pp. 452, 463, n. 37.

[202] Cf. PNA 1/I (p. 178a s.v. Aššūr-da''in-aplu); PNA 2/I (p. 593b s.v. Kabtî, no. 9).

[203] See Postgate, FNALD, p. 6. For more details on writing materials and languages used in the Neo-Assyrian Empire, see S. Parpola, SAA I, pp. xv–xvi; R.P. Dougherty, "Writing upon Parchment and Papyrus among the Babylonians and Assyrians," *JAOS* 48 (1928), pp. 109–135.

[204] See the discussion in Chapter 2.1 s.v. *kirku*.

[205] See the discussion in Chapter 2.1 s.v. *miglu*.

[206] See, for instance, S. Parpola, "Assyrian Royal Inscriptions and Neo-Assyrian Letters," in F.M. Fales (ed.), *Assyrian Royal Inscriptions: New Horizons, in Literary, Ideological, and Historical Analysis: Papers of a Symposium Held in Cetona (Siena) June 26–28, 1980* (Rome 1981), p. 123, n. 9; M.P. Streck, "Keilschrift und Alphabet," in D. Borchers et al. (eds.), *Hieroglyphen – Alphabete – Schriftreformen: Studien zu Multiliteralismus, Schriftwechsel und Orthographieneuregelungen* (Göttingen 2001), p. 77; K. Radner, "Schreiberkonventionen im assyrischen Reich: Sprachen und Schriftsysteme," in J. Renger (ed.), *Assur – Gott, Stadt und Land: 5. Internationales Colloquium der Deutschen Orient-Gesellschaft 18. – 21. Februar 2004 in Berlin* (Wiesbaden 2011), p. 389; S. Görke, "Aramäischer Einfluss in Assyrien," in M. Novák, F. Prayon & A-M. Wittke (eds.), *Die Außenwirkung des späthethitischen Kulturraumes: Güteraustausch – Kulturkontakt – Kulturtransfer* (Münster 2004), p. 327.

[207] See PNA 3/I (p. 1134a s.v. Sīn-iddina, no. 5).

official had asked permission to send the king letters written in Aramaic. The letter (SAA XVII 2:15–22), reads as follows:[208]

> *k*[*i*]-[*i* IGI LUG]AL *maḫ-ru ina* ŠÀ *si-ip-ri* / [KUR].*ár-m*[*a-a-a lu-u*]*s-pi-ir-ma a-na* LUGAL / [*l*]*u-še-bi-la mi-nam-ma ina ši-pir-ti* / *ak-ka-da-at-tu la ta-šaṭ-ṭar-ma* / *la tu-šeb-bi-la kit-ta ši-pir-tu* / *šá* [[]] *ina* ŠÀ-*bi ta-šaṭ-ṭa-ru* / *ki-i pi-i a-gan-ni-tim-ma i-da-at* / *lu-ú šak-na-at*
>
> 'If it is acceptable [to the ki]ng, let me write and send (my messages) to the king on Aram[aic] leather-scrolls' – why would you not write and send me messages in Akkadian? Really, the message which you write in it must be drawn up in this very manner – this is a fixed regulation!

It is obvious from the king's response above that the king firmly declines the request and insists that Sîn-iddina should write in Akkadian. It has been suggested by Parpola that tradition may have dictated that cuneiform was the proper medium of communication with Sargon II, and that the political administration of the Assyrian empire still preferred cuneiform writing above alphabetic.[209] It may also have been for security reasons, because intercepted Aramaic documents would have been easier to read.[210]

Another case in point is found in the undated letter SAA XVI (63:13–14), sent to Esarhaddon from the West, concerning crimes in Gūzāna. A passage in the letter reveals that two versions of the same list of taxes due from the provinces were composed, one in Assyrian and the other in Aramaic, a case of double registration.[211] The passage reads as follows: *ṣarap iškāri ša rāʾē ina libbi nibzi aššūrāya / ina libbi nibzi armāya issaṭarū* "They wrote the silver quota of shepherds on an Assyrian document (and) on an Aramaic document."[212]

For Aramaic text written on ostracon, potsherds used as writing materials, probably as a substitute for leather or papyrus, we have the so-called Assur Ostracon (see fig. 7 below), which was sent from Babylon to Assyria.[213] This is a letter from the reign of Assurbanipal which was unearthed in a private house near

---

[208] Cf. Parpola, ibid., p. 123, n. 9; idem, SAA I, p. xvi. Cf. SAA XVII, p. xv.

[209] See S. Parpola, *The Correspondence of Sargon II, Part I: Letters from Assyria and the West* (Helsinki 1987), p. xvi.

[210] Ibid.

[211] See F.M. Fales, "Multilingualism on Multiple Media in the Neo-Assyrian Period: A Review of the Evidence," *SAAB* 16 (2007), p. 108.

[212] See F.M. Fales, "The Tablets from Tell Shioukh Fawqani/Burmarina in the Context of Assyro-Aramaic Studies," in G. del Olmo Lete & J.-L. Montero Fenollós (eds.), *Archaeology of the Upper Syrian Euphrates, the Tishrin Dam Area: Proceedings of the International Symposium Held at Barcelona, January 28th–30th 1998* (Barcelona 1999), p. 628.

[213] See M. Lidzbarski, "Ein aramäischer Brief aus der Zeit Ašurbanipals," *ZA* 31 (1917/1918), pp. 193–202; idem, *Altaramäische Urkunden aus Assur* (Leipzig 1921), pp. 5–15; R.A. Bowman, "An Interpretation of the Asshur Ostracon," in L. Waterman (ed.), *Royal Correspondence of the Assyrian Empire* (New York 1936), Part IV, pp. 275–282; A. Dupont-Sommer, "L'ostracon araméen d'Assour," *Syria* 24 (1944), pp. 24–61; O. Pedersén, ALA II, N 23 and p. 114, n. 1; M.F. Fales, "Aramaic Letters and Neo-Assyrian Letters: Philological and Methodological Notes," *JAOS* 107 (1987), pp. 451–469; idem, "New Light on Assyro-Aramaic Interference: The Assur Ostracon," in F.M. Fales & G.F. Grassi (eds.), *CAMSEMUD 2007: Proceedings of the 13th Italian Meeting of Afro-Asiatic Linguistics, Held in Udine, May 21st–24th, 2007* (Padova 2010), pp. 189–204.

the western town wall of the city of Assur and is preserved in six fragments of a large white-glazed clay sherd written in ink in Aramaic.[214] It is not dated, but can be assigned from its historical context to ca. 650 B.C.[215] The letter was written by Bēl-ēṭir, a cohort commander who was active in Babylonia, for his "brother," Pir᾽-Amurru in Assur, reporting on events in Babylonia during the Šamaš-šumu-ukīn revolt. This piece of evidence also attests to the use of Aramaic as a communication medium between Assyrian high officials in the Assyro-Babylonian area.[216]

Figure 7. The Assur Ostracon (VA 8384), from ca. 650 B.C. From: M. Lidzbarski, *Altaramäische Urkunden aus Assur* (Leipzig, 1921), pl. I.

Another ostracon (ND 6231), unearthed in 1957 at fort Shalmaneser in Calah/Nimrud, contains two lists, in Aramaic script, of West-Semitic proper names of men written on the convex and the concave sides of the ostracon, attesting to the use of Aramaic script in the palace. It has been demonstrated that the two lists of names are the work of different handwritings and the paleographic evidence indicates with fair certainty that the two texts were written sometime between the years of 725 and 675 B.C. (see fig. 8 below).[217]

---

214 For the findspot of Assur Ostracon, see O. Pedersén, ALA II, pp. 113f.

215 See PNA 3/I (p. 995b s.v. Pir᾽-Amurru); V. Hug, *Altaramäische Grammatik der Texte des 7. und 6. Jh.s v.Chr.* (Heidelberg 1993), pp. 19f., Assurbrief (AssB), l. 5.

216 It is appropriate to mention that Aramaic writing is also found in Assyria proper on items that were acquired as booty or tribute from the western provinces of the Assyrian empire. Examples of such items are the well-known Nimrud bowls and ivory plaques. Cf. J.E. Curtis, & J.E. Reade (eds.), *Art and Empire: Treasures from Assyria in the British Museum* (London 1995), p. 191; A.R. Millard, "Alphabetic Inscriptions on Ivories from Nimrud," *Iraq* 24 (1962), pp. 41–51.

217 See J.B. Segal, "An Aramaic Ostracon from Nimrud," *Iraq* 19 (1957): 139–145; W.F. Albright, "An Ostracon from Calah and the North-Israelite Diaspora," *BASOR* 149 (1958), pp. 33–36; A.R. Millard, "Assyrians and Arameans," *Iraq* 45 (1983), p. 102.

Figure 8. The convex side of the Aramaic ostracon from Calah/Nimrud (ND 6231), containing six lines of text written in Aramaic, ca. 725–675 B.C. From: J.B. Segal, "An Aramaic Ostracon from Nimrud," *Iraq* 19 (1957), pl. XXXIV, fig. I.

Still further evidence for the use of Aramaic in Assyria proper comes from the so-called bullae, round clay seals usually bearing an inscription written in Aramaic. It is generally assumed that these bullae might have been attached to official documents of papyrus.[218] For example, we have a stamp seal from Dūr-Šarrukēn (Khorsabad), from the reign of Sargon II, ca. 710 B.C., with a clearly Assyrian name of the owner (see fig. 9 below). The seal reads as follows: [*l*] *pnʾsr* / [*l*]*mr srs z*[!] / *srgn* "[belonging to] Pān-Aššūr-lāmur, eunuch of Sargon." Apparently, the owner of this stamp seal was a high ranking official at the Sargon's court.[219]

[218]This assumption was challenged by Herbordt, who argued that bullae functioned as labels attached to containers, see S. Herbordt, *Neuassyrische Glyptik des 8.–7. Jh. v. Chr.* (Helsinki 1992), pp. 16f. For examples of clay bullae fastened to jars from the Neo-Assyrian period, see J.N. Postgate, *The Governor's Palace Archive* (London 1973), nos. 233–235 and the commentary on p. 223.

[219] See M. Sprengling, "An Aramaic Seal Impression from Khorsabad," *AJSL* 49 (1933), pp. 53–55; Tadmor, *Aramaization*, pp. 450, 461 n. 23; S.A. Kaufman, "The History of Aramaic Vowel Reduction," in M. Sokoloff (ed.), *Arameans, Aramaic and the Aramaic Literary Tradition* (Ramat-Gan 1983), p. 53–54; idem, "Assyro-Aramaica," *JAOS* 109 (1989), p. 97, n. 1; K. Watanabe, "Neuassyrische Siegellegenden," *Orient* 29 (1993), p. 116; PNA 3/I (p. 983 s.v. Pan-Aššūr-lāmur, no. 4); Herbordt, ibid., p. 170, Ḫorsabad 1, pl. 27, 3.

Figure 9. A clay bulla from Dūr-Šarrukēn/Khorsabad, representing a stamp seal of an Assyrian official and bearing inscription written in Aramaic: *[l]pn'sr* / *[l]mr srs z*! / *srgn* "(belonging to) Pān-Aššūr-lāmur, eunuch of Sargon." From: M. Sprengling, "An Aramaic Seal Impression from Khorsabad," *AJSL* 49 (1932), p. 54.

The use of Aramaic is also implied in association with oracular queries placed before the god Shamash, the lord of the oracles, in an act of extispicy.[220] It seems that oracular queries were often joined with a papyrus document including the name of the petitioner (usually Esarhaddon) and/or other relevant details, as the cuneiform tablets often refer to "the man whose name is written on this *niāru* or *urbānu*," i.e., "papyrus," rather than "on this *ṭuppu*," which would refer to a clay tablet. Most likely the information written on papyrus was in Aramaic. An attestation to the use of *niāru* "papyrus," is found for instance in SAA IV (156:2): *[a-me-l]u šá* MU-*šú i-na ni-ia-a-ri an-na-a šá-aṭ-ru-ú-ma* "[the ma]n whose name is written on this papyrus."[221] A reference for the use of *urbānu*, "papyrus," for writing comes from SAA IV (108:3): *[ša] i-na* Ú.*ur-ba-an-ni an-ni-⸢i⸣ šaṭ-ru-ma* "[wh]ich are written in this papyrus." The papyrus documents referred to may have contained another kind of text written in Aramaic as well. Unfortunately, Aramaic queries written on papyrus, a perishable material, did not survive. An extant query, SAA IV (162:7′), written on clay tablet in Neo-Assyrian cuneiform, bears an Aramaic script, namely *nbwšlm 'q*[*r'*], obviously the signatures of Nabû-šallim and Aqar-Aia, both diviners at the court of Nineveh from the reign of Esarhaddon.[222] It is quite interesting that although both diviners have Akkadian names they put their signatures on the clay tablet in Aramaic. Another query (SAA IV 58 r.8–11) asks Shamash whether Esarhaddon should send his messenger with an Aramean scribe. This also attests to the employment of Aramean scribes in the royal service. Of special interest in this genre of texts is a

---

[220] See H. Tadmor, "Assyria and the West: The Ninth Century and its Aftermath," in H. Goedicke & J.J.M. Roberts (eds.), *Unity and Diversity. Essays in the History, Literature, and Religion of the Ancient Near East* (Baltimore 1975), p. 43; I. Starr, *Queries to the Sungod: Divination and Politics in Sargonid Assyria* (Helsinki 1990), p. 359a s.v. *urbānu* "papyrus."

[221] For additional examples, see I. Starr, ibid., p. 343a s.v. *niāru* "papyrus."

[222] See Tadmor, ibid.

query (SAA IV 144:9) where the Assyrian and the Aramean scribes are listed successively: [LÚ.DUB.SAR].MEŠ *aš-šur*.KI-*a-a lu-ú* LÚ.DUB.SAR.MEŠ *ár-ma-a-a*, "the Assyrian [scribes], or the Aramean scribes."

It is clear that during the 8th and 7th centuries B.C., the Assyrian scribes not only produced bilingual texts written in Neo-Assyrian and Aramaic, but also produced text written solely in Aramaic. It appears that the two scribes, *ṭupšarru aššūrāya* and *ṭupšarru armāya*, enjoyed equal prestige during the last two centuries of the Neo-Assyrian empire.[223]

From two cuneiform texts excavated at Nineveh and one cuneiform text excavated at Calah/Nimrud, we deduce that the scribes who wrote the texts were undoubtedly bilingual and spoke Aramaic as their first language. The first instance is a copy of the first tablet of the Epic of Gilgamesh, which was produced for the library of Assurbanipal. In it we find that the scribe made a mistake of a sort only expected from an individual who spoke Aramaic as his first language.[224] The scribe erroneously utilized the cuneiform sign "lord" for writing the word "son," due to the homophonic similarity between Aramaic *mar'* (definite state: *mar'ā*), meaning "lord," and Assyrian *mar'u* (construct state: *mār*) "son."[225]

A rather similar lapse is found in a Neo-Assyrian letter (SAA I 220:3) sent by an official named Arīḫu during the time of Sargon II (ca. 721–705 B.C.) and concerning the corn tax of the Samarians.[226] The letter was unearthed in Nineveh; originally it was probably dispatched from the province of Lāqê in the middle Euphrates region. SAA I 220:1–3 reads as follows: *a-na* ^{md}PA–BÀD–PAB / IM ^{m}*a-ri-ḫi lu* DI-*mu* / *a-na* ⌜DUMU⌝-*ia* "A letter from Ariḫu to Nabû-duru-uṣur. Good health to my lord!" In NA the logogram DUMU normally denotes *mar'u* "son, boy." However, rendering DUMU as "son, boy," does not make sense in the context of this NA letter. Therefore, it is considered to be a slip, most likely due to the Aramaic influence, that the logogram DUMU denotes here the word "lord."[227] A similar mistake is found in a NA letter (SAA XIX 13:3, 5) from the 8th century B.C., which was unearthed at Calah/Nimrud.[228] The semantic variation of DUMU, "son, boy" versus "lord," has been explained a result of the homophonic similarity between the NA *mar'u* "son, boy" and the contemporary Aramaic word *mar'* or *mar'ā* "lord."[229]

The textual material provides another type of evidence attesting to the use of Aramaic alongside Akkadian in the heartland of Assyria. This kind of evidence consists of Aramaic loanwords that are found in NA, SB and NB texts excavated

---

[223] See R.P. Dougherty, "Writing upon Parchment and Papyrus among the Babylonians and Assyrians," *JAOS* 48 (1928), p. 130.

[224] See S. Parpola, *The Standard Babylonian Epic of Gilgamesh* (Helsinki 1997), p. 74, l. no. 242 (ms. D) // l. no. 265 (ms. A2); idem, "Assyrians after Assyria," *JAAS* 12 (2000), p. 12; idem, "The Neo-Assyrian Ruling Class," in T.R. Kämmerer (ed.), *Studien zu Ritual und Sozialgeschichte im Alten Orient / Studies on Ritual and Society in the Ancient Near East: Tartuer Symposien 1998–2004* (Berlin 2007), pp. 265f. Cf. A.R. George, *The Babylonian Gilgamesh Epic: Introduction, Critical Edition and Cuneiform Texts* (Oxford 2003), pp. 802f n. on l. 259.

[225] Ibid.

[226] See PNA 1/I (p. 131a s.v. Arīḫu, no. 1).

[227] See the discussion in chapter 2.1 below s.v. *mar'u*.

[228] Ibid.

[229] Ibid.

in Assyria proper. Loanwords are a useful tool for detecting the vernacular used at the time of direct contact between the donor/source language and the recipient language. In our case, a particularly telling example is the Aramaic loanword *kiqillutu* "dung heap, dunghill, refuse dump," which is attested in two NA legal documents (SAA VI 200:5; SAA VI 31 r.3), and in a NA letter (SAA X 294:15).[230] These NA texts originate from Nineveh. This loanword is coined along the lines of *qīqilta*, which is found in the later dialects of Aramaic.[231] In comparison, a more literary form of the same Aramaic word is found as *qlqlt'* in the Old Aramaic of Tell Fekherye inscription.[232] Since a more colloquial form of this Aramaic word was borrowed into NA, it stands to reason that Aramaic was probably used alongside Akkadian as a spoken language in the Assyrian heartland.[233]

1.9.2 Visual evidence

The narrative reliefs of the Assyrian kings, beginning with Shalmaneser III (858–824 B.C.), portray scribes accompanying the army on campaigns.[234] However, from the time of Tiglath-pileser III (744–727 B.C.), there are numerous depictions on the Assyrian palace reliefs of two scribes standing next to each other, holding different type of writing equipment, and in the act of writing. They are usually portrayed counting captives and recording booty.[235] One scribe is writing with a stylus on a clay tablet or on a wax-coated, ivory or wooden hinged writing board; the other scribe is writing with a pen or brush on papyrus or a leather scroll (see figs. 10–12 below).[236] One pictorial instance, namely the wall painting from Til-

[230] See the discussion in chapter 2.1 below s.v. *kiqillutu*.

[231] See J.C. Greenfield & A. Shaffer "Notes on the Akkadian-Aramaic Bilingual Statue from Tell Fekherye," *Iraq* 40 (1983), p. 116.

[232] Cf. A. Abou-Assaf, P. Bordreuil & A.R. Millard, *La statue de Tell Fekherye et son inscription bilingue assyro-araméenne* (Paris 1982), pp. 23f, l. 22 and p. 36; E. Lipiński, *Studies in Aramaic Inscriptions and Onomastics, II* (Leuven 1994), pp. 70f.

[233] See J.C. Greenfield & A. Shaffer, "*qlqlt', tubkinnu*, Refuse Tips and Treasure Trove," *AnSt* 33 (1983), p. 125.

[234] See J.M. Russell, *Sennacherib's Palace without Rival at Nineveh* (Chicago 1991), pp. 28–31; K. Radner, "Schreiberkonventionen im assyrischen Reich: Sprachen und Schriftsysteme," in J. Renger (ed.), *Assur – Gott, Stadt und Land: 5. Internationales Colloquium der Deutschen Orient-Gesellschaft 18.–21. Februar 2004 in Berlin* (Wiesbaden 2011), p. 388, n. 12.

[235] The images representing Assyrian scribes in pairs also come from the reigns of Shalmaneser V (726–722 B.C.), Sargon II (721–705 B.C.), Sennacherib (704–681 B.C.), and Assurbanipal (668–627 B.C.). There are other similar images which are ascribed to the reign of Sinsharrishkun (ca. 627–612 B.C.). However, in the images from the reign of Assurbanipal, none of the two scribes is writing with a pen or brush on papyrus or a leather scroll. See J.M. Russell, ibid., p. 706.

[236] For additional instances of this sort of visual evidence and a catalogue of illustrations of Neo-Assyrian scribes, see J. Reade "Visual Evidence for the Status and Activities of Assyrian Scribes," in G.B. Lanfranchi et al. (eds.), *Leggo! Studies Presented to Frederick Mario Fales on the Occasion of His 65th Birthday* (Wiesbaden 2012), pp. 702–704 and 712–716; J.M. Russell, *Sennacherib's Palace without Rival at Ninevxeh* (Chicago 1991), p. 321 n. 36. See also S. Parpola, "National and Ethnic Identity in the Neo-Assyrian Empire and Assyrian Identity in Post-Empire Times," *JAAS JAAS* 18/2 (2004), p. 9, n. 21. For the view that there is no attestation in the Neo-Assyrian textual material of the preparation of skin or leather for writing purposes, see F.M. Fales, "The Use and

Barsip (see fig. 12 below), provides additional detailed information by tinting brown the tablet held by one scribe, most probably to make it resemble a clay tablet, while the sheet held by the other scribe is tinted white, undoubtedly to resemble papyrus or leather.[237]

Messerschmidt concludes from these depictions of pairs of scribes on the Assyrian narrative reliefs that the official documents must have been produced in duplicate, one in cuneiform written on a clay tablet and the other in Aramaic alphabet written on papyrus.[238]

A different interpretation of the visual evidence has been put forward by Madhloom who has argued that the person holding a scroll was not a scribe but an artist preparing rough sketches that would be used as models for carving palace reliefs in Assyria.[239] He states that the Assyrian textual records clearly refer to an artist (*ēṣiru*) who is described as sketching on leather.[240] Tadmor, on the other hand, believes that conclusive evidence against Madhloom's opinion is furnished by a fresco from Til-Barsip (Tell Aḥmar), a major Assyrian administrative center in the western part of the Empire, which portrays two scribes facing the king, one writing on a tablet and the other on a sheet of papyrus (see fig. 10 below).[241]

Function of Aramaic Tablets," in G. Bunnens (ed.), *Essays on Syria in the Iron Age* (Louvain 2000), pp. 123f, n. 181.

237 See A.R. Millard, "Assyrians and Arameans," *Iraq* 45 (1983), p. 101. Cf. R.P. Dougherty, "Writing upon Parchment and Papyrus among the Babylonians and Assyrians," *JAOS* 48 (1928), p. 129.

238 See L. Messerschmidt, *Zur Technik des Tontafel-Schreibens* (Berlin 1907), p. 6.

239 See T.A. Madhloom, *The Chronology of Neo-Assyrian Art* (London 1970), pp. 121f; idem, "The Influence of Foreign Societies as Shown in Assyrian Art," in J. Harmatta & G. Komoróczy (eds.), *Wirtschaft und Gesellschaft im Alten Vorderasien* (Budapest 1976), p. 385; idem, "*al-fannān al-'āšūrī yurāfiq al-ḥamalāt al-'askarīyah*," in *Researches on the Antiquities of Saddam Dam Basin Salvage and Other Researches* ([Baghdad] 1987), pp. 245–248.

240 See Madhloom, ibid. For other opinions relating to Madhloom's interpretation, see J. Reade, "Neo-Assyrian Monuments in Their Historical Context," in F.M. Fales (ed.), *Assyrian Royal Inscriptions: New Horizons, in Literary, Ideological, and Historical Analysis: Papers of a Symposium Held in Cetona (Siena) June 26–28, 1980* (Rome 1981), p. 162; idem, *Assyrian Sculpture* (London 1983), p. 34; idem, "Visual Evidence for the Status and Activities of Assyrian Scribes," in G.B. Lanfranchi et al. (eds.), *Leggo! Studies Presented to Frederick Mario Fales on the Occasion of His 65th Birthday* (Wiesbaden 2012), p. 711; U. Seidl, "Assurbanipals Griffel," *ZA* 97 (2007), p. 119. For textual evidence concerning drawings made on leather, see S. Parpola, "The Royal Archives of Nineveh," in K.R. Veenhof (ed.), *Cuneiform Archives and Libraries: Papers read at the 30e Rencontre Assyriologique Internationale Leiden, 4–8 July 1983* (Istanbul 1986), p. 225, n. 18; SAA XV 136 r.15–18.

241 See H. Tadmor, "On the Role of Aramaic in the Assyrian Empire," in M. Mori (ed.), *Near Eastern Studies Dedicated to H.I.H. Prince Takahito Mikasa on the Occasion of His Seventy-Fifth Birthday* (Wiesbaden 1991), p. 420, n. 8.

Figure 10. A fresco from Til-Barsip (Tell Aḥmar), ascribed to Shalmaneser V (726–722 B.C.), representing Assyrian scribes at the royal court. The scribe to the right is writing on a clay tablet, in cuneiform, in Assyrian, and the scribe on the left side is probably writing on papyrus, in alphabet script, in Aramaic. From: F. Thureau-Dangin & M. Dunand, *Til-Barsib* (Paris, 1936), pl. L.

According to Tadmor, the scene in the above-mentioned fresco is not associated with a military campaign abroad but with a ceremony at the Assyrian court, and therefore the person holding the sheet of papyrus must be a scribe recording the royal instructions in Aramaic.[242] Also opposing Madloom's interpretation, Fales has pointed out that the circumstances where an individual with a brush and a scroll stands next to a scribe writing in cuneiform frequently depict the act of registering booty, making it unlikely that he is an artist drawing sketches.[243]

[242] Ibid. For similar counterarguments to Madhloom's interpretation, see K. Watanabe, Review of "The Correspondence of Sargon II, Part I, Letters from Assyria and the West," by S. Parpola, *BiOr* 48 (1991), p. 202; F.M. Fales, "Assyrian-Aramaic Cultural Interrelation: Older and Newer Results," in L. Bachelot & F.M. Fales (eds.), *Tell Shiukh Fawqani 1994–1998, II* (Padova 2005), p. 603, n. 40. Cf. J. Reade "Visual Evidence for the Status and Activities of Assyrian Scribes," in G.B. Lanfranchi et al. (eds.), *Leggo! Studies Presented to Frederick Mario Fales on the Occasion of His 65th Birthday* (Wiesbaden 2012), pp. 711f.
[243] See Fales, ibid.

Figure 11. A stone relief from Calah/Nimrud (BM 118882) depicting an Assyrian official and two scribes recording booty during one of the campaigns of Tiglath-Pileser III (744–727 B.C.). The scribe to the left is writing in cuneiform on a clay tablet or on a hinged writing-board, and the other is probably writing Aramaic in alphabetic script on leather. From: F.M. Fales & J.N. Postgate, SAA XI, p. 96.

Figure 12. A stone relief from the reign of Assurbanipal or later (BM 124596) depicting Assyrian scribes recording booty. The scribe to the right is writing Assyrian on a hinged writing-board in cuneiform and the scribe to the left is probably writing Aramaic on papyrus or a leather scroll in alphabetic script. From: F.M. Fales & J.N. Postgate, SAA VII, p. 126.

The textual/visual evidence and scholarly research reviewed above attest to the fact that Aramaic was indeed utilized alongside Akkadian in the Assyrian empire from the time of Tiglath-pileser III (744–727 B.C.) onward.[244] It was recognized

[244] See R.A. Bowman, "Arameans, Aramaic, and the Bible," *JNES* 7 (1948), p. 75; H. Tadmor, "Assyria and the West: The Ninth Century and its Aftermath," in H. Goedicke & J.J.M. Roberts (eds.), *Unity and Diversity* (Baltimore 1975), p. 42; F.M. Fales, AECT, p. 44.

as a second official language alongside Akkadian, at least in the western provinces of the Neo-Assyrian Empire.[245]

The frequent Aramaic personal names attested in different Neo-Assyrian texts stemming from Assyria proper confirm the presence of Arameans in the heartland of Assyria during the first millennium B.C. We know, based on their occupational titles, that many of them held high positions within Assyrian society. It is certain that a large majority of those Arameans were originally deported to the Assyrian heartland. However, as the records reveal, many Arameans as well as other non-Assyrians assumed Assyrian names in the second generation and afterwards. Undoubtedly this happened for the purpose of prestige and as a result of the accelerated process of Assyrianization.[246] Nevertheless, based on the extant prosopographical data, Zadok has concluded that the predominantly Assyrian character of Assyria proper was maintained until the very end of the Assyrian empire.[247] On the other hand, the prosopographical data shows that the large majority of the population in the western provinces of the empire, namely the Gozan-Harran area, constituted of the bearers of West-Semitic names whereas the bearers of Assyrian names in the same area were only 30%.[248]

Geller believes that Aramaic was already widely spoken in Assyria during the Neo-Assyrian period.[249] Postgate remarks that by the 7th century the main records of corn and commodity transactions in Assyria were in Aramaic, but currency loans were recorded in Assyrian.[250] According to many scholars, it was in the Neo-Assyrian empire that Aramaic was first recognized as the second official language of a great power and became a *lingua franca*.[251]

Parpola states that the Assyrian rulers imposed Aramaic as a *lingua franca* through a carefully calculated policy aimed at unifying different nations and languages of the vast Empire to create a unified national identity.[252] He also points out that from the reign of Sargon and before we have a large number of letters received from provincial governors, but we completely lack this kind of

[245] See H. Tadmor, "On the Role of Aramaic in the Assyrian Empire," in M. Mori (ed.), *Near Eastern Studies Dedicated to H.I.H. Prince Takahito Mikasa on the Occasion of His Seventy-Fifth Birthday* (Wiesbaden 1991), p. 419; idem, *Aramaization*, p. 451; J.A. Fitzmyer, *A Wandering Aramaean: Collected Aramaic Essays* (Chico 1979), p. 59.

[246] See R. Zadok, "The Ethno-Linguistic Character of the Jezireh and Adjacent Regions in the 9th–7th Centuries (Assyrian Proper vs. Periphery)," in M. Liverani (ed.), *Neo-Assyrian Geography* (Rome 1995), p. 278.

[247] See Zadok, ibid., p. 281.

[248] Ibid., p. 278. Cf. F.M. Fales, *Censimenti e catasti di epoca neo-assira* (Rome 1973), pp. 106f, and n. 90.

[249] See M.J. Geller, Review of "A Sketch of Neo-Assyrian Grammar," by J. Hämeen-Anttila, *BSOAS* 65 (2002), p. 563.

[250] See J.N. Postgate, "Middle Assyrian to Neo-Assyrian: The Nature of the Shift," in H. Waetzoldt & H. Hauptmann (eds.), *Assyrien im Wandel der Zeiten* (Heidelberg 1997), p. 161.

[251] See the discussion above in Section 1.8 under Old Aramaic and Official Aramaic.

[252] See S. Parpola, "The Neo-Assyrian Ruling Class," in T.R. Kämmerer (ed.), *Studien zu Ritual und Sozialgeschichte im Alten Orient / Studies on Ritual and Society in the Ancient Near East: Tartuer Symposien 1998–2004* (Berlin 2007), p. 262; see also idem, "Assyrians after Assyria," *JAAS* 12 (2000), pp. 1–16.

letters from the reigns of Esarhaddon and the later kings.[253] Parpola suggests that probably from the reign of Sennacherib the provincial governors switched to sending letters written in Aramaic on perishable material, such as papyrus or parchment, which is now lost forever.[254]

The status of Aramaic as an official language was maintained afterwards by the succeeding Babylonians and Persians. It is no wonder that we find in a LB tablet from the reign of Cyrus (Cyr. 364:16), a reference, in a broken context, to a scribe (of Aramaic), who most likely was an Assyrian from southern Mesopotamia as identified by the nominal pattern and the theophoric element in his name, and was employed in the royal service: ^{m}IGI–AN.ŠÁR-*lu-mur* ^{lú}*si-pi-ri* ⌜DUMU–LUGAL⌝ "Pān-Aššūr-lūmur, scribe (of Aramaic), of *the son of the king*."[255] Interestingly, Pān-Aššūr-lūmur's occupational title is not *ṭupšarru*, but *sepīru*, which means he was a scribe specialized in writing Aramaic.

Zadok states: "Aramaic texts were generally written in Aramean political entities before 720 B.C. Later on, with the final conquest of these entities by the Assyrians, Aramaic became the *lingua franca* of the Assyrian empire. Therefore, an Aramaic text in a given place after 720 B.C. is not necessarily an indication of the presence of Arameans there."[256] Zadok iterates later saying:

> Aramaic inscriptions appear in the Jezireh as early as the 9th century. Their number increases and their geographical distribution widens in the ensuing centuries. However, from the end of 8th century, Aramaic became a communication language in most parts of the Assyrian empire thereby ceasing to be an indication of the presence of ethnic Arameans. Hence most of the pertinent direct evidence ceases after the liquidation of the last Aramean polities in Syria towards the end of the 8th century.[257]

Brock expresses almost a similar view, stating: "Only in the early centuries of its recorded history has Aramaic been tied to a specific ethnic group, the Arameans, for it was soon adopted as a spoken or as a literary language (or as both) by peoples of many ethnic and religious backgrounds."[258]

Prior to Zadok and Brock, Bowman described one of the aspects of the Aramaic language as follow:

> Part of the difficulty in the study of Aramaic lies in the fact that the language is usually not definitely tied to any single national or ethnic group. Most Aramaic we

[253] See S. Parpola, "Assyrian Royal Inscriptions and Neo-Assyrian Letters," in F.M. Fales (ed.), *Assyrian Royal Inscriptions: New Horizons, in Literary, Ideological, and Historical Analysis: Papers of a Symposium Held in Cetona (Siena) June 26–28, 1980* (Rome 1981), pp. 122f.

[254] Ibid. Cf. Fales, "The Use and Function of Aramaic Tablets," in G. Bunnens (ed.), *Essays on Syria in the Iron Age* (Louvain 2000), pp. 123f.

[255] See R.P. Dougherty, "Writing upon Parchment and Papyrus among the Babylonians and Assyrians," *JAOS* 48 (1928), pp. 118f, n. 56; J.N. Strassmaier, *Inschriften von Cyrus, König von Babylon (538–529 v. Chr.)*, (Leipzig 1890), p. 216.

[256] See R. Zadok, "On the Onomasticon of the Old Aramaic Sources," *BiOr* 48 (1991), p. 25.

[257] See R. Zadok, "The Ethno-Linguistic Character of the Jezireh and Adjacent Regions in the 9th–7th Centuries (Assyrian Proper vs. Periphery)," in M. Liverani (ed.), *Neo-Assyrian Geography* (Rome 1995), p. 218.

[258] See S. Brock, "Three Thousand Years of Aramaic Literature," *ARAM Periodical* 1 (1989), p. 11.

> possess was not written by Arameans or within any particular Aramean state. The specifically "Aramean" kingdoms that we know were all relatively small and rather unimportant politically, and most of them were located in areas as yet but poorly worked by archeologists. The influence of the Aramaic language has been out of all proportion to the political importance of the people who spoke it, for Aramaic soon became a cultural element at home almost everywhere in the ancient world.[259]

In later periods the Aramaic script was called in Greek *Assyria grammata* "Assyrian characters," in Demotic it was called *sẖ ʾIšr* "script of Assyria," and in Talmudic literature the term *kṯāḇʾaššūrī* "Assyrian writing" is used for the Aramaic form of the alphabet, i.e., the "square" Jewish script that replaced the ancient Hebrew script.[260] All this was, perhaps, due to the association of the Aramaic language and script with Assyria and the Assyrians.

The centuries' long coexistence and language contact between Akkadian (Assyrian and Babylonian) and Aramaic led to a mutual influence between the two languages. They vied for dominance, and eventually Akkadian, the native language of Mesopotamia, was replaced by Aramaic which became the medium of communication in the entire ancient Near East.[261] Much later, in the same region, Aramaic met with a similar fate as that of Akkadian, and was ultimately replaced by Arabic in the wake of the Islamic conquest in the 7th century A.D.

1.10 The scheme for presentation of data

The analysis of the proposed Aramaic loanwords in Neo-Assyrian which is put forward in Chapter 2 is presented and arranged as follows:

A. The order of the lemmata:

The headwords are listed in the order of the Latin alphabet and following the generally accepted convention by which the dotted letters (*ṣ*, *ṭ*) follow the undotted letters, and *š* follows *ṣ*. The headwords are entered in bold character followed by other existing forms of the word entered in italics. They consist of the proposed Aramaic loanwords that are cited in their Neo-Assyrianized lexical forms as they appear in *Assyrian-English-Assyrian Dictionary* (AEAD),[262] and are generally listed in the nominative singular form of nouns. For *plurale tantum*, the

---

[259] See R.A. Bowman, "Arameans, Aramaic, and the Bible," *JNES* 7 (1948), p. 66.

[260] See R.C. Steiner, "Why the Aramaic Script Was Called 'Assyrian' in Hebrew, Greek, and Demotic," *Or* 62 (1993): 80–82, with references to previous discussions on this subject. See also J.C. Greenfield, "The Aramaic Legal Texts of the Achaemenian Period," *Transeuphratène* 3 (1990), p. 88; R. Schmitt, "Assyria grammata und ähnliche: Was wußte die Griechen von Keilschrift und Keilschriften?" in C.W. Müller, K. Sier and J. Werner (eds.), *Zum Umgang mit fremden Sprachen in der griechisch-römischen Antike* (Stuttgart 1992), pp. 21–35; G. Rubio, "Writing in Another Tongue: Alloglottography in the Ancient Near East," in S.L. Sanders (ed.), *Margins of Writing, Origins of Cultures* (Chicago 2006), p. 51.

[261] See Kaufman, AIA, p. 2.

[262] See S. Parpola et al. (eds.), *Assyrian-English-Assyrian Dictionary* (Helsinki 2007).

lexical form is indicated as plural. In the case of verbs, the Neo-Assyrian infinitive is listed. Where a lexical form is reconstructed, an asterisk precedes it. Grammatical information, e.g., syntactic category, is provided immediately after the headword. The verbal stems are abbreviated as follows: The basic stem, *Grundstamm*, (G); the doubled stem (D); the causative stem or the Š-stem (Š); the passive stem or N-stem (N). A brief gloss follows on the same line as the headword. English translations are enclosed in double quotation marks, e.g., *durā'u* n. "arm, forearm"; definitions are enclosed in parentheses, e.g., *siprītu* (a textile).

B. Attested forms and citations:

The attested Neo-Assyrian word form(s) of a proposed Aramaic loanword and its textual reference(s) are given immediately under the headword. They serve as the accumulated evidence of usage. Whenever possible, the textual citations and their renditions quoted in CAD, AHw., or von Soden's articles on Aramaic loanwords in Neo-Assyrian and Neo- and Late-Babylonian are replaced by the new editions of the same texts that appeared in SAA volumes I–XIX, or in other current Neo-Assyrian text editions appearing for instance in CTN, StAT, SAAB and BATSH. Detailed information is provided on the NA texts that include proposed Aramaic loanwords, to investigate whether there are any pattern(s) in the groups of texts and the loanwords studied. The relevance of geographical and chronological factors in the extant NA texts containing Aramaic loanwords can now be investigated. The information is presented in table format and is arranged in six columns containing the following details:

(1) *Loanword*: This comprises all the forms attested for a given Aramaic loanword in NA. Since Neo-Assyrian employs cuneiform signs for writing, the transliteration of the attested forms cited is given sign-by-sign in the Latin alphabet following the conventions of the SAA series. The logograms are written in capitals.
(2) *Reference*: This provides the textual references for the NA texts cited. As for the line numbering of the NA texts quoted, the method of line numbering in the SAA series and the State Archives of Assyria Project's electronic database, Corpus of Neo-Assyrian Texts (CNA), is followed. Texts that are royal letters are referred to as (RL).
(3) *Provenance*: This indicates the geographical location where the NA text cited was excavated.
(4) *Origin*: This indicates the geographical location where the NA text was initially written or composed (if known). Conjectural suggestions are given in italics. Unknown origin is marked (–).
(5) *Genre*: This refers to the type of the NA text which contains an Aramaic loanword. For indicating the type of the NA text, the following abbreviations are used: (AD) administrative document; (AR) astrological report; (D) decree; (Inscr.) inscription; (L) letter; (LD) legal document;

(LL) lexical list; (LT) literary text; (MC) mystical & cultic; (P) prophecy; (R) ritual; (T) treaty; (TL) textile list; (WL) wine list.

(6) *Date*: All the dates of the NA texts cited refer to B.C. In addition, the following abbreviations and symbols are utilized:

Adn	= Adad-nērārī III (810–783 B.C.)
Asb	= Assurbanipal (668–627 B.C.)
Asn	= Ashurnasirpal II (883–859 B.C.)
Esh	= Esarhaddon (680–669 B.C.)
Sg	= Sargon II (721–705 B.C.)
Shalm. III	= Shalmaneser III (858–824 B.C.)
Sn	= Sennacherib (704–681 B.C.)
Tgl	= Tiglath-pileser III (744–727 B.C.)
PC	= post-canonical (648*–609* B.C.)
–	= not dated *or* date lost
*	= a reconstructed post-canonical date.[263]

C. Assessment of the loan hypothesis:

The loan hypothesis is provided under the attested word forms and textual citations. A number of operators are utilized as follows: (⇒) to indicate a loan direction; (=▷) to indicate a semantic loan; (;) to indicate independent co-receptors of a loan; (// //) to mark a previous loan hypothesis that is now considered false; [?] to indicate a possible but questionable loan.

D. The source word:

All the Aramaic words from different Aramaic languages/dialects which may contribute to identifying the possible Aramaic source words borrowed into Neo-Assyrian are quoted for the sake of discussion and analysis of the loan hypothesis. The words include, when possible, Old Aramaic (OAram.), Official Aramaic (OffAr.), Nabatean (Nab.), Palmyrene (Palm.), Biblical Aramaic (BA), Jewish Literary Aramaic (JLA), Qumran Aramaic (QA), Palestinian Targumic Aramaic (PTA), Jewish Palestinian Aramaic (JPA), Galilean Aramaic (Gal.), Christian Palestinian Aramaic (CPA), Samaritan Aramaic (Sam.), Syriac (Syr.), Late Jewish Literary Aramaic (LJLA), Jewish Babylonian Aramaic (JBA), Mandaic (Ma.), and Sūret (a.k.a. NENA).

E. Discussion and analysis of the proposed loanword:

Discussions previously put forward by scholars which are pertinent to a proposed loanword, as well as any related controversy, are noted, analyzed and contrasted

[263] The sequence of *limmu* dating follows A. Millard, *The Eponyms of the Assyrian Empire 910–612 BC* (Helsinki 1994). The post-canonical (PC), eponyms are based on the provisional order by S. Parpola, in K. Radner (ed.), *The Prosopography of the Neo-Assyrian Empire, 1/I, A* (Helsinki 1998), pp. xviii–xxi.

with each other. The main objective is to present the evidence that leads to establishing or rejecting a proposed loanword as clearly and comprehensively as possible.

F. The translations of the Neo-Assyrian passages quoted:

If not clearly stated otherwise, the translations of the NA passages quoted in this study for the sake of discussion are the same as those given in SAA volumes I–XXI, or in other current Neo-Assyrian text editions appearing in CTN, StAT, SAAB and BATSH. Uncertain and conjectural translations are indicated by italics.

2. ANALYSIS OF LOAN HYPOTHESES

All the proposed Aramaic loanwords in Neo-Assyrian are discussed and analyzed in this chapter. Here the evidence put forward to establish the borrowing for each proposed loanword is analyzed and re-assessed, and a conclusion is reached about whether to accept or dismiss the loan hypothesis. The proposed loanwords are categorized into two groups. The first group, discussed in (2.1), consists of words that are recognized as Aramaic loanwords or possible Aramaic loanwords in Neo-Assyrian. The second group, discussed in (2.2), consists of the proposed Aramaic loanwords that, according to the conclusions drawn by this study, should be rejected and no longer considered Aramaic loanwords in Neo-Assyrian.

2.1 Analysis of the proposed Aramaic loanwords in Neo-Assyrian

This group of the proposed Aramaic loanwords in Neo-Assyrian consists of those words that, after analyzing the evidence required to establish the borrowing, are judged to be certainly borrowed from Aramaic. Also included here are those proposed Aramaic loanwords whose loan relationship is considered to be possible but questionable. An explanation of the scheme for presentation of data, including a clarification of a number of operators and abbreviations used here to facilitate the discussion, is given in section (1.10) above.

adê n. pl. tant. "(vassal) treaty, covenant, pact, pledge of allegiance"[264]

Loanword	Reference	Provenance	Origin	Genre	Date
a-de	StAT 2 169 r.8	Assur	Daria *or* Assur	LD	641*
	StAT 3 64 r.1 ⸢*a*⸣-*de*	Assur	Assur	LD	PC
a-de-e	AfO 32 42 r.6 (= BM 122698)	Assur	Assur	LD	620*
	BATSH 6/2 199 e.10	Dūr-Katlimmu	Dūr-Katlimmu	LD	620*
	CTN III 30 r.1	Calah	Calah	LD	617*

[264] See AEAD (p. 4a s.v. *adê*). The lexical form is given as plural for the words that are *plurale tantum*. For lengthening the final vowel in this word by a circumflex (^), see Luukko, SAAS XVI, § 1.4. For recent literature discussing the institution of *adê*, see M. Liverani, *Assyria: The Imperial Mission* (Winona Lake, 2017), pp. 132–137; J. Lauinger, "The Neo-Assyrian *adê*: Treaty, Oath, or Something Else?" *ZAR* 19 (2013), p. 99, n. 1. See also Kaufman, AIA, p. 33, n. 10; H. Tadmor, "Assyria and the West: The Ninth Century and its Aftermath," in H. Goedicke & J.J.M. Roberts (eds.), *Unity and Diversity* (Baltimore 1975), p. 48, n. 54; D. Pardee, Review of "Textbook of Syrian Semitic Inscriptions, vol. 2. Aramaic Inscriptions, Including Inscriptions in the Dialect of Zenjirli," by John C.L. Gibson, *JNES* 37 (1978), pp. 196f; DNWSI (p. 824f s.v. *ʿd_1*). In CAD, *adû* A and *adû* B should be subsumed under one lemma, as in AHw.

CTN III 31 r.2	Calah	Calah	LD	630*
CTN III 34 r.6	Calah	Calah	LD	638*
CTN III 36:12	Calah	*Calah*	LD	622*
CTN III 47 r.10	Calah	*Calah*	LD	–
CTN III 63 r.4	Calah	Calah	LD	653
CTN III 64 r.1	Calah	*Calah*	LD?	613*
SAA I 8 r.20	Nineveh	Assyria	L	Sg
SAA I 76:6	Nineveh	Assur	L	Sg
SAA II 1 e.15′	Nineveh	*Nineveh*	T	825?
SAA II 2 i 13′, 15′, 24′, r. iv 17, 29′, r. v 8, 14, 16, 24′	Nineveh	*Nineveh*	T	754?
SAA II 6:1, 10, 12, 41, 64, 96, 104, 132, 153, 175, 283, 289, 291, 351, 358, 382, 387, 390, 398, 400, 513, 526, 573, 616, 666	Calah	Calah	T	672
SAA II 8:9	Nineveh	*Nineveh*	T	669?
SAA II 12:1	Assur	–	T	625?
SAA VI 95 r.5	Nineveh	*Nineveh*	LD	–
SAA IX 3 ii 27, 36; iii 11, 14	Nineveh	*Nineveh*	P	Esh
SAA X 5 r.1	Nineveh	*Nineveh*	L	673?
SAA X 6:9, 19, r.10, 17	Nineveh	*Nineveh*	L	672
SAA X 7:13, r.3	Nineveh	*Nineveh*	L	672
SAA X 199 r.19′	Nineveh	Nineveh	L	670
SAA X 273:12	Nineveh	Nineveh	L	672?
SAA X 316:22, e.25	Nineveh	*Nineveh*	L	670?
SAA X 354:21	Nineveh	Babylon	L	670*
SAA XIII 32:10	Nineveh	*Assur*	L	672?
SAA XIV 96 r.2	Nineveh	*Nineveh*	LD	7th c.
SAA XIV 459 r.4′	*Nineveh*	*Assur*	LD	635*
SAA XV 90:8, r.19	Nineveh	*Kār-Šarrukīn*	L/T	Sg
SAA XV 98 r.4′	Nineveh	*Kār-Šarrukīn*	L	Sg
SAA XV 196:4′	Nineveh	Northern Babylonia	L	Sg
SAA XVI 21:9, r.5	Nineveh	Babylon	L	Esh
SAA XVI 59:4	Nineveh	*Nineveh*	L	Esh
SAA XVI 60:5	Nineveh	*Nineveh*	L	Esh
SAA XVI 61:5	Nineveh	–	L	Esh
SAA XVI 71 r.3	Nineveh	–	L	Esh
SAA XVI 126:19, 25	Nineveh	Phoenicia	L	Esh
SAA XVI 150:8′	Nineveh	–	L	Esh
SAA XVI 171:11′	Nineveh	–	L	Esh
SAA XVI 243 r.6′	Nineveh	–	L	Esh
SAA XIX 28:4	Calah	Ṣimirra?	L	Tgl
SAAB 2 9 r.5′	Nabula	Nabula	LD	–
SAAB 5 59 r.10	Assur	Assur	LD	617*
SAAB 9 71 r.13	Assur	Assur	LD	650
Rfdn 17 3 r.1	Assur	Assur	LD	621*
Rfdn 17 10 r.12	Assur	*Assur*	LD	612*

	a-de-(e)				
	Rfdn 17 30:11	Assur	Assur	LD	638*
	StAT 2 33 e.6′	Assur	*Assur*	LD	–
	StAT 2 145 r.10	Assur	Assur	LD	Asb?
	StAT 2 146:13	Assur	Assur	LD	Asb
	StAT 2 164 r.7, 13	Assur	Assur	LD	675
	StAT 2 242 r.4	Assur	Assur	LD	612?
	StAT 2 266 r.3′	Assur	*Assur*	LD	648*
	StAT 2 272 r.2	Assur	*Assur*	LD	647*
	StAT 3 2:15	Assur	Assur	LD	648*
	StAT 3 59 r.7	Assur	*Assur*	LD	634*
	StAT 3 60 r.6	Assur	Assur	LD	631*
	StAT 3 76 r.5′	Assur	Assur	LD	637*
	StAT 3 88 r.12′	Assur	*Assur*	LD	638*
	StAT 3 103 r.3	Assur	*Assur*	LD	622*
	T i 1, 13, 19, 46′, v 7, 15, 22, 46, 53, 56, 62, 64, 69, viii 66	Kullanīa	*Calah*	T	672
a-de-e-ka	SAA XVI 59:5	Nineveh	–	L	Esh
a-de-e-ku-nu	SAA II 6:292	Calah	Calah	T	672
a-de-ka	SAA XVI 60:5	Nineveh	*Nineveh*	L	Esh

Aram. ⇒ NA; NB; LB

OAram., *ʿdyʾ* n. m. pl. tant. "pact, treaty, treaty-stipulations" DNWSI 824; Brauner 447ff; CAL. Nab., *ʿdyʾ* n. m. pl. tant. "contractual agreements" CAL.

The use of the term *adê* for treaties is attested for the first time in the Assyrian sources in a vassal treaty imposed by Aššūr-nērāri V (754–745 B.C.) on Matīʾ-ilu, king of Arpad, an Aramaic city-state north of Aleppo.[265] The treaty was probably concluded in the very first year of the Assyrian king's reign.[266] The word appears in Aramaic in the emphatic pl. עדיא and absolute pl. עדן, as well as in construct pl. עדי.[267]

AHw. (p. 14a s.v. *adû* I) lists this word in the sense of "Eid." The editors of CAD (A/I, p. 131b s.v. *adû* A) define the word as (a type of formal agreement). Neither of the two dictionaries provides an etymology for this word. In DNWSI (pp. 824f. s.v. *ʿd*$_1$), the direction of borrowing is unresolved and the word is considered to be either a loan from Akkadian or a loan into Akkadian.

---

[265] See SAA II 2.

[266] For a presentation of the Neo-Assyrian corpus of Treaties and Loyalty Oaths, see S. Parpola & K. Watanabe (eds.), *Neo-Assyrian Treaties and Loyalty Oaths* (Helsinki 1988), pp. xv–lv; K. Watanabe, *Die adê-Vereidigung anlässlich der Thronfolgeregelung Asarhaddons* (Berlin 1987), pp. 6–25. See some cursory observations by Tadmor, *Aramaization*, pp. 455–458. See also S. Ponchia, "The Neo-Assyrian *Adê* Protocol and the Administration of the Empire," in S. Gaspa, et al. (eds.), *From Source to History: Studies on Ancient Near Eastern Worlds and Beyond Dedicated to Giovanni Battista Lanfranchi on the Occasion of His 65th Birthday on June 23, 2014* (Münster 2014), pp. 501–525. For another term, namely *adê ša šarri* "(loyalty) oath to king," see K. Deller, "Zur Terminologie neuassyrischer Urkunden," *WZKM* 57 (1961), pp. 31f.

[267] See J.A. Fitzmyer, *The Aramaic Inscriptions of Sefire* (Rome 1995), p. 57.

Von Soden was of the opinion that this word occurs as *a-di-an-ni* in a MA text from El-Amarna.[268] However, the same text is quoted in CAD, and the correct reading of the same word appears as *a-di an-ni* in the sense of "until now."[269] In discussing international treaties known so far in Aramaic, Lipiński has rejuvenated the attempt to push the attestation of the word back to a MA private document.[270] He mentions the emendation *a-di-a-*(*na*) proposed for the MA word in CAD (A/I, p. 134a s.v. *adû* A), but apparently subscribes to a reading and translation of the same word by Postgate as *a-di-a* "stipulation."[271] Abraham and Sokoloff, however, consider both the date of the document and the fact that it concerns a private rather than a political matter to speak against Lipiński's opinion.[272]

Tadmor states that *adê* does not occur in MA and that the listing of the alleged MA singular form **adû* in current Akkadian dictionaries is incorrect, being based either on an erroneous reading or a reconstruction made at the time when its etymology was not yet known.[273] He asserts that the origin of *adê* is Aramaic and it was borrowed into Akkadian.[274]

Greenfield also affirms that *adê* is an Aramaic loanword in Neo-Assyrian suggesting that it may in turn be a loanword in Aramaic from a Canaanite dialect, and associating it with the Hebrew root עדו "to see, witness," or with Hebrew עדים* "treaty."[275]

In an excursus on *adê*, Parpola considers this word a loan from Aramaic in NA which replaced the MA word *riksu/rikiltu* "treaty."[276] He regards it as an interesting phenomenon which falls within the general framework of Assyro-Aramaic ethnolinguistic contact.[277] Parpola, unlike Tadmor, does not consider the loyalty oath or vassal treaty, as an institution, to have been a late western innovation in Assyria; rather it had constituted an essential part of all Mesopotamian imperial systems since the earliest times.[278] Durand, on the other

---

[268] This is an Assyrian (royal) letter (VAB 2, 15, 9) quoted in AHw. (p. 14a s.v. *adû* I).

[269] See CAD (A/I, p. 119b s.v. *adi* A, mng. g, 2′).

[270] See E. Lipiński, *The Aramaeans: Their Ancient History, Culture, Religion* (Leuven 2000), pp. 596f, n. 258.

[271] See Lipiński, ibid. See also J.N. Postgate, "More 'Assyrian Deeds and Documents'," *Iraq* 32 (1970), p. 147, n. 10.

[272] See Abraham & Sokoloff, *Reassessment*, p. 25, n. 35.

[273] See Tadmor, *Aramaization*, pp. 455, 468 n. 113. However, prior to Tadmor, B. Volkwein, "Masoreitisches *'ēdūt, 'ēdwōt, 'ēdōt* – 'Zeugnis' oder 'Bundesbestimmungen'?" *BZ* 13 (1969), p. 33, n. 115, had already shown that there are no certain attestations of *adû* in MA as claimed by von Soden.

[274] See Tadmor, ibid., p. 455.

[275] See J.C. Greenfield, "Some Glosses on the Safire Inscriptions," *Maarav* 7 (1991), p. 142. See also Kaufman, AIA, p. 33, n. 11; HALOT (p. 787 s.v. עֵד*). Cf. D. Pardee, Review of *Textbook of Syrian Semitic Inscriptions, Vol. 2. Aramaic Inscriptions, Including Inscriptions in the Dialect of Zenjirli*, by John C.L. Gibson, *JNES* 37 (1978), p. 196.

[276] See S. Parpola, "Neo-Assyrian Treaties from the Royal Archives of Nineveh," *JCS* 39 (1987), pp. 180–183.

[277] Ibid.

[278] See Parpola, ibid. See also J.A. Fitzmyer, *The Aramaic Inscriptions of Sefire* (Rome 1995), p. 59. Cf. Tadmor, *Aramaization*, p. 455; idem, "Assyria and the West: The Ninth Century and its Aftermath," in H. Goedicke & J.J.M. Roberts (eds.), *Unity and Diversity* (Baltimore 1975), pp. 42f.

hand, suggests an Akkadian etymology for the word *adê*, which he connects with the Akkadian word *adû(m)* "work assignment, duty."[279]

Chronologically, it has been shown that there is no conclusive evidence for the occurrence of *adê* in Akkadian texts prior to the NA and NB periods. The oldest attestation of *adê* in Aramaic texts is its frequent occurrence in the Aramaic inscriptions of Sefire, which were contemporaneous with Aššūr-nērāri V (754–745 B.C.).

Phonologically, the Aramaic word appears to be derived from the root ʿDY. It is important to point out that there is no indication whatsoever of the preservation of *ʿayin* in first-millennium Akkadian, and no solid proof of any Northwest Semitic borrowing from an Akkadian word with an initial vowel being represented by /ʿ/.[280] Also, when NA words with initial vowel are borrowed into Aramaic, they are written with an initial aleph.[281] Hence, the word is not a borrowing from Akkadian into Aramaic.

A further phonological consideration is that the original Semitic voiced pharyngeal fricative /ʿ/ was already reduced in Akkadian and appears from about 2000 B.C. as a glottal stop ʾ (hamza). The latter, then, as a result of the reduction of /ʿ/, disappears totally, causing an *e*-coloring of the neighboring **a*, i.e., an umlaut of *a* > *e*.[282] In our case, the lack of *e*-coloring in the word *adê* also points to a borrowing into NA.[283]

The lack of a satisfactory etymology for the word *adê* in Akkadian, the phonological evidence, and the occurrence of *adê* only in NA, NB and LB, taken together all point to a loan from Aramaic into NA.

adrāʾu n. "forearm"; (see the discussion below s.v. *durāʾu*)

Aram. ⇒ NA

agappu, *aqappu*, *akappu* n. "wing"

Loanword	Reference	Provenance	Origin	Genre	Date
a-gap-pi	SAA I 51:5	Nineveh	*Nineveh*	L	Sg
a-gap-pi-ia	SAA IX 2 iii 27′	Nineveh	*Arbela*	P	Esh
a-kap-pi	SAA V 293:7	Nineveh	*Nineveh*	L	Sg
	SAA IX 2 ii 6′	Nineveh	*Arbela*	P	Esh
a-qa-pu-šú	SAA IX 1 i 7′	Nineveh	*Arbela*	P	Esh
UZU.*a-gap-pa-a-ni*	SAA XII 68:36	Assur	–	D	9th c. ?

279 See J.-M. Durand, "Précurseurs syriens aux protocoles néo-assyriens," in D. Charpin & F. Joannès (eds.), *Marchands, diplomates et empereurs: études sur la civilisation mésopotamienne offertes à Paul Garelli* (Paris 1991), p. 70 n. 167. For a concurring remark, see J. Lauinger, "The Neo-Assyrian *adê*: Treaty, Oath, or Something Else?" *ZAR* 19 (2013), p. 115.

280 See Kaufman, AIA, pp. 33, 142.

281 See Hämeen-Anttila, SAAS XIII, § 2.1.4.

282 See above, n. 64.

283 Cf. J.A. Fitzmyer, *The Aramaic Inscriptions of Sefire* (Rome 1995), p. 59.

Aram. ⇒ NA; SB [?]

JPA, LJLA *ʾgp*, *ʾgpʾ* n. m. "wing" DJPA 34b; Jastrow 13b; CAL. JBA *gpʾ* n. m. "wing; feather" DJBA 297a. Ma., *gpʾ* n. m. "wing" MD 78a. Sam., *gp*, *gpʾ* n. m. "wing" DSA 156b; CAL. Syr., *gpʾ* "wing" Audo 157a; Manna 120b; SL 253b; PSm. 76b. JPA *gp* n. m. "wing" DJPA 134b.

Neither AHw. (p. 15b s.v. *agappu*(*m*)), nor the editors of CAD (K, p. 185a s.v. *kappu* A), consider *agappu* a loanword. From OB on, the word *kappu* was used to indicate a "wing." It is derived from the Semitic root KNP, which in Akkadian exhibits regressive assimilation of the cluster *nC*.[284] The occurrence of this root in Aramaic and Hebrew, and also as KNF in Arabic, all in the sense of "wing," makes this a plausible Common Semitic meaning, but its other meanings such as "hand," "side," "bosom," "protection," etc., are secondary semantic developments shared by some or only found in one of the individual Semitic languages. There exists another *kappu*, a homophone which belongs to the Semitic root KPP or KPʾ, attested in NA in the sense "drinking bowl; dish; list."[285]

In NA *agappu* is used as a new word denoting "wing." This word has two variants, *aqappu* and *akappu*. About the former, Parpola states that this unusual NA by-form is undoubtedly an alloform of *agappu*, in spite of the fact that no other explicit spellings of the word with *q* instead of *g* are attested other than that found in SAA IX 1 i 7.[286] Another word attested already in MA, namely *gappu* "wing," is also found in NA.[287] From older periods *agappu* is only attested lexically in OB in the sense "wing" (of door).[288]

However, the word *agappu* in the sense "wing," was identified by Zimmern as an Aramaic loanword in Akkadian.[289] He tentatively considered the Akkadian *agappu* "wing," which he described as "späteres u. selteneres Wort," as a loan from Aramaic *ʾagappā*.[290] Parpola also considers *agappu* to be a loanword from Aramaic characteristic of NA.[291] Both scholars seem to have based their conclusions on the attested word *ʾgp* "wing," in later Aramaic, but provide no argument in support of the loan identification.

On phonological grounds, we may reason from the existence of *ʾgp* and *gp* in later Aramaic texts, both with the meaning "wing," that *ʾgp* is *Lectio difficilior*, hence the older form. It is possible that the Aramaic *ʾgp* is a reflection of the Neo-Assyrian *agappu*, since it is known that Akkadian words having an initial

---

[284] See G. Buccellati, *A Structural Grammar of Babylonian* (Wiesbaden 1996), § 5.2, 3.

[285] In CAD these two homophones of *kappu* ought to be entered under separate headings as in AHw. For *kappu* as "drinking bowl," see SAA XIII 50 r.3; SAA XI 34:6; SAA VII 62 i 4, iii 11, iv 7, 14; SAA VII 71:2; SAA VII 75 r.5; SAA VII 78:3, 5; SAA VII 81:1, 2; SAA VII 91 r.3; SAA VII 127 r.2; SAA VII 174:6; StAT 2 184:9. For *kappu* as "bowl, dish," see SAA XVII 122:10; SAA III 14 r.12; SAA 1 34:11, r.5; SAA 1 158:14, 16. For *kappu* as "edge, bank," see SAA XVII 201 r.3. For *kappu* as "list?" see SAA XVI 50:1.

[286] See n. ad SAA IX 1 i 7; GAG § 8h, 3. Cf. Hämeen-Anttila, SAAS XIII, pp. 15f.

[287] See *gap-pi* in SAA XIII 47:3′; AHw. (p. 281b s.v. *gappu*).

[288] See AHw. (p. 15b s.v. *agappu*(*m*)).

[289] Zimmern, AF, p. 48.

[290] Ibid.

[291] See SAA IX, p. lxvii.

vowel do carry an initial /ʾ/ when borrowed into Aramaic.[292] On the other hand, it is difficult to explain why, if such is the case, the NA *gappu*, attested already in MA, would take an onset vowel, i.e., *gappu* > *agappu*, unless it is a borrowing.[293]

Based on the chronology and distribution of the Aramaic *ʾgp* "wing," it is somewhat problematic to consider it the source word for NA and SB *agappu* "wing." Etymologically, on the other hand, the existence of an Akkadian etymon cannot be ruled out, in view of the existence of a potential OB predecessor, namely *agappu* "wing (of door)." Nevertheless, the occurrence of *agappu* only in NA and SB and its phonological peculiarity also points to the possibility of a borrowing from Aramaic.

akê adv. "so, thus"

Loanword	Reference	Provenance	Origin	Genre	Date
a-ke-e	SAA X 72 r.1	Nineveh	Nineveh	L	670?
	SAA X 322:13	Nineveh	Nineveh	L	Esh
	SAA XIII 19 r.5[294]	Nineveh	Assur	L	Esh
	ZA 73 13:8	*Nineveh*	*Assur*	L	7th c.

Aram. ⇒ NA

JBA *hky* (*hākē*) adv. "in this manner, thus, such, so" DJBA 382b; Jastrow 350b; Dalman 106b. OffAr., Hatran, JBA, JPA *hkyn* (*hākēn*) adv. "so, thus" DNWSI 279; DJBA 382b; DJPA 165a; CAL.[295] Syr. *hākan* "so, thus" SL 342b; Manna 173b; PSm. 103b.

From OA and OB, the word *akê* in Akkadian represented an interrogative meaning "how."[296] However, based on the context, *akê* occurs in the NA instances provided above as an adverb meaning "so." A form corresponding to the NA term is the JBA word הָכֵי or האכי, which is an adverb with the meaning "in this manner, thus, such, so." According to DJPA, the Aramaic word is a compound consisting of the following: הא כן > הכן, i.e., the interjection הָא "behold!" and the adverb כֵּן "so, thus."[297] Nevertheless, in JBA the word is also attested as הָכֵי or האכי, i.e., with elision of the final *n*. It is possible that a similar elision had also occurred in Aramaic during a period prior to that when it is attested, and from there the form was borrowed into NA without the final *n*.

Etymologically, the most salient feature in favor of a borrowing from Aramaic into NA is that the source word in Aramaic is an analyzable complex, i.e., הא כן > הכן > הכ, but as a single unit its internal structure was lost after entering NA. In

---

292 See Kaufman, AIA, p. 142.
293 Cf. GAG § 14a.
294 See LAS II ad no. 252:13. Cf. TCAE, pp. 291f.
295 Cf. CPA *hkn* (*hākan*) adv. "so, thus" LSp. 51a; CAL. Cf. Syr., *hkn* (*hāḵan*, *hāḵanā*) adv. "so, thus" SL (p. 342b s.v. ܗܳܟܰܢ).
296 See CAD (A/I, p. 266a s.v. *akê*; K, p. 320b s.v. *kî*, mng. f). Cf. AEAD (p. 5b s.v. *akē*).
297 Cf. DJPA (p. 165a s.v. הכן); Jastrow (p. 350b s.v. הָכֵי).

other words, the Aramaic source word is a compound consisting of two morphemes, but its compound nature was no longer recognizable when it had entered NA as a monomorphemic word, *akê*. The initial voiceless laryngeal fricative *h* of the Aramaic word הָכֵי was completely dropped and was not reinforced by voiceless velar fricative *ḫ* when the word was borrowed into NA.[298] Unlike Aramaic, which consistently has *g* for the NA intervocalic *k*,[299] the NA word *akê* retains the *k* of the Aramaic word.

anēnu, *anīni*, *anīnu* personal pron. "we"

Loanword	Reference	Provenance	Origin	Genre	Date
a-né-en-nu	SAA X 289 r.9′	Nineveh	Nineveh	L	672?
	SAA XVI 140 r.5	Nineveh	*Der*	L	Esh
a-né-en-nu-ni	SAA X 289 r.14′ (RL)	Nineveh	Nineveh	L	672?
a-né-e-nu	SAA XV 92 r.3′	Nineveh	*Kār-Šarrukīn*	L	Sg
	SAA XV 98:6	Nineveh	*Kār-Šarrukīn*	L	Sg
	SAA XV 100:6	Nineveh	*Kār-Šarrukīn*	L	Sg
	SAA XVI 63 r.5	Nineveh	Gūzāna	L	Esh
an-e-nu	SAA XV 76 r.9	Nineveh	*Sumurzu*	L	Sg
a-ni-in-nu	SAA VIII 163:6	Nineveh	Nineveh	MC	7th c.
	SAA X 259 r.8	Nineveh	Nineveh	L	670?
	SAA X 289:9, 14	Nineveh	Nineveh	L	672?
a-ni-in-nu-ma	SAA X 241:9	Nineveh	Nineveh	L	670?
a-ni-ni	SAA XXI 117 r.3′	Nineveh	–	L	–
	SAA II 9:15′, r.3′	Nineveh	Nineveh	T	Asb
	SAA X 3:8	Nineveh	Nineveh	L	679?
	SAA XV 78:3′	Nineveh	–	L	Sg
	SAA XV 116 r.5′, 9′, 15′	Nineveh	*Der*	L	Sg
	SAA XV 130:21, 23	Nineveh	*Der*	L	Sg
	SAA XV 131:18	Nineveh	*Der*	L	Sg
	SAA XV 136 e.27	Nineveh	Laḫīru	L	Sg
	SAA XV 199:3, r.5	Nineveh	Darati	L	Sg
	SAA XIX 98:11, 22, r.5, 10, 17	Calah	Babylonia	L	Tgl
[a-n]i-ni-i-ni	SAA XV 136:12	Nineveh	Laḫīru	L	Sg
a-ni-nu	SAA XXI 104 r.3 (RL)	Nineveh	*Babylon*	L	7th c.
	HAF 91	Assur	*Assur*	L	Esh
	KAV 215 r.19	Assur	Assur	L	7th c.
	NABU 02/90 r.9[300]	–	–	L	–
	SAA I 54 r.14	Nineveh	*Nineveh*	L	Sg
	SAA I 63 r.4	Nineveh	*Nineveh*	L	Sg
	SAA I 71:9	Nineveh	*Nineveh*	L	Sg
	SAA II 6:494, 507	Calah	Calah	T	672

298 Cf. Table 3 above.
299 See Kaufman, AIA, p. 139.
300 See V. Donbaz, "A Neo-Assyrian Text of unknown Provenance," *NABU* 2002/90.

	SAA III 14:2	–	–	LT	–
	SAA III 16:22	Ḫuzīrīna	*Ḫuzīrīna*	LT	–
	SAA V 2:12	Nineveh	Amidi	L	Sg
	SAA V 21:14	Nineveh	*Tīdu*	L	Sg
	SAA V 105:12	Nineveh	*Kumme*	L	Sg
	SAA V 108 r.28	Nineveh	*Kumme*	L	Sg
	SAA V 149 r.21	Nineveh	–	L	Sg
	SAA V 160:12′	Nineveh	–	L	Sg
	SAA V 182 r.5′	Nineveh	–	L	Sg
	SAA VI 133 e.10	Nineveh	Nineveh	LD	694
	SAA VIII 3 r.4	Nineveh	*Nineveh*	AR	668?
	SAA VIII 60:4	Nineveh	Nineveh	AR	7th c.
	SAA IX 2 i 8′	Nineveh	*Arbela*	P	Esh
	SAA X 50 r.7	Nineveh	Nineveh	L	670?
	SAA X 51 r.15	Nineveh	Nineveh	L	670?
	SAA X 185:13	Nineveh	Nineveh	L	672?
	SAA X 214:9	Nineveh	Nineveh	L	669?
	SAA X 221 r.8	Nineveh	Nineveh	L	669?
	SAA X 226 r.11	Nineveh	Nineveh	L	666?
	SAA X 228 r.2	Nineveh	Nineveh	L	666?
	SAA X 236:9	Nineveh	Nineveh	L	672?
	SAA X 289 r.13′ (RL)	Nineveh	Nineveh	L	672?
	SAA X 368:9	Nineveh	Babylonia	L	Esh
	SAA XIII 146:10	Nineveh	–	L	7th c.
	SAA XIII 172 r.8′	Nineveh	*Babylon*	L	Esh?
	SAA XV 3:6, 7	Nineveh	Arrapḫa	L	Sg
	SAA XV 78:3′	Nineveh	–	L	Sg
	SAA XV 91 r.8	Nineveh	*Kār-Šarrukīn*	L	Sg
	SAA XV 104 r.12′	Nineveh	–	L	Sg
	SAA XV 150 r.2	Nineveh	–	L	Sg
	SAA XVI 42 r.7	Nineveh	–	L	Esh
	SAA XVI 79:9	Nineveh	Nineveh	L	Esh
	SAA XVI 95 r.6′, 13′	Nineveh	*Assur*	L	Esh
	SAA XVI 243 r.5′	Nineveh	–	L	Esh
	SAA XIX 33 r.15	Calah	North-Western Province	L	8th c.
	SAA XIX 90:5′	Calah	Eastern Provinces	L	8th c.
	StAT 2 163 r.10	Assur	Assur	L	Sn
	VAT 9770:4	Assur	Assur	L	Asb?
a-ni-nu-ni	SAA XXI 104 r.4 (RL)	Nineveh	*Babylon*	L	7th c.
	SAA V 95:13	Nineveh	Kumme	L	Sg
an-ni-nu	SAA I 172 r.32, 36e	Calah	Damascus	L	Sg
	SAA V 53 r.7	Nineveh	*Province of the Treasurer*	L	Sg

Aram. ⇒ NB ⇒ NA

OAram.,[301] OffAr., JBA, JPA *ʾnḥn* (*ʾanaḥnā*) personal pron. "we" DNWSI 81; DJBA 144b; DJPA 65a; Jastrow 82b; CAL. Syr., *ʾnḥnn* (*ʾanaḥnan*) personal pron. "we" (archaic form of *ḥnan*) SL 60b; PSm. 21a; Manna 28a. Syr., *ʾanḥnan*, *ʾaḥnan*, *ʾaḥnū* personal pron. "we" Manna 28a.

From OA and OB on, the word *nīnu* (also *nēnu*, *nīni*) "we" is used to indicate the independent first person plural pronoun.[302] However, NA and NB make use of a different form, namely *anē/īnu* "we."[303] As for the latter, von Soden states that *anē/īnu* is a new formation in NA and NB and he considers it to be a loanword from Aramaic *anaḥnā* "we."[304]

In his notes on von Soden's Grammar, *Grundriss der akkadischen Grammatik* (Rome 1952), Gelb discusses the problems of morpheme chronology in reference to *anīnu*, saying:

> V.S.'s observation that *anīnu* is of later date in Akk. than *nīnu* is quite right, but the conclusion that because of chronological attestation *anīnu* was developed secondarily from *nīnu* runs counter to the reconstruction of historical grammar, according to which the Semitic prototype should be **ʾan-ʾa-n-u*; ... If *anīnu* is to be considered older than *nīnu* on grounds of morphemic development, then the fact that *anīnu* is later from the point of chronological attestation can be explained only if it is taken to be a borrowing, either from a related Semitic language or from a dialect of Akk. lying off the path of evolution of the classical dialect.[305]

The original Semitic pharyngeal /*ḥ*/ is reduced in early Akkadian to a glottal stop ʾ (hamza). The latter, as a result of the reduction of /*ḥ*/ then disappears completely, causing an *e*-coloring of the neighboring **a*, i.e., an umlaut of *a* > *e*. Since, following Gelb, the Semitic *ʾnḥn* is *lectio difficilior*, we can posit the following development for the OA and OB *nēnu*: PS **(ʾ)anaḥnu* > **anaḥnu* > **naḥnu* > **neʾnu* > *nēnu*. In Akkadian, as well as in NA, the word-initial glottal stop ʾ (hamza) is not written, leaving the word with an initial vowel. The latter undergoes aphesis, i.e., the loss of a short unstressed vowel at the beginning of a word, principally in nouns, pronouns and adverbs.[306] The voiceless pharyngeal fricative *ḥ* at the end of the first syllable is reduced to a glottal stop, **naʾnu*, which later is dropped and replaced by compensatory lengthening of the syllable vowel. This in turn changes from *ā* > *ē*, producing the final shorter form *nēnu*.[307] The shorter form of **(ʾ)anaḥnu*, *nḥn*, is also attested in other Semitic languages. In Arabic, for instance, it is نَحْنُ, and in Syriac ܚܢܢ.

---

301 According to Kaufman the Aramaic pronoun *ʾanaḥnā* "we" can be ascribed to Common Aramaic, see S.A. Kaufman, "Aramaic," in R. Hetzron (ed.), *The Semitic Languages* (London 1997), p. 121. See also CAL s.v. *ʾnḥnh*.
302 See CAD (N/II, p. 239a s.v. *nīnu*).
303 For variation between the vowels *i* and *e* in Akkadian, see GAG § 8b.
304 See von Soden, *Or* 35 (1966), p. 6:5; idem, *Or* 46 (1977), p. 184:5; AHw. (p. 51b s.v. *anī/ēnu*); GAG § 41i, j 15. See also CDA (p. 17b s.v. *anīnu*). Cf. CAD (A/II, pp. 122f s.v. *anīni*), which does not comment on the form *anīni* and only connects it with Akkadian *nīnu*.
305 I.J. Gelb, "Notes on von Soden's Grammar of Akkadian," *BiOr* 11 (1955), § 14a.
306 See Luukko, SAAS XVI, § 4.12. Cf. E. Reiner, *A Linguistic Analysis of Akkadian* (The Hague 1966), p. 38; GAG § 14a, b.
307 See GAG § 24e.

Hence, the longer form of the pronoun with an extra initial syllable is attested in Aramaic as *ʾnḥn* (*ʾanaḥnā*), and NA and NB as *anē/īnu*. It is also attested in Hebrew as אֲנַחְנוּ "we,"[308] and Phoenician as *ʾnḥn* (*ʾanaḥnū*) "we,"[309] as well as in Syriac as ܐܢܚܢܢ, ܐܚܢܢ, ܐܚܢ and ܐܢܚܢ.[310] According to Huehnergard, the extra syllable at the front of the independent first person plural pronoun "is presumably secondary, the result of levelling from the other first and second forms in the paradigm."[311] Gelb had almost the same understanding of the extra syllable at the front of the pronoun for which he adduced the element *ʾan* in **ʾan-ta*, **ʾan-ti*.[312]

It is obvious that Akkadian *nē/īnu* and Aramaic *ʾanaḥnā* are cognates. The existence of *nēnu* in older stages of Akkadian vis-à-vis *anē/īnu* in NA and NB makes it more plausible to envisage a borrowing of *anē/īnu* in NA and NB than to assume instead an internal development in these later dialects of Akkadian. Thus, the pronoun *anēnu* in NA with the initial vowel *-a* must be considered a loan from Aramaic. Its form, however, is only partially adapted to the NA phonological system. There is no room here for archaism, since the older form of this pronoun in Akkadian is not attested other than with the loss of the initial (ʾ) and with the aphesis of the initial vowel. However, when borrowing from Aramaic into NA, the Aramaic pharyngeal /*ḥ*/ is usually rendered <*ḫ*>, a phenomenon actually corroborated by the representation of non-Assyrian phonemes in NA transcriptions of Aramaic names.[313]

Although a shorter pronoun, namely *nēnu*, is also attested in NA,[314] its form is considered to be only a stylistic variation of *anē/īnu*.[315] The final *-i* in NA *a-ni-ni* is due to progressive vowel assimilation, because a long and stressed penultimate syllable of a word may bring about an optional qualitative assimilation of the vowel of the last syllable, rendering it similar to its own vowel.[316] Assuming that von Soden is correct that NA *anēnu* is a loan from Aramaic *ʾnḥn*, the lack of a reflex of the Aramaic voiceless pharyngeal fricative /*ḥ*/ in the NA word must be accounted for. This problem may be solved by considering the Aramaic loan to be a trans-NB borrowing into NA.

Recently, Abraham and Sokoloff argued that von Soden's interpretation that the NA and NB *anē/īnu* is a loanword from Aramaic *anaḥnā* is very unlikely because "the vowel in Akk[adian] is *ī/ē* as in *nīnu*, and not *a* as in Aram[aic], and

---

308 See Dalman, p. 24a.

309 See P.-A. Beaulieu, "Aspects of Aramaic and Babylonian Linguistic Interaction in First Millennium BC Iraq," *Journal of Language Contact* 6 (2013), p. 364.

310 Manna, p. 28a.

311 See J. Huehnergard, "Features of Central Semitic," in A. Gianto (ed.), *Biblical and Oriental Essays in Memory of William L. Moran* (Rome 2005), pp. 166f. For the term "levelling," see P.H. Matthews, *The Concise Oxford Dictionary of Linguistics* (Oxford 1997), p. 203.

312 See Gelb, ibid.

313 For the representation of Aramaic *ḥ* by NA *ḫ*, see E. Salonen, "Über den Laut H im Akkadischen," *StOr* 46 (1975), p. 293, 3; J. Tropper, "Akkadisch *nuḫḫutu* und die Repräsentation des Phonems /*ḥ*/ im Akkadischen," *ZA* 85 (1995), pp. 61ff.; J. Huehnergard, "Akkadian *ḫ* and West Semitic **ḥ*," in L. Kogan (ed.), *Studia Semitica, FS A. Militarev* (Moscow 2003), pp. 102–119. Cf. GAG § 8i, Anm; PNA 1/I, p. xxiv.

314 The form *né-e-nu* is attested in a NA letter (SAA I 133 r.7′).

315 See Luukko, SAAS XVI, § 4.12.

316 See K. Deller & S. Parpola, "Progressive Vokalassimilation im Neuassyrischen," *Or* 36 (1967), pp. 337f; Luukko, ibid., § 4.5, 2.

there is no reflex in Akk[adian] of the *ḥ* which would still have been pronounced in Aram[aic] at the time of the borrowing."[317] Beaulieu also subscribes to Abraham and Sokoloff's conclusion, and adds that their argument is supported by the fact that pronouns in general exhibit intense resistance to borrowing.[318]

The problems with the loan hypothesis put forward by Abraham and Sokoloff can be solved in two ways: either we are dealing with a "lehnbildung" based on Akkadian *nēnu* and expanded by the initial *a* in parallel with Aramaic,[319] or *anē/īnu* is phonologically integrated into Akkadian whereby *anaḥnā* becomes *anē/īnu* according to Akkadian sound rules. It is known that a sound change in Akkadian, known as *e*-coloring, is caused by the influence of certain consonants on the neighboring vowel *a*, resulting in an umlaut *a* > *e*. This happens, for instance, in syllables where *a* is adjacent to a glottal stop ʾ (hamza) that has developed from a PS **ḥ* when this ʾ occurs at the beginning or end of a syllable before being completely dropped. In addition, the Aramaic word is most likely a trans-NB borrowing into NA, which is why there is no reflex of the Aramaic *ḥ* which is expected to appear as *ḫ* in the NA word.

In general, personal pronouns are considered to be the most "hard-to-borrow" lexical item because they are deeply rooted within the linguistic system of the language.[320] However, in researching the question of borrowability of personal pronouns, and based on a rich body of evidence from different parts of the world, Thomason and Everett concluded that pronoun borrowing, not unlike the other contact phenomena, is subject to intentional and conscious choices decided by speakers of different languages, and that the common assumption that pronouns must be inherited because they are hardly ever borrowed is untenable.[321]

anīna, *anīnu* int. "hear me!"[322]

Loanword	Reference	Provenance	Origin	Genre	Date
a-ni-na	SAA III 16 r.3	Ḫuzīrīna	*Ḫuzīrīna*	LT	–
	SAA IX 3 ii 13	Nineveh	*Nineveh*	P	Esh
	SAA XVI 32 r.7	Nineveh	*Nineveh*	L	Esh?
	SAA XVI 70:5	Nineveh	*Nineveh*	L	Esh?
a-ni-nu	SAA XVI 59:8, 12	Nineveh	*Nineveh*	L	Esh
	SAA XVI 60 r.18′, s.1	Nineveh	*Nineveh*	L	Esh

Aram. ⇒ NA

[317] Abraham & Sokoloff, *Reassessment*, p. 26:12.

[318] See P.-A. Beaulieu, "Aspects of Aramaic and Babylonian Linguistic Interaction in First Millennium BC Iraq," *Journal of Language Contact* 6 (2013), p. 363.

[319] M.P. Streck (personal communication).

[320] See S.G. Thomason & D.L. Everett, "Pronoun Borrowing," *Proceedings of the Annual Meeting of the Berkeley Linguistics Society* 27 (2001), p. 301.

[321] Ibid., p. 313.

[322] See AEAD (p. 8a s.v. *anīna*). Cf. the Glossary of SAA III (p. 127b s.v. *anina*), where the word *anīna* attested in the NA literary text SAA III 16 r.3, and in a broken context in SAA III 52:4′, is rendered "please."

OAram., Palm., *'ny* v. "to grant, to answer someone's prayer" DNWSI 875f. JBA, JPA, Sam., CPA *'ny* v. "to respond, answer" DJBA 871b; DJPA 412b; Jastrow 1093a; DSA 647a; LSp. 149b; DCPA 314b. Syr., *'ny* v. "to answer, respond; to hearken, hear" PSm. 419a; SL 1116a; Manna 551b; Audo 733b. Ma., *ana*, *'na* v. "to answer, reply, respond" MD 24a.

AHw., and CAD differ as to the meaning and classification of this word. In AHw. (p. 51b s.v. *anīna*), the word is approximately glossed as meaning "siehe doch!"[323] The editors of CAD (A/II, p. 122b s.v. *anīna* B) consider it an adverb with the meaning "now." However, a different interpretation of the word is put forward by Parpola who regards *anīna* as an interjection meaning "hear me!" and considers it to be a loanword from Aramaic.[324] Parpola adduces the Aramaic word *'an'/y* "to answer, respond; hearken, hear," which he considers to fit all attestations of the word in NA, and for a comparative usage he quotes the Syriac phrase ܥܢܝܢܝ ܡܪܝܐ "hear me, O Lord!"[325] Parpola explains that the substitution of the final *-i* with *-a* in the NA word corresponds to the change in NA *udīni* > *udīna* "yet," and that it probably occurred to avoid the clash of homonyms, i.e., to avoid confusion with NA *anīni* "we."[326] He rules out connecting the word with Aramaic *ḥanīnā* "pity, mercy, compassion," arguing that the latter is normally spelled with an initial *ḫa* in NA names.[327]

Parpola's reasoning that the replacement of the final *-i* with *-a* was probably meant to avoid the clash of homonyms is possible, however it is somewhat hampered by the attested alternative spelling of the word, *anīnu* "hear me!" The latter, in turn, might also be confused with the other form of the NA word *anīni*, namely *anīnu* "we." The risk of this kind of confusion is hinted at by Nissinen in his rendering of the word *anīnu* attested in ABL (1217: 8, 12), where he notes: "The word *anīnu* ... is hardly to be understood as a personal pronoun of 1p. pl. but rather as an interjection similar to *anīna* or *annû* "behold."[328]

Chronologically, the Syriac word *'ny* with the meanings "to hearken, hear," has a forerunner in Old Aramaic *'ny* "to grant, to answer someone's prayer."[329] The onset *'ayin* in the Aramaic word makes it impossible for it to be a loan from Akkadian, as there is no evidence of the preservation of this pharyngeal in first-millennium dialects of Akkadian.[330] On the other hand, the initial voiced pharyngeal fricative ' is reduced in Akkadian to a glottal stop ' (hamza) which is ultimately dropped. The sense "hear me!" derived from the context is unattested before NA. The variation in the NA forms *anīna*, *anīnu* suggests that the

323 Cf. CDA (p. 17b s.v. *anīna*), which renders the word in the sense "now."
324 See n. ad SAA IX 3 ii 13.
325 Ibid.
326 Ibid.
327 Ibid.
328 See SAAS VII, p. 110, n. 428. Note that ABL 1217 is now re-edited as SAA XVI 59.
329 See the reference to the 9th-century inscription of Zakkūr king of Hamath given as KAI 202A l. 11 in DNWSI (p. 875f s.v. *'ny*$_1$ mng. no. 2). See also J.A. Emerton, "New Evidence for the Use of *Waw* Consecutive in Aramaic," *VT* 44 (1994), p. 255.
330 See Kaufman, AIA, p. 142.

Aramaic accusative pronominal suffix *-ni* for the 1p. sg.,[331] as in ܫܡܥܢܝ, was probably not clearly understood by the Assyrian scribes. Taken together these considerations make it simpler to account for *anīna* "hear me!" as an Aramaic loanword in NA.[332]

aqqabu, (pl. *aqqabāni*) n. "lower part, hind part"; (see also the discussion below s.v. *gammīdutu*)

Loanword	Reference	Provenance	Origin	Genre	Date
aq-qa-ba-ni	SAA VII 115 r. ii 17	Nineveh	Nineveh	AD	Sg

Aram. ⇒ NA [?]

JPA, CPA, Sam., *ʿqb*, *ʿqbʾ* (*ʿqeḇ*, *ʿeqbā*) n. m. "end" DJPA 416a; LSp. 151a; DCPA 318a; DSA 655b. JBA *ʿqbʾ* n. m. "end, bottom part" DJBA 858b; Jastrow 1104b. Syr., *ʿeqḇā* n. m. "lower part, bottom; end, extreme part" SL 1128f; PSm. 424a. Syr., *ʿeqḇ* n. m. & f. "end, rear; hind part; base, bottom; lowest part" Audo 743b; Manna 559b.[333] Ma., *ʿqbʾ* n. m. "heel, hinder part" MD 356b.

The word *aqqabāni* is a *hapax legomenon* in NA, and the plausibility of etymology proposed for it is determined by the sentence context. The word occurs in association with the term *gammīdu*-garments in a NA administrative document (SAA VII 115 r. ii 17), in an account detailing the consumption of flax and wool allocated to different administrative parties and localities, and for other specific purposes.[334] The passage where the word occurs (SAA VII 115 r. ii 17–18) reads as follows:

> 2 MA *a-na aq-qa-ba-ni* / *ša ga-me-da*!*-te*
>
> 2 minas for the *hind-part* of the ..-garments.

The editors of CAD (A/II, p. 207a s.v. *aqqabu* (or *aqqabānu*)), consider the word to be a substantive of unknown meaning. In AHw. (p. 62b s.v. *aqqabu*), the word is followed by a question mark signifying uncertainty of meaning. Later, in the addenda and corrigenda section of AHw. (p. 1544a s.v. *aqqab*(*ān*)*u*), the word is glossed "Überbleibsel," and considered to be an Aramaic foreign word in NA

---

331 See V. Hug, *Altaramäische Grammatik der Texte des 7. und 6. Jh.s v.Chr.* (Heidelberg 1993), p. 59.

332 The word under discussion is referred to in Abraham & Sokoloff, *Reassessment*, p. 24, n. 31 no. 1.

333 Cf. DNWSI (pp. 881f s.v. *ʿqb_2* and *ʿqb_5*).

334 See also S. Gaspa, "Garments, Parts of Garments, and Textile Techniques in the Assyrian Terminology: The Neo-Assyrian Textile Lexicon in the 1st-Millennium BC Linguistic Context," in S. Gaspa et al. (eds.), *Textile Terminologies from the Orient to the Mediterranean and Europe, 1000 BC to 1000 AD* (Lincoln, 2017), p. 79 s.v. *aqqābu*, and n. 540.

and NB. In his articles on Aramaic loanwords, von Soden connects the word with Aramaic עֲקָבָא.[335] Also, the editors of CDA (p. 21b s.v. *aqqabu*), tentatively render this word as "remainder," and consider it to be an Aramaic loanword in NA. In DNWSI (pp. 881f s.v. *ʿqb*$_5$), von Soden's interpretation is considered to be highly uncertain. However, a different interpretation is found in the glossary of SAA VII (p. 209a s.v. *aqqābu*), where the meaning of *aqqabāni* (SAA VII 115 r. ii 17) is regarded as uncertain, but perhaps indicating "hind part." Accordingly, in AEAD (p. 9a s.v. *aqbu* (*aqqabu*)), the word is glossed "heel; lower part, extremity."

Nevertheless, in his review of SAA VII 115, von Soden reiterates his previous standpoint on *aqqabāni*. He states that *aq-qa-ba-ni* is likely an Aramaic foreign word, which in NA is associated with remnants of garments, but he remarks that a word form as עֲקָבָא in the sense "remainder," is unattested in Aramaic.[336] He also refers to a NB passage (CT 54 433:4), which supposedly has a similar word: *aq-qa-bu-ú ša aklē* "remnants of bread."[337]

However, the NB instance (CT 54 433:4) quoted by von Soden has recently been edited in SAA XVIII 121:4, where, unlike von Soden's rendering, the word [*a*]*q-qa-bu-ú* is taken to be a verb with the sense "I spoke up," derived from *qabû* "to say, speak, tell, command." This, in turn, dismisses the assumed NB attestation corresponding to the NA word under discussion. Abraham and Sokoloff also confirm that no Aramaic word as עֲקָבָא in the sense "remainder" exists in the Aramaic dictionaries.[338]

Admittedly, interpreting *aqqabānu* is problematic. It is itself a *hapax legomenon* and occurs in a passage together with an Aramaic loanword, namely *gammīdāte* n. f. pl. "mangled garment." Most likely, *aqqabānu* stands in plural, similar to *gammīdāte*. However, *aqqabāni* seems to be of the nominal form *PaRRaS*, m. pl., with doubling of the second radical indicative of an intensified adjective, possibly meaning "(extreme lower) hind parts." The word is followed by the masculine plural ending *-āni*, and is taken to be from Aramaic *ʿqb* "lower part, bottom; end, extreme part," as attested, for instance, in Syriac.

Semantically, the word *eqbu* in the sense "heel, hoof," occurs only in SB.[339] It is cognate with Aramaic, Hebrew and Arabic *ʿqb* "heel, hoof."[340] Accordingly, the PS root can be reconstructed as *ʿQB. However, the meanings found in the later dialects of Aramaic as "hind part, lower part, bottom; end, extreme part" seem to fit the NA context.

Phonologically, the form of the word in NA with initial *a* points to a borrowing, as there is no *e*-coloring of the neighboring *a*, i.e., no umlaut of *a* > *e* as expected from the reduction and ultimate total disappearance of the voiced

---

335 See also von Soden, *Or* 35 (1966), p. 6:7; idem, *Or* 46 (1977), p. 184:7.

336 See W. von Soden, Review of "Imperial Administrative Records, Part I," by F.M. Fales & J.N. Postgate, *WO* 25 (1994), p. 137.

337 Ibid.

338 See Abraham & Sokoloff, *Reassessment*, p. 26:13, n. 64. However, Abraham & Sokoloff erroneously attribute the review of SAA 7, to Jursa instead of to von Soden.

339 See CAD (E, p. 248b s.v. *eqbu*).

340 Von Soden (AHw., p. 231b), glosses *eqbu*(*m*) as "Ferse, Absatz," and defines it as a Common Semitic word except for Ethiopic. Furthermore, he considers the usage of *eqbu* in the expression *ina eq-bi-in-ni*, "in unserer Nachfolge (gab er)," in LB to be a loan from Aramaic.

pharyngeal fricative ʿ of the PS *ʿQB.[341] Even the Assyrian vowel harmony does not seem to be operating in the NA word. Hence, the evidence points to a possible borrowing from Aramaic. Interestingly, our text includes two confirmed Aramaic loanwords as *šapīnāte* "boats," and *gammīdāte* "mangled garments." It also includes two possible Aramaic loanwords as *maqaṭṭu* "gown," and *ša-ṣallīšu* "dealer in leather hides."

aṣūdu, (pl. *aṣūdātu*) n. "kneading bowl, fruit bowl; fruit offering";[342] also in *rab aṣūdi* "fruit-bowl master"[343]

Loanword	Reference	Provenance	Origin	Genre	Date
a-ṣu-da-ti-ku-nu	SAA II 6:447	Calah	Calah	T	672
a-ṣu-di	ND 5461:2 (Iraq 19, 1957, pl. 29)	Calah	Calah	LD	668
	SAA XVI 92:8	Nineveh	Nineveh	L	Esh
	SAA IX 3 iii 32 *a-ṣu*!*-di*	Nineveh	*Nineveh*	P	Esh
a-ṣu-du	SAA XVI 41 r.14	Nineveh	*Nineveh*	L	Esh
	SAA XVI 212 r.3	Nineveh	*Nineveh*	L	Esh
	CTN I 35 r.1 18′	Calah	Calah	AD	–
	SAAB 9 77:11	Assur	Assur	LD	–
	SAAB 9 82:2′ [*a-ṣ*]*u-du*	Assur	Assur	LD	617?
	SAAB 9 94:4	Assur	Assur	LD	613
	VAT 8667 (= Ass 14232t) *a-ṣu-d*[*u*]	Assur	Assur	AD	614
a-ṣu-u-di	CTN III 14 r.2	Calah	Calah	LD	–
DUG.*a-ṣu-da-a-te*	SAA VII 125:3	Nineveh	Nineveh	AD	Esh?
DUG.*a-ṣu-du*	SAA VII 208 r.5′	Nineveh	Nineveh	AD	Esh?
	SAA VII 209 r.4	Nineveh	Nineveh	AD	Esh?
	SAA VII 215 r.4 D[UG.*a-ṣ*]*u-du*	Nineveh	Nineveh	AD	Esh?
	SAA VII 216 r.7 [DU]G.*a-ṣu-du*	Nineveh	Nineveh	AD	Esh?
	SAA VII 217 r.5	Nineveh	Nineveh	AD	Esh?
	SAA VII 218 e.7′ [DUG].*a-ṣu-du*	Nineveh	Nineveh	AD	Esh?
LÚ.GAL–*a-ṣu-de*	BATSH 6/2 8 r.12	Dūr-Katlimmu	Dūr-Katlimmu	LD	633*

Aram. ⇒ NA [?]

Syr., Sam., JLA *ʾṣw*, *ʾṣwtʾ* (*ʾāṣū*, *ʾāṣūṯā*) n. f. "kneading trough" PSm. 27a; Manna 37a; Audo 46a; SL 91a; DSA 58a; Jastrow 110b, 1102a (*ʿāṣūtā*); Dalman

[341] See GAG § 9a; L. Kogan, "ġ in Akkadian," *UF* 33 (2001), pp. 263f; J. Huehnergard, *A Grammar of Akkadian* (Atlanta 1997), p. 38, § 6.1 and p. 587.
[342] See AEAD (p. 10b s.v. *aṣūdu*).
[343] Ibid. See also, n. ad BATSH 6/2 8 r.12.

35b, 305b (*ʿāṣūtā*); CAL. JPA, Syr., CPA *ʾṣw*, *ʾṣwt*ʾ (*ʾāṣū*, *ʾāṣūṯā*) n. f. "dough, batch" DJPA 72a; PSm. 27a; Manna 37a; Audo 46a; SL 91a; DCPA 26b.

The editors of CAD (A/II, p. 385a s.v. *aṣūdu*), define this word as (a dish of food of liquid consistency), and provide no etymological discussion other than a reference to von Soden. In AHw. (pp. 77b, 1545a s.v. *aṣūdu*), this word is glossed "ein Speisegefäß," and is tentatively considered to be an Aramaic foreign word in NA.[344] In his discussion of *aṣūdu*, von Soden states that the interpretation of this word is uncertain and explains the difficulty encountered in associating it with Aramaic as follows: "*aṣūdu*, Pl. *aṣūdātu* (AHw. 77b) ist vermutlich mit aram. *āṣūṯā* (jaram. auch *ʿāṣūṯā*) 'Backtrog' gleichzusetzen, obwohl ich das *d* für aram. *ṯ* nicht erklären kann. Ist das *ṯ* des jüngeren Aramäischen aus älterem *ḏ* entstanden??"[345]

That the NA *aṣūdu* is a kind of vessel is confirmed by the determinative DUG occasionally prefixed to it, which is used before names of receptacles, containers and bowls. The word is used, for instance, in Aššūr temple offerings (SAA VII 208 r.5′) to refer to a bowl with certain ingredients and fruit, but it is also used on other occasions, such as Esarhaddon's succession treaty (SAA II 6:447), where it refers to a bowl in connection with dough.

However, the NA word *aṣūdu* is semantically fairly congruent with the Aramaic meaning. It has no etymology in Akkadian and is only attested in NA.[346] The attested forms of the word in NA are consistently written syllabically, an unusual characteristic for a noun inherent in the Akkadian lexicon. In Syriac the word is written ܐܨܘܬܐ, and in Jewish Aramaic it is written אָצוּתָא, but also as עָצוּתָא.[347] Even though *aṣūdu* is attested several times in NA, any possibility that this word was borrowed into Aramaic from NA is ruled out due to phonological difficulties. Specifically, in a scenario of a borrowing from NA into Aramaic we cannot account for the change *d* > *t*. Also, we cannot account for the initial *ʿayin* attested in the variant Jewish Aramaic form עָצוּתָא.[348] In NA, on the other hand, the existence of a voiced environment, such as an intervocalic position, facilitates the voicing of the voiceless dental plosive: *t* > *d*.[349] The change (*t* > *d*), in NA is found, for example, in the word *biādu* < *biātu* "to stay overnight," which is cognate with Syriac ܒܬ, ܒܝܬ "to spend the night,"[350] and Arabic بَاتَ "to pass the night," and أَبَاتَ "to lodge, put up for the night."[351] It seems that in the NA *aṣūdu* the *d* had become the normal variant instead of *t*.

---

344 Cf. CDA (p. 27a s.v. *aṣūdu*). Cf. also Abraham & Sokoloff, *Reassessment*, p. 27:18.

345 See von Soden, *Or* 35 (1966), p. 7:9; See also, idem, *Or* 46 (1977), p. 184:9.

346 Note that the word *kallaṣūdi* (a plant or a drug), attested in SB text from Assyria (AMT 41, 1 iv 28), is probably connected with the word *aṣūdu*. Probably it is a compound consisting of (*kallu* + *aṣūdu*?). The word *kallu* has the sense "(kind of) bowl for liquids, food." Cf. CAD (K, p. 79a s.v. *kallaṣūdi*); AHw. (p. 425b s.v. *kallaṣūdi*).

347 See Dalman, pp. 35b, 305b; Jastrow, pp. 110b, 1102a. From the other Semitic languages, Arabic عَصِيدَة "porridge, gruel; a thick paste made of flour and clarified butter," may be related to *aṣūdu*. Cf. Elias & Elias (p. 442a s.v. (عصد)); Wehr-Cowan, p. 616a.

348 Cf. Kaufman, AIA, p. 142.

349 See Hämeen-Anttila, SAAS XIII, § 2.1.6.1, esp. p. 16; Luukko, SAAS XVI, pp. 69f.

350 See SL (p. 132a s.v. ܒܝܬ); Manna (p. 57b s.v. ܒܬ).

351 See Elias & Elias, p. 83b.

badāqu v. (G) "to repair"

Loanword	Reference	Provenance	Origin	Genre	Date
ba-di-qu-nu	SAA XVI 126 r.22′	Nineveh	Phoenicia	L	Esh

Aram. ⇒ NA; NB? [?]

Syr., *bdq* v. "to repair, restore" SL 120a; PSm. 35b; Manna 52b; Audo 59b. Syr., *bədāqā* n. m. "repairing, restoring; place needing repair" SL 120b; PSm. 36a; Audo 59b; CAL.

This word is a *hapax legomenon* which occurs in a mostly broken NA letter sent by Itti-Šamaš-balāṭu, an Assyrian official active in northern Phoenicia, to the Assyrian king Esarhaddon reporting on the completion of certain products by carpenters. This occurrence of the word is not entered in AHw., or CAD. In the glossary section of SAA XVI (p. 179b s.v. *batāqu*), the word is glossed "to cut off, parcel out; to repair." AEAD (p. 12a), on the other hand, lists a separate heading as *badāqu* in the sense "to repair," as well as *badqu* "repair work," with a sub-entry *bēl badqi* "repairer, restorer."[352] The meaning "to repair," in our case is suggested by the context, and is taken by Luukko and Van Buylaere to correspond to the Syriac word *bdq* "to repair, restore."[353] A cognate in Hebrew is the word בֶּדֶק "repair, attendance."[354] SAA XVI 126 r.21′–24′ reads:

> *a-a-i dul-lu ša* LUGAL *be-lé e-pu-su-su-nu* / *ù ba-di-qu-nu ma-ri dul-lu*!!*-nu* / *ša* LUGAL *be-lí ep-pa-su-nu* / *gab-bi-šú da-mu-qi*
>
> What work has the king, my lord, done, that would have been repaired? All the work the king, my lord, performs, is well made!

It is possible that *badāqu* is a variant form of *batāqu* in which the voiceless stop *t* became voiced, i.e., *t* > *d*, because of its position between vowels or by assimilating to the voiced phonetic environment represented by the preceding voiced stop *b*.[355] It also appears that the sense "to repair," is not restricted to *badāqu* in NA, because the word *batqu*, a derivative of *batāqu*, is also attested in NB in the sense "repair (work)."[356]

In our case, the word seems to be inflected as a stative in the G-stem of the root BDQ, forming the subjunctive in a relative clause and ending with the NA extra

---

[352] Cf. AEAD, p. 14b, which provides a heading *rab batqi* in the sense "official in charge of levy." Cf. also AHw. (p. 115a s.v. *batqu(m)* I, mng. no. 6), which provides a derivative of the word *batāqu* attested in NA as *bat-qí* and in LB as *bat-qu*, both in the sense "Reparatur." Furthermore, in AHw. (p. 115b s.v. *batqu(m)* I, mng. no. 7), the expression *rab batqi* is rendered "Inspektor der Reparaturen."

[353] See n. ad SAA XVI 126 r.22.

[354] See Jastrow, p. 141b; Dalman, p. 46b.

[355] Cf. Luukko, SAAS XVI, § 4.1.1.

[356] See, for instance, *ba-taq-šú* "its repair work" in SAA XVIII 124 r.1; *bat-qí* "the repairs" in SAA XVIII 187:10. See also the Glossary of SAA XVIII (p. 179a s.v. *batqu*). Cf. the etymological note on the word *batqu* in CAD (B, p. 168a s.v. *batqu*, mng. no. 3d).

particle *-ni*.[357] Furthermore, the word seems to have undergone a progressive vowel assimilation due to the long and stressed penultimate syllable, hence *-ūni* > *-ūnu*. This progressive vowel assimilation is optional.[358]

Kaufman does not subscribe to the view that Jewish Aramaic or Mandaic *bdq* "to burst," not to mention the more common Aramaic meanings "to search; to repair," is strongly influenced by Akkadian. He notes:

> Indeed Akk. *batāqu* (and the BH hapax *btq*) appears at first to be the unexpected form in the group of roots composed of a labial, dental, and velar stop meaning "to split": Arab., Ethiopic *btk*; Arab., Ar. *f/ptq*; Ar., Heb. (and Ug. *bdqt*?) *bdq*. But *batāqu* is in fact the correct Akkadian reflex of original *bdq*; cf. GAG *Ergänz*., p. 8**, § 51*d*.[359]

The first part of the statement above presumably implies, as far as Akkadian is concerned, that Akkadian would actually not tolerate the root combination BTQ. It is true that the valid sound laws for root formation in Akkadian do not allow for more than one consonant of the same place of articulation to occur in the root, but none of the consonants *b*, *t*, and *q* have the same place of articulation.[360] Also, it is not clear what Kaufman meant by writing, "but *batāqu* is in fact the correct Akkadian reflex of original *bdq*." The reference that he adduced for comparison, i.e., GAG (Ergänz., p. 8**, § 51d), maintains the following:

> Wurzelauslautendes *d* wird nach stimmhaftem Verschlusslaut als 2. oder 1. Radikal zu *t* (z.B. in *abātum* "zugrunde richten," *kabātum* "schwer sein," *galātum* "erschrecken" usw.), in jüngeren Texten aus Assyrien aber oft wiederhergestellt (s. die Lexika auch zu *nābutum* "fliehen").[361]

But, in our case, the radical *d* of the word *badāqu* does not occupy the root's final position. Instead it constitutes the root's second radical.

Nevertheless, phonologically, it is not problematic to analyze the NA *badāqu* as variant form of *batāqu* as explained above. Chronologically and semantically, the sense "to repair," is only attested in NA and possibly also in NB. Accordingly, the meaning "to repair" attested in Aramaic which fits into the context of the NA text points to a possible borrowing from Aramaic.

***baru** n. "son"

Loanword	Reference	Provenance	Origin	Genre	Date
bur!	SAA VI 173:6	Nineveh	Nineveh	LD	685

[357] Cf. *ep-pa-su-nu* on l. no. r.23′ of the same text.
[358] See Luukko, SAAS XVI, p. 92 s.v. (ʾpš) and (*dullu*).
[359] See Kaufman, AIA, pp. 41f s.v. *batāqu*, n. 52.
[360] Cf. GAG § 51c.
[361] See W. von Soden, *Ergänzungsheft zum Grundriss der akkadischen Grammatik* (AnOr 33), (Rome 1969), p. 8**.

Aram. ⇒ NA

OAram., OffAr., Palm., JBA, JPA, Sam., CPA, Ma., Syr., *br*, *br'* (*bar*, *ber*, *brā*) n. m. "son" Brauner 111; DNWSI 188ff; DJBA 231b; Jastrow 188b; DJPA 97a; DSA 103b; LSp. 30a; DCPA 58b; MD 68b; SL 177b; PSm. 53a; Manna 79b; Audo 98a; CAL. Sūret *brōnā* n. m. "son" Maclean 38b.[362]

This word occurs a single time in NA, and as a *hapax legomenon* its semantic connection is determined from the context. It occurs as *bur*! in a legal transaction (SAA VI 173:6), which is a deed concerning the purchase of an estate. Kwasman and Parpola, the editors of SAA VI, did not comment on this word, but in the glossary section of SAA VI (p. 293a s.v. *bar*), they rendered it as "son," and defined it as (Aramaic word). Also, the editors of CDA (p. 49b s.v. *buru*), glossed the word as "son," and considered it a borrowing from Aramaic. The passage where the word is attested (SAA VI 173:4–7) reads as follows:

> É 20 ANŠE A.ŠÀ *ú*!-*gar*!-*ru* / GIŠ.SAR *ša* Ú.SAR ⸢*ša*⸣ ^{m}NUMUN-*i* / *bur*! ^{md}PA–SIG$_5$ MÍ-*su*-*šú*! / 1 DUMU.MÍ *x*[*xx*]*x* [*xxxxx*]
>
> An estate of 20 hectares of land, an irrigated field, a vegetable garden belonging to Zarî son of Nabû-dammiq, his wife, one daughter [......].

In his review of SAA VI, Jursa considers the use of the Aramaic word *bar* "son," in the case of *bur*, in a filiation statement in Akkadian, to be very surprising and wonders if the reading obtained by collation, i.e., *bur*!, is really accurate.[363]

The term *bar* "son," is a Common Aramaic word. As is well known, however, it has the radical *r* instead of the expected *n*, as with its cognates in the other Semitic languages, for instance, the Hebrew בֵּן,[364] Akkadian *bīnu/binnu*,[365] the orthographic form *bn* in Phoenician and Ugaritic, and the Epigraphic South Arabian *bn* as well as the Literary Arabic اِبْن.[366] Nevertheless, in Aramaic *br* is always used in the singular and *bn* is always used in the plural. Hence, the form *br* for the word "son," in Aramaic, in contrast to *bn* in the other Semitic languages, is considered to be one of the hallmarks of the Aramaic lexicon. A counterpart of the Aramaic phenomenon is found in Modern South Arabian (MSA), where *ber* stands for "son."[367] This remarkable parallel between the Aramaic and MSA is considered a dissimilation occurring as a result of a regular

---

362 In Sūret, the word *brōnā* "son," represents a diminutive form.

363 See M. Jursa, Review of "Legal Transactions of the Royal Court of Niniveh [*sic*], Part I. Tiglath-Pileser III through Esarhaddon," by K. Theodore & S. Parpola, *WZKM* 84 (1994), p. 207 ad 173. Cf. Abraham & Sokoloff, *Reassessment*, p. 24, n. 31 no. 2.

364 See Dalman, p. 55b. Cf. M. Wagner, *Die lexikalischen und grammatikalischen Aramaismen im alttestamentlichen Hebräisch* (Berlin 1966), p. 37:46.

365 See AHw. (p. 127a s.v. *binu*(*m*)); CAD (B, p. 242b s.v. *bīnu* B).

366 The Arabic form has a prosthetic vowel: *'ibn* < *bn* "son." See Lipiński, *Semitic Languages*, § 27.17.

367 See D. Testen, "The Significance of Aramaic *r* < **n*," *JNES* 44 (1985), p. 144.

sound change applied independently to the phonology of these two cognate languages.[368]

In OAkk., the word for "son" is *mar'um*, in OA *mer'um* and in MA and NA *mar'u*, but in Babylonian it is *māru(m)*.[369] However, another word, namely *bīnu(m)/binnu* "son," is found in OAkk., OA and SB. In addition, *bīnu* "son" is also attested in a NA personal name: Nabû-bīna-ukīn "Nabû has established a son."[370]

The word *bur*, on the other hand, is only attested in our NA text and appears only to be explicable as a loan from Aramaic *bar* "son." In addition, the word *bur* appears in many NA personal names, for instance Bur-Aia "Son of Ea," Bur-Anate "Son of Anat," and Bur-Zināni "Son of Zinanu."[371]

It is worth mentioning here that the Aramaic *br* "son" is attested in an Aramaic caption on the edge of a NA conveyance text from Nineveh (SAA VI 284 e.16) from 671 B.C. (reign of Esarhaddon), concerning the sale of a slave woman and her son. The Aramaic caption (SAA VI 284 e.16–17) reads as follows:[372]

> [*x x x*] *br*⌜*h*⌝ [*x x x x x*] / [*x x x*]*d nb*!*w*![*blṣr x x*] (Aramaic caption)
>
> [*Marqiḫitâ and*] her son [...], [...] Nabû-[*bēlu-uṣur*].

The Aramaic *br* "son" is also attested in NA texts excavated at Dur-Katlimmu (Tell Šēḫ Ḥamad). For instance, it is found in an Aramaic caption on the left edge of a NA legal document (BATSH 6 53 l.e.2) from ca. 641* B.C. (reign of Assurbanipal), concerning the sale of two slave women.[373] The Aramaic caption (BATSH 6 53 l. e.1–2) reads as follows:

> *dnt 'mtšlmn 'mt 'tḥrsr*!*ṣr / br ssḥṣr* (Aramaic caption)
>
> Deed of Amat-Salmanu, the slave woman of 'Atḫar-šarru-uṣur, son of Šamaš-aḫu-uṣur.

These Aramaic captions present additional evidence of the spreading of bilingualism among the Assyrian scribes during the Neo-Assyrian period and speaks for the possibility of borrowing the Aramaic *br* "son" into NA.

Phonologically, the CVC sign BUR may also have represented the sound values (bar) and (bir).[374] Otherwise, the vowel /u/ in *bur* has to be explained as an

---

[368] Ibid. See also S.E. Fassberg, "The Forms of 'Son' and 'Daughter' in Aramaic," in H. Gzella & M.L. Folmer, (eds.), *Aramaic in its Historical and Linguistic Setting* (Wiesbaden 2008), pp. 41f and 44; W.R. Garr, "The Comparative Method in Semitic Linguistics," *AuOr* 25 (2005), p. 18.

[369] For the possibility that Aramaic *bar* "son" might be etymologically related to Babylonian *māru*, OA *mer'um* and MA as well as NA *mar'u*, see Lipiński, *Semitic Languages*, § 11.6 and § 63.8.

[370] See PNA 2/II (p. 819a s.v. Nabû-bīna-ukīn).

[371] For further names, see PNA 1/II, pp. 353–356.

[372] See also F.M. Fales, AECT, pp. 161ff. no. 14.

[373] Additional instances of Aramaic *br* "son," attested in the NA texts excavated at Dur-Katlimmu (Tell Šēḫ Ḥamad), are: BATSH 6 55 l.e.1 *b*[*r*]; 65 e.1; 200 l.e.1.

[374] See M.P. Streck, "Keilschrift und Alphabet," in D. Borchers et al. (eds.), *Hieroglyphen – Alphabete – Schriftreformen: Studien zu Multiliteralismus, Schriftwechsel und Orthographieneuregelungen* (Göttingen 2001), p. 81, no. 3.1. For LB, cf., idem, *Zahl und Zeit.*

allophone of /a/. The /a/ > /u/ occurs in NA in closed syllables ending in *r* (often near a labial).[375]

basālu v. (G) "to melt"

Loanword	Reference	Provenance	Origin	Genre	Date
ba-si-li	SAA XI 26 r.2	Nineveh	*Harran*	AD	7th c.

Aram. ⇒ NA [?]

Syr., *bšl* v. "to melt" PSm. 56b; Manna 84a. Syr., *bšl* v. "to smelt" CAL. Syr., *bešālānā* n. m. "gold-smelting workshop" SL 195a. Syr., *bšln, bšlnʾ* n. m. "gold smelter" CAL. Syr., *bašlā* adj. "melted" Manna 84a. JBA *bšl* v. Pa. "to bake (in the furnace) the earthen vessel" Jastrow 199a.

The word *basālu* has a single occurrence in a NA record of merchants' transactions. As a *hapax legomenon*, its semantic connection must be determined from the context where it occurs, but that is not entirely clear due to a minor break immediately after the determinative sign NA_4 which usually appears before stone names.

AHw. (p. 110a s.v. *basālu*) is uncertain about the reading of this word and defines it as (Stein). The editors of CAD (B, p. 133a s.v. *basālu*) express uncertainty about the meaning of *basālu*, but based on the Hebrew and Aramaic *psl*, tentatively suggest the rendering "has not been wrought."[376] AEAD does not list a word *basālu*. A word *pasālu* in the sense "to turn around, to twist," is found in OB, MA and SB, but this meaning does not fit the context where the NA word occurs. On the other hand, the editors of CDA (p. 40a s.v. *basālu*), consider the meaning of the word to be unknown, but for a possible source word they refer tentatively to the Akkadian word *bašālu* "to be cooked; become ripe." In SAA XI 26, the expression *la ba-si-li* is translated "genuine," but in the glossary section of SAA XI (p. 160a), the word *ba-si-li* is listed under the headword *bašālu* "to cook, boil." SAA XI 26 r.1–4, reads:

> 1 GÚ.UN 6 MA.NA DÀG.GAZ NA_4.[*x x*] / *la ba-si-li ina* ŠÀ 1 MA.NA 10 GÍN [KUG.UD *ina* ŠU.2] / [m]*ba-la-si* DUMU–KÁ.DINGIR.RA.KI *ina qa-*⸢*ab-si*⸣ / URU.KASKAL *la-qi ma-a e-ti*[!]*-qu* ⸢*šú-u*[!]⸣

Grammatik der Numeralia und des Verbalsystems im Spätbabylonischen (Groningen 1995), n. 245 and 554.

375 See Luukko, SAAS XVI, p. 84; Hämeen-Anttila, SAAS XIII, § 2.4.1. Cf. S.E. Fassberg, "The Forms of 'Son' and 'Daughter' in Aramaic," in H. Gzella & M.L. Folmer, (eds.), *Aramaic in its Historical and Linguistic Setting* (Wiesbaden 2008), pp. 44 and 47ff.

376 Cf. Nab., *pšl* "to sculpt"; Palm., *psl* "to sculpt"; Pun., *pslh* "hewn stone"; Syr., *psl* "to quarry, hew (stone)."

> 1 talent 6 minas blocks of genuine [...]-stone purchased for 1 mina 10 shekels [of *silver from*] Balassu, citizen of Babylon inside the city of Harran – he says: 'He was *passing through.*'

The suggested Aramaic or West-Semitic *psl* "to cut, hew," for rendering the NA word, as indicated in CAD, is problematic, because during the relevant period of language contact, the Aramaic or West-Semitic *psl* is expected to appear in NA as *pšl* or *bšl.*[377] In other words, we would expect that the Aramaic or West-Semitic source word would be either *pšl* or *bšl.*[378] The only feasible way for NA to keep the sibilant of the supposed Aramaic *psl* would have been through a trans-NB or trans-SB Aramaic loan in NA, but *psl* in the sense "to cut, hew," is not attested in NB or SB.

If, instead, the NA *ba-si-li* denotes "to melt," then we have to assume a borrowing from Aramaic *bšl* "to melt, smelt," for only then we can explain the sibilant's change *š* > *s*. In MA and NB *bašālu* is used in the G-stem to mean "fuse, melt (referring to the ingredients of glass)" and in OA it is used in the Š-stem to denote melting of metal (silver). In another NA text (StAT 2 164:9), we have the word *bašlu* in the G-stem meaning "refined (silver)" derived from *bašālu* "to refine (silver)."[379] StAT 2 164:9, reads:

> 1/3 MA.NA KÙ.BABBAR *ba-áš-lu*
>
> One-third mina of refined silver

The form of the NA word *basīli* can be analyzed as a substantivized verbal adjective of the Semitic pattern **QaTīL*, but this pattern is not productive in Akkadian, has no adjectival usage and serves mostly for substantives.[380] Besides, the NA form of this pattern may undergo a vowel assimilation resulting in **QiTīL.*[381] In fact, the proper NA pattern in this case would be **QaTL*, a contracted form of **QaTiL*, as in *bašlu* in the example given above.

It is more likely then that *basīli* reflects the Aramaic pattern *QaTīL* with adjectival usage,[382] combined with the NA progressive vowel assimilation, i.e., *basīlu* > *basīli.*[383] Accordingly *la ba-si-li* in our text can be rendered "not melted," referring to a crude or untreated stone most probably rich in a certain metal.[384] Most likely, the form of the NA word points to a borrowing from Aramaic.[385]

---

377 See above, n. 71.

378 Ibid. For variation between *b* and *p* in Neo-Assyrian, see Luukko, SAAS XVI, § 4.1.1. Cf. I.J. Gelb, "Notes on von Soden's Grammar of Akkadian," *BiOr* 12 (1955), § 25d.

379 See the Glossary of StAT2 (p. 224b s.v. *bašālu*). Cf. CAD (B, p. 140a s.v. *bašlu*, mng. no. 3).

380 See J. Fox, *Semitic Noun Patterns* (Winona Lake 2003), pp. 187ff.

381 See GAG § 55i.

382 See Fox, ibid., p. 187. Cf. the Syriac *bašīlā* "melted, cooked" in Manna (p. 84a s.v. ܒܫܝܠܐ).

383 Cf. Luukko, SAAS XVI, § 4.5, 2.

384 A passage that might serve to support this rendering is found in a NB text (GCCI 2 369:2), quoted in CAD (B, p. 136 s.v. *bašālu*, d). It reads: 1-*et* NA_4.LAGAB *a-na ba-šá-lu*, and is translated "one lump of stone for melting(?)."

385 Cf. Nili, p. 135:30.

bašā'u v. (G) "to despise, disdain, scorn; to neglect"

Loanword	Reference	Provenance	Origin	Genre	Date
ba-ši-i'	SAA V 46:16′	Nineveh	*Bīt-Zamāni*	L	Sg

Aram. ⇒ NA [?]

JPA, JBA, CPA, Syr., Ma., *bsy* v. "to despise, disdain, scorn; to neglect, to be negligent" DJPA 106a; DJBA 223b; Jastrow 178a; Lsp. 27b; DCPA 52b; SL 163b; PSm. 48a; Manna 70a; Audo 82b; MD 67b.

This word occurs only once in a NA letter (SAA V 46:16′), and as a *hapax legomenon* its semantic connection is determined from the context. Lanfranchi and Parpola tentatively translate the word *ba-ši-i'* as "to no avail."[386]

> SAA V 46:12′–e.19′ read as follows:
>
> *a-šab-bar muk a-le-e mì-li*[*k-ka* 0] / *ṭè-mu-ma la i-šak-kan* LÚ*.*kal*-[*la-bu*] / *ša ina* IGI-*ia* LUGAL *ip-q*[*i-du*]-*ni* [0] / 3-*šú* 4-*šú* TA LÚ*.A–KIN-*iá* [*a-sa-bar*] / *ba-ši-i' ṭè-mu-ma la* [*iš-kun*] / *a-na* LÚ*.A–KIN-*iá ú-ti*-[*ra*] / *ma a-ṣa-bat ina* ŠÀ *si*-⌜*bar*⌝-[*ri*] / *e-si-ip-ka*
>
> I keep writing: "Where is [your] sense?" but he does not give any *reason*. [I have] many times over [sent] the *kal*[*lāpu*] whom the king ap[poin]ted in my service with my messenger, but *to no avail*. [He has not given] any *explanation* but has retur[ned] my messenger, (saying): "I will seize you and wrap you up in iron chains!"

Based on the context, however, it seems that the meanings "to neglect; to despise" fit better for the word under discussion and, as such, it is more likely a borrowing from Aramaic *bsy* "to despise; to neglect."[387] If this is the case, the borrowing must have happened prior to the development of the Aramaic root III' > IIIī in the 8th century B.C., i.e., before the estimated date of the NA letter.[388] Otherwise, the Akkadian root BŠ' is only attested in the word *bašû*(*m*) in the sense "to exist, to be in existence and available, to be on hand," which does not fit into the context of the NA word.[389] The change *s* > *š* from the Aramaic alphabetic writing into the Neo-Assyrian cuneiform rendering is to be expected.[390] Syntactically the form of the NA word *ba-ši-i'* points to a G-stem verb of the *a*-class in the stative with a passive significance and ought to be rendered with the sense "was neglected; was despised," in reference to *kallāpu* "(armored)

[386] However, in the Glossary of SAA V (p. 220a s.v. *bašā'u*), the meaning of this word is defined as (unknown).
[387] Cf. AEAD (p. 14a s.v. *bašā'u*).
[388] Cf. V. Hug, *Altaramäische Grammatik der Texte des 7. und 6. Jh.s v.Chr.* (Heidelberg 1993), § 9.2.5; T.H. Robinson, *Paradigms and Exercises in Syriac Grammar* (Oxford 1962), § 29.
[389] See CAD (B, p. 144a s.v. *bašû*); AHw. (p. 112b s.v. *bašû*(*m*)).
[390] See n. 71 above.

horseman, knight, outrider."[391] The Aramaic word *bsy* "to despise, disdain, scorn," is probably cognate with the Arabic word بسا, despite the fact that the latter has quite the opposite meanings, namely "to treat amicably; to be intimate, be on familiar terms (ب with)."[392]

bēt zibli n. "dump; lavatory"; (see the discussion below s.v. *ziblu*)

Aram. ⇒ NA

bunbullu n. "cone?"

Loanword	Reference	Provenance	Origin	Genre	Date
bu-un-bu-ul-li	SAA XVI 63:22	Nineveh	*Gūzāna*	L	Esh
bu-un-bu-ul-lu	SAA III 7:3	Nineveh	Nineveh	LT	Asb

Aram. ⇒ NA; SB [?]

Sūret *bambūlā, banbūlā* n. m. "an icicle; the spout (of a vessel, jug)" Maclean 34a. Sūret *banbūlā* n. m. "faucet, a device fixed to a pipe to control the flow of liquid from it" Oraham 56b. Sūret *balbūltā, banbūltā* n. m. "tap; nozzle (of a pitcher)" Ashitha 48a. NENA *balbulka* n. m. "spout" Sabar 110b.

This enigmatic word is a *dis legomenon* in NA and a *hapax legomenon* among *materia medica* in a SB text stemming from Assyria.[393] Its semantics can therefore only be determined from context. CAD (B, p. 317a s.v. *bunbullu*) gives no translation for its three citations of *bunbullu*, but comments: "None of the contexts cited is sufficiently preserved to permit even a guess at the meaning of the word."[394] AHw. (p. 138a s.v. *bunbullu*) on the other hand, defines *bunbullu* as (wohl ein Gegenstand) of unknown origin. In AEAD (p. 18a s.v. *bunbullu*), the word is tentatively glossed "cone(?)."

The attestation *bu-un-bu-ul-li* occurs in a letter (ABL 633) written by an official to the Assyrian king Esarhaddon concerning crimes in Gūzāna. This letter was first edited by Fales, who leaving this word untranslated rendered the passage where *bunbulli* occurs as follows: "Qurdî, the charioteer, mistreats the horses of the deposit of the palace. On the *bunbullu* [of one horse(?)] he set his hands, saying: 'Let's check our strokes'."[395]

The same letter has now been re-edited as SAA XVI (63:21–23) by Luukko and Van Buylaere, who tentatively render *bunbullu* as "cone," based on the Sūret

[391] See AEAD (p. 45a s.v. *kallāpu*).
[392] See Wehr-Cowan (p. 57b s.v. بسا).
[393] For SB, see AMT 4, 1:3, *bu-un-bu-ul-l*[*i/a*].
[394] CAD (B, p. 317a s.v. *bunbullu*).
[395] See F.M. Fales, "New Assyrian Letters from the Kuyunjik Collection," *AfO* 27 (1980), pp. 142ff, 12; idem, CLNA, pp. 118–125.

expression *banbūlā dəgdīlā* "icicle."[396] They translate the same passage as follows:

> [ᵐ*qur-d*]*i-i* LÚ*.*mu-kil*–KUŠ.*a-pa-a-ni* ANŠE.KUR.RA.MEŠ *na-kam-te* / [0? É].GAL *ú-ka-ba-as ina* UGU *bu-un-bu-ul-li* / [*ša* ᵈ15?] Á.2-*šú i-sa-kan ma-a maḫ-ṣi-ni né-mur*
>
> [Qurd]î, the chariot driver of the treasury horses, is treading on (the authority of) the [Pa]lace. He has laid his hands on the *cone* [of Ištar], saying: "Strike (f. sg.) me! Let's see (what happens)!

The other attestation, i.e., *bu-un-bu-ul-lu*, occurs in a literary text written in NA representing a hymn by Assurbanipal to goddess Ištar of Nineveh. The text has been re-edited by Livingstone, and the passage where this word occurs (SAA III 7:2–3) reads:

> *šar-ḫat šu-ru*!*-ḫat el-let* ᵈIŠ.TAR.MEŠ [0] / NINA.KI *bu-un-bu-ul-lu šá-kin ša ina* ŠÀ-*bi l*[*a x x x*]
>
> She is glorious, most glorious, the finest of the goddesses! Nineveh is set with *bunbullu* decorations, within which there is no [...].

Livingstone, in his effort to explain the word *bunbullu* attested in the passage above, refers to Fales' translation of the other NA text where *bunbulli* is attested and notes the following:

> In view of the present occurence [*sic*], and the episode in CT 53 46:21–6 where the *bunbullu* is to be cut from the side of a horse ......, one could suppose that it was a kind of decoration. If it was a plume or feathers, this would also explain its appearance among *materia medica* (AMT 4,1:3).[397]

Another scholar who is in favor of an Aramaic origin is Kwasman, who in a short article on *bunbullu* takes into consideration all the three instances where this word is attested, but elaborates more on the attestation in the SB text and, based on Fales' translation, draws the following conclusion:

> A definition that would fit all the contexts would have to be a plant that could be crushed, dried and softened, as *bu-un-bu-ul-*[*li*] is mentioned as one of five plants: ZÉ GU₄ GI₆ ZÉ GÍR.TAB ZÉ PEŠ *bu-un-bu-ul-*[*li*] ᵁ*su-a-di* TUR-*ár* SÚD 5 Ú ḪI.A ŠEŠ.MEŠ DIRI-*ma*. A gloss is written over *su-a-di*: ZÉ MUŠ. Three of the five plant names have *Decknamen* (excrement of a black ox, excrement of a scorpion, excrement of mouse) and the gloss has added the *Deckname* of *su-a-di* (excrement of a snake). Together they are described clearly as 5 Ú.ḪI.A ŠEŠ.MEŠ which supports Köcher's explanation that the substances of the *Dreckapotheke* are secret names of plants;....... In ABL 633:22, *bunbullu* was used to decorate a horse or alternatively represented a decoration that resembles a plant (see F.M. Fales

[396] See n. ad SAA XVI 63:22. Cf. Oraham, p. 57a.
[397] See n. ad SAA III 7:8.

AfO 27 (1980) 142ff). The plant could well have been used for ritual purposes i.e. ABRT 1 7 :3. The Neo-Aramaic word *bunbūla* [*bumbūla*] has the meaning "cone" see R. Macuch, E. Panoussi, *Neusyrische Chrestomatie*, Wiesbaden 1974 21. Hence, *bunbullu* with the meaning "cone" appears to fit the above mentioned contexts.[398]

Symbolically, objects resembling a bucket and a pine cone, also interpreted as a fir cone (*Pinus brutia*), which seem to be associated with purification, are depicted in Neo-Assyrian art, often together with the stylized tree.[399] However, both Livingstone and Kwasman base part of their conclusion on Fales' rendering of the passage where *bunbullu* occurs in one of the NA texts. But that passage suffers a minor break and its reconstruction is conjectural. While Fales' reconstruction is, *bunbullu* [of one horse(?)], Luukko and Van Buylaere re-edited the entire text anew and reconstructed the same break as *cone* [of Ištar].

Shifting focus to the supposedly Aramaic source word, we find that it is attested as *bambūlā*, *banbūlā*, *bunbūlā* (*bumbūlā*),[400] *balbūltā*, *banbūltā* and *balbulka*, in masculine and in feminine with the meanings as listed under the comparative data above. However, none of these meanings include the rendering "cone," in a botanical sense, as interpreted by Kwasman. The Sūret word consists of the radicals BN/MBL or BLBL. A parallel term, which semantically corresponds to the Sūret word, is the Arabic *bulbulah* n. f. "snout; nozzle" derived from the root BLBL.[401] Since Neo-Aramaic and Arabic share the radicals BLBL, but not BN/MBL, the former is expected to be the source of the word, provided that no loan relationship exists between the two languages. But if BLBL were the source of the Sūret word, one would expect a phonological development of the so-called "starke Dissimilation," to take place.[402] This means the total disappearance of a radical through dissimilation especially with reduplicated roots, leading to the following development *balbūltā* > *babūltā*.

Semantically, the word *banbūlā*, *bunbūlā* in Sūret also implies a "cone," but only in a geometric sense. Hence, the expression *banbūlā dəgdīlā* "icicle, a pendent, and usually conical, mass of ice, formed by the freezing of dripping water."[403] In English, on the other hand, the word "cone" has a geometric meaning as well as a botanical meaning. In German "Zapfen" has the meaning "spigot (for a barrel)" as well as the botanical meaning "cone." The former meaning, i.e., a "cone," in the geometric sense, is what is meant by *banbūlā* in Sūret. In Classical Syriac the word *qōnōs* in the sense "cone; cedar cone" is utilized, and is a loan from the Greek κῶνος.[404] Consequently, if the NA *bunbullu* is connected etymologically with the Sūret *banbūlā*, the meaning "cone," in its

398 See T. Kwasman, "*bunbullu*," *NABU* 1999/60.

399 Cf. J. Black & A. Green, *Gods, Demons and Symbols of Ancient Mesopotamia: An Illustrated Dictionary* (London 1992), p. 46.

400 See R. Macuch & E. Panoussi (eds.), *Neusyrische Chrestomathie* (Wiesbaden 1974), p. 21 s.v. *bunbūlā* [*bumbūla*] "Zapfen," pl. *bunbulē dgdīlā* "Eiszapfen."

401 See Elias & Elias, p. 73a.

402 See K. Tsereteli, *Grammatik der modernen assyrischen Sprache (Neuostaramäisch)* (Leipzig 1978), § 2.5.5.

403 See Oraham, p. 57a.

404 See SL, p. 1336b.

botanical sense has to be ruled out, but "cone," in the geometric sense remains a possibility.

būṣīnu, *būṣinnu* n. "lamp"

Loanword	Reference	Provenance	Origin	Genre	Date
bu-ṣi-ni	SAA VII 88 r.15	Nineveh	Nineveh	AD	7th c.?
É.*bu-*⸢*ṣi*⸣*-ni*	Iraq 23 33 (= ND 2490+ r.13)[405]	Calah	Calah	AD	–
GIŠ.*bu-ṣi-(in)*	SAA III 39:32	Assur	Assur	MC	7th c.
GIŠ.*bu-ṣi-ni*	CTN II 141:7	Calah	Calah	AD	–

Aram. =▷ NA; SB [?]

OffAr., Ma., Syr., *bwṣyn, bwṣyn'* (*bō/ūṣīn, bō/ūṣīnā*) n. m. "mullein" CAL; SL 128b. JPA, JBA, CPA, Sam., Syr., *bwṣyn, bwṣyn'* (*būṣīn, būṣīnā*) n. m. "a plant; wick; lamp" DJPA 88a; DJBA 192a; Jastrow 147b; Dalman 48a; LSp. 23b; DCPA 42b; DSA 86b; PSm. 39a; Audo 65a; Manna 56b; SL 128b; CAL. Ma., *būṣīnā* n. m. "pumpkin" MD 56b.[406]

This word in Nuzi refers to (a plant). In OAkk, OB, SB and NA, it refers to a "wick (made from *verbascum* leaves)." In MB and SB it means "mullein, *verbascum*." Only in NA and SB the word designates a "lamp." The term is probably the name of the plant *verbascum thapsus* (English "mullein"), the leaves of which were used to make wicks for candles and lamps.[407]

In AHw. (p. 143a s.v. *buṣīnum, buṣinnu*), the word is considered to be a borrowing from Akkadian into Aramaic with the meaning "Lampe; Königskerze."[408] In CDA (p. 50b s.v. *buṣinnu*) no borrowing relationship is suggested. Zimmern considers the Aramaic word *būṣīnā*, which was borrowed into Persian as *būzīn* and Armenian as *bucin*, to be a loan from Akkadian *būṣinnu* in the sense "Docht; Licht."[409] He also regards the Akkadian *būṣinnu* in the sense "Königskerze, Verbascum," to be borrowed into Syriac as *būṣīnā* from which it was borrowed into Arabic as *būṣīr*.[410] Kaufman considers the term to be foreign in both languages based on its distribution in Aramaic, and the *-innu* ending which in Akkadian indicates foreign words.[411]

---

405 See B. Parker, "Administrative Tablets from the North-West Palace, Nimrud," *Iraq* 23 (1961), pp. 33f. The transliteration É.*bu-*⸢*ṣi*⸣*-ni* and the line numbering are taken from the Corpus of Neo-Assyrian Texts (CNA).
406 Cf. DNWSI (p. 148 s.v. *bwṣyn* "gourd, cucumber"). Cf also I. Löw, *Aramäische Pflanzennamen* (Leipzig 1881), pp. 66, 331.
407 See the comment in CAD (B, p. 348a s.v. *buṣinnu*, mng. no. 3).
408 See also SL (p. 128b s.v. ܒܘܨܝܢܐ); DJPA (p. 88a s.v. בּוֹצִין); DJBA (p. 192a בּוֹצִינָא).
409 See Zimmern, AF, pp. 35f., 56.
410 Ibid., p. 56.
411 See Kaufman, AIA, p. 45, n. 68. See also GAG § 58b.

Nevertheless, only in few NA texts and one SB from Assyria the word *būṣīnu* is attested in the sense "lamp." In one NA administrative document (Iraq 23 33 = ND 2490+ r.13) which comes from Calah/Nimrud, the text consists of a list of inventory including objects mainly made of wood or metal such as a (copper lamp). Here, the word *būṣīni* is preceded by the logogram É which stands for the word *bētu* "house; container." Hence, the combination *bēt būṣīni* "lamp."[412] The NA text (Iraq 23 33 = ND 2490+ r.13) reads as follows:

1 É.*bu*-⌜*ṣi*⌝-*ni* URUDU

One copper lamp.

In the SB text from Assyria, the word *būṣīni* is also preceded by the logogram É. Together they form the expression *bēt būṣīni* which has a variant as *bēt būṣinni* "lamp."[413] The term is mentioned among the booty taken from Urartu. The context where the SB word is attested (Sg TCL III 365) reads as follows:[414]

É.*bu-ṣi-ni* AN.BAR

An iron lamp.

In the NA administrative text from the Governor's Palace Archive at Calah/Nimrud (CTN II 141:7), the word is attested as GIŠ.*bu-ṣi-ni*, i.e., is preceded by the logogram GIŠ.[415] The latter stands for the Akkadian word *iṣu/ēṣu* "wood," but can also serve as a determinative before names of trees, wood and devices.[416] The NA text (CTN II 141:6–7) reads as follows:

2? MA.NA URUDU *ša* Ì.MEŠ / *ša* GIŠ.*bu-ṣi-ni*

2 minas of copper for oil for the lamp(s).

Postgate comments on GIŠ.*bu-ṣi-ni* (CTN II 141:7) saying that this term would strictly refer to a certain plant, probably mullein or the wick produced from it, but here it is undoubtedly an abbreviation for *bēt būṣinni* "lamp."[417] He adds that *bēt* is also left out in another NA text (ADD 964 r.15 = SAA VII 88 r.15).[418]

In CTN II 141:7 and SAA III 39:32 where the word under discussion is preceded by the logogram GIŠ, the contexts do not allow interpreting the logogram as *iṣu/ēṣu* "wood." It is more likely that GIŠ in the two texts represents a determinative indicating a device which in both cases must have been a (lamp). Since the word *būṣīnu* "lamp" is only attested in NA and SB, and based on its

412 See CAD (B, p. 348b s.v. *buṣinnu*, no. 3).
413 Ibid.
414 See F. Thureau-Dangin, *Une relation de la huitième Campagne de Sargon* (Paris 1912), p. 56:365. See also CAD (B, p. 348b s.v. *buṣinnu*, no. 3).
415 The same is also attested in GIŠ.*bu-ṣi-*(*in*) in (SAA III 39:32).
416 See Borger, ABZ, no. 296.
417 See n. ad CTN II 141:7.
418 Ibid.

distribution in Aramaic, it is more likely that the meaning of the word as "lamp" was borrowed from Aramaic. The borrowing in this case is merely a semantic extension of the word in NA and SB based on the meaning of an Aramaic cognate.

darāsu v. (G) "to expound, interpret, debate"; (D) "to thresh"

Loanword	Reference	Provenance	Origin	Genre	Date
ad-di-ris	SAA X 235 r.15	Nineveh	Nineveh	L	673?
lu-du-ri-[su]	SAA XIX 53 r.9′	Calah	Naṣibina	L	Tgl

Aram. ⇒ NA

JBA, LJLA, Syr., *drš* v. "to interpret, to expound" DJBA 353b; Manna 162f; Audo 217a; PSm. 98a; CAL. Syr., *drš* v. Pe. & Pa. "to thresh, tread" Manna 162f; Audo 217a; CAL. JPA, JBA, Sam., *drs* v. "to tread, press, trample" DJPA 156a; DJBA 353a; Jastrow 324b; DSA 194b; CAL.

The Akkadian word *darāsu* bears the meanings "to trample upon, to throw over or back, to press hard, to treat harshly."[419] It is cognate with Jewish Aramaic דְּרַס "to tread, stamp,"[420] Hebrew דָּרַס "tread, stamp,"[421] Syr., ܕܪܫ "to tread; step or walk on,"[422] and Arabic دَرَسَ "to thrash or thresh (harvest)."[423] In one NA letter from Nineveh (SAA X 235 r.15), the word occurs as *addiris*, but the usual Akkadian meanings of *darāsu* do not fit the context.[424] The NA letter, possibly related to funerary rites, was written to Esarhaddon by Marduk-šākin-šumi, an Assyrian scholar who later became the chief exorcist during the reign of Assurbanipal.[425]

CAD (D, p. 110b s.v. *darāsu* mng. no. 1c) considers the meaning of *addiris* to be obscure. AHw. (pp. 163b, 1550b s.v. *darāsu(m)*) defines *ad-di-ris* as meaning (beiseite gestoβen warden), and tentatively takes it to be in the preterit of the N-stem. Parpola, on the other hand, cites the West-Semitic root DRŠ in the sense "to examine, expound, interpret" as a possible etymology for *addiris*, noting thus: "*addiris*: tentatively connected with rabbinical *drš* 'to examine, expound, interpret' (Jastrow Dict. 325b) rather than Akkadian *drs* 'to trample, press hard,' which is otherwise not attested in NA."[426] The expression *addalaḫ addiris* is interpreted as a hendiadys,[427] i.e., a rhetoric term expressing a single complex idea. The passage where *addiris* occurs (SAA X 235 r.10–15), reads as follow:

---

419 CAD (D, p. 110a s.v. *darāsu*, 1, c).
420 See Jastrow, p. 324b; Dalman, p. 99b.
421 Ibid.
422 See Manna, p. 162b.
423 See Elias & Elias, p. 212a.
424 For a previous bibliography treating the text, see Parpola, LAS II, p. 195, no. 198.
425 See PNA 2/II (p. 722b s.v. Marduk-šākin-šumi, no. 2b, 1′).
426 See n. ad SAA X 235 r.15. For Parpola's first edition of ABL 379, see LAS I & II, no. 198.
427 See SAA X 235, ibid. Cf. SAA XIII 28 r.15 and 29 r.7′.

> *ina ti-ma-li te-gír-tú* / *ina* UGU *la da-ga-li* / *as-sa-kan* / *ú-ma-a* / *ad-da-làḫ* / *ad-di-ris*
>
> Yesterday I *made an excuse* for (its) not being seen; now I have *made a quick commentary to it.*

As a *hapax legomenon* in NA, the meaning of *addiris* can be determined only from the context in which the notions "to expound, interpret, debate," of the West-Semitic root DRŠ seem to fit nicely. Syntactically and phonologically, *addiris* is taken as 1p. preterit of *darāsu* in the Gt-stem, resembling the Assyrian form *aptiqid* as opposed to the Babylonian *aptaqid.* The *t* of the *-ta-* infix is fully assimilated to the preceding dental *d.*[428] The sound change of the West-Semitic *š* into NA *s* is unproblematic.[429] The purpose of the NA letter and the homiletical connotation associated with the root DRŠ in Aramaic, as well as the extremely limited distribution of the NA word, together point to a loan, most likely from Aramaic, which exhibits a wider range of semantics for the root DRŠ.

In another NA letter from Calah/Nimrud (SAA XIX 53 r.9′), reign of Tiglath-pileser III, the word occurs as *lu-du-ri-*[*su*]. Also here, the usual Akkadian meaning of *darāsu* does not fit the context. The passage where the word is attested (SAA XIX 53 r.5′–11′) reads as follows:

> *an-n*[*u-rig*] / *ša* ^{md}U.GUR–*ú-bal-liṭ* 2-[*e*] / *an-na-ka liq-bu-ni-šú-*[*nu*] / GUD.MEŠ-*šú-nu lil-lik-ú-*⸢*ni*⸣ / ŠE$^{!}$.BURU$_{14}$-*šú-nu lu-du-ri-*[*su*] / *li-in-tu-ḫu ina* ŠÀ UR[U] / *lu-še-ri-bu* [0]
>
> Right [now] (men) of the deputy governor Nergal-uballiṭ are here. Let th[em] be told that their oxen should come and that they should thre[sh] their harvest, fetch it and bring it into the ci[ty].

In the instance given above, *lu-du-ri-*[*su*] is taken to be in the D-stem with the meaning "to thresh."[430] If the word is correctly interpreted, it constitutes a *hapax legomenon* in NA.[431] As such, however, the word should also be considered a borrowing from Aramaic. The Aramaic source word with the meaning "to thresh" is found in the Syriac word ܕܪܫ, which in both the Pe. and Pa. tenses has the additional meaning "to thresh."[432] In this sense, the Syriac word is cognate with the above-mentioned Arabic word دَرَسَ "to thrash or thresh (harvest)."

---

[428] See Hämeen-Anttila, SAAS XIII, § 2.2.3.1. Cf. Luukko, SAAS XVI, § 4.2.3.

[429] See n. 71 above.

[430] See the Glossary of SAA XIX (p. 232b s.v. *darāsu*). Note that in the precative, the form of the word *lu-du-ri-*[*su*] is expected to be *lu-da-ri-*[*su*], i.e., with an *a* instead of the *u* in the second syllable.

[431] See n. ad SAA XIX 53 r.9.

[432] See Manna, p. 162f; Audo, p. 217a.

durā'u, *adrā'u* n. "arm; foreleg"

Loanword	Reference	Provenance	Origin	Genre	Date
ad-ra-'i	SAA XIX 88:4, 6	Calah	Eastern Provinces	L	Tgl?
du-ra-'i	SAA VII 73:3, 6, 11 [*d*]*u-ra-'i*, e.16 *du-ra-*[*'i*], r.4, 9	Nineveh	Nineveh	AD	Sg?
UZU.*du-ra-'u*	KAR 33:25 (= TuL 75, 25)	Assur	Assur	MC	–
	SAA XX 19 r. ii 21′	Assur	Assur	MC	–

Aram. ⇒ NA

OffAr., *zr'* n. m. "arm" DNWSI 342.[433] JBA, CPA *dr'*, *dr''* (*drā'*, *drā'ā*) n. m. "arm" DJBA 353a; Jastrow 324b; LSp. 48b; CAL. Syr., *drā'ā* n. m. "arm; shoulder; forequarter (of an animal)" SL 324b; PSm. 98a; Manna 162b; Audo 216a. Ma., *dra* n. m. "arm" MD 114a. JLA, Gal., PTA, CPA, Sam., Ma., LJLA *'dr'*, *'dr''* (*'eḏrā'*, *'eḏrā'ā*) n. m. "arm" DJPA 37a; Jastrow 19a; MD 8a; DSA 10b; LSp. 48b; DCPA 5b; CAL.

This word appears in NA in two forms, namely *durā'u* and *adrā'u*.[434] In AHw. (p. 177b s.v. *durā'u*), the word is approximately glossed in the sense "Fuβ mit Fuβgelenk," and its origin is considered unknown. Later in the addenda and corrigenda section of AHw. (p. 1551b s.v. *durā'u*), the term is considered to be an Aramaic foreign word meaning "Arm; Vorderbein," and is regarded as a borrowing from Aramaic *drā'ā*.[435] The editors of CAD (D, pp. 190f s.v. *dura'u*), render the word as "arm, foreleg," and consider it to be a West-Semitic loanword in NA. They note that "the Aram. *dəra'* and Heb. *zərō^a'* offer a meaning which fits the references so well that one has to assume a borrowing."[436]

As for the NA form *adrā'i*, Saggs notes that this NA noun is hardly *adru* "threshing floor," because despite the fact that a cognate occurs in Aramaic as *'adr'* "threshing floor," the NA normally has no glottal stop, and semantically the meaning "threshing floor" would not make sense in the NA context.[437] Abraham and Sokoloff point out that the word appears six times in a NA administrative document (SAA VII 73), in the phrase 1 *šabīru du-ra-'i ḫurāṣi* "1 arm-ring of gold," and since the same text also refers to 1 *šabīru rit-te ḫurāṣi* "1 hand-ring of gold," the suggested meaning "arm," as derived from Aramaic *dr'*, is quite possible.[438]

---

433 See DNWSI, p. 342 s.v. *zr'*3.
434 For *adrā'u*, see n. ad SAA XIX 88:4, 6.
435 See also von Soden, *Or* 35 (1966), p. 7:16; idem, *Or* 46 (1977), p. 185:16; CDA (p. 62b s.v. *durā'u*); AEAD (p. 22b s.v. *durā'u*).
436 CAD (D, pp. 190f s.v. *dura'u*).
437 See CTN V, p. 262, notes on l. 4, 6.
438 See Abraham & Sokoloff, *Reassessment*, p. 29:40, n. 127.

Etymologically, the existence of the Hebrew זְרוֹעַ, Aramaic דרע/זרע, Syriac ܕܪܥܐ, Arabic ذِرَاع, and Ethiopic *mazrā'ṯ*, all with the sense "arm," points to a cognate and a derivation from a common PS root *ḎR'. However, the word *durā'u* or *adrā'u* seems to be a borrowing, based on chronology and the limited distribution of the word in NA. The evidence based on the comparative method as applied to the Semitic sound laws is in favor of a borrowing from Aramaic where the first radical is *d* < *z* vis-à-vis the *z* in Hebrew and Ethiopic and *ḏ* in Arabic. It is very likely that the development *z* > *d* in Aramaic occurred earlier than the period in which it is attested, i.e., earlier than 500 B.C.

Phonologically, the difference in the first vowel *u* in the NA *durā'u* vis-à-vis the Aramaic *ə* is difficult to explain. Parpola suggests that "NA <*u*> here is rendered phonetically /ə/ ~ /œ/, not /u/."[439] The form of the NA *adrā'u* has a prosthetic vowel, most likely to disjoin the initial two-consonant cluster *dr*.[440] Probably, the NA form *adrā'u* corresponds to Aramaic *'eḏrā'ā* n. m. "arm," with the initial glottal stop ' (hamza).

The nominal form of the NA *durā'u* is that of **QuTāL*. This nominal pattern is rare in Semitic languages. In Akkadian it is attested in some isolated nouns or in a few substantivized genuine adjectives that may belong to the diminutive category.[441] Perhaps the use of the **QuTāL* pattern in the NA *durā'u* was intended to give emphasis to the diminutive aspect, i.e., in the sense that a "foreleg," is shorter in length or smaller in size than a "hind leg." The third radical ' of the Aramaic word is represented in the NA word by the glottal stop ' (hamza).[442]

Eber nāri, *Ebir nāri* n. cp. "Across the river, Transeuphratia" (land west of the Euphrates)

Loanword	Reference	Provenance	Origin	Genre	Date
e-bir–ÍD	TCAE p. 376ff. (= ND 2451:9)	Calah	Calah	AD	707
	Iraq 23, p. 45f. (= ND 2727:4)	Calah	Calah	AD	–
	Iraq 23, p. 55ff. (= ND 2803 r. i 9)	Calah	Calah	AD	Sg?
	SAA II 5 iv 9′	Nineveh	Nineveh	T	676*
	SAA XI 21 r.7′	Nineveh	*Nineveh*	AD	–
KUR.*e-bir*–ÍD	CT 53 336:5′ KUR.*e-bir*–[ÍD]	Nineveh	Nineveh	L	Sg
	SAA I 204 r.10	Nineveh	Raṣappa	L	Sg
	SAA XIII 102 r.6	Nineveh	Calah	L	Esh?

439 S. Parpola (personal communication).
440 See Lipiński, *Semitic Languages*, § 27.17.
441 See GAG § 55k; J. Fox, *Semitic Noun Patterns* (Winona Lake 2003), pp. 229ff.
442 See Table 3 above.

Aram. =▷ NB ⇒ NA; LB

BA, JLA, PTA, Syr., LJLA *ʿbr nhr*, *ʿbr nhrʾ* n. m. "land across the river (i.e., Transeuphratia)" CAL; SL 1066b.[443] Syr., *ʿbar nahrā* n. m. "crossing the river" PSm. 399a.[444]

As a toponym, seen from the Mesopotamian perspective, *Eber nāri* in NA, NB and LB, as well as *ʿbr nhrʾ* in Aramaic, meant "across the river; beyond the river," referring to the region beyond the west bank of the Euphrates, which roughly corresponded to the Levant.[445] This term appears, for instance, in a treaty between the Assyrian king Esarhaddon and Baal, king of Tyre.[446] Later, in 535 B.C., the Persian king Cyrus the Great organized most of the newly conquered territories of the former Neo-Babylonian Empire into a single satrapy, "Babylonia and *Eber nāri*."[447] The satrap resided in Babylon and there were sub-governors in *Eber nāri*, one of whom was Tettenai, mentioned in both the Bible and Babylonian cuneiform documents.[448] This arrangement remained unchanged until at least 485 B.C., (Xerxes 1st reign), but before c. 450 B.C., the "mega-satrapy" was split into two, Babylonia and *Eber nāri*.[449]

No discussion on the origin of this geographical term is provided in AHw. (p. 181b s.v. *Eber nāri*), or CAD (E, p. 8a s.v. *eber nāri*). The editors of CDA (p. 64b s.v. *Eber nāri*) consider the term to be a compound consisting of the Akkadian words *ebēru* "to cross over" and *nāru* "river." However, von Soden states in his articles on Aramaic loanwords that *Eber nāri*, "the far shore, Syria," is certainly a Babylonized version of the Imperial Aramaic *ʿab̲ar nahrā*.[450] He argues that a substantive *ebru* cannot be derived from the Akkadian word *ebēru* "to cross over."[451] Based on data provided in CAD, Abraham and Sokoloff argue that the term under discussion had a strictly Mesopotamian usage in the sense "far bank."[452] They conclude that *Eber nāri* is originally Akkadian, and that the Aramaic phrase עֲבַר נַהֲרָא is an etymological calque from Akkadian.[453]

Nevertheless, the first part of the term *Eber nāri*, namely *eber* is a construct of the substantive **ebru* and, as von Soden argued, a substantive *ebru* cannot be derived from the Akkadian verb *ebēru* "to cross over." It is, therefore, more likely that *eber* has been formed in accordance with Aramaic *ʿebar*, which, in

---

[443] Cf. DNWSI (p. 823 s.v. *ʿbr*$_5$).

[444] See PSm., (p. 399a s.v. ܥܒܪܐ).

[445] Although our study focuses on lexemes as the smallest distinctive units, the term *Eber nāri* is included and analyzed because it has previously been discussed by other scholars as a borrowing from Aramaic into NA and NB.

[446] See SAA II 5 iv 9′. See also S.S. Tuell, "The Southern and Eastern Borders of Abar-Nahara," *BASOR* 284 (1991), p. 51; S. Parpola, *Neo-Assyrian Toponyms* (Neukirchen-Vluyn 1970), p. 116.

[447] M.A. Dandamayev, "Eber-Nāri," in E. Yarshater (ed.), *Encyclopaedia Iranica* (London 1994), vol. 7, pp. 654f.

[448] See A.T. Olmstead, "Tettenai, Governor of Across the River," *JNES* 3 (1944), p. 46.

[449] See M.W. Stolper, "The Governor of Babylon and Across-the-River in 486 B.C.," *JNES* 48 (1989): 283–305; Dandamaev, ibid.

[450] See von Soden, *Or* 35 (1966), p. 8:17; idem, *Or* 46 (1977), p. 185:17.

[451] Ibid.

[452] See Abraham & Sokoloff, *Reassessment*, p. 30:41.

[453] Ibid.

turn, is a construct of the Aramaic *ʿebrā* "farther bank."[454] Also in Arabic, the term عَبْرِ النهرِ means "across the river."[455] Hence, the case of *Eber nāri* is a borrowing which represents the so called "Lehnbildung," i.e., formation of a NA word after the pattern of an Aramaic word.

That the form *eber* represents a Babylonian construct is confirmed by the epenthetic vowel *e* as opposed to the usually expected *a* in the Assyrian construct forms.[456] However, *eber* is also possible alongside *ebar* in NA.[457] The second part of the term consists of the Akkadian substantive *nāru* "river," which stands in the genitive.

gabdi, *gabdu* adj. "beside, next to, adjoining"

Loanword	Reference	Provenance	Origin	Genre	Date
gab-di	CTN III 55:5, 6, 7, 8, 9	Calah	Calah	LD	625*
	Iraq 15, p. 142 (= ND 3430:7, r.2)	Calah	Calah	LD	650
	SAA VI 33:1′	Nineveh	*Nineveh*	LD	706
	SAA VI 22:4, 5, 6, 7	Nineveh	*Nineveh*	LD	729
	SAA VI 154:6, 7, e.8	Nineveh	Nineveh	LD	678
	SAA XI 219 r. iv 7	Nineveh	Harran	AD	Sg
	SAA XIV 35:8, 10, 11	Nineveh	Nineveh	LD	630*
	SAA XIV 41:7, 8, 9, 11, r.1′, 3′, 4′, 6′, 7′	Nineveh	*Qurubi*	LD	625*
	SAA XIV 42:4, 5, 6, 7, 8, 9, 10, 11, 12, 13, 14, 15, 16, 17, 18, 19, 20, 21, 22, 24, 25, 28, r.2, 3, 4, 5, 6, 7, 8, 9, 10, 11	Nineveh	*Abi-ilaʾi*	LD	625*
	SAA XIV 43:10	Nineveh	*Nineveh*	LD	624*
	SAA XIV 44:5, 7, 8	Nineveh	*Bit-abi-ilaʾi*	LD	623*
	SAA XIV 109:7, 8, 9	Nineveh	*Nineveh*	LD	637*
	SAA XIV 111:10, e.11, 12	Nineveh	Nineveh	LD	636*?
	SAA XIV 117:6, 7, 8, 9	Nineveh	*Dayyan-Adad*	LD	633*
	SAA XIV 131:6′	Nineveh	–	LD	666
	SAA XIV 168:9′	Nineveh	–	LD	620*
	SAA XIV 248:8	Nineveh	–	LD	–
	SAA XIV 257:5′, 7′	Nineveh	–	LD	–
	SAA XIV 392:5′	Nineveh	–	LD	–
	SAA XIV 468:5, 7,	Nineveh	*Hulî*	LD	Sg

[454] Cf. SL (p. 1066b s.v. ܥܶܒܪܳܐ "farther bank").
[455] See Elias & Elias, p. 422a.
[456] GAG § 64f.
[457] Cf. NA *nēmel* ~ *nēmal* "because, since" and *mišil* ~ *mišal* "demi-, hemi-." See Luukko, SAAS XVI, p. 83. I am thankful to Prof. Simo Parpola for calling my attention to this NA variation.

	8, 9, 12, 13, 14, 17, e.19, 20, 21, 22, r.1				
	SAAB 2 7:10, 11	Girnavaz	Girnavaz	LD	631*
	SAAB 7 1:4, 5, 6, 8	Dūr-katlimmu	*Dūr-katlimmu*	LD	603
	SAAB 7 2:6, 7, 10, 11, 13	Dūr-katlimmu	*Dūr-katlimmu*	LD	602
	SAAB 7 3:6, 7, 8	Dūr-katlimmu	*Dūr-katlimmu*	LD	602
	SAAB 7 4:8, 10	Dūr-katlimmu	*Dūr-katlimmu*	LD	600
	BATSH 6/2 48:7	Dūr-katlimmu	*Dūr-katlimmu*	LD	645*
	BATSH 6/2 113:6, 7, 8	Dūr-katlimmu	*Dūr-katlimmu*	LD	673
gab-du	SAAB 3 66:6, 7	*Balaṭ*	*Balaṭ*	LD	646*
	SAAB 5 33:8, 11	Assur	*Assur*	LD	Asb?
	StAT 2 207:7, 8, 9, 10, 11	Assur	Assur	LD	618*
	StAT 2 263:13, 14, 15, 16, 17	Assur	Assur	LD	622*

Aram. ⇒ NA

Palm., JBA, JPA, CPA, Ma., Syr., *gb*, *gb'* (*gab*, *geb*, *gabbā*) n. m. "side, flank" DNWSI 207; DJBA 254a; DJPA 118a; Jastrow 203a; LSp. 39a; DCPA 66a; MD 77a; SL 198b; PSm. 58a; CAL. Gal., PTA, CPA, JBA, Ma., LJLA *gb*, *gby* (*gab*, *gabbē*) prep. "near, next to" CAL. OAram., OffAr., *zy* prep. "of, (genitive particle)" DNWSI 310ff; CAL. Com., *dy* prep. "of, (genitive particle)" DNWSI 310ff; PSm. 81a; Manna 131a; CAL.

The term *gabdi* is frequently attested in legal documents of the Neo-Assyrian period concerned with the buying or selling of fields or houses. It is used when describing the location and boundaries of the fields or houses in relation to adjacent properties or some distinctive feature, such as a road, a wall, a river or a wadi.

As for the Akkadian vocabularies, the term is only listed in AEAD (p. 29a s.v. *gabdi*) as an adjective meaning "beside, next to, adjoining." Nevertheless, it is relevant to point out that there is another Akkadian term which functions quite similarly to *gabdi*, namely the word *ṭēḫi* (construct of *ṭēḫu* "adjoining, adjacent to, close to, next to, near"), which is attested from OA and OB on, and for which a pseudo-logogram SUḪUR is occasionally used in MA and NA.[458] Even so, it seems that a certain distinction between the two terms *gabdi* and *ṭēḫi* can be deduced from the texts where they occur together.[459] The former seems to be associated more with buying and selling houses in urban centers, while the latter seems to apply to large parcels of land in rural areas, where a property was more difficult to demarcate from other plots.[460]

---

[458] See CAD (Ṭ, p. 81b s.v. *ṭēḫu*); AHw. (p. 1383b s.v. *ṭē/īḫu(m)*); Borger, ABZ, no. 403. Cf. Radner, SAAS VI, p. 277, n. 1555.
[459] See Postgate, FNALD, § 2.2.1; SAA XIV 468.
[460] See Fales, CCENA, p. 62, n. to l. 7. For the reading of the pseudo-logogram SUḪUR, see C. Saporetti, "Intorno a *VDI* 80 (2/1962) 71," *Or* 35 (1966), p. 276.

Fales notes that the previously suggested reading GABA.DI is not established and that we should not exclude the possibility that the word is an Aramaism in NA, taken from Aramaic *gb* "side," and the genitive particle *dy* "of."[461] However, based on the attestation of a variant spelling of the NA word as *gabdu*, Finkel argues against the interpretation of *gabdi* as derived from Aramaic *gb dy*.[462] In contrast, Fales and Jakob-Rost consider the other form of the word, *gabdu*, to be no more than a variant of *gabdi*.[463] The final <*u*> here is probably an allophone of <*i*>.[464]

The origin of the Aramaic word *gb* "side" is the root GNB.[465] In Syriac, the word ܓܒ "side" is sometimes written ܓܢܒ, and in Mandaic the word is *ganba*.[466] In the other Semitic languages cognates are found, in Arabic, جَنْب "beside, next to, near," and in Ethiopic *gabbo*.[467] Accordingly, the word is derived from the PS root *GNB. The Aramaic combination *gb dy* with the meaning "at the side of," is attested, for instance, in a Palmyrene phrase: *bsṭrʾ gbʾ dy smlʾ* "at the north side," as part of a tomb construction.[468] In Syriac, the expression *gb dy* meaning "on the side of" is attested, for example, in the phrase ܡܢ ܓܒܐ ܕܦܪ̈ܝܫܐ "on the Pharisees' side."[469] On the other hand, the root GNB with the meanings "side; beside, next to" is not attested in Akkadian.

Based on semantic and morphological evidence, the word is certainly a borrowing from Aramaic in NA.[470] It seems, however, that the internal structure of the Aramaic expression *gb dy* was lost after it entered NA. It was no longer analyzable as a complex, but instead was regarded as a single word, *gabdi*. Nevertheless, it is still necessary to explain the Aramaic genitive particle *dy*, which at the time of language contact between NA and Aramaic had the form *zy*. Etymologically, the origin of the consonant *z* in this genitive particle is the PS voiced interdental fricative **ḏ*.[471] Hence, the development in Aramaic was as follows: **ḏy* > *zy* > *dy*. As mentioned previously, it is very likely that the development *z* > *d* in Aramaic occurred earlier than the period in which it is attested, i.e., earlier than 500 B.C.[472] On the other hand, the voiced interdental **ḏ* in NA is expressed either by *z* or *d*.[473]

---

461 See Fales, ibid. Cf. R. Degen, *Altaramäische Grammatik der Inschriften des 10.–8. Jh. v.Chr.* (Wiesbaden 1969), § 27. Cf. also R.A. Brauner, *A Comparative Lexicon of Old Aramaic* (Ann Arbor 1974), p. 113 s.v. *gb*.

462 See I.L. Finkel, "A Neo-Assyrian Exchange Contract," *SAAB* 3 (1989), p. 65.

463 See F.M. Fales & L. Jakob-Rost, "Neo-Assyrian Texts from Assur: Private Archives in the Vorderasiatisches Museum of Berlin, Part 1," *SAAB* 5 (1991), p. 76.

464 Cf. Luukko, SAAS XVI, § 4.3.4.

465 See R. Degen, ibid., p. 44, n. 2.

466 See PSm., (p. 58a s.v. ܓܒ); Manna (p. 87a s.v. ܓܒ). For Mandaic, see MD (p. 77 s.v. *ganba*, no. 1).

467 For Arabic, see Wehr-Cowan (p. 139a s.v. جنب).

468 See DNWSI (p. 207 s.v. gb_1, p. 1162 s.v. $šml_1$ mng. no. 2). See also CAL s.v. *gb*, *gbʾ* mng. no. 1.

469 See PSm., ibid.

470 Cf. Abraham & Sokoloff, *Reassessment*, p. 24, n. 31, no. 4.

471 See S. Moscati (ed.), *An Introduction to the Comparative Grammar of the Semitic Languages* (Wiesbaden 1964), § 13.36. See also Degen, ibid., § 40.

472 See the discussion above on p. 93 s.v. *durāʾu*.

473 See Tables 1 and 3 above. Cf. DNWSI (pp. 310ff s.v. *zy*).

gab'u n. "lair(?), pit(?)"; (compare the discussion below s.v. *gubbu*)

Loanword	Reference	Provenance	Origin	Genre	Date
gab-'i	SAA X 294:39	Nineveh	Nineveh	L	Esh

Aram. ⇒ NA [?]

Nab., Palm., JPA, Sam., CPA, Ma., Syr., *gwb*, *gwb'* (*goḇ*, *gubbā*) n. m. "well, cistern; pit, den" DNWSI 207;[474] DJPA 122a; DSA 134a; DCPA 69a; MD 82a; Manna 87a; Audo 125a; PSm. 62b; SL 210b; CAL. Sam., *gb'*, *gb''* n. m. "hill" DSA 126a; CAL. LJLA *gb'h*, *gb't'* n. f. "hill" CAL. Sry., *geḇ'əṯā* n. f. "hill, mount" Manna 89b.

This word is attested as a *hapax legomenon* in NA. It occurs in a letter (SAA X 294:39) consisting of a petition possibly sent by the royal exorcist Urad-Gula to the Assyrian king. AHw. (pp. 272b s.v. *gab'u*) lists the word as meaning "Gipfel,"[475] and also adduces a NA instance as *gab-'u* (ABL 1285:38),[476] the meaning of which is considered unclear. The editors of CAD (G, p. 6b s.v. **gab'u*) gloss this word as "height," and comment that this rendering is based on Hebrew etymology. CAD does not refer to the NA instance *gab-'i* in (ABL 1285). The word is also listed in AEAD (p. 29a s.v. *gab'u*), with the sense "lair, pit." Since the word *gab'u* is a *hapax legomenon*, the possibility of determining its meaning and then its etymology is determined by the sentence context. The passage where the word occurs (SAA X 294:39) reads as follows:

> [*x x x x x* UD]-*mu ù* MI *ina* IGI[!] *gab-'i ša* UR.MAḪ ⸢LUGAL[!] *ú*[!]⸣-*ṣal*-[*la*]
>
> [......] Day and night I pray to the king in front of the lion's pit.

The interpretation of *gab'u* as "pit" was suggested by Parpola, who in a textual note took the term tentatively to be a loanword from Aramaic *gōb* "pit (of lions)."[477] Furthermore, discussing the style of the NA letter, Parpola draws significant parallels between the passage quoted above, which reveals the petitioner's predicament, and the story of Daniel in the lion's den (Dan. 6:12–27).[478] Parpola asks: "Is this a mere coincidence, or is the passage rather a literary topos already current in the Sargonid era, like the 'half my kingdom' topos attested in LAS no. 171?"[479] Zadok, on the other hand, connects our word with

---

474 See DNWSI (p. 207 s.v. gb_2).

475 Cf. CDA (p. 87b s.v. *gab'u*).

476 ABL 1285 is now re-edited as SAA X 294:39.

477 See S. Parpola, "The Forlorn Scholar," in F. Rochberg-Halton (ed.), *Language, Literature, and History: Philological and Historical Studies Presented to Erica Reiner* (New Haven 1987), p. 276, n. on l. 39.

478 Ibid., p. 274. The passage (Dan. 6:12–27) is in the Book of Daniel in the Old Testament.

479 Ibid. For Parpola's re-edition of the same text, see SAA X 294.

West-Semitic *gb*ʿ "hill; peak," and states that the ancient Aramaic form of the word is rendered by the NA *gab-*ʾ.[480]

Nevertheless, the etymology suggested by Parpola for *gab-ʾi*, namely the Aramaic *gōb* 'pit," must be rejected on purely phonological grounds. In fact, it is difficult to elucidate how the NA word *gabʾu* is taken from Aramaic *gōb*, given that the latter is derived from a *mediae geminatae* root GBB, or –the hollow root GWB.[481] Semantically, the Aramaic *gubbā* "pit, den" fits the context of our passage nicely, but phonologically it is not feasible to derive the NA word from it. More viable is Zadok's attempt to connect the NA word with Aramaic *gb*ʿ "hill; peak," but this meaning does not fit the context of the NA passage.

Considering the difficulties encountered above, Parpola suggests that the NA spelling *gab-*ʾ could be a hypercorrection for a word borrowed from Aramaic *gubbā* "pit, den," to prevent a clash or confusion with the homonym word *gabbu* "all."[482] According to Parpola, the source of the hypercorrection could be sought in IIIʾ verbs, where the glottal stop ʾ (hamza), undergoes a complete assimilation to the preceding radical in 3p. m. pl., e.g., *ittabbū* < *ittabʾū* "they got up."[483]

gaddāiu n. "pruner(?); reed- or wood-cutter(?)"

Loanword	Reference	Provenance	Origin	Genre	Date
LÚ.*gad-a-*[*a*]	StAT 2 141 r.13	Assur	*Assur*	LD	623*
LÚ.*ga-da-a-*[*a*]	SAA XII 69 r.20	Assur	Assur	T	809
LÚ*.*gad-da-a-a*	SAA XII 83 r.9	Calah	Calah	AD	7th c.
LÚ.GAL–*gad-da-a-a*	SAA XII 86 r.31	Assur	Assur	AD	684?

Aram. ⇒ NA [?]

JPA, PTA, Sam., *gd*ʿ v. Pa. "to hew off, to cut off, cutting down" DJPA 121a; Jastrow 214a; DSA 131a; CAL. Syr., *gd*ʿ v. Pe. "to prune, lop off" SL 207a. Syr., *gd*ʿ v. Pe. and Pa. "to cut off" Manna 93a; Audo 120a.

This word appears in NA as *gaddāiu*, as well as in the compound *rab gaddāi*. AHw. (pp. 273a, 1555a s.v. *gaddāja*) has an entry for this word only for LB of the Seleucid period, defining it as (ein Funktionär), and in the etymology section considers it a foreign word of unknown origin. The editors of CAD (G, pp. 7b–8a s.v. *gadāʾa*) define this word as (an official), attested only in LB, and consider it possibly to be an Old Persian word. AEAD (p. 29a s.v. *gaddāiu*), defines the

480 See R. Zadok, "NA *ga-ba-*ʾ = West Semitic *gb*ʿ," *NABU* 1989/47. For Hebrew, see Jastrow (p. 208a s.v. גִּבְעָה). Notice the conjectural restoration *ga-ba-a*ʾ suggested by Kwasman in his re-edition of the NA deed (ADD 628:7), for which, see Kwasman, NALDK, p. 35, no. 25, and p. 36, n. on l. 7. In the latest re-edition of ADD 628 as (SAA XIV 117:7), the word in question is not transliterated, but is replaced by ⌜*x x x*⌝ to indicate broken or undeciphered signs.

481 Jastrow (p. 216b s.v. גּוּב), etymologizes the word as from the root GBB. CAL subsumes the Aramaic *gob*, *gubbā* "well, cistern; cave, den," under the root GWB.

482 S. Parpola (personal communication).

483 Ibid. Cf. Luukko, SAAS XVI, § 4.2.2; Hämeen-Anttila, SAAS XIII, p. 13.

word as (a profession). On the other hand, for the meaning and etymology of this word, the editors of CDA (p. 87b s.v. *gaddāya*, p. 91b s.v. *gaṭṭa'a*), refer to another word, namely *gaṭṭa'a*, which they tentatively render as "reed- or wood-cutter." They consider it to be a loanword from Aramaic in NA and NB.[484]

In a textual commentary in a joint article, Deller and Millard comment concerning the word LÚ*.*gad-da-a-a*, which occurs in a NA edict appointing Nergal-apil-kumu'a to a position in Calah/Nimrud (BM 36711 r.9), that the earlier assumption that it is "possibly an Old Persian word," can no longer be maintained.[485] They add that it can be inferred from the NA context that the word refers to either leather workers or cattle herders.[486] In a lexical note on the word *gaddāiu*, Zadok writes:

> *gaṭṭa'a* < *qaṭṭā'ā*, hitherto known (and registered as *gaddāja*) only from Hellenistic Uruk (*AHw*., p. 273a), is mentioned (in recently published documents) as early as 544/3 B.C. (1. [lú]*ga-aṭ-ṭa-a-a*, *CT* 55, 426, 2) and 524/3 B.C. (2. [lú]*qàṭ-ṭa-a-a*, *VAS* 20, 49, 20). With the former reading (*gaddāja*) it looks as if it renders *gadday*, Aram. 'lucky' ..., but the contexts suggest an occupation rather than a title. *Gaṭṭa'a* could originate from Aram. *qaṭṭā'ā* 'cane cutter, woodcutter' which is otherwise represented by N/LB (3) *qé-et-ta-u*, (4) [lú]*qa-ṭe-e* ... and probably (5) [lú][*k'a(!)-ṭa-a-a* (*AnOr* 9, 9, ii, 20; mentioned among other occupations). All these spellings, except for (4), are with a dissimilation of one emphatic due to the presence of another emphatic. (3) and (5) are with *ṭ* > *t* and *q* > *k* respectively, whereas (1) exemplifies the shift *q* > *g* which is more common in Babylonia and is one of the features that the ancient Aramaic dialect of Babylonia – the assumed forerunner of Mandaic – shares with the latter... Mandaic has many forms which had originally had two emphatics, but underwent a dissimilation expressed by *q*- > *g*-.[487]

Zadok's reading of the word as *gaṭṭa'a* instead of *gaddāia* meets with difficulties as far as NA is concerned, because the evidence from the NA orthography does not allow for such a reading. For instance, the NA examples LÚ.*gad-a-*[*a*], LÚ*.*gad-da-a-a* and LÚ.GAL–*gad-da-a-a*, would require invoking an *ad hoc* NA sound value *gaṭ* for the first syllable *gad*. Besides, we need to explain the dissimilation of the initial *q* > *g* in NA, if the word were borrowed from the Aramaic word *qṭ'*.[488]

---

[484] Cf. von Soden, *Or* 37 (1968), p. 264:121; idem, *Or* 46 (1977), p. 192:121; Abraham & Sokoloff, *Reassessment*, p. 47:184; Nili, pp. 209:90 and 211:92.

[485] See K. Deller & A.R. Millard "Die Bestallungsurkunde des Nergal-āpil-kūmūja von Kalḫu," *BaM* 24 (1993), p. 231, n. on l. 9. Cf. R. Zadok, Review of "The Chicago Colloquium on Aramaic Studies, Journal of Near Eastern Studies Vol. 37, No. 2, April 1978," *WO* 12 (1981), p. 198 s.v. *G–D–D*. Cf. E.Y. Kutscher, "Aramaic," in T.A. Sebeok (ed.), *Current Trends in Linguistics*, 6. *Linguistics in South West Asia and North Africa* (The Hague 1970), p. 357. Note that the NA text (BM 36711), was later re-edited as SAA XII 83, where the word LÚ*.*gad-da-a-a* is left untranslated, but in the Glossary of SAA XII (p. 131a s.v. *gaddāiu*), the word is defined as (a profession or occupation).

[486] See Deller & Millard, ibid.

[487] See R. Zadok, "Assyro-Babylonian Lexical and Onomastic Notes," *BiOr* 41 (1984), p. 34. Cf. DNWSI (p. 214 s.v. gdy_3).

[488] Cf. Table 2 above.

A different approach, suggested here to solve the difficulties encountered above, is to account for the available data in a more economical way by viewing the word *gaddāia* as borrowed not from the Aramaic root QṬʿ "to cut," as proposed earlier,[489] but rather from the Aramaic root GDʿ "to prune, lop off; to cut off." This etymology seems to be more fitting phonologically. The Aramaic root GDʿ is cognate with the Hebrew root GDʿ "abhacken, verstümmeln,"[490] and the Arabic root ǦDʿ "to dock, cut off, amputate; to maim, mutilate (esp. some part of body)."[491]

The form of the word *gaddāia*, with the doubling of the second radical, is that of the Akkadian nominal pattern *PaRRāS* which denotes a member of a profession, in this case most likely "a pruner; reed- or wood-cutter."[492] On the other hand, the Aramaic root QṬʿ "to cut," probably entered NB as a loanword in the form of *qāṭû* "wood-cutter," and LB in the form of *qettāʾu* "reed- cane-cutter."[493]

gadiu n. "male kid (of 1–2 years of age)"

Loanword	Reference	Provenance	Origin	Genre	Date
ga-de-e	SAA II 6:636c	Calah	Calah	T	672

Aram. ⇒ NA; NB ⇒ LB

Com., *gdy*, *gdy*ʾ (*gḏē*, *gaḏyā*) n. m. "kid, goat" CAL. OAram., *gdy* n. m. "kid" Brauner 118.[494] JBA, JPA, Sam., CPA *gdy* n. m. "young goat, kid" DJBA 260b; DJPA 121a; Jastrow 211b; DSA 129a; LSp. 34a; DCPA 68a. Syr., *gadyā* n. m. "kid" SL 205a; PSm. 60b; Manna 92a; Audo 118b. Ma., *gadia* "kid, young goat" MD 73b.

In NA the word *gadiu* is a *hapax legomenon* attested in a treaty between Esarhaddon and Baal, king of Tyre (SAA II 6). The word is interpreted as a "male kid,"[495] and the passage where it occurs (SAA II 6:636A–636C) reads as follows:

> *a-na ka-a-šú-nu* MÍ.MEŠ-*ku-nu* ŠEŠ.MEŠ-*ku-nu* / DUMU.MEŠ-*ku-nu* DUMU.MÍ.MEŠ-*ku-nu* / *ki-i* UDU.NIM *ga-de-e lu-*⌜*x x x*⌝-[*ku-nu*]

---

489 See von Soden, ibid.
490 See Dalman (p. 68b s.v. גָּדַע); Jastrow (p. 213b s.v. גָּדַע).
491 See Elias & Elias (p. 107a s.v. جَذَعَ); Wehr-Cowan (p. 114b s.v. جدع).
492 For the nominal form *PaRRāS*, see GAG § 55o.
493 See von Soden, ibid. Cf. Register Assyriologie, *AfO* 42/43 (1995/1996), p. 441a s.v. *gaddaju* and p. 441b s.v. *gaṭṭāʾu*.
494 Brauner (p. 118 s.v. *gdh*), remarks that the form of the word in Old Aramaic *gdh* is the absolute singular of *gdy*ʾ, which can be compared with the Hebrew *gdy*.
495 See the Glossary of SAA II (p. 89a s.v. *gadiu*).

> May they [*slaughter*] you, your women, your brothers, your sons, and your daughters like a spring lamb and a kid.

The word *gadû* in the sense "kid, young goat" is attested in Hebrew as גְּדִי, Ugaritic *gdy*, Phoenician *gd'* and Arabic جَدْي.[496] AHw. (pp. 273a, 1555a s.v. *gadû*) glosses the word as "Böckchen (1–2 Jahre)," and considers it to be a loan from Aramaic.[497] The editors of CAD (G, p. 9a s.v. *gadû*) consider this word to be a West-Semitic borrowing into NB. Abraham and Sokoloff state that the distribution of this word throughout almost all of the Semitic languages suggests that it is more likely to be a cognate.[498]

The word is common in Aramaic, but is a *hapax legomenon* in NA. Hence, the chronological and distribution evidence points to a borrowing into NA. It is more likely that *gadû* was borrowed from Aramaic, with which the later dialects of Akkadian had closer contact than with the other West-Semitic languages.

galītu n. f. "deportation"; (see the discussion below s.v. *galû*)

Loanword	Reference	Provenance	Origin	Genre	Date
ga-li-te	SAA V 203 s.1	Nineveh	Māzamua (Lullumê)	L	Sg
	SAA XV 55:10, 12 *[ga-l]e-e-te*	Nineveh	Parsua	L	Sg
	SAA XV 106 r.3′ *[ga]-⸢li⸣-tú*	Nineveh	*Kār-Šarrukīn*	L	Sg
	SAA XIX 3 s.2 *g[a-l]i-⸢ti⸣*	Calah	Calah	L	8th c.

Aram. ⇒ NA

galû v. (G) "to go into exile, emigrate, migrate"; (Š) "to carry away, deport, exile, lead into exile"; (see also above s.v. *galītu*)

Loanword	Reference	Provenance	Origin	Genre	Date
i-ga-li-ú	SAA XIX 87 r.9	Calah	Eastern provinces	L	Tgl
[i]g-da-⸢al⸣-ú	SAA XIX 127 r.8′	Calah	*Babylonia*	L	Tgl
ig-lu-u-ni	SAA I 194:18e	Nineveh	Harran	L	Sg
lu-šag-li-a-šú	SAA XV 169:10	Nineveh	Northern	L	Sg

---

[496] See A. Militarev & L. Kogan (eds.), *Semitic Etymological Dictionary, Vol. II, Animal Names* (Münster 2005), p. 113:76, **gady-* "kid."

[497] Cf. von Soden, *Or* 35 (1966), p. 8:19; idem, *Or* 46 (1977), p. 186:19; CDA (p. 87b s.v. *gadû*); A. Salonen, Review of "Akkadisches Handwörterbuch. Lieferungen 3–5," by W. von Soden, *AfO* 21 (1966), p. 97.

[498] See Abraham & Sokoloff, *Reassessment*, p. 30:44.

			Babylonia		
nu-sag-li	SAA XV 40 r.6′	Nineveh	*Hamrin area*	L	Sg
nu-šag-la	SAA XV 40 r.2′	Nineveh	*Hamrin area*	L	Sg
nu-šag-la-a-ma	SAA XV 40 r.3′	Nineveh	*Hamrin area*	L	Sg
nu-šag-li	SAA XV 40 r.7′	Nineveh	*Hamrin area*	L	Sg
ša-ga-la-ni	SAA XIX 87 e.12′	Calah	Eastern provinces	L	Tgl
[*šá*]-*ga-lu-u-ni*	SAA V 54:4′	Nineveh	*Rab Šaqê Province*	L	Sg
[*š*]*ag-lu-ú-ni*	SAA XIX 127:11′	Calah	*Babylonia*	L	Tgl
ta-ga-lu-ni	SAA II 2 iv 33′	Nineveh	*Nineveh*	T	754?
ul-te-eg-lu-ma	SAA II 1:6′	Nineveh	*Nineveh*	T	825?
ú-⸢*sa*⸣*-ag-*[*li*]	SAA XIX 127 r.3′	Calah	*Babylonia*	L	Tgl
ú-sa-ag-li-ú-šú	SAA XIX 23:13	Calah	Western provinces	L	Tgl
ú-sa-ga-li-ia	SAA I 234:12	Nineveh	*Gūzāna*	L	Sg
[*ú-s*]*a-ga-li-u*	SAA XV 314 r.3′	Nineveh	–	L	Sg
ú-sa-ga-li-uš	SAA I 204 r.11	Nineveh	Raṣappa	L	Sg
⸢*ú*⸣*-sag-*⸢*li*⸣*-šú-nu*	SAA XIX 127 r.7′	Calah	*Babylonia*	L	Tgl
ú-šá-gal-na-ši-ni	SAA I 190 r.6′	Nineveh	Harran	L	Sg
ú-šá-ga-lu-ka-nu-ni	SAA XXI 50 r.4 (RL)	Nineveh	*Nineveh*	L	Asb
ú-šá-gal-u-šú-nu	SAA V 112 r.2	Nineveh	*Kumme*	L	Sg
ú-šá-ga-lu-šú-nu	SAA V 105:23	Nineveh	*Kumme*	L	Sg
[*ú-šag*]*-la-na-a-ši*	SAA I 256:3′	Nineveh	–	L	Sg
[*ú*]*-šag-la-na-ši*	SAA I 261:4′	Nineveh	–	L	Sg
ú-šag-ga-lu-na-ši	SAA XV 221:3′, r.8	Nineveh	Babylonia	L	Sg

Aram. ⇒ NA; NB ⇒ LB; SB

JBA, JPA, JA, Syr., Ma., *gly* v. Pe. “to go into exile” DJBA 286a; DJPA 129b; DNWSI 223; Jastrow 248a; DJA 38b; PSm. 69b; SL 235a; Manna 105b; MD 92b; CAL. Syr., *gly* v. Pa. “to lead or go into captivity or exile” SL 235b; PSm. 69b; Audo 139b. JPA, JBA, CPA, Syr., Ma., *glw, glwtʾ* n. f. (*gālū, gālūtā*) “exile, captivity” DJPA 129a; DJBA 285b; LSp. 37a; DCPA 73a; SL 234a; PSm. 70b; Manna 106b; MD 93b; CAL.

In AHw. (pp. 275b, 1556a s.v. *galû* II) this word is glossed “in die Verbannung gehen,” and is considered to be a borrowing from Aramaic.[499] In CAD (Š/III, p. 201a s.v. *šuglû*, (*galû*)), the word is rendered “to go into exile; to deport, to exile,” and is also considered to be a loanword from Aramaic. However, it seems that Saggs, with his attempt to render the words *ša-ga-la-ni* and *i-ga-li-ú* (NL 5:12′, 24′), was the first who connected *galû* with Aramaic, pointing out that it has no Akkadian etymon.[500]

[499] Cf. von Soden, *Or* 35 (1966), p. 8:21; idem, *Or* 46 (1977), p. 186:21. Cf. CDA (p. 88b s.v. *galû* II); DNWSI (p. 223 s.v. *gly* mng. no. 2).

[500] H.W.F. Saggs, “The Nimrud Letters, 1952 – Part I,” *Iraq* 17 (1955), p. 34, n. on l. 12′and 24′. For later editions of the same text, see H.W.F. Saggs, *The Nimrud Letters, 1952* (London 2001), pp. 25f; SAA XIX 87.

The attested derivatives of *galû* in NA are *galītu* "deportation; (coll.) deportees, settlers,"[501] *šaglû* "deported; deportee,"[502] *šaglûtu* "deportation,"[503] as well as an occupational designation *rab šaglûti* "deportation officer," which is attested in the form of a compound word, namely LÚ.GAL *šag-lu-te*.[504] The proposed Aramaic source word גלי "to go into exile," is cognate with Hebrew גלה "to go into exile,"[505] Ugaritic *gly/w* "to set off (on foot), go,"[506] Arabic جَلَا "to banish; expel; drive away,"[507] and Ethiopic *tagalgala* "he was taken into exile."[508]

As to the NA forms of *galû* with anaptyctic vowel, von Soden states that in view of the fact that NA often inserts a vowel between two consecutive consonants, a form such as *ú-šá-ga-lu-ka-nu-ni* does not indicate the existence of a root ŠGL.[509] The editors of CAD, on the other hand, note that "spellings with anaptyctic vowels are variants of expected forms of *šuglû*, and do not necessitate positing a lemma **šuggulu*."[510] In fact, the NA anaptyctic vowel in *ú-šá-ga-lu-ka-nu-ni* is not to be interpreted orthographically, but rather phonetically, because for instance in nouns the main function of anaptyctic vowel was probably to leave the rhythm of the language undisturbed.[511] As for the form of the word *[i]g-da-⸢al⸣-ú*, attested in SAA XIX 127 r.8′, it exhibits the NA regular partial assimilation of *t* in the perfect forms of the G/D-stem verbs with *g* as their first root consonant, i.e., *g* + *t* > [*gd*].[512]

Held notes that sometimes, mostly in NA letters, the word *galû*/*šuglû* "to go into exile, to exile, deport," replaces the widely attested *nasāḫu* "to banish, expel," but because of the obscure contexts and fragmentary condition of most of the NA letters in which *galû* occurs, we cannot quite be certain whether it is the

---

501 See AHw. (p. 1555b s.v. *galītu*); CDA (p. 88a s.v. *galītu*); AEAD (p. 29a s.v. *galītu*). The word *galītu* does not have an entry in CAD. For the connection of *galītu* with Aramaic *gly* "to go into exile, to be deported," see K. Deller, "The Neo-Assyrian Epigraphical Remains of Nimrud," *Or* 35 (1966), p. 194.

502 See AHw. (p. 1127b s.v. *šaglû*); CAD (Š/III, p. 200b s.v. *šuglû*); CDA (p. 380b s.v. *šuglû*); AEAD (p. 108a s.v. *šaglû*).

503 See AHw. (p. 1125b s.v. *šagalûtu*); CAD (Š/III, p. 202a s.v. **šuglûtu*); CDA (p. 345b s.v. *šagalûtu*); AEAD (p. 108a s.v. *šaglûtu*).

504 For the term *rab šaglûti* "deportation officer," see CTN III 102 iii 23′; AEAD (p. 90b s.v. *rab šaglûti*, and p. 108a s.v. *šaglûtu*). Cf. רֵישׁ גָּלוּתָא "Oberhaupt der (babylon.) Exulanten," in Dalman (p. 75a s.v. גָּלוּתָא).

505 See E. Klein, *A Comprehensive Etymological Dictionary of the Hebrew Language for Readers of English* (New York 1987), p. 99 s.v. גלה; David J.A. Clines (ed.), *The Concise Dictionary of Classical Hebrew* (Sheffield 2009), p. 66b s.v. גלה; Jastrow (p. 247b s.v. גלי); H. Tawil, *An Akkadian Lexical Companion for Biblical Hebrew* (Jersey City 2009), p. 66a s.v. גלה.

506 See J. Tropper, *Kleines Wörterbuch des Ugaritischen* (Wiesbaden 2008), p. 35 s.v. √*gly/w*; J. Aistleitner, *Wörterbuch der Ugaritischen Sprache* (Berlin 1963), p. 66 s.v. *gli*.

507 See Elias & Elias, p. 120a s.v. جَلَا; Wehr-Cowan, p. 132a.

508 Klein, ibid.

509 See von Soden, *Or* 35 (1966), p. 8:21. Cf. GAG § 18d.

510 CAD (Š/III, pp. 200f s.v. *šuglû*).

511 For anaptyctic vowels in NA nouns and finite verb forms, see Luukko, SAAS XVI, § 4.8 and § 4.8.1, esp. s.v. (gl). See idem, § 4.6 esp. p. 96 s.v. (glī Š), for regressive vowel dissimilation *u* > *a* in the suffixed pronominal form *-kanu-*, i.e., *-kunu-* > *-kanu-*.

512 See Luukko, SAAS XVI, § 4.2.3; Hämeen-Anttila, SAAS XIII, § 2.2.3.1; K. Deller, *Lautlehre des Neuassyrischen* (Wien 1959), § 42b; S. Ylvisaker, *Zur babylonischen und assyrischen Grammatik* (Leipzig 1912), § 2b.

exact equivalent of *nasāḫu.*[513] Abraham and Sokoloff find it difficult to understand why the Assyrians would have had to borrow the Aramaic term *galû*, which signifies the act of deportation or exile, when the Assyrians were the ones who initiated the use of exile as a political strategy.[514] Usually a new word is borrowed to denote something entirely new to the borrowing language. However, psycholinguistic factors unknown to us may be involved in the process of borrowing, and may possibly explain why a certain word was borrowed.[515]

The fact that this loanword is attested in NA in the causative Š-stem as *šaglû* and *šaglûtu*, while the suggested Aramaic etymon גלי is never inflected in the Šaf'el mode, is a clear indication that this loanword is completely integrated into the NA morphological system. It also indicates that the Šaf'el mode was not yet functioning in Aramaic during the period of contact with NA.[516]

No verbs of type III*w* or III' exist in Aramaic or Syriac because they all have merged into the verbal group III*y*, so the evidence points to a borrowing specifically from Aramaic. Interestingly, two of the NA texts listed above, namely SAA XIX 3 s.2 and SAA XXI 50:4′, r.4 (= ABL 541:4′, r.4),[517] in which derivatives of this Aramaic loanword occur, are in fact royal letters (*abat šarri*). This attests to the fact that even royal scribes occasionally utilized Aramaic loanwords in writing royal letters.

gammīdutu n. f., *gammīdu* n. m. "mangled garment"

Loanword	Reference	Provenance	Origin	Genre	Date
ga-me-da[!]*-te*	SAA VII 115 r. ii 18	Nineveh	Nineveh	AD	Sg
ga-mid	SAA VII 104:6′	Nineveh	Nineveh	AD	–
ga-mì-di	SAAB 1 2 ii 13′	Nineveh	Nineveh	AD	–
TÚG.*ga-me-da-a-te*	FNALD 14:25 (= ND 2307:25)	Calah	Calah	LD	PC
TÚG.*ga-me-da-te*	CTN II 1:12′	Calah	Calah	TL	–
	StAT 1 39:3	Assur	Assur	AD	–
	StAT 3 1:14	Assur	Assur	TL	–
TÚG.*ga-me-de-te*	StAT 1 39 r.10	Assur	Assur	AD	–
TÚG.*ga-me-du-tú*	ND 2687:1, 7 (= Iraq 23, p. 43)	Calah	Calah	AD	Sg?
	PVA 248	Assur	Assur	LL	–
TÚG.*ga-mid*	SAA VII 97 r.8	Nineveh	Nineveh	AD	–

Aram. ⇒ NA; LB

[513] See M. Held, "On Terms for Deportation in the OB Royal Inscriptions with Special Reference to Yaḫdunlim," *JANES* 11 (1979), p. 56, n. 29.
[514] See Abraham & Sokoloff, *Reassessment*, p. 30:46. See also B. Oded, *Mass Deportations and Deportees in the Neo-Assyrian Empire* (Wiesbaden 1979).
[515] See Kaufman, AIA, p. 16.
[516] See also below s.v. *paḫāzu*.
[517] See Waterman, RCAE, part I, p. 382 no. 541, and part III, p. 190 no. 541.

OffAr., *gmydh* n. f. "certain type of garment" DNWSI 226; CAL.[518] Syr., *gmd* v. "to mangle (clothes), press heavily" PSm. 71b; SL 239b. Syr., *gāmūdūtā* n. f. "mangling or smoothing (linen)" PSm. 72a. Sūret *gāmūdūtā* n. f. "mangling; the act of cutting or bruising with repeated blows or strokes; pressing heavily" Oraham 87b. JBA *gmd* adj. "shrunk (in connection with felt)" DJBA 289a; CAL.

The two major Akkadian dictionaries differ as to the origin of *gammīdutu*.[519] The editors of CAD (G, p. 36b s.v. *gammidu*) define this word as (a cloth), and consider it probably to be a loan from Aramaic. AHw. (pp. 279b, 1556a s.v. *gammidatu*) defines it as (ein Gewand), referring for an etymology to the Akkadian word *kamādu*(*m*), which probably means "to beat cloth."[520] On the other hand, AEAD (p. 29b s.v. *gammīdu*, *gammīdutu*) glosses the words as "mangled garment." A different etymology was proposed by Salonen who, in his review of the installment 3–5 of AHw., tentatively analyzed *gammīdutu*/*gammīdu* as, "spätes Wort, viell. < aram. *garmīdā* 'Elle(nbogen) > Kleidungsstück'."[521] Kaufman rules out an Akkadian borrowing into Aramaic saying: "Probably an old Aramaic loanword in Akkadian, but certainly not an Akkadian word."[522] Fales and Postgate do not consider *gammīdu* to be a kind of clothing but a type of rug or blanket. [523] Parpola connects *gammīdutu/gammīdu* with Syriac ܓܡܰܕ "to mangle/smooth (linen)" and considers it to be obviously derived from the Aramaic passive participle *gammīd* and hence possibly to mean "smooth gown or cloak."[524]

As for Salonen's suggested Aramaic etymology, which is found in Syriac as ܓܪܡ ܐܝܼܕܐ "arm, forearm; length of two outstretched arms," [525] the total assimilation of the liquid *r* to the following consonant is unusual in Akkadian and is rarely attested in NA.[526] Salonen's suggested Aramaic etymology has no obvious connection with "cloth, garment" as material, apart from being a means of measurement and probably related to Hebrew גּוֹמֶד "gomed, a length-measure, supposed to be the cubit less the hand's length; arm."[527] The posited development "Elle(nbogen) > Kleidungsstück," though not unlikely, remains a speculative and far-fetched analogy which weakens the loan hypothesis.

The word *gammīdutu* in NA and LB surely designates some kind of cloth or garment, because it is usually preceded by the determinative TÚG which stands before articles of clothing. The word is also listed as TÚG.*ga-me-du-tú* in the cloak section of the Practical Vocabulary of Assur (PVA 248). On the other

---

[518] Cf. DNWSI (p. 225 s.v. *gmd*).

[519] The readings *gamerāte* in AHw. (p. 62b s.v. *aqqabu*?), and *ga-me-ra-te* in CAD (A/II, p. 207a s.v. *aqqabu*), ought to be corrected to *ga-me-da*!*-te*.

[520] Cf. CDA (p. 143b s.v. *kamādu*(*m*)).

[521] See A. Salonen, Review of "Akkadisches Handwörterbuch. Lieferungen 3–5," by W. von Soden, *AfO* 21 (1966), p. 97.

[522] For previous literature commenting on the word, see Kaufman, AIA, p. 51 s.v. *gammidatu*, n. 96.

[523] See SAA VII, p. xxix.

[524] See S. Parpola, "Cuneiform Texts from Ziyaret Tepe (Tušḫan), 2002–2003 (Plates I–XXV)," *SAAB* 17 (2008), p. 57.

[525] Cf. Manna (p. 126a s.v. ܓܪܡ ܐܝܼܕܐ).

[526] Cf. Luukko, SAAS XVI, § 4.2.1.

[527] See Jastrow, p. 223a.

hand, the Akkadian word *kamādu(m)* "to weave and prepare cloth in a specific way,"[528] is certainly cognate with Arabic كَمَدَ "to make thin or fine (a process applied to cloth by the fuller)"[529] as well as with Syriac ܟܡܰܕ "to make smooth, remove the wrinkle or crease (of a cloth by the fuller)."[530]

The Akkadian word *kamādu(m)* might be considered a plausible native Akkadian etymon for *gammīdutu*, but the latter is never attested in NA or LB with the initial voiceless velar plosive *k*. This leaves no room for considering the spelling with initial *g* as a by-form. Thus, we are left with the proposed Aramaic etymology in the sense "mangled garment," derived from the root GMD, as found in the Syriac word, as the best plausible etymology for *gammīdutu*.

According to Gaspa, it is not clear whether the two forms of the word in NA, i.e., the masculine *gammīdu* and the feminine *gammīdutu*, refer to two varieties of the same item of clothing, as probably based on different sizes.[531] However, the two different forms of the word may indicate uncertainty about the original form of the word and, hence, point to a borrowing. Noticeably, in writing this word in LB, the doubling of the second radical is orthographically clearly marked, for instance, TÚG.*ga-am-mi-da-tu* or TÚG.*gam-mi-da(-a)-ti*. This fact can be taken as a case where LB, and maybe also NA, could double the second root consonant of a loanword, just like the tendency exhibited in Aramaic.[532] The forms of the word as TÚG.*ga-me-de-te* and TÚG.*ga-me-du-tú* in NA exhibit the so-called Assyrian vowel harmony.

gammuzu v. (D only) "to jib, balk, move restively (of horse)"; (see also the discussion below s.v. *burbāni*)

Loanword	Reference	Provenance	Origin	Genre	Date
ga-mu-zu!	SAA V 64 r.4	Nineveh	*Rab Šaqê Porvince*	L	Sg

Aram. ⇒ NA

Syr., *gmḏ* v. Pe. & Pa. "to jib, balk, move restively (of horse)" Manna 110b.[533]
Syr., *gmd* v. Pa., Af. "to resist, stand firm; to remain" CAL; SL 239b; PSm. 71b.

The word *gammuzu* occurs as a *hapax legomenon* in a NA letter (SAA V 64), where it is followed by the word *burbāni* which, in turn, is a *dis legomenon* in

---

[528] See CAD (K, p. 108b).
[529] See *Al-munǧidu*, p. 698a.
[530] See Manna, p. 879b.
[531] Cf. S. Gaspa, "Garments, Parts of Garments, and Textile Techniques in the Assyrian Terminology: The Neo-Assyrian Textile Lexicon in the 1st-Millennium BC Linguistic Context," in S. Gaspa et al. (eds.), *Textile Terminologies from the Orient to the Mediterranean and Europe, 1000 BC to 1000 AD* (Lincoln, 2017), p. 70 s.v. *gammīdu*.
[532] Cf. Mankowski, ALBH, p. 25.
[533] Cf. Audo (p. 145a s.v. ܓܡܕ).

NA, as discussed below in chapter 2.2. AHw. (p. 1556a s.v. *ga-mu-zu*) remarks that this word is related to horses, but states that its meaning is unclear.[534] The word is not entered in CAD. In AEAD (p. 30a s.v. *gammuzu*), the word is tentatively glossed as "to press hard," and it is indicated that it is attested in the D-stem only. The NA passage where this word occurs (SAA V 64 r.4–6), reads as follows:

i-se-niš ANŠE.KUR.RA.ME / *ga-mu-zu*! / *lip-šu-ḫu* / *bur-ba-a-ni*

All the same, the horses have been *heavily pressed*; the *foals* should rest.

In his attempt to provide an etymology for *gammuzu*, Parpola renders this word tentatively as "to press hard."[535] Commenting on it and the following word *burbāni*, he says: "Both *ga-mu-zu* and *bur-ba-a-ni* seem to be Aramaic loanwords; cf. Syr. *gmz* 'to mangle clothes, press heavily' (Payne Smith, pp. 71f) and *bar bānā* 'calf, bullock that has not yet been yoked' (ibid. 53b)."[536] Taking a closer look at the Syriac word in question, we find that *gəmad* (ܓܡܕ) "to mangle clothes, press heavily," was erroneously read as *gmz*. Furthermore, it seems that the meaning "press heavily," associated with the word *gəmad*, refers to a process mainly applied by a fuller to a garment to remove its rumples.[537]

On the other hand, the root GMD in Syriac denotes, among other things, "to jib, balk, move restively (of horse)."[538] In view of that, we may assume the existence of an Old Aramaic word **gmz* with the same sense, that served as a forerunner of the Syriac *gmd*, which would have been the source word for the NA *gammuzu*. The origin of the assumed Old Aramaic **gmz* would have been a PS *GMḎ. Phonologically, the representation of the relevant consonantal phonemes would be compatible with the evidence for borrowing; i.e., Old Aramaic **ḏ* > *z* is represented by the NA *z*.[539] This suggestion seems plausible in connection with the meaning "shackle?" proposed in chapter (2.2) below for the word *bur-ba-a-ni*, which follows in the NA phrase. Accordingly, the word *ga-mu-zu* in our text would be read as *gammuzū* "are restive," with reference to horses, and is to be considered a loanword from Aramaic, standing in the D-stem, stative, 3p. m. pl. of *gammuzu* "to jib, balk, move restively (of horse)."

***garīṣtu**, **girīṣtu*, (pl. *gariṣāte*, *giriṣāte*) n. f. "round flat loaf of bread"

Loanword	Reference	Provenance	Origin	Genre	Date
ga-ri-ṣa-te	SAA VII 161 i 1, 12, ii 1, r. i 1, 11, r. ii 1, 10	Nineveh	*Nineveh*	AD	Asb?

[534] See also CDA (p. 89b s.v. *gamuzu*).
[535] See n. ad SAA V 64 r.4, 6.
[536] Ibid.
[537] See SL (p. 239f s.v. ܓܡܕ).
[538] See Manna (p. 110b s.v. ܓܡܰܕ).
[539] Cf. Tables 1 and 3 above.

gi-ri-ṣa-te	SAA VII 159 i 7, 8, r. i 2′	Nineveh	*Nineveh*	AD	–

Aram. ⇒ NA; LB

PTA *gərīṣətā* n. f. "bread or cake formed of slices twisted together or layers above one another" Jastrow 269a. JBA *gərīṣtā* n. f. "loaf of bread or cake" DJBA 301b. Syr., *gərīṣtā*, pl. *gərīṣātā* n. f. "a round flat loaf (of bread); a lump of dough; loaf" Manna 128a; Audo 162a; SL 260b. Syr. *gārṣā*, *gerṣā*, *gərīṣā*, pl. *gərīṣē* n. m. "a round flat loaf (of bread)" Manna 128a, Audo 162a. Sam., *griṣh* n. f. "cake" DSA 158a, CAL. JBA *grṣ'* n. m. "dough" DJBA 305a; CAL. Syr., *grṣ* v. "to grind, mill" Manna 128a.

The word **garīṣtu* and its variant **girīṣtu* are attested only in f. pl. forms as *garīṣāte* and *girīṣāte* respectively, and occur a number of times in two different NA imperial administrative documents recording temple offerings in the form of food offerings from officials. The word is also attested in a plural form in LB. The editors of CAD (G, p. 51a s.v. **gariṣtu*) gloss the word as "loaf of bread." They do not assume a borrowing for this word, but refer for comparison to Syriac ܓܪܝܨܬܐ "loaf of bread."[540] AHw. (p. 282a s.v. *ga/irīṣ(t)u*) renders the word as "Brotlaib," and considers it to be a borrowing from Aramaic *gərīṣ(t)ā*.[541]

In his articles, von Soden considers *girīṣ(t)u* "Brotlaib," a borrowing from Aramaic and states that the NA word, f. pl. *garīṣāte*, has a variant *giriṣātu* with vowel harmony.[542] The change of the vowel in the first syllable from /*a*/ to /*i*/ is due to the NA phonological variation in vowels whereby /*a*/ > /*i*/ takes place in an open syllable before stressed /*i*/.[543] Accordingly, we can posit the following development: **garīṣtu* > **girīṣtu* > f. pl. *girīṣātu*.

Abraham and Sokoloff are of the opinion that the word under discussion is identical with Aramaic גריצתא, which signifies a type of bread, and they rightly point out the occurrence of the word in parallel to *kusīpu* "flat thin bread," in a LB text (TCL 9 117:22).[544] They note that if the Semitic root *QRṢ is the origin of Syriac ܓܪܝܨܬܐ, as suggested by Brockelmann (LS, p. 135b), then the Syriac word exhibits a dissimilation of the first of the two emphatic consonants, i.e., *q* > *g*.[545] They add that this phonetic change signifies an Akkadian origin, although, in keeping with Geers' law, the change of the first emphatic consonant in Akkadian

[540] Note that the reference **gurruṣu* B, given for comparison in CAD (G, p. 51a s.v. **gariṣtu*; p. 141b s.v. **gurruṣu* B), can no longer be regarded as correct. For a revised reading, see SAA VI 62:2, where the word **gurruṣu* is read as ⌜m⌝*ga-ru-ṣu* and is interpreted as a personal name, i.e., Garruṣu. See PNA 1/II (p. 421b s.v. Garruṣu, no. 2).
[541] Cf. CDA (p. 90b s.v. *gariṣ(t)u*); DNWSI (p. 236 s.v. *grṣh*).
[542] See von Soden, *Or* 35 (1966), p. 8:24; idem, *Or* 46 (1977), p. 186:24.
[543] See Luukko, SAAS XVI, § 4.3.1.
[544] See Abraham & Sokoloff, *Reassessment*, p. 30:49. Note that the LB text (TCL 9 117:22), is quoted in CAD (G, p. 51b s.v. **gariṣtu*, a; K, p. 585a s.v. *kusīpu* A). Cf. CDA (p. 170a s.v. *kusīpu* I, m. & f. pl. "bread (crumbs)").
[545] See Abraham & Sokoloff, ibid., p. 31, n. 145.

is expected to be *q* > *k*.[546] Unlike von Soden, Abraham and Sokoloff conclude that the direction of the borrowing appears to be from Akkadian to Aramaic.[547]

In his review of CAD (vol. D), Edzard comments on the change of the consonants *g/k/q* in Akkadian in comparison with the other Semitic languages.[548] He compares the Akkadian word *garīṣtu* "Brotfladen," with Syriac *gərīṣtā*, Arabic *qurṣa* and Mishnaic Hebrew *qrṣ*.[549] Edzard points out that, in accordance with Geers' law, the root QRṢ in Akkadian must become KRṢ, and adds that the latter is in fact attested in Akkadian as *karāṣu* "to pinch off."[550] He also asked whether *garīṣtu* is a loanword in Akkadian based on the shape of the word.[551] According to Fraenkel, the Aramaic word as in Syriac and Jewish Aramaic has already transformed its original *q* into *g*, while the Mishnaic Hebrew form of the same word still retains the original *q*.[552]

The Semitic root GRṢ in Akkadian gives us the word *garāṣu* (CAD G, p. 49b), which is defined as (to pinch off clay), and the word *karāṣu* (CAD K, p. 209b), which is glossed "to pinch off (clay)." In the other Semitic languages, we have Hebrew גְּרִיצָה "bread or cake formed of slices twisted together or layers above one another, twists,"[553] and JBA גְּרִיצְתָא, pl. גְּרִיצָן n. f. "loaf of bread or cake," as well as גרצא n. m. "dough."[554] From the root GRṢ, we have in Syriac the verb ܓܪܨ "to grind, mill," and the word ܓܪ̈ܨܐ, ܓܝܪܨܐ, ܓܪܝܨܐ n. m. "round flat loaf of bread."[555] We also have the word ܓܪܝܨܬܐ n. f. "round flat loaf of bread; a lump of dough."[556]

Cognate words also seem to be found in the Semitic root QRṢ, such as in Arabic قَرَصَ "to pinch," alongside قَرَّصَ "to make dough into flat loaves" and قُرْصَة "round flat loaf of bread."[557] A corresponding word in Syriac is the verb ܩܪܨ "to pinch; to cut dough in round lump, to flatten and widen the dough," as well as ܩܪ̈ܨܐ "round flat loaf of bread."[558] Apparently, the Semitic roots QRṢ and GRṢ are related. Furthermore, the Syriac words ܓܪ̈ܨܐ and ܩܪ̈ܨܐ are probably just variants.

Semantically, the root GRṢ in Akkadian provides no satisfactory sense for the NA and LB word *garīṣāte/girīṣāte*. Phonologically, according to Audo, the emphatic voiceless velar plosive *q* and the voiced velar plosive *g* are interchangeable in both Syriac and Arabic.[559] Indeed, the word قُرْصَة "round flat

---

546 Ibid.
547 Ibid., p. 30:49.
548 See D.O. Edzard, Review of "The Assyrian Dictionary of the Oriental Institute of the University of Chicago," by A.L. Oppenheim et al., *ZA* 53 (1959), p. 295. Cf. Section 1.6.1.2 and Table 2 above.
549 Edzard, ibid.
550 Ibid.
551 Ibid.
552 See Fraenkel, pp. 35f.
553 See Jastrow (p. 268b s.v. גְּרִיצָה). Cf. Dalman (p. 82b s.v. גְּרִיצָה).
554 See DJBA, pp. 301b, 305a.
555 See Manna (p. 128a); Audo (p. 162a s.v. ܓܪܝܨܐ).
556 Ibid.
557 See Wehr-Cowan, p. 756b; Elias & Elias, p. 534a; *Al-munğidu*, p. 620a.
558 See Manna (p. 707a, b); Audo (p. 957a).
559 See the remark on the word ܓܪܝܨ in Audo (p. 957a s.v. ܩܪܨ).

loaf of bread," for instance, is pronounced with an initial *g*, i.e., *gurṣat* in Baghdadi colloquial Arabic or in the Bedouin Arabic of Iraq. Most importantly, if the NA and LB *garīṣāte* were derived from the root QRṢ, the form of the word clashes with the well-known Geers' law whereby *qrṣ* is expected to appear in Akkadian and its dialects as *krṣ* not as *grṣ*.[560] The evidence points to a borrowing from Aramaic into NA and LB.

gaṭṭaʾa n. "reed- or wood-cutter"?; (see the discussion above s.v. *gaddāiu*)

gazālu v. (G) "to steal, carry off"

Loanword	Reference	Provenance	Origin	Genre	Date
ig-da-az$^?$*-lu*	CTN II 119 r.19	Calah	–	AD	8th c.

Aram. ⇒ NA [?]

JBA, JPA, JLA, Gal., PTA, LJLA, Ma., *gzl* v. "to rob" DJBA 275b; DJPA 125b; Jastrow 230b; CAL; MD 86b. Syr., *glz* v. "to rob" SL 234b; Manna 107b; Audo 142a; PSm. 70b.

This word is a *hapax legomenon* in NA. It is not in CAD, AHw., or CDA. It is listed in AEAD (p. 30b s.v. *gazālu*), with the meaning "to steal, carry off." As with other *hapax legomena*, the possibility of establishing the meaning of *gazālu* is determined by the sentence context, here CTN II 119 r.18–19, which reads:

> PAP-*ma* 11 LÚ.*sa-ru-ti*.MEŠ / 70 UDU.MEŠ *ig-da-az*$^?$*-lu*
>
> All in all, 11 criminals — they carried off 70 sheep.

Postgate rendered the word *ig-da-az*$^?$*-lu*, from the passage above, in the sense, "to carry off."[561] In a textual note he invoked the West-Semitic root GZL to explain it, saying: "The verb here posited, **gazālu*, is not attested in Akkadian; however, the general meaning is clear, and my translation can seek support in the West Semitic root *gzl*, well attested in Biblical Hebrew and occurring in Aramaic."[562] Von Soden, quoting the same passage above, rendered the word *gazālu* as "rauben," and interpreted it to be an Aramaic loanword in NA, referring to the Jewish Aramaic and Mandaic word *gəzal*.[563] He, however, offered no argument on the loan relationship he proposed.

---

[560] Cf. Section 1.6.1.2 and Table 2 above.
[561] See CTN II 119. Note that CNA reads the word as *ig-da-⸢az⸣-lu*.
[562] See n. ad CTN II 119, 19.
[563] See von Soden, *Or* 46 (1977), p. 186:181. Note that Abraham & Sokoloff, *Reassessment*, did not include or treat this word in their article. Cf. DNWSI (p. 219 s.v. *gzl*$_1$). See further the words section of Register Assyriologie of *AfO* (1974/1977), p. 434b s.v. **gazālu*.

Nevertheless, if we take the third cuneiform sign of *ig-da-az*$^{?}$*-lu* to be *az*, then we are surely dealing with a loanword simply because the root GZL is not operative in Akkadian. Phonologically, the form of the word in the NA text displays the progressive partial assimilation of the voiceless dental plosive *t* of the infixed *-ta-* of the perfect form to the preceding voiced velar plosive *g*. Hence, the following development took place: *g* + *t* > [*gd*].[564] This partial assimilation is a regular NA feature exhibited in the perfect forms of G/D-stems of verbs that have the voiced velar plosive *g* as their first root consonant.[565] Although not dated, our text seems to stem from the 8th century B.C., based on details provided in the text.[566] This estimated date makes it more likely that the borrowing occurred from Aramaic, rather than from the other West-Semitic languages, due to the intensive language contact between Neo-Assyrian and Aramaic at that period of time. In Syriac, in comparison with the other dialects of Aramaic, the term "to rob," is expressed by the word ܓܠܙ, which displays the metathesis of consonants vis-à-vis *gzl*. This is probably done to resolve a clash of homonyms. Instead, the root GZL in Syriac is assigned to denoting, "to split, tear; deprive."[567]

gazāru v. (G) "to cut"

Loanword	Reference	Provenance	Origin	Genre	Date
[*i*]-˹*g*˺*e-zi-ir*$^{!}$	SAA XX 30 r.15′	Assur	Assur	R	–

Aram. ⇒ NA [?]

OAram., JPA, JBA, CPA, Syr., Ma., *gzr* v. "to cut" DNWSI 220; DJPA 126a; DJBA 276a; LSp. 36a; DCPA 71b; SL 226a; PSm. 67b; Manna 102a; Audo 133b; MD 87a. Sam., *gzr* n. m. "cutting" DSA 140b.

This word is a *hapax legomenon* in NA. It occurs a single time in a ritual text from Assur concerning the banquet of Gula (SAA XX 30 r.15′). Based on the NA attestation above, the word is listed in AEAD (p. 30b s.v. *gazāru*) as a verb of *i*-class with the meaning "to cut." As with other *hapax legomena*, the possibility of establishing the semantics and etymology of [*i*]-˹*g*˺*e-zi-ir*$^{!}$ is determined by the sentence context. The passage where it occurs (SAA XX 30 r.13′–15′) reads as follows:

> [*x x*] ˹*ki*˺*-is-pi ina up*$^{!}$*-ni-šú-nu* GAR-*an* L[Ú$^{!}$.SAN]GA$^{!}$ KUŠ$^{?}$.[*x*] *a-*˹*na*$^{!}$˺ *na*$^{!}$*-*˹*ṣi*$^{?}$˺*-x*[*x x x*] / [*x*] ˹*ú*˺*-qar-rab ki-is-*˹*pi*$^{!}$ *i*$^{!}$*-ma*˺*-ḫar*$^{!}$*-šú-nu* A.MEŠ *a-na* ŠU.2-*šú-nu* SUM-*an ni-ip-šu ša* U[GU$^{!}$ *x x*] / [*i*]-˹*g*˺*e-zi-ir*$^{!}$ *ina* IZI *i-ka*[*r*$^{!}$*-á*]*r*$^{!}$

---

564 Cf. Luukko, SAAS XVI, § 4.2.3.

565 See Ibid; S. Ylvisaker, *Zur babylonischen und assyrischen Grammatik* (Leipzig 1912), § 2b; K. Deller, *Lautlehre des Neuassyrischen* (Wien 1959), § 42b; Hämeen-Anttila, SAAS XIII, § 2.2.3.1.

566 See PNA 2/I (p. 485b s.v. Iada'-il, no. 3).

567 See Manna (p. 101a s.v. ܓܙܠ).

> [...] puts the [funerary off]erings in the palms of their hands. T[he priest] offers [……], receives the funerary offerings, and gives water for their hands. He *curls* a tuft of [… wool], th[ro]ws it into the fire.

Parpola, who edited SAA XX 30, tentatively translated [*i*]-⌜*g*⌝*e-zi-ir*! as "he curls," and took it to be derived from the word *gezēru* "to curl."[568] However, the root GZR is not operative in Akkadian.[569] Probably the word [*i*]-⌜*g*⌝*e-zi-ir*! is a loan from Aramaic גזר "to cut," also found in Syriac as ܓܙܪ "to cut." Cognates with the same meaning are found in Hebrew and Ugaritic.[570] In Arabic, a cognate is found in the word جَزَرَ "to slaughter, kill, butcher."[571] It is difficult, however, to explain the vowel *e* in *igezzir*, which otherwise is expected to appear in NA as *a*, i.e., *igazzir*. Probably the /*e*/ here is an allophone of /*a*/. In NA, the change /*a*/ > /*e*/ occurs in a closed syllable before /*r*/.[572]

gidlu n. "braid, plait, twining"

Loanword	Reference	Provenance	Origin	Genre	Date
gi-dil	SAA VII 62 iv 2′	Nineveh	Nineveh	AD	–
	SAA VII 63 i 1, 9	Nineveh	Nineveh	AD	–
	SAA VII 72 r.15′	Nineveh	Nineveh	AD	–
	gi!*-dil*				
	SAA VII 118 i 9, 12, 13, 16	Nineveh	Nineveh	AD	663?

Aram. ⇒ NA [?]

JBA, CPA, Syr., Ma., *gdl* v. "to twist, twine, braid, plait hair" DJBA 261b; Jastrow 213a; LSp. 34a; DCPA 68a; PSm. 61a; SL 205b; Manna 92a; Audo 119a; MD 80b. Syr., *giḏlā* n. m. "braid, plait, twining" Audo 119a; Manna 92a. Ma., *gdlh, gdlt'* (*gḏālā, gḏāltā*) n. f. "plait, braid" MD 80a; CAL.

Zimmmern considered *gidlu, giddīlu* in the sense "Geflecht, Gebinde (von Zwiebeln)" to be a late word in Akkadian and perhaps a borrowing from Aramaic.[573] AHw. (287b s.v. *gidlu*(*m*)) lists this word for OB, LB and NA in the sense "gedrehte Schnur," pointing out that in OB and LB the word refers to a "plait," of onions used as measure, but in NA designates a kind of gold

---

568 See the Glossary of SAA XX (p. 174a s.v. *gezēru*).

569 For possible attestations of the root GZR in Akkadian, see M. Dietrich & O. Loretz, "*GZR* 'Abschneiden, Abkneifen' im Ugar. und Hebr.," *UF* 9 (1977), pp. 55–56. However, cf. the word *gu-zi-ru* in SAA III 16:26, for which see the Glossary of SAA III (p. 133a s.v. *guzīru*). Cf. also the word *ga-zi-ri* (T viii 56), for which see J. Lauinger, "Esarhaddon's Succession Treaty at Tell Tayinat: Text and Commentary," *JCS* 64 (2012), p. 122, n. on l. viii 56.

570 See Dietrich & Loretz, ibid.

571 See Elias & Elias, p. 113b.

572 See Luukko, SAAS XVI, § 4.3.1; Hämeen-Anttila, SAAS XIII, § 2.4.1. Cf. GAG § 96b, for the Babylonian dialect.

573 Zimmern, AF, p. 35.

ornament.[574] In CAD (G, p. 66a s.v. *gidlu*), the word is listed for OB and NB in the sense “string (of garlic)” and for NA in the sense “torque (of gold)” but in the commentary section it states that the NA meaning is possibly connected with Aramaic *gədiltā* “braided rope.” This term is attested only once in OB.

The word is certainly cognate with Aramaic גדל and Syriac ܓܕܠ “to twist, to twine, to braid,” and ܓܕܠܐ “braid, plait, twining.”[575] It is also cognate with Hebrew גְּדִיל “twisted thread,” and גָּדַל “to plait, dress the hair,”[576] as well as with Arabic جَدَلَ “to twist, twine (rope); to plait, braid (hair)” and جَدِيلَة “braid, plait.”[577] The single OB occurrence proves the existence of the word in the sense “string (of garlic)” at an early stage of the Akkadian language.[578] However, the West-Semitic distribution points to an early West-Semitic loan in Babylonian, which resurfaced in LB also with the meaning “string (of garlic).” In NA, on the other hand, the word is probably a later borrowing, specifically from Aramaic, meaning “braid, plait.”

gubbu, (pl. *gubbāni*) n. “cistern, well; pit”; (compare the discussion above s.v. *gab'u*).

Loanword	Reference	Provenance	Origin	Genre	Date
gu-bi	TH 57:6	Gūzāna	Gūzāna	AD	9th c.
gu-ub-ba-a-ni	Streck Asb.72 viii 102 (= Asb. A viii 102)	Niveveh	Nineveh	Inscr.	Asb.
gu-ub-bu	SAA V 15:12	Nineveh	Amidi	L	Sg
	SAA XI 202 i 7′ *gu-ub-*[*bu*]	Nineveh	Harran	AD	Sg
	SAA XII 3:4′, 5′	Assur	Assur	AD	9th c.
[*gu*]*-ub-bi*	SAA XI 210 r. iv 7′	Nineveh	Harran	AD	Sg
[*gub*]*-bi*	SAA XI 209 r. i 3′	Nineveh	Harran	AD	Sg

Aram. ⇒ NA; NB ⇒ LB

Nab., Palm., JPA, Sam., CPA, Ma., Syr., *gwb*, *gwb'* (*gob̲*, *gubbā*) n. m. “well, cistern; pit, den” DNWSI 207;[579] CAL; DJPA 122a; DSA 134a; DCPA 69a; MD 82a; Manna 87a; Audo 125a; PSm. 62b; SL 210b. Syr., *gūbā* n. m. “press (for oil)” Manna 87a; Audo 125a.

An early discussion of the origin of this word was presented by Zimmern who considered *gubbu* “cistern” to be perhaps borrowed from Akkadian into Aramaic as *gubbā*, and from Aramaic further borrowed into other languages such as Arabic

[574] See also CDA (p. 92b s.v. *gidlu*(*m*)).
[575] See Manna (p. 92a s.v. ܓܕܠ).
[576] See Jastrow (p. 212a s.v. גְּדִיל, p. 213a s.v. גָּדַל II).
[577] See Elias & Elias, p. 107b.
[578] See the OB evidence given in CAD and AHw.
[579] See DNWSI (p. 207 s.v. gb_2).

جُبّ, Ethiopic *gebb*, as well as Armenian *gub*.[580] Zimmern, however, erroneously considered the origin of *gubbu* "cistern" to be the root GB'.[581] In contrast, the editors of CAD (G, p. 117b s.v. *gubbu* A) glossed the word as "well," but considered it probably to be a West-Semitic loan in NA. In AHw. (pp. 295a, 1557a s.v. *gubbu*) the term is glossed "Zisterne," and is considered to be perhaps an Aramaic loanword in NA and NB. However, in his articles on Aramaic loanwords, von Soden more decisively argues that this word is a borrowing from Aramaic *gubbā*.[582] Abraham and Sokoloff are of the opinion that *gubbu* may in fact be a borrowing from Aramaic into NA and NB.[583]

Fales, in his treatment of the NA expression *gu-bi ša* GEŠTIN.MEŠ (TH 57:6), which he renders "wine-cisterns," remarks that the expression has no parallel in NA texts, and concurs with von Soden on the direction of the borrowing of *gubbu*.[584] Perhaps, in this regard, one should take into consideration the meaning "cavity in winepress," as found in the JPA word גּוּבָּה "pit; cistern; cavity in winepress."[585] As for the reading of ⌜É?⌝ *gu-ub-bu* (SAA V 15:12), Lanfranchi and Parpola take it to be two separate words, namely *bīt* "property," and *gubbu* "well," but von Soden, based on an attestation in a LB text (YOS 7, 191:25), considers it to be a single expression *bīt gubbu*, meaning "Pflugland."[586]

According to Manna, Syriac has the verb ܓܒ "to dig, cut; to make convex,"[587] and the noun ܓܘܒܐ "cistern, well; pit."[588] In Arabic, from the root ǦBB we have the verb جَبَّ "to excise; cut off *or* out," and the noun جُبّ "pit; (deep) well."[589] According to Al-munǧidu, the word جُبّ, which means "a deep well," is so called because it is dug by cutting; i.e., it is derived from the root ǦBB "to cut."[590] However, it seems that JPA גּוּבָּה "pit, cistern," Syriac ܓܘܒܐ "cistern, well; pit," Arabic جُبّ "(deep) well; pit," Hebrew גּוֹב "pit"[591] and NA *gubbu* "cistern, well, pit,"[592] are all cognates.

The suggested Aramaic source word is derived from a *mediae geminatae* root GBB or the hollow root GWB.[593] The nominal form of the NA *gubbu* is that of

580 See Zimmern, AF, p. 44.
581 Ibid. Note that Kaufman, AIA, does not treat the word *gubbu*.
582 See von Soden, *Or* 35 (1966), p. 8:28; idem, *Or* 46 (1977), p. 186:28. Cf. CDA (p. 95a s.v. *gubbu*).
583 See Abraham & Sokoloff, *Reassessment*, p. 31:54.
584 See F.M. Fales, "Studies on Neo-Assyrian Texts I: Joins and Collations to the Tell Halaf Documents," *ZA* 69 (1979), p. 208, n. on l. 6. Cf. J. Friedrich et al. (eds.), *Die Inschriften vom Tell Halaf: Keilschrifttexte und aramäische Urkunden aus einer assyrischen Provinzhauptstadt* (Osnabrük 1967), p. 38, no. 57, n. on l. 6.
585 See DJPA (p. 122a s.v. גּוּב).
586 See von Soden, Review of "The Correspondence of Sargon II, Part II: Letters from the Northern and Northeastern Provinces," by G.B. Lanfranchi & S. Parpola, *WO* 25 (1994), p. 134. See also von Soden, *Or* 46 (1977), p. 186:28. Cf. DSA (p. 88b), for the Samaritan Aramaic expression בית גוב "prison."
587 See Manna (p. 86b s.v. ܓܒ).
588 Ibid., p. 87a.
589 See Elias & Elias (p. 104a s.v. جَبَّ and جُبّ).
590 See *Al-munǧidu* (p. 77b s.v. جبّ).
591 See Jastrow, p. 216b.
592 See AEAD (p. 31 s.v. *gubbu*).
593 Jastrow (p. 216b s.v. גּוֹב), etymologizes the word as of the root GBB. CAL subsumes the Aramaic *goḇ*, *gubbā* "well, cistern; cave, den," under the root GWB.

PuSSu, which points to a derivation from a root with a doubling of the second radical.[594] In Akkadian no satisfactory etymology is found for this word and its shape and meaning point to a borrowing. While a logogram PÚ is usually used in Akkadian for the words *būru* and *būrtu*, in the sense of "cistern, well; pit,"[595] the word *gubbu*, on the other hand, is never written logographically, but only syllabically, which is a characteristic unusual for a noun inherent in the Akkadian lexicon. Altogether, the evidence is in favor of a borrowing from Aramaic.

gulēnu n. "cloak, tunic"[596]

Loanword	Reference	Provenance	Origin	Genre	Date
gul-IGI.2!	SAA VII 113:4	Nineveh	Nineveh	AD	–
	SAA VII 105:2′ *gul*-IGI.[2]	Nineveh	Nineveh	TL	–
	Iraq 23, pp. 18f. (= ND 2097:8) [*gu*]*l*-IGI.2	Calah	Calah	TL	–
	SAA VII 107 r.8′ [*gu*]*l*-IGI.2	Nineveh	Nineveh	TL	–
TÚG.*gu*-IGI-*ni*	FNALD 14 r.1[597]	Calah	Calah	LD	PC
TÚG.*gul*-IGI	Iraq 23, p. 44 (= ND 2691:9)	Calah	Calah	AD	–
	SAA VII 98:8′	Nineveh	Nineveh	TL	–
	SAA XI 28:11 TÚG.*gul*!-IGI	Nineveh	Nineveh	AD	–
TÚG.*gul*-IGI.2	SAA VII 96:5′	Nineveh	Nineveh	TL	–
	SAA VII 117 r.4	Nineveh	Nineveh	AD	–
	SAA VII 94:2 ⸢TÚG⸣.*gul*-IGI.2	Nineveh	Nineveh	TL	681
	SAA VII 98:12′ [TÚG].*gul*-IGI.2	Nineveh	Nineveh	TL	–
	SAA VII 113:1 TÚG.*gul*!-IG[I.2]	Nineveh	Nineveh	TL	–
TÚG.*gul*-IGI.2.MEŠ	SAA I 193: r.6, TÚG.*gul*-IGI.2. M[EŠ] 193 r.2, TÚG.*gul*-IGI.2.[MEŠ] 193:4′	Nineveh	*Nineveh*	L	8th c.
TÚG.*gu-l*[*i*]-⸢*na-a-te*⸣	CTN II 154 r.2′	Calah	Calah	AD	–
	Billa 89:2′ TÚG.[*gu-li*]-*na-a-te*, 7′ [TÚG.*g*]*u-li-na-a-te*[598]	Šibanība	Šibanība	AD	–

[594] Cf. GAG § 541.

[595] See Borger, ABZ, no. 511; W. Schramm, *Akkadische Logogramme* (Göttingen 2003), p. 128.

[596] The plural form of this word is both m. & f. Cf. AEAD (p. 31b s.v. *gulēnu*).

[597] The reading TÚG.*gu*-IGI.2 in FNALD is faulty, see n. ad FNALD 14:25. The reading TÚG.*gu*-IGI-*ni* is taken from the Corpus of Neo-Assyrian Texts (CNA).

TÚG.*gu-li-na-te*	CTN II 1:11′	Calah	Calah	AD	–
	TH 63 e.7 TÚG.*gu-li-na*(*-te*)	Gūzāna	Gūzāna	AD	–
TÚG.*gu-li-ni*	SAA XI 36 ii 13	Nineveh	Nineveh	AD	–
	TH 48:10 TÚG.*gu-l*[*i-ni*]	Gūzāna	Gūzāna	AD	–
TÚG.*gu-li-nu*	PVA 246	Assur	Assur	LL	–
	TH 52 r.5 TÚG.*gu-li-nu*	Gūzāna	Gūzāna	AD	–
	TH 54 r.2 [TÚG.*g*]*u-li-nu*	Gūzāna	Gūzāna	AD	–

CW? ⇒ Aram. ⇒ NA; LB [?]

JPA, JBA, Syr., JLA, Gal., LJLA *glym*, *glym'* n. m. "cloak, mantle" DJPA 130b; DJBA 287b; Jastrow 249a; SL 237b; PSm. 71a; Manna 109a; Audo 144a; CAL.[599]

The word under discussion is often prefixed by the determinative TÚG which signifies garments.[600] In NA the term is frequently written with the cuneiform sign *gul* plus the pseudo-logogram IGI, alone or followed by a dual sign, i.e., IGI.2. Whether followed by the dual sign or not, the pseudo-logogram IGI has sound values such as *ēnu* and *īnu*.[601] AHw. (p. 296b s.v. *gulē/īnu*) defines this word as (ein Obergewand), and compares it with Aramaic *gəlī/aimā* and Hebrew *gəlōm*. The editors of CAD (G, p. 127a s.v. *gulēnu*) define this entry as (a coat), and consider it to be possibly related to Aramaic *gəlīma*, *gəlaimā* and Hebrew *gəlōm*.

A corresponding word is attested in Jewish Babylonian Aramaic as גְּלִימָא with the sense "garment, cloak," and in Syriac as ܓܠܝܡܐ, ܓܠܝܡܐ with the sense "cloak, mantle, a garment made of wool or goats' hair." In Hebrew, we have the term גְּלוֹם n. m. "mantle, cloak," which is considered possibly to be a foreign word.[602] A parallel is also found in Persian as *gilīm* (گليم), meaning "a garment made of goats' hair or wool; a carpet or rug to lie down upon; a blanket."[603] The Arabic words جَلَمَ "to shear, cut (wool)" and جَلَم "shears" are probably cognates.[604]

It seems that Tallqvist was the first to connect this word with Hebrew *gəlōm* and Aramaic *gəlī/aimā*.[605] In a philological note on *gulēnu*, Langdon considers the word to be a loan in Assyrian because it is only attested in the late period, and argues that a different reading, such as *gul*-LIM, might indicate an original

598 The transliteration of Billa 89 is taken from the Corpus of Neo-Assyrian Texts (CNA).
599 According to CAL (s.v. *glym*), the feminine form of the entry cited in DJPA as גלימה is incorrect, and the Syriac form ܓܠܝܡܐ is known only from the lexical tradition and ought to be vocalized with long /i/ as in the other Aramaic traditions.
600 See Borger, ABZ, no. 536.
601 Ibid., no. 449.
602 See W. Gesenius, *Wilhelm Gesenius' Hebräisches und Aramäisches Handwörterbuch über das Alte Testament* (Leipzig 1915), p. 141a.
603 See F. Steingass, *A Comprehensive Persian–English Dictionary: Including the Arabic Words and Phrases to be Met with in Persian Literature* (London 1963), p. 1096b.
604 See *Al-munğidu* (p. 98c s.v. جلم); Elias & Elias (p. 120a s.v. جَلَمَ).
605 See K.L. Tallqvist, *Die Sprache der Contracte Nabû-nâ'ids (555–538 v. Chr.) mit Berücksichtigung der Contracte Nebukadrezars und Cyrus'* (Helsinki 1890), p. 60.

gulēmu.[606] Furthermore, he states that the *ō* of the Hebrew גְּלוֹם is attributable to the labial *m*, and also adds that the development *gulīmu* > *gulīnu* would be a case of progressive assimilation, i.e., *l–m* > *l–n*, while a dissimilation might also have taken place, i.e., *gulīnu* > *gulīmu*.[607] Weidner defines *gulēnu* as follows: "Es dürfte sich um das bis zu den Knien reichende, *kurzärmelige Gewand* handeln, das an den Hüften von einem doppelten Gürtel zusammengehalten wird und über dem der Bogenschütze mitunter das Brustkoller trägt."[608] In his article on Assyrian uniforms, Postgate suggests translating *gulēnu* as "shirt."[609] Gaspa, on the other hand, suggests that the NA and NB form of the word is probably derived from another West-Semitic textile designation found in Syriac as *gallōn*, *gallōnā* "garment," which is derived from the Syriac word *gallā* "covering; cloak; horse-blanket, saddle."[610] However, Gaspa's suggestion is unlikely because the NA and NB word seems to be derived from the root GLN, but the suggested Syriac etymon *gallōn*, *gallōnā*, is derived from the root GLL and the *n* at the end of the word is only part of the diminutive ending *-ōnā*.

Nevertheless, in many instances, as cited above, our word is written syllabically as TÚG.*gu-li-nu*, which in turn dismisses the reading *gul*-LIM suggested by Langdon. That the NA and LB words end with the voiced dental nasal *n*, as opposed to the labial nasal *m*, in Aramaic and Hebrew is problematic. However, the change *m* > *n* is attested even in final position in Akkadian, Aramaic and Hebrew.[611] The first vowel *u* of the NA and LB words is also difficult to explain in comparison with that of Aramaic and Hebrew. Probably the NA <*u*> here is rendered phonetically /ə/ ~ /œ/, not /*u*/.

The word under discussion lacks an obvious Semitic etymology. It is probably an old culture term of indeterminate origin with the meaning "cloak," which is shared by the later dialects of Akkadian, Aramaic, Hebrew and Persian. The evidence points to a separate development of the possibly inherited culture word.

gumāru n. "live coal, coal"

Loanword	Reference	Provenance	Origin	Genre	Date
gu-ma-ru	SAA XX 33 ii 9	Nineveh	Nineveh	R	–

[606] See S. Langdon, "Philological Notes," *RA* 28 (1931), p. 13. Cf. Borger, ABZ, no. 449.
[607] See Langdon, ibid.
[608] See n. ad TH 48:10.
[609] See J.N. Postgate, "Assyrian Uniforms," in W.H. van Soldt (ed.), *Veenhof Anniversary Volume: Studies Presented to Klaas R. Veenhof on the Occasion of his Sixty-Fifth Birthday* (Leiden 2001), p. 385.
[610] See S. Gaspa, "Garments, Parts of Garments, and Textile Techniques in the Assyrian Terminology: The Neo-Assyrian Textile Lexicon in the 1st-Millennium BC Linguistic Context," in S. Gaspa et al. (eds.), *Textile Terminologies from the Orient to the Mediterranean and Europe, 1000 BC to 1000 AD* (Lincoln, 2017), p. 70 s.v. *gulēnu*. See also SL (pp. 231f s.v. ܓܠܐ, p. 233b s.v. ܓܠܘܢܐ). A cognate to the Syriac word is found in Arabic as جَلَّ "to cover, spread over," see Elias & Elias (p. 119b s.v. جَلَّ).
[611] See Lipiński, *Semitic Languages*, § 11.7.

Aram. ⇒ NA

QA, JA, CPA, JBA, Syr., Ma., LJLA, *gwmrh*, *gmwrtʾ* (*gumrā*, *gmurtā*) n. f. "coal" CAL; LSp. 38b; DCPA 70a; Jastrow 223a; PSm. 72a; SL 240b; Manna 113a; Audo 148a; MD 83b. JBA *gwmrtʾ* n. f. "live coal" DJBA 269b. JPA *gwmrh* n. f. "coal, carbuncle" DJPA 123b. Syr., *gūmrā* n. m. "live coal" Manna 112b. Ma., *gumra* n. m. "coal, glowing coal" MD 83b. Syr., *gmr* v. Pa. "to set fire to, to set on fire, inflame" Manna 112b. Syr., *gmr* v. Pa. "to heat over red-hot coals" PSm. 73a; SL 243a; CAL. Syr., *gmr* v. Af. "to make a live coal" SL 243a. CPA *gmr* v. Af. "to burn incense" LSp. 38b; DCPA 70b; CAL.

This word appears a single time in a NA text consisting of a protocol for the royal dinner. As a *hapax legomenon*, its meaning is determined by the sentence context. The passage where *gu-ma-ru* is attested (SAA XX 33 ii 6–10 = MVAeG 41/3 pl. 2:8–10) reads as follows:

> LÚ*.*šá*–É–2-*i* 1-*en* T[A *pu-ú-te*] / *a-na ma-ṣar-t*[*e š*]*á* ITI.AB *iz-za-az né-su-*˹*pu*˺ [AN.BAR] / *mu-te-er-ru ma-šá-a-nu* AN.BAR *ina* ŠU.2-*šú šum-ma pe-ʾe-et-*˹*tu*˺ / *lu-u gu-ma-ru* TA* UGU *ka-nu-nu it-tu-qu-ut* / *er-ra-ba i-mat-taḫ ina* UGU *ka-nu-ni i-kar-ra-ar*
>
> One *sp*[*ecial*] lackey keeps watch over the brazier with an [iron] shovel and an iron rake and tongs in his hands. If an ember or a coal falls from the brazier, he enters, picks it up and puts it back on the brazier.

In light of two corresponding Semitic terms, namely Aramaic גּוּמַרְתָּא "live coal, coal" and Arabic جَمْرَة "live coal," the editors of CAD (G, p. 133a s.v. *gumāru*), tentatively render the NA word as a substantive in the sense "ember," and consider *gumāru* and *piʾittu* to be designating a fuel, probably different kinds of charcoal. They add that "the word may well have been borrowed by Aram. and Arabic, and has most likely no connection with the root GMR." AHw. (p. 298a s.v. *gumāru*) renders the word as "verkohltes Holz." CDA (p. 96a s.v. *gumāru*) glosses it as "carbonized wood, charcoal."

In his articles on Aramaic loanwords, von Soden considers this NA word to be a borrowing from Aramaic.[612] Müller compares *gumāru* with Aramaic גּוּמְרָא, גּוּמַרְתָּא and Syriac ܓܘܡܪܐ, ܓܘܡܪܬܐ "coal," as well as with Arabic جَمْرَة "live coal," but states that *gumāru* in the NA passage cannot be interpreted as "live coal," i.e., with a meaning similar to that of the corresponding Semitic terms.[613] He argues that since the stove is heated with wood, *gumāru* cannot mean "charcoal which has not burnt yet"; rather, it means "burnt or charred wood."[614] He adds that this interpretation is corroborated by the root GMR, which occurs in the same text as *gam-mu-rat* and *ug-da-ta-me-ru*, where it appears to mean "to

[612] See von Soden, *Or* 35 (1966), p. 9:31; idem, *Or* 46 (1977), p. 186:31. See also DNWSI (p. 227 s.v. *gmr*₃). Cf. Abraham & Sokoloff, *Reassessment*, p. 32:58.
[613] See K.F. Müller, *Das Assyrische Ritual, Teil I: Texte zum assyrischen Königsritual* (Leipzig 1937), p. 76, n. on l. 9.
[614] Ibid.

burn up, burn down."[615] The following are the contexts where the two occurrences are attested:

> SAA XX 33 ii 4–6, reads:
>
> [*šum-m*]*a* ŠEM.MEŠ *ug-da-ta-me-ru* L[Ú.*šá*–É–2-*i ú-ṣa*] / [*a*]-*na né-si-pi* AN.BAR *ú-še-ra-ba* [*ina* ŠÀ-*bi* ŠEM.MEŠ] / [*š*]*ar-pu-ú-te ú-še-ṣa*
>
> [I]f the aromatics run out, t[he lackey goes out], brings in an iron shovel and removes the burnt [aromatics with it].
>
> SAA XX 33 r. i 37′–40′, reads:
>
> *ina* IGI [d]UTU-*ši ra-bé-e si-me-en* GIŠ.*ziq-tú* GIŠ.*zi-qa-a-te* / *ú-šá-an-mu-ru ina* É.GAL *ú-še-ru-bu* LÚ*.*šá*–É–2-*i* / *a-na ma-ṣar-te iz-za-az* GIM GIŠ.*zi-iq-tu gam-mu-rat giš-gi-ri* / *ú-ša-an-mar ú-še-rab il-da-a-te i-maḫ-ḫar ú-še-ṣa*
>
> Before sunset, at torch time, torches are lit and brought into the palace. A lackey keeps watch. As soon as a torch is burnt out, he lights a torchwood, brings it in, collects the stumps and takes them out.

In Akkadian, the conjunction *lū* is used in the expression (X *lū* Y) to mean "either X or Y."[616] Hence, *gumāru* in the NA passage (*pe'et'tu' lū gumāru*), in association with a brazier (*kanūnu*), undoubtedly refers to some kind of fuel, and designates a substance comparable to *pe'ettu* "amber." The M/NA word *pe'ettu* "amber," which from OB on is known as *pēmtu*(*m*), is derived from the PS root *PḤM. A cognate is found in Arabic as فَحْم "charcoal, coal,"[617] and in Syriac as ܦܚܡܐ "coal."[618]

On the other hand, the word גוּמַרְתָּא n. f. "coal" is attested in different dialects of Aramaic.[619] It is also attested in the masculine form as in Mandaic and, rarely, in Syriac as ܓܘܡܪܐ.[620] Audo defines the Syriac ܓܘܡܪܬܐ as (a coal of timber that is in a fire and the burning elements of which are not yet consumed).[621]

Morphologically, the nominal form of the NA word is that of *PuRāS*. This nominal pattern in Akkadian is only found in some few isolated nouns that may belong to the diminutive category and in a small semantic group of nouns for "prayer."[622] However, no diminutive sense seems to be associated with the NA *gumāru* in the context where it occurs. The form of the NA word with the vowel *u* in the first syllable is similar to that of the Aramaic, with the first vowel as *u*.[623] In

---

615 Ibid.
616 See A. Ungnad, *Akkadian Grammar* (Atlanta 1992), § 97.
617 See Wehr-Cowan (p. 699a s.v. فحم); *Al-munğidu* (p. 494b s.v. فَحْم).
618 The Syriac word is probably a borrowing from Arabic, see SL (p. 1179b s.v. ܦܚܡܐ). Cf. DJPA (p. 428a s.v. פחם).
619 See CAL, s.v. *gmr*.
620 See MD (p. 83b s.v. *gumra*); Manna (p. 112b s.v. ܓܘܡܪܐ).
621 See Audo (p. 148a s.v. ܓܘܡܪܬܐ).
622 See J. Fox, *Semitic Noun Patterns* (Winona Lake 2003), pp. 229f. See also GAG § 55k.
623 But cf. M. Kalinin & S. Loesov, "Lexical *Sondergut* of Neo-Assyrian," *SAAB* 23 (2017), p. 9, 1.4.1. Contra Kalinin & Loesov, ibid, if the word had a short vowel in the second syllable i.e.,

contrast, the first vowel in the Arabic word is *a*. The wider distribution of the word in Aramaic, in contrast to its single occurrence in NA, points to a borrowing from Aramaic. The motivation for borrowing the word *gumāru* was probably due to the need for a synonym with a semantic nuance to increase the expressive capacity of NA.[624] Accordingly, it fits well to render the phrase (*šumma pe'ettu lū gumāru*) as "If an ember or a coal."

As for the Akkadian verb *gamāru(m)*, it means, among other things, "to complete, finish; to destroy; to annihilate."[625] It has a cognate in Aramaic as גמר, in the sense "to complete, to fulfill; to consume; to destroy,"[626] and in Hebrew as גָּמַר, in the sense "to finish; to complete; to destroy."[627] Most important, however, is that Aramaic has another verb as גמר, which is a denominative from גּוּמַרְתָּא "live coal, coal."[628] It has meanings in the Pa''el mode as "to heat with burning coals; to set on fire, to inflame,"[629] in the Af'el mode as "to make live coal; to burn incense," and in the Etpe'el mode as "to be perfumed with incense; to be turned into coal(?)."[630] This Aramaic verb has a cognate in Hebrew as גָּמַר, which also is a denominative verb with the meaning "to perfume (clothes) with burned spices."[631] In the Aramaic and Hebrew lexica, this denominative verb is entered under a separate lemma of גמר.[632] Another cognate is found in Arabic, as a verb in Form II, namely جَمَّرَ "to roast (meat)" and in Form VIII, namely إِجْتَمَرَ "to burn incense."[633] In Akkadian, on the other hand, only the NA instance attested here as *gam-mu-rat* (SAA XX 33 r. i 39′), appears to be a stative in the feminine of the verb *gamāru* in the D-stem with the meaning "to burn."[634] This semantic usage of the NA *gamāru*, is certainly a borrowing from the equivalent Aramaic denominative verb גמר, and ought to be listed under a new lemma in the Akkadian lexicon. Otherwise, the Akkadian language usually uses terms such as *ḫamāṭu*, *kabābu*, *qamû* and *šarāpu*, for expressing "to burn." It is known that Akkadian, unlike the other Semitic languages, hardly forms denominative verbs.[635]

**gumaru*, the vowel *a* would not have been assimilated, rather it would have been elided and the word would have appeared as *gumru*.

[624] AEAD, p. 32a, glosses *gumāru* as "(live) coal, ember." See also the Glossary of SAA XX (p. 174b s.v. *gumāru* "coal, ember").

[625] See CAD (G, p. 25a s.v. *gamāru*); AHw. (p. 276b s.v. *gamāru*(*m*) II).

[626] See CAL, s.v. *gmr*.

[627] See Jastrow (p. 255a s.v. גָּמַר II).

[628] See PSm., (p. 73a s.v. ܓܡܰܪ).

[629] See PSm., ibid; SL (p. 243a s.v. ܓܡܪ); Manna (p. 112b s.v. ܓܰܡܰܪ); CAL, s.v. *gmr* mng. no. 3.

[630] See SL, ibid; CAL, ibid.

[631] See Jastrow (p. 254b s.v. גָּמַר I).

[632] See CAL, s.v. *gmr* no. 3. See also Jastrow (p. 254b s.v. גָּמַר I). Cf. Dalman (p. 77b s.v. גָּמַר). Note that Syriac does not distinguish between the two verbs of ܓܡܰܪ, and subsumes them under one heading.

[633] See Wehr-Cowan (p. 134a s.v. جمر II); *Al-munǧidu* (p. 100c s.v. جَمَّرَ).

[634] Cf. CAD (G, p. 25a s.v. *gamāru*); AHw. (p. 276b s.v. *gamāru*(*m*) II).

[635] See G. Buccellati, *A Structural Grammar of Babylonian* (Wiesbaden 1996), pp. 72f.

ḫalābu, *ḫalāpu* v. (G) "to milk"; (see also below s.v. *ḫilpu*)

Loanword	Reference	Provenance	Origin	Genre	Date
i-ḫal-li-bu-ni	SAA III 34:33	Assur	Assur	LT	–
ta-ḫal-lip	SAA III 13 r.8	Nineveh	Nineveh	LT	Asb

Aram. ⇒ NA

JBA, JPA, Syr., *ḥlb* v. "to milk" DJBA 461a; DJPA 201b; Jastrow 464a; Dalman 138b; SL 451b; PSm. 142b; Manna 239a; Audo 339b; DNWSI 372. OffAr., JBA, JPA, Sam., CPA, Ma., Syr., *ḥlb*, *ḥlb'* (*ḥalḇ*, *ḥalḇā*) n. m. "milk" DNWSI 372; DJBA 461a; DJPA 201b; Jastrow 464a; Dalman 138b; DSA 270a; LSp. 64a; DCPA 130a; MD 121a; SL 452a; PSm. 142b; Manna 239a; Audo 339b.

The verb *ḫalāb/pu* "to milk" is a *dis legomenon* in NA. In addition, a related word, namely *ḫilpu* "milk," is attested in NA as *hapax legomenon.*[636] In AHw. (p. 309b s.v. *ḫalābu*), this word is glossed "melken," and in the etymology section it is considered to be a denominative verb from *ḥala/īb* "Milch." The editors of CAD (Ḫ, p. 36b s.v. *ḫalāpu* B), gloss this word as "to milk." In CDA (p. 101a), on the other hand, the word *ḫalābu* "to milk" is considered to be a Semitic loan in NA. Also in CDA (p. 116a), the word *ḫilpu* "milk" is considered to be a West-Semitic loan in NA.

Zimmern notes that Meiβner and, probably independently, Langdon, have correctly identified the NA word *ḫalābu* with the meaning "to milk," as in Arabic حَلَبَ "to milk," despite the initial *ḫ*.[637] In his review of CAD Ḫ, Edzard adduces the West-Semitic word *ḥlb* for comparison and states that the words *ḫalāp/bu*, *ḫilap/bānu*[638] and *ḫilpu*, which bear the basic meaning of "milk; to milk," are first attested in Akkadian in the 1st millennium B.C., and are probably not originally Akkadian.[639]

Von Soden does not indicate in AHw. that the NA terms *ḫalāb/pu* and *ḫilpu* are loanwords. However, in his articles on Aramaic loanwords, he rightly points out that the Akkadian word for "milk" is *šizbu*, from which, as far as we know, no denominative verb is attested.[640] He states that the NA words *ḫilpu* "milk" and *ḫalāb/pu* "to milk," as well as the SB word *ḫilabānu* (a plant with milky sap), are probably borrowed from Aramaic *ḥalbā* "milk" and *ḥlb* "to milk."[641]

---

636 See AHw., p. 345b; CAD Ḫ, p. 187a. See also below, p. 136 s.v. *ḫilpu*. For "milk" and its products in Akkadian, see RlA 8, pp. 189ff.

637 See H. Zimmern, "Babylonische Mysterien und kein Ende," *ZA* 36 (1925), p. 85, n. 1. See also W. von Soden, "Gibt es ein Zeugnis, daβ die Babylonier an Marduks Wiederauferstehung glaubten?" *ZA* 51 (1955), p. 146, comment on l. 33.

638 Cf. CAD (Ḫ, p. 184a s.v. *ḫilabānu*, p. 185a s.v. *ḫilapānu*).

639 See D.O. Edzard, Review of "The Assyrian Dictionary of the Oriental Institute of the University of Chicago, Vol. VI 'Ḫ'," by I.J. Gelb et al., *ZA* 53 (1959), p. 298.

640 See von Soden, *Or* 35 (1966), p. 11:53.

641 See von Soden, *Or* 46 (1977), p. 188:53. Cf. AHw. (p. 345a s.v. *ḫilabānu*); Cf. DNWSI (p. 372 s.v. *ḥlb*₁). For the suggestion that even the NB word *ḫu*?*-li-bi*, which is attested in a medical recipe, is perhaps a further loan from Aramaic חֲלָב "a viscous substance, glair," see I.L. Finkel, "On Late

Abraham and Sokoloff state that *ḥlb* "milk" is a common West-Semitic word known in both Hebrew and Aramaic, and is most probably a loanword in Akkadian, but they remark that in all of the Aramaic dialects the nominal form of the word is *ḥalb* and not **ḥilb*.[642] Based on the form of the NA word as *ḫilpu*, Kalinin and Loesov state that *ḫilpu* was not borrowed directly from Aramaic in the sense "milk," rather it was derived in NA from the verb *ḫalāpu* "to milk," and must mean "milking" or "that which was obtained by milking, milk yield."[643]

Nevertheless, the plausibility of etymologies suggested for the NA *ḫalāb/pu* and *ḫilpu* are established on the basis of the sentence context.

SAA IX 7 r.7–11, reads:

ma-a ki-i ta-ri-ti ina UGU *gi-iš-ši-ia* ÍL$^{!}$*-ši-ka / ma-a* GIŠ.ḪAŠḪUR$^{!}$.KUR.RA *ina bi-rit* UBUR.MEŠ*-ia a-šak-kan-ka / šá mu-ši-ia e-rak an-ṣar-ka šá kal*–UD*-me ḫi-il-pa-ka ad-dan / šá kal-la-ma-ri un-na-ni-ka ú-ṣur ú-ṣur up-pa-áš-ka /* ⸢*ma-a*⸣ *at-ta la ta-pal-làḫ mu-u-ri šá ana-ku ú-rab-bu-u-ni*

I will carry you on my hip like a nurse; I will put you between my breasts (like) a pomegranate. At night I will stay awake and guard you; in the daytime I will give you milk; at dawn I will play '*watch, watch your …*' with you. As for you, have no fear, my calf, whom I (have) rear(ed).

SAA III 34:33, reads:

ši-iz-bu ša ina IGI ^{d}15 *ša* NINA.KI *i-ḫal-li-bu-ni né-mi-il ši-i tu-ra-bu-šú-ni re-e-mu ú-ka-li-im-šú-*[*ni*]

The milk which they milk in front of Ištar of Nineveh is (milked) because she brought him up *and* showed compassion to him.

SAA III 13 r.6–8, reads:

ṣe-eḫ-ru at-ta ^{m}AN.ŠÁR–DÙ–A *ša ú-maš-šir-u-ka ina* UGU ^{d}*šar-rat*–NINA.KI / *la-ku-u at-ta* ^{m}AN.ŠÁR–DÙ–A *ša áš-ba-ka ina bur-ki* ^{d}*šar-rat*–NINA.KI / *er-bi zi-ze-e-šá ina pi-ka šak-na* 2 *te-en-ni-iq* 2 *ta-ḫal-líp ana pa-ni-ka*

You were a child, Assurbanipal, when I left you with the Queen of Nineveh; you were a baby, Assurbanipal, when you sat in the lap of the Queen of Nineveh! Her four teats are placed in your mouth; two you suck, and two you milk to your face.

The use of *ḥlb* to designate "milk" is found in most of the West-Semitic languages and it is common in Aramaic. The postulated PS ancestor of the word is **ḥalab* "milk."[644] It is attested in Syriac as ܚܠܒܐ, in Hebrew as חָלָב and in

Babylonian Medical Training," in A.R. George & I.L. Finkel (eds.), *Wisdom, Gods and Literature: Studies in Assyriology in Honour of W.G. Lambert* (Winona Lake 2000), p. 172, n. on l. 17:9.

642 See Abraham & Sokoloff, *Reassessment*, p. 33:69. See also L. Kogan, *Genealogical Classification of Semitic: the Lexical Isoglosses* (Berlin 2015), p. 83 no. 20.

643 See M. Kalinin & S. Loesov, "Lexical *Sondergut* of Neo-Assyrian," *SAAB* 23 (2017), p. 8, 1.1.1.

644 See Kogan, ibid.

Arabic as حَلَب and حَلِيب.[645] It is also attested in Ugaritic as *ḥlb* and in modern South Arabic as *ḥelob*, as well as occurring in Mehri as *ḥəlēb* "milking," and in Geʿez as *ḥalab* "sour milk," and *ḥalīb* "milk."[646] As for *ḥalīb*, which is found in Arabic and Geʿez, it is probably a secondary form constructed on the schema of passive noun.[647] A denominative verb *ḥlb* "to milk; give milk" is known in Aramaic, Hebrew and Arabic. Obviously, the reconstructed PS root of this word is expected to be *ḤLB.

In Akkadian, the unusual substantive *ḫilpu* "milk," and the rare verb *ḫalāb/pu* "to milk," are only attested in NA. In fact, a nominal pattern corresponding to *QiTLu* < *QiTaL*, as in *ḫilpu*, is very rare in Akkadian and is not productive.[648] Otherwise, the usual Akkadian word for "milk" continued to be *šizbu*, which in NA has the form *zizibu*.[649] On the other hand, to express "milking," the verb GÍD, i.e., *šadādum* "to draw" is utilized.[650] In NB, the verb *ṣabātu* "to draw (milk)" is also used to express "milking."[651]

Semantically, the Akkadian verb *ḫalāpu* with the meanings "to slip in or through; to cover, clothe; to be intertwined (said of trees); to coat (with bronze)" does not fit the contexts of the NA texts above.[652] Furthermore, this Akkadian verb is of the semantic class *u/u*, from which it is expected to yield an inflection in the present tense 2p. m. sg. *taḫallup*, not *taḫallip*. The latter represents the semantic class *i/i* of the G-stem, as in SAA III 13 r.8 above.[653]

Phonologically, the most salient Akkadian feature which corroborates the loan hypothesis in this case is the initial voiceless velar fricative *ḫ*, which stands for the voiceless pharyngeal fricative *ḥ* of the West-Semitic words. Had the NA words *ḫilpu* and *ḫalābu* been directly derived from a PS root *ḤLB, the initial *ḥ* would have been reduced to a glottal stop and eventually dropped. On the other hand, the West-Semitic pharyngeal /*ḥ*/ is usually rendered <*ḫ*> in NA.[654] The first vowel *i* in *ḫilpu* "milk," instead of the expected *a*, is probably an allophone of the latter. The change /*a*/ > /*i*/ in NA occurs in a closed syllable before /*l*/.[655] Another possibility is that the first vowel *i* in *ḫilpu* occurs by analogy with the vowel *i* in the corresponding usual Akkadian word for milk *šizbu*, which in NA takes the form *zizibu*.

The occurrence of the voiceless bilabial plosive *p* instead of the voiced bilabial plosive *b* in the NA variant form *ḫalāpu*, as in *ta-ḫal-líp*, can be explained as a

---

645 See SL (p. 452a s.v. ܚܠܒܐ); Jastrow (p. 464a s.v. חָלָב); Elias & Elias (p. 162a s.v. حَلِيب).
646 See G.J. Botterweck & H. Ringgren (eds.), *Theological Dictionary of the Old Testament, Vol. 4, z–ebh–hms* (Grand Rapids 1980), p. 386.
647 Ibid.
648 For the nominal pattern *QiTaL* > *QiTLu* in Akkadian, see J. Fox, *Semitic Noun Patterns* (Winona Lake 2003), p. 213.
649 See AEAD, p. 134b.
650 See RlA 8, p. 191b § 4.3.
651 See YOS VII 79:9; CAD (Š/III, p. 150a s.v. *šizbu*).
652 See AHw. (p. 310a s.v. *ḫalāpu*(*m*) I); CAD (Ḫ, p. 35a s.v. *ḫalāpu* A).
653 See H. Zimmern, "Babylonische Mysterien und kein Ende," *ZA* 36 (1925), p. 85, n. 1.
654 For the representation of Aramaic *ḥ* by NA *ḫ*, see n. 313 above.
655 See Luukko, SAAS XVI, § 4.3.1. For a comparison of the "isolated nouns" of the pattern *QiTL* in Akkadian and West-Semitic, see J. Fox, *Semitic Noun Patterns* (Winona Lake 2003), p. 141, n. 4.

variation between the two consonants in NA.[656] The fact that the West-Semitic *ḥalab* "to milk" is a denominative verb provides additional corroboration of the borrowing of the word into NA. The Akkadian language, unlike the other Semitic languages, hardly forms denominative verbs.[657] Obviously, the verb *ḫalāb/pu* "to milk" fills a semantic gap in NA. It is more likely that *ḫilpu* and *ḫalāb/pu* were borrowed from Aramaic into NA because language contact between NA and Aramaic during the first millennium B.C., was more intensive than with the other Semitic languages.

ḫalīdu n. "cavity, burrow(?)"

Loanword	Reference	Provenance	Origin	Genre	Date
ḫa-li-di$^{!}$	SAA XIV 477:4	Nineveh	Nineveh	LD	664

Aram. ⇒ NA [?]

Syr., *ḥld* v. "to dig; to burrow; to drive a mine underground" PSm. 142b; Manna 240a; Audo 340b. CPA, Syr., *ḥld* v. to penetrate" LSp. 64a; DCPA 130a; SL 453a.

This word is not listed in AHw., CAD or CDA. On the other hand, it is listed as a substantive in AEAD (p. 33b s.v. *ḫalīdu*), in the sense "cavity, burrow(?)." The word occurs as a *hapax legomenon* in NA and is attested in a broken context in a legal document from 664 B.C. concerning a land purchase. As with other *hapax legomena*, the meaning of *ḫalīdu* is determined by the context where the word occurs (SAA XIV 477:1–6), which reads as follows:

> [*x x x x x x* (*x*)]$^{!}$ EN A.ŠÀ SUM-*ni* / (cylinder seal impression) / [*x x x x x x*]*x* ⌜*x x*⌝-*ba-al ina* URU.*mi*[*r*$^{!}$-*x x x*] / [*x x x x*]–MAN$^{!}$–PAB SUḪUR URU.*la-ḫi-x*[*x x*] / [*x x x x*]*x* SUḪUR *ḫa-li-di*$^{!}$ [*x x*] / [*x x x* (*x*) ^{m}]^{d}*aš-šur*–EN–LAL [0] / [*x x x* SUḪ]UR$^{!}$ ^{m}*di-d*[*i*]-⌜*i*$^{!}$⌝ [*x x x*]
>
> [Seal of NN], owner of the field being sold. (cylinder seal impression) […]… in the town of Mi[r…], [*adjoining* DN]-šarru-uṣur, adjoining Laḫi[…, …], adjoining a *cave* […, *adjoining*] Aššūr-bēlu-taqqin, […, adjoin]ing Didî, […].

Mattila, who edited SAA XIV 477, tentatively translates *ḫa-li-di*$^{!}$ as a "cave," but regrettably no discussion about this interpretation was put forward.[658] The word is probably taken to be a borrowing from Aramaic *ḥld* "to dig; to burrow

---

[656] See S. Ylvisaker, *Zur babylonischen und assyrischen Grammatik* (Leipzig 1912), § 4; von Soden, "Zur Laut- und Formenlehre des Neuassyrischen," *AfO* 18 (1957), pp.121f. For the difficulty encountered in explaining this kind of variation, see Luukko, SAAS XVI, § 4.1.1, esp. p. 73. Note that the last sign *líp* has an additional sound value as *líb* (Borger, ABZ, p. 131 no. 322), which allows for a transliteration of the word as *ta-ḫal-líb*, but this sign usage is not attested in NA.

[657] See G. Buccellati, *A Structural Grammar of Babylonian* (Wiesbaden 1996), pp. 72f.

[658] Note that the word *ḫalīdu* is not listed in the Glossary of SAA XIV.

(ground)." However, in addition to Aramaic, the word is attested in Hebrew as חָלַד "to undermine, cave, dig."[659] In Syriac a passive participle ܚܠܝܕܐ "being dug?" is attested,[660] as well as a substantive ܚܘܠܕܐ "mole."[661] In Arabic a cognate of the latter is the substantive خُلْد "mole-rat, mole."[662] According to the evidence at hand, we can reconstruct the expected PS root of the word in question as *ḪLD.

Nevertheless, on the basis of the Aramaic meaning and the context of the NA word, a derivation from Aramaic as a loanword in NA is possible; especially because the root ḪLD is not productive in Akkadian. However, it must be pointed out that no substantive of the root ḤLD is attested in Aramaic with the meaning "cavity, burrow."

ḫalputu, (gen., *ḫalpete*) n. f. "successor"

Loanword	Reference	Provenance	Origin	Genre	Date
ḫal-pe-te	SAA IX 7:4	Nineveh	Nineveh	P	Esh

Aram. ⇒ NA

OAram., *ḥlp* n. "successor" Brauner 200. OffAr., *ḥlyph, ḥlypt'* (*ḥlīpā, ḥlīptā*) n. f. "substitute; replacement; equivalent" DNWSI 374; CAL. Sam., *ḥlyph* n. f. "successor" DSA 274b; CAL. Syr., *ḥəlapṯā* n. f. "successor, substitute; caliph" Manna 243a; Audo 345a. Syr., *ḥelpā* n. m. "successor, substitute; caliph" Manna 243a. Syr., *ḥlīptā* (< Ar.) n. m. "substitute, caliph" SL 456b. Syr., *ḥlp* v. "to change; to exchange, substitute" SL 458b; Manna 242a; Audo 344a; PSm. 144a.

The NA word *ḫalputu* is a *hapax legomenon* attested in a prophetic text (SAA IX 7:4) addressed by the prophetess Mullissu-kabtat to the Assyrian crown prince Assurbanipal. In CAD (Ḫ, p. 48b s.v. **ḫalpatu*) the meaning of this NA word is given as unknown. AHw. (p. 313a s.v. *ḫalpatu*) expresses uncertainty about the meaning of this word.[663] Also, CDA (p. 102b s.v. **ḫalpatu*) considers the meaning of this NA word to be unknown. However, interpreting the word as meaning "successor" is suggested by the NA context (SAA IX 7:2–6), which reads as follows:

> [*ma*]-*a a-bat* LUGAL ᵈNIN.LÍL *ši-i ma-a la ta-pal-làḫ* ᵐ*aš*ˈ-*šur*ˈ–DÙ–A / [*ma*]-*a a-di ki-i šá aq-bu-u-ni ep-pa-šu-u-ni ad-da-nak-kan-ni* / [*ma*]-⌜*a*⌝ *a-di ina* UGU

[659] See Jastrow (p. 464b s.v. חָלַד); Dalman (p. 139a s.v. חָלַד).
[660] See Audo, p. 340b.
[661] See Manna, p. 240b. Cf. PSm., p. 142b. Cf. also Jastrow (p. 464b s.v. חַלְדִּין n. m. pl. "cave-dwellers").
[662] See Elias & Elias, p. 195b; Wehr-Cowan, p. 254a.
[663] Cf. AHw. (p. 313a s.v. *ḫalpu* III), where the LB word *ḫalpu* "Ersatzmann" is considered to be a borrowing from Aramaic *ḥalpā*. See also von Soden, *Or* 35 (1966), p. 9:43; idem, *Or* 46 (1977), p. 187:43; CDA (p. 102b s.v *ḫalpu* II). Cf. Abraham & Sokoloff, *Reassessment*, p. 34:75.

DUMU.MEŠ *šá šá*–SU_6.MEŠ *ina* UGU *ḫal-pe-te šá* LÚ.SAG.MEŠ / [*at-t*]*a* LUGAL-*u-tú ina* UGU-*ḫi-šú-nu tu-up-pa-šú-u-ni* / [*a-ḫa-ṣ*]*i*[!]-*in*[!]-*ka ina* É–UŠ-*u-ti*

This is the word of Queen Mullissu: Fear not, Assurbanipal! Until I have done and given to you what I promised, until you rule as king over the sons of the bearded courtiers and the successors of the eunuchs, [I will look af]ter you in the Palace of Succession.

Parpola comments on the passage quoted above noting that it refers to "the new government of the future king, the sons of the uncastrated officials taking the place of their fathers, and new eunuchs replacing their predecessors, who could not have sons."[664] He considers *hal-pe-te* definitely to be an Aramaic loanword in NA and adducing Syriac *ḥalpətā* [*sic*] "something given in exchange, a substitute,"[665] derived from *ḥlp* "to exchange, substitute," and also citing Arabic *ḫalīfa* "deputy; successor; caliph."[666]

The Official Aramaic חליפה "substitute; equivalent," the Samaritan Aramaic חליפה "successor," Syriac ܚܠܦܬܐ "successor, caliph, substitute," Hebrew חֲלִיפָא n. f. "replacement, substitution,"[667] and Arabic خَلِيْف, خَلِيفَة "successor; caliph"[668] are all cognates. On the other hand, the Syriac word ܚܠܝܦܬܐ n. m. "substitute, caliph" is considered to be a borrowing from Arabic خَلِيفَة.[669] The latter is a masculine noun despite ending with the feminine marker, the *tā' marbūṭa* (التاء المربوطة).[670] It is attested that Semitic languages have some instances where masculine names carry feminine gender morphemes.[671]

The cognates adduced above are imperative for our investigation because they help in determining the radicals of the PS root from which they were presumably derived. From these cognates, we infer that the first radical must have been the voiceless velar fricative /*ḫ*/. Accordingly, the reconstructed PS root would be *ḪLP. This fact is important to realize because, as we know, the /*ḫ*/ was maintained in Akkadian but was merged with /*ḥ*/ in Aramaic, and if we only had the NA and Aramaic evidence, it would have been difficult to determine whether the initial /*ḫ*/ of the NA word is original or not.[672]

Etymologically, Akkadian has the verbs *ḫalāpu* "to slip in or through; to cover, clothe; to be intertwined (said of trees); to coat (with bronze)," in addition to another *ḫalāpu* in the sense "to milk,"[673] but none of these meanings fits the NA context for the word *ḫal-pe-te*. In comparison, Syriac has the verb *ḥlp* "to change; to substitute," Pa. "to change, replace."

---

664 See n. ad SAA IX 7:4.
665 The form of the Syriac word cited by Parpola as *ḥalpətā* is actually ܚܠܦܬܐ. See PSm., p. 145a.
666 See n. ad SAA IX 7:4. See also LAS II, pp. 20f., and p. 117, n. ad LAS II 129:8.
667 See Jastrow, p. 469a; Dalman, p. 140b.
668 See Elias & Elias, p. 198a; Wehr-Cowan, p. 257b.
669 See SL, p. 456b.
670 See W. Wright, *A Grammar of the Arabic Language* (Cambridge 1967), § 290d.
671 See S. Moscati (ed.), *An Introduction to the Comparative Grammar of the Semitic Languages* (Wiesbaden 1964), § 12:34.
672 Cf. Kaufman, AIA, p. 19.
673 See CAD (Ḫ, p. 35a s.v. *ḫalāpu* A, p. 36b s.v. *ḫalāpu* B).

Nevertheless, assuming a loan from Aramaic חליפה "successor" is untenable because we cannot account for the loss of the semivowel *y* in the NA word *ḫalputu*. The only plausible source of borrowing would be from a nominal form such as that attested in Syriac, namely ܚܠܦܬܐ "successor, caliph, substitute." The *ṯ* of the Syriac word stands for an original *t*. Even so, the derivation is still problematic because from *ḥəlapṯā* we must first reconstruct a NA m. sg. as **ḫalpu*, and then from the latter we can derive the NA f. sg. *ḫalputu*. Accordingly, we can posit the following development: **ḫalapu* > **ḫalpu* > **ḫalpatu* > *ḫalputu*.

This means that from the nominal pattern *PaRaS* a noun **ḫalapu* in the singular masculine is obtained. This undergoes contraction due to the elision of the short unstressed vowel between single consonants, yielding the form **ḫalpu*. To the latter the feminine marker *-at* is added to form a feminine noun **ḫalpatu*,[674] which in turn undergoes the so-called Assyrian vowel harmony and becomes *ḫalputu*, but when standing in the genitive appears as *ḫalpete*.[675] Despite the difficulties mentioned above, this NA *hapax legomenon* is undoubtedly a loanword from Aramaic. The pharyngeal /*ḥ*/ of the loanword is represented by <*ḫ*> in NA.[676]

ḫālu n. "vinegar"

Loanword	Reference	Provenance	Origin	Genre	Date
ḫa-li	SAA VII 119 i 12′ ⸢*ḫa-li*⸣, ii 8′	Nineveh	Nineveh	AD	–
ḫa-lu	PVA 188	Assur	Assur	LL	–

Aram. ⇒ NA; LB; SB[677]

JBA, JPA, Sam., CPA, Syr., *ḥl*, *ḥl'* (*ḥal*, *ḥallā*) n. m. "vinegar" DJBA 460b; DJPA 201a; Jastrow 463b; DSA 271a; DCPA 129b; LSp. 64a; SL 451b; PSm. 142a; DNWSI 372; CAL. Ma., *hala* n. m. "vinegar" MD 121a.

The meaning of this word was originally suggested by Meissner who tentatively rendered it as "Essig," and connected it with Arabic خل "vinegar."[678] In NA, the word occurs as *tris legomenon*, and is found twice in an administrative document and once in a lexical list. In AHw. (p. 312b s.v. *ḫallu* IV) this word is glossed

674 GAG § 60b.
675 See Hämeen-Anttila, SAAS XIII, § 2.4.5.
676 For the representation of Aramaic *ḥ* by NA *ḫ*, see n. 313 above.
677 The word is probably attested as *ḫa-a-li* in a SB text (Asb IIT:161). See A. Fuchs, "Kapitel VII: Die Inschrift vom Ištar-Tempel," in R. Borger, *Beiträge zum Inschriftenwerk Assurbanipals. Die Prismenklassen A, B, C = K, D, E, F, G, H, J und T sowie andere Inschriften* (Wiesbaden 1996), pp. 259–296.
678 See B. Meissner, *Supplement zu den assyrischen Wörterbüchern* (Leiden 1898), p. 38a s.v. *ḫalla*.

"Essig," and is considered to be a borrowing from Aramaic.[679] The editors of CAD (Ḫ, p. 43a s.v. *ḫallā*) render the word as "vinegar," and consider it to be a loanword from Aramaic.[680] Abraham and Sokoloff deem that *ḫallu* "vinegar" certainly seems to be a borrowing from Aramaic into NA and LB for the reason that the word חל is attested in most of the Aramaic dialects and the regular corresponding word in Akkadian is *ṭābātu*.[681]

Indeed, the normal Akkadian word for "vinegar," attested from OB on, is *ṭābātu*(*m*), which is a *plurale tantum* and is written not only syllabically, but also logographically as A.GEŠTIN.NA.[682] Although not attested in NA, the existence of *ṭābātu*(*m*) "vinegar" in the other dialects of Akkadian should by no means prevent NA from borrowing a new word from another language with a meaning similar to that of a native one.[683]

A clear indication, however, that *ḫālu* in NA is a substance connected with wine is that it is listed in a lexical list where it stands for the logogram GEŠTIN.MEŠ KA.[684] In NA, GEŠTIN or GEŠTIN.MEŠ reads *karānu*, "wine." On the other hand, the NA expression ⌜GEŠTIN? *ḫa-li*⌝, which can be transcribed as *karān ḫāli*, probably means "wine vinegar,"[685] similar to the Syriac expression ܚܠܐ ܕܚܡܪܐ "vinegar made from wine."[686]

The JBA חַלָּא "vinegar," and the Syriac ܚܠܐ, with the same meaning, are cognate with the Arabic word خَلّ "vinegar."[687] Accordingly, we can deduce that the Aramaic and Arabic words were derived from a common PS root *ḪLL, because, as we know, the /ḫ/ was maintained in Arabic but merged with /ḥ/ in Aramaic. Nevertheless, the derivatives of this root in Akkadian provide no satisfactory sense that would fit the context for *ḫālu* as attested in the NA texts cited above. Therefore a borrowing from Aramaic is almost certain. In Syriac, the origin of ܚܠܐ "vinegar" is taken to be from the verb *ḥll* "to tear asunder, cut apart."[688]

Phonologically, the initial voiceless velar fricative *ḫ* in *ḫālu* occurs in accordance with the representation of the West-Semitic voiceless pharyngeal fricative *ḥ* in NA.[689] The form of the NA word, *ḫālu*,[690] as opposed to *ḫallu* of LB, indicates that a closed syllable was replaced by a long open syllable, i.e., *ḫallu* > *ḫālu*. Although not very common in NA, it seems that the two different types of

---

679 See also von Soden *Or* 35 (1966), p. 9:42; idem, *Or* 46 (1977), p. 187:42; CDA (p. 102b s.v. *ḫallu* IV). Cf. DNWSI (p. 372 s.v. *ḥl*$_6$).

680 Cf. CAD (K, p. 205b s.v. *karānu*, 1, d, 3′), where the occurrence of, GEŠTIN.MEŠ KA = *ḫa-lu*, attested in PVA, p. 330:188, is considered a special designation for wine. Cf. also CAD (Ḫ, p. 53b s.v. *ḫalu*), where the meaning of *ḫalu* in the formula above is considered uncertain.

681 See Abraham & Sokoloff, *Reassessment*, p. 34:74.

682 See AHw. (p. 1376a s.v. *ṭābātu*(*u*)); CAD (Ṭ, p. 4a s.v. *ṭābātu*). See also Borger, ABZ, no. 579, p. 198.

683 Cf. Kaufman, AIA, p. 16.

684 See PVA, p. 330:188.

685 See SAA VII 119 i 12′; AEAD (p. 34a s.v. *ḫālu*). See also Abraham & Sokoloff, *Reassessment*, p. 34, n. 220.

686 See PSm., (p. 142a s.v. ܚܠ).

687 See Elias & Elias, p. 199a; Wehr-Cowan, p. 252a.

688 See SL (p. 451b s.v. ܚܠܐ, p. 457a s.v. ܚܠܠ no. 3).

689 For the representation of Aramaic *ḥ* by NA *ḫ*, see n. 313 above.

690 See AEAD, p. 34a.

syllable are in free variation with one another.[691] Hence, the long vowel *ā* appears instead of the expected gemination of *l* in the NA form of the word.

ḫangaru n. "dagger"; (see the discussion in chapter 2.2 s.v. *akku*)

Loanword	Reference	Provenance	Origin	Genre	Date
ḫa-an-ga-ru	SAA IX 1 iv 7	Nineveh	–	P	Esh

CW? ⇒ Aram. ⇒ NA [?]

Syr., *ḥngr*, *ḥngr'* (*ḥangrā*) n. m. "dagger" SL 470a; CAL.[692] Sūret *ḫanğār* (< poss. Ar.) n. f. "dagger" Maclean 102b.

The Akkadian words which denote "dagger" are *marqantu*, attested in a SB synonym list,[693] and *uṣultu*, attested in SB and NA.[694] However, there is another word meaning "dagger," namely *ḫangaru* which occurs as a *hapax legomenon* in NA in an oracle of Ištar of Arbail to Esarhaddon (SAA IX 1 iv 7). AEAD also lists an adjective, namely *ḫangarānu* "dagger-like," which is attested as a personal name.[695] As a *hapax legomenon*, the meaning of *ḫangaru* is suggested by the context. The passage where the word occurs (SAA IX 1 iv 5–10), reads as follows:

> ᵐ*aš-šur*–PAB–AŠ *ap-lu* / *ke-e-nu* DUMU ᵈNIN.LÍL / *ḫa-an-ga-ru ak-ku* / *ina* ŠU.2-*ia* / LÚ.KÚR.MEŠ-*ka* / *ú-qa-at-ta*
>
> Esarhaddon, rightful heir, son of Mullissu! With an angry dagger in my hand I will finish off your enemies.

The editors of CAD (Ḫ, p. 79b s.v. *ḫangaruakku*) include *ḫangaru* together with the word *akku*, which immediately follows it, as one word, i.e., *ḫangaruakku*, and define its meaning as unknown, but also suggest the possibility of reading the word as *ḫanga ru'akku* or *ḫangaru akku*. AHw. (pp. 321a, 1559a s.v. *ḫangaru*) considers the meaning of this term to be unclear, but lists it as an Aramaic foreign word and refers to von Soden's discussion on its origin and meaning. CDA (p. 105b s.v. *ḫangāru*) glosses the word tentatively as "dagger," and considers it to be a borrowing from Aramaic into NA.

In his article on Aramaic loanwords, von Soden renders *ḫangāru* as "Dolch," and regards it a borrowing from an Aramaic word, as found in Syriac *ḥangərā*

691 See Luukko, SAAS XVI, § 4.14.1. Cf. K. Deller, *Lautlehre des Neuassyrischen* (Wien 1959), § 38.
692 See also, R. Payne Smith, et al. (eds.), *Thesaurus Syriacus* (Hildesheim 1981), p. 1314.
693 See CAD (M/I, p. 284b s.v. *marqantu*). Cf. AHw. (p. 612a s.v. *marqantu*).
694 See AEAD (p. 131a s.v. *uṣultu*). Cf. CAD (U/W, p. 290b s.v. *uṣultu*).
695 See AEAD (p. 34b s.v. *ḫangarānu*). Cf. PNA 2/I (p. 453a s.v. Ḫangarānu).

"Dolch."[696] Parpola concurs with von Soden's interpretation, citing as a corresponding expression, Ištar's "pointed sword" (*namṣaru zaqtu*), which is attested in an inscription of Assurbanipal (Streck Asb., p. 116:55).[697]

Nevertheless, in addition to Sūret, the word *ḫanǧar* in the sense "dagger" is attested in many other modern languages such as Arabic, Turkish and Persian.[698] The word in Sūret is certainly a borrowing, as revealed by the third radical *ǧ*, and as a loanword its gender is considered to be feminine although it does not end with the feminine marker *t*. Almost all loanwords in Sūret are syntactically considered to be feminine. According to Sokoloff's *Syriac Lexicon* (SL), both Syriac ܚܢܓܪܐ and Arabic خَنْجَر, in the sense "dagger," are loanwords from the New Persian term خنجر "dagger."[699] Note, however, that the instance given in SL as *ḥangrta* for Christian Palestinian Aramaic with the meaning "dagger" is incorrect and instead means "throat."[700] Zadok is of the opinion that the Arabic word is a loan from Syriac. In his words: "Syr. *ḥangrā* > Arab. *ḫanjar* 'dagger' should be added to Fränkel, Fremdw., 239f. where other terms for daggers and swords of non-Arabic origin are discussed."[701] In contrast, Asbaghi considers خنجر in the sense "Kandschar, groβes Dolchmesser, Dolch" to be a Persian loanword in Arabic.[702]

On the other hand, the word is attested in Parthian as *ḫenǧer* "dagger."[703] It is also attested in New Persian as خنجر.[704] The latter has been etymologized as being derived from the Persian words (خون کار), literally (blood *and* act).[705] But based on phonological difficulties, this explanation seems to be unlikely.

Etymologically, neither Aramaic nor Arabic provides a native etymon for the word under discussion here. However, the semantic and phonetic agreement of the NA *ḫangaru* with the Syriac *ḥangrā* is perfect. The fact that the Assyrian vowel harmony is not operative in the NA *ḫangaru* is itself a strong indication that the term is a loanword in NA. Hence, the word is phonologically not integrated into NA. Nevertheless, the lack of a convincing Semitic etymology, or for that matter even a Persian one, obliges us to look somewhere else for the origin of *ḫangaru*. Perhaps the term was a culture word, which, most likely, entered NA via Aramaic.

---

696 See von Soden, *Or* 46 (1977), p. 187:188. Cf. DNWSI (p. 387 s.v. *ḥngr*). Cf. also Abraham & Sokoloff, *Reassessment*, p. 34:78.
697 See n. ad SAA IX 1 iv 7.
698 See Maclean, p. 102b.
699 See SL (p. 470a s.v. ܚܢܓܪܐ).
700 Ibid. See DCPA (p. 118b s.v. **ḥgra*).
701 See R. Zadok, Review of "The Chicago Colloquium on Aramaic Studies, Journal of Near Eastern Studies Vol. 37, No. 2, April 1978," *WO* 12 (1981), p. 199 s.v. *Ḫ–G–R*. Cf. Fraenkel, pp. 239f.
702 See A. Asbaghi, *Persische Lehnwörter im Arabischen* (Wiesbaden 1988), p. 113.
703 See D.-M. Desmond, *Dictionary of Manichaean Middle Persian and Parthian* (Turnhout 2004), p. 363b s.v. *xnjyr, hynjyr*.
704 See F. Steingass, *A Comprehensive Persian–English Dictionary: Including the Arabic Words and Phrases to be Met with in Persian Literature* (London 1963), p. 476a.
705 See J.B. Al-Qinai, *Morphophonemics of Loan-words in Translation*. Online 15/09/2022: http://img2.timg.co.il/forums/75882210.pdf

ḫannīu dem. pron. "this"

Loanword	Reference	Provenance	Origin	Genre	Date
ḫa-an-ni-e	SAA I 15:7′ (RL)	Nineveh	Nineveh	L	Sg
	SAA II 6:531, 548, 580, 623, 629, 638	Calah	Calah	T	672
	SAA VIII 55 r.7	Nineveh	Nineveh	AR	666?
	SAA XIII 29:4	Nineveh	Assur	L	Asb
ḫa-an-ni-i	SAA I 7:10′ (RL)	Nineveh	Nineveh	L	Sg
	SAA I 10:10 (RL)	Nineveh	Nineveh	L	Sg
	SAA II 6:604	Calah	Calah	T	672
	SAA V 204:10	Nineveh	Māzamua	L	Sg
	SAA X 202 r.10′	Nineveh	Nineveh	L	670?
	SAA X 241 r.12	Nineveh	Nineveh	L	670?
	SAA XVI 99:6′	Nineveh	*Nineveh*	L	9th c. ?
ḫa-an-ni-i-e	SAA X 45 r.9	Nineveh	Nineveh	L	670?
	SAA X 56:15	Nineveh	Nineveh	L	669?
ḫa-an-ni-ma	SAA V 25:10	Nineveh	*Tīdu*	L	Sg
	SAA X 227 e.29, r.17	Nineveh	Nineveh	L	666?
ḫa-an-nim-ma	SAA X 221 r.1	Nineveh	Nineveh	L	669?
ḫa-an-ni-tú	SAA I 1 r.52 (RL)	Calah	Calah	L	Sg
	SAA XV 306:6′	Nineveh	*Nineveh*	L	Sg
ḫa-an-ni-u	SAA I 21 r.1 (RL)	Nineveh	Nineveh	L	Sg
	SAA X 8 r.14	Nineveh	Nineveh	L	672?
	SAA XIII 155 r.2	Nineveh	*Assur*	L	Asb
ḫa-an-ni-ú	SAA I 18 r.9′ (RL)	Nineveh	Nineveh	L	Sg
	SAA XV 129 e.40	Nineveh	*Babylonia*	L	Sg
ḫa-an-nu-ti	CT 53 816:8′	*Nineveh*	–	L	–
	SAA I 1:29 (RL)	Calah	Calah	L	Sg
	SAA I 5:4 (RL)	Nineveh	Nineveh	L	Sg
	SAA I 10:5 (RL)	Nineveh	Nineveh	L	Sg
	SAA XVI 4:3	Nineveh	*Nineveh*	L	Esh?
ḫa-an-nu-tú	SAA I 72:6′	Nineveh	*Calah*	L	Sg
ḫa-an-nu-um-ma	SAA II 6:60	Calah	Calah	T	672
ḫa-ni-e	SAA V 121 r.10	Nineveh	Kurba'il	L	Sg
	SAA V 199:13	Nineveh	Māzamua	L	Sg
ḫa-ni-i	SAA XIX 35:9	Calah	Northwest	L	Tgl?
ḫa-ni-ma	SAA XIII 138 r.10	Nineveh	Arbela	L	Asb
	SAA XIX 156:22	Calah	*Calah*	L	Tgl?
ḫa-nim-ma	SAA XVI 37 r.8′	Nineveh	*Nineveh*	L	Esh?
	SAA XVI 126:13	Nineveh	Phoenicia	L	Esh
ḫa-ni-ti	SAA I 183:18′	Nineveh	Carchemish	L	Sg
ḫa-ni-tu	StAT 2 315 r.3	Assur	Assur	L	Asb?
ḫa-ni-u	SAA V 53:15	Nineveh	*Province of the Treasurer*	L	Sg
	SAA V 154 r.6′	Nineveh	Northeastern frontier	L	Sg
	SAA X 319:10	Nineveh	Nineveh	L	Esh
ḫa-nu-te	SAA I 99:6	Nineveh	Assur	L	Sg

	SAA I 176 r.16	Calah	Ḫamāt	L	Sg
	SAA V 121 r.19	Nineveh	Kurba'il	L	Sg
ḫa-nu-u-te	SAA V 121:8	Nineveh	Kurba'il	L	Sg

Aram. ⇒ NA

OffAr., JAB, CPA, Syr., *hn'* (*hānā*) dem. pron. m. "this" DNWSI 287; DJBA 385a;[706] LSp. 52a;[707] SL 346b; PSm. 104b; Manna 170a; Audo 236a; CAL.[708]

For the near deixis, NA often employs *annīu* pron. m. sg. "this." However, another form of the same word, namely *ḫannīu*, is also used in the same sense.[709] The latter may be written as *ḫannī'u*, as implied in writings such as *ḫa-an-ni-i-e*. These two variant forms of this demonstrative pronoun, (*ḫ*)*annīu*, can even occur simultaneously in a single text, for instance, the two occurrences in a NA letter (SAA X 8:23, r.14) written to the king by Issār-šumu-ēreš, the chief scribe/astrologer at the court of Nineveh (reigns of Esarhaddon and Assurbanipal), concerning astronomical matters:

an-ni-u	SAA X 8:23
ḫa-an-ni-u	SAA X 8 r.14

The two major dictionaries, AHw. (p. 53b s.v. *annû*(*m*) I),[710] and CAD (A/II, p. 136a s.v. *annû*), do not indicate a possible Aramaic influence on the form *ḫannīu* in NA. However, in his articles on Aramaic loanwords, von Soden attributes the reinforcement of an initial *h* in the NA *ḫannīu* to the influence of Aramaic *hānā* "this."[711] Lipiński similarly regards it as probable that on the synchronic level Aramaic influence can be detected in the NA form *ḫa-an-ni-e*, for the dem. pron. *anniu* "this."[712] Hämeen-Anttila and also Luukko consider the other form of the NA *anniu*, i.e., the one with the initial *ḫ*, possibly to be due to Aramaic influence.[713]

On the other hand, Kutscher criticizes von Soden's suggestion that the form of the NA word *ḫanniu* "this," with the initial *ḫ*, is due to the influence of Aramaic *hānā* "this," arguing that the latter is only attested in Syriac.[714] He adds: "Therefore it is at least problematic whether the Neo-Assyrian (before 600 B.C.) *ḫanniu* owes its existence to the S[yriac] *hānā* (several hundred years later)."[715]

---

706 The JBA instance הנא is a borrowing from Syriac.
707 According to LSp., the attestation in CPA is only a Syriacism by scribal correction. See CAL, s.v. *hn'*.
708 Cf. OAram., *hny* pron. 3p. f. pl. "these, those, they" Brauner 145.
709 The feminine form is (*ḫ*)*annītu*. See Luukko, SAAS XVI, p. 134; Hämeen-Anttila, SAAA XIII, p. 14 and § 3.1.4.1.
710 Cf. also CDA (p. 18b s.v. *annû*(*m*) I).
711 See von Soden, *Or* 35 (1966), p. 6:6; idem, *Or* 46 (1977), p. 184:6. Cf. GAG § 23a*, § 24a, § 25a, § 45b. Cf. E. Salonen, "Über den Laut H im Akkadischen," *StOr* 46 (1975), p. 298.
712 See Lipiński, *Semitic Languages*, § 19.9 and § 36.33.
713 See Hämeen-Anttila, SAAA XIII, p. 15. See also Luukko, SAAS XVI, p. 89, n. 283.
714 See E.Y. Kutscher, "Aramaic," in T.A. Sebeok (ed.), *Current Trends in Linguistics*, 6. *Linguistics in South West Asia and North Africa* (The Hague 1970), p. 357.
715 Ibid. Cf. Section 1.6.8 above.

Abraham and Sokoloff also regard von Soden's suggestion to be implausible because the Aramaic form he adduces is only found in the first millennium A.D., in Syriac ܗܢܐ "this."[716]

Usually in Akkadian, as well as in NA, word-initial laryngeal *h* is reduced to a glottal stop ʾ (hamza), which is ultimately dropped.[717] However, in his discussion of the gutturals, Ylvisaker calls attention to the representation of the voiceless laryngeal fricative *h* in NA, adducing some examples, among other things, the words with initial *ḫ*, such as *ḫannīu* "this," and *ḫannāka* "here."[718] He notes that this is certainly not a pure *ḫ*, but probably only an attempt by the NA scribe to reproduce a spoken ה.[719] Concerning the pronunciation of the word-initial *ḫ* in *ḫannīu*, Hämeen-Anttila also points out that, "*h* (velar [*ḫ*]), has probably been changed in NA to pharyngeal *ḥ* or even to laryngeal *h*."[720] Moscati remarks that it is likely that the *h* reappears in NA, since *anniu* "this," is frequently spelt *ḫannīu*.[721]

An objection can be raised against the view that the form *ḫannīu* in NA is probably due to Aramaic influence, because the other cognate words in NA, such as *annāka* "here," and *annēša* "hither," also have variants with initial *ḫ*, namely *ḫannāka* and *ḫannēša*, but lack parallels in Aramaic from which an influence could have played a role in the NA forms with initial *ḫ*. However, since *annīu* is cognate with the words *annāka* and *annēša*, by the rule of analogy, their variant forms *ḫannāka* and *ḫannēša* might be explained as being influenced by the variant of *annīu*, i.e., *ḫannīu*.

As Semitic words, the Aramaic dem. pron. הנא and the Syriac ܗܢܐ in the sense "this," as well as NA *annīu* "this," are certainly cognates and point to the fact that the Aramaic/Syriac form with the initial voiceless laryngeal fricative *h* represents a *Lectio difficilior*. Hence, based on chronological grounds, the form of the NA dem. pron. *ḫannīu* with the initial *ḫ* is most likely due to Aramaic influence.[722]

ḫarbutu, *ḫarbūtu* n. f. "ruin"

Loanword	Reference	Provenance	Origin	Genre	Date
ḫar-bat.MEŠ	KAV 197:16 (= TCAE, p. 363)	Assur	Assur	L	–

[716] See Abraham & Sokoloff, *Reassessment*, p. 34:79. Cf., however, the Aramaic comparative data above.
[717] Hämeen-Anttila, SAAA XIII, § 2.1.4.
[718] S. Ylvisaker, *Zur babylonischen und assyrischen Grammatik* (Leipzig 1912), § 1 and § 14c.
[719] Ibid., p. 7, n. 1.
[720] See Hämeen-Anttila, ibid., p. 15.
[721] See S. Moscati (ed.), *An Introduction to the Comparative Grammar of the Semitic Languages* (Wiesbaden 1964), § 8.54. Cf. W. von Soden & W. Röllig, *Das Akkadische Syllabar* (Rome 1967), pp. xxii–xxiii.
[722] On the question of pronoun borrowing, see S.G. Thomason & D.L. Everett, "Pronoun Borrowing," *Proceedings of the Annual Meeting of the Berkeley Linguistics Society* 27 (2001), pp. 301–315. Interestingly, among the modern dialects of Aramaic, Sūret has the dem. pron. *ʾannā/ē* "these," for the m. & f. pl. near deixis, as well as *ʾanā/ē/ō* "those," for the m. & f. pl. far deixis, both forms without the initial *h*.

ḫar-bu-u-tú	SAAB 9 73:7	Assur	Assur	LD	698

Aram. ⇒ NA

JBA, CPA, Syr., JLA *ḥrbh, ḥrbt'* (*ḥarbā, ḥarbṯā*) n. f. "ruin" DJBA 481b; LSp. 69b; DCPA 138a; PSm. 155f; Manna 260b; Audo 369b; SL 486b; CAL. Syr., *ḥrbh, ḥrbt'* (*ḥarbā, ḥarbəṯā*) n. f. "waste, desert" PSm. 155b; Manna 260b; SL 486b. Syr. *ḥrbw, ḥrbwt'* (*ḥarbū, ḥarbūṯā*) n. f. "ruin, desolation" Manna 260b; CAL.

This *dis legomenon* has two different forms in NA. According to AHw. (p. 325a s.v. *ḫarbūtu(m)*), the word occurs in OB and SB with the meaning "Verödung." CAD (Ḫ, p. 99a s.v. *ḫarbūtu*) lists the word, from OB on, with the sense "devastation." AEAD (p. 35a s.v. *ḫarbāti*) lists the word as n. f. pl. meaning "ruins," and (p. 35b s.v. *ḫarbūtu*) glosses the word only in the sense "untilled land."[723] However, according to the two NA contexts, the words *ḫarbātu* and *ḫarbūtu* indicate "ruin."

> KAV 197:14–17, reads:[724]
>
> [m]*aš-šur-na-din* [m]IGI.LÁ-*aš-šur* / *a-ta-a ip-ḫi-zu at-ta qa-la-ka* / É.MEŠ *gab-bu a-na ḫar-bat*.MEŠ *ú-ti-ru* / *uḫ-ta-li-qu-na-ši ina* ŠÀ ŠU[II]-*ka*
>
> Why do you remain silent when Aššūr-nādin and Amur-Aššūr are acting unjustly? They have turned all (our) houses into ruins, and lost us from out of your charge.
>
> SAAB 9 73:2–8, reads:[725]
>
> É *ep-šu a-di* GIŠ.ÙR.MEŠ-*šú* GIŠ.IG.MEŠ-*šú* / É *dan-ni* É KI.NÁ TÙR É-*a-ni* / É ⌜2⌝-*e* É TU₅ É *mu-ṣa-lu-tú* / É-ŠU.2 *ina* ŠÀ-*bi* É-ŠU.2 *ina* TÙR È-*e* / KÁ NINDU[?] É *ubu-sa-a-te* **ṭiḫḫi* É [I]URUDU[?]-*a-nu* / **ṭiḫḫi* É [I]*ta-*⌜*din*⌝–15 **ṭiḫḫi ḫar-bu-u-tú ša* É / [I]*ṣa-bu*[?] **ṭiḫḫi su-qa-qu la-pi-u*
>
> A fully built house with its beams and its doors, a main building, a bedroom, a courtyard, private quarters, a service building, a bathroom, an *afternoon building*, a service building therein, a service building in the courtyard, a ..., a storehouse – adjacent to the house of *Eriānu*, adjacent to the house of Tadin-Ištar, adjacent to the ruins of the house of *Ṣabu*, adjacent to the circular road.

The verb *ḫarābu* is found in MB, LB and SB with the meaning "to lie waste, to be(come) deserted."[726] The root *Ḫ/ḤRB with the same sense is Common

---

[723] The meaning "ruin" ought to be added to AEAD (p. 35b s.v. *ḫarbūtu*).
[724] The translation is that of TCAE, p. 363. Cf. F.M. Fales, "People and Professions in Neo-Assyrian Assur," in H. Waetzoldt & H. Hauptmann (eds.), *Assyrien im Wandel der Zeiten* (Heidelberg 1997), p. 39f; K. Radner, StAT 1, p. 31, n. 96.
[725] See K. Deller et al., "Neo-Assyrian Texts from Assur Private Archives in the Vorderasiatisches Museum of Berlin," *SAAB* 9 (1995), pp. 33ff.
[726] See AHw. (p. 322b s.v. *ḫarābu* I); CAD (Ḫ, p. 87a s.v. *ḫarābu* A); CDA (p. 106b s.v. *ḫarābu*).

Semitic except for Ethiopic.[727] In Syriac, we have usages such as: ܠܚܪܒܬܐ ܢܒܢܘܢ ܕܐܚܪܒܘ ܒܚܛܗܝܗܘܢ "they will build the ruin which they destroyed by their sins,"[728] and ܚܪܒܬܗ ܕܐܘܪܫܠܡ "the ruins of Jerusalem."[729] The corresponding term in Arabic is the word خَرَابَة "ruin."[730] However, the usual words for "ruin," in NA are *ḫarbītu* in the singular and *ḫarbānāti* or *ḫarbāti* in the plural.[731] Taking in consideration the forms of the word in Syriac as *ḥarbəṯā* and *ḥarbūṯā*, the other two NA forms of the word *ḫarbātu* and *ḫarbūtu*, indicate a borrowing from Aramaic.

ḫilpu n. "milk"; (see the discussion above s.v. *ḫalābu*)

Loanword	Reference	Provenance	Origin	Genre	Date
ḫi-il-pa-ka	SAA IX 7 r.9	Nineveh	Nineveh	P	Esh

Aram. ⇒ NA

ḫulūṭu n. (a meal made of a mixture of different grains(?))

Loanword	Reference	Provenance	Origin	Genre	Date
ḫu-lu-ṭi	SAA VII 207 r.3′ *ḫu-l*[*u*!*-ṭi*]	Nineveh	*Nineveh*	AD	Esh?
	SAA VII 208 r.4′	Nineveh	*Nineveh*	AD	Esh?
	SAA VII 210 r.6	Nineveh	*Nineveh*	AD	Esh?
	SAA VII 215 r.2 *ḫu-l*[*u-ṭi*]	Nineveh	*Nineveh*	AD	Esh?
	SAA VII 216 r.6	Nineveh	*Nineveh*	AD	Esh?
	SAA VII 217 r.4	Nineveh	*Nineveh*	AD	Esh?
	SAA VII 218 e.5′	Nineveh	*Nineveh*	AD	Esh?
ḫu-lu-ṭí	SAA VII 209 r.3	Nineveh	*Nineveh*	AD	Esh?

Aram. ⇒ NA

OffAr., *ḥlṭ* n. "mixtures(?)" DNWSI 374. Syr., *ḥalūṭā* n. m. "a mixture (especially of grain)" Manna 241a. Syr., *ḥilṭā* "mixed grain" Manna 241a; PSm. 143a. JPA, JLA *ḥlyṭh* (*ḥlīṭā*, *ḥlīṭṭā*) n. f. "dumpling" DJPA 202b; Jastrow 468b; CAL. Syr., *ḥəlīṭṭā* n. f. "porridge prepared from ground wheat" SL 455b; Manna 241a; Audo 341b. Sūret *ḥilṭā* n. m. (a folk-meal made of a mixture of different grains) Ashitha 177b. Syr., JLA *ḥlṭ* v. "to mix" Manna 240b; SL 454a; Audo 341a; PSm. 143a; Jastrow 466b; CAL.

---

727 See AHw., ibid.
728 See SL (p. 486b s.v. ܚܪܒܬܐ no. 2).
729 See PSm., (p. 155f s.v. ܚܪܒ).
730 See Wehr-Cowan, p. 231b.
731 See AEAD, p. 35a, b.

In AHw. (pp. 355a, 1562a s.v. *ḫulūṭu*), the word is first tentatively defined as (ein Getränk), and later, in the addenda and corrigenda section, is said to be an Aramaic foreign word. In CDA (p. 120a s.v. *ḫulūṭu*), the word is defined as (a mixed? drink), and is considered to be a loanword from Aramaic. The editors of CAD (Ḫ, p. 233b s.v. *ḫulūṭu*) do not suggest an etymology for this word, but define it as (a foodstuff). In AEAD (p. 38b s.v. *ḫulūṭu*), the word is tentatively rendered as "dumpling."

All the attested occurrences of *ḫulūṭu* come from administrative texts which appear to represent inventories of offerings presented in the Temple of Aššūr.[732] The word always comes together with the term *marmēna*, which is defined as (a drink; a milk product?).[733] In SAA VII, the two words are rendered slightly differently as "yoghurt" and "*marmena*-yoghurt." For instance, SAA VII 218 e.5′–6′, reads as follows:

> DUG.*ma-si-tú ḫu-lu-ṭi* / DUG.*ma-si-tú mar-me-na.*
>
> A flagon of *yoghurt*; a flagon of *marmena*-yoghurt.

While there is some agreement among scholars that *ḫulūṭu* designates a foodstuff or a drink; there is little agreement over the speculated meaning of this word. In his articles on Aramaic loanwords, von Soden considers NA *ḫulūṭu* probably to be derived from the Aramaic root ḤLṬ "to mix," and thinks that it designates a "Mischtrank."[734] Abraham and Sokoloff point out that it is impossible to infer from the context what kind of food is meant and that von Soden's rendering "Mischtrank," based on Aramaic חלט "to mix," is merely a conjecture.[735] They note, however, that *ḫuluṭu* may refer to a different sort of mixture and still be an Aramaic loanword.[736]

In Syriac the word ܚܠܝܛܐ means "a mixture (especially of grain)," and is derived from ܚܠܛ "to mix."[737] In Arabic we have خَلَطَ "to mix, mingle, blend,"[738] and in Hebrew חָלַט "to mix."[739] On the other hand, the Sūret word ܚܠܝܛܐ designates a folk-meal made of a mixture of different grains.[740] The Iraqi colloquial Arabic word مَخلوطة has a similar meaning as that of Sūret. In view of this, we may reconstruct a PS root *ḪLṬ "to mix." As is known, in Old Aramaic the phoneme *ḫ* had already merged with *ḥ*.

Most important, however, is that the root ḪLṬ is not productive in Akkadian. In addition, the term *ḫulūṭu* is limited to NA. Accordingly, the evidence points to a borrowing from Aramaic into NA. Phonologically, the initial *ḫ* of the NA

---

[732] See G. van Driel, *The Cult of Aššur* (Assen 1969), p. 207.
[733] See CDA (p. 198a s.v. *marmēnu*); AEAD (p. 61a s.v. *marmēna*). In the glossary section of SAA VII (p. 212b s.v. *ḫuluṭu*), the word is tentatively defined as (a milk product?).
[734] See von Soden, *Or* 35 (1966), p. 11:54; idem, *Or* 46 (1977), p. 188:54.
[735] See Abraham & Sokoloff, *Reassessment*, p. 36:93.
[736] Ibid., p. 36, n. 262.
[737] See Manna, p. 241a.
[738] See Elias & Elias, p. 196b; Wehr-Cowan, p. 255b.
[739] See Jastrow, p. 466b; Dalman, p. 140a.
[740] See Ashitha, p. 177b.

ḫulūṭu, represents *ḫ* of a assumed Aramaic source word *ḥalūṭā*.[741] On the other hand, the first syllable of the NA *ḫulūṭu* is expected to have the short vowel *a*, as that of the proposed Aramaic source word. Parpola suggests that NA <*u*> here is rendered phonetically /ə/ ~ /œ/, not /u/.[742] Morphologically, one has to bear in mind that the nominal pattern *QuTūL* (corresponding to *PuRūS*) is rare in Akkadian, and in Aramaic it merged with **qatūl*.[743] As it stands, the evidence at hand settles the question of borrowing into NA fairly decisively.

ḫurbānu n. pl. tant. "deserted places/regions"

Loanword	Reference	Provenance	Origin	Genre	Date
ḫur-ba-nu-šá	SAA XX 40 r. iii 35′	Nineveh	Nineveh	R	7th c.
ḫur-ba-nu-šú	SAA XX 42 r. iii 13′	Assur	Assur	R	PC

Aram. ⇒ NA

Syr., *ḥurbānāyā* adj. "deserted" SL 433a; CAL. JBA, JPA, CPA, Sam., *ḥrbn*, *ḥrbn*ʾ (*ḥurbān*, *ḥurbānā*) n. m. "destruction" CAL; DNWSI 403; DJBA 442b; DJPA 214a; Jastrow 439b; LSp. 69b; DCPA 138a; DSA 293b. Ma., *hurbana* n. m. "destruction" MD 137b. Syr., *ḥarbānā* n. m. "destruction, demolition; deserted region" Manna 260a. Syr., *ḥarbānā* n. m. "destruction, demolition" SL 486b; PSm. 156a; Audo 369b.

In AHw. (p. 358b) the word *ḫurbu* is glossed "Wüste," and is considered to be a borrowing from Aramaic in LB.[744] A single reference is given (Dar. 435:3), part of which reads: *ina su-ú-qu šá ḫu-ur-bi*.[745] However, von Soden considers *ḫurbu*, in the instance quoted above, to be borrowed from Aramaic *ḥu/orbā* "desert," and distinguishes it from the original Akkadian word *ḫarbu* "waste land."[746] In contrast, the editors of CAD (Ḫ, p. 220a s.v. *ḫubūru* A; M/2, p. 216b s.v. *mūradu*, b) take the LB word *ḫu-ur-bi*, referred to above, to be a metathesis for *ḫubur*, and list it under the heading *ḫubūru* A, which they define as (a large vat for beer). Abraham and Sokoloff also consider the single LB attestation *ḫu-ur-bi* to be a misspelling for *ḫubur*, pointing out that the *Ḫubur* street, namely "street of the *ḫubūru*-beer vat makers," in Babylon, is identified from many other NB archival texts.[747]

As for NA, the word *ḫurbānu* is attested as a *dis legomenon*. It occurs in a *tākultu*-ritual for Assurbanipal (SAA XX 40 r. iii 35′) written by Issār-šumu-ēreš,

[741] For the representation of Aramaic *ḥ* by NA *ḫ*, see n. 313 above.
[742] S. Parpola (personal communication).
[743] See J. Fox, *Semitic Noun Patterns* (Winona Lake 2003), pp. 209, 212.
[744] See also CDA (p. 121b s.v. *ḫurbu*).
[745] See J.N. Strassmaier, *Inschriften von Darius, König von Babylon (521–485 v. Chr.)*, (Leipzig 1892–1897).
[746] See von Soden, *Or* 35 (1966), p. 11:55; idem, *Or* 46 (1977), p. 188:55. Cf. CAD (Ḫ, p. 98b, v.s. *ḫarbu* B; p. 249b s.v. *ḫurbū*); DNWSI (p. 403 s.v. *ḥrb*₃).
[747] See Abraham & Sokoloff, *Reassessment*, p. 36:94.

chief scribe/astrologer at the court of Nineveh. It also occurs in another *tākultu*-ritual (SAA XX 42 r. iii 13′) containing prayers for the benefit of the Assyrian king Aššūr-etel-ilāni (ca. 630–627 B.C.). The editors of CAD (Ḫ, p. 248b) list the word *ḫurbānu* as a substantive pl. tant. meaning "deserted places."[748]

SAA XX 40 32′–36′, reads:

ṣa[!]*-x* KUR–*aš-šur* URU.MEŠ-*šá* / BARAG.MEŠ-*šá* / *ma-ṣa-ra-tú-šá* / *ḫur-ba-nu-šá* / *ti-la-nu-šá*

The ... of Assyria, its cities, its daises, its garrisons, its wastelands and its mounds.

SAA XX 42 r. iii 11′–13′, reads:

KUR–[d]*a-šur* BÀD.MEŠ-[*šú* BARAG.MEŠ-*šú*] / *du-na-tu-šu ma-ad-ga-l*[*a-tu-šu*] / *ur-pa-nu-šú ḫur-ba-nu-šú*

The land of Aššūr, [its] city walls, [daises], strongholds, watchtow[ers], uncultivated fields, wastelands.

Etymologically, the Akkadian word *ḫarābu*, which is attested in MB, SB and LB, means "to lie waste."[749] Other cognate words in Akkadian are *ḫarībatu*(*m*) "waste land," in OB, MA and SB, and *ḫuribtu* "desert," in MB, SB and LB, as well as SB *ḫurbū* n. pl. tant. "waste land, deserted place."[750] Cognates are also found in other Semitic languages. In Arabic خَرَبَ "to ruin, destroy, lay in ruins, wreck," and خَرْبان "out of order."[751] Hebrew has חָרֵב "to be burned, ruined, waste,"[752] and חוּרְבָּה "ruin, ruins, desert building."[753] In JBA there is חוּרְבָּא "ruined building, ruin," and in Syriac ܚܘܪܒܐ "devastation; desert; wilderness."[754]

The context where the two NA instances occur indicates, through analogy with the neighboring words, that *ḫurbānu* stands in plural. However, the morpheme -*ānu*, which precedes the final pronominal suffix -*ša* or -*šu*, is difficult to explain. Usually, the Semitic nominal pattern extended by the suffix -*ān* occurs in abstracts, adjectives and diminutives.[755] Of course, a particular Akkadian type of the patterns with the suffix -*ānu* is used to refer to a special person in a specific condition.[756] But, this does not seem to be the case here. On the other hand, if -*ānu* is representing a substantive in the plural masculine, it is expected to appear

748 Cf. AEAD (p. 39a s.v. *ḫurbu* "desert(ed place), wasteland"); The Glossary of SAA XX (p. 175a s.v. *ḫurbu*).
749 See AHw. (p. 322b s.v. *ḫarābu* I); CAD (Ḫ, p. 87a s.v. *ḫarābu* A).
750 See CAD (Ḫ, p. 249b s.v. *ḫurbū*).
751 See Elias & Elias, p. 182a.
752 See Dalman, p. 150b. Cf. Jastrow, p. 498a.
753 Ibid., p. 439b.
754 See DJBA, p. 442b; SL, p. 433a.
755 For Semitic nominal patterns extended by the suffix -*ān*, see S. Moscati, *An Introduction to the Comparative Grammar of the Semitic Languages: Phonology and Morphology* (Wiesbaden 1964), § 12.21. Cf. Lipiński, *Semitic Languages*, § 29.35. Also cf. R. Degen, *Altaramäische Grammatik der Inschriften des 10.–8. Jh. v.Chr.* (Wiesbaden 1969), § 30, 2.
756 See A. Ungnad, *Akkadian Grammar* (Atlanta 1992), § 38e.

in NA as *-āni*.[757] Nevertheless, the word *ḥurbānā* n. m. sg. "destruction," is common in Aramaic. It appears exceptionally as *ḥarbānā* in Syriac, but also in the sense of "deserted region." Hence, based on the distribution and form of NA *ḫurbānu*, the evidence points to a borrowing from Aramaic. Interestingly, NA employs two other cognate words which are attested only in plural, namely *ḫarbānāti* n. f. pl. "ruins" and *ḫarbāti* n. f. pl. "ruins."[758] It was probably also in analogy to these two cognates that the borrowed NA word *ḫurbānu* was taken as representing a plural noun.

iābilu n. "ram"

Loanword	Reference	Provenance	Origin	Genre	Date
ia-bi-li	PVA 331:306	Assur	Assur	LL	–

Aram. ⇒ NA

OAram., *ybl* n. m. "ram" CAL. JBA, JPA *ywbyl'* n. m. "ram" DJBA 528b; DJPA 237a; Jastrow 567b.

The word for "ram" in NA is consistently written logographically as UDU.NITÁ in the singular and UDU.NITÁ.MEŠ in the plural.[759] Thus far, it is attested only once, written syllabically in a plural form as *ia-bi-li*, and as such it constitutes a *hapax legomenon* in NA.[760] It is found in a lexical list, the so-called "Practical Vocabulary of Assur," where its semantic connection is determined by the equation UDU.NITÁ.MEŠ = *ia-bi-li*.[761]

Landsberger and Gurney, the editors of the aforementioned lexical list, equate NA *iābilu* to the Hebrew word יוֹבֵל "ram."[762] Zadok rules out the possibility that the Jewish Aramaic יוֹבְלָא "ram" is a loanword from Hebrew, arguing that there are indications that the word might have existed in Old Aramaic.[763] In fact, according to CAL, the word *ybl* n. m. "ram" is already attested in Old Aramaic from Zinçirli (Sam'al). A cognate is also found in Punic as *ybl* "ram."[764] The editors of CAD (I/J, p. 321a s.v. *jabilu*) gloss the word as "ram," but attempt no etymology for it. AHw. (p. 411a s.v. *jabilu*) lists this word in the sense "Widder,"

757 See Hämeen-Anttila, SAAS XIII, § 3.9.2. Cf. GAG § 61i–j and the nominal paradigm, p. 3*.

758 See AEAD, p. 35a.

759 The logogram UDU.NITÁ is usually rendered "ram, sheep." See W. Schramm, *Akkadische Logogramme* (Göttingen 2003), p. 164; Borger, ABZ, p. 188 no. 537.

760 Note that Fales suggests further possible NA attestations of *iābilu* "ram," which are written as *ib-li* in TH 59:3, 6, e. 8 and TH 79:4′, 6′. See n. ad TH 59:3, in F.M. Fales, "Studies on Neo-Assyrian Texts I: Joins and Collations to the Tell Halaf Documents," *ZA* 69 (1979), p. 202.

761 See PVA, p. 331:306.

762 See the philological remark in, PVA, p. 340:306. Cf. Nili, p. 194:54.

763 See R. Zadok, Review of "The Chicago Colloquium on Aramaic Studies, Journal of Near Eastern Studies Vol. 37, No. 2, April 1978," *WO* 12 (1981), p. 200 s.v. *Y–B–L*.

764 See DNWSI (p. 433 s.v. *ybl*$_2$).

and considers it to be a borrowing from Canaanite *yōbēl*.[765] CDA (p. 440a s.v. *yābilu*) regards the word as a loan from West-Semitic in general. Parpola, on the other hand, considers *iābilu* to be an Aramaic loanword in NA.[766]

Phonologically, the most telling factor indicating that the NA *iābilu* is a loanword is the preservation of the initial semivowel *y* represented in the word-initial ligature I+A. The original initial semivowel *y* is almost always dropped in Akkadian, and is very rarely preserved in initial position, notably in the pronominal forms of the first person singular *iāši*, *iāti* "me," as well as in loanwords.[767] Nevertheless, it is difficult to explain the vowel *-a* in the first syllable of the NA word in the light of the *-w* of the first syllable of the corresponding West-Semitic words, including the later form of the Aramaic word. However, it is more likely that *iābilu* was borrowed from Aramaic because the latter had closer contact with NA.

ianūqu n. "suckling animal, animal before being weaned"

Loanword	Reference	Provenance	Origin	Genre	Date
ia-nu-qi	SAA XI 106 r.2	Nineveh	*Nineveh*	AD	–
[UZU].*ia-nu-qu*	SAA XX 33 r. i 30′	Nineveh	Nineveh	R	–

Aram. ⇒ NA

Syr., LJLA *ynq*ʾ n. m. "suckling animal" CAL. Sūret *yānūqā* n. m. "suckling; a young child or animal before being weaned" Oraham 204b. OffAr., JBA, Ma., Syr., *ynq*, *ynq*ʾ (*yāneq*, *yānqā*, *yānōqā*) n. m. "child, suckling child" DNWSI 462; DJBA 537b; MD 186b; SL 576b; PSm. 193b; Manna 313a. OAram., OffAr., JBA, JPA, Sam., CPA, Ma., Syr., *ynq* v. "to suckle, nurse, suck" Brauner 250; DNWSI 461; DJBA 538b; DJPA 242b; Jastrow 581b; DSA 349b; LSp. 84b; DCPA 164a; MD 192b; PSm. 193b; SL 577a; Manna 313a; Audo 434b.

This word has two occurrences in NA and as such it is a *dis legomenon*. It is attested as [UZU].*ia-nu-qu* in a broken context in an instruction for preparing a cultic meal (SAA XX 33 r. i 30′). It also occurs in a note concerned with Oxen (SAA XI 106 r.2), where six persons are mentioned in the text followed by the

---

765 Cf. ibid.

766 See S. Parpola, "Neo-Assyrian Treaties from the Royal Archives of Nineveh," *JCS* 39 (1987), p. 183.

767 See GAG § 22c; Hämeen-Anttila, SAAS XIII, § 2.1.3; S. Parpola, *Letters from Assyrian Scholars to the Kings Esarhaddon and Assurbanipal, II* (Winona Lake 2007), p. 139 esp. n. 278. For further analysis of the semivowel *y* in Akkadian, see E. Reiner, "The Phonological Interpretation of a Subsystem in the Akkadian Syllabary," in R.D. Biggs & J.A. Brinkman, (eds.), *Studies Presented to A. Leo Oppenheim* (Chicago 1964), pp. 174ff.; I.J. Gelb, "Comments on the Akkadian Syllabary," *Or* 39 (1970), pp. 536ff.

words, *ša šizbē* "milk," *ša saliāte* "*nets*," and the two enigmatic words *ša qa-ru-ḫi*, *ša ia-nu-qi*, and the word *ša gušūrē* "beams."[768]

SAA XX 33 r. i 29′–31′, reads:

[*x x x x x x x x x*] ⸢*x* UZU.*si-ir*⸣-[*x x x*] / [*x x x x x x* UZU].*ia-nu-qu* UZU.*ḫal-la-nu* UZ$^{!}$.MUŠEN$^{!}$ / [*x x x*.MUŠEN TU.GU]R$_{4}^{!}$.MUŠEN *ak-bi-ri nap-tu-nu am–mar ša par-ṭu*

[......], ...-meat, (30) [...-meat], *iānuqu*-[meat], hind legs, goose, [...-bird, turtl]edove, jerboas. All the meal that was served.

SAA XI 106:1–r.3, reads:

^{m}*tab*-URU-*a-a* GUD / ^{m}*dan-nu*–U.GUR :. / ^{md}PA–NUMUN–DÙ :. / ^{m}MAN–IGI.LAL-*a-ni* :. / ^{mP}PA–*šal-lim* :. / ^{m}EN–PAB-*ir* :. / 0! PAB *an-nu-te* / *ša* GA.MEŠ / *ša sa-li-a-te* / *ša qa-ru-ḫi* / *ša ia-nu-qi* / *ša* GIŠ.ÙR.MEŠ

Tabālāyu – an ox, Dannu-Nergal – ditto, Nabû-zēru-ibni – ditto, Šarru-ēmuranni – ditto, Nabû-šallim – ditto, Bēl-nāṣir – ditto, All these – of milk, of *nets*, of ..., of *a suckling*, of beams.

In AHw. (p. 412a s.v. *janūqu*) this word is first considered to be of unknown origin and is rendered "eine Fleischsorte," in cultic context, but in the addenda and corrigenda section of AHw. (p. 1565b), the word is tentatively rendered "Lamm," and is thought to be an Aramaic foreign word.[769] In CAD (I/J, p. 324b s.v. *janūqu*), this word is tentatively considered to be foreign and its meaning is given as unknown. In CDA (p. 440b s.v. *yanūqu*), the word is tentatively glossed "ram," and is considered to be an Aramaic loanword in NA. On the other hand, in AEAD (p. 39a s.v. *ianūqu*), the word is defined as (a meat), and tentatively rendered as "milk chicken."

In his article on Aramaic loanwords, von Soden interprets the two enigmatic words *qa-ru-ḫi* and *ia-nu-qi*, as borrowings from Aramaic and connects them with Jewish Aramaic קָרוֹחַ "bald," in reference to an old animal, and יָנוּקָא "suckling, infant," in reference to a young animal.[770] Later, he rendered *ianūqu* as "Lamm."[771] Referring to von Soden, Fales and Postgate tentatively render *ia-nu-qi* as "suckling," and consider it undoubtedly to be a borrowing from Aramaic.[772] But, against von Soden's interpretation, Abraham and Sokoloff argue that the Aramaic term, i.e., יָנוּקָא, refers only to children, not animals, and that the real meaning of the word *ianūqu* in Akkadian is in doubt.[773] Nevertheless, they note

---

768 For the words *qa-ru-ḫi* and *sa-li-a-te*, see the discussions below s.v. *qarūḫu* and *salītu* respectively.
769 Cf. DNWSI (p. 462 s.v. *ynq*$_2$).
770 See von Soden, *Or* 37 (1968), 270:169, 170. Cf. Jastrow, pp. 581a and 1413b.
771 See von Soden, *Or* 46 (1977), p. 188:169.
772 See n. ad SAA XI 106:8–r.3. However, in the Glossary of SAA XI, p. 161b and SAA XX, p. 175a, the meaning of *ianūqu* is defined as (unknown).
773 See Abraham & Sokoloff, *Reassessment*, p. 56:270. Cf. the discussion on the word **uniq-t-um?* by D. Testen, "An Akkadian-Arabic Cognate-Pair and the Formation of Stem-Based Diminutives in

that "if this Akk[adian] word is in fact connected with the meaning of sucking, its phonetic form with *ya-* points to its being a loanword."[774] According to CAL, however, the word *ynq'* in the sense "suckling animal," occurs in Syriac and LJLA. Furthermore, in Sūret the word ܝܢܘܩܐ means "a young child or animal before being weaned."[775]

In Akkadian, from Old-Babylonian on, the root YNQ is attested in the word *enēqu(m)* "to suck." The latter is cognate with the Ugaritic, Hebrew and Aramaic word ינק, which also means "to suck." However, the form of the word in NA, *ianūqu*, makes a loan virtually certain because the semivowel *y*, here the first part of the ligature (I+A), is very rarely preserved in initial position.[776]

In SAA XI 106, as cited above, the word *ia-nu-qi* is preceded by the word *qa-ru-ḫi*. The latter probably means "young sheep that has no horns," and as such it is possibly a borrowing from Aramaic *qərāḥā* "a young sheep, lamb, yearling (that has no horns)."[777] Then, by analogy, the word *ia-nu-qi* probably means "lamb before being weaned," referring to a younger animal.[778] Thus, the sequence *ša qa-ru-ḫe, ša ia-nu-qe* would likely refer to a young sheep that has no horns and a lamb before being weaned. If such is the case, the terms *qarūḫu* and *ianūqu* would explicitly indicate the approximate age of the animal.

im–magāni adv. "gratuitously, gratis, in vain"[779]

Loanword	Reference	Provenance	Origin	Genre	Date
im–ma-ga-a-ni	SAA XXI 63:5 (RL)	Nineveh	Nineveh	L	Asb

Indo-Iranian ⇒ Ugaritic? ⇒ Aram. ⇒ NA; LB

JBA, JPA, CPA, Sam., Syr., LJLA *mgn* (*maggān*) adv. "gratis; for nothing, in vain, without reason" DJBA 641b; DJPA 291a; Jastrow 729b; LSp. 106b; DCPA 209a; PSm. 250b; DSA 450b; SL 709b; Audo 524a; Manna 385b; CAL. Palm., *mgn* n. "gift" DNWSI 593.

The word *im–magāni* occurs as a *hapax legomenon* in NA. It is attested in a letter (SAA XXI 63:5) sent by the Assyrian king Assurbanipal to Tammarītu II, king of Elam (ca. 652–649 B.C.). In AHw. (574b s.v. *mag/kannu*, mng. no. 2a), the NA *im–magāni* is considered to be an Aramaic foreign word meaning "umsonst, grundlos."[780] The editors of CAD (M/I, p. 31b s.v. *magannu* A, mng. no. 2)

Early Semitic," in G. Deutscher & N.J.C. Kouwenberg (eds.), *The Akkadian Language in Its Semitic Contexts: Studies in the Akkadian of the Third and Second Millennium BC* (Leiden 2006), pp. 140f.

[774] Abraham & Sokoloff, ibid., p. 56, n. 727.

[775] See Oraham, p. 204b.

[776] Cf. Hämeen-Anttila, SAAS XIII, § 2.1.3.

[777] See the discussions below s.v. *qarūḫu*.

[778] Cf. Oraham (p. 204b s.v. ܝܢܘܩܐ).

[779] See AEAD (p. 57b s.v. *magānu*).

[780] In LB the expression *ana magānu* "gratis," is also considered an Aramaic foreign word. Cf. CDA (p. 188b s.v. *magannu* I); DNWSI (pp. 593f s.v. *mgn*$_3$).

consider the origin of *magannu* "gift, present," to be a borrowing from Indo-Iranian, transmitted via Hurrian.

According to von Soden, the word under discussion here was first borrowed from Hurrian into the early Akkadian of Nuzi and the MB of Ugarit with the sense of "gift," but it was later borrowed from Aramaic into NA and LB with the meaning "gratis; grundlos."[781] He regards the origin of the word to be a combination of the Vedic Sanskrit word *maghá(m)* "rich gift" + *-nnu*.[782] He also considers the attestation *im–magāni* in NA in the sense "for nothing, in vain," and *ana magānu* in LB in the sense "gratis," to be foreign words from Aramaic *maggān*, but remarks that it is not known whether the word entered Aramaic by way of Ugaritic or through another medium.[783] In contrast to von Soden, O'Connor argues that the instances of the corresponding word in Hurrian reveal a borrowing from the Semitic languages into Hurrian.[784] Abraham and Sokoloff state that the transmission of this word into Aramaic and the late dialects of Akkadian cannot be determined with certainty.[785]

Since the word is a *hapax legomenon* in NA, the plausibility of etymology proposed for it is determined by the sentence context, here SAA XXI 63:4–5, which reads as follows:

> *ina* UGU *e-mu-qí an-nu-ti ša i*[*p*$^{!}$*-ṭu-ru-ni*] / *la im–ma-ga-a-ni ip-paṭ-r*[*u x x*]
>
> Concerning these forces which were dis[solved], they were not dis[solved] gratuitously – […].

The word is also attested in Punic as *mgn* "gift,"[786] in JPA as מגן "for nothing, in vain," in Syriac as ܡܓܢ "in vain, without reason," and in Arabic as مَجّانًا "gratis, for nothing, free (of charge), gratuitously."[787] However, the NA word *im–magāni* "gratis; for nothing" is a compound consisting of the preposition *ina* "in" and *magāni*, which is the genitive form of the borrowed word *magannu*/*magānu* "gratis; for nothing." Hence, the NA *im–magāni* represents a case of external sandhi. The last vowel of the preposition *ina* is dropped and the remaining consonant *n* at the end of the preposition is affixed to the following word *magāni*, resulting in total assimilation of the dental nasal *n* of the preposition to the first consonant *m* of the following word.[788] The word *magānu* has no Akkadian etymology. In fact, the lack of a Semitic etymology generally indicates a foreign origin. On the other hand, the advanced Indo-Iranian etymology is convincing. Also, in favor of a borrowing from Aramaic into NA is the distribution of the

---

781 See von Soden, "Vedisch *magham*, 'Geschenk' – neuarabisch *maǧǧānīja*, 'Gebührenfreiheit': Der Weg einer Wortsippe," *JEOL* 18 (1964), pp. 339–344.
782 Ibid.
783 Ibid., p. 340. Cf. von Soden, *Or* 35 (1966), p. 15:83; idem, *Or* 46 (1977), p. 189:83. Cf. also Kaufman, AIA, p. 67 s.v. *magannu*.
784 See M. O'Connor, "Semitic **mgn* and its Supposed Sanskrit Origin," *JAOS* 109 (1989), p. 30.
785 See Abraham & Sokoloff, *Reassessment*, p. 40:125.
786 DNWSI (p. 593 s.v. *mgn*$_3$).
787 See Elias & Elias, p. 644b; Wehr-Cowan, p. 894a.
788 Cf. Luukko, SAAS XVI, § 4.11; Hämeen-Anttila, SAAS XIII, § 2.2.2.1.

word in the former and the fact that the usage of the word in NA is perfectly congruent with that of Aramaic.

kadāru v. (G) “to toil, to be wearied, to be burdened”

Loanword	Reference	Provenance	Origin	Genre	Date
ka-da-a-ru	SAA X 294:29	Nineveh	Nineveh	L	Esh

Aram. ⇒ NA [?]

Syr., *kdr* v. “to be wearied, tired” Manna 327b; Audo 452b; PSm. 205b; SL 600b; CAL. Ma., *kdr* v. Pe. “to be heavy, weighty, hard” MD 204a; CAL. Ma. *kdr* v. Etpe. “to be weighed down, burdened” MD 204b; CAL.

The word *kadāru* in the sense “to toil” is attested as a *hapax legomenon* in NA. It occurs in a broken context in a long and bitter letter of complaint sent probably by Urdu-Gula, the royal exorcist from Nineveh, to Esarhaddon.

In AHw. (p. 419a s.v. *kadāru(m)* II), the word is glossed “sich aufbäumen,” but for the NA attestation (ABL 1285:29), which is discussed here, the word is taken to have the sense “Unterwerfung.” In contrast, in CDA (p. 141a s.v. *kadāru* IV), the word in the G-stem is tentatively glossed “to labour,” and also tentatively considered to be a denominative verb from *kudurru* “(earth-carrying) labour (obligation).”[789] In CAD (K, p. 30a s.v. *kadāru* A, no. 1), the NA word is taken to have the meaning “to be overbearing, arrogant, spirited.” On the other hand, in AEAD (p. 44b s.v. *kadāru* B), the word is glossed “to toil.” The context where the NA word occurs (SAA X 294:26–30), reads as follows:

> MU ˹*la*! SIG$_5$!˺ [*l*]*i-iḫ-šú ù še-eṣ-ṣu-ú ša a-bi-ti iz-zi-ʾa-ár* / *ik*!-[*ki*]-˹*bi*! *ša*! LUGAL! EN˺-*ia at-ta-aṣ-ṣar* LÚ.EN.MEŠ–MUN *la-a aṣ-ba-ta* / *dib*-˹*bi*! *x x x*˺ [*x*]-*ú-tu as-sa-ad-da-ad ma-az-za-as-su nu-bat-tu* / *x*[*x*] ˹*x x x ú*!˺ *ka-na-a-šú ka-da-a-ru ù pu-luḫ-tu ša* É.GAL / ˹LÚ.ARAD!˺.MEŠ *ša*–˹*ziq*!-*ni*!˺ *ù* LÚ.SAG.MEŠ *us-sa-am-mid mi-i-nu ina* Š˹À-*b*˺*i*
>
> Improper conduct, whispering about and revealing a secret are detestable things; I guarded the privileges of the king my lord, but I did not find benefactors, I endured [...] words, [I made] (my) office (my) night’s resting place, I taught the servants, the non-eunuchs and eunuchs alike, submission, *toil* and fear of the palace, and what did I get for it?

In a textual note in his earlier edition of the same NA letter (ABL 1285:29 = SAA X 294:29), Parpola writes that the rendition of *ka-da-a-ru* as “to toil” seems to be certain on the basis of the context, despite the fact that no other attestations

[789] See CDA (p. 165a s.v. *kudurru* I).

in this sense are entered in the dictionaries.[790] Furthermore, referring to (CAD K 496), he takes *ka-da-a-ru* to be probably a denominative verb from *kudurru* B "corvée service."[791]

As a substantive in Akkadian, *kadāru* is attested lexically in SB, and probably indicates (a reed fence).[792] As a verb, however, it means "to rear up, rise in opposition, be insubordinate; to be overbearing, arrogant, spirited."[793] It can also mean "to delimit, to establish a border (by means of a boundary stone), to set up a boundary stone."[794] However, none of these different meanings fits the context for the word *kadāru* in SAA X 294:29. From the West-Semitic languages, the verb ܟܕܪ in Syriac means "to be wearied," and in Mandaic *kdr* means "to be weighted down, burdened." In Arabic the verb كَدَرَ means "to be troubled, disturbed."[795] According to Drower and Macuch, these West-Semitic words are cognate with Akkadian *kudurru* "slavery."[796] In Akkadian, the latter means a "basket to carry earth or brick," and indicates corvée service.[797] However, it is possible that this NA word is a borrowing from Aramaic, in which it survived in its later dialects Syriac and Mandaic with the meanings "to be wearied, tired; to be weighed down, burdened."

kandu n. "pitcher; vessel, pot"

Loanword	Reference	Provenance	Origin	Genre	Date
DUG.*kan-du*!	SAA VII 130:9	Nineveh	Nineveh	AD	7th c.

Aram. ⇒ NA; LB

OffAr., JBA, JPA, QA *kd, kd'* (*kaḏ, kaddā, kandā*) n. m. "vessel, pot; pitcher, jar" DNWSI 487, 518; DJBA 553a, 587b; DJPA 250b; Jastrow 612a; Dalman 191b; DJA 56a; CAL. Syr., LJLA *kdn, kdn'* (*kaddān, kaddānā, kəḏānā*) n. m. "small pitcher with narrow neck" Manna 327a; Audo 452b; SL 600b; PSm. 205b; Jastrow 614a; Dalman 183b; CAL.

This word is a *hapax legomenon* in NA. It occurs in an administrative document mentioning various food contributions from officials to the Lady of the House. The word is preceded by the determinative DUG which signifies vessels or containers. AHw. (p. 436b s.v. *kandu* II) lists this word as meaning "Krug," and

---

790 See S. Parpola, "The Forlorn Scholar," in F. Rochberg-Halton (ed.), *Language, Literature, and History: Philological and Historical Studies Presented to Erica Reiner* (New Haven 1987), p. 276, n. on l. 29.

791 Ibid. Cf. CAD (K, p. 496a s.v. *kudurru* B, mng. 1b).

792 See AHw. (p. 419a s.v. *kadāru* I); CAD (K, p. 30a s.v. *kadāru*).

793 See AHw. (p. 419a s.v. *kadāru(m)* II); CAD (K, p. 30a s.v. *kadāru* A); CDA (p. 140b s.v. *kadāru(m)* II).

794 See AHw. (p. 419a s.v. *kadāru* III); CAD (K, p. 30b s.v. *kadāru* B).

795 See Elias & Elias, p. 584a; Wehr-Cowan, p. 817a.

796 See MD (p. 204a s.v. KDR I).

797 CAD (K, p. 496b s.v. *kudurru* B, b).

considers it to be a borrowing into LB from Aramaic *kandā*.[798] In CAD (K, p. 148b s.v. *kandu*), the word is defined as (a container of earthenware or silver, mainly for wine), and is regarded as a West-Semitic word in NB.

Referring to the Hebrew words *kad*, *kadd-*, and Aramaic *kaddā*, *kaddānā*, Zimmern suggests that *kandu* is probably a West-Semitic borrowing in Akkadian meaning "Krug."[799] Von Soden, in his articles on Aramaic loanwords, regards *kandu* as a borrowing from Aramaic into LB with the sense "Krug."[800] Abraham and Sokoloff concur with von Soden and argue that the word in West-Semitic was so far only attested as *kd* in Biblical Hebrew, Ugaritic and different Aramaic dialects, but now is also attested with dissimilation of *n* in Official Aramaic כנד as a container for wine.[801] The word is also attested in Phoenician and Punic as *kd* in the sense "pitcher, jar."[802] The context where the NA *kandu* occurs (SAA VII 130:5–9) reads as follows:

> [1] UDU.NITÁ *ša* ^md^PA–*ku-ṣur-a-ni* / ⌜LÚ⌝.NAM URU.*ár-zu-ḫi-na* / [1 *tar-m*]*a-zi-li*.MUŠEN [[ ]] / [*ša* ^md^*x*]–SU LÚ*.SAG–MAN / [*x x x x*] DUG.*kan-du*! GIŠ.GEŠTIN
>
> [1] male sheep – of Nabû-kuṣuranni, the governor of Arzūḫina; [1 *tarm*]*azilu* bird – [of …]-eriba, eunuch of the king; […] vessel of wine.[803]

Although the word is attested as *kd* in the other West-Semitic languages, including different dialects of Aramaic, the fact that the word occurs as כנד in Official Aramaic and as כַּנְדָּא in JBA makes it certain that Aramaic is the donor of the loanword into NA and LB. The form כנד displays the following dissimilation: *-dd-* > *-nd-*, i.e., *kaddā* > *kandā*.[804] The Syriac word ܟܢܕܐ "small pitcher with narrow neck" is probably cognate with כנד, taking in consideration the possibility of a metathesis occurring in the Syriac word.

kannušu v. (D only) "to assemble, collect, gather (people, harvest); "to die; to bury, inter"; (see the discussion below s.v. *kinăltu*)

Loanword	Reference	Provenance	Origin	Genre	Date
ka-ni-ši	StAT 2 163 r.11	Assur	Assur	L	Sn
kan-nu-šú	SAA I 1 r.59 (RL)	Calah	Calah	L	Sg
ka-nu-šá	SAA XIX 19:6	Calah	*Calah*	L	Sg
lu-ka-ni-šú-u-ni	SAA X 227 r.13 (= "to bury, inter")	Nineveh	Nineveh	L	666?
nu-ka-na-šú-ú-ni	SAA V 3 r.20	Nineveh	Amidi	L	Sg
tú!-*ka-na-šú-ni*	KAV 214:27	Assur	*Assur*	L	Asb?

[798] Cf. CDA (p. 145b s.v. *kandu*).
[799] See Zimmern, AF, p. 33. .
[800] See von Soden, *Or* 35 (1966), p. 12:62; idem, *Or* 46 (1977), p. 188:62.
[801] See Abraham & Sokoloff, *Reassessment*, p. 36:101. Cf. HALOT, p. 461b; DUL, p. 429.
[802] See DNWSI (p. 487 s.v. kd_1).
[803] Note that in the Glossary of SAA VII p. 214a, the word *kandu* is glossed "pitcher."
[804] See DNWSI, ibid; DJBA (p. 553a s.v. כַּדָּא; p. 587b s.v. כַּנְדָּא).

[*ú*]-*kan-na-áš*	SAA XIX 164 r.11′	Calah	*Calah*	L	Sg
ú-kan[!]*-ni-šú-u-ni*	SAA X 227 r.12 (= "to bury, inter")	Nineveh	Nineveh	L	666?
uk-ta-ni-iš	SAA XV 286:13′	Nineveh	*Arzūḫina*	L	Sg

Aram. ⇒ NA; NB[805]

OffAr., JBA, JPA, Sam., CPA, QA, Ma., Syr., *knš* v. Pe. & Pa. "to gather, collect, assemble" DNWSI 520; DJBA 589b; DJPA 264a; Jastrow 651b; DSA 398a; LSp. 95a; DCPA 181a; MD 220a; SL 637a; PSm. 219a; Manna 344a; Audo 470b; CAL. Syr., *knš* v. Pe. & Pa. "to shroud, dress for the grave; to bury, inter, entomb, inhume; to die; to put to death, to cause to die" Manna 344a; Audo 470b; PSm. 219a. Syr., *knš* v. Etpe. "to be interred (of a dead person)" SL 637b. JPA *knš* v. Etpe. "to die (calque < Biblical Hebrew)" DJPA 264a.

One of the general meanings of the Akkadian word *kanāšu* is "to submit (to)."[806] It has a fricativized variant in NA as *ḫanāšu*.[807] According to Hämeen-Anttila, the root KNŠ in NA has been limited to the sense "to assemble," but its fricativized variant ḪNŠ has maintained its initial meaning of "to submit."[808] However, this understanding is now challenged by Luukko, who argues that *knš* in NA was not restricted to the meaning "to assemble," because there are many instances where *knš* is also used in the sense "to submit."[809] In fact, the NA *kanāšu* in the D-stem is attested in the sense "to assemble, collect, gather," with reference to people or a harvest, as is the case in the textual references given above. The fricativization of the initial *k* > *ḫ*, as in *kanāšu* > *ḫanāšu*, has been recognized as a dialectal variation in NA.[810]

AHw. (p. 436b s.v. *kanāšu* II) lists this NA word under a new heading as *kanāšu* II with the meaning "einsammeln," and considers it to be a loanword from Aramaic *knš* "sammeln."[811] In his articles on Aramaic loanwords, von Soden states that *kanāšu* in the sense "(ein)sammeln" is so far only attested in the D-stem and as such is a loanword from Aramaic.[812] Abraham and Sokoloff remark that NA *kanāšu* "to gather in" is considered to be a loanword from Aramaic כנש

805 See CDA (p. 145b s.v. *kanāšu* II). Cf. von Soden, *Or* 46 (1977), p. 188:61, where he gives references for Late-SB.

806 See AHw. (p. 435b s.v. *kanāšu(m)* I); CAD (K, p. 144a s.v. *kanāšu*).

807 See Hämeen-Anttila, SAAS XIII, § 2.1.6.2. Cf. GAG § 25d; Lipiński, *Semitic Languages*, § 18.5. Cf. also E.E. Knudsen, "Spirantization of Velars in Akkadian," in M. Dietrich & W. Röllig (eds.), *lišān mitḫurti* (Neukirchen-Vluyn 1969), p. 155; Kaufman, AIA, pp. 116f, n. 2 & 3.

808 Hämeen-Anttila, ibid.

809 Luukko, SAAS XVI, p. 71. The word *knš* in the sense "to submit," is attested in the following NA letters: SAA X 33 r.16; SAA X 174:16; SAA X 294:29; SAA XV 230:15; SAA XVI 127:12 and CTN V 179 (= ND 2676:7′), whereas *ḫnš* is attested in SAA V 78:9, 12, r.12; SAA V 149:7; SAA V 184:6′; SAA V 286:3.

810 See Hämeen-Anttila, ibid. Cf. Luukko, ibid., pp. 71f. Cf. also I.J. Gelb, "Notes on von Soden's Grammar of Akkadian," *BiOr* 12 (1955), p. 102b, § 25d.

811 Cf. CDA (p. 145b *kanāšu* II); DNWSI (p. 520 s.v. $knš_1$). Cf. also AEAD (p. 46a s.v. *kannušu*). However, the NA verbal forms of *knš* in the sense "to gather in barley, to collect, assemble persons" are listed under *kummusu* in CAD (K, 116a s.v. *kamāsu* A, 4).

812 See von Soden, *Or* 35 (1966), p. 12:61; idem, *Or* 46 (1977), p. 188:61.

and that it replaced the earlier Akkadian word *kamāsu* with a similar sense.[813] The word *kanāšu* in the sense "to assemble" is also found in the NA word *kināltu* "congregation," which is also a loanword from Aramaic.[814]

The Aramaic word כְּנַשׁ "to collect, gather," is cognate with the Hebrew words כָּנַס (and only once as כָּנַשׁ) "to collect, gather."[815] However, the West-Semitic root KNŠ in the sense "to collect, gather" does not seem to be related to the Akkadian root KNŠ "to submit; to bend down, to bow down." Semantically, the meanings "to assemble, collect, gather" are not found in Akkadian *kanāšu* before NA and NB, while in Aramaic, *knš* "to gather, collect, assemble" is well attested. The evidence points to a borrowing from Aramaic into NA and NB.[816]

Interestingly, in a NA letter (SAA X 227 r.12, 13) addressed by the Assyrian scholar Adad-šumu-uṣur to Assurbanipal, the word *knš* occurs twice, namely as *ú-kan*$^{!}$*-ni-šú-u-ni* and *lu-ka-ni-šú-u-ni*, but none of the meanings of the word *kanāšu* "to submit (to)" or the borrowed meaning from Aramaic, "to assemble, collect, gather" fits the context. The context where the word occurs in the NA letter (SAA X 227 r.10–13) reads as follows:[817]

> *a-ki ša* TA* LUGAL *be-lí-iá ke-na-ku-u-ni / ina mu-ti šim-ti la-mu-ut* LUGAL *be-lí liš-pu-ra*$^{!!}$ */ ki-i*$^{!}$ *ša*$^{!}$ *a-na*$^{!}$ $^{m!}$*da*$^{!}$*-da*$^{!}$*-a ú-kan*$^{!}$*-ni-šú-u-ni a-na a-a-ši / lu-ka-ni-šú-u-ni*
>
> May I die at my time according to how loyal I have been to the king, my lord. May the king, my lord, *send word that* just as Dadâ was 'harvested,' so may I be 'harvested.'

In editing the text given above, Parpola tentatively renders these two occurrences, *ú-kan*$^{!}$*-ni-šú-u-ni* and *lu-ka-ni-šú-u-ni*, as "harvested."[818] In a textual note in a previous edition of the same letter, Parpola refers to the same instances quoted above, explaining that they perhaps denote the writer's funeral expressed through a metaphor taken from rural life.[819] He adds that *kannušu* was an agricultural term in the sense "to harvest," and its usage in the passage above is analogous with an expression in Babylonian, where *kms* D "to collect (grain, persons)" also means "to prepare for burial."[820]

In fact, it fits better to translate the two occurrences of the word *kanāšu* in SAA X 227 r.12, 13 with the meaning "to bury, inter, entomb, inhume," taken as a

---

813 See Abraham & Sokoloff, *Reassessment*, p. 36:99.

814 See the discussion below s.v. *kināltu*.

815 See Jastrow (p. 649a s.v. כָּנַס, p. 651b s.v. כָּנַשׁ). Cf. J.C. Greenfield, "Three Related Roots: *KMS*, *KNS* and *KNŠ*," in Sh.M. Paul, M.E. Stone & A. Pinnick (eds.), *'Al Kanfei Yonah: Collected Studies of Jonas C. Greenfield on Semitic Philology*, Vol. II (Leiden 2001), pp. 840–846, n. 9.

816 For further attestations, see K. Deller, "Getreidekursangaben in neuassyrischen Rechtsurkunden," *Or* 33 (1964), p. 260, n. 2.

817 This NA letter (ABL 358 = SAA X 227) is entered under *kunnušu* in CAD (K, p. 146b s.v. *kanāšu*, 5a, 4′).

818 See also the Glossary of SAA X (p. 340a s.v. *kanāšu* B).

819 See LAS II ad no. 122 r.11–13.

820 Ibid. Cf. K. Deller, "Die Briefe des Adad-šumu-uṣur," in W. Röllig & M. Dietrich (eds.), *Lišān mitḫurti: Festschrift Wolfram Freiherr von Soden zum 19.4.1968 gewidmet von Schülern und Mitarbeitern* (Neukirchen-Vluyn 1969), pp. 50f.

loanword from Aramaic *knš*. This etymology is based on the other meanings of the Aramaic word found in Syriac, namely "to shroud, dress for the grave; to bury, inter, entomb, inhume; to die; to put to death, deprive of life."[821] In Syriac, we find expressions such as: ܟܢܫܗ ܐܠܗܐ ܠܘܬ ܐܒܗܘܗܝ "he died," literally "God *assembled* him to his forefathers"; ܟܢܫ ܦܓܪܗ ܕܡܝܬܐ "he buried the corpse of the dead"; ܐܬܟܢܫ ܡܢ ܥܠܡ ܒܝܫܐ "he passed away."[822] CAL offers the following passage from epigraphic JPA: טב ליה לההוא צדיק מתכנש בשלום "it is better that that righteous man should die in peace."[823] This borrowed sense of NA *kannušu* occurs twice in the same text.

Phonologically, the sibilant *š* of the Aramaic word *knš* is expected to appear as *s* when borrowed into NA.[824] Accordingly, we would have anticipated the following development: Aramaic *knš* > NA *kns*. This rule, however, is not observed in this case, most likely because *kanāšu* is already found in Akkadian and NA although in another sense.

katāru v. (G) "to wait; hesitate"

Loanword	Reference	Provenance	Origin	Genre	Date
ak-te-tir	SAA XXI 155:10	Nineveh	Nineveh	L	Asb
i-kàt-te-ru	SAA X 239 r.7′	Nineveh	Nineveh	L	Esh
li-ik-te-ru	SAA X 242 r.8	Nineveh	Nineveh	L	670
ni-ik-te-ti-[*ir*]	SAA V 249:5′	Nineveh	Nineveh	L	Sg
ni-kàt-tir	SAA X 221 r.4	Nineveh	Nineveh	L	669?

Aram. ⇒ NA; NB[825]

Syr., *ktr* v. Pe. "to remain, stay (obsolete *or* rare usage)" Manna 360b. OffAr., CPA, Ma., Syr., *ktr* v. Pa. "to remain, stay; wait for, continue" DNWSI 548; Jastrow 682b; LSp. 99b; DCPA 188a; MD 225b; PSm. 231b; SL 663a; Audo 492a; Manna 360b. Syr., *ktr* v. Pa. "to be amazed *or* astonished; to hesitate" Manna 360b. Sam., *ktr* v. Pa. "to delay, stay; to tarry" DSA 417a; CAL.

The word *katāru* in the sense "to help, aid, assist, get as help, recruit as ally," is attested in NA and SB.[826] It is probably a denominative verb of *kitru* "help, aid, assistance; ally; auxiliary troops; cooperation."[827] Yet, none of these meanings of *katāru* fits the context of the NA letters cited above. Nevertheless, for some of these NA letters, the editors of CAD (K, p. 304a s.v. *katāru* B) list another *katāru*

---

821 For references, see under the comparative data above.
822 For these expressions and some more, see Audo (pp. 470ff s.v. ܟܢܫ).
823 See CAL, s.v. *knš*.
824 See n. 71 above.
825 For a possible attestation of the word under discussion in NB as *ak-te-ra-ma*, see S.W. Cole, *Nippur IV: The Early Neo-Babylonian Governor's Archive from Nippur* (Chicago 1996), no. 63 r.20, and p. 147, n. on l. 20. Cf., however, Abraham & Sokoloff, *Reassessment*, p. 37, n. 302.
826 See AHw. (p. 465a s.v. *katāru* I); CAD (K, p. 303b s.v. *katāru* A); AEAD (p. 48b s.v. *katāru*).
827 See AHw., ibid. Cf. AEAD (p. 51a s.v. *kitru*).

that always occurs in the G-stem, and which they cautiously gloss as "to think, hesitate(?)." AHw. (p. 465a s.v. *katāru* II) also lists another *katāru* in the G-stem in the sense "warten," which is considered to be a loanword from Aramaic *kattar*.[828]

Von Soden, in his articles on Aramaic loanwords, suggests that *katāru* with the meaning "wait" is a borrowing from Aramaic *kattar*, which is in the D-stem of a group of verbs of praying and waiting.[829] He states that the NA forms of the verb are either based on a misunderstanding of the Aramaic D-stem forms as present tense or, as he thinks more likely, is an indication that Old Aramaic also used the verb in the G-stem.[830] Referring to von Soden's loan hypothesis, Parpola renders *katāru* as meaning "to wait, hesitate," and takes it to be a loanword from Aramaic.[831] Abraham and Sokoloff remark that the NA *katāru*, which von Soden connects with later Aramaic כתר, is attested only in the G-stem, unlike the Aramaic word, which is always attested in the D-stem.[832]

As is known, there exist in Akkadian a number of verbs, some of which are intransitive, that imply a durative meaning and are only attested in the D-stem. To these belongs a group of usually weak verbs of waiting, praying and searching, e.g., *qu''û(m)* "to await; wait for," *sullû(m)* "to pray to," and *bu''û(m)* "to look for, search."[833] In our case, all the citations attested for *katāru* in NA with the meaning "to wait, hesitate" are inflected in the G-stem. However, the Aramaic *kattar*, as von Soden points out, is in the D-stem of the group of verbs of praying and waiting. It appears that von Soden's assumption that Old Aramaic probably also used the verb כתר in the G-stem is tenable. His assumption can be substantiated by the rarely attested Syriac *ktr* "to remain, stay" in the Pe'al mode.[834] Although *ktr* in the Pe'al mode is considered to be rare or obsolete in Syriac, it is possible that it represents an archaic usage that was preserved from older stages of Aramaic.

It remains to be mentioned that it seems to fit the context best in the NA letter (SAA X 221 r.4) to render *ni-kàt-tir* with the sense "to hesitate."[835] This meaning of *katāru* is also attested in Syriac, as is indicated in the comparative data above.

kinältu n. f. "congregation, assembly"; (see the discussion above s.v. *kannušu*)

Loanword	Reference	Provenance	Origin	Genre	Date
˹LÚ.*ki*˺-*na*-˹*al*˺-*ti*	SAA XVI 20:5	Nineveh	Nineveh	L	Esh
	SAA XI 155 e.7	Nineveh	*Nineveh*	AD	7th c.

828 Cf. CDA (p. 153b s.v. *katāru* II); DNWSI (p. 548 s.v. *ktr*₁).
829 See von Soden, *Or* 35 (1966), p. 12:66; idem, *Or* 46 (1977), p. 188:66.
830 Ibid.
831 See LAS II ad no. 237.
832 See Abraham & Sokoloff, *Reassessment*, p. 37:106.
833 See GAG § 88h.
834 See Manna (p. 360b s.v. ܟܬܰܪ).
835 Note that CAD (K, p. 304a s.v. *katāru* B), which quotes the same NA letter (ABL 362 r.4 = SAA X 221 r.4), tentatively glosses this word as "to think, hesitate(?)." Cf. AEAD (p. 48b s.v. *katāru* B), which glosses the word as "to wait, hesitate."

	LÚ.*ki-na-al*?-*ti*!				
LÚ*.*ki-na-a*[*l-t*]*i*	SAA XIX 1:3 (RL)	Calah	Calah	L	729?

Aram. ⇒ NB ⇒ NA;[836] LB

JPA *knyšh*, *knyšt'* n. f. "gathering, assembly, synagogue" DJPA 263a. JBA *knyšt'* n. f. "synagogue, congregation" DJBA 588a. Sam., QA, JLA, LJLA *knšh*, *knšt'* n. f. "gathering, assembly" DSA 399a; DJA 57a; Jastrow 652a; CAL. Syr., *knwšt'* (*knuštā*) n. f. "congregation, assembly" PSm. 218a; SL 634a; Manna 345a; Audo 471b.

This word occurs as a *tris legomenon* in NA, where its form is always attested as *kināltu.* [837] AHw. (p. 480b s.v. *kiništu*, *kinaš/ltu*) glosses the word as "Priesterkollegium," and considers it to be a borrowing in NB and LB from Aramaic *kni/uštā*.[838] In CAD (K, p. 386a s.v. *kiništu*, (*kinaštu*, *kinaltu*, *kinartu*)) the word is defined as (class of priests of a low status (concerned with the preparation of food offerings)), and is considered to be an Aramaic loanword in NA and NB.

Saggs renders the word as meaning "congregation," and considers it to be a variant spelling of *kiništu* and *kinaštu*.[839] In his articles on Aramaic loanwords, von Soden also renders *kiništu* and *kinaš/ltu* in the sense "Priesterkollegium" and considers it to be a borrowing from Aramaic *kništā*.[840] On the other hand, Abraham and Sokoloff consider von Soden's rendering of *kiništu* as "priesthood, religious staff" to be untenable because the word denotes an assembly, with a civic capacity, of temple affiliated people.[841] Instead, they consider the word probably to be a borrowing from Aramaic כנישה, as attested in the Jewish Aramaic dialects with the sense "assembly, synagogue."[842] However, the precise meaning and association of *kiništu* has been widely debated by scholars, and it has been rendered differently as "the prebendaries of a temple organization,"[843] or as "temple council."[844]

Interestingly, two of the NA texts cited above in which this loanword occurs are royal letters. The first one (SAA XVI 20:5) is almost certainly a letter sent by the crown prince Assurbanipal to Esarhaddon. The second (SAA XIX 1:3) is a

---

[836] The word also occurs as LÚ.*ki-na-al-ti* in an inscription of Aššūr-etel-ilāni to Marduk (B6 Aei 02:16); see the Corpus of Neo-Assyrian Texts (CNA), s.v. *kinaltu*. See also E. Ebeling, "Eine Weihinschrift Aššureṭililânis für Marduk," *AnOr* 12 (1935), p. 72:15.

[837] See AEAD (p. 50a s.v. *kin, ltu*). Note that in the Glossary of SAA XVI, p. 185b and SAA XIX, p. 238a, the word *kinaltu* is glossed "congregation, assembly," but in SAA XI, p. 163a, *kinaltu* is defined as (a priest).

[838] See also CDA (p. 158b s.v. *kiništu*); DNWSI (p. 520 s.v. *knšh*).

[839] See H.W.F. Saggs, "The Nimrud Letters, 1952–Part V: Administration," *Iraq* 21 (1959), p. 164, n. on l. 3. (NL 54 = ND 2438).

[840] See von Soden, *Or* 35 (1966), p. 13:69; idem, *Or* 46 (1977), p. 189:69.

[841] See Abraham & Sokoloff, *Reassessment*, p. 37:109.

[842] Ibid.

[843] See A.C.V.M. Bongenaar, *The Neo-Babylonian Ebabbar Temple at Sippar: Its Administration and its Prosopography* ([Istanbul] 1997), pp. 150ff.

[844] See *passim* in T. Boiy, *Late Achaemenid and Hellenistic Babylon* (Leuven 2004).

royal letter (*abat šarri*) sent by the Assyrian king Tiglath-pileser III, probably in the year 729 or 720 B.C.

SAA XVI 20:1–7, reads:

a-na MAN EN-˹*ia*˺ [ARAD-*ka* ^{m}*aš-šur*–DÙ–A] / *lu-u* DI-*mu a-na* [MAN EN-*ia*] / ^{d}PA *u* ^{d}AMAR.UTU *a-n*[*a* MAN EN-*ia*] / *lik-*˹*ru*˺*-bu* / ˹*x* LÚ.*ki*˺*-na-*˹*al*˺*-ti* / *ša* ^{m}EN–*šal-lim* LÚ.GAL–KAR / ˹*ur-ta-am*˺*-m*[*e*]

To the king, my lord: [your servant Assurbanipal]. Good health to [the king, my lord]! May Bēl and Nabû bless [the king, my lord]. I rejected the [...] assembly of Bēl-šallim, the chief of trade.

SAA XIX 1:1–8, reads:

a-bat LUGAL / *a-na* LÚ*.TU.ME[Š]–[É] / LÚ*.*ki-na-a*[*l-t*]*i* / LÚ*.SAG.KAL.MEŠ ˹*ša*˺ [*x x*]*x* / *a-na* LÚ*.TIN.TIR.K[I.ME]Š / DI-*mu ia-a-ši* / DI-*mu a-na* KUR–*aš-šur* / ŠÀ-*ku-nu lu* DÙG.GA-*ku-nu*

The king's word to the clergymen, the congrega[ti]on, the leaders of [...] (and) to the citizens of Babylon: I am well, Assyria is well – you can be glad.

Etymologically, the word under discussion here is related to the word *kannušu* "to assemble, gather (people)" which, in turn, is an Aramaic loanword in NA.[845] The Aramaic word occurs in JBA as כְּנִישְׁתָּא "congregation, synagogue," and in Syriac as ܟܢܘܫܬܐ "congregation; synagogue; church." The latter was borrowed into Arabic as كَنِيسَة "church; synagogue, temple."[846] As for the form of the word in NA and NB, from MB and MA on, the sibilant *š* becomes *l* before the dental *t*; i.e., the following development takes place: *št* > *lt*.[847] The *š* is frequently preserved, however, before the *t* of the feminine ending. Hence, the borrowed word is attested as *kinaltu*, but also as *kinaštu*, as in LB.[848] In NA, the *lt* that arises from *št* further develops to *ss*.[849] Accordingly, we expect to see the form of the word in NA to be *kinassu*. Since *kinaltu* is not entirely integrated phonologically into NA, it is likely that this Aramaic loanword is a trans-NB borrowing into NA.

kiqillutu n. f. "dung heap, dunghill, refuse dump"

Loanword	Reference	Provenance	Origin	Genre	Date
ki-qí$^{!}$*-il-te*	SAA VI 200:5	Nineveh	Nineveh	LD	Sn?
ki-qil-li-ti	SAA X 294:15	Nineveh	Nineveh	L	Esh

[845] See the discussion above s.v. *kannušu*. Cf. CDA (p. 158b s.v. *kiništu*).
[846] See *Al-munǧidu* (p. 700b s.v. الكَنِيس); Elias & Elias, p. 605a.
[847] See GAG § 30g.
[848] See AHw. (p. 480b s.v. *kiništu*).
[849] See GAG § 30h, § 34d; Hämeen-Anttila, SAAS XIII, § 2.2.3.2; Luukko, SAAS XVI, § 4.2.4.

ki-qi-lu-tu	SAA VI 31 r.3	Nineveh	Nineveh	LD	709

Aram. ⇒ NA

JBA, JPA, Gal, JLA, LJLA, Syr., CPA *qyqlh*, *qyqlt'* (*qīqlā*, *qīqalṯā*) n. f. "garbage heap, dunghill" DJBA 1015b; DJPA 491b; Jastrow 1367b; PSm. 505a; SL 1365b; Manna 697a; Audo 944b; DCPA 372b. Ma., *qiqla*, *qiqilta* n. f. "dung (heap), dunghill, infamy" MD 412a. OAram., JLA, LJLA *qlqlh*, *qlqlt'* n. f. "garbage heap, garbage dump" DNWSI 1012; Jastrow 1382b; CAL.

This word occurs as a *tris legomenon* in NA. It is first attested in 709 B.C. in a contract (SAA VI 31 r.3), by which Nabû-kabti-aḫḫēšu, scribe of Sargon II, buys land with a plot described as *ki-qi-lu-tu*. In addition, it occurs in a contract (SAA VI 200:5) from the early 7th century B.C., probably during the reign of Sennacherib. The contract mentions a *kí-qí*[!]*-il-te* in the description of a house being purchased. The word is also found in a letter (SAA X 294:15) in which probably the Assyrian scholar Urdu-Gula writes a plea to king Esarhaddon who has lifted him *issu libbi ki-qil-li-ti*, "from the dung heap."

In CAD (K, p. 401a s.v. *kiqillatu*) the word is given as uncertain.[850] In AHw. (p. 483b s.v. *kiqillatu*), the origin of this word is considered to be unknown and its meaning is hesitatingly rendered as "Zwangsverkauf." In contrast, the editors of CDA (p. 159b s.v. *kiqillutu*) gloss the word as "rubbish dump," and consider it to be an Aramaic loanword in NA.[851] In AEAD (p. 50a s.v. *kiqillutu*), the word is glossed "dung heap, dunghill, refuse dump." Actually, rendering *kiqillutu* in the sense "dunghill" was first suggested by Postgate based on a NA context.[852]

The Old Aramaic word *qlqlt'* "garbage heap, garbage dump," in its reduplicated form, is attested for the first time in the Akkadian-Aramaic bilingual inscription from Tell Fekherye.[853] Kaufman points out that *qlqlt'* in this bilingual inscription ought to be taken as plural, since its equivalent in the Akkadian text, i.e., *tubkinnāte*, is in plural.[854] Greenfield and Shaffer highlight that *kiqillutu* is an Aramaic loanword in NA.[855] They add that the form of this loanword in NA resembles a form found in the later dialects of Aramaic, *qīqla*, *qīqilta*.[856] In addition, they call attention to the fact that, in its reduplicated form, *qlqlt'* is also attested in various Targumic texts, but its usual form in the Palestinian,

[850] Cf. K. Deller, W.R. Mayer & J. Oelsner, "Akkadische Lexikographie: *CAD* Q," *Or* 58 (1989), p. 262 ad [252].
[851] Cf. DNWSI (p. 1012 s.v. *qlqlh*).
[852] See Postgate, FNALD, p. 195a s.v. *kiqilūtu* (*kiqillutu*).
[853] See A. Abou-Assaf, P. Bordreuil & A.R. Millard, *La statue de Tell Fekherye et son inscription bilingue assyro-araméenne* (Paris 1982), pp. 23f, l. 22 and p. 36.
[854] See S.A. Kaufman, "Reflections on the Assyrian-Aramaic Bilingual from Tell Fakhariyeh," Maarav 3 (1982), p. 173. Cf. J.N. Postgate, "The Ownership and Exploitation of Land in Assyria in the 1st Millennium B.C.," in M. Lebeau & Ph. Talon (eds.), *Reflets des deux fleuves: Volume de mélanges offerts à André Finet* (Leuven 1989), p. 143, n. 28.
[855] See J.C. Greenfield & A. Shaffer "Notes on the Akkadian-Aramaic Bilingual Statue from Tell Fekherye," *Iraq* 40 (1983), p. 116; idem, "*qlqlt'*, *tubkinnu*, Refuse Tips and Treasure Trove," *AnSt* 33 (1983), p. 125.
[856] Ibid.

Babylonian, Syriac and Mandaic dialects of Aramaic is *qīqlā* in the absolute form and *qīqiltā* in the determined form.[857] Additionally, Greenfield and Shaffer state: "Thus both the more literary *qlqlt'* has been found in the Tell Fekherye inscription and the more colloquial *kiqillutu* in Neo-Assyrian texts. This is added evidence for the use of Aramaic as spoken language in Assyria."[858]

Steiner, referring to Greenfield and Shaffer's statement above to illustrate how transcriptions and loanwords are extremely effective in detecting the vernacular that has been concealed by well-trained scribes, provides the following interesting comment on their statement:

> They could have added that it is also evidence for the antiquity and amazing tenacity of the distinction between written and spoken Aramaic. It appears that well-trained scribes succeeded in suppressing a colloquial form for a millennium until the old norms broke down in Late Aramaic. We know this now thanks to a cuneiform scribe whose career did not depend upon mastering the correct, historical spelling of this word. There is a certain amount of poetic justice in this example. Scholars are always turning to the *sēpiru*, the Aramaic scribe, to find out how Akkadian was pronounced; for once we can thank a *ṭupšarru*, an Akkadian scribe, for information about the pronunciation of Aramaic.[859]

The Aramaic word *qlqlt'* is most likely derived from the quadrilateral verb *qlql* "to defile, to despise, disdain; to ruin," which is formed by duplication of the initially monosyllabic root QYL.[860] However, the shorter form of the Aramaic word, which is attested in the later dialects of Aramaic, i.e., *qīqiltā*, shows, owing to the weakness of the liquids, the dropping of the medial *l*, which is compensated by a lengthening of the preceding vowel.[861] Hence, the following development took place: *qīqiltā* < *qilqiltā*. Greenfield and Shaffer correctly observe that the NA form *kiqillutu* follows the Aramaic form *qīqla*, *qīqilta*. Nevertheless, the doubling of the liquid *l* in the NA form is orthographically clearly marked, as in *ki-qil-li-ti*, which probably occurs as a result of the influence of the longer Aramaic form of the word, or of the word's stress. Furthermore, the initial velar plosive *q* of the Aramaic word exhibits dissimilation to *k* in the NA word. This dissimilation (*q*...*q* > *k*...*q*), is a regular feature of NA.[862] Obviously, the so-called Assyrian vowel harmony is in force here, yielding: *kiqillutu* < *kiqillatu*. Certainly, the Old Aramaic word *qlqlt'* is a case of *Lectio difficilior*. Hence,

---

[857] See J.C. Greenfield & A. Shaffer, "*qlqlt'*, *tubkinnu*, Refuse Tips and Treasure Trove," *AnSt* 33 (1983), p. 123. Cf. Abraham & Sokoloff, *Reassessment*, p. 38:110.

[858] See Greenfield & Shaffer, ibid., p. 125.

[859] R.C. Steiner, "Papyrus Amherst 63: A New Source for the Language, Literature, Religion, and History of the Aramaeans," in M.J. Geller et al. (eds.), *Studia Aramaica: New Sources and New Approaches* (Oxford 1995), pp. 202f.

[860] See E. Lipiński, *Studies in Aramaic Inscriptions and Onomastics, II* (Leuven 1994), p. 70, comment on lines 22b–23. See also Manna (p. 676b s.v. ܩܠܩܠ "to despise, disdain, slight, look down upon," p. 677b s.v. ܩܠܐ "to despise, disdain"). Cf. CAL, s.v. *qlql* "to ruin."

[861] See Lipiński, *Semitic Languages*, § 17.2.

[862] See Hämeen-Anttila, SAAS XIII, § 2.2, § 2.3. Cf. E.E. Knudsen, "Cases of Free Variants in the Akkadian *q* Phoneme," *JCS* 15 (1961), p. 85; GAG § 26b*. See also Table 2 above.

based on chronological grounds, etymology and the distribution of the word, the NA *kiqillutu* must be a borrowing from Aramaic.[863]

Perhaps, the word *kiqillutu* "dung heap" is the origin of the NA personal name K/Qiqillāni. According to PNA, the meaning of this name is possibly connected with NA *kiqillutu.*[864] However, it is known that some children in ancient Mesopotamia were given opprobrious names to protect them against malignant spirits. The form of this personal name as Kiqillāni/u agrees with the NA regular dissimilation (*q…q* > *k…q*), as mentioned above. However, Greenfield and Shaffer correctly note that the form of the name as Qiqillāni is inconsistent with Geers' law.[865]

kirku n. "scroll, roll"

Loanword	Reference	Provenance	Origin	Genre	Date
ki-ir-ki	CTN II 144:4	Calah	*Calah*	LD	711
	CTN II 145:3	Calah	*Calah*	LD	710
	SAA I 34 r.19′	Nineveh	Nineveh	L	Sg
ki-ir-ku	PVA 269	Assur	Assur	LL	–
ki-ri-ka	FNALD 14:23	Calah	Calah	LD	PC

Aram. ⇒ NA; LB

JBA *krk'* n. m. "roll, scroll" DJBA 602b. Syr., *krk'* (*kerkā*) "a written roll; scroll; volume, tome" PSm. 227b; Audo 484a; Manna 353a; SL 654a. JPA, JBA, Sam., CPA, Ma., Syr., *krk* v. "to wrap up; wrap around, roll; go around" DJPA 269b; DJBA 601b; DSA 410a; Jastrow 668b; LSp. 97b; DCPA 185a; MD 223a; Manna 352b; Audo 483b; PSm. 226b; SL 652b; CAL.

AHw. (p. 468a s.v. *kerku* II) lists this word in the meaning "Rolle," and considers it to be a loan from Aramaic.[866] The editors of CAD (K, p. 408a s.v. *kirku* B) list this word in the sense "roll," and tentatively consider it to be a borrowing from Aramaic. In NA, *kirku* in the sense "scroll (of papyrus)" occurs in a letter from Nineveh (SAA I 34 r.19′) concerned with distributing tribute and audience gifts. It occurs in the meaning "roll" in association with cloth (FNALD 14:23) and is also listed in the garment section of a lexical list (PVA 269). It is also attested in the sense "roll," probably in connection with gold-leaf used as inlay (CTN II

[863] The rendering "Zwangsverkauf," in AHw., ought to be rejected.
[864] See PNA 2/I (p. 618a s.v. Kiqillānu). In AHw. (p. 483b s.v. *kiqillatu*) the PN *Qi-qi-la-a-ni* is erroneously considered as occurring in MA. The same error is quoted in J.C. Greenfield & A. Shaffer, "*qlqlt'*, *tubkinnu*, Refuse Tips and Treasure Trove," *AnSt* 33 (1983), p. 125, n. 12. Cf. Postgate, TCAE, p. 344; K. Deller, W.R. Mayer & J. Oelsner, "Akkadische Lexikographie: *CAD* Q," *Or* 58 (1989), p. 263 ad [268b].
[865] See Greenfield & Shaffer, ibid.
[866] See also von Soden, *Or* 35 (1966), p. 13:67; idem, *Or* 46 (1977), p. 188:67. Cf. DNWSI (p. 536 s.v. *krk*$_2$); CDA (p. 155a s.v. *kerku* II); AEAD (p. 50a s.v. *kirku*).

144:4; CTN II 145:3), which most probably was rolled to make it easier to store and transport.[867]

Abraham and Sokoloff point out that the essential meaning of the Aramaic word כרך is "to roll," from which a substantive with the sense "scroll" was derived.[868] They dismiss the possibility of deriving NA and LB *kirku*, meaning "roll," from Akkadian *karāku*, because the latter has an entirely different meaning.[869] In Syriac, the expression ܟܪܟܐ ܕܕܗܒܐ refers to a "roll of gold(-leaf); gold plate (to overlay with)."[870] This may be parallel to a usage found in the NA legal document (CTN II 145:1–4), which reads as follows:

> 2 GÍN KUG.GI / TA* ŠÀ *gi-za-a-ti / a-na ki-ir-ki / ša tam-lit*
>
> 2 shekels of gold, out of the clippings, for rolls for the inlay.

Semantically, from the root KRK in Akkadian there is a verb found in NA, SB and LB as *karāku* with the sense "to obstruct, to dam (a canal or waterway); to immerse, soak, intertwine."[871] There is also a substantive found in OB and LB as *kirku* with the meaning "regulated water in a canal."[872] However, these meanings of *karāku* and *kirku* in Akkadian do not fit the context of the NA occurrences quoted above. Hence, our word must be a borrowing from Aramaic.

kurḫu n. "a separate little dwelling; a hut, cabin"

Loanword	Reference	Provenance	Origin	Genre	Date
˹É.*kur*˺-*ḫi*	As 12002:4 (= VAT 19511)	Assur	Assur	LD	621*
	StAT 2 263:8 É.*kur*$^{?}$-*ḫi*	Assur	Assur	LD	622*
É.*ku-ur-ḫu*	CTN III 2:3	Calah	Calah	L	7th c.
É.*kur-ḫu*	CTSHM 30:8 (= Ass 13955gl)	Assur	Assur	LD	7th c.
	Rfdn 17 10:8 É.*kur*$^{!}$-*ḫu*	Assur	Assur	LD	612*
˹É˺.*kur*-˹*ḫu*˺	StAT 3 14:4	Assur	Assur	LD	8th c.
	StAT 2 98 r.2 É.˹*kur*$^{?}$-*ḫu*˺	Assur	Assur	LD	615*
	StAT 3 3:7 É$^{?!}$.*kur*$^{?}$-*ḫ*[*u*]$^{?!}$	Assur	Assur	LD	PC

Aram. ⇒ NA

---

867 See n. ad CTN II 144:4.
868 See Abraham & Sokoloff, *Reassessment*, p. 37:106.
869 Ibid.
870 See Audo (p. 484a s.v. ܟܪܟܐ).
871 See CAD (K, p. 199a s.v. *karāku*). Cf. AHw. (p. 446a s.v. *karāku*); CDA (p. 148a s.v. *karāku*).
872 See CAD (K, p. 408a s.v. *kirku* A). Cf. AHw. (p. 468a s.v. *kerku*(*m*) I).

Syr., *krḥ*, *kwrḥ'* (*kūraḥ*, *kūrḥā*) n. m. "a hut, shed, hovel, cabin; a (hermit's) cell, a separate little dwelling" PSm. 211a; SL 613a; Manna 351b; Audo 482b. Hatran *krḥ* n. m. "enclosing wall(?)" DNWSI 535; CAL. Syr., *kūrḥōnā* n. m. "small cell" SL 613a. Syr., *kurḥāyā* adj. "one who lives in a cell, a hermit" PSm. 211a; Manna 351b; Audo 482b.

The word É.*kur-ḫu* is so far attested in several texts from Assur and one text from Calah. It is only listed in AEAD (p. 52a s.v. *kurḫu*), in the sense "workshop." The textual evidence from Assur points to the fact that É is here the determinative which designates buildings.[873]

Based on CTN III 2:3: É.*ku-ur-ḫu*, Radner points out that the reading of the cuneiform sign (kur) in the other NA instances of this word would either give the sound value *kur* or *qúr*.[874] Furthermore, she argues that in searching for an Akkadian etymology, a reading such as É.*qúr-ḫu* > *qurḫu* in the sense "ice house," with a nominal form *PuRS-*, connected to Akkadian *qarāḫu* "to freeze," and *qarḫu* "ice," would make sense.[875] Nevertheless, she dismisses such an interpretation due to the complete lack of words such as **qur-ḫu* or **qu-ur-ḫu* in Akkadian.[876] Radner adds that the other possible reading of the word is *kurḫu*, which seems to be related to the term *kirḫu* or *kerḫu* "citadel, fortified area within a city; circumvallation, enclosure wall of a sanctuary," but such a connection cannot be safely determined or rejected.[877]

In Radner's opinion *kurḫu* is most likely derived from a Hurrian verbal root known as *kur*, which has been tentatively rendered as "to manufacture, produce."[878] She points out that the Nuzi texts contain an expression, namely *bēt kurdi*, the latter part of which has been tentatively analyzed as *kur=di* in the sense "workshop."[879] According to Radner, *kurḫu* can now be interpreted as a Hurrian loanword in NA with the sense "workshop," consisting of *kur=ḫi*, where *=ḫi* is a suffix meaning "belonging to."[880] She adds that, regrettably, the numerous attestations now available cannot shed light on the purpose of *kurḫu* and thereby prove the suggested interpretation given above; the fact remains however that it can be easily deduced from the evidence at hand that *kurḫu* is connected with "workshop."[881]

Against Radner's hypothesis above one can point out that the interpretation of the Hurrian verbal root KUR is not firmly established and therefore it cannot guarantee the validity of conclusions based on it. Also the interpretation provided in the form of *kur=di* "workshop," is only tentative. Radner's explanation of *=ḫi* as a suffix meaning "belonging to" is unclear. Hence, the proposed Hurrian

---

873 See K. Radner, SAAS VI, p. 274, n. 1532. See also VAT 19511:4: 3-*su ša* ˹É.*kur*˺-*ḫi*; StAT 2 263:8, *meš-lu* TÙR *šá* É.*kur*?-*ḫi*.
874 See Radner, ibid., p. 274.
875 Ibid.
876 Ibid. pp. 274f.
877 Ibid. See further AHw. (pp. 467f s.v. *kerḫu*(*m*)); CAD (K, pp. 404f s.v. *kirḫu*). In CAD, *kirḫu* is considered to be a foreign word.
878 See Radner, ibid., p. 275.
879 Ibid.
880 Ibid.
881 Ibid.

etymology is by no means certain and the connection postulated between NA *kurḫu* and the assumed Hurrian source word *kur* is highly doubtful. Actually, nothing in the NA textual contexts gives reason for rendering *kurḫu* as "workshop."

As mentioned above, NA *kurḫu* lacks a satisfactory Akkadian etymology. According to the attested NA evidence, *kurḫu* may designate an independent construction[882] or a part of a house.[883] In addition, it is usually connected with a courtyard (*tarbāṣu*).[884] In one case, *kurḫu* is situated in a courtyard,[885] and in another instance the courtyard is described as belonging to the *kurḫu*-building.[886] A highly possible etymological suggestion is to consider *kurḫu* a loanword from Aramaic *kurḥā* n. m. "a separate little dwelling; a hut, cabin." In fact, both the meaning and the form of the Aramaic word attested in Syriac ܟܘܪܚܐ "a hut, a separate little dwelling," bear a close resemblance to those of the NA *kurḫu*, which also refers to some type of construction. The Syriac word is borrowed into Arabic as الكِرْخ "a (hermit's) cell."[887] Phonetically, the Aramaic pharyngeal /*ḥ*/ is usually rendered <*ḫ*> in NA.[888]

kuribtu n. f. "a plowed field?"

Loanword	Reference	Provenance	Origin	Genre	Date
ku-ri-bat[!]	SAA VI 137:4	Nineveh	Nineveh	LD	693

Aram. ⇒ NA [?]

JPA, JBA, Ma., Syr., *krb*, *krb'* (*krāb*, *krābā*) n. m. "plowing; furrow, plowed or tilled field" DJPA 268a; DJBA 213b; Jastrow 663b; MD 222b; SL 646b, Manna 350b, Audo 480a; PSm. 224b. JBA, Ma., Syr., *krb* v. "to plow, till (the ground)" DJBA 598b; Jastrow 663b; MD 223a; SL 646b; PSm. 224a; Audo 479b; Manna 350a.

This term occurs only once in a NA legal document concerning a copper loan guaranteed by a pledge of land (SAA VI 137:4), where the meanings of the Akkadian word *karābu* "to pray, bless, greet" do not fit the context. Hence, it is a *hapax legomenon*, and the plausibility of etymologies proposed for it is determined by the sentence context. The context where the word occurs (SAA VI 137:2–4) reads as follows:

---

882 CTN III 2:3; StAT 3 3:7; StAT 3 14:4; As 12002:4.
883 StAT 2 263:8, 11; Rfdn 17 10:8; CTSHM 30:8.
884 StAT 3 14:4; As 12002:4; StAT 2 263:8, 11; CTSHM 30:8; Rfdn 17 10:8.
885 Rfdn 17 10:8, TÙR É.*kur*[!]-*ḫu ina* ŠÀ-*bi* "A courtyard: a *kurḫu* within (it)."
886 StAT 2 263:8, *meš-lu* TÙR *šá* É.*kur*[?]-*ḫi* "half of the courtyard of the *kurḫu* building," 11, TÙR É.[*kur-ḫi*] "the courtyard of the *kurḫu* building."
887 See *Al-munǧidu* (p. 680a s.v. كرخ).
888 For the representation of Aramaic *ḥ* by NA *ḫ*, see n. 313 above.

> É 1 ANŠE ˹5BÁN$^{?}$˺ / ˹É$^{!}$˺ 1 ANŠE 5BÁN *ina* SAG$^{!}$ *ka-pi* É *x*[*x*] / ˹É$^{!}$˺ 1 ANŠE *ku-ri-bat*$^{!}$ *ina* UGU *na-*[*ḫal-li*]
> An estate of 1 hectare *5* decares (of land), an estate of 1 hectare 5 decares on top of an embankment, an estate of x[…], and an estate of 1 hectare of *plowed* (*field*) on the w[adi].

This word is not listed in AHw., CAD or CDA.[889] It is, however, included in AEAD (p. 52a s.v. *kuribtu*), where it is defined as (a kind of field). Kwasman and Parpola, the editors of SAA VI, tentatively translate the word *ku-ri-bat* as "plowed (field)" and suggest connecting it with Aramaic **krb* "to plow," which they reconstruct based on Syriac ܟܪܳܒܐ "furrow, fallow ground."[890] However, Jursa rejects considering *kuribtu* (*ku-ri-bat*) a loanword, stating that neither such a word nor the nominal form *PuRiSt* is attested in Aramaic.[891] Abraham and Sokoloff point out that no feminine nominal form of the root KRB "plowing, furrow" occurs in Aramaic.[892]

The Aramaic verb כרב "to plow, till (the ground)" is borrowed into Arabic as كَرَبَ "to till the land."[893] Akkadian has a the term *miḫṣu* meaning "plowed land," but this term is not attested in NA.[894] However, the form of *kuribtu* is that of *PuRiSt*, which probably functions as the Akkadian nominal pattern *PuRīSt*, with a diminutive or pejorative sense.[895] This nominal form is possibly used here to indicate "a small plowed (field)." Semantically, the meanings of the Akkadian root KRB do not fit the context of the NA text. Hence, the borrowing is based on the meaning of the Aramaic word. The word's nominal form, on the other hand, is that of Akkadian.

leḫmu n. "bread; food, victuals"

Loanword	Reference	Provenance	Origin	Genre	Date
liḫ-mu	SAA XIII 147 r.6	Nineveh	*Nineveh*	L	7th c.

Aram. ⇒ NA

OAram., OffAr., Palm., JPA, JBA, CPA, Sam., Syr., *lḥm*, *lḥm*ʾ (*lḥem*, *laḥmā*) n. m. "bread, food" DNWSI 572; DJPA 280b; DJBA 622b; Jastrow 704a; LSp. 102b; DCPA 198b; DSA 433a; SL 685b; PSm. 240b; Manna 375a; Audo 509b; CAL. Ma., *lhm*ʾ (*lahma*) n. m. "bread, food, subsistence, livelihood" MD 227a. Syr. *lḥm* v. Pa. "to bake" Manna 374b.

---

889 Cf. Zimmern, AF, p. 40 s.v. *kirubū*; Kaufman, AIA, p. 85 s.v. *qarbatu*.

890 See n. ad SAA VI 137:4. Cf. PSm., (p. 224b s.v. ܟܪܳܒܐ). Cf. also n. ad NALDK 397:4.

891 See M. Jursa, Review of "Legal Transactions of the Royal Court of Niniveh [*sic*], Part I. Tiglath-Pileser III through Esarhaddon," by K. Theodore & S. Parpola, *WZKM* 84 (1994), p. 207 ad 137.

892 See Abraham & Sokoloff, *Reassessment*, p. 24, n. 31 no. 11.

893 See Fraenkel, pp. 126f. Cf. *Al-munğidu* (p. 679b s.v. كَرَبَ no. 3).

894 See CAD (M/II p. 62a s.v. *miḫṣu* no. 7).

895 See GAG § 55k, for the SB and NA example *butiqtu* "(little) dam breach." Cf. CDA (p. 50b s.v. *butiqtu* "(water-flow from) dam breach"); AEAD (p. 18b s.v. *butiqtu* n. f. "water conduit(?)").

This word is a *hapax legomenon* in NA. It occurs in a letter concerning Ištar of Arbela sent by a priest to either Esarhaddon or Assurbanipal. The letter mentions that the goddess has gone up to the divine 'party' in Arbela. The context where *leḫmu* is attested (SAA XIII 147 r.2–8) reads as follows:

> ANŠE.KUR.RA *ina* É.GAL / *liš-ši-ú* / *un-qu ina* UGU LÚ.GAL*–da-ni-bat* / *lid-di-nu-u-ni* / *liḫ-mu lid-di-na* / *ku-um* ^{d}15 / *ta-du-kan*$^{!}$*-ni*$^{!}$*-ni*
>
> They should take a horse from the palace and give me a sealed order concerning the chief victualler (to the effect) that he should give me *sacrificial bread*, lest Ištar kill me.

The word *leḫmu* is not listed in AHw., CAD or CDA. It is, however, included in AEAD (p. 55a s.v. *leḫmu*) with the sense "food, victuals." Deller transliterates the word as *laḫ-mu* and, in light of a Biblical Hebrew instance, suggests that this NA word is related to Hebrew and Aramaic *lḥm* in the sense "bread."[896] Cole and Machinist, the editors of the NA letter (SAA XIII 147), refer to Deller and translate the word *leḫmu* tentatively as "sacrificial bread."[897]

The Semitic root LḤM is found in Phoenician as a verb in the sense "to eat, devour."[898] It is also attested in Punic, Hebrew and Aramaic as a noun with the meaning "bread, food."[899] However, in Arabic the word لَحْم, of the same root, means "meat; flesh."[900]

In Akkadian, a reflex of the Semitic root LḤM is found in the verb *lêmu* "to consume, eat and drink," for which we can posit the following development: **laḥāmum* > *le'ēmum* > *lêmu*(*m*). The word occurs in Old Akkadian as *le'ēmum*, which exhibits replacement of the voiceless pharyngeal fricative /*ḥ*/ by the expected glottal stop ' (hamza). In NA it is attested as *liāmu* "to taste."[901] Instead, NB and LB utilize the word *laḫāmu*/*leḫēmu* in the sense "to consume, eat, taste."[902] The latter is attested for instance in two NB letters (SAA XVII 140 r.7′ *il-ḫi-mu*; SAA XIX 130:12′ *al-ḫi-im*). This *laḫāmu*/*leḫēmu* is most likely a borrowing from Aramaic as attested in Syriac ܠܚܡ "to eat."[903]

As mentioned above, *lḥm* as a noun meaning "bread, food" is attested in some West-Semitic languages, including Aramaic. However, based on the postulated phonological development of the root LḤM in Akkadian, as seen above in the

---

[896] See K. Deller, "Marginalien zu den Rechtsurkunden aus Balawat," *Or* 34 (1965), p. 169.

[897] See n. ad SAA XIII 147 r.6. However, in the Glossary of SAA XIII, p. 187a, the meaning of *liḫmu* is considered uncertain.

[898] See DNWSI (p. 572 s.v. *lḥm*$_2$). According to PSm., (p. 240a s.v. ܠܚܡ), a verb *lḥm* is also attested in Syriac with the meaning "to eat."

[899] See DNWSI (p. 572 s.v. *lḥm*$_4$).

[900] See Wehr-Cowan, p. 861b.

[901] See AEAD (p. 55b s.v. *liāmu*); E. Ebeling, "Kultische Texte aus Assur," *Or* 20 (1951), p. 402 ii 19.

[902] See P.-A. Beaulieu, "Aspects of Aramaic and Babylonian Linguistic Interaction in First Millennium BC Iraq," *Journal of Language Contact* 6 (2013), pp. 372f.

[903] See the Glossary section of SAA XVII (p. 181a s.v. *laḫāmu*); SAA XIX (p. 239a s.v. *leḫēmu*). See also CAD (p. 38b s.v. *laḫāmu*, p. 116a s.v. *leḫēmu*, p. 126a s.v. *lêmu*); AEAD (p. 55a s.v. *leḫēmu*); CDA (p. 179b s.v. *leḫēmu*); PSm. (p. 240a s.v. ܠܚܡ); Manna (p. 374b s.v. ܠܚܡ).

verb *lêmu*, the form of the NA word *leḫmu* strongly points to a borrowing from West-Semitic, most likely from Aramaic. The first cuneiform sign *liḫ* of the NA word *liḫ-mu* can also be read as *laḫ*,[904] which would lead to a reading such as *laḫmu*. The form of the latter, with the vowel *a*, would also point to a loan from Aramaic, as there would be no *e*-coloring, i.e., an umlaut of *a* > *e*, as expected from the usual reduction of *ḥ* > ʾ and ultimately complete disappearance of the glottal stop ʾ (hamza).[905] Phonologically, the Aramaic pharyngeal /*ḥ*/ is usually expressed by <*ḫ*> in NA.[906]

madbar, *midbar*, *mudābur* n. "desert, plateau, steppe"

Loanword	Reference	Provenance	Origin	Genre	Date
mad-bar	SAA I 176 r.9 *⸢mad!⸣-bar*, 15 *mad!-bar*	Calah	Ḫamāt	L	Sg
	SAA I 178 r.4 *mad-bar!*	Nineveh	*Ṣūpat*	L	Sg
	SAA I 256:4′	Nineveh	–	L	Sg
	SAA V 139:6	Nineveh	Eastern Provinces	L	Sg
	SAA XI 206 i 12′ *mad!-bar*	Nineveh	Harran	AD	Sg
	SAA XII 50 r.33′	Nineveh	Nineveh	AD	Asb
mad-bar-ma	SAA V 139:9	Nineveh	Eastern Provinces	L	Sg
mid-bar	SAA I 13:15′ (RL)	Nineveh	Nineveh	L	Sg
mu-da-⸢bir⸣	SAA XIX 12 r.8′	Calah	Calah	L	8th c.
	CTN II 188:5 *m*[*u*]*-da-bir*	Calah	Assur	L	8th c.
mu-da-bi-ri	SAA X 294 r.17	Nineveh	Nineveh	L	Esh
	SAA XI 227:2, 5	Nineveh	*Nineveh*	AD	7th c.
	SAA XV 53 e.12 *mu!-da-bi-r*[*i*]	Nineveh	Parsua	L	Sg
	SAA XIX 37 r.13′	Calah	Western Provinces	L	Tgl
mu-da-bur	CTN II 188:9	Calah	Assur	L	8th c.
[KUR.*m*]*u!-da-bar!*	SAA V 256 r.5′	Nineveh	–	L	Sg
[KU]R.*mu-da-bir*	SAA I 105 r.1	Nineveh	Assur	L	Sg
KUR.*mu-da-bi-ri*	SAA XIX 19:13[907]	Calah	*Calah*	L	Sg
	SAA XIX 3:12 (RL) ⸢KUR⸣.*mu-⸢da-bir⸣*	Calah	Calah	L	8th c.
	SAA XIX 3:15 (RL) KUR.*⸢mu-da⸣-bi-ri*	Calah	Calah	L	8th c.

[904] See Deller, ibid. Cf. Borger, ABZ, no. 381.
[905] See GAG § 9a.
[906] For the representation of Aramaic *ḥ* by NA *ḫ*, see n. 313 above.
[907] For the interpretation that *mudabiru* (*madbaru*, AHw, 275a) must have meant the corn-growing plain, rather than specifically desert, or may have become a toponym, see n. ad ND 2355:13 (CTN V, p. 194).

Aram. ⇒ NA; LB; SB

W.Sem. ⇒ OB; Mari; MA; MB

OAram., OffAr., JBA, JPA, CPA, Sam., Syr., *mdbr*, *mdbr'* (*madbar*, *madbrā*) n. m. "desert, wilderness, steppe" Brauner 327; DNWSI 595; DJBA 642a; DJPA 291a; Jastrow 731b; LSp. 42a; DCPA 209b; DSA 168a; SL 712a; PSm. 251b; Manna 135b; Audo 174a; CAL.

In AHw. (p. 572a s.v. *madbaru*), this word is glossed "Steppe, Wüste," and its source is considered to be the Ugaritic, Canaanite or Aramaic *mi/adbar*. The editors of CAD (M/I, p. 11b s.v. *madbaru*) render this word as "steppe, desert," but provide no etymological discussion or loan hypothesis and only refer to von Soden's analysis of this word. CDA (p. 187b s.v. *mabaru(m)*), on the other hand, tentatively considers this word to be a borrowing from West-Semitic.

The borrowing of this word into Akkadian was already suggested by Delitzsch, who connected it with Syriac ܡܕܒܪܐ "wasteland, steppe."[908] Zimmern too considered this word a loan from West-Semitic.[909] Deller, on the other hand, argued that this term should probably be regarded as a West-Semitic loanword in Akkadian due to its sound shape, which contains an *m*-prefix in a root which has a labial.[910] Likewise, von Soden states that because of the prefix *ma-* in a labial-containing root, the word *madbaru* "desert, steppe," as well as its Assyrian variant *mud(a)baru* and its genitive form with a vowel harmony *mudabiri*, are certainly not Akkadian.[911] He adds that the attested MA form of the word, *mudbaru*, from the time of Tiglathpileser I (ca. 1115–1077 B.C.), may be borrowed from Canaanite or Old Aramaic, but the later form, namely *madbaru*, is certainly borrowed from Aramaic.[912] Abraham and Sokoloff provide a reference to the attestation of this word in Mari, from which they conclude that the word was probably borrowed into Akkadian in two different periods.[913]

The native word for "steppe, desert" in Akkadian is *ṣēru*. However, NA only utilizes the word *madbar* "steppe, desert" and its other forms, i.e., *midbar*, *mudābur*. The latter is indeed a very early West-Semitic loanword in Akkadian, and is now also attested in OB.[914] The word occurs in Ugaritic as *mdbr*,[915] in Hebrew as מִדְבָּר,[916] and in Syriac as ܡܕܒܪܐ,[917] all in the sense "desert." Moreover,

[908] See F. Delitzsch, *Assyrisches Handwörterbuch* (Leipzig 1896), p. 393a s.v. *mudbaru*.
[909] See Zimmern, AF, p. 43.
[910] See K. Deller, *Lautlehre des Neuassyrischen* (Wien 1959), § 19h.
[911] See von Soden, *Or* 35 (1966), p. 15:80; idem, *Or* 46 (1977), p. 189:80. Cf. DNWSI (p. 595 s.v. *mdbr*); Tadmor, *Aramaization*, pp. 455, 467 n. 100.
[912] See von Soden, ibid.
[913] See Abraham & Sokoloff, *Reassessment*, p. 39, n. 342 and 343. See also J.-M. Durand, *Archives épistolaires de Mari I/1* (Paris 1988), p. 114, n. b) ad no. 14:10.
[914] For the OB attestation, see M.P. Streck, *Das amurritische Onomastikon der altbabylonischen Zeit*: Vol. I (Münster 2000), p. 103.
[915] See DUL, p. 525.
[916] See Jastrow, p. 731a; Dalman, p. 214a.
[917] See SL, p. 712a.

the word in NA is also attested in the form of the masculine personal name Mudabirāiu "Steppe-dweller."[918] It is worth mentioning that the word occurs as מדברא on the fifth line of an Aramaic letter from the time of Assurbanipal (ca. 650 B.C.), known as Assur Ostracon, unearthed in a private house near the western town wall of the city of Assur.[919]

Etymologically, the root DBR is very rare in Akkadian and the meaning of its derivative, *dabāru*, is unknown.[920] However, the most salient evidence that the word under discussion here is borrowed into Akkadian is its nominal prefomative *ma-*. According to "Barth's law," the initial *m* of the nominal preformative *m*^{a}*/e-* dissimilates in Akkadian and becomes *n*^{a}*/e-* when prefixed to roots containing a labial radical (*b*, *p*, or *m*).[921] Accordingly, the form of the word in Akkadian is expected to appear as **nadbaru*.

The first vowel *u* instead of the expected *a*, in *mudabir* and *mudabur*, is probably caused by the open syllable having the initial labial nasal *m*.[922] The first vowel *i* instead of the expected *a*, in *mid-bar*, is probably the result of using Akkadographic spelling for writing an Aramaic word, i.e., the use of an Akkadian word spelled syllabically to stand for an Aramaic lexeme in a NA text. In this case, the first syllable *mid* is written with the CVC-sign (bat), which when occurring in the first position in a NA word has, among other things, the sound value (mid).[923]

It is more likely that our word was borrowed into NA specifically from Aramaic because language contact between NA and Aramaic in the first millennium B.C., was more intensive than the language contact between NA and the other West-Semitic languages.

magguru v. (D only) "to tear down"[924]

Loanword	Reference	Provenance	Origin	Genre	Date
tu-un-ʾtaʾ-gi-ir	SAA XIX 100 r.13′	Calah	Babylonia	L	Tgl
un-ta-gír	SAA I 179:12	Nineveh	*Ṣūpat*	L	Sg

[918] See PNA 2/II (p. 759a s.v. Mudabirāiu). For a possible Syriac parallel, see SL (p. 712a s.v. ܡܕܒܪܝܐ n. m. "one living in the desert").

[919] See M.F. Fales, "New Light on Assyro-Aramaic Interference: The Assur Ostracon," in F.M. Fales & G.F. Grassi (eds.), CAMSEMUD 2007: Proceedings of the 13th Italian Meeting of Afro-Asiatic Linguistics, Held in Udine, May 21st–24th, 2007 (Padova 2010), p. 195, l. 5. See also Figure 7 on p. 47 above.

[920] See AHw. (p. 147b s.v. *dabāru*); CAD (D, p. 14a s.v. *dabāru*). Cf. E. Lipiński, "'Leadership' The Roots DBR and NGD in Aramaic," in M. Dietrich & I. Kottsieper (eds.), "Und Mose schrieb dieses Lied auf" (Münster 1998), pp. 501, 506.

[921] See J. Barth, "Das Nominalpräfix *na* im Assyrischen," *ZA* 2 (1887), pp. 111ff. See also W.C. Delsman, "Das Barth'sche Gesetz und Lehnwörter," *UF* 11 (1979), pp. 187f; GAG § 31b, § 56b; Kaufman, AIA, p. 20.

[922] Cf. Hämeen-Anttila, SAAS XIII, § 2.4.1; Luukko, SAAS XVI, p. 84; K. Deller, *Lautlehre des Neuassyrischen* (Wien 1959), § 19–21.

[923] See Luukko, SAAS XVI, § 3.14, especially p. 52 s.v. bat. See also Borger, ABZ, no. 69.

[924] See AEAD (p. 58a s.v. *magguru*). See also the Glossary of SAA I, p. 219a; SAA XIX (p. 240a s.v. *magguru*).

ú-ta-gi-i[*r*]	SAA XIX 196:2′	Calah	–	L	8th c.

Aram. ⇒ NA

OffAr., BA, JLA, LJLA *mgr* v. Pa. "to overthrow; to drag down; to diminish, destroy" DNWSI 594; Jastrow 730a; CAL. JBA *mgr* v. "to vanquish" DJBA 641b. Syr., *mgr* v. "to fall" SL 710b; Manna 931a; CAL.

In Akkadian, the word *magāru* in the G-stem has the meanings "to consent, agree, accept, be in agreement, obey; to grant a person something; to favor." In the D-stem, it is attested in OA in the sense "to bring to agreement, to make agree, make obey," and in SB in the sense "to reconcile."[925] However, *magāru* in the D-stem is attested in three different NA letters, as listed above, but in all the three instances the Akkadian meanings of *magāru* do not fit the context. For instance, in one of the NA letters (SAA I 179:12), the word occurs in the D-stem as *un-ta-gír* but none of the Akkadian meanings mentioned above fit the context. Parpola translates *un-ta-gír* as meaning "I have torn down," and considers it to be a loanword from Aramaic *mgr* in the D-stem with the meaning "to overthrow."[926] The editors of CDA (p. 215a s.v. *mugguru*) list a verb in the D-stem as *mugguru* with the meaning "to tear down (building)" and consider it to be a borrowing from Aramaic into NA. The following are the three instances of the NA word under discussion. SAA XIX 100 r.12′–13′, reads:

> *ši-*⸢*i*⸣ [*a*]-⸢*na*⸣ *qa-ni ta-at-t*[*u-ṣ*]*i* / *i-*⸢*si*[!]⸣*-t*[*ú*] *ša* GIŠ.SAR *tu-un-*⸢*ta*⸣*-gi-ir*
>
> She we[nt] out and demolished the tower of the orchard.
>
> SAA I 179:8–12, reads:
>
> LÚ*.ENGAR LÚ*.NU.GIŠ.SAR / [*ša* ᵐ*a-mi*]*–li-i'-ti* DUMU ᵐ*a-me-ri* / [TA* ŠÀ U]RU.MEŠ*-ia uk-ta-ši-di* / [*x x-t*]*ú ši-i ša* UDU.MEŠ *ša ir-ṣip-u-ni* / *un-ta-gír*
>
> I have driven the farmer(s) and gardener(s) [of Ammi]li'ti son of Amiri [out of] my towns and torn down a […] of sheep he had constructed.
>
> SAA XIX 196:2′–4′, reads:
>
> *a-tu-r*[*i*]-⸢*di* URU⸣.MEŠ *ú-ta-gi-i*[*r*] / *a-sa-rap* ŠE.P[A]D.MEŠ *a-ta-ta-ḫa* / *ina* URU.⸢*bir-ti*⸣ [*a*]*k-ta-ra-ra*
>
> I wen[t d]own, razed the towns and burnt them, lifted the ba[rl]ey and [p]iled it up in the fort.

Semantically, the meanings of the Aramaic word *mgr* "to destroy, overthrow" fit the contexts of the three NA texts quoted above. Also, the usage of the NA

[925] See CAD (M/I, p. 34b s.v. *magāru*); AHw. (575a s.v. *magāru*(*m*)).
[926] See n. ad SAA I 179:12. Cf. n. ad SAA XIX 100 r.13.

magguru in the D-stem inflection with the meaning “to tear down” matches that of the Aramaic intensive inflection Pa‘‘el. The evidence points to the word being a borrowing from Aramaic, and as such it is a *tris legomenon* in NA. The forms of the NA words *un-ta-gír* “I have torn down” and *tu-un-⸢ta⸣-gi-ir* “she demolished” display partial assimilation of the first radical, the labial nasal *m*, to the following voiceless dental plosive infix *-t*, resulting in: *m* + *t* > *nt*.[927] On the other hand, the form of the word *ú-ta-gi-i*[*r*] “I have torn down” shows a complete regressive assimilation, i.e., *m* + *t* > *tt*.[928] Hence, all the three borrowing instances show that this loanword is phonologically integrated into NA. However, based on the semantic range of the root MGR in Akkadian and Aramaic, it seems that this root is not a cognate in these two Semitic languages.

makaḫalūtu n. f. “kohl pen, eyeliner”

Loanword	Reference	Provenance	Origin	Genre	Date
ma-ka-ḫa-lu-u-tú	Iraq 16, p. 37f. (= ND 2307 r.16)	Calah	Calah	LD	622*

Aram. ⇒ NA [?]

JBA, Syr., *mkḥl*, *mkḥl*’, *mkḥlt*’ (*maḵḥāl*, *maḵḥālā*, *makəḥalətā*) n. m. & f. “the stick or style used in applying kohl to the eyes” DJBA 675b; Jastrow 782a; Dalman 224b; PSm. 271b; SL 757b; Manna 334b; Audo 460b; CAL. JBA, JPA, Syr., *kḥl* v. “to paint the eyelids (for medical or for cosmetic purposes)” DJBA 568a; DJPA 255b; Jastrow 629a; PSm. 212b; SL 617b; Manna 334a; Audo 460a; CAL.

The word *makaḫalūtu* occurs as a *hapax legomenon* in NA. It is attested in a list cataloguing a rich dowry of jewelry, clothing, furniture and utensils in a marriage contract between a bride’s mother and the groom. The context where the word is mentioned (ND 2307 r.13–16)[929] reads as follows:

> 1 NA_4.*bu-ra*$^?$*-a-li* / 2 *da-na-a-ni ša ri-qí-i* / 2 GIŠ.*pu-ru-si-a-te ša* MUN$^?$ / *ma-ka-ḫa-lu-u-tú*
>
> 1 beryl, 2 large containers of aromatics, 2 (offering) bowls of *salt*, a kohl pen.

Postgate defines *makaḫal(l)ūtu* as (an object, possibly “koḥl-container”).[930] The word is not listed in AHw., CAD or CDA. It is, however, listed in AEAD (p. 58b s.v. *makaḫalūtu*), with the sense “kohl pen, eyeliner.”

---

927 Cf. Luukko, SAAS XVI, § 4.2.3; Hämeen-Anttila, SAAS XIII, § 2.2.1.
928 Cf. Luukko, SAAS XVI, § 4.2.1.
929 ND 2307 was published by B. Parker, “The Nimrud Tablets, 1952–Business Documents,” *Iraq* 16 (1954), pp. 37f. The same text was discussed by Postgate, FNALD, p. 103 no. 14.
930 See Postgate, ibid., p. 197b.

From the Akkadian lexical inventory, a cognate that comes closest to the NA word under discussion is the word *guḫlu*, which denotes antimony paste or kohl used as eye paint, and is attested in several historical and literary texts from Assyria written in SB,[931] as well as in a NB letter (ABL 791) addressed by Bēl-ibni to Assurbanipal.[932] It is certainly related to the Semitic word *kuḥl* in the same sense, even though its initial radical is *g* instead of *k*. Zimmern considered the origin of the Akkadian *guḫlu* and the Aramaic *kuḥlā*, both in the sense of "antimony," to be uncertain.[933] Additionally, he pointed out that the Aramaic word was borrowed into the Late Hebrew as כָּחַל and into Arabic as كُحْل.[934]

In Aramaic a feminine noun, namely מִכְחַלְתָּא is attested, indicating a stick used for painting the eye.[935] Also in Arabic a feminine substantive مُكْحُلَة "a kohl jar, kohl bottle, kohl container, vessel for keeping kohl" is found.[936] In comparison, the form of the NA word *makaḫalūtu* is rather strange. It consist of a nominal form with the preformative *ma-*, which forms Semitic nouns of place or instrument, but it ends with the afformative *-ūt* which, despite denoting feminine nouns, often has an abstract or collective meaning.[937] The several attestations of the cognate word *guḫlu* in SB and LB with the voiced velar plosive *g* as the first radical, as opposed to the voiceless velar plosive *k* of *kuḥl* in the other Semitic languages, points to the borrowing of *makaḫalūtu* from Aramaic into NA. Phonetically, the Aramaic pharyngeal /*ḥ*/ is usually rendered <*ḫ*> in NA.[938]

maqarrutu (pl. *maqarrātu*) n. f. "bale (a measure for straw or reeds)"

Loanword	Reference	Provenance	Origin	Genre	Date
ma-qa-ra-a-te	ZA 74 80 r.16[939]	–	–	AD	–
[m]a-qa-rat	SAA I 27:5′	Nineveh	Nineveh	L	Sg
ma-qa-ra-te	SAAB 5 9:2	Assur	Assur	LD	641*
	ZA 74 80 e.18[940] *ma-qa-ra-⌜te⌝*	–	–	AD	–
ma-qar-a-te	Iraq 16, p. 34 (= ND 2088:8)	Calah	Calah	LD	625*
ma-qar-ra-a-ti	SAA XIX 9:8	Calah	*Til-Basip / Gūzāna*	L	Tgl
ma-qar-rat	SAA XI 24 r.5, 7, 9, 11e	Nineveh	–	AD	–
	CTN III 2:4	Calah	Calah	L	7th c.
	TH 108:1	Gūzāna	Gūzāna	LD	625

931 See AHw. (p. 296b s.v. *guḫlu*); CAD (G, p. 125a s.v. *guḫlu*).
932 See PNA 2/I (p. 479b s.v. Ḫundāru, no. 2b).
933 See Zimmern, AF, p. 61.
934 Ibid.
935 See Jastrow (p. 782a s.v. מִכְחָלָא).
936 See Elias & Elias, p. 583b; Wehr-Cowan, p. 817a.
937 See Lipiński, *Semitic Languages*, § 29.20 and § 29.46. See also GAG § 56b, § 56s.
938 For the representation of Aramaic *ḥ* by NA *ḫ*, see n. 313 above.
939 See K. Deller and I.L. Finkel, "A Neo-Assyrian Inventory Tablet of Unknown Provenance," *ZA* 74 (1984), pp. 78ff.
940 Ibid.

	StAT 2 133 e.6 *ma-qar-*⸢*rat*?⸣	Assur	Assur	AD	Asb?
	StAT 3 39:2 *ma-qar-*⸢*rat*⸣	Assur	Assur	LD	647*
	StAT 3 38:1 ⸢*ma*⸣*-[qa]r-[rat]*	Assur	Assur	LD	647*
ma-qar-rat.MEŠ	SAA XIV 32 e.8	Nineveh	*Šiddi-asika*	LD	618
	FNALD 32:9	Calah	Calah	LD	656
ma-qa-ru-tú	SAA XIV 32:5	Nineveh	*Šiddi-asika*	LD	618
	SAA I 105:4′ *ma-*⸢*qa*⸣*-ru-tú*	Nineveh	*Assur*	L	Sg
ma-qar-ru-tú	StAT 1 49:1	Assur	Assur	AD	7th c.
	CTN III 43:3	Calah	Calah	LD	627*
	SAA XIX 10:11, r.3 *m[a-qar]-ru-tú* (RL)	Calah	*Til-Basip* / *Gūzāna*	L	Tgl
ma-qir-te	SAA XI 25:2′	Nineveh	Nineveh	AD	–
ŠE.*ma-qa-ra-te*	TCAE 399ff (= ND 3467:5, 12)	Calah	*Calah*	L	–
ŠE.*ma-qa-ru-tú*	SAA I 236 r.2	Nineveh	Naṣibina	L	Sg
TÚG.*ma-qar-rat*	SAA I 26:2 (RL)	Calah	Calah	L	Sg
TÚG.*ma-qar-rat*.MEŠ	CTN III 16:1	Calah	Calah	LD	639*
	CTN III 15 e.1 TÚG.*ma-qar-rat*.[M]EŠ	Calah	*Quri'*	LD	639*

Amorite ⇒ OB [?] / Aram. ⇒ NA; NB [?]

OAram., *mqrh* n. f. "(of straw) bundle, bale" CAL.

In AHw. (p. 605b s.v. *maqarrūtu*), the word is defined as (ein Maß für Stroh). The editors of CAD (M/I, p. 240a s.v. *maqarrutu*) tentatively render the word as "bundle(?)" and define it as (a measure for straw or reeds). Neither of the two dictionaries provides an instance of the word in NB.[941] On the other hand, CDA (p. 196a s.v. *maqarratu*) considers the meaning of this word in NA and NB to be "bale (of straw)." AEAD (p. 60a s.v. *maqarrutu*) glosses the word as "bale." AHw. lists the word with the long vowel *ū*, i.e., *maqarrūtu*, but the attested forms of the word do not support such a transcription.[942]

The term *maqarrutu* means a "bale," and is most often used as a unit of volume for measuring straw (*tibnu*). It is also used for measuring reed (*kuppû*). The latter is attested in a NA letter (SAA XIX 10 r.3–4): 90 *m[a-qar]-ru-tú / ša ku-up-[p]e-e* "90 b[al]es of reed." It is also attested in another NA letter (SAA XIX 9:8): 36 *ma-qar-ra-a-ti ša ku-pe-e* "36 bales of reed."[943]

[941] For a NB attestation of the word, see S.W. Cole, *Nippur IV: The Early Neo-Babylonian Governor's Archive from Nippur* (Chicago 1996), p. 340 s.v. *maqarratu* "bundle."
[942] See M.P. Streck, "Die Nominalformen *maPRaS(t)*, *maPRāS* und *maPRiS(t)* im Akkadischen," in N. Nebes (ed.), *Neue Beiträge zur Semitistik: Erstes Arbeitstreffen der Arbeitsgemeinschaft Semitistik in der Deutschen Morgenländischen Gesellschaft* (Wiesbaden 2002), p. 246, n. 203.
[943] For the interpretation that *kuppû* ought to be taken here as "ice" or "snow," see Postgate, FNALD, § 6.3.5; K. Radner, "Salmanassar V. in den *Nimrud Letters*," *AfO* 50 (2003/2004), pp. 98f, n. ad no. 2 (= ND 2792:8). Against the interpretation of Postgate and Radner, see M. Luukko, SAA

The word is preceded three times by the determinative ŠE, which comes before the names of cereals, and three times by the determinative TÚG, which comes before the names of garments.[944] In a NA legal document from Calah (CTN III 15:1–3), the bale (*maqarrutu*) is defined as "Assyrian." The passage where it occurs reads: 5 TÚG.*ma-qar-rat*.[M]EŠ / *ša* ŠE.IN.NU / *ina lib-bi aš-šur-i-te* "5 bales of straw according to the Assyrian (bale)."

None of the Akkadian lexica cited above, however, provide an etymology for the word *maqarrutu*. The root Q/GRR in Akkadian gives the word *q/garāru(m)* in the sense "to flow, to overflow; to spry, sprinkle; to writhe; to grovel; to undulate; to be wavy."[945] Semantically, these meanings do not fit the contexts where the NA word *maqarrutu* is attested.[946] In Aramaic, the equivalent of *maqarrutu* is the word *mqrh* "bale." It is attested in two triangular loan dockets of Śehr-nūrī (O 3671:1; O 3715:1), which come from Maʾallanāte, concerning loans of straw (*tbn*).[947]

In an attempt to solve the etymology of the word under discussion, Lipiński states that the Aramaic word *mqrh* is a borrowing from the NA *maqarrutu*, and that the latter is derived from the root *QRN, which is prefixed by the nominal performative *ma-*, suffixed by *-atu*, and undergoes the total progressive assimilation *rn* > *rr*.[948] He adds that the word is already attested in OB.[949] Lipiński points out that in Aramaic the root provides the word *qrn* "the capital, principal (of a loan)," and in Akkadian, the word *qarānu* "to accumulate; to amass," which has a cognate in Arabic as قَرَنَ "to combine."[950] As for the Aramaic form of the word, Lipiński believes that the spelling *mqrh* indicates that the word was certainly pronounced as *maqarrā*, with the loss of the *-t* ending.[951] Against Lipiński's interpretation, the editors of CAL consider the NA *maqarrutu* "bundle, bale (of straw)" to be almost certainly a borrowing from Aramaic, and that the OB attestation of the word was borrowed from Amorite.[952]

However, no satisfactory meanings are found in the Akkadian or Aramaic roots QRN and QRR that would fit the contexts where the word under discussion is

XIX, pp. li, lxvi, n. 233. See also H.W.F. Saggs, *The Nimrud Letters, 1952* (London 2001), pp. 204f, n. ad ND 2792:8; K. Deller and L. Finkel, "A Neo-Assyrian Tablet of Unknown Provenance," *ZA* 74 (1984), p. 86, n. on l. 18–19.

944 See Borger, ABZ, nos. 367 and 536.

945 See CAD (Q, p. 127a s.v. *qarāru* (*garāru*)); AHw. (p. 902a s.v. *q/garāru(m)*; CDA (p. 285a s.v. *qarāru(m)*); AEAD (p. 87a s.v. *qarāru*).

946 See Streck, ibid., p. 246 s.v. *maqarratu*.

947 See E. Lipiński, *Studies in Aramaic Inscriptions and Onomastics*, III, *Maʿālānā* (Leuven 2010), pp. 175ff.

948 Ibid., p. 171.

949 Ibid. For the OB attestation, see J. van Dijk, *Texts in the Iraq Museum* II (Wiesbaden 1965), no. 158:2′–3′; L. Cagni, *Altbabylonische Briefe in Umschrift und Übersetzung* 8, *Briefe aus dem Iraq Museum* (TIM II), (Leiden 1980), pp. 102–103, no. 158.

950 See E. Lipiński, *Studies in Aramaic Inscriptions and Onomastics*, III, *Maʿālānā* (Leuven 2010), pp. 171 and 258.

951 See E. Lipiński, "Straw in the Neo-Assyrian Period," in E. Wardini (ed.), *Built on Solid Rock: Studies in Honor of Professor Ebbe Egede Knudsen on the Occasion of His 65th Birthday April 11th 1997* (Oslo 1997), p. 189; idem, *Semitic Languages*, § 27.28. For a different interpretation of the loss of the final *t* in the Aramaic word *mqrh*, see CAL, s.v. *mqrh* and *rsh*.

952 See CAL, s.v. *mqrh*.

attested. Lipiński's suggested total progressive assimilation *rn* > *rr*, does not seem to be operative in NA.[953] Hence, the etymology of *maqarrutu*, and the possible direction of its borrowing remain obscure.[954]

maqartu n. f. "cooling (vessel)?"

Loanword	Reference	Provenance	Origin	Genre	Date
ma-qar-te	SAA I 34:9, r.3′, 6′	Nineveh	Nineveh	L	Sg
ma-qur-ti	TCAE 387f (= ND 2672:9)[955]	Calah	Calah	AD	–

Aram. ⇒ NA; LB [?]

OAram., JA, Gal., JPA *mqrh, mqrt'* (*maqqərā, maqqartā*) n. f. "cooling place, store room" CAL; Jastrow 833b; Dalman 239a; DJPA 327a. Syr., *maqrānā* n. m. "small jug of clay; vessel for cooling water" Manna 697b, 974a. Syr., *maqrānā, maqrānīṯā* n. m. & f. "cooling, cooling vessel, a water cooler, refrigerant" SL 823a; PSm. 297b; Audo 945a.

AHw. (p. 605b s.v. *maqartu*) defines this word as (ein Gefäβ), gives only an attestation from LB, and cautiously suggests connecting it with Aramaic *məqartā* "Kühlung?" The editors of CAD (M/I, p. 240a s.v. *maqartu*), define this word as (a vessel), and tentatively consider it to be an Aramaic loanword in NB. AEAD (p. 60a s.v. *maqartu*) considers the meaning of this word to be "cooling." CDA (p. 196a s.v. *maqartu*), on the other hand, states that this word perhaps denotes a "cooling (vessel)," and considers it to be a borrowing from Aramaic into NA and NB.

As for NA, however, AHw. and CAD quote the two NA instances under an erroneous heading, namely *lamaqartu.*[956] Salonen too compares the word *maqartu* with the purportedly NA word *lamaqartu*.[957] In his articles on Aramaic loanwords von Soden suggests translating LB *ma(q)qartu* as "Kühlgefäss," and takes it to be a loanword from Aramaic consisting of a feminine participle in the Afʿel of the root QRR "kühl sein."[958] Parpola also connects NA *maqartu* with Aramaic *maqartā* "cooling."[959] He points out that the NA phrase (DUG.LA *ma-*

---

[953] See GAG § 33, § 35; Hämeen-Anttila, SAAS XIII, § 2.2.2.2; Luukko, SAAS XVI, § 4.2.2. See also Lipiński, *Semitic Languages*, § 27.3.
[954] For Aramaic, see ibid., s.v. *mqrh*, and *qrr*.
[955] The transliteration *ma-qur-ti* is taken from the Corpus of Neo-Assyrian Texts (CNA). Cf. B. Parker, "Administrative Tablets from the North-West Palace, Nimrud," *Iraq* 23 (1961), pl. XXII.
[956] See AHw. (p. 532b s.v. *lamaqa/urtu*); CAD (L, p. 60a s.v. *lamaqartu*, p. 112b s.v. *lattu*); CDA (p. 177a s.v. *lamaqartu*).
[957] See A. Salonen, *Die Hausgeräte der alten Mesopotamier nach sumerisch-akkadischen Quellen: eine lexikalische und kulturgeschichtliche Untersuchung. Teil II; Gefäße* (Helsinki 1966), p. 399.
[958] See von Soden, *Or* 35 (1966), p. 18:89; idem, *Or* 46 (1977), p. 190:89. Cf. DNWSI (p. 681 s.v. *mqrh*, p. 1036 s.v. *qrr*$_1$). Cf. also Abraham & Sokoloff, *Reassessment*, p. 41, n. 378.
[959] See n. ad SAA I 34:9.

qar-te) is written with an apparent space between LA and *ma*.[960] This means, of course, that *ma-qar-te* is not preceded by a determinative. On the other hand, Nili rejects von Soden's loan hypothesis, arguing that the Aramaic etymology cannot be accepted because there is no term attested in Aramaic that designates a vessel and is derived from a root QRR "to be cold."[961] She adds that the word *maqartu* should not be included in the list of words of West-Semitic origin, because the above mentioned Aramaic etymology is not acceptable, and also because it is possible to derive the word under discussion from another NA word, namely *lamaqartu*, which denotes a vessel used for measuring temple offerings.[962] Abraham and Sokoloff also reject von Soden's loan hypothesis, stating that there is no proof of the existence of the alleged Aramaic source word and that the possible JPA *hapax* מקרת is uncertain.[963]

In all the NA instances quoted above, *maqartu* is preceded by the logogram DUG.LA, which stands for the word *ḫaṣbu* "clay pot, pot, crock, sherd; pottery, terracotta."[964] This indicates that the word *maqartu* which follows is some kind of a pot. The following LB context of Nebuchadnezzar II also suggests that *maqartu* is a vessel or a pot: 2 DUG *ma-qar-tu*₄ (Nbk. 457:16).[965] The root QRR in the sense "to be cold" is Common Semitic except for Akkadian. In Hebrew we have קָרַר "to be cold,"[966] in Syriac ܩܪ "to be cold, frosty,"[967] and in Arabic قَرَّ "to be chilly, very cold."[968] On the other hand, the Akkadian word *qarāru* in the sense "to flow, to overflow; to pour; (D) to spray, sprinkle" does not fit into the NA context, and therefore the NA word lacks a plausible Akkadian etymology.[969]

Interestingly, from the root QRR "to be cold," Syriac has the word ܡܩܪܢܐ n. m. "small jug of clay; cooling, cooling vessel, a water cooler, refrigerant."[970] Also a feminine form of the same word, namely ܡܩܪܢܝܬܐ is found.[971] In Arabic, from the root QRR we have the word مَقَرَّة meaning "Jar, earthen vessel."[972] The evidence at hand points to a possible borrowing from Aramaic into NA. The vowel variation /a/ vs. /u/ in the two NA forms, i.e., *maqarte* and *maqurte*, probably represents an allophone caused by the closed syllable ending in *r*.[973] Nevertheless, the entry *lamaqartu* ought to be stricken from the dictionaries.

---

960 Ibid.
961 See Nili, p. 268:95.
962 Ibid.
963 See Abraham & Sokoloff, *Reassessment*, p. 41:134. See also DJPA (p. 327a s.v. מקרה), where the word is hesitatingly glossed as "cooling place," and it is stated that this word may possibly be a geographical name. Cf., however, CAL, s.v. *mqrh*.
964 See SAA I, p. 205 s.v. DUG.LA and p. 214b s.v. *ḫaṣbu*; AEAD (p. 36a s.v. *ḫaṣbu*). Cf. CAD (Ḫ, p. 132a s.v. *ḫaṣbu*). Cf. also Borger, ABZ, no. 55.
965 The LB instance is quoted in AHw. (p. 605b s.v. *maqartu*) and CAD (M/I, p. 240a s.v. *maqartu*).
966 See Jastrow (p. 1427b s.v. קָרַר II).
967 See SL, p. 1417a.
968 See Elias & Elias, p. 533a.
969 See CAD (Q, p. 127a s.v. *qarāru*).
970 See Manna, p. 697b; SL p. 823a; PSm., p. 297b.
971 See Audo (p. 945a s.v. ܡܩܪܢܐ). Note that in the addenda section of Manna (p. 974a s.v. ܩܪ) a word ܡܩܪܢܘܬܐ, with the meaning "refrigerant," is also listed, but this term is probably a neologism.
972 See *Al-munğidu* (p. 616c s.v. قَرَّ).
973 Cf. Luukko, SAAS XVI, § 4.3.1.

maqaṭṭu n. m. *or* f. "(short) gown"; (see the discussion below s.v. *maqaṭṭutu*)

maqaṭṭutu, (pl. *maqaṭṭāte*) n. f. "(short) felt-gown"; (see above s.v. *maqaṭṭu*)

Loanword	Reference	Provenance	Origin	Genre	Date
ma-qa-ṭí	Iraq 15, p. 138 (= ND 3407:5′)	Calah	Calah	TL	–
	SAA VII 104:1′ ⸢*ma*⸣-*qa-ṭ*[*í*!], 2′, 3′, 4′	Nineveh	Nineveh	TL	–
	SAA VII 108 r. ii′ 3′	Nineveh	Nineveh	TL	–
	SAA VII 109 iii 2′, r. ii 2′ *ma-qa-ṭ*[*í*], 4′ 6′	Nineveh	Nineveh	TL	–
	SAA VII 115 ii 9	Nineveh	Nineveh	AD	Sg
TÚG.*ma-qa*	SAA VII 95:1, 2 [TÚ]G.*ma-qa*, 6 [TÚ]G.*ma-qa*	Nineveh	Nineveh	TL	–
TÚG.*ma-qa-aṭ-a-ti*	SAA VII 112:10′	Nineveh	Nineveh	TL	7th c.?
TÚG.*ma-qa-ṭa-te*	SAA VII 111:1	Nineveh	Nineveh	TL	7th c.
TÚG.*ma-qa-ṭí*	SAA VII 93:1	Nineveh	Nineveh	TL	658
	SAA VII 94:4	Nineveh	Nineveh	TL	681
	SAA VII 97 r.1, 3, 5	Nineveh	Nineveh	TL	–
	SAA VII 99:2	Nineveh	Nineveh	TL	–
	SAA VII 103 r.2′ TÚG.*ma-q*[*a-ṭí*]	Nineveh	Nineveh	TL	–
	SAA VII 119 r. ii′ 4′ TÚG.*ma-qa-*[*ṭí*]	Nineveh	Nineveh	TL	–
	VAT 9849:15 (= Ass 3070)	Assur	Assur	TL	–
TÚG.*ma-qa-ṭu*	Iraq 23, p. 43 (= ND 2687:3)	Calah	Calah	TL	–
TÚG.*ma-qa-ṭu-tu*	Iraq 23, p. 20 (= ND 2311:5)	Calah	Calah	TL	–
TÚG.*ma-qa-ṭu-tú*	PVA 249	Assur	Assur	LL	–
	SAAB 17 8:2 (= ZTT I 8:2)	Tušḫan	Tušḫan	TL	–
TÚG.*mu-qa-ṭu-tu*	VAT 8659:2 (= Ass 1384ae)	Assur	Assur	TL	–
TÚG.*mu-qa-ṭu-tú*	StAT 2 164:12	Assur	Assur	LD	675
	StAT 2 255:6′ [TÚ]G.*mu-qa-ṭu-tú*	Assur	Assur	AD	–

Aram. ⇒ NA [?]

Syr., *məqaṭṭaʿtā* n. f. "a short garment" Manna 671b. JPA, JBA, Sam., CPA, Syr., *qṭʿ* v. Pe. "to cut off, to cut down," Pa. "to cut off; to divide into sections" DJPA 487b; DJBA 1007b; DSA 772a; LSp. 178a; DCPA 369a; SL 1354b; PSm. 501b; Manna 671a.

This word is listed as TÚG.*ma-qa-ṭu-tú* in the cloak section of the Practical Vocabulary of Assur.[974] In AHw. (p. 607b s.v. *maqāṭu*, *maqāṭatu*), it is defined as (ein Gewand), and its origin is considered to be unknown.[975] The editors of CAD (M/I, p. 251a s.v. *maqāṭu*) define the word as (a piece of apparel) made mostly of wool or linen. On the other hand, in AEAD (p. 60a s.v. *maqaṭṭu* and *maqaṭṭutu*), the two entries for the word are glossed as "(short) gown," and "(short) felt-gown" respectively.[976]

The word *maqaṭṭutu* is also attested in the spelling *muqaṭṭutu*, and has a basic variant as *maqaṭṭu*.[977] Both *maqaṭṭu* and *maqaṭṭutu* are often mentioned alongside the word *urnutu*, which designates "(dressing) gown, frock."[978] Parpola considers this NA word to probably designate a short gown made of felt or linen, and takes it to be a Paʿʿel present participle of the Aramaic verb *qṭʿ*, "to cut short," and proposes the following development: *məqaṭaʿ/məqaṭʿā* > *maqaṭʾu* > *maqaṭṭu*, in the sense "cut-off, shortened (gown or mantle)."[979] He also adduces two Jewish Palestinian Aramaic instances relating to garments, namely קטע קטעך "cut your cutting! (spoken to a tailor)" and הוה חבריה קטע פלגא דגולתיה "his friend would cut off (*qṭʿ*) half of his garment."[980] Parpola adds that his interpretation is supported by a variant of the NA word attested as TÚG.*mu-qa-ṭu-tu/tú*, occurring in StAT 2 164:12 and Ass 1384ae = VAT 8659:2, which was obviously realized as a D-stem participle, as well as by the fact that the word has distinct masculine and feminine forms that apparently indicate the grammatical gender of the sort of gown "cut short."[981]

The most salient feature of *maqaṭṭu* or *maqaṭṭutu* that is suggestive of a borrowing into NA is that phonologically the forms of this word do not fulfill the requirements of Geers' law advocating the dissimilation of one of the two emphatic consonants in any given Akkadian root, which in our case is expected to lead to the following development: *q – ṭ* > *q – t*.[982] Interestingly, as mentioned above, Syriac has a n. f. ܡܩܛܥܬܐ with the meaning "a short dress or garment."[983] A parallel is also found in Arabic attested as مُقَطَّعَة and مُقَطَّعَات in the sense "short garments."[984]

974 See PVA, p. 331:249.

975 See also CDA (p. 196b s.v. *maqāṭu*).

976 Cf. the Glossary of SAA VII (p. 216b s.v. *maqāṭu*).

977 See S. Gaspa, "Garments, Parts of Garments, and Textile Techniques in the Assyrian Terminology: The Neo-Assyrian Textile Lexicon in the 1st-Millennium BC Linguistic Context," in S. Gaspa et al. (eds.), *Textile Terminologies from the Orient to the Mediterranean and Europe, 1000 BC to 1000 AD* (Lincoln, 2017), p. 71 s.v. *maqaṭṭu*.

978 See AEAD (p. 130b s.v. *urnutu*). Cf. J.N. Postgate, "Assyrian Uniforms," in W.H. van Soldt (ed.), *Veenhof Anniversary Volume: Studies Presented to Klaas R. Veenhof on the Occasion of his Sixty-Fifth Birthday* (Leiden 2001), pp. 386f.

979 See S. Parpola, "Cuneiform Texts from Ziyaret Tepe (Tušḫan), 2002–2003 (Plates I–XXV)," *SAAB* 17 (2008), pp. 56f.

980 See ibid. See also DJPA (p. 488a s.v. קטע no. 1:4).

981 See Parpola, ibid., p. 57.

982 See F.W. Geers, "The Treatment of Emphatics in Akkadian," *JNES* 4 (1945): 65–67; A. Ungnad, *Akkadian Grammar* (Atlanta 1992), § 21a; GAG § 51e. See also Section 1.6.1.2, and Table 2 above.

983 See Manna (p. 671b s.v. ܡܩܛܥܬܐ).

984 See *Al-munǧidu* (p. 641b s.v. المُقَطَّعَة).

marāsu v. $^{i/i}$ (G) "to mash, squash, squeeze"[985]

Loanword	Reference	Provenance	Origin	Genre	Date
li-im(var. *lim*)*-ri-is-ku-nu*	SAA II 6:602	Calah	Calah	T	672

Aram. ⇒ SB ⇒ NA

JPA, JBA, Syr., *mrs* v. Pe. "to crush, press" DJPA 331b; DJBA 710b; Jastrow 845a; CAL; SL 836b; PSm. 302b; Manna 418a; Audo 563a. Ma., *mrs* v. "to crush down, squash" MD 279a. Syr., *mrs* v. Pe. & Pa. "to squash, squeeze" Manna 418a. JBA, Syr., *mrs* v. Pe. "to rub" DJBA 710b; Jastrow 845a; Manna 418a.

This word occurs as a *hapax legomenon* in NA and is attested in Esarhaddon's succession treaty. In AHw. (p. 609a s.v. *marāsu*, mng. no. 2), this word in the sense "zerdrücken" is tentatively considered to be an Aramaic foreign word in NA. Referring to von Soden, the editors of CAD (M/I, p. 269a s.v. *marāsu* B) gloss this word as meaning "to squash," but list it under a new heading and consider it to be an Aramaic loanword in NA. As with other *hapax legomena*, the possibility of determining the meaning and the origin of *marāsu* is determined by the sentence context, here SAA II 6:601–602, which reads:

> *ki-i zu-um-bi ina* ŠU.2 LÚ.KÚR-*ku-nu le-pa-šu-ku-nu* / LÚ.KÚR-*ku-nu li-im-ri-is-ku-nu*
>
> May they make you like a fly in the hand of your enemy, and may your enemy squash you.

In his articles on Aramaic loanwords, von Soden states that Akkadian *marāsu* in the sense "(in Flüssigkeit) durchrühren," is a verb of the so-called "ablaut class," with the thematic vowels *a/u* (*imarras, imrus*).[986] He adds that the other *marāsu* with the thematic vowels *i-i* meaning "zerdrücken," which is attested in the NA treaty of Esarhaddon, should certainly be considered an Aramaic loanword, based on its semantic affiliation.[987] Note that *marāsu* with the thematic vowels *i-i* is also attested in SB.[988]

Nili agrees with von Soden's suggested borrowing from Aramaic and corroborates the meaning of the NA word under discussion by referencing a proposal by Chaim Cohen that the meaning of *marāsu* "to crush, squash" is parallel to the meaning of the word *mês/šu* "to crush, squash" attested in the following passagc (Borgcr Esarh. 76:19): *kullat nākirīya lumīš kulbābiš* "let me

---

985 In AEAD (p. 60b s.v. *marāsu*), the thematic vowels of this word ought to be given as *i/i*.
986 See von Soden, *Or* 35 (1966), p. 18:91; idem, *Or* 46 (1977), p. 190:91. Cf. AHw. (p. 609a s.v. *marāsu*, 1); CAD (M/I p. 269a s.v. *marāsu* A); DNWSI (p. 694 s.v. *mrs*).
987 See von Soden, ibid.
988 See AHw. (p. 1573b s.v. *marāsu*).

squash all my enemies like ants."[989] Abraham and Sokoloff state that a borrowing from Aramaic is likely if the Aramaic root MRS "to crush," which is known from its later dialects, is not cognate with Akkadian MRS.[990]

The root MRS, which is found in Hebrew as מָרַס "to crush; to rub; to stir,"[991] is cognate with Syriac ܡܪܰܣ "to crush; to press; to squash, squeeze; to rub; to macerate, steep." It is also cognate with Arabic مَرَسَ "to macerate, steep in a liquid, soak (in water); to rub,"[992] and probably also with the Arabic word مَرَثَ "to mash, reduce to a soft pulpy state by beating or rubbing; to macerate, soften by steeping in a liquid."[993] According to *Al-munǧidu*, the Arabic مَرَثَ is a variant of مَرَسَ.[994] Certainly this West-Semitic root MRS in the sense "to stir, to macerate, steep in a liquid," is cognate with Akkadian *marāsu* "to stir into a liquid."[995]

However, the Akkadian meaning of *marāsu* "to stir into a liquid," does not fit the context of the NA *li-im-ri-is-ku-nu*. On the other hand, the meaning associated with *mrs* "to crush; to squash," found in the later dialects of Aramaic, fits the NA context perfectly. A possible parallel to the NA usage of *marāsu* "squash" is found in the following Syriac Etpaʿʿal instance: ܐܝܟܢܐ ܕܝ ܦܪܐ ܕܡܐ ܕܡܬܡܪܣܝܢ ܦܪ̈ܘ ܒܢܝܗ̇ "as in the case of a bird when its chicks are crushed."[996] Interestingly, the word *marāsu* "squash" also occurs as a *hapax legomenon*, namely *i-ma-ri-su*, in a fragmentary context of a SB text from Assyria (SAA III 38:46).[997] The evidence at hand points to a borrowing from Aramaic into NA and SB.

Phonologically, however, the form of the NA word is problematic because it does not comply with the known phenomenon whereby the NA *š* is used to write Aramaic *s*.[998] In other words, the borrowed NA *marāsu* is expected to appear as **marāšu*. To account for the form of the NA word, one may postulate that the word is a trans-SB borrowing from Aramaic, in which case no change of the sibilant is required. There is no room here for semantic extension because of the difference in the two verbs' thematic vowels, *marāsu* (*a/u*) vs. *marāsu* (*i/i*).

marʾu, *māru* n. "lord"

Loanword	Reference	Provenance	Origin	Genre	Date
DUMU-*ia*	SAA XIX 13:3, 5	Calah	Calah	L	8th c.
	SAA I 220:3 ⸢DUMU⸣-*ia*	Nineveh	Lāqê	L	Sg

[989] See Nili, p. 202:75. The phrase is quoted in CAD (K, p. 501b s.v. *kulbābiš*, M/II, p. 36a s.v. *mêsu*, mng. no. 1.b).
[990] See Abraham & Sokoloff, *Reassessment*, p. 41:137.
[991] See Jastrow, p. 845a; Dalman, p. 242b.
[992] See Wehr-Cowan, p. 903a; Elias & Elias, p. 651b; *Al-munǧidu*, p. 755c.
[993] See Elias & Elias, p. 649b; *Al-munǧidu*, p. 754b.
[994] See *Al-munǧidu*, ibid.
[995] See AHw., ibid; CAD, ibid.
[996] See CAL, s.v. *mrs*.
[997] See the Glossary of SAA III (p. 139b s.v. *marāsu*). See also AHw. (p. 1573b s.v. *marāsu*).
[998] See n. 71 above.

Aram. ⇒ NA

Com., *mr*ʾ, *mry*ʾ (*mārā*, *māryā*) n. m. "lord, master" Brauner 364; DNWSI 682; DJPA 329b; DJBA 707a; Jastrow 834a; DSA 484a; LSp. 115b; DCPA 245b; SL 823b; PSm. 298a; Manna 415b; Audo 560a; MD 251a; DJA 64a; CAL.

The word *mar*ʾ*u* in the sense "lord" is a *tris legomenon* in NA. In fact, the logogram DUMU stands in NA for the word *mar*ʾ*u* or *māru* "son, boy."[999] The word is occasionally written syllabically as *ma-a-ru*. In contrast, *mr*ʾ is a common Aramaic word in the sense "lord." Etymologically, however, the Hebrew מַר "man, lord, master,"[1000] and Syriac ܡܪܐ "master," as well as Arabic مَرْء (إمْرِئ، أمْرُؤ) "man,"[1001] are cognates with the Akkadian word *māru*(*m*) or *mar*ʾ*u*(*m*) "son." Nevertheless, it does not make sense in the two NA letters cited above to render DUMU as "son, boy." Instead, it fits better if DUMU is interpreted as "lord."

SAA XIX 13:1–7, reads:

IM ^{m}L[U]GAL–B[ÀD$^{?}$] / *a-na* LÚ*.A.˹BA˺–É.GAL / *lu* ˹DI˺-*mu a-na* DUMU-*ia* / ^{md}PA–SUM–PAB.MEŠ / *ina* UGU DUMU-*ia* / *a-sa-par* / ˹*i*˺–*da-a-ti*

A tablet of Šarru-*d*[*ūrī*] to the palace scribe. Good health to my lord! I sent Nabû-nādin-aḫḫē to my lord; afterwards [……].

SAA I 220:1–3, reads:

a-na ^{md}PA–BÀD–PAB / IM ^{m}*a-ri-ḫi lu* DI-*mu* / *a-na* ˹DUMU˺-*ia*

A letter from Arīḫu to Nabû-dūru-uṣur. Good health to my lord!

Parpola convincingly explains that using DUMU to denote "lord" is a scribal error caused by the homophonic similarity between Aramaic *mr*ʾ "lord" and Assyrian *mar*ʾ*u* "son."[1002] Similarly, Luukko states that as a result of Aramaic influence, the logogram DUMU, which in NA usually denotes *mar*ʾ*u* "son, boy," may exceptionally be taken as "lord."[1003] He renders DUMU-*ia* in the NA letter (SAA XIX 13:3, 5), as "my lord," but notes, based on the usual letter hierarchy, that in this particular case it can be claimed that the interpretation "my son" was intended, since the sender was a superior Assyrian official, namely Šarru-dūrī the governor of Calah (later 8th century B.C.).[1004] According to the normal letter

[999] Cf. Borger, ABZ, no. 144.
[1000] See Jastrow, p. 834a.
[1001] See Elias & Elias, p. 649a; Wehr-Cowan (p. 901b s.v. امرء).
[1002] See S. Parpola, "The Neo-Assyrian Ruling Class," in T.R. Kämmerer (ed.), *Studien zu Ritual und Sozialgeschichte im Alten Orient / Studies on Ritual and Society in the Ancient Near East: Tartuer Symposien 1998–2004* (Berlin 2007), pp. 265f.
[1003] See Luukko, SAAS XVI, § 7.3.
[1004] See n. ad SAA XIX 13:3, 5. See also Luukko, ibid., p. 179, n. 531 and p. 241, notes to Appendix B no. 31; PNA 3/II (p. 1233b s.v. Šarru-dūri, no. 1:b). Cf. the previous interpretation of DUMU-*ia* as "my son," in CTN V, p. 241.

formulae, the individual with the higher ranking position in the Assyrian official hierarchy is always mentioned first regardless of whether he/she is the sender or the receiver of the letter.[1005] It seems more likely that the scribe of this NA letter (SAA XIX 13) made a mistake by utilizing the logogram "son" for writing the word "lord."

A similar lapse is found in another NA letter (SAA I 220:3), which was sent by Arīḫu, an official in Lāqê from the time of Sargon II (ca. 721–705 B.C.), concerning the corn tax of the Samarians.[1006] The letter was unearthed in Nineveh, but it probably was originally dispatched from the province of Lāqê in the middle Euphrates region.

A reverse slip also occurred due to the homophonic similarity between Aramaic *mr'* "lord," and NA *mar'u* "son," and is attested in a copy of the first tablet of the Epic of Gilgamesh, which was made for the library of Assurbanipal. According to Parpola, the scribe made a mistake by using the cuneiform sign "lord" in writing the word "son."[1007]

This use of DUMU in the sense "lord" is also attested in some NA personal names such as Mār-bi'dī "The Lord is behind me," which is written as ᵐ*mar–bi-i'-di*, but also as ᵐDUMU–*bi-i'-di*.[1008] Similarly we find the names: Mār-larīm "May the Lord be exalted," Mār-nūrī "[The] Lord is my light," and Mār-sūrī "[The] Lord is my bulwark."[1009] The Aramaic component of these personal names, i.e., "[The] Lord...," is occasionally written with the DUMU sign in NA sources. Fales labels this phenomenon as "improper coding."[1010]

This kind of lapse, dabbed onto clay tablets by the styli of Assyrian scribes more than two and a half millennia ago, may perhaps be an ancient example of code-switching in writing.[1011]

maṣû v. (Š only) "to overcome"

Loanword	Reference	Provenance	Origin	Genre	Date
ú-šá-an-ṣa-ka	SAA IX 2 ii 12′	Nineveh	Nineveh	P	Esh

Aram. =▷ NA [?]

1005 See Luukko, ibid.
1006 See PNA 1/I (p. 131a s.v. Arīḫu, no. 1).
1007 See S. Parpola, "Assyrians after Assyria," *JAAS* 12 (2000), p. 12; idem, *The Standard Babylonian Epic of Gilgamesh* (Helsinki 1997), p. 74, l. no. 242 (ms. D) // line 265 (ms. A2). See also A.R. George, *The Babylonian Gilgamesh Epic: Introduction, Critical Edition and Cuneiform Texts* (Oxford 2003), pp. 802f n. on l. 259.
1008 See PNA 2/II (p. 702b s.v. Mār-bi'dī).
1009 See PNA 2/II (p. 740b s.v. Mār-larīm and Mār-liḫia, p. 741a s.v. Mār-nūrī and Mār-sūrī).
1010 See F.M. Fales, "On Aramaic Onomastics in the Neo-Assyrian Period," *OrAnt* 16 (1977), p. 61.
1011 Note that "code-switching in writing" occurs much less frequently than in conversation. For the term "code-switching," and even a related term "code mixing," see P.H. Matthews, *The Concise Oxford Dictionary of Linguistics* (Oxford 1997), p. 58; D. Crystal, *The Penguin Dictionary of Language* (London 1999), p. 60. For studies on "code-switching in writing," see M. Sebba et al. (eds.), *Language Mixing and Code-Switching in Writing: Approaches to Mixed-Language Written Discourse* (London 2012).

OffAr., *šnṣy* v. Shaphʿel "to succeed" DNWSI 1177. JBA *mṣy* v. "to overpower, overcome" DJBA 699f.[1012] Syr., *mṣy* v. "to be able to overcome" SL 812a. Syr., *mṣy* v. Etpe. "to prevail over, overcome" PSm. 293b; Manna 412b; CAL.

According to CAD (M/I, p. 349b s.v. *maṣû*, mng. no. 8), this NA word in the Š-stem means "to be able," and is mostly used in hendiadys.[1013] However, the word occurs in a NA oracle (SAA IX 2 ii 12′) delivered by Lā-dāgil-ili, a prophet from Arbail,[1014] to Esarhaddon, on behalf of the Lady of Arbail who promises to protect the king and keep him safe in his palace. The oracle is part of a collection of oracles concerning Babylon and the stabilization of the king's rule. SAA IX 2 ii 11′–12′, reads:

> *ina* É.GAL-*ka ú-ta-qa-an-ka / ni-kit-tu ni-ir-ri-ṭu ú-šá-an-ṣa-ka*
>
> I will keep you safe in your palace; I will make you overcome anxiety and trembling.

Semantically, the usual meanings of *maṣû* in Akkadian including "to be able," do not fit the context of this NA text. Parpola translates the word *ú-šá-an-ṣa-ka*, in the text quoted above, as "to overcome." He points out that *maṣû* is normally intransitive in NA, but in the present case it has a transitive usage parallel to that of Syriac *mṣy*, which in the Etpe. has the meanings "to be able," and "to prevail over, overcome."[1015] The following usage in the Etpe. is found in Syriac: ܐܬܬܚܪܬ ܥܡ ܡܠܐܟܐ ܘܥܡ ܒܪܢܫܐ ܘܐܬܡܨܝ ܒܗ ܚܝܠܐ "you strove with an angel and with a man and prevailed," as well as in the expression ܘܐܬܡܨܝ ܒܗ ܫܠܛܘܢ ܘܟܒܫܘ ܐܢܘܢ "they prevailed and conquered them."[1016]

As with many semantic studies, establishing the exact nuance of a word often relies heavily on the semantic context. In addition, the syntactical context is also required in analyzing the role that a certain word plays in the sentence and thereby establishing its grammatical function. Given that *maṣû* as a transitive verb meaning "overcome" is attested only once in NA, i.e., is a *hapax legomenon*, the evidence at hand points to a semantic borrowing from Aramaic. The Aramaic evidence, however, comes solely from two Eastern Aramaic dialects, namely JBA and Syriac. In our case, the borrowing from Aramaic would merely be considered a semantic extension of the already existing NA *maṣû*.

1012 See DJBA (p. 700a s.v. מצי 2, mng. no. 3).
1013 Cf. AHw. (pp. 621f s.v. *maṣû(m)*, Š, 6); Luukko, SAAS XVI, § 6.8. Cf. also DNWSI (p. 1177 s.v. *šnṣy*).
1014 See PNA 2/II (p. 649b s.v. Lā-dāgil-ili, no. 2).
1015 See n. ad SAA IX 2 ii 12′.
1016 See CAL, s.v. *mṣy*. Cf. Kaufman, AIA, p. 104 s.v. *šunṣû*. Cf. also the Mandaic usage: *mṣia bhailẖ* "can defeat him, is as strong as he" MD (p. 276b s.v. MṢA I).

miāru v. (G) "to buy, deal in"

Loanword	Reference	Provenance	Origin	Genre	Date
i-me-ru	SAA I 178:12	Nineveh	*Ṣūpat*	L	Sg
	SAA I 179:7	Nineveh	*Ṣūpat*	L	Sg
ma-a-ri	SAA XIX 48:15, 20	Calah	Western Provinces	L	8th c.
me-e-ru	SAA XIX 12 r.9′	Calah	Calah	L	8th c.

Aram. ⇒ NA; NB; LB

Syr., *mwr* v. Pe. "to buy, purchase; to barter, exchange" Manna 390a; Audo 530a; PSm. 259a; SL 728b. JBA *mwr* v. Af. "to exchange" DJBA 649a; Jastrow 748b; Dalman 217b; CAL. Sam., *mwr* v. Pe. "to procure food" DSA 457a.

In AHw. (p. 616b s.v. *mâru*), this term is tentatively glossed as "kaufen," and is considered to be an Aramaic loanword in NB and LB.[1017] The editors of CAD (M/I, p. 317a s.v. *mâru*) gloss the term as "to buy," and consider it to be an Aramaic loanword in NB. In his articles on Aramaic loanwords von Soden regards this word to be a borrowing from Aramaic and states that despite the fact that NB/LB *mâru* "to buy," is a middle weak verb with *ī* as the theme vowel, it can hardly be separated from Aramaic *mūr* "to buy."[1018] Luukko also considers *mâru/miāru* to be an Aramaic loanword in the sense "to deal in corn, to supply, transport or import provisions, to buy corn."[1019] Abraham and Sokoloff accept the loan hypothesis, but consider the direction of the borrowing to be uncertain.[1020]

Nevertheless, the usual terms used in Akkadian to express "to buy," are the words *šâmu/šiāmu*, *laqû* and *qanû*. On the other hand, the essential meanings of מור in Aramaic are "to exchange valuables; to buy, purchase." The vowel *ī* of the NA word, rather than the vowel *ū* of the Aramaic source word, is difficult to explain. The *r* probably brings about the change *ū* > *ī*. Most important, however, is the fact that "the majority of the Akkadian loanwords in Aramaic have what must be considered the correct reflex of the posited Akkadian form, both as to vowel quality and quantity."[1021] Since there is a difference in vowel quality between NA *mâru/miāru* and Aramaic *mūr*, the evidence points to a borrowing from Aramaic into NA.

[1017] Cf. CDA (p. 199a s.v. *mâru*); DNWSI (p. 605 s.v. *mwr*$_1$).

[1018] See von Soden, *Or* 35 (1966), p. 18:92; idem, *Or* 46 (1977), p. 190:92. Cf. the discussion below s.v. *šiāḫu*.

[1019] See n. ad SAA XIX 48:15, 20. See also the Glossary of SAA XIX (p. 242a s.v. *miāru*).

[1020] See Abraham & Sokoloff, *Reassessment*, p. 41:138.

[1021] See Kaufman, AIA, p. 146.

miglu n. "scroll"

Loanword	Reference	Provenance	Origin	Genre	Date
mi-ig-li	SAA XIII 28 r.4	Nineveh	Assur	L	Asb?

Aram. ⇒ NA

OffAr., JBA, JPA, Syr., Ma., *mglh*, *mglt'* (*mga/illā*, *mga/ilṯā*) n. f. "scroll" DNWSI 593; DJBA 641a; DJPA 836a; Jastrow 729a; SL 709b; PSm. 250b; Manna 104b; Audo 524a; MD 238b; CAL. Syr., *məgallā* n. m. "scroll" Manna 104b; PSm. 250b.

The word *miglu* "scroll," is a *hapax legomenon* in NA and is only listed in AEAD (p. 64b s.v. *miglu*). In AHw. and CAD, on the other hand, the word *magallatu* "parchment scroll, leather scroll (as writing material)" is listed as a loanword from Aramaic into SB and LB.[1022] The NA word occurs in a report sent to the Assyrian king concerning gold and silver work for the temple of Sîn. As with other *hapax legomena*, the etymology proposed for *miglu* is determined by the sentence context. The context where the NA word occurs (SAA XIII 28 r.3–5) reads as follows:

> *ù* 1 GÚ.UN KUG.UD *ina* KALAG-*te* / *mi-ig-li* NA_4.KIŠIB *ša* ^{md}30–I GAL–SIMUG.KUG.GI / *ina* UGU-*ḫi*
>
> Furthermore, there is one talent of silver by the heavy standard (= 60 kg) with a scroll (bearing) the seal of Sîn-na'di, chief goldsmith, attached to it.

The identification of the NA *mi-ig-li* with Aramaic *mglh* was made by Deller and Millard, who transcribed the words *mi-ig-li* NA_4.KIŠIB as (*migilli kunukki*), and rendered it "Siegelabrollung."[1023] Cole and Machinist refer to Deller and Millard, but render *mi-ig-li* in the sense "scroll," without explaining the peculiar form of the word.[1024]

Etymologically, the Aramaic word *mglh* or *mglt'* "scroll" is derived from the root GLL "to roll, turn round; to make round."[1025] The Aramaic word is borrowed into Arabic as مَجَلَّة "magazine, periodical."[1026] In Hebrew, the word is attested as מְגִלָּה "roll, scroll," and in Syriac as ܡܓܰܠܬܳܐ "scroll; bonds, promissory note."[1027] As mentioned above, the term has entered SB and LB as a loanword in the form of *magallatu* "leather scroll (as writing material)." Abraham and Sokoloff state that *magallatu* was foreign to Mesopotamian cuneiform culture and is obviously a

[1022] See AHw. (p. 574b s.v. *magallatu*); CAD (M/I, p. 31a s.v. *magallatu*). Cf. von Soden, *Or* 35 (1966), p. 15:82; idem, *Or* 46 (1977), p. 189:82. Cf. also DNWSI (p. 593 s.v. *mglh*).
[1023] See K. Deller & A.R. Millard, "Zwei Rechtsurkunden aus Aššur im British Museum," *AfO* 32 (1985), p. 47.
[1024] See n. ad SAA XIII 28 r.3–5. See also the Glossary of SAA XIII (p. 188b s.v. *miglu*).
[1025] Cf. SL (p. 709b s.v. ܡܓܰܠܬܳܐ).
[1026] See Fraenkel, pp. 247f. Cf. Wehr-Cowan, p. 129a.
[1027] See Jastrow, p. 729a; Dalman, p. 213a. See also SL, p. 709b.

borrowing from Aramaic into Akkadian.[1028] The NA *miglu* "scroll" is certainly also borrowed from Aramaic. However, the form of the NA word *mi-ig-li* is that of the nominal pattern *PiRS*, which is difficult to explain in light of the Aramaic source word. The *i* here probably represents an original *a*, and the change *a* > *i* occurred due to the closed syllable before *l*.[1029] The masculine gender of the NA word corresponds to that found in Syriac as ܡܓܠܬܐ.[1030]

***mil'u**, (pl. *mil'āni*) n. "flood"

Loanword	Reference	Provenance	Origin	Genre	Date
mì-il-'a-a-ni	SAA I 36 r.7′	Nineveh	Nineveh	L	Sg

OB ⇒ Aram. ⇒ NA [?]

Syr., LJLA n. m. *ml'* (*mel'ā*) n. m. "flood, inundation" Manna 402a; Psm. 275a; SL 763b; Audo 544b; CAL.

The unusual plural form *mil'āni* occurs in a NA letter (SAA I 36 r.7′), sent by the crown prince Sennacherib to king Sargon, concerning floods in central Assyria. As such, it occurs as a *hapax legomonon* in NA. The Akkadian word *mīlu*(*m*) < **mil'u*(*m*) "flood"[1031] has a *PiRSu* nominal form and is derived from *malû*(*m*) < **malā'u*(*m*) "to be(come) full; fill up."[1032] Its plural form is *mīlū*, and in NA *mīlē*.[1033] However, in the NA letter mentioned above, the plural form of the word is written differently, as *mil'āni*.[1034]

The Akkadian *malû* "to be(come) full; fill up," and West-Semitic *ml'*, which has the same meaning, are cognates. Accordingly, the expected reconstruction of the PS word would be **ml'*. Kaufman is of the opinion that Akkadian *mīlu* "flood" probably exerted some influence on the form of the Syriac *melyā* "flood."[1035] He further calls attention to a possible Aramaic influence on the NA form *mil'u*.[1036] According to another assumption, put forward by Worthington, the

---

[1028] See Abraham & Sokoloff, *Reassessment*, p. 40:124.
[1029] Cf. Luukko, SAAS XVI, § 4.3.1.
[1030] See Manna 104b; PSm., 250b.
[1031] See GAG § 15b and § 55c, ii. Cf. I.J. Gelb, "Notes on von Soden's Grammar of Akkadian," *BiOr* 12 (1955), p. 100, § 15b; B. Kouwenberg, "The Reflexes of the Proto-Semitic Gutturals in Assyrian," in G. Deutscher & N.J.C. Kouwenberg (eds.), *The Akkadian Language in its Semitic Context: Studies in the Akkadian of the Third and Second Millennium BC* (Leiden 2006), p. 164, n. 40.
[1032] See AHw. (p. 597a s.v. *malû*(*m*) IV, p. 652b s.v. *mīlu*(*m*), p. 653a s.v. *mil'u* II); CAD (M/I, p. 174b s.v. *malû*, M/II, p. 69b s.v. *mīlu* A).
[1033] See, for instance, *mi-i-li* in SAA X 226:11.
[1034] Cf. Luukko, SAAS XVI, § 5.3 and p. 138 s.v. (*mīlu*).
[1035] See Kaufman, AIA, p. 72. Cf. C. Brockelmann, *Lexicon Syriacum* (Hildesheim 1995), p. 389a; Zimmern, AF, p. 44.
[1036] See Kaufman, ibid. Cf. Luukko, SAAS XVI, § 3.5 and p. 28 s.v. (*mīlu*); Hämeen-Anttila, SAAS XIII, p. 13.

unusual spelling of *mì-il-'a-a-ni* "floods" in NA may be morphographemic; i.e., it may give precedence to etymology over pronunciation.[1037]

Taking into consideration the reconstruction of historical grammar concerning morphemic development, the NA *mil'āni* with an ' (hamza) resembles the shape of an older form of the word. Since *mil'āni* is chronologically attested later, the most logical way to explain its form is to consider it a borrowing from Aramaic. However, the NA *mil'āni* is attested only once, and the available Aramaic evidence comes solely from Syriac and LJLA.

natānu v. (G) "to give"

Loanword	Reference	Provenance	Origin	Genre	Date
li-te-nu-ni	SAA V 17 r.1	Nineveh	*Amidi*	L	Sg
	SAA XV 50:6′	Nineveh	*Hamrin area*	L	Sg

Aram. ⇒ NA [?]

OAram., OffAr., JPA, JBA, Sam., CPA, Ma., *ntn* v. "to give" Brauner 414; DNWSI 766ff; DJPA 362b; DJBA 780b; DSA 554a; LSp. 129a; DCPA 274a; MD 307b; CAL.

The irregular verb *tadānu* in NA is used instead of *nadānu* in the sense "to give."[1038] Nevertheless, as cited above, there exists a *dis legomenon* in NA as *li-te-nu-ni*, whose form and context, albeit fragmentary, reveal a precative of 3p. m. pl. of *natānu*, a verb of *i*-class in the sense "to give." Hence, we have the following development: *lū* + *intenū* > *lū* + *ittenū* > *littenū*. The latter is followed by the pronominal suffix *-ni* of the 1p. sg. in the accusative, and becomes *littenūni* "let them give me."

SAA V 17 r.1, reads:

[*x x x x*]*x* UD.MEŠ *li-te-nu-ni*

[... in x] days let them *give me*.[1039]

1037 See M. Worthington, "Some New Patterns in Neo-Assyrian Orthography and Phonology Discernible in Nouns with Monosyllabic Stems," *JNES* 69 (2010), p. 188, n. 44.

1038 See AHw. (p. 1300a s.v. *tadānu(m)*); CAD (N/I, p. 42a s.v. *nadānu*); AEAD (p. 70b s.v. *nadānu*; p. 120b s.v. *tadānu*). However, *nadānu* is also attested in NA; see, for instance, SAA XIII 1:19; SAA X 89 r.6.

1039 Note that the word *li-te-nu-ni* in SAA V 17 r.1, is tentatively translated as "alternate," and is taken to be from *enû* "to change." See the Glossary of SAA V (p. 223a s.v. *enû*). Cf. n. ad SAA XV 50:6; Hämeen-Anttila, SAAS XIII, p. 98 n. 94. Cf. also the Glossary of SAA XV (p. 241a s.v. *natānu*).

SAA XV 50:6′–8′, reads:

[*x x x an-n*]*i-tú li-te-nu-ni* / [*x x x x*]*x-pa dul-lu* LUGAL / [*x x x x x*]*-uš*

Let them *give* me [th]is [..., and I *will* ...... d]o the king's work.

Referring to the same NA texts cited above, Parpola tentatively suggests that the NA *tadānu* "to give" occasionally appears as *natānu*.[1040] Also referring to the same NA texts, Luukko states that "the verb *tadānu* 'to give' may have had, possibly owing to Aramaic influence, a variant root NTN as two precative forms of the third-person plural indicate."[1041]

The root NTN with the meaning "to give" is attested in Aramaic as נתן and in Hebrew as נָתַן.[1042] In Ugaritic and Phoenician, on the other hand, it occurs as YTN. However, Syriac utilizes the word ܢܬܠ "to give,"[1043] which is a combination of (**ntn + l- > ntl*), and displays the assimilation of the *n* to the following *l*.[1044]

Nonetheless, due to the fact that *li-te-nu-ni* occurs in two rather fragmentary NA passages, additional and contextually more solid evidence would certainly be welcomed to further collaborate the NA *natānu* in the sense "to give."

nibzu, (pl. *nibzāni*) n. "(clay) tablet, document"

Loanword	Reference	Provenance	Origin	Genre	Date
IM.*ni-ib-zi*	SAA IV 290 r.6	Nineveh	Nineveh	P	Asb
	SAA IV 305:9′	Nineveh	Nineveh	P	650
ni-ib-za-a-ni	SAA X 365:8′	Nineveh	Babylonia	L	669?
ni-ib-zi	O 3698:1	Ma'allanāte	Ma'allanāte	AD	7th c.
	SAA IV 311 r.2	Nineveh	Nineveh	P	–
	SAA XVI 63:13, 14	Nineveh	–	L	Esh
ni-ib-zu	SAA X 365:10′, 12′	Nineveh	Babylonia	L	669?
	SAA XV 122:4	Nineveh	Der	L	Sg
	SAA XV 247:7′	Nineveh	Babylonia	L	Sg
	StAT 1 53 e.7	Assur	Assur	L	7th c.

Aram. ⇒ NA [?]

OffAr., *nbz* n. m. "document, receipt" DNWSI 711, CAL. JPA, CPA, Sam., *nbz* n. m. "lot" DJPA 339a; LSp. 118b; DCPA 255a; DSA 494b. Ma., *nbz* n. m. "piece, portion" MD 296b.

1040 See S. Parpola, Review of "Akkadisches Handwörterbuch. Vols. II & III/1 (Lfg. 7–12)," by W. von Soden, *OLZ* 74 (1979), p. 27 ad 701a.

1041 See Luukko, SAAS XVI, p. 149. Cf. Hämeen-Anttila, SAAS XIII, § 3.14.1.

1042 See Jastrow, p. 944b; Dalman, p. 267b.

1043 See PSm., p. 354b; Audo, p. 608b; Manna, p. 470b. Note, however, that in Syriac the irregular verb *yhb* "to give" is also utilized.

1044 See SL (p. 955b s.v. ܢܬܠ).

In AHw. (p. 786a s.v. *nibzu*), this word is rendered "Dokument, Urkunde," and is considered to be a borrowing from Old Aramaic *nbz* into NA and NB.[1045] The editors of CAD (N/II, p. 206a s.v. *nibzu*) gloss this word as "tablet, document," and cautiously consider it to be a loanword from Aramaic into NA and NB. Actually, the term *nibzu* is only attested in NA, and all supposedly NB references (PRT 124:9 and PRT 139 r.6), cited in AHw. and CAD, are in fact also NA.[1046]

Earlier, Zimmern considered this term to be a loanword from Akkadian *nibzu* "Urkunde" into Aramaic in the sense "Quittung."[1047] In contrast, von Soden considered Old Aramaic *nbz* to be a loanword into NA and NB in the sense "Dokument, Urkunde."[1048] The editors of DNWSI regard the origin and etymology of the Aramaic *nbz* "document, receipt" to be uncertain.[1049] Kaufman states that the etymology of *nibzu* "document, receipt" is unknown, but emphasizes without elaborating that it is a loanword in Akkadian.[1050] Cowley, on the other hand, takes the Official Aramaic נבז to be a loanword from the Persian term نوشتن "a (written) receipt."[1051] On the other hand, the editors of DNWSI regard the origin and etymology of the Aramaic *nbz* "document, receipt" to be uncertain.[1052]

Some scholars are of the opinion that *nibzu* designates the triangular shaped NA clay tablets often referred to in English as dockets.[1053] In contrast, Parpola states that translating *nibzu* as "document" is unnecessarily narrow; rather, *nibzu* was used for various kinds and purposes of clay tablets and seems to have been identical in meaning with *ṭuppu* "tablet."[1054]

Etymologically, however, the root NBZ in Akkadian is only attested in SB as *nabāzu* "to bleat (said of goats)."[1055] The latter, however, does not fit the context of the NA texts cited above, for which an etymology for *nibzu* must be sought elsewhere. In Arabic, from the root NBḎ, we have the substantive نَبْذَة or نُبْذَة, which denotes "note; paragraph; small piece, part, section; a separate part of

---

[1045] Cf. CDA (p. 252a s.v. *nibzu*).

[1046] The two supposedly NB texts, i.e., PRT 124:9 and PRT 139 r.6, which are cited in AHw. and CAD, are now re-edited respectively as (SAA IV 305:9′ and SAA IV 290 r.6). These two texts are written in the NA script and are regarded as NA texts. See also Radner, SAAS VI, § iv. 6; Abraham & Sokoloff, *Reassessment*, p. 43, n. 427.

[1047] Zimmern, AF, p. 19.

[1048] See von Soden, *Or* 37 (1968), p. 261:103; idem, *Or* 46 (1977), p. 191:103. Cf. E.Y. Kutscher, "Aramaic," in T.A. Sebeok (ed.), *Current Trends in Linguistics*, 6. *Linguistics in South West Asia and North Africa* (The Hague 1970), p. 357. Cf. also Abraham & Sokoloff, *Reassessment*, p. 43:155.

[1049] See DNWSI (pp. 711f s.v. *nbz*).

[1050] See Kaufman, AIA, p. 77.

[1051] See A. Cowley, *Aramaic Papyri of the Fifth Century B.C.* (Oxford 1923), p. 34. Cf. Y. Muffs, *Studies in the Aramaic Legal Papyri from Elephantine* (Leiden 1969), p. 186.

[1052] See DNWSI (pp. 711f s.v. *nbz*).

[1053] See M.W. Stolper, Review of "Fifty Neo-Assyrian Legal Documents," by J.N. Postgate, *BASOR* 239 (1980), p. 79b; Tadmor, *Aramaization*, pp. 453f, n. 64; S. Dalley & J.N. Postgate, *The Tablets from Fort Shalmaneser* (Oxford 1984), p. 63; F.M. Fales, AECT, pp. 21–24. For a discussion on dockets, see Postgate, FNALD, § 1.2.3.

[1054] See Parpola, LAS II, ad no. 288:8′; idem, SAA I, p. xxiv, n. 10; idem, Review of "Akkadisches Handwörterbuch. Vols. II & III/1 (Lfg. 7–12)," by W. von Soden, *OLZ* 74 (1979), p. 29 ad 786a. See also Radner, SAAS VI, pp. 65f.

[1055] See AHw. (p. 697b s.v. *nabāzu*); CAD (N/I, p. 24b s.v. *nabāzu*). For *z* as the third radical of a root in Akkadian, see GAG § 51d.

something (such as a book)."[1056] This Arabic word is probably cognate with Mandaic *nibza* "piece, portion, apportioned piece (said of prayer)." [1057] Accordingly, we may reconstruct a PS root as *NBḎ with the meaning "note; section, part (of a text)." Probably, *nibzu* initially meant "note." Since the word is only attested in NA, it is most likely a borrowing from Aramaic, or a trans-Aramaic borrowing, in which case its origin and etymology cannot yet be determined.

niqittu n. f. "revenge"

Loanword	Reference	Provenance	Origin	Genre	Date
ni-qi-it-te	SAA XVI 62 r.1′	Nineveh	–	L	Esh?

Aram. ⇒ NA [?]

JPA, Sam., CPA, JLA, Gal., LJLA, Syr., *nqmh, nqmt*ʾ (*neqmā, nqamṯā/neqməṯā*) n. f. "revenge, vengeance" DJPA 360b; DSA 547b; LSp. 128a; DCPA 272b; SL 947b; PSm. 351b; Manna 465a; Audo 603a; Jastrow 933a; Dalman 265a; DNWSI 759; CAL. OffAr., *nqmn* n. m. "avenger" DNWSI 758. OAram., JPA, Sam., JBA, CPA, Syr., *nqm* v. "to take revenge, avenge" Brauner 409; DNWSI 758; DJPA 360b; DSA 547a; DJBA 775b; LSp. 128a; DCPA 272b; SL 947a; PSm. 351b; Manna 465a; Audo 603a; Dalman 265a; CAL.

In AHw. (p. 792b s.v. *niqittu* II), this term is rendered in the sense "Vergeltung, Genugtuung," and is considered to be a loanword in NA from Aramaic *nqm*.[1058] Two instances are adduced, namely *ni-qit-ti* (ABL 455:13) and *ni-qit-tu* (TI pl. II ii 12). The editors of CAD (N/II, p. 251b s.v. *niqittu*), define the meaning of this term as uncertain and, consider it to be a West-Semitic loanword in NA. CAD also refers to *ni-qit-ti* (ABL 455:13).

However, the first text (ABL 455:13), is now edited as (SAA XV 30:13), and according to the context, the word in question is read differently, as *ni-kit-ti*, and is translated in the sense "beat (of heart)."[1059] The second text, i.e., (TI pl. II ii 12), is now also edited as (SAA IX 2 ii 12′), and in relation to the context, the word in question is read and rendered differently, as *ni-kit-tu* "anxiety."[1060]

1056 See *Al-munğidu* (p. 785b s.v. نبذ); Wehr-Cowan (p. 938b s.v. نبذة); Elias & Elias (p. 684a s.v. نُبْذَة). Cf. A. Cowley, *Aramaic Papyri of the Fifth Century B.C.* (Oxford 1923), p. 34.

1057 See MD (p. 296b s.v. *nibza*). According to MD, however, the root NBZ is secondary from BZA "to split, cleave, rend, slit, tear, make a hole."

1058 See also von Soden, *Or* 37 (1986), p. 261:104; idem, *Or* 46 (1977), p. 191:104. Cf. CDA (p. 254b s.v *niqittu* II); DNWSI (p. 759 s.v. *nqmh*), albeit citing *miqittu* [*sic*] for *niqittu*.

1059 See n. ad SAA XV 30:13. Cf. the Glossary of SAA XV (p. 241a s.v. *nikittu* "fear, worry"). However, the word *nikitti* in the meaning "beating of heart" seems to be a substantive in the feminine in construct of *nakādu* "to beat, throb, palpitate."

1060 See the Glossary of SAA IX (p. 50b s.v. *nikittu* "fear, worry"). Cf. Nili, p. 275:117; Abraham & Sokoloff, *Reassessment*, p. 43:158.

Hence, in keeping with the new editions of the aforementioned texts, the two NA instances *ni-qit-ti* and *ni-qit-tu* should be read *ni-kit-ti* and *ni-kit-tu* respectively, and ought to be listed in AHw. and CAD under the heading *nikittu* "beat (of heart); anxiety," and regarded as derivatives of *nakādu* "to beat, throb, palpitate; to worry, to fear, to be anxious about."[1061]

On the other hand, there is a NA word *ni-qi-it-te* (SAA XVI 62 r.1′) which occurs as a *hapax legomenon* in a broken context. The word is tentatively translated as "revenge." The broken passage where the word occurs (SAA XVI 62 r.1′), reads as follows:

> [*x x x x x x*]-*li*? *šá ni-qi-it-te šu*-[*u*]
>
> [……] is of *revenge.*

Although it is difficult to draw a reliable conclusion concerning the meaning of *ni-qi-it-te*, keeping in mind the somewhat fragmentary condition of the passage where it occurs, the context as a whole suggests rendering it as "revenge." As such, *ni-qi-it-te* is taken to be a loanword from Aramaic *neqmətā* "revenge, vengeance." The form of the word in NA indicates a complete regressive assimilation of the labial nasal *m* to the following dental plosive *t*, suggesting the following development: *m* + *t* > *tt* and *niqimte* > *niqitte*.[1062] Corresponding words are found in Syriac as ܢܩܡܬܐ "vengeance,"[1063] Arabic as نِقْمَة "vengeance, revenge, vendetta,"[1064] and Hebrew as נְקָמָה "revenge."[1065]

paḫāzu v. (G) "to be insolent, be loose, be reckless; to boast, brag"; (Š) "to leave loose"

Loanword	Reference	Provenance	Origin	Genre	Date
ip!-*ḫi-zu*!	KAV 197:15[1066]	Assur	Assur	L	–
⸢*i*!⸣-*pa-aḫ-ḫi-iz*	SAA X 72 r.15	Nineveh	Nineveh	L	670?
pa-ḫa-a-z[*u*]	SAA III 35:25	Nineveh	Nineveh	LT	–
ú-šap-ḫu-zu	SAA X 95 r.15′	Nineveh	Assur	L	Esh?
	SAA X 353 r.5	Nineveh	Babylonia	L	670

Aram. ⇒ NA; NB

JPA, Syr., Gal., PTA, LJLA *pḥz* v. Pe. & Pa. "to be lewd, wanton, boisterous, reckless, heedless" DJPA 427b; SL 1177b; PSm. 441a; Manna 582a; Audo 773b; Dalman 316a; CAL. Ma., *phz* v. "to be reckless, heedless, wanton" MD 366b.

1061 Cf. AHw. (p. 717a s.v. *nakādu*(*m*)); CAD (N/I, p. 153a s.v. *nakādu*).
1062 Cf. Luukko, SAAS XVI, § 4.2.1.
1063 See Manna (p. 465a s.v. ܢܩܡܬܐ); SL, p. 947b. In Akkadian it is only attested as a West-Semitic word in El-Amarna texts; see CAD (N/I, p. 328b s.v. **naqāmu*).
1064 See Elias & Elias, p. 731b; Wehr-Cowan, p. 996b.
1065 See Jastrow, p. 933b; Dalman, p. 265a.
1066 See Postgate, TCAE, pp. 363–367. Cf. the Corpus of Neo-Assyrian Texts (CNA).

JPA, Syr., *pḥz'* (*peḥzā*) n. m. "wantonness, lewdness, recklessness" DJPA 427b; SL 1177b; PSm. 441a; Manna 582a; Audo 733b; CAL.

In AHw. (pp. 811b, 1581a s.v. *paḫāzu*), this word is rendered approximately as "anmaβend auftreten," and is regarded as an Aramaic foreign word in NA and NB.[1067] In contrast, in CDA (p. 261a s.v. *paḫāzu*), the meaning is considered unclear and no etymology or loan hypothesis is provided for the word. The editors of CAD (P, p. 32b s.v. *paḫāzu*) entered it in the sense "to be arrogant, high-handed; to allow to be arrogant, improper," and considered it to be a West-Semitic loanword in NA and NB.[1068] In AEAD (p. 79a s.v. *paḫāzu*), the word in the G-stem is glossed "to be insolent, be loose, be reckless, run wild; to boast, brag, swagger," and in the Š-stem "to leave loose."

The word in the G-stem in NA is translated "to act unjustly," (KAV 197:15), and "to boast," (SAA X 72 r.15), as well as being translated tentatively as "to be insolent" (SAA III 35:25). In the Š-stem, on the other hand, it is translated "to leave loose" (SAA X 95 r.15′; SAA X 353 r.5). In NB an adjective, *paḫḫuzû* in the sense "insolent" (SAA XVIII 102:9′), and a substantive, *piḫzu* "insolence" (SAA XVII 39:8), are attested.

Further words in this connection are found in the NA terms such as *pāḫizu* and *paḫḫizu*, and the plural *pāḫizāni*, which occur preceded by the determinative LÚ that indicates a profession or an occupation.[1069] We have only one tentative translation, given as "insolent person, boaster" (SAA III 35:25).[1070] AHw. (p. 811b s.v. *pāḫizu*), cautiously renders the word as "aufdringlich," and CAD (P, p. 33b s.v. *pāḫizu*) defines the word as (a profession or status). However, AEAD (p. 79a) lists two separate entries, the first a substantive, namely *paḫḫizu* "boaster, braggart; grotesque performer," and the second, also a substantive, *pāḫizu* "comic actor, comedian, buffoon."[1071] Nevertheless, the word *pāḫizu/paḫḫizu* does not seem to be a direct borrowing from Aramaic, but rather derived from the NA *paḫāzu*.[1072]

Chronologically, the word *paḫāzu* is not attested prior to NA and NB. Semantically, the NA meanings deduced contextually reveal a connection with Aramaic פחז "boisterous, reckless, heedless," and point to a borrowing from the latter. In addition to Aramaic, the root PḤZ/FḪZ is also attested in the other Semitic languages.[1073] In Arabic, فَخَرَ has the meanings "to boast, magnify

[1067] See also von Soden, *Or* 37 (1968), p. 262:108; idem, *Or* 46 (1977), p. 191:108. Cf. DNWSI (p. 905 s.v. *pḥz*₁); Abraham & Sokoloff, *Reassessment*, p. 44:162.
[1068] Cf. H. Tawil, *An Akkadian Lexical Companion for Biblical Hebrew* (Jersey City 2009), p. 294a.
[1069] See, LÚ.*pa-ḫi-za-ni* (CTN I 13 r.12′); [L]Ú.*pa-ḫi-za-*⸢*ni*⸣ (CTN I 25 s.3); LÚ.*pa-ḫi-zu* (SAA XVI 30:3); LÚ.*pa-ḫi-z*[*a-(a)-ni*] (CTN III 134:4′); [LÚ.*pa*]-*aḫ-ḫi-zu* (SAA III 35:25).
[1070] See also the Glossary of SAA III (p. 143a s.v. *paḫḫizu*).
[1071] Cf. von Soden, ibid; J.V. Kinnier-Wilson, *The Nimrud Wine Lists* (London 1972), pp. 86f.
[1072] See CDA (p. 261a s.v. *paḫāzu*).
[1073] For a discussion concerning this root, see J.C. Greenfield, "the Meaning of פחז," in Y. Avishur & J. Blau (eds.), *Studies in the Bible and the Ancient Near East Presented to Samuel E. Loewenstamm, on His Seventieth Birthday* (Jerusalem 1978), pp. 35–40, esp. p. 39.

oneself,"[1074] and in Biblical Hebrew פָּחַז means "to be haughty, elated, heedless."[1075]

The fact that this loanword in NA also occurs in the causative Š-stem as *ú-šap-ḫu-zu*, whereas the proposed Aramaic etymon פחז is not attested in the Šafʿel mode, is a clear indication that this loan is completely integrated into the NA morphological system. This is another instance which shows that the Šafʿel mode was not yet functioning in Aramaic during the period of its contact with NA.[1076] The causative conjugation in Aramaic, as in the other West-Semitic languages, was usually expressed by the -ה prefix. Hence, the meaning "to leave loose," associated with *paḫāzu* in the Š-stem appears to be restricted to NA.

parāḫu v. (D) "to squander"; (N) "to depart(?)"

Loanword	Reference	Provenance	Origin	Genre	Date
ip-par-ri-ḫi	SAA XVI 5 r.11 (RL)	Nineveh	Nineveh	L	Esh
⸢par⸣-ru-ḫa-at	KAV 215:10 (= VAT 9874)	Assur	*Assur*	L	7th c.

Aram. ⇒ NA [?]

Syr., *prḥ* v. Pa. "to squander, dissipate (riches, possessions)" PSm. 459b; SL 1235f; Manna 608b; Audo 815b; CAL. JBA *prḥ* v. Pe. "to depart" DJBA 931a.

In CAD (P, p. 145a s.v. *parāḫu*), the word is listed as a verb in SB, with the meaning "to sprout; to ferment."[1077] This, however, is cognate with the Syriac verb ܦܪܚ "to spring up, bud, put or bring forth leaves or flowers"[1078] and the Arabic verb فَرَّعَ "to put forth branches."[1079] On the other hand, AEAD (p. 80b s.v. *parāḫu*) lists a NA verb in the G-stem as "to flee," and in the D-stem as "to squander."

The word *parāḫu* occurs as a *dis legomenon* in NA. It is attested as *⸢par⸣-ru-ḫa-at* in a letter (KAV 215:10),[1080] sent by Nabû-šulmu-ēreš, from Assur, to his mother Bāia. The letter concerns the managing of family's property which, perhaps, was inherited from a deceased *paterfamilias*, and was being exploited

[1074] See *Al-munğidu* (p. 571c s.v. فخز). For the etymology of فخز in Arabic, see Greenfield, ibid., p. 39, n. 26.

[1075] See Jastrow, p. 1152a.

[1076] See also above s.v. *galû*.

[1077] Cf. AHw. (p. 827b s.v. *parāḫu* I); CDA (p. 265a s.v. *parāḫu*).

[1078] See PSm. p. 463a; SL p. 1247a. See also Jastrow (p. 1236a s.v. פְּרַע II).

[1079] See Wehr-Cowan (p. 707a s.v. فرع); Elias & Elias (p. 500b s.v. فَرَّعَ الشجر).

[1080] In CAD (P, p. 159b s.v. *parāku*), the word *⸢par⸣-ru-ḫa-at* is taken to be derived from *parāku*, no. 5, c, 2′, in the sense "to place athwart, crosswise, to block, hinder." See also CAD (R, p. 131b s.v. *rammû*, c).

arbitrarily by other members of the family.[1081] The NA letter (KAV 215:6–10) reads as follows:[1082]

> GIŠ.IG / *ina* IGI-*ki li-ip-te-ú / lik-nu-ku me-me-ni ina* É / *lu la i-rab a*ˡ*-nu-te-ni* / ⸢*par*⸣*-ru-ḫa-at ra-mu-at*
>
> Let them open and reseal the door in your (f.) presence. Nobody should enter the house; our property has been squandered and neglected.

The word ⸢*par*⸣*-ru-ḫa-at* is most likely a borrowing from Aramaic *prḥ* v. Pa. in the sense "to squander (riches, possessions)," which fits the context of this NA letter. It is to be interpreted as consisting of the verb *parāḫu* in the D-stem, stative, 1p. f. sg., in the sense "is squandered." The Syriac verb ܦܰܪܰܚ in the Pa‘‘el mode is used together with the words ܥܘܬܪܐ "riches," and ܩܢܝ̈ܢܐ "possessions," in the sense "to squander, dissipate."[1083] For instance, the expressions ܒܪܐ ܕܦܰܪܰܚ ܥܘܬܪܗ, "the son who squandered his riches = the prodigal son,"[1084] and ܥܘܬܪܐ ܠܥܓܠ ܦܠܒܠܟܒܬ ܦܪܣܝܢ "the riches dissipate quickly,"[1085] as well as ܦܰܪܰܚ ܩܢܝ̈ܢܟܝ "(he) squandered your possessions."[1086] The occurrence of *anūteni* "our possessions" in the NA letter, together with *parruḫat* in the D-stem, is parallel to the combination found in Syriac. The NA usage and the distribution point to a borrowing from Aramaic.

Furthermore, *parāḫu* is attested in NA as *ip-par-ri-ḫi* in a broken context in a royal letter (SAA XVI 5) concerning settling accounts and preparing for a royal visit to Harran. SAA XVI 5 r.10–11 reads as follows:

> *man-nu-ma* ⸢*lu*ˀ *la*ˀ⸣ *i-*⸢*sa*ˀ⸣*-ma-*[x]*-a / lu*ˡ ⸢*la*⸣ *ip-par-ri-ḫi*
>
> May nobody be unreliable and make difficulties!

Luukko and Buylaere, the editors of SAA XVI 5, translate *ip-par-ri-ḫi* as "make difficulties," and take it to be from *parāḫu* "to obstruct(?)."[1087] Moreover, they note, albeit with a question mark, that the word is alternatively derived from *parāku* "to oppose; to be obstructed," in the N-stem.[1088]

A different interpretation would be to consider *ip-par-ri-ḫi* a loanword from Aramaic *prḥ* "to depart." An instance of the latter is found in JBA: פוקו ופרחו מן אבא בר בריכתא "go out and depart from PN."[1089] In that case, *ipparriḫi* may be analyzed as consisting of the verb *parāḫu* "to depart," in the N-stem, present, 1p. m. sg., with the final *-i*, representing the so-called "überhängendem Vokal."[1090]

[1081] See PNA 1/II (p. 253a s.v. Bāia, no. 7).
[1082] The transliteration of KAV 215:6–10 is taken from the Corpus of Neo-Assyrian Texts (CNA).
[1083] See PSm., (p. 459b s.v. ܦܪܚ, Pa. b).
[1084] Cf. ibid.
[1085] See SL (p.1236a s.v. ܦܪܚ, Pa. 2a).
[1086] Cf. ibid.
[1087] Cf. the Glossary of SAA XVI (p. 190a s.v. *parāḫu*).
[1088] See n. ad SAA XVI 5 r.11.
[1089] See DJBA (p. 931 s.v. פרח).
[1090] See GAG § 82e.

Together with the preceding NA prohibitive expression *lū lā*, the phrase *lū lā ipparriḫi* may be rendered as "let nobody depart!"[1091] Maybe, this meaning of *parāḫu*, "to depart," better fits the contexts of the NA letter, and a borrowing from Aramaic is possible.

parāmu v. (N) "to shred (of shoes)"

Loanword	Reference	Provenance	Origin	Genre	Date
li-par-ma	SAA II 6:658	Calah	Calah	T	672

Aram. ⇒ NA; NB; SB [?]

JBA, Syr., *prm* v. "to cut, chop, hack down" DJBA 934b; SL 1242b; PSm. 461b; Manna 610b; Audo 818b. Syr., *prm* v. Pa. "to cut apart, tear to pieces, slice up" SL 1242b; PSm. 461b; Manna 610b; Audo 818b. Sam., *prm* v. "to rend" DSA 704a. Syr., *prmyn, prmyt'* n. f. pl. "torn shoes, worn out shoes" SL 1242b; CAL. JBA *prm'* n. m. "chopped food" DJBA 905b.

The word *parāmu* occurs as a *hapax legomenon* in NA. It is not listed in AHw. In contrast, in CDA (p. 265a s.v. *parāmu*), it is listed only for NA in the N-stem with the meaning "to shred (of shoes)," and is tentatively considered to be an Aramaic loanword in NA. In CAD (P, p. 161a s.v. *parāmu*), the word is listed in the G-stem with the meaning "to rend, to slice through." It is only entered for SB and NB, and no borrowing is suggested. The following attestations are provided in CAD: *ša pa-ar-mu* "which are in tatters," *pa-ri-im napištu* "who cuts the throat," and *ta-par-ra-am* "you will chop."

On the other hand, the single NA instance of *parāmu* expresses a curse in the vassal treaty of Esarhaddon. The context where the word occurs (SAA II 6:656–658) reads as follows:

> [*k*]*i-i šá* KUŠ.E.SÍR *šal-qa-tu-u-ni* / *ina kaq-qar pa-qut-ti* [KUŠ.E.SÍR.ME]Š-*ku-nu* / *li-par-ma ina* UG[U *xx-k*]*u-nu x*[*x x x*]
>
> Just as (these) shoes are split, so may your [shoes] be torn in a region of brier. [*Go around barefooted!*].

In an earlier edition of the same treaty, Watanabe suggests reading the NA word as *li-par-ma*, and connects it semantically with Akkadian *šalāqu*(*m*) "to cut open (sheep, leather bottle, shoe)."[1092] She transcribes the word as *lipparmā* and analyzes it as 3p. f. pl. in the precative of N-stem of **prm* "to be cut/slashed, to be torn."[1093] She explains that so far the word can be found in the dictionary only in

[1091] Cf. GAG § 81h.
[1092] See K. Watanabe, *Die adê-Vereidigung anlässlich der Thronfolgeregelung Asarhaddons* (Berlin 1987), p. 209, § 103.
[1093] Ibid.

the nominal form *PiRiSt*, namely *pirindu* < **pirimtu*, which probably means "slice (of pomegranate; as food)," attested in SB and NB.[1094] Watanabe connects the NA word under discussion with the Aramaic and Hebrew root PRM "to cut," and wonders whether the NA word is a borrowing from Aramaic.[1095]

In fact, the root PRM is not attested in the older dialects of Akkadian. Usually, NA uses the words *šalāqu* to express "to cut, slit open; to lacerate," and *batāqu* to express "to cut, cut off, amputate; to hew." In the West-Semitic languages, in addition to Aramaic פְּרַם "to cut, chop; to tear to pieces, slice up," and Hebrew פָּרַם "to tear open; to strip,"[1096] the root PRM is also found in Arabic as فَرَمَ in the sense "to cut into small pieces (meat), mince, chop."[1097] Interestingly, in Syriac usage, the word ܦܪ̈ܡܝܬܐ indicates n. f. pl. "worn out shoes, torn shoes."[1098] Hence, the lack of *parāmu* in the older dialects of Akkadian, its narrow distribution in NA, NB and SB, and the existence of a possible related Syriac usage, taken together all point to a loan from Aramaic.

pašāqu v. (D) "to explain"

Loanword	Reference	Provenance	Origin	Genre	Date
up-ta-ši-iq	SAA XVI 121:12	Nineveh	*Nineveh*	L	Esh

Aram. =▷ NA [?]

Palm., Ma., Syr., *pšq* v. Pa. "to explain, expound, make clear; to interpret, translate" DNWSI 946; MD 383a; SL 1262b; PSm. 468b; Manna 620b; Audo 838a.

The word *pašāqu* in the D-stem, with the meaning "to explain," occurs as a *hapax legomenon* in NA. It is attested in a letter (SAA XVI 121) addressed by Bēl-nāṣir, a royal official, to Esarhaddon. The context where the word is attested (SAA XVI 121:11–13) reads as follows:

> ⌜*ana*⌝-*ku a-ba-ak-ka la aq-ri-i*[*b*] / *up-ta-ši-iq a-na*! LUGAL EN-*iá* / *aq-ṭi-bi mu-uk ta-ri-iṣ*
>
> Weeping, I didn't arrive; I *explained* and told the king, my lord, that it was right (to do so).

In AHw. (p. 841b s.v. *pašāqu*(*m*)), the meaning of this word is considered to be unclear. It is, however, tentatively considered to be a borrowing from Aramaic

---

1094 Ibid. See also AHw. (p. 866a s.v. *pirindu* "Fruchtschnitz ?"); CDA (p. 275a s.v. *pirindu* ~ "slice"). Cf. CAD (P, p. 398a s.v. *pirindu* (a vegetable foodstuff)).

1095 See Watanabe, ibid.

1096 See Jastrow, (p. 1230a s.v. פָּרַם, פְּרַם).

1097 See Wehr-Cowan (p. 710a s.v. فرم); Elias & Elias (p. 502b s.v. فَرَمَ اللحم).

1098 See SL, p. 1242b; CAL, s.v. *prmyn, prmyt'*.

paššeq in the sense "erklären." CAD (P, p. 545a s.v. *puššuqu*), provides the meaning "to explain," and refers for comparison to West-Semitic *pšq* "to explain." Luukko and Van Buylaere, the editors of SAA XVI 121, tentatively render the word under discussion as meaning "to explain," following the interpretation of CAD.[1099]

However, the usual meanings of *pašāqu* in Akkadian, "to be narrow; be difficult," do not fit the context of the NA passage. On the other hand, the Aramaic meaning of *pšq* "to explain," which is attested in the D-stem in Syriac and Palmyrene, fits better in the passage quoted above. Interestingly, Syriac *pšq* in the G- and D-stems has the additional meaning "to make easy," which is the opposite of its Akkadian cognate *pašāqu* "to be difficult." These cognates with opposite meanings seem to be an additional example of the inter-Semitic phenomenon known as *ḍidd* (ضدّ).[1100] If the rendering of our word as meaning "to explain," is correct, it remains difficult to determine the direction of the borrowing. Nevertheless, based on the distribution, our assumption inclines towards a borrowing from Aramaic into NA.

Phonologically, the sibilant *š* of the Aramaic word *pšq* is expected to appear as *s* when borrowed into NA.[1101] Accordingly, we would have anticipated the following development: Aramaic *pšq* > NA *psq*. This rule, however, is not observed here, most likely because *pašāqu* is a native Akkadian word also attested in OB. Hence, the borrowing in NA only involves the semantic extension of a native word.

pispisu n. "bedbug, bug"

Loanword	Reference	Provenance	Origin	Genre	Date
pi-is-pi-su	SAA II 6:603	Calah	Calah	T	672

Aram. ⇒ NA [?]

Syr., *pšpš'* n. m. (*pešpəšā*, *pašpəšā*) "(small reddish) bug, bedbug, tick" Manna 620b; Audo 837b; SL 1262b; PSm. 468b; CAL. Syr., *pašpūšā* n. m. "bug, bedbug, tick" Manna 620b; Audo 837b; SL 1262b. Syr., *pūšpāšā* n. m. "bird lice, small vermin infesting birds" Manna 620b; PSm. 440b.

This word occurs as a *hapax legomenon* in NA. It is attested in Esarhaddon's succession treaty (SAA II 6:603). In AHw. (p. 867b s.v. *pispisu*), the word is followed by a question mark and left untranslated. On the other hand, CDA (p. 275b s.v. *pispisu*) renders the word tentatively as "bug." The editors of CAD (P, p. 425b s.v. *pispisu*) define the word as (an insect). The NA passage where *pispisu* occurs (SAA II 6:603) reads as follows:

1099 See n. ad SAA XVI 121:12; The Glossary of SAA XVI (p. 190b s.v. *pašāqu*).
1100 See *Al-munğidu* (p. 447b s.v. ضدّ).
1101 See n. 71 above.

> *ki-i šá pi-is-pi-su (an-ni-u) bi-ʾi-šu-u-ni / ki-i ḫa-an-ni-i ina* IGI DINGIR *u* LUGAL *a-me-lu-te / ni-piš-ku-nu lib-ʾi-iš*
>
> Just as (this) bug stinks, just so may your breath stink before god and king (and) mankind.

In his editio princeps *The Vassal-Treaties of Esarhaddon*, Wiseman translated *pispisu* as "urine."[1102] Reiner, on the other hand, translates the same word as "bedbug."[1103] Watanabe subscribes to Reiner's interpretation and considers *pispisu* an Aramaic loanword in NA.[1104] Watanabe argues that by analogy with the preceding lines, where insects such as locusts, lice, caterpillars, other field pests, and flies are referred to as means for inflicting mishaps upon and belittling anyone who breaks Esarhaddon's treaty, one would expect *pispisu* to be an insect.[1105] She cites the Encyclopaedia Britannica (vol. 3 (1963), p. 361a), which states that "the peculiar disagreeable odour of bedbugs is due to the secretion of the scent, or stink, glands so characteristic of heteropterous insects."[1106]

Alongside the Syriac ܦܫܦܫܐ, this word, in the sense "bedbug," is also attested in Mishnaic Hebrew as פישפש, and is borrowed into Arabic as فَسْفَس.[1107] The nominal pattern of this NA word discloses a normal reduplication of a biconsonantal root, *PiSPiS*.[1108] Phonologically, the NA *s* instead of the Aramaic *š* accords with the fact that NA <*s*> is used to represent West-Semitic /*š*/.[1109] On the whole, the evidence points to a borrowing from Aramaic into NA.

purṣīnu, (pl. *purṣīnāte*) n. "pomegranate seed; kernel of grapes"

Loanword	Reference	Provenance	Origin	Genre	Date
pur-ṣi-na-[te]	CTN III 87 s.2	Calah	Calah	AD	8th c.
GIŠ.*pur-ṣi-⸢na⸣-te*	CTN III 87 r.15 [GIŠ.*pur-ṣ*]*i-na-te*, 17	Calah	Calah	AD	8th c.
Ú.*pur-ṣi-na-te*	CTN III 87 r.20	Calah	Calah	AD	8th c.

Aram. ⇒ NA [?]

1102 See Wiseman, VTE, p. 76:603.

1103 E. Reiner, "The Vassal-Treaties of Esarhaddon," in J.B. Pritchard (ed.), *Ancient Near Eastern Texts Relating to the Old Testament* (Princeton 1969), p. 540:87.

1104 K. Watanabe *Die adê-Vereidigung anlässlich der Thronfolgeregelung Asarhaddons* (Berlin 1987), p. 204 § 87.

1105 Watanabe, ibid. Cf. S. Parpola & K. Watanabe, *Neo-Assyrian Treaties and Loyalty Oaths* (Helsinki 1988), p. 55:603 and the Glossary (p. 99a s.v. *pispisu*).

1106 Quoted in Watanabe, ibid.

1107 See the reference in SL p. 1262b. Cf. LS p. 613b. See also Jastrow, p. 1248b; Dalman, p. 339b.

1108 See GAG § 57a.

1109 See n. 71 above.

Sam., JLA *pwrṣn, pwrṣn'* n. m. "kernels of grapes, a pomace of kernels" DSA 677b; Jastrow 1148b;[1110] CAL. JBA, TA *pwrṣnt'* n. f. "stone or kernel of fruit (esp. of grapes)" DJBA 893a; Dalman 337a. Syr., *prṣnt'* (*parṣentā*) n. f. "pomegranate seed; grain of a seed" SL 1250b; Manna 614a; Audo 825b. Syr., *parṣānā, parṣentā* n. m. & f. "a grape stone, pomegranate seed" PSm. 464b.[1111]

This word has no entry in AHw., CAD or CDA. In AEAD (p. 85a s.v. *purṣīnu*), it is listed as meaning "pomegranate seed." It is attested at least three times in a single administrative text concerning *ilkakate*-payments related to contributions (of food), or dues.

Kinnier Wilson reads the word as *burṣināte*, and suggests rendering it as "door socket," based on a possible connection with the term *burṣimtu* applied to doors.[1112] Postgate, on the other hand, suggests the reading *burṣināte* or *purṣināte*, considering it perhaps to be connected to the word *pursandu* (an oil-producing substance) or the word *buṣin*(*nu*), a plant used for making wicks.[1113] In addition, he points out that Kwasman suggested a connection with Aramaic *purṣana* "kernels of grapes."[1114]

Notably, this NA word is written in three different ways in the same text. It occurs as GIŠ.*pur-ṣi-*⸢*na*⸣*-te*, i.e., is preceded by the determinative GIŠ, which comes before the names of trees and devices made of wood. It is also attested as Ú.*pur-ṣi-na-te*, i.e., preceded by the determinative Ú, which comes before the names of plants. However, it also occurs without a preceding determinative, namely as *pur-ṣi-na-*[*te*]. These three different ways of writing the same word in a single text indicate, most likely, the scribe's uncertainty about how to write the word, obviously because it was not a genuine Akkadian word. In addition to *purṣīnāte*, other things are mentioned in the context, such as leeks, pistachios and grapes. All these things together indicate that *purṣīnāte* almost certainly refers to a vegetable or a fruit. The evidence at hand points to a loanword meaning "pomegranate seed; kernel of grapes," most probably borrowed from Aramaic.

pusku,[1115] *pušku* n. "span, handbreadth, palm (as a linear measure: $^{1}/_{6}$ cubit = ca. 8 cm.)"

Loanword	Reference	Provenance	Origin	Genre	Date
pu-⸢*su*!*-ku*!⸣	SAA V 295 e.26	Nineveh	–	L	Sg
pu-us-ki	SAA XVI 197:4′	Nineveh	–	L	Esh
pu-uš-ki	CTN III 95 r.7, 21	Calah	Calah	AD	PC?
pu-uš-ku	CTN II 212:9′	Calah	Calah	AD	–
	CTN III 95 r.27	Calah	Calah	AD	PC?

1110 See Jastrow (p. 1148b s.v. פּוּרְצְנָא "kernels of grapes, a pomace of kernels").
1111 According to Manna (p. 614a s.v. ܦܪܨ), a denominative verb ܦܪܨ "to loosen the seeds of pomegranate" is attested in Sūret.
1112 See CTN I, pp. 107f.
1113 See n. ad CTN III 87:42, 45, 50.
1114 Ibid.
1115 See AEAD (p. 85a s.v. *pusku*).

pu-uš-ka-a-a	CTN II 1:5′	Calah	Calah	TL	–
	StAT 3 1 r.5	Assur	Assur	TL	–

Aram. ⇒ NA; LB

OffAr., JBA, JPA, TA, Syr., *pšk*, *pšk'* (*pšak*, *pe/ukšā*) n. m. "handbreadth, palm (1/6 cubit, 4 fingers)" DNWSI 946; DJBA 894a; DJPA 453b; Jastrow 1149a; Dalman 339b; SL 1261b; PSm. 468b; Manna 619b; Audo 836a; CAL. Syr., *pšk* v. Pe. & Pa. "to measure with span" Manna 619b; Audo 836b.

In AHw. (pp. 883b, 1583b s.v. *pušku*), this word is considered to be an Aramaic foreign word in NA and LB with the meaning "Handbreite; 1/6 Elle."[1116] The editors of CAD (P, p. 542b s.v. *pušku* A) list the word as meaning "handbreadth, palm (one sixth of a cubit)," and consider it to be an Aramaic loan in NA and NB.[1117]

The context where *pusku/pušku* occurs shows that it indicates a linear measure. It is equivalent to a sixth part of cubit, i.e., an approximate metric equivalent of 8 cm.[1118] However, the root PŠK is not operative in Akkadian. Therefore, we must look elsewhere for the etymology, and the available evidence points to a borrowing from Aramaic. The NA form *pusku*, with an *s* instead of *š*, is in accordance with the fact that NA <*s*> is used to represent West-Semitic /*š*/.[1119] On the other hand, it is difficult to account for the NA form *pušku*. A trans-NB Aramaic loan in NA would allow the form *pušku*, but the latter is, so far, only attested in LB. As for *puškāyē*, which in both cases occurs in the genitive, i.e., *ša pu-uš-ka-a-a*, von Soden considers it to be the same word, but in a still unexplained special use.[1120] It seems, however, that *ša pu-uš-ka-a-a* is used in qualifying textiles "that are each a palm wide."[1121]

pušku n. "handbreadth, palm"; (see the discussion above s.v. *pusku*)

puṭuru n. "mushroom, fungus"

Loanword	Reference	Provenance	Origin	Genre	Date
pu-ṭu-ri	SAA VII 130:1	Nineveh	Nineveh	AD	7th c.

Aram. ⇒ NA

[1116] See also von Soden, *Or* 37 (1968), p. 263:116; idem, *Or* 46 (1977), p. 192:116. Cf. CDA (p. 280a s.v. *pušku*).
[1117] See also Postgate, FNALD, § 6.6.2; M.A. Powell, "Masse und Gewichte," *RlA* 7 (1987–1990), pp. 470ff; Abraham & Sokoloff, *Reassessment*, p. 45:173.
[1118] See Postgate, ibid., § 6.6.0. Cf. Powell, ibid., pp. 470f., § I.4b.
[1119] See F.M. Fales, "Two Neo-Assyrian Notes," *RA* 75 (1981), p. 67, n. 2. See also n. 71 above.
[1120] See von Soden, *Or* 46 (1977), p. 192:116. Cf. n. ad StAT 3 1:22.
[1121] See CAD (P, p. 542b s.v. *pušku* A, b).

JBA *pyṭwr'* n. m. "fungus" DJBA 899a; Jastrow 1162a; CAL. Syr., *pṭwrt'* (*peṭōrtā*) n. f. "mushroom, fungus" SL 1181a; PSm. 442a; Manna 585a; Audo 777b.

This word occurs as a *hapax legomenon* in NA. It is attested in an administrative text (SAA VII 130:1) containing an inventory of various gifts of food from officials to the Lady of the House. It has en entry in CAD (P, p. 555a s.v. *puṭūru*), where it is defined as (a foodstuff). The word is not entered in AHw., however, it is listed in CDA (p. 280b s.v. *puṭūru* I), and is hesitatingly defined as (a mushroom). In AEAD (p. 85b s.v. *puṭuru*), the word is listed with the meaning "champignon, fungus, mushroom, truffle." Furthermore, an adjective, namely *puṭrānu* "fungous, spongy," is also entered in AEAD.[1122] Fales and Postgate, the editors of SAA VII 130, tentatively render *pu-ṭu-ri* as "truffles."[1123]

SAA VII 130:1–2, reads as follows:

[1] *sa-lu pu-ṭu-ri* [*x x x*] / *ša* ⸢LÚ$^{!}$⸣.NAM$^{!}$ KUR$^{!}$.*ba*[*r*]-⸢*ḫa*$^{?}$⸣-[*z*]*i*

[*1*] basket of *truffles* [...] – of the governor of Barḫalzi.

As stated above, the contents of the text (SAA VII 130) consist of various provisions contributed by the officials. These include sheep, lamb, birds, wine and *spray* of pomegranates. This leads us to conclude that *pu-ṭu-ri* must have been some kind of foodstuff.

Semantically, the Akkadian verb *paṭāru* in the G-stem means "to loosen, unite; to clear away; to uncover; to release, free; to discontinue," and in the D-stem it means "to unhitch; to separate; to clear away; to dismantle; to dispel, break; to release." From this verb a substantive, *puṭūru*, is derived with the sense "release, ransom," which is found in NB as well as lexically in SB.[1124] However, neither this substantive nor the other meanings of the Akkadian verb *paṭāru* fits the context where the NA word *pu-ṭu-ri* is attested.

In the other Semitic languages, a related root PṬR/FṬR is also known.[1125] From this root, the word ܦܛܘܪܬܐ "mushroom," is attested in Syriac[1126] and the word פִּיטוּרָא "fungus," is found in JBA.[1127] In Syriac, the verb ܦܛܪ in the Afʿel tense means "to shoot out, thrust out."[1128] In Arabic, from the root FṬR, we have a substantive with the first vowel *i/u*, i.e., الفُطْر/الفِطْر "mushroom," and the verb فَطَّرَ "to split, cleave," as well as the expression تَفَطَّرَت الأرضُ بالنباتِ, which approximately means "the earth was cracked by the plant."[1129] In Mishnaic

[1122] See AEAD (p. 85b s.v. *puṭrānu*).

[1123] In the Glossary of SAA VII (p. 219b s.v. *puṭuru*), the word is listed as meaning "fungus, mushroom, truffle."

[1124] See AHw. (p. 885a s.v. *puṭūru*); CDA (p. 280b s.v. *puṭūru* II).

[1125] See AHw. (p. 849a s.v. *paṭāru*(*m*)).

[1126] See SL, p. 1181a.

[1127] See DJBA, p. 899a.

[1128] See PSm., pp. 442f.

[1129] See *Al-munǧidu* (p. 587c s.v. فطر). Cf. Wehr-Cowan (p. 719b s.v. فطر).

Hebrew there is the word פִּטְרִיּוֹת meaning "mushrooms."[1130] In contrast, the word "truffle," as is known from some Semitic languages, is *km'* or *kmhh*. For instance, in Syriac we have the word ܟܡܐܬܐ "truffle,"[1131] and in JPA, כמהה*, pl. כמהין.[1132] In Arabic it is attested as كَمْءٌ (pl. كَمْأَةٌ) "truffle."[1133]

In CAD and CDA the word is listed as *puṭūru*, i.e., with the nominal form *PuRūSu*. The latter is an Akkadian nominal pattern which does not fall into a specific semantic range.[1134] On the other hand, AEAD lists the word as *puṭuru* with the nominal form *PuRuSu*. The attested plene writing *pu-ṭu-ri* suggests a transcription such as *puṭuru* for the nominative. Also, the Syriac and Arabic evidence does not exhibit a doubling of the second radical *ṭ*. Therefore, a development in NA such as *puṭṭuru* > *puṭūru* is not expected.

It is difficult to explain the vowel *u* in the first syllable of the NA word in view of the corresponding vowel *i* of the suggested Aramaic source word. Most likely, the change *i* > *u* in the NA word is a vowel assimilation triggered by the neighboring bilabial plosive *p*, as well as by the vowel *u* of the second syllable. Altogether, the evidence is in favor of a borrowing from Aramaic into NA.

***qallīlu**, (f. *qallīssu*) adj. "unimportant; little, small"

Loanword	Reference	Provenance	Origin	Genre	Date
qa-li-su	SAA X 194 r.11′	Nineveh	Nineveh	L	670
qàl-li-su	SAA XVI 62:4	Nineveh	–	L	671?

Aram. =▷ NA

OffAr., *qlyl* adj. "light (> despised); small (used as a nickname)" DNWSI 1011. Syr., *qlyl* adj. "light, small, minor; swift; reckless" Manna 677a. JBA, JPA, Syr., *qlyl* adj. "light, small, minor; swift" DJBA 1018b; DJPA 493b; Jastrow 1376b; SL 1370b; PSm. 506b; Audo 921b. OffAr., *qll* v. "(to be light >) to be less respected, despicable" DNWSI 1011. Sam., *qll* v. "to be little, unimportant" DSA 779a; CAL. Sam., *qll* adj. "little worth" DSA 778b.

This word is only attested in its feminine form and occurs as a *dis legomenon* in NA. The passages where it is attested are as follows:

SAA X 194 r.10′–11′, reads:[1135]

MÍ.*ṣu-uḫ-ru* / *qa-li-su bi-la-a-ni*

Get me *the small/little* (girl) Ṣuḫru.

[1130] See for reference, SL (p. 1181a s.v. ܦܛܪܝܬܐ). Cf. Jastrow (p. 1158b s.v. פִּטְרִיּוֹת).
[1131] See Manna, p. 330b; SL, p. 619a s.v. no. 2.
[1132] See DJPA (p. 262a s.v. כמהה).
[1133] See Elias & Elias, p. 602b.
[1134] See J. Fox, *Semitic Noun Patterns* (Winona Lake 2003), p. 209.
[1135] The translation differs slightly from that provided in SAA X 194.

SAA XVI 62:4–5, reads:

a-bu-tu-u qàl-li-su / ši-i

Is it an insignificant matter?

In AHw. (p. 894a s.v. *qallissu*), this word is rendered "eilige (Sache), baldigst," and is taken to be from Aramaic *qallīlā*. The editors of CAD (Q, p. 61b s.v. **qallilu*) render this word as "unimportant, small," and consider it possibly to be an Aramaic loanword in NA. In CDA (p. 283a s.v. *qallissu*), this word is translated as "slave girl; urgent; slight," and is tentatively considered to be a borrowing from Aramaic *qallīlā*.[1136] The word *qallu* (f. *qallatu*) as an adjective with the meaning "light; of low standing, of little value; small, young," is attested from OB onward.[1137]

Von Soden translated the two instances of *qallīssu* in the sense "eilig," and considered the word to be taken from Aramaic *qallīlā* "leicht; schnell, rasch."[1138] He regarded Parpola's rendering of the word *qallissu* in (MÍ.*ṣu-uḫ-ru / qa-li-su bi-la-a-ni*), as "slave girl," hardly to be correct, pointing out that the development *qallatu* > *qallissu* is impossible.[1139] Later, Parpola concurred with von Soden's argument and conceded that the feminine of Akkadian *qallu* "slave" would have been *qallutu*.[1140] Parpola, however, translated *qallīssu* in (*a-bu-tu-u qàl-li-su ši-i*), in the sense "unimportant matter," and considered von Soden's rendering of the same word as "swiftly" to be unwarranted.[1141] Recently, Abraham and Sokoloff have argued that this word may be an original form in Akkadian, saying that in the latter "the *QaṬṬīL*-pattern is also employed for adjectival forms, especially for verbs with the thematic vowel *i*, which is the case here."[1142] However, they point out that the regular Akkadian adjective from QLYL is *qallalu*.[1143]

Clearly, the NA feminine of **qallīlu*, i.e., **qallīltu* undergoes the well-known NA sound change *-lt* > *-ss-*, which leads to *qallīssu* < **qallīltu*.[1144] However, the fact is that the known Akkadian adjective of QLL for masculine in the D-stem is *qallalu* (NA *qallulu*) "very small, very little." This means that it takes the pattern *PaRRaS*, and its reconstructed NA feminine form would be **qallussu* < **qallultu*.[1145]

1136 Cf. the Glossary of SAA X (p. 354a s.v. *qallissu* "slave girl").
1137 See CAD (Q, p. 62a s.v. *qallu*).
1138 See von Soden, *Or* 37 (1968), p. 263:117.
1139 See von Soden, *Or* 46 (1977), p. 192:117. Cf. Parpola, LAS I, 151:11′.
1140 See LAS II ad no. 151 r.11′.
1141 Ibid. See also, S. Parpola, Review of "Akkadisches Handwörterbuch. Vols. II & III/1 (Lfg. 7–12)," by W. von Soden, *OLZ* 74 (1979), p. 31 ad 894a.
1142 See Abraham & Sokoloff, *Reassessment*, p. 45:175. Cf. GAG § 55m.
1143 Abraham & Sokoloff, ibid.
1144 See K. Deller, *Lautlehre des Neuassyrischen* (Wien 1959), § 43b; GAG § 34d; Hämeen-Anttila, SAAS XIII, § 2.2.3.2., c; Luukko, SAAS XVI, § 4.2.4.
1145 For adjectival forms of **qll* in NA, see K. Deller, W.R. Mayer & J. Oelsner "Akkadische Lexikographie: *CAD* Q," *Or* 58 (1989), p. 257 ad [60b]; von Soden, *Or* 37 (1968), p. 263:117. See also CAD (Q, p. 60a s.v. *qallalu*, p. 62a s.v. *qallu*).

As for SAA X (194 r.10′–11′), the name Ṣuḫru "Youth," is derived from the Akkadian word *ṣeḫēru(m)* "to be(come) small, young, little."[1146] On the other hand, we have *qlyl* attested in Official Aramaic as an adjective meaning "small, used as a nickname."[1147] Apparently, there is a semantic connection between the name Ṣuḫru and the word *qallīssu* which follows it. The combination *Ṣuḫru qallīssu* probably meant "Ṣuḫru the small/little." It is possible that the girl had a small stature and that is why she was called Ṣuḫru.[1148] As regards SAA XVI (62:4–5), the translation of *abutu qallīssu* as "insignificant matter" has an interesting parallel in JBA, i.e., מילי קליליתא "minor matters."[1149] Hence, despite the fact that the *PaRRiS* pattern is attested in Akkadian, the occurrence of *qallīssu* in NA in the sense "unimportant; small, little," can best be explained as a borrowing from Aramaic or as influenced by it.[1150]

qamāru v. (G) "to strap(?)"

Loanword	Reference	Provenance	Origin	Genre	Date
i-qa-mar	SAAB 5 12:4 (= VAT 14453 = ALA N9(13))	Assur	Assur	LD	681

Old Persian? ⇒ Aram. ⇒ NA [?]

Syr., *qmr* v. Pe. & Pa. "to tie; to strap, to gird, girdle, to put on a belt; to swathe, bind tightly; to fetter, chain" PSm. 509a; Manna 683b; Audo 929b. LJLA *qmr* v. Pa. "to tie; to put on a belt" Jastrow 1387a; CAL. JBA, Syr., Ma., *qmr*, *qmr*ʾ (*qmar*, *qamrā*) n. m. "belt, girdle" DJBA 1026b; Jastrow 1387a; SL 1379a; PSm. 509a; Manna 683b; Audo 929b; MD 401b; CAL.

This word is attested as a *hapax legomenon* in a NA note or receipt of debts pertaining to a commercial enterprise. The word is listed only in AEAD (p. 86b s.v. *qamāru*), where it is cautiously rendered "to strap(?)." The plausibility of any etymology proposed for this *hapax legomenon* is determined by the sentence context (SAAB 5 12:1–e.7), which reads as follows:[1151]

> [L]Ú*.TUR *ša* ᵐ*da-*⸢*da–aḫ*⸣ / ANŠE.NITÁ *a-di e-bi-si-šú* / *ša* EN–KASKAL-[MEŠ (*x*)] / *ma-a*ʾ*-da i-qa-mar* [*x*] / 1 MA.NA KUG.UD-MEŠ *ḫi-bi-la-a-*⸢*te*⸣ / ᵐ*da-da–aḫ* / TA ŠÀ-*bi* ⸢ÍL⸣

1146 See PNA 3/I (p. 1178a s.v. Ṣuḫru). Cf. AHw. (p. 1087a s.v. *ṣeḫēru(m)*); CAD (Ṣ, p. 120b s.v. *ṣeḫēru*).

1147 See DNWSI (p. 1011 s.v. *qlyl*, mng. no. 3).

1148 Cf. LAS II, ad no. 151 r.11′.

1149 See DJBA (pp. 1018f s.v. קְלִיל, mng. no. 5); Abraham & Sokoloff, ibid. Cf. DSA (p. 778b s.v. קלל).

1150 Cf. Abraham & Sokoloff, ibid.

1151 The transliteration of the texts cited is taken from the Corpus of Neo-Assyrian Texts (CNA). The translation of *i-qa-mar* as "he straps" is tentative.

> *A dependent/subordinate* of Dād-aḫ̮ḫ̮ē – *a* male donkey, including its bundles, of the expedition chiefs, *he straps* exceedingly; (thus) Dād-aḫ̮ḫ̮ē has taken away one mina of silver as compensation therefrom.

Fales and Jakob-Rost point out that despite a comprehensive collation the issue in this text (SAAB 5 12), is not entirely clear.[1152] They transliterate the word under discussion as *i*-QA-MAR and explain that the meaning of the expression (*ma-a'-da i*-QA-MAR) in line 4 is uncertain, but they take it as a verbal clause denoting an excess (*ma-a'-da*) of sorts in the treatment of a donkey.[1153] They point out that Deller, however, reads the word differently, as *i-qa-rad*! in the sense "kardätischt er (zu) sehr" arguing that this reading refers to an existing verb, unlike **qmr* which needs to be introduced into the Akkadian dictionary.[1154] Nevertheless, Fales and Jakob-Rost comment on Deller's suggested reading and rendering above saying that "the action implied by the verb has little bearing with a description of a donkey, 'including its bundles'."[1155]

As a matter of fact, the root QMR is not productive in Akkadian. Therefore, it is possible that this *hapax legomenon* in NA is a borrowing from somewhere else. Arabic has the words قَمَرَ v. "to gamble; to rob" and قَمَرُ n. m. "moon."[1156] Aramaic provides the word קמר "to tie; to strap, to gird, girdle; to bind tightly." We have the JBA קַמְרָא, Syriac ܩܡܪܐ and Mandaic as *qmr*ʾ n. m. "belt, girdle."[1157] Also, a denominative verb is attested in Syriac ܩܡܪ and LJLA קַמֵּר with the meanings "to tie; to girdle."[1158] In contrast, the Akkadian language, as opposed to the other Semitic languages, does not tend to form denominative verbs.[1159] The Aramaic meanings would fit the context of this NA text if the action implied by the verb concerned the packing on the donkey.

However, the Aramaic substantive is considered to be a borrowing from Middle Persian *kamar* "belt."[1160] The latter was also borrowed, apparently independently, into Arabic as كَمَر "belt (of hair)."[1161] Hence, the suggested source word belongs to the chronological period of Aramaic, which corresponds to Middle Persian. Phonologically, the use of the emphatic voiceless velar plosive *q* for rendering Iranian voiceless velar plosive *k* became standard only in the stage of Middle Aramaic, particularly in Jewish Babylonian Aramaic, Syriac and

---

1152 See F.M. Fales & L. Jakob-Rost, "Neo-Assyrian Texts from Assur Private Archives in the Vorderasiatishes Museum of Berlin, Part 1," *SAAB* 5 (1991), p. 41, n. on l. 1ff.
1153 Ibid.
1154 See n. ad SAAB 5 12:4.
1155 Ibid.
1156 Scc *Al-munǧidu* (p. 653b s.v. قمر).
1157 See DJBA (p. 1026b s.v. קַמְרָא); SL (p. 1379a s.v. ܩܡܪܐ).
1158 See Manna (p. 683b s.v. ܩܡܪ); Audo (p. 929b s.v. ܩܡܪ); Jastrow (p. 1387a s.v. קַמֵּר).
1159 See G. Buccellati, *A Structural Grammar of Babylonian* (Wiesbaden 1996), pp. 72f.
1160 See C.A. Ciancaglini, *Iranian Loanwords in Syriac* (Wiesbaden 2008), pp. 248f s.v. ܩܡܪܐ; C. Bartholomae, *Altiranisches Wörterbuch* (Strassburg, 1904), p. 440b s.v. *kamarā*; H. Hübschmann, *Armenische Grammatik*, I Teil, *Armenische Etymologie* (Leipzig 1897), p. 164 no. 296; DJBA 1026b s.v. קַמְרָא. Cf. DNWSI (p. 1013 s.v. qmr_2).
1161 See *Al-munǧidu* (p. 698a s.v. كَمَر).

Mandaic.[1162] In the Achaemenian and Hellenistic period, this was never the case.[1163]

On the other hand, while Old Persian was the vernacular language of the Achaemenid monarchs, it was certainly spoken for a few centuries prior to the rise of the Achaemenid dynasty. It is plausible, despite the chronological and phonological difficulties referred to above, that the word *kamar* "belt," already existed in Old Persian and was borrowed into the earlier dialects of Aramaic from which it entered NA. If such were the case, then *qamāru* must be considered a trans-Aramaic loanword in NA. In addition, the NA *qamāru* would represent a case where we can retrieve an Old Persian word. It would also point to an early representation of Old Persian *k* by Aramaic *q*.

qanū'āte n. m. *or* f. pl. "reeds"

Loanword	Reference	Provenance	Origin	Genre	Date
qa-nu-a-te	Rfdn 17 15:5	Assur	Assur	LD	633*

Aram. =▷ NA [?]

OffAr., JBA, JPA, CPA, Syr., *qnh*, *qany'* (*qanyā*, pl. *qənayyā*, *qanyē*, *qənāwāṯā*) n. m. "reed" DNWSI 1014; DJBA 1028b; DJPA 496b; LSp. 181a; DCPA 376b; Manna 685a; Audo 932b; SL 1383b; PSm. 510b; Jastrow 1392a. Ma., *qaina* (by metathesis) n. m. "reed, cane, stalk, rod" MD 400a, 411b.

The word used to designate "reed" in Akkadian is *qanû*. Its usual plural form in NA is *qanê*, but it is also attested as *qanāti*.[1164] However, the word has an additional plural form in NA, *qanū'āte* "reeds," which occurs as a *hapax legomenon* in a legal document (Rfdn 17 15:5) concerning loan of various commodities. The line where the word occurs reads as follows: [*m*]*a*?-SAR-*a-te* *qa-nu-a-te* "... reeds."[1165] Cognates of the word are attested in different Semitic languages. For instance, in Biblical Hebrew it is קָנֶה n. m. "reed," in Syriac ܩܢܝܐ n. m. "a cane, reed" and ܩܢܘܬܐ n. f. pl. "reeds," and in Arabic قَنَاةٌ n. f. "(bamboo) lance."[1166]

[1162] See S. Shaked, "Iranian Words Retrieved from Aramaic," in D. Weber (ed.), *Languages of Iran: Past and Present: Iranian Studies in Memoriam David Neil MacKenzie* (Wiesbaden 2005), p. 173.

[1163] Ibid.

[1164] See AEAD (p. 86b s.v. *qanû*); AHw. (p. 898a s.v. *qanû*(*m*) I); CAD (Q, p. 85a s.v. *qanû*). Cf. the expression LÚ*.*šá*–UGU–*qa-na-te* "overseer of reeds," in SAA XIV 81 r.9.

[1165] The reading of the line (Rfdn 17 15:5) comes from the State Archives of Assyria Project's electronic database, Corpus of Neo-Assyrian Texts (CNA). Cf. A.Y. Ahmad, "The Archive of Aššur-mātu-taqqin Found in the New Town of Aššur and Dated Mainly by Post-Canonical Eponyms," *Al-Rāfidān* 17 (1996), p. 246, n. on l. 5.

[1166] See Jastrow, p. 1388b; Manna (p. 685a s.v. ܩܢܝܐ); Wehr-Cowan, p. 794a.

Zadok points out that the NA form of the word *qa-nu-a-te* "reeds" corresponds to Akkadian *qa-na-(a-)te*, but ends with an Aramaic plural.[1167] He adduces some instances of Aramaic substantives with a similar plural form, among other things the Old Aramaic word in Zakkūr Stele *mḥnh*, *mḥnt*ʾ n. f. "army, camp," which in the plural construct form appears as *mḥnwt*.[1168] In its plural form, however, the word is attested in OA as *qanuʾe*.[1169] On the basis of the latter, Streck poses the question of whether the form of the OA *qanuʾe* is related or has some bearing on the form of the NA *qanūʾāte*.[1170] A potential corresponding form is found in the Syriac *qənāwāṯā*. The Aramaic influence, in this case, would be classified as "Lehnbildung," i.e., formation of a NA word after the pattern of an Aramaic word.

qapīru n. (a container or measure for fish and dates)

Loanword	Reference	Provenance	Origin	Genre	Date
DUG.*qa-pi-ra-ni*	SAA XIII 157 r.4	Nineveh	*Calah*	L	7th c.
qa-bir	SAA VII 136 ii′ 3′	Nineveh	Nineveh	AD	7th c.
qa-pi-ru	SAA XI 37:2	Nineveh	*Nineveh*	AD	7th c.

Aram. ⇒ NA [?]

OffAr., Syr., *qpyr*, *qpyr*ʾ (*qpīrā*) n. m. (a certain measure, a measure of capacity), SL 1392a; DNWSI 1020; CAL.

This word is a *tris legomenon* in NA. In AHw. (p. 898b s.v. *qapīru*), it is defined as (ein Hohlmaβ), and is considered to be an Aramaic foreign word in NA. The editors of CAD (Q, p. 91b s.v. *qapīru*) define this word as (a container), and refer to a Syriac cognate. In CDA (p. 284a s.v. *qapīru*), the word is defined as (a container (for fish, dates)), and is considered to be a borrowing from Aramaic.

In his article on Aramaic loanwords, von Soden considered *qapīru* to be an Aramaic borrowing into NA and referred for an etymology to the Syriac word *qəpīrā*, which denotes a certain measure of capacity.[1171] Brockelmann, on the other hand, tentatively suggested that the Syriac word should perhaps be read as ܩܦܝܕܐ.[1172] According to CAL, all instances of the rare term *qəpīrā* ought to be connected with the well-known term *qpyz*, which designates (a measure of

[1167] See R. Zadok, "On aromatics and reeds," *NABU* 1997/55, no. 3). Cf. the designation LÚ*.*šá*–UGU–*qa-na-te* "overseer of reeds," (AR 660:23 = SAA XIV 81 r.9), in AHw. (p. 898a s.v. *qanû*(*m*) I, mng. no. 1, e).

[1168] See ibid. See also R. Degen, *Altaramäische Grammatik der Inschriften des 10.–8. Jh. v.Chr.* (Wiesbaden 1969), p. 52 s.v. *mḥnwt*, p. 53, n. 20.

[1169] See the OA spelling *qá-nu-e* in AHw. (p. 898a s.v. *qanû*(*m*) I, meaning no. 1, a)).

[1170] M.P. Streck (personal communication).

[1171] See von Soden, *Or* 46 (1977), p. 192:199. Cf. DNWSI (p. 1020 s.v. *qpyr*$_2$).

[1172] See LS (p. 686a s.v. ܩܦܝܪܐ); SL (p. 1392a s.v. ܩܦܝܪܐ). See also Abraham & Sokoloff, *Reassessment*, p. 46:176.

capacity), and which in Official Aramaic is read as *qpyd* and in Syriac as *qpyz*.[1173] The Syriac word *qəpīzā*, in turn, is borrowed into Arabic as قفيز.[1174] Interestingly, however, there exists an Arabic word, namely قفير "basket; beehive," which is probably cognate with the NA *qapīru* and Aramaic *qpyr'*.[1175] Nevertheless, based on the evidence at hand, a borrowing from Aramaic into NA cannot be determined with complete certainty.

qarābu n. "battle, fight, combat"

Loanword	Reference	Provenance	Origin	Genre	Date
qa-ra-a-bu	SAA II 6:311	Calah	Calah	T	672
qar-a-bi	SAA XV 113:18	Nineveh	Der	L	Sg
	SAA XV 130:14, 22	Nineveh	*Der*	L	Sg
qa-ra-bi	SAA I 1:8 *qa-ra-bi*! (RL)	Calah	Calah	L	Sg
	SAA V 3 r.4	Nineveh	Amidi	L	Sg
	SAA XVI 77 r.5	Nineveh	Nineveh	L	Esh
qa-rab-šú-nu	SAA III 17:14	Ḫuzīrīna	*Ḫuzīrīna*	LT	9th c.
qar-a-bu	SAA XV 130:20	Nineveh	Der	L	Sg
qa-ra-bu	SAA III 34:23, 69	Assur	Assur	LT	–
	SAA III 35:29, 41	Nineveh	Nineveh	LT	–
	SAA XV 69:14	Nineveh	Šingibūtu	L	Sg
	SAA XV 101:13	Nineveh	Kār-Šarrukīn	L	Sg
	SAA XVI 243 r.2′ *qa-ra-b*[*u*]	Nineveh	–	L	Esh
	SAA XIX 25:4	Calah	Ṣimirra?	L	Tgl
	SAA XIX 71 r.1	Calah	Urarṭian frontier	L	Tgl
	SAA XIX 125:27′	Calah	Babylonia	L	Tgl

Aram. ⇒ NA ⇒ SB?

OffAr., JBA, JPA, Sam., CPA, Syr., Ma., *qrb*, *qrb'* (*qrāḇ*, *qrāḇā*) n. m. "war, battle" DNWSI 1030; DJBA 1038b; DJPA 502a; DSA 796b; LSp. 184a; DCPA 381a; SL 1401b; PSm. 517b; Manna 700b; Audo 948a; MD 415a, 356b. Syr., *qrb* v. Af. "to make war, fight, join battle" SL 1401a; PSm. 517b; Manna 700a.

In Akkadian the word *tāḫāzu*(*m*), is generally used to mean "battle, combat."[1176] Also, the word *mitḫuṣu* in the sense "fight, combat," is used in MA and SB.[1177] However, in NA another word, namely *qarābu* is also used to mean "battle, combat." The equation (*mit-ḫu-ṣu* = *qa-ra-bu*) is attested in a SB synonym list

---

[1173] See CAL, s.v. *qpyz*. See also DNWSI (p. 1020 s.v. *qpyr*₂, *qpr*₁); SL (p. 1391a s.v. ܩܦܝܙܐ). Cf. R.K. Ritner, "The Earliest Attestation of the *kpḏ*-Measure," in P.D. Manuelian (ed.), *Studies in Honor of William Kelly Simpson* (Boston 1996), pp. 683–688.
[1174] See Fraenkel, p. 207.
[1175] See *Al-munğidu* (p. 646a s.v. القفير). Cf. Wehr-Cowan, p. 781a.
[1176] See CAD (T, p. 42a s.v. *tāḫazu*); AHw. (p. 1301a s.v. *tāḫāzu*(*m*)).
[1177] See CAD (M/II, p. 138b s.v. *mitḫuṣu*); AHw. (p. 662b s.v. *mitḫuṣu*).

from Assyria.[1178] In AHw. (p. 901b s.v. *qarābu* I), this word, glossed as "Kampf," is considered to be a borrowing from Aramaic into NA and SB.[1179] In CAD (Q, p. 125b s.v. *qarābu*), the word is glossed "battle, fight," and considered to be a borrowing from Aramaic into NA.

Zimmern was of the opinion that while the general meaning of QRB "to approach" is Common Semitic, the special military meaning of QRB "to fight," as well as of *qərāb*, *qərābā* "battle, war," in later Hebrew and Aramaic is perhaps a borrowing from Akkadian.[1180] Von Soden in his articles on Aramaic loanwords considered the word *qarābu* meaning "Kampf," to be a borrowing from Aramaic into NA and SB.[1181] Mankowski doubts an Eastern Semitic origin of this word, and points out that as early as ca. 510 B.C., the word *qarābu* is attested in Imperial Aramaic in the Behistun inscription, whereas the analogous Akkadian passage uses the usual term *tāḫāzi*.[1182] Abraham and Sokoloff also argue in support of a loanword from Aramaic into NA saying that the Akkadian verb is *qerēbu*, and the majority of the derived nouns in Akkadian have an *e* vowel, whereas the substantive *qarābu* in NA has two *a* vowels, as in Aramaic.[1183]

However, one might argue that *qerēbu* is the form of the verb in Babylonian vis-à-vis the Assyrian *qarābu*,[1184] of which the substantive is expected to take either a short vowel, i.e., *qarbu*, or a long vowel, i.e., *qarābu*. The latter is a substantivized infinitive of the G-stem. Interestingly, the word קְרָב "Kampf" in the Hebrew of the Old Testament is considered to be a lexical Aramaism.[1185] However, based on distribution of the word and the Behistun inscription, the evidence points to borrowing from Aramaic into NA. In fact, one might speak of a semantic extension of the NA root QRB under the influence of its Aramaic cognate. It remains to be pointed out that the word *qarābu* ought also to be listed in AEAD as a separate lemma as a substantive meaning "battle."[1186]

qarāḫu v. (G) "to freeze";[1187] (see the discussion below s.v. *qarḫu*)

Loanword	Reference	Provenance	Origin	Genre	Date
i-qar-ra-ḫu-ni	SAA XIII 127 r.17	Nineveh	Babylonia	L	Esh
iq-ru-ḫu	SAA V 272 r.3	Nineveh	–	L	Sg

Heb. ⇒ Aram. ⇒ NA [?]

[1178] See W. von Soden, LTBA 2, 2:238f.
[1179] Cf. DNWSI (p. 1030 s.v. *qrb₃*); CDA (p. 285a s.v. *qarābu*).
[1180] Zimmern, AF, p. 13.
[1181] See also von Soden, *Or* 37 (1968), p. 264:119; idem, *Or* 46 (1977), p. 192:119. Cf. Kaufman, AIA, p. 30; S. Parpola, "Neo-Assyrian Treaties from the Royal Archives of Nineveh," *JCS* 39 (1987), p. 183.
[1182] Mankowski, ALBH, pp. 133f.
[1183] See Abraham & Sokoloff, *Reassessment*, p. 46:178.
[1184] See GAG § 9b. See also AHw. (p. 915b s.v *qerēbu(m)*); CAD (Q, p. 228a s.v. *qerēbu*).
[1185] See M. Wagner, *Die lexikalischen und grammatikalischen Aramaismen im alttestamentlichen Hebräisch* (Berlin 1966), p. 103:270.
[1186] See AEAD (p. 87a s.v. *qarābu*, p. 150a s.v. "battle"). Cf. CDA (p. 285a s.v. *qarābu*).
[1187] See AHw. (p. 902a s.v. *qarāḫu*); CAD (Q, p. 126b s.v. *qarāḫu*); AEAD (p. 87a s.v. *qarāḫu*).

qarḫu, (pl. *qarḫāte*) n. "ice, frost"; (see also above s.v. *qarāḫu*)

Loanword	Reference	Provenance	Origin	Genre	Date
qar-ḫa-a-te	SAA XV 41:9′	Nineveh	–	L	Sg
qar-ḫu	SAA V 105 r.6	Nineveh	*Kumme*	L	Sg
	SAA V 272 r.2	Nineveh	–	L	Sg
	SAA XIII 127 r.17	Nineveh	Babylonia	L	Esh

Heb. ⇒ Aram. ⇒ NA; SB[1188]

Sam., BabMBK,[1189] LJLA *qrḥ*, *qrḥ'* (*qārəḥā*, *qariḥā*) n. m. "ice, frost, hail" DSA 798b; CAL; Jastrow 1415b; Dalman 371b.[1190]

In NA, the word *qarḫu* "ice" is used instead of the Akkadian word *šurīpu* "ice."[1191] The equation (*šu-ri-pu* = *qar-ḫu*) is attested in a SB synonym list.[1192] Also, a denominative verb, namely *qarāḫu* "to freeze," occurs in conjunction with *qarḫu* in two paranomastic expressions: *a-di qar-ḫu la i-qar-ra-ḫu-ni* "before it ices up" (SAA XIII 127 r.17); *šúm-mu qar-ḫu / ina* UGU-*ḫi-šú* : *la iq-ru-ḫu* "If ice does not form on it" (SAA V 272 r.2–3).

Von Soden states that in the case of NA *qarḫu* "ice" the borrowing question cannot be answered with certainty.[1193] He explains that the sense "kalt werden, gefrieren" is expressed in Aramaic by the roots QRR and QRŠ, and their derivatives, but the variant QRḤ in Aramaic is only attested as a nominal root in *qarḥā*.[1194] Abraham and Sokoloff state that if the NA and SB *qarḫu* "ice" were related to the West-Semitic word for ice, a borrowing into NA and SB would seem likely.[1195] They add that the word קֶרַח "ice" is well known in Biblical Hebrew, but a similar word is lacking in Aramaic.[1196]

As for the Aramaic dialects, in fact Samaritan Aramaic has the words קרח "frost, ice" and קורח "ice."[1197] According to CAL, *qrḥ* "ice" is also attested in Babylonian Magic Bowl Koine Aramaic (BabMBK), as well as in a Late Jewish

---

[1188] See AHw. (p. 903b s.v. *qarḫu*); CDA (p. 285b s.v. *qarḫu*).

[1189] According to CAL, incantation bowls (*or* magic bowls) are usually written in a formal standardized literary Eastern Aramaic, but occasionally they are written in a "koine" of Southern Babylonian Aramaic.

[1190] See CAL s.v. *qrḥ*, mng. no. 5. See also Jastrow (p. 1415b s.v. קַרְחָא); Dalman (p. 371b s.v. קַרְחָא).

[1191] See AHw. (p. 903b s.v. *qarḫu*); CAD (Q, p. 131b s.v. *qarḫu*); AEAD (p. 87a s.v. *qarḫu*). Cf. K. Radner, "Salmanassar V. in den *Nimrud Letters*," *AfO* 50 (2003/2004), pp. 101f. Cf. also M.P. Streck, "Schnee," in M.P. Streck et al. (eds.), *Reallexikon der Assyriologie und Vorderasiatischen Archäologie, vol., 12: Šamuḫa–Spinne* (Berlin 2009/2011), pp. 241f.

[1192] See W. von Soden, LTBA 2, 2:311. Cf. B. Landsberger, "Lexikalisches Archiv," *ZA* 42 (1934), p. 157.

[1193] See von Soden, *Or* 37 (1968), p. 264:120; idem, *Or* 46 (1977), p. 192:120. Cf. DNWSI (p. 1032 s.v. *qrh*$_2$ and *qrḥ*$_2$). Cf. also Tadmor, *Aramaization*, pp. 455 and 467, n. 105.

[1194] von Soden, ibid.

[1195] See Abraham & Sokoloff, *Reassessment*, p. 46:179.

[1196] Ibid.

[1197] See DSA (p. 798b s.v. קורח).

Literary Aramaic text (LJLA).[1198] However, CAL states that the word *qrḥ* "ice" entered the Aramaic dialects from Hebrew.[1199] Perhaps, the Hebrew קֶרַח "frost, ice, hail"[1200] is somehow connected etymologically with the Syriac words ܩܪܣ "to freeze, be frozen; to become cold,"[1201] and ܩܪܫ "to freeze, be frozen; to become cold,"[1202] as well as with the Arabic word قَرَس "severe *or* biting cold."[1203] However, Parpola points out that the NA *qarḫu* "ice" is already attested in the reign of Sargon II (721–705 B.C.), only a few years after the fall of Samaria, which does not allow sufficient time for a Hebrew loanword to spread into NA as a result of language contact between the two Semitic languages, given that the Israelite deportees were employed by the Assyrian army in the construction of Dūr-Šarrukēn after 720 B.C.[1204]

qarūḫu adj. "white-spotted (of animal); hornless (ram); bald (of an old animal)"

Loanword	Reference	Provenance	Origin	Genre	Date
qa-ru-ḫi	SAA XI 106 r.1	Nineveh	*Nineveh*	AD	–

Aram. ⇒ NA

JLA, PTA, Sam., LJLA *qrwḥ* adj. "white-spotted" DJPA 503b; Jastrow 1413b; Dalman 371b; DSA 798a; CAL. Sam., *qrwḥ* adj. "bald" DSA 798a; Dalman 371b; CAL. Syr., *qərāḥā*, *qarḥā* adj. "bald; spotted" SL 1405a; Manna 702a. Syr., *qərāḥā*, *qūrḥā* adj. "bald; having a white spot on the forehead; hornless (ram)" Manna 702a; Audo 951b, 952a; PSm. 518b. JBA, JPA, Sam., CPA, Syr., *qrḥ* v. "to become bald" DJBA 1039a; DJPA 504a; DSA 798a; SL 1404b; PSm. 518b; Manna 702a; Audo 951b.

This enigmatic word is attested as *qa-ru-ḫi* in a NA note (SAA XI 106 r.1) concerning oxen. It occurs as a *hapax legomenon* in a context which includes other terms that are suggested to be loanwords from Aramaic.[1205] In the edition of the note the word *qa-ru-ḫi* is left untranslated.[1206] Unfortunately, the text of the

1198 See CAL (s.v. *qrḥ*, mng. no. 5).
1199 See CAL, ibid.
1200 Cf. HALOT (p. 1140a s.v. קֶרַח).
1201 See Manna, p. 705b; Audo, p. 955b.
1202 See Manna, p. 710a; Audo, p. 959a.
1203 See Elias & Elias, p. 534a; Wehr-Cowan, p. 756a; *Al-munǧidu* (p. 619b s.v. قَرِسَ). Cf. HALOT (p. 1140a s.v. קֶרַח); H. Tawil, *An Akkadian Lexical Companion for Biblical Hebrew: Etymological-Semantic and Idiomatic Equivalents with Supplement on Biblical Aramaic* (Jersey City 2009), p. 345a s.v. קֶרַח.
1204 S. Parpola (personal communication).
1205 See n. ad SAA XI 106:8–r.3. See also the discussion above s.v. *ianūqu*, and below s.v. *salītu*.
1206 Note that in the Glossary of SAA XI, p. 166a, the word *qa-ru-ḫi* is listed under the heading *qarāḫu* "to freeze."

note is very brief and the context does not elucidate the meaning of our word.[1207] The note (SAA XI 106:1–r.3), reads as follows:

> ᵐ*tab*-URU-*a-a* GUD / ᵐ*dan-nu*–U.GUR :. / ᵐᵈPA–NUMUN–DÙ :. / ᵐMAN–IGI.LAL-*a-ni* :. / ᵐᵖPA–*šal-lim* :. / ᵐEN–PAB-*ir* :. / 0! PAB *an-nu-te* / *ša* GA.MEŠ / *ša sa-li-a-te* / *ša qa-ru-ḫi* / *ša ia-nu-qi* / *ša* GIŠ.ÙR.MEŠ
>
> Tabālāyu – an ox, Dannu-Nergal – ditto, Nabû-zēru-ibni – ditto, Šarru-ēmuranni – ditto, Nabû-šallim – ditto, Bēl-nāṣir – ditto, All these – of milk, of *nets*, of *a hornless (ram)*, of *a suckling*, of beams.

The major lexical tools offer contrasting proposals as regards the rendering and etymology of *qa-ru-ḫi*. AHw. (p. 905b s.v. *qarruḫu*, 2) lists it with the sense "kahlköpfig, altes Tier," and considers it to be an Aramaic foreign word in NA.[1208] The editors of CAD (Q, p. 126b s.v. *qarāḫu*; p. 145b s.v. *qarruḫu*) list the word under the heading *qarāḫu* "to become iced up," and tentatively translate it as "sherbet," noting that the form of *qa-ru-ḫi*, most likely represents an infinitive of the D-stem.

Von Soden connects *qa-ru-ḫi* with the word that follows it, namely *ia-nu-qi* (SAA XI 106 r.2), and interprets them in the sense of the Jewish Aramaic words *qrūḥā* "kahlköpfig" and *yānōqā* "Säugling" respectively as meaning "old animal" as opposed to "young animal."[1209] Fales, on the other hand, referring to Lipiński, suggests that the Aramaic term *q*(*y*)*r*(*w*)*ḥ* "spotted" probably underlies the NA cuneiform writing *qa-ru-ḫi*, which would provide a better sense in relation to oxen than does the rendering "kahlköpfig."[1210] However, no etymology for *qa-ru-ḫi* is found in Akkadian and a borrowing from Aramaic is likely. It is probably better to interpret our word in accordance with the Samaritan Aramaic term קרוח, which is attested in the nominal form *QāṬōL* in reference to an animal and with the meaning "(white) spotted."[1211]

qūbāti n. pl. "ague(?)"

Loanword	Reference	Provenance	Origin	Genre	Date
qu-ba-te-šú-nu	SAA V 156 r.6	Nineveh	Northeastern frontier	L	Sg

Aram. ⇒ NA [?]

[1207] See Abraham & Sokoloff, *Reassessment*, p. 46:181.

[1208] Cf. DNWSI (p. 1032 s.v. *qrḥ*₃). In CDA (p. 285b s.v. *qarruḫu*), the word is tentatively rendered "bald? (of old animal)." In AEAD (p. 87b s.v. *qarūḫu*), the word is rendered "bald, old animal."

[1209] See von Soden, *Or* 37 (1968), p. 270:169–170; idem, *Or* 46 (1977), p. 192:170.

[1210] See F.M. Fales, "On Aramaic Onomastics in the Neo-Assyrian Period," *OrAnt* 16 (1977), p. 68. Cf. E. Lipiński, *Studies in Aramaic Inscriptions and Onomastics, vol. I* (Leuven 1975), p. 122.

[1211] See DSA (p. 198a s.v. קרוח). Cf. Jastrow (p. 1413b), which provides the words קָרוּחַ, קֵרוֹחַ, in the sense "bald; white-spotted."

OAram., *qbbh* n. "shivering fit(?)" Brauner 515.[1212] Syr., *qwbb*, *qwbb'* (*qūbbāḇ*, *qūbbāḇā*) n. m. "ague, shivering fit" PSm. 491b; SL 1322a; Manna 651b; Audo 882b; CAL. Syr. *qbby*, *qbbyt'* (*qabbāḇī*, *qabbāḇīṯā*) n. f. "shivering fit, shudder, shuddering from fever" Audo 882b; Manna 651b; SL 1309a; PSm. 487a.[1213] Syr., *qbb* v. Pa. & Etpa. "to suffer fever, to shiver feverishly" Audo 882b; Manna 651b; SL 1308b; PSm. 486b.

This word is a *hapax legomenon* in NA and occurs as *qu-ba-te-šú-nu* in a letter (SAA V 156 r.6) addressed to king Sargon II concerning inspection of deportees.[1214] Since the word is a *hapax legomenon*, the plausibility of etymologies proposed for it is determined by the sentence context. The passage where the word occurs (SAA V 156 r.1–7) reads as follows:

> UN.MEŠ *e-ta-[an-šú]* / *a–dan-[niš]* / ⸢*šá*?⸣-*ár*!-*bu* *la*[*m*?-*šú-nu*] / *e-ta-kal* KUR.⸢MEŠ⸣-[*ni*] / [*i*]*m*!-*tar-qu-šú-nu* / *qu-ba-te-šú-nu* / *il-la-ku-u-ni*.
>
> The people are ve[ry] we[ak]; *weather* has eaten up [their] *loo*[*ks*] and the mountains have crushed them. They are coming *ague-stricken*.

In AHw. (p. 925b s.v. *qu*(*b*)*batu*) and CAD (Q, p. 291b s.v. *qubbātu*), the meaning of this word is given as unknown. In AEAD (p. 89a s.v. *qūbāti*), on the other hand, it is tentatively listed as having the sense "ague." Lanfranchi and Parpola tentatively translate the expression *qūbātišunu* as "ague-stricken."[1215] They suggest that *qūbāti* may be an Aramaic loanword and compare it to Syriac *qūbābā* "ague, shivering fit."[1216]

The form of the NA word developed as follows: *qūbāti* < *qubbāti*. AHw. analyzes *qu-ba-te-šú-nu* as a predicate in the plural masculine, but considers it to be unclear.[1217] It seems that the word consists of a noun in the plural plus a pronominal suffix of 3p. m. pl., functioning as copula, i.e., *qūbātišunu* < *qūbāti* + *-šunu* in the sense "they are *ague-stricken*." However, while the context of the passage supports the interpretation "ague-stricken," the rendering and the loan hypothesis remain speculative due to the somewhat fragmentary condition of the text.

[1212] Cf. R.A. Brauner, *A Comparative Lexicon of Old Aramaic* (Ann Arbor 1974), p. 527 s.v. *qqbt* "partridge(?)."

[1213] A word corresponding to Syriac ܩܒܒܝܬܐ in JPA is עבביתה n. f. "shivering fit," i.e., with initial ʿ instead of *q*. See DJPA (p. 391a s.v. עבבי).

[1214] Cf. the NA word [*q*]*u-ub-ba-tú*, which, if the reading is correct, occurs in a broken context in a commentary to the Assyrian cultic calendar (SAA III 40:20).

[1215] See SAA V 156, and the Glossary (p. 233b s.v. *qubbāti*). Cf. R. Zadok, "Assyro-Babylonian Lexical and Onomastic Notes," *BiOr* 41 (1984), p. 36:10.

[1216] See n. ad SAA V 156 r.6.

[1217] See AHw. (p. 925b s.v. *qu*(*b*)*batu*).

qumbutu n. f. "vault, arch, dome"

Loanword	Reference	Provenance	Origin	Genre	Date
qu-um-ba-t[*e*]	CTDS 7:5′	Dūr-Šarrukēn	Dūr-Šarrukēn	AD	7th c.
qu-um-bu-tú	SAA XIV 63:1′	Nineveh	Nineveh	LD	669

Aram. ⇒ NB? ⇒ NA [?]

Palm., Syr., Ma., LJLA *qwbh*, *qwbt*ʾ (*qubbā*, *qubbəṯā*) n. f. "vault, vaulted room, dome, arch" DNWSI 978; PSm. 491b; SL 1324a; Manna 652a; Audo 882a; MD 405b; Jastrow 1324a; CAL. JBA, JLA, Syr., *qwbh*, *qwbt*ʾ (*qubbā*, *qubbəṯā*) n. f. "pavilion" DJBA 989b; PSm. 491b; SL 1324a; Manna 652a; CAL. Ma., *qumba* n. m. and *qumbta* n. f. "vault, dome; arch, bow" MD 408b.

This word is a *dis legomenon* in NA. It is only listed in AEAD (p. 89a s.v. *qumbutu*), where it is defined as (a building). The plausibility of etymologies proposed for *qumbutu* is determined by the sentence context, here:

CTDS 7:1′–9′, reads:[1218]

[É *ep-šú a-di* GIŠ].˹ÙR˺.MEŠ-*šú a-di* / [GIŠ.IG.MEŠ-*šú a-na g*]*i-mir-ti-šú* / [*x x x x x x* S]UḪUR É [m]KÁ.DINGIR-*a-a* / [*x x x x x x* SIL]A *ša* É LÚ.EN.NAM / [*x x x x x x* S]UḪUR É *qu-um-ba-t*[*e*] / [*x x x x x x* SU]ḪUR SILA *ša* É [m]*ab-da-a* [0] / [*x x x x x x*]*x* É N[I]M *ina* ŠÀ-*bi* / [*x x x a-na* [d]A]G EN-*šu* / [*x x x x x x*]*x-ma* BA-*eš*

[A built house with its be]ams and [its doors in its e]ntirety, [...... a]djoining the house of Bābilāiu, [and adjoining the stree]t of the house of the governor, [...... a]djoining the *vault/arch*, [...... ad]joining the street of the house of Abdâ, [......], with an upper floor in it, [... *to* the god Na]bû, his lord [......] was donated.

SAA XIV 63:1′–11′, reads:[1219]

1 É *qu-um-bu-tú* ˹*x*˺ [*x x x x*] / ˹*x x x x x x x*˺ [*x x x x*] / É *tal-pi-tú a-na gi-m*[*ir-ti-šá*] / *ina* URU.ŠE [m]DÙG.GA–*pa-x*[*x x*] / É 20 ANŠE A.ŠÀ.MEŠ *x*[*x x x*] / *ad-ri* GIŠ.SAR ˹*x x*˺[*x x x*] / *ú-piš-ma* [m]PAB-*bu*-[*u x x*] / [*ina*] ŠÀ-*bi* 1 MA.NA 15 GÍN [KUG.UD] / [*ina*] 1 MA.NA-*e ša* URU.*gar*-[*ga-miš*] / [T]A *pa-an* [m]SUḪUŠ–[d]PA [*il-qi*] / [*kas-p*]*u ga-*˹*mur ta-din*˺

1 *vault/arch*, a *barnyard* to [its] enti[rety] in the village of Ṭab-pa[...]. An estate of 20 hectares of land [...], threshing floor, orchard [...] – Aḫ-abû, [...] has contracted and [bought f]or one mina 15 shekels of [silver by] the mina of Car[chemish fr]om Urbu-Nabû. [The mone]y is paid completely.

[1218] The transliteration of CTDS 7:1′–9′ given above is taken from the Corpus of Neo-Assyrian Texts (CNA). See PNA 1/I (p. 4a s.v. Abdâ, no. 16); PNA 1/II (p. 245b s.v. Bābilāiu, no. 33).

[1219] In SAA XIV 63, the word *qu-um-bu-tú* is not translated, and in the Glossary section (p. 326b s.v. *qumbutu*), the meaning of this word is considered uncertain.

In both NA texts quoted above, the evidence indicates that *qu-um-ba-t*[*e*] or *qu-um-bu-tú* designates a certain kind of building, structure or construction, especially because the word is preceded by the logogram É, which is a determinative used before buildings. The contexts, as well, point to the same conclusion.

Etymologically, the roots QMB and QNB are not productive in Akkadian. The nominal form of NA *qumbutu* must be that of *PuSSaT*, i.e., derived from a root consisting of a doubling of the second radical,[1220] such as QBB which is, likewise, not productive in Akkadian. This fact directs us to look somewhere else for the etymology of this NA word. A potential candidate for the source word for borrowing is the word *qubbəṯā* or *qumbəta* "vault, dome, arch," which is found in different dialects of Aramaic. It is perhaps borrowed into Arabic as قُبَّة "cupola, dome; dome-shaped edifice."[1221] It is probably also borrowed into Persian as *gunbad* "vault, dome, cupola," with the *g* instead of the initial *q*, and the dissimilation of the double *-bb-*, i.e., *bb* > *nb*.[1222] The Aramaic word provides a satisfactory meaning which fits the contexts where the word occurs. In Syriac, the verb ܩܒ݂ means, among other things, "to over-arch, form a dome," and in Pa. "to vault."[1223] According to Audo, this Syriac verb, i.e., *qbb*, seems to be exactly the same as the Syriac verb *kpp* "to curve, bow," but since the latter was pronounced hard, i.e., not aspirated, it changed even in writing, whereby the following developments took place: *k* > *q* and *p* > *b*.[1224] If Audo's interpretation is true, it would mean that the Syriac or Aramaic verb *qbb* "to over-arch, form a dome," is cognate with the Akkadian verb *kapāpu* "to bend, curve."[1225] The latter is Common Semitic except for Ethiopic.[1226]

Phonologically, the shape of the NA word *qumbutu* displays the so-called Assyrian vowel harmony. However, it also displays a dissimilation *bb* > *mb*, which is unusual in NA.[1227] In comparison, in the Babylonian dialect after OB, a long voiced consonant, especially *bb*, *dd*, *gg*, *zz*, i.e., a voiced doubled consonant, is often resolved into *m* + labial, or *n* + dental or sibilant (nasalization).[1228] According to Buccellati, this is a case of homorganic dissimilation.[1229] An instance of *bb* > *mb* comes from the word *nabû*(*m*) "to name," namely *ibbī* beside *imbī* "he called." This Babylonian tendency to dissimilate the double consonants

---

1220 See GAG § 541.
1221 See Wehr-Cowan, p. 737b; SL (p. 1324a s.v. ܩܘܡܒܬܐ).
1222 See Th. Nöldeke, *Persische Studien* (Wien, 1888), p. 41 s.v. گنبد; S. Shaked, "Aramaic Loan-words in Middle Persian," *Bulletin of the Asia Institute, N.S.*, 19, (2005), p. 160a s.v. *gunbad*.
1223 See PSm. (p. 486b s.v. ܩܒ݂); Manna (p. 651a s.v. ܩܒ݂); Audo (p. 882a s.v. ܩܒ݂). Cf. SL (p.1309a s.v. ܩܒܒ, mng. no. 2).
1224 See Audo (p. 882a s.v. ܩܒ݂).
1225 See CAD (K, p. 175a s.v. *kapāpu*).
1226 See AHw. (p. 442a s.v. *kapāpu*(*m*)).
1227 On the related subject of nasalization, see GAG § 32b; K. Deller, "Old Assyrian *Kanwarta*, Middle Assyrian *Kalmarte*, and Neo-Assyrian *Garmarte*," *JEOL* 29 (1985–1986, Leiden 1987), p. 48.
1228 See G. Buccellati, *A Structural Grammar of Babylonian* (Wiesbaden 1996), p. 39 § 5.2.8; A. Ungnad, *Akkadian Grammar* (Atlanta 1992), § 22c.
1229 See Buccellati, ibid.

dd, *bb*, and *zz* has been preserved as a phonetic feature in Mandaic.[1230] It can be seen, for instance, in the word *hmbl* < *hbbl* "to destroy." The same applies to the Mandaic *qumba* < *qubba*; *qumbta* < *qubbta* "vault, dome."

Taking into consideration the lack of an etymon in Akkadian and the phonological peculiarity associated with NA *qumbutu*, the evidence points to a borrowing into NA. However, the only feasible way by which this word could have entered NA is through the medium of the Babylonian dialect, i.e., a trans-NB loan from Aramaic, but so far no word *qumbatu* is attested in NB. Another possibility is to consider a direct borrowing from Aramaic into NA, but this requires the existence of a form of the word similar to that of Mandaic *qumbta* in at least one of the earlier dialects of Aramaic. Interestingly, a place name attested as *Qumbatu* occurs twice as URU.*qu-um-ba-te* in a NA legal document (SAA XIV 44:4, 6), and bears a resemblance to the NA word under discussion here.[1231] Whether there is some kind of connection between the two remains unclear.

rab šaglûti n. "deportation officer"; (see the discussion above s.v. *galû*)

Loanword	Reference	Provenance	Origin	Genre	Date
LÚ.GAL *šag-lu-te*	CTN III 102 iii 23′	Calah	*Calah*	AD	711?

Aram. ⇒ NA

radāpu, *radābu* v. (G) "to pursue, chase; to hurry, urge"; (see below s.v. *ridpu*)

Loanword	Reference	Provenance	Origin	Genre	Date
ar-ti-di-pi	CTN II 207:3′	Calah	–	L	–
ir[!]*-di-pa*	SAA X 273:14	Nineveh	Nineveh	L	672?
ir-ti-di-bi	SAA V 53:19	Nineveh	*Province of the Treasurer*	L	Sg
ir-ti-di-ip	SAA I 244:16	Nineveh	Naṣībina	L	Sg
ir-ti-di-p[*i*?]	CTN II 207:6′	Calah	–	L	–
ni-⸢*ir*⸣*-ti-di-pi*	SAA I 175 r.12	Calah	Ḫamāt	L	Sg
⸢*ni*⸣*-ir-ti-di-ip-šú-n*[*u*]	SAA XIX 26:11′	Calah	–	L	Sg?
ra-da[!]*-bi*	SAA V 47:13	Nineveh	Bit-Zamani	L	Sg

Aram. ⇒ NA; NB; LB

JBA, JPA, Sam., CPA, Ma., Syr., *rdp* v. Pe. "to pursue, follow after; to urge, drive on" DJBA 1060b; DJPA 517a; Jastrow 1453b; DNWSI 1061; DSA 819b; LSp. 190a; DCPA 391a; MD 425b; SL 1438b; PSm. 530b; Audo 977a; Manna 724b. Syr., *rdp* v. Etpa. "to be hurried" PSm. 530b. Ma., *radpa* n. m. "pursuit"

[1230] See T. Nöldeke, *Mandäische Grammatik* (Halle 1875), § 68:3.
[1231] Cf. n. ad NALDK, Appendix I, 4.

MD 418b. Syr., *rəḏāpā* n. m. "pursuit" Audo 977a. Ma., *ridpa* n. m. "persecution, oppression" MD 432b; CAL.

In AHw. (p. 941a s.v. *radāpu*), the word is glossed "verfolgen," and is considered to be a borrowing from Aramaic.[1232] The editors of CAD (R, p. 59b s.v. *radāpu*) listed the word in the sense "to pursue," and only referred to von Soden for an Aramaic cognate. However, in addition to Aramaic, the root RDP is found in Biblical Hebrew as רָדַף "to run, to pursue," and in Arabic as رَدَفَ "to come next, follow, succeed."[1233] Von Soden rightly remarks that the Semitic root RDP is unusual in Akkadian, and with regard to its usage, it is found as an Aramaic loanword in NA, NB and LB.[1234] Only in one NA instance (SAA X 273:14) is *radāpu* attested in hendiadys with *alāku*, in the sense "to hurry, do quickly."[1235] Von Soden considers this second meaning of *radāpu* to be also borrowed from Aramaic and comments saying thus: "Wir haben keinen Anlass zu bezweifeln, dass auch diese zweite Verwendungsweise altaram. ist."[1236] In fact, the verb *rdp* in the Etpa. with the meaning "to be hurried on a journey," is also attested in Syriac.[1237]

SAA X 273:13–15, reads:

ina UGU-*ḫi mi-i-ni* ^{m}*šu-ma-a* / *ir*$^{!}$*-di-pa* TA* URU.*kal-làḫ* / *il-li-ka*.

Why on the earth did Šumaya hurry up from Calah?

Chronologically, the word under discussion is not attested in Akkadian before the first millennium B.C. Phonologically, the forms of the verb *rdp* in NA exhibit alternation of the third radical between the voiced *b* and the voiceless *p*, but that is entirely in accordance with the NA phonological traits.[1238] This alternation, together with the construction of the perfect tense, for instance *artidip* "I pursued," with the NA infix (*-ti-* < *-ta-*), points to the fact that this loanword is phonologically and morphologically fully integrated into NA.[1239]

The related NA substantive *ridpu* "pursuit, chase" is an Akkadian nominal formation derived from *radāpu*, and is considered to be an Aramaic foreign

[1232] Cf. DNWSI (p. 1061 s.v. *rdp*).
[1233] See Jastrow (p. 1453a s.v. רָדַף); Wehr-Cowan, p. 335a.
[1234] See von Soden, *Or* 37 (1968), p. 265:124; idem, *Or* 46 (1977), p. 193:124. Cf. Abraham & Sokoloff, *Reassessment*, p. 47:190.
[1235] See CAD (R, p. 59b s.v. *radāpu*, b); CDA (p. 295a s.v. *radāpu*). See also von Soden, *Or* 37 (1968), p. 265:124; LAS II ad no. 211:14. Cf. SAA V 53:18, and the Glossary section p. 234a s.v. *radāpu*.
[1236] See von Soden, *Or* 37 (1968), p. 265:124.
[1237] See PSm. (p. 530b s.v. ܪܕܰܦ). Cf. Manna (p. 724b. s.v. ܪܕܰܦ no. 7).
[1238] See K. Deller, *Lautlehre des Neuassyrischen* (Wien 1959), § 47a and § 47d; Luukko, SAAS XVI, § 4.1.1., esp. p. 72 s.v. (*rdp*).
[1239] Cf. M.P. Streck, "Akkadian and Aramaic Language Contact," in S. Weninger (ed.), *The Semitic Languages: An International Handbook* (Berlin 2011), p. 420, § 2.2.5.

word.[1240] A corresponding parallel to the NA *ridpu*, is found in Mandaic as *radpa* "pursuit."[1241]

rad(d)īdu n. (a textile or garment, perhaps "veil")

Loanword	Reference	Provenance	Origin	Genre	Date
rad-di-di	SAA VII 96:6′	Nineveh	*Nineveh*	AD	7th c.?
	SAA VII 98:11′	Nineveh	*Nineveh*	AD	7th c.?
ra-⸢di⸣-d[u]	SAA VII 105:3′	Nineveh	*Nineveh*	AD	7th c.?
ra-di-du.MEŠ	SAA VII 105:3′	Nineveh	*Nineveh*	AD	7th c.?

CW? ⇒ Aram. ⇒ NA [?]

PTA, LJLA, Syr., *rdyd*, *rdyd'* (*rəḏīḏ*, *rəḏīḏā*) n. m. "(thin) veil, bridal veil, a thin cloak" DJPA 517a; Jastrow 1452b; PSm. 530b; SL 1438b; Audo 977a; Manna 723b; CAL. Syr., *arḏīḏā* n. m. "veil; cloak" SL 1438b; PSm. 530b; Manna 723b. Syr., *rəḏīdtā* n. f. "vestment of deacon without sleeves" SL 1438b; PSm. 530b; Manna 723b. Syr., *rdd* v. Pa. "to take off (e.g., clothes)" Manna 723b.

In AHw. (p. 941a s.v. *raddi/adu*), this word is defined as (ein Kleidungsstück), and in CAD (R, p. 60a s.v. *raddidu*), it is defined as (a garment). According to Zadok, *radīdu* may be the same word as Biblical Hebrew רְדִיד "a (female's) wrap of fine texture, veil."[1242] He adds that the term probably was a culture word that entered Hebrew via Aramaic, since chronologically it is not attested in Hebrew prior to the period of the divided kingdom.[1243] Arabic cognates might be the word رِدَاء "loose outer garment, cloak, robe; (lady's) dress, gown" and the words تَرَدَّى, إِرْتَدَى "to wear, put on, be clothed in."[1244] In Syriac, the substantive ܪܕܝܕܐ n. m. "light veil," has a second form with an initial ʾ (hamza), namely ܐܪܕܝܕܐ.[1245] The latter is *Lectio difficilior*, hence the older form of the word. The NA instances occur in three different lists enumerating different types of textile. The word *rad(d)īdu* is not attested in Akkadian prior to the first millennium B.C., and it does not occur in NB or LB. It is probably a culture word that entered NA through Aramaic.

[1240] See von Soden *Or* 37 (1968), p. 265:124; idem, *Or* 46 (1977), p. 193:124; AHw. (p. 981a s.v. *ridpu*). Cf. CAD (R, p. 324a s.v. *ridpu*); AEAD (p. 94b s.v. *ridpu*). Cf. also Nili, p. 284:141.
[1241] For Hebrew, cf. H. Tawil, *An Akkadian Lexical Companion for Biblical Hebrew* (Jersey City 2009), p. 359a s.v. רדף.
[1242] See R. Zadok, "Assyro-Babylonian Lexical and Onomastic Notes," *BiOr* 41 (1984), p. 37:12; Jastrow (p. 1452b).
[1243] See Zadok, ibid.
[1244] See Wehr-Cowan, p. 336a; Elias & Elias, p. 247b.
[1245] See SL (p. 1438b s.v. ܪܕܝܕܐ); PSm., (p. 530b s.v. ܪܕܝܕ); Manna (p. 723b s.v. ܪܕܝܕܐ).

***raʾsu**, **reʾsu*, (pl. *reʾsāni*) n. "chieftain"[1246]

Loanword	Reference	Provenance	Origin	Genre	Date
LÚ*.*re-eʾ-sa-ni*	SAA XIX 87:5′	Calah	Eastern Provinces	L	Tgl

Aram. ⇒ NB; NA ⇒ SB

OAram., *rʾš* n. m. "head" Brauner 536. Palm., Nab., JBA, JPA, Syr., *rʾš*, *ryšʾ* (*rēšā*, *rēšānā*) n. m. "chief, leader, prince, prefect, superior" DNWSI 1043; CAL; DJBA 1079a; DJPA 510b; PSm. 540a; SL 1463a; Manna 731b; Audo 1021b. Syr., *ršn*, *ryšn* v. "to make chief, to make ruler" Manna 731b; Audo 1021b; PSm. 540b; SL 1465b, 1492b. Syr. *rēšānā* n. m. (pl. *rēšānē*) "chief, leader" Manna 732b; Audo 1021b.

In AHw. (p. 959a s.v. *raʾsu*), this term is considered to be an Aramaic foreign word in the sense "(Kaldäer-)Häuptling."[1247] In CAD (R, p. 182b s.v. **raʾsu*), it is glossed in the sense "tribal chief," and is regarded as an Aramaic loanword. The word occurs as a *hapax legomenon* in a NA letter which was sent to the Assyrian king Tiglath-Pileser III (744–727 B.C.). The letter was unearthed in Kalḫu (Calah/Nimrud), and concerns power struggles between Chaldean leaders. The passage where the word occurs (SAA XIX 87:5′–6′) reads as follows:

> *ma–at-ta-a ina* ŠÀ LÚ*.*re-eʾ-sa-ni ša* KUR.*kal-di* / [*ša r*]*e-ḫa-ka-ni*
>
> Who do you think you are among the chieftains of Chaldea who are [l]eft for you?

The earliest attestations of the designation *raʾsāni* or *reʾsāni* in reference to Chaldean tribal chiefs come from the time of Tiglath-Pileser III, and occur in the stereotyped phrase: LÚ.*ra-aʾ-sa-a-ni ša* KUR.*kal-di* "Chaldean chiefs."[1248] In comparison, the title *nasīku*, meaning "sheikh, tribal leader," is usually used in the Assyrian textual sources, especially from the time of the Sargonids, to designate the head of an Aramean clan.[1249]

The substantive *rʾš* in the sense "head" is Common Semitic. In Biblical Hebrew it is ראשׁ, in Syriac ܪܫܐ / ܪܝܫܐ and in Arabic رَأْس, all meaning "head." In Phoenician, it occurs in a personal name, Raʾsūnu "He of the head; chief."[1250] In Akkadian the word is *rēšu/rāšu* "head."[1251] Arabic utilizes the word رَئِيس in the sense "chieftain, leader, chief, boss."[1252]

[1246] See AEAD (p. 93a s.v. *raʾsu*).
[1247] See also CDA (p. 299b s.v. *raʾsu*). Cf. DNWSI (pp. 1042ff s.v. $r'š_1$, esp. p. 1044).
[1248] See J.A. Brinkman, *A Political History of Post-Kassite Babylonia 1158–722 B.C.* (Rome 1968), p. 265, n. 1705.
[1249] See the discussion on Section 2:2 below s.v. *nasīku*; Brinkman, ibid., p. 274.
[1250] See PNA 3/I (p. 1033b s.v. Raʾsūnu).
[1251] See AHw. (p. 973b s.v. *rēšu(m)*); CAD (R, p. 277a s.v. *rēšu*).
[1252] See Wehr-Cowan, p. 318a.

Von Soden, in his article on Aramaic loanwords, considered the term to be a borrowing from Aramaic into NA and NB.[1253] Abraham and Sokoloff affirm that *ra'su* is a West-Semitic loanword in NA, SB and NB.[1254] In fact, they classify the word as a "Fremdwort," which refers specifically to non-Akkadian, mainly non-urban, institution.[1255] However, based on phonological considerations they dismiss the claim that the word is definitely derived from Aramaic, maintaining that the word occurs in Aramaic only in one nominal pattern, as **ri'š*.[1256] Furthermore, Abraham and Sokoloff note that **ri'š* may be a secondary form from Common Semitic **ra'š*.[1257] They also note that no plural form with the ending *-ānīn* is attested for this word in any dialect of Aramaic.[1258] In contrast, the editors of CAL list a Syriac and LJLA word *ryšn*, *ryšn'* (*rēšān*, *rēšānā*) with the sense "chief, ruler," and consider it to be a back-formation from the individuating plural form of *ryš*, i.e., *rēšānīn*.[1259]

In SB the term is attested as LÚ.*ra-a'-sa-a-ni*, but in NB as LÚ.*ra-šá-a-nu* and LÚ.*ra-šá-ni* or LÚ.*ra-šá-a-ni*. In NA, on the other hand, the term occurs as LÚ*.*re-e'-sa-ni*.[1260] Because of the preservation of the glottal stop ' (hamza), it is obvious that the forms *re'sāni/ra'sāni* were borrowed from West-Semitic. Phonologically, the original *š* of the Aramaic or West-Semitic word is represented by *s* in NA and SB, but in NB it is preserved as *š*.[1261] It looks as if the form of the word in SB was influenced by that in NA. However, the form of the NA word *re'sāni* seems to be borrowed from a form such as **re'š*. This points to a borrowing from Aramaic. In Syriac, for instance, the change *a* > *e* often takes place under the influence of a sibilant, hence: **ra'ša* > *rē(y)šā* "head."[1262]

ridpu n. "pursuit, chase"; (see the discussion above s.v. *radāpu*)

Loanword	Reference	Provenance	Origin	Genre	Date
ri-di-pi	SAA V 53:18	Nineveh	Province of the Treasurer	L	Sg
ri-id-pu	SAA V 53 r.7	Nineveh	*Province of the Treasurer*	L	Sg

Aram. ⇒ NA

[1253] See von Soden, *Or* 46 (1977), p. 193:207.
[1254] See Abraham & Sokoloff, *Reassessment*, p. 48:193.
[1255] Ibid., p. 24 and n. 27.
[1256] Ibid., p. 48:193.
[1257] Ibid., p. 48 n. 541.
[1258] Ibid., p. 48 n. 540.
[1259] See CAL, s.v. *ryšn*. Cf. Manna (p. 732b s.v. ܪ̈ܫܢܐ); Audo (p. 1021b s.v. ܪ̈ܫܢܐ).
[1260] See AHw. (p. 959a s.v. *ra'su*); CAD (R, p. 182f s.v. **ra'su*).
[1261] See n. 71 above.
[1262] Cf. C. Brockelmann, *Grundriss der vergleichende Grammatik der semitischen Sprachen*, vol. 1 (Berlin 1908), § 76c.

sādiu, (pl. *sādiāti*) n. "slinger"

Loanword	Reference	Provenance	Origin	Genre	Date
LÚ*.*sa-di-a-*˹*ti*˺	TH 17 r.5	Gūzāna	Gūzāna	AD	Adn

Aram. ⇒ NA [?]

Syr., *šdy*, *šdyʾ* (*šddāy*, *šddāyā*) n. m. "a thrower of stones, an archer" PSm. 560b; Manna 770a; Audo 1039b; CAL. Syr., *šdwy*, *šdwyʾ* (*šāḏōy*, *šāḏōyā*) n. m. "archer, bowman, hurler" Manna 770a; Audo 1039a; PSm. 560b; CAL. Syr., *mšdy* (*mašdē* (const. in compounds with shot item)) n. f. "shooting, range of shooting, range of a bowshot, arrow shot, stone's throw" PSm. 304b; SL 841a; Manna 770a; CAL. Syr., *šdytʾ* (*šāḏītā*) n. m. "sling stone; spear, javelin" PSm. 560b; SL 1513b. OffAr., Palm., JBA, JPA, CPA, Ma., Syr., v. *šdy* "to throw, shoot" DNWSI 1111; DJBA 1109b; DJPA 538a; Jastrow 1524b; LSp. 201b; DCPA 413b; MD 449a; SL 1512b; PSm. 560a. Syr., *šdy* v. "to shoot an arrow, cast a stone, sling" PSm. 560a; SL 1512b; Audo 1039a; Manna 769b.

This word is attested in its plural form and occurs as a *hapax legomenon* in a NA administrative document (TH 17 r.5). The document is fragmentary and difficult to interpret. Most likely, it comes from the archive of Mannu-kī-māt-Aššūr, the governor of Gūzāna, who was the eponym of the year 793 B.C. (reign of Adad-nērārī III). The document lists names of personnel at the palace and designates their profession as LÚ*.*sa-di-a-*˹*ti*˺, which probably means "(stone-)slingers."

The editors of CAD (S, p. 19a s.v. *sādiʾu*) consider the meaning of the word under discussion to be unknown and comment that it possibly refers to a profession. The word is not listed in AHw. and CDA. In AEAD (p. 96a s.v. *sādiu*), it is glossed "slinger." The NA document (TH 17:1′–r.6), reads as follows:[1263]

> [*x x x*] / [*x x x*] KA [*x x x*] / [*x x x*] GÀR$^{?}$ *x* [*x x x*] / [*x x x*] MAN NU NU [*x x x*] / [*x x x*] Á [*x x x*] / [*x x x*] *x* [*x x x*] / [PAP n] ˹*ša*˺ ^{m}*man-nu-*[*x x x*] / ^{m}10-*ba-á*$^{?!}$*-d*[*i x x x*] / ^{m}*a-ši-ri* [*x x x*] / [^{m}*ṭ*]*ab*$^{!}$*-la*$^{!}$*-ku-nu* // [^{m}*x*]-TA$^{?}$-^{d}30 / [^{m}*b*]*a-ri-ku* / [PAP] 5 *ša* É [*x x x*$^{?}$] / *ina* É.GAL / LÚ*.*sa-di-a-*˹*ti*˺ / [*ša* (*x x x*) ^{m}(*x*)]*-ar x* [*x x x*] / [*x x x*]

> [total] of Mannu-[...]. Adda-biʾd[ī ...], Ašīru [...], [Ṭ]āb-la-kunu, [...]-issi-Sîn, [B]arīku. [total] 5 of the house of Bēt-[...] in the palace; (they are) *slingers* [(...) of] P[N].

[1263] The transliteration and the translation of TH 17 given above is taken from A. Dornauer, *Das Archiv des assyrischen Statthalters Mannu-kī-Aššūr von Gūzāna/Tall Ḥalaf* (Wiesbaden 2014), p. 49. For a previous edition of TH 17, see J. Friedrich et al. (eds.), *Die Inschriften vom Tell Halaf: Keilschrifttexte und aramäische Urkunden aus einer assyrischen Provinzhauptstadt* (Osnabrük 1967), p. 22, no. 17. However, the Corpus of Neo-Assyrian Texts (CNA) transliterates TH 17 as follows: [*x x x x x x*] / [*x x*] *ša* ^{m}*man-nu–*[*ki–*KUR*–aš-šur*] / ^{m}10*–ba-aʾ-d*[*i*$^{!}$] / ^{m}*a-ši-ri* [0] / ^{m}*tab*$^{?}$*-la*$^{!}$*-ku-nu* // [^{m}*x*]*-ta–*^{d}30 / [^{m}]*ba-ri-ku* / [PAB] 05 *ša* É / [*i*]*na* É.GAL / [L]Ú*.*sa-di-a-n*[*i*] / [*x x x x*]*x*[*x x x*] / (Rest broken away).

Weidner does not provide a translation for LÚ*.*sa-di-a-*⌜*ti*⌝, and states that he is not aware of any additional attestations similar to it, and that the word can hardly be compared with the term *sa-da-a-ti* "pasture, meadow," which occurs in the myth of Etana.[1264] Dornauer proposes an interpretation of the NA word suggested by Parpola, who reads it differently as [L]Ú*.*sa-di-a-*[*ni*], suggesting it is probably a borrowing from Aramaic *šdy* in the sense "slingers," as attested in the Syriac word ܫܕܐ "to hurl, throw, shoot an arrow, cast a stone, sling," and ܫܕܘܝܐ "hurler, shooter of an arrow."[1265] Dornauer adds that the usual Middle Assyrian term *ša-ušpi* "slinger," is completely absent in NA, and that another term for the frequently depicted slingers in pictorial representations does not exist.[1266]

The NA word *sa-di-a-*⌜*ti*⌝ is preceded by the determinative LÚ*, which clearly indicates that the term designates a profession. Etymologically, it is difficult to find a source word in Akkadian from which the NA word might have been derived. On the other hand, the Aramaic root ŠDY "to throw; to sling," could be a possible etymon for the NA word. The word ܫܕܝܐ or ܫܕܝܐ n. m. "a thrower of stones, an archer," is found, for instance, in Syriac.[1267]

Phonologically, the initial radical *s* in *sādiāti* complies with the expected *š* ⋛ *s* interchange between alphabetic and NA cuneiform renderings.[1268] As a substantive, the NA *sādiāti* ends with *-āti* of the m. pl. The Aramaic word *šdy* is probably also borrowed into NB, but as *šadû* in the sense "to be rejected."[1269]

saḫaru n. "tower(?)"

Loanword	Reference	Provenance	Origin	Genre	Date
sa-ḫa-⌜*ru*⌝	SAA VI 217:10	Nineveh	Nineveh	LD	7th c.

Aram. =▷ NA [?]

Syr., *ṣḥrh*, *ṣḥrt*ʾ (*sāḥrā*, *sāḥartā*, *səḥartā*) n. f. "citadel, walled enclosure, palace; court, courtyard; large public room" SL 994b; PSm. 372b; Manna 489b; Audo 628a; CAL. Syr., *sḥrt*ʾ (*səḥartā*) n. f. "valley" SL 994b; CAL. Ma., *sahra* n. "tower, watch-tower; enclosure" MD 310b. OAram., Sam., *sḥrh* (*sāḥrā*) n. f. "surroundings, environs" Brauner 417; DNWSI 783; DSA 579b; CAL.

This *hapax legomenon* occurs in a NA legal document (SAA VI 217) concerning the purchase of a plot of land. The description of the boundaries of the plot purchased is retrieved from a broken context; therefore the meaning of *sa-ḫa-*⌜*ru*⌝

1264 See E.F. Weidner, in J. Friedrich et al., ibid., n. on l. 10. Cf. AHw. (p. 1002a s.v. *sādu* I).
1265 See Dornauer, ibid., p. 50, n. on l. 15. Cf. PSm. (p. 560 s.v. ܫܕܐ and ܫܕܘܝܐ).
1266 See Dornauer, ibid.
1267 See PSm. (p. 560b s.v. ܫܕܝܐ mng. b); Manna (p. 770b s.v. ܫܕܝܐ).
1268 See n. 71 above.
1269 See von Soden, *Or* 37 (1968), p. 267:142; idem, *Or* 46 (1977), p. 195:142. See also AHw. (p. 1125a s.v. *šadû* IV); DNWSI (p. 1111 s.v. *šdy*₁); Abraham & Sokoloff, *Reassessment*, p. 52:231.

which occurs there cannot be decided with absolute certainty. In AHw. (p. 1009a s.v. *saḫḫāru*), the word is glossed "Turm," and is considered to be a borrowing from Aramaic.[1270] In CAD (S, p. 55b s.v. *saḫḫāru*), the term is listed as meaning "tower," and is also regarded to be a loanword from Aramaic. In CDA (p. 311a) and AEAD (p. 96b) the word is entered as *saḫaru*. In the addenda and corrigenda section of AHw. (p. 1586b s.v. *saḫaru*), the term is considered to be an Aramaic foreign word in NA. As with other *hapax legomena*, the possibility of establishing the semantics and etymology for *saḫaru* is determined by the sentence context. The passage where the word occurs (SAA VI 217:4–10) reads as follows:

> É 30 ANŠE A.Š[À *x x x*] / *ša* A.MEŠ É 2 AN[ŠE *x x x*] / *ša* ŠE.GIŠ.Ì : *ina x*[*x x x*] / *i-na-ra-šu-*[*x*(*x*)] / *ina* URU.*ḫa-me-*[*e*] / SUḪUR ÍD SUḪUR [*x x*] / SUḪUR *sa-ḫa-*⸢*ru*⸣ [*x x*].
>
> An estate of 30 hectares of la[nd, ...] of water; an estate of 2 hect[ares ...] of sesame in ...[...], ...[...] in the city of Ḫamê adjoining the river, [...], and a *tower* [...].

Zimmern stated that the Akkadian word *siḫirtu*, presumably meaning "Ringmauer einer Stadt, eines Palastes," may be the origin of the Syriac word *səḥartā* "Burg," and probably even of the Hebrew word *sôḫērā*.[1271] Kaufman considers the Syriac *sḥrt*ʾ and Mandaic *sʾhr*ʾ, both with the sense "walled enclosure; palace," to be borrowed from Akkadian *sāḫertu* meaning "Ummauerung."[1272] He points out that the verb *sḥr* in Aramaic, on the other hand, is used to mean "to go around peddling."[1273] In contrast, von Soden, in his article on Aramaic loanwords, considers NA *saḫaru* to be a borrowing from an Aramaic word meaning "Turm," and refers to Mandaic *sahra* and Jewish Aramaic and Syriac *sḥartā*.[1274] Mankowski doubts the supposedly Akkadian origin of the Biblical Hebrew word סֹחֵרָא, which is tentatively rendered as "rampart, fortress."[1275]

It seems that NA *saḫaru*, Hebrew סֹחֵרָא, Syriac ܣܚܪܬܐ, and Mandaic *sahra* are cognates. Even the Arabic word صَرْح "palace, castle, edifice, imposing structure,"[1276] is probably related to the other Semitic instances given above, if we assume that a metathesis took place in the Arabic word and that the initial *ṣ* stands for *s*.[1277] As for the NA *saḫaru*, despite the fragmentary condition of the passage where it occurs, the context implies some kind of construction or landmark in connection with the word "river," which precedes it.

1270 Cf. DNWSI (p. 782 s.v. $sḥr_4$).
1271 Zimmern, AF, p. 14.
1272 Kaufman, AIA, p. 90.
1273 Ibid.
1274 See also von Soden, *Or* 46 (1977), p. 193:210.
1275 Mankowski, ALBH, pp. 110ff.
1276 See Elias & Elias, p. 511a.
1277 Cf. Syriac ܣܒܪ, and Arabic صَبَرَ, both in the sense "to be patient."

Phonologically, the form of *saḫaru* in NA clashes with the so-called Assyrian vowel harmony.[1278] The fact that the Assyrian vowel harmony does not work in *saḫaru* is in itself a strong indication that the term is a borrowing into NA. However, if a suggested source word such as **sḥr* came from Aramaic or another West-Semitic language, it would be expected to appear in NA as *šaḫuru*, i.e., with the change *s* > *š* and the Assyrian vowel harmony. Parpola is of the opinion that *saḫaru* is a loanword from Aramaic and argues convincingly that the sibilant *s* of the NA word is explained by association of the word with the Akkadian root SḪR "to go around."[1279] Nevertheless, the source word cannot at present be established with absolute certainty.[1280] Perhaps one ought to look for an etymology in other words as well, such as Syriac ܫܚܘܪ̈ܬܐ, ܫܚܘܪ̈ܬܐ and ܫܚܘܪܐ all meaning "a rugged and rocky road; perilous and difficult place."[1281]

salītu n. f. "(fishing) net"

Loanword	Reference	Provenance	Origin	Genre	Date
sa-li-a-te	SAA XI 106:9	Nineveh	*Nineveh*	AD	–

Aram. ⇒ SB ⇒ NA; LB [?]

JBA *sylyh*, *sylyt'* (*sīlītā*) n. f. "snare, net" DJBA 804b; CAL. Ma., *sylyt'* (*silita*) n. f. "a circular fishing-net weighted with leads" MD 326b. Syr., *ṣly*, *ṣlyt'* (*ṣālīṯā*, *ṣəlīṯā*) n. f. "trap, snare, net" SL 1289a; PSm. 479b; Manna 637a; Audo 864b; CAL.

This word occurs as a *hapax legomenon* in a NA administrative document (ADD 909:9) which consists of a note concerning oxen. The document is now re-edited as (SAA XI 106:9), and the word in question is tentatively translated as "*nets*."[1282] The context where the word occurs (SAA XI 106:1–r.3) does not offer much to establish its meaning. It reads as follows:

> ^m^*tab*-URU-*a-a* GUD / ^m^*dan-nu*–U.GUR :. / ^md^PA–NUMUN–DÙ :. / ^m^MAN–IGI.LAL-*a-ni* :. / ^mp^PA–*šal-lim* :. / ^m^EN–PAB-*ir* :. / 0! PAB *an-nu-te* / *ša* GA.MEŠ / *ša sa-li-a-te* / *ša qa-ru-ḫi* / *ša ia-nu-qi* / *ša* GIŠ.ÙR.MEŠ
>
> Tabālāyu – an ox, Dannu-Nergal – ditto, Nabû-zēru-ibni – ditto, Šarru-ēmuranni – ditto, Nabû-šallim – ditto, Bēl-nāṣir – ditto, All these – of milk, of *nets*, of …, of *a suckling*, of beams.

1278 Perhaps the lack of the Assyrian vowel harmony in *sa-ḫa-*⌈*ru*⌉ was the reason which prompted the editors of CAD and AHw., to transcribe the word as *saḫḫāru*.

1279 S. Parpola (personal communication).

1280 Cf. DNWSI (p. 782 s.v. $sḥr_4$); Abraham & Sokoloff, *Reassessment*, p. 49:201; Nili, p. 284:144.

1281 See Manna (p. 784b s.v. ܫܚܘܪ̈ܬܐ); SL (p. 1541a s.v. ܫܚܘܪ̈ܬܐ); Audo (p. 1055a s.v. ܫܚܘܪܐ and ܫܚܘܪ̈ܬܐ).

1282 Cf. the Glossary of SAA XI (p. 167a s.v. *salītu*).

In AHw. (p. 1016a s.v. *salītu*), the word is glossed "Netz," and is considered to be an Aramaic foreign word in NA, SB and LB.[1283] The editors of CAD (S, p. 104a s.v. *salītu*), on the other hand, render the word as meaning "(fishing) net," but restrict this rendering to the occurrences in SB and NB. In CAD (S, p. 217b s.v. *sellu*, 1, 1′), they list the word *sa-li-a-te*, which occurs in NA (ADD 909:9), under the word *sellu* with the meaning "basket."[1284]

In his article on Aramaic loanwords, von Soden lists the term as "Netz," and considers it to be a borrowing from Aramaic into SB, NA and LB.[1285] For an etymology he refers to Mandaic *silita* and Syriac *ṣəlīṯā*, but with the latter he marks the word's initial *ṣ* with an exclamation mark.[1286] Fales and Postgate express their opinion as to the origin of this word, saying: "There do not appear to be any solid reasons for deriving this word from *sallu* 'a (fruit) basket' rather than *salītu* 'a net,' also perhaps Aramaic."[1287] In contrast, Abraham and Sokoloff acknowledge the attestation of סלית in all of the eastern Aramaic dialects, but state that it has no obvious Aramaic etymology.[1288] According CAL, the relationship among the forms סיליתא, ܨܠܝܬܐ and Akkadian *salītu* is not at all as clear as is suggested in DJBA (p. 804b s.v. סִילִיתָא no. 1).[1289]

The proposed Aramaic etymon, if it is the same word in its different dialects, is written differently. In Syriac it is written ܨܠܝܬܐ n. f. "net, snare," i.e., with initial *ṣ*. Brockelmann derives this substantive from the Syriac verb ܨܠ, which is more common as ܨܠܐ, in the sense "to lay or set a trap."[1290] A corresponding Arabic word is مِصْلَاة "trap," and its denominative verb is صَلَى "to set a trap."[1291] The Mandaic word is *silita*, which Nöldeke renders as "hook," and for which he adduces the corresponding Arabic words سُلًّى, سُلِّيَّة, سُلّاء, and JBA סִילִיתָא, all in the sense "thorn."[1292]

Semantically, it is possible that a development in meaning was involved in the Aramaic word, i.e., thorn > hook > snare/trap/net. Still, if the Mandaic, JBA and Syriac words have the same origin, it is difficult to explain why the initial consonant is *ṣ* in Syriac. Phonologically, a salient problem with the loan hypothesis lies in the absence of the change *s* > *š*, which is expected to take place when borrowing from Aramaic into NA, unless, of course, the Aramaic loanword entered NA via SB. In addition, the first vowel in the NA word is an *a* instead of the expected *i*, as is the case in the suggested Aramaic source word. This is probably another NA example where the expected <*i*> is replaced by <*a*>, which

---

1283 See also CDA (p. 314a s.v. *salītu*).

1284 Cf. DNWSI (p. 787 s.v. *slyt*).

1285 See von Soden, *Or* 46 (1977), p. 193:211.

1286 Ibid.

1287 See n. ad SAA XI 106:9.

1288 Abraham & Sokoloff, *Reassessment*, p. 49:203.

1289 See CAL, s.v. *ṣly*.

1290 See C. Brockelmann, *Lexicon Syriacum* (Hildesheim 1995), p. 628a s.v. ܨܠܐ. See also Manna (p. 636a s.v. ܨܠ and ܨܠܐ). Cf. Abraham & Sokoloff, ibid., p. 49, n. 568.

1291 See *Al-munǧidu* (p. 434a s.v. صَلَى). For the relationship of this Arabic word with Syriac, see Fraenkel, p. 120.

1292 See T. Nöldeke, *Mandäische Grammatik* (Halle 1875), p. 103; MD (p. 326b s.v. *silita*); DJBA (p. 804a s.v. סִילְוָא, p. 812a s.v. סלוא). Cf. *Al-munǧidu* (p. 343a s.v. سلا).

in turn stands for an *e*.[1293] The fact that the word *sa-li-a-te* is immediately followed by two other Aramaic loanwords in NA, namely *qarūḫu* "white-spotted (of animal); bald (of an old animal)" and *ianūqu* "suckling animal, animal before being weaned," speaks in favor of the word being borrowed from Aramaic.[1294]

salṭu, (pl. *salṭāni*) n. "quiver, bow-and-arrow case"

Loanword	Reference	Provenance	Origin	Genre	Date
KUŠ.*sa-al-ṭa-ni*	SAA XI 27:7	Nineveh	Nineveh	AD	7th c.
sa-al-ṭa-ni	SAA III 36 r.1	*Nineveh*	*Nineveh*	MC	–
sa-al-ṭi-šú	SAA III 36 r.2	*Nineveh*	*Nineveh*	MC	–
sal-ṭu!	SAA VII 64 i 1	Nineveh	Nineveh	AD	–
	SAAB 1 3 ii′ 14′	Nineveh	Nineveh	AD	7th c.

Aram. ⇒ NA; NB; LB

Syr., *šlṭ*ʾ (*šalṭā* pl. *šalṭē*) n. m. "quiver; long thin arrow; weapon; girdle" PSm. 579b; SL 1563a; Manna 793b; Audo 1064a; CAL. QA, JLA *šlṭ*, *šlṭ*ʾ (*šlāṭ*, *šlāṭā*, *šilṭā*) n. m. "quiver" Jastrow 1581b; CAL.

Zimmern tentatively rendered this word as "Schild; Köcher," and connected it with Hebrew שֶׁלֶט and Syriac ܫܰܠܛܳܐ in the same sense, without specifying the loan direction, which he thought remains uncertain.[1295] In his monograph on the weapons of the ancient Mesopotamians, Salonen defined this word as (eine Art Schild aus Leder).[1296] Von Soden considered this word a borrowing from Aramaic into LB with the meaning "Lederschild."[1297] In contrast, Borger was able to show, based on Akkadian texts and visual evidence depicted on sculptured reliefs, that *šalṭu* means either a "quiver," or "bow case."[1298] Later in AHw. (p. 1151a s.v. *šalṭu* III), von Soden listed this entry as an Aramaic foreign word in LB meaning "Bogenfutteral."[1299]

Syriac ܫܰܠܛܳܐ "quiver; long thin arrow; weapon; girdle," is certainly cognate with Biblical Hebrew שֶׁלֶט "armor, shields," and Arabic سِلْطة "long thin arrow."[1300]

[1293] Cf. Luukko, SAAS XVI, § 4.3.2.

[1294] See the discussion above s.v. *qarūḫu* and *ianūqu*.

[1295] Zimmern, AF, p. 12.

[1296] E. Salonen, *Die Waffen der alten Mesopotamier: eine lexikalische und kulturgeschichtliche Untersuchung* (Helsinki 1965), pp. 130ff.

[1297] See von Soden, *Or* 37 (1968), p. 267:144.

[1298] R. Borger, "Die Waffenträger des Königs Darius: Ein Beitrag zur alttestamentlichen Exegese und zur semitischen Lexikographie," *VT* 22 (1972): 385–398. See also M. Sokoloff, *The Targum to Job from Qumran Cave XI* (Ramat-Gan 1974), p. 156, with previous literature.

[1299] See also von Soden, *Or* 46 (1977), p. 195:144. Cf. CAD (Š/I, p. 271b s.v. *šalṭu*); CDA (p. 352a s.v. *šalṭu* III); DNWSI (p. 1142 s.v. $šlṭ_2$); S. Parpola, "Neo-Assyrian Treaties from the Royal Archives of Nineveh," *JCS* 39 (1987), p. 183.

[1300] See Jastrow (p. 1581b); H. Tawil, *An Akkadian Lexical Companion for Biblical Hebrew* (Jersey City 2009), pp. 400f; *Al-munğidu* (p. 344c s.v. السَلِط).

In MB and NA the word *azannu*, was used to mean "quiver."[1301] Also, the word *išpatu/išputu* "quiver; bow case," was used in OB, SB and NA.[1302] However, as shown above, the NB and LB word *šalṭu*, which in NA appears as *salṭu*, is also used to mean "quiver." Phonologically, the initial radical *s* in *salṭu* complies with the expected *š* ⋛ *s* interchange between alphabetic and NA cuneiform renderings.[1303] The appearance of the word in the later dialects of Akkadian, as well as the form of the word, i.e., *šalṭu* in NB and LB, as opposed to *salṭu* in NA, taken together support the loan hypothesis.[1304]

sapāku, **sabāku* v. (D) "to seize; to assail, attack, overwhelm"; (N) "to ensnare, seize, catch in"

Loanword	Reference	Provenance	Origin	Genre	Date
is-sa-pa-ku-u-ni	SAA II 6:589	Calah	Calah	T	672
⸢*ú*⸣*-sa-pa-ak*	SAA IX 2 i 11′	Nineveh	*Assur*	P	Esh

Aram. ⇒ NA [?]

Syr., *sbk* v. Pe. "to assail, attack; to entangle, cling," Pa. "to cling, seize, lay hold, catch in"; Af. "to attack, overwhelm" PSm. 357b; Manna 473b; SL 962b; Audo 611b; CAL. JBA *sbk* v. "to attach" DJBA 783b. Ma., *sbk* v. "to interweave, interlace" MD 316a. OffAr., Syr., JLA *sbk*, *sbk*ʾ (*sḇak/sḇāḵ*, *seḇḵā/sḇāḵā*) n. m. "net, curtain" DNWSI 774; CAL.

This verb is attested as a *dis legomenon* in NA. It occurs once in the N-stem in Esarhaddon's succession treaty (SAA II 6:589), and once in the D-stem in an oracle to Esarhaddon (SAA IX 2 i 11′), proclaimed by Nabû-ḫussanni, the prophet of the Inner City, concerning the stabilization of the king's rule.

SAA II 6:588–590, reads:

ki-i šá ḫa-e-ru-uš-ḫi ú-ma-mu ina kip-pi / is-sa-pa-ku-u-ni a[*t-t*]*u-nu* [MÍ.MEŠ]*-ku-nu* ŠEŠ.MEŠ*-ku-nu* DUMU.MEŠ*-ku-nu* / DUMU.MÍ.MEŠ*-ku-nu ina* ŠU.2 LÚ.KÚR*-ku-nu na-aṣ-bi-ta*

Just as a … beast is caught in a snare, may you, your [women], your brothers, your sons and your daughters be seized by the hand of your enemy!

SAA IX 2 i 10′–12′, reads:

[1301] See CAD (A/II, p. 526b s.v. *azannu* B).
[1302] See CAD (I/J, p. 257a s.v. *išpatu*).
[1303] See n. 71 above.
[1304] Cf. Abraham & Sokoloff, *Reassessment*, p. 52:234.

[m]*aš-šur*–PAB–AŠ MAN KUR–*aš-šur* / [LÚ.KÚR.MEŠ-*ka*] ⸢*ú*⸣*-sa-pa-ak* / [*ina* GÌR.2-*ia*] *ú-kab-ba-as*

Esarhaddon, king of Assyria! I will seize [your enemies] and trample [them under my foot].

In AHw. (p. 1025a s.v. *sapāku*), the attested N-stem of this verb is hesitatingly defined as (sich winden?). In contrast, CDA (p. 317a s.v. *sapāku*) glosses the word in the N-stem approximately as "to be ensnared." According to AHw., and CDA, no G-stem is attested for *sapāku*. The editors of CAD (S, p. 157a s.v. **sapāku*) define the meaning of this word as uncertain, but render the NA attestation in the N-stem in the sense "to be caught in," and consider it probably to be a loan from Aramaic *spq*. On the other hand, AEAD (p. 96a s.v. *sabāku*) lists the word differently, as *sabāku* instead of *sapāku*, and renders it in the G-stem as "to assail," and in the D-stem as "to seize, catch in."[1305]

In his edition of Esarhaddon's succession treaty, Wiseman translated the NA verb *sapāku* in the N-stem as "is caught in."[1306] In fact, the NA verb is preceded in the text by the word *kippu* "snare, loop, trap," which substantiates Wiseman's translation. We have a comparative usage of *kippu* from SB, albeit in connection with the verb *ṣabātu* "to seize, catch," in relation to catching wild animals: 4 *pīrī balṭūti aṣbat* 5 *ina kippi aṣbat* "I caught four elephants alive, five (more) I caught with snares."[1307] This further validates the translation of *sapāku* as "to catch" in connection with *kippu*.

As for NA *sapāku* in the D-stem, Parpola renders "to seize," based on the Syriac word *sbk*, and he provides references for the devoicing of the middle radical, i.e., *sbk* > *spk*, which coincides with the alternation between *b* and *p* in NA.[1308] Parpola considers it impossible, and rejects taking NA ⸢*ú*⸣*-sa-pa-ak* to be derived from *šapāku* "to pour," as suggested by Parrot and Nougayrol.[1309]

The origin of the Syriac word ܣܒܟ is the Semitic root *ŚBK "net; to entwine": *sbk* < **śbk*.[1310] Hence, the Official Aramaic *sbk* "(fishing) net," Syriac ܣܒ̈ܟܬܐ "net covering (for head)"[1311] and Hebrew סְבָכָה/שְׂבָכָה "a gold embroidered hair net,"[1312] as well as Arabic شَبَكَة "net"[1313] are certainly cognates.[1314] Also, the OB word *sabāku(m)* "to interweave," is cognate with Hebrew *śbk*, Syriac *sbk*, and Arabic *šbk*.[1315] Semantically, the Syriac meanings of *spk* "to assail, attack, overwhelm," and "seize, lay hold, catch in," fit the contexts of the two NA instances. For one

---

1305 Cf. the Glossary section of SAA II (p. 101a s.v. *sapāku*).
1306 See VTE, p. 74:588–589.
1307 See CAD (K, p. 399b s.v. *kippu*).
1308 See n. ad SAA IX 2 i 11. See also Hämeen-Anttila, SAAS XIII, § 2.1.6.1; Luukko, SAAS XVI, § 4.1.1, specially p. 73 s.v. (*sbk D).
1309 See n. ad SAA IX 2 i 11. Cf. A. Parrot & J. Nougayrol, "Asarhaddon et Naqi'a sur un bronze du Louvre (AO 20, 185)," *Syria* 33 (1956), pp. 158f, n. 6.
1310 See SL (p. 961b s.v. ܣܒܟ).
1311 SL (p. 962a s.v. ܣܒ̈ܟܬܐ). Cf. DJBA (p. 783b s.v. סבכתא).
1312 See HALOT (p. 1301b s.v. *שׂבך and *סבך); Jastrow (pp. 950a, 1515a s.v. שְׂבָכָה).
1313 See Elias & Elias, p. 332b.
1314 See LS (p. 454b s.v. ܣܒܼܟ).
1315 AHw. (p. 999a s.v. *sabāku(m)*).

of the instances we can reasonably assume the following semantic development: *sbk* "to entangle, catch in" > *sbk* "to ensnare." We assume that **śbk* is the etymon of the word *sbk* in the later dialects of Aramaic.[1316] This, then, explains the form of the borrowed NA word, i.e., *sapāku* < **sabāku*, which did not require the otherwise expected *š* ≷ *s* interchange between alphabetic and NA cuneiform renderings.[1317] In light of the foregoing discussion, the suggested Aramaic etymon *spq*, given in CAD is certainly wrong.

sapāqu v. (G) "to suffice, be enough, be sufficient"

Loanword	Reference	Provenance	Origin	Genre	Date
i-sa-ap?*-[pi]-qa*	SAA XVI 5 r.4 (RL)	Nineveh	Nineveh	L	Esh
i-sa-pi-qu	SAA XV 142 r.2	Nineveh	*Der*	L	Sg

Aram. ⇒ NA

JBA, PTA, JLA, Syr., CPA, Sam., LJLA *spq* v. Pe. "to be sufficient, to suffice, be enough; to be able" DJBA 827b; DJPA 386a; SL 1033a; PSm. 386a; Manna 508a; Audo 658a; LSp. 138b; DCPA 291b; DSA 605a; Jastrow 1016a; CAL.

This verb is attested as a *dis legomenon* in NA. In AHw. (p. 1026a s.v. *sapāqu*), it is considered to be an Aramaic foreign word in NA with the meaning "genügen," and in LB with the meaning "vermögen."[1318] The editors of CAD (S, p. 161a s.v. *sapāqu*) list the word for NA and SB with the meaning "to be sufficient," and compare it to Hebrew *śpq* in addition to referring to von Soden for a suggested Aramaic etymology. The LB instance appears in a commentary on a medical text in the equation: *ta-sa-pi-iq* : *tu-dan-na-an*.[1319] However, based on semantic grounds, Abraham and Sokoloff reject considering the LB instance as a borrowing from Aramaic, and argue that it is equated with the verb *danānu* in the D-stem with the meaning "to reinforce."[1320] The two NA instances are as follows:

SAA XVI 5 e.26–r.4, reads:

ŠE.PAD.MEŠ *ša ina pu-u-ḫi // ta-di-na-ni pu-ru-us / šup-ra a-na-ku ina* ŠU.2 LÚ*.EN–*pi-qit-tú-ia / lu-ba-ʾi-a* TA IGI UN.MEŠ-*ia / i-sa-ap*?*-[pi]-qa* ⸢*at*!⸣*-ta qa-la-ka*

Determine the barley given as a loan, write to me, (and) I will call my official to account. It will be sufficient *for* my people, and you will keep silent.

[1316] See Lipiński, *Semitic Languages*, p. 150.
[1317] See n. 71 above.
[1318] See also CDA (p. 317a s.v. *sapāqu*); DNWSI (p. 798 s.v. spq_1, spq_2).
[1319] See H. Hunger, *Spätbabylonische Texte aus Uruk*, I (Berlin 1976), p. 60 no. 50:31.
[1320] See Abraham & Sokoloff, *Reassessment*, p. 49:207.

SAA XV 142:5′–r.2, reads:

> *ù* LÚ*.*qe-e-pu / ša* URU.*de-e-ri / is-sa-pa-ra ma-a / 2-lim* LÚ*.ERIM.MEŠ / *še-bi-la ù* ERIM.MEŠ / TA* *an-na-ka // a-na* URU.ḪAL.ṢU.MEŠ / *la i-sa-pi-qu*
>
> Further: the legate of Der has written to me: 'Send me 2,000 men!' But the men from here do not suffice (even) for the fortresses!

Waterman translated *i-sa-pi-qu* (ABL 868 r.2 = SAA XV 142 r.2), as "assembled," deriving it from the Akkadian word *šapāku* "to heap up."[1321] Von Soden dismissed Waterman's rendering for failing to account for the *q* of the NA word.[1322] Instead, he analyzed the word as *sapāqu* in the sense "genügen," and considered it a borrowing from Aramaic *spq*.[1323]

Von Soden's suggested rendering fits well in the context of the two NA texts quoted above. A usage comparable to NA *lā isappiqū* "they do not suffice" (SAA XV 142 r.2) would be the Syriac expression ܠܐ ܣܦܘܩܐ ܒܐܝܕܘܗܝ "he has not enough."[1324] Certainly, the origin of the proposed Aramaic source word *spq* "to suffice, be enough" is the PS root *ŚPQ. A cognate word in Hebrew is ספק/שׂפק "to be sufficient."[1325] The Old South Arabic word *šfq* "abundant," is also a cognate.[1326] It is likely that the ancestor of *spq* in the later dialects of Aramaic was realized as **śpq* in Old Aramaic, i.e., with an initial voiceless dental fricative *ś*.[1327] It is possible, therefore, that the form of the NA word *sapāqu* did not require the change *s* > *š*, which otherwise is expected to take place when borrowing from Aramaic into NA.[1328] The Aramaic etymon and the distribution of the word in NA as well as the usage of its equivalent in Syriac point to a borrowing from Aramaic into NA.

sarābu, (pl. *sarabāte*) n. "heat; sultry wind, hot wind; drought"

Loanword	Reference	Provenance	Origin	Genre	Date
sa-rab-a-te	SAA IX 9:13	Nineveh	*Arbela*	P	650

Aram. ⇒ NA [?]

Syr., LJLA *šrb, šwrb'* (*šreḇ, ša/urbā, šarābā, šərābā*) n. m. "sultry wind, hot wind, the simoom" PSm. 597a; SL 1600b; Manna 819a; Jastrow 1627b; CAL. JPA, CPA, Sam., *šrb, šwrb'* (*šreḇ, ša/urbā*) n. m. "heat" DJPA 566a; LSp. 215b;

1321 See Waterman, RCAE, part II, pp. 102f., and part III, p. 250.

1322 See W. von Soden, "Zum akkadischen Wörterbuch. 61–66," *Or* 24 (1955), p. 145.

1323 Ibid. See also von Soden, *Or* 37 (1968), p. 265:129; idem, *Or* 46 (1977), p. 194:129. See the Glossary section of SAA XV (p. 244b s.v. *sapāqu*), and SAA XVI (p. 192b s.v. *sapāqu*).

1324 See PSm. (p. 386a s.v. ܣܦܩ).

1325 See HALOT (p. 765b s.v. II ספק, p. 1349a s.v. II שׂפק).

1326 See A.F.L. Beeston, "On the Correspondence of Hebrew *s* to ESA s^2" *JSS* 22 (1977), p. 56.

1327 See Lipiński, *Semitic Languages*, p. 150, § 20.

1328 Cf. above, n. 67.

DCPA 422a; DSA 930a; CAL. Syr., *šrb* (*šərāḇā*) n. m. "drought" PSm. 597a; Audo 1092b. Ma., *širba* n. m. "dry heat, dryness, aridity" MD 463a. JPA *šrbrwby*, *šrbrwbyt'* n. f. "heat" DJPA 566a; CAL. Syr., *šrb* v. Pe. "to become dry," Pa. "to dry something up" SL 1600a; PSm. 596b; Manna 818b; Audo 1092a.

The word *sarābu*, attested in its plural form as *sarabāte* and supposedly meaning "heat; sultry wind, hot wind; drought," occurs as a *hapax legomenon* in NA. It is found in a prophetical text consisting of an oracle of Ištar of Arbela and Mullissu to Assurbanipal proclaimed by Dunnaša-āmur, a prophetess from Arbela. In AHw. (p. 1029a s.v. *sarbu*(*m*), mng. no. 1), the word is listed in the sense "Nässe." In CAD (Š/II, p. 60b s.v. *šarbu* A), it is rendered "rainy season, cold." In contrast with AHw., in CDA (p. 317b s.v. *sarabu*, p. 360b s.v. *šarbu* II) the word is given as meaning "rainy season, cold." The meaning "Nässe," was suggested by Landsberger and was accepted in AHw. and CAD.[1329] The word is listed in AEAD (p. 98b s.v. *sarābu*) with the sense "drought."[1330] The NA text, where the word is attested, is re-edited by Parpola, and the passage where the word occurs (SAA IX 9:10–14) reads as follows:[1331]

> ⌜*e-ta*⌝*-na-at-ti-iq* KUR.MEŠ-*e ḫur-sa-a-ni* / ⌜*e-ta*⌝*-nab-bir* ÍD.MEŠ *ka-li-ši-na* / *e*-⌜*ta*⌝*-nak-kal-a-ni ia-a-ši* / *ṣe-*[*t*]*a-a-te sa-rab-a-te* / *il-ta-nap-pa-ta ba-nu-ú la-a-ni*
>
> I traverse mountains and mountain chains; I cross over all rivers. Droughts and showers consume me and affect my beautiful figure.

CAD (Ṣ, p. 152a s.v. *ṣētu*, mng. no. 1. e) quotes part of the same passage and translates it as follows: *ētanattiq šadê ḫursāni ētanabbir nārāti kališina ētanakkalanni iāši ṣētāte sarabāte* "I pass to and fro through the hills and mountains; I am ever crossing all the rivers; the weather and the rains constantly cut me."[1332] Hence, *sarabāte* is rendered "rains."

However, scholars differ as to the interpretation and meaning of this *hapax legomenon*. Parpola now suggests that the translation "showers," which he provided for *sa-rab-a-te* in SAA IX 9:13, ought to be replaced by "droughts," which can be taken as a borrowing from Aramaic *šərābā* "drought."[1333] His argument is cited here in full:

> The translation of *sa-rab-a-te* with "showers" in SAA 9 (based on the rendering "Nässe" introduced by Landsberger, ZA 42 161f, and accepted in AHw. 1029a and CAD Š/2 60) is incompatible with the implications of the context, which states, in conformity with Gilg. IX 126 and X passim, that the prophet's face had been "eaten" by the *s*. Showers do not "eat" one's face, but droughts and continuous

---

[1329] See B. Landsberger, "Lexikalisches Archiv," *ZA* 42 (1934), pp. 161f; idem, "Jahreszeiten im Sumerisch-Akkadischen," *JNES* 8 (1949), p. 252, n. 30.
[1330] Cf. AEAD (p. 98b s.v. *sarabu*, p. 112b s.v. *šarbu* "rainy weather, cold").
[1331] In the Glossary of SAA IX (p. 51a s.v. *sarbu*), the word is glossed "cold rain, shower; squash."
[1332] Cf. CAD (Š/II, p. 60b s.v. *šarbu* A); H. Zimmern, "Gilgameš-Omina und Gilgameš-Orakel," *ZA* 24 (1910), p. 169:13.
[1333] S. Parpola (personal communication). See PSm. (p. 597a s.v. ܫܪܒܐ "drought", p. 596b s.v. ܫܪܒ "to become dry"); Dalman (p. 414a s.v. שַׁרְבָא, שְׁרָבָא "Sonnenglut, Hitze").

> excessive exposure to sunshine do. Hence the appearance of *sa-rab-a-te* in hendiadys with *ṣētāte* "sultry weather, open sun, sunburn" in the text. The rendering "drought" was introduced in *AEAD* and should replace the translation "showers" in SAA 9, although the meaning "rainy season" is well attested lexically for Akk. *šarbu*.[1334]

A different interpretation is suggested by Streck, who does not subscribe to Parpola's rendering of *sa-rab-a-te* as "droughts" rather than "rainy season, cold." Streck formulates his argument as follows:

> However, Parpola's argument … does not hold: In Gilg. there is nothing of *akālu* "to eat," but the text speaks of *qummû* "to burn," fitting *ṣētu*, but also *šarbu*, etymologically connected with *šarāpu* "to burn." In SAA IX 9 *sa-rab-a-te* could well go only with the second verb *iltanappatā* "to affect," to "touch," fitting well a subject "rain," or the like. Moreover, lex. texts equate the word with Sum. *šèg* "rain," Akk. *zanānu* "to rain," *ḫalpû* "ice."[1335]

Semantically, the evidence points to the fact that the NA *sa-rab-a-te* ought to be taken as a borrowing form Aramaic *šarābā* "sultry wind, hot wind; heat," or *šərābā* "drought," which better fits the context. A cognate of the Aramaic word is found in Hebrew as שָׁרָב "heat of the sun, dry heat," or שָׁרַב "to glow; be dry."[1336] Another cognate also found in Arabic is شَرَبَة pl. شَرَب and شَرَبات "extreme heat."[1337] Most importantly, the evidence in support of this loan identification is found in the following Targumic Aramaic expression: בִּימָמָא אֲכַלְנִי שָׁרָבָא "during the day the heat wore me out."[1338] The usage of the NA *ētanakkalanni…sarabāte* (from *akālu* "to eat" and *sarābu* "hot wind; heat; drought"), is obviously identical with that of Aramaic אֲכַלְנִי שָׁרָבָא. Phonologically, the change *š* > *s* from the Aramaic alphabetic writing into the NA cuneiform rendering is appropriate.[1339]

sarḫu adj. "enraptured, ravished"

Loanword	Reference	Provenance	Origin	Genre	Date
sa-ar-ḫa-at	SAA XVI 59 r.3′	Nineveh	*Nineveh*	L	Esh

Aram. ⇒ NA [?]

Syr., *šrḥ* v. Pe. & Pa. "to be overjoyed, ravished with joy; to enrapture, fascinate, captivate; to make wanton, inflame with passion" Manna 820b; Audo 1093b; PSm. 598a; SL 1603b. CPA *šrḥ* (*ʾšrḥw*) v. "to misbehave, behave wantonly"

1334 S. Parpola, ibid. For allusion to Gilgamesh, see n. ad SAA IX 9:12–14. Cf. AEAD (p. 112b s.v. *šarbu* (*sarabu*) "rainy weather, cold").
1335 M.P. Streck (personal communication).
1336 See Dalman, p. 414a; Jastrow, p. 1627a.
1337 See *Al-munǧidu* (p. 380c s.v. شَرِبَ). Cf. MD (p. 463a s.v. *širba*).
1338 Quoted in CAL s.v. *šrb*, mng. no. 1.
1339 See n. 71 above.

CAL. Syr., *šrḥ* (*šrīḥā*) adj. "shameless, immoderate, unrestrained; lascivious" Manna 820b; Audo 1094a; SL 1607a; PSm. 598a; CAL.

The word *sa-ar-ḫa-at* occurs in a NA letter (SAA XVI 59) sent to Esarhaddon by Nabû-reḫtu-uṣur, an official who warns of a conspiracy against the king. In the letter the official quotes a prophetic oracle of Nusku proclaimed on the outskirts of Harran by a slave girl of Bēl-aḫu-uṣur, according to which the divine appoints Sāsî as a challenger to the throne and the name and seed of Sennacherib will be destroyed.

Luukko and Van Buylaere, the editors of SAA XVI 59, tentatively translate the word *sa-ar-ḫa-at* as meaning "enraptured."[1340] The word is listed in CAD (S, p. 171b s.v. *sarāḫu*), but its meaning is considered to be uncertain. In AHw. (p. 1028a s.v. *sarāḫu(m)*), it is rendered in the sense "zerstören." On the other hand, AEAD (p. 98b s.v. *sarḫu*) lists it as an adjective *sarḫu* meaning "ecstatic, rapturous."[1341]

SAA XVI 59 r.2′–5′, reads:

GEMÉ *šá* ᵐEN–PAB–PAB *ina*ᶦ *q*[*a-n*]*i šá* ˹URU˺.K[ASKAL].2 *ina* U[GU *x x x x*] / *ma-a* TA* ŠÀ ITI.SIG₄ *sa-ar-ḫa-at ma-a da-ba-bu* SIG₅ *ina* UGU-*ḫi* / *ta-da-bu-bu ma-a a-bat* ᵈPA.TÚG *ši-i ma-a* LUGAL-*u-tu a-na* ᵐ*sa-si-i* / *ma-a* MU NUMUN *šá* ᵐᵈ30–PAB.MEŠ–SU *ú-ḫal-la-qa*

"A slave-girl of Bēl-aḫu-uṣur […] upon […] in a su[bur]b of H[arran]; since Sivan (III) she is *enraptured* and speaks nice words about him: 'It is the word of Nusku: The kingship is for Sasî. I will destroy the name and seed of Sennacherib!'"

Couey rightly points out that although this letter does not utilize the standard language for prophecy in reference to the event, the slave girl's speech can be classified as a prophetic oracle, because in her introductory statement she attributes her words to Nusku, saying: *abat Nušku šî* "It is the word of Nusku."[1342] Couey notes that "the slave-girl does not appear to be a professional prophet, but the phenomenon of lay prophecy is attested at Mari (e.g., a servant girl who falls into an ecstatic trance….) and would certainly have been possible in Assyria."[1343] He also notes that the word *sarḫat*, from Akkadian *sarāḫu*, which is translated as "enraptured," is not the usual word for prophetic ecstasy in Neo-Assyrian, where another Akkadian word, namely *ragāmu* "shout, proclaim" is used.[1344] Parpola interprets *sarḫat* as a G-stem stative, 3p. f. sg. meaning "she is enraptured" and

---

1340 Note that the Glossary of SAA XVI, p. 192b, lists a verb *sarāḫu* and tentatively renders it as "to be enraptured(?)."

1341 Cf. AEAD (p. 98b s.v. *sarāḫu*).

1342 See J.B. Couey, "Amos vii 10–17 and Royal Attitudes Toward Prophecy in the Ancient Near East," *VT* 58 (2008), p. 307. See also Nissinen, SAAS VII (1998), pp. 108–153, esp. p. 151.

1343 Couey, ibid., n. 16.

1344 Ibid. Cf. AEAD (p. 98b s.v. *sarāḫu*).

corresponding to the Syriac verb *šrḥ* "to rage," which in its Af'el mode has the meanings "to ravish, enrapture, fascinate, captivate."[1345]

Semantically, the Akkadian verb *sarāḫu* has the meanings "to destroy, ruin."[1346] However, these senses do not fit the context of the NA letter. Most likely, therefore, the NA word *sa-ar-ḫa-at* is a borrowing from Aramaic *šrḥ* "to enrapture." A cognate is found in Arabic, شَرَحَ "to delight, gladden,"[1347] and إِنْشَرَحَ "to be or become delighted, glad, happy, pleased, to rejoice."[1348] Phonologically, the initial radical *s* complies with the expected *š* ⪌ *s* interchange between alphabetic and NA cuneiform renderings.[1349] In addition, the Aramaic pharyngeal /*ḥ*/ is usually rendered <*ḫ*> in NA.[1350] As a borrowing from Aramaic, *sa-ar-ḫa-a* in the sense "is enraptured," is only attested once in NA, hence it is a *hapax legomenon*.

supīrātu n. f. pl. "clippings(?), trimmings(?)"

Loanword	Reference	Provenance	Origin	Genre	Date
su-pi-ra-ti	Iraq 15, 146 (= ND 3468:5′)	Calah	Calah	AD	7th c.

Aram. ⇒ NA [?]

Syr., *sūpārūṯā* n. f. "clippings" Manna 510a. Syr., *sūpārtā* n. f. "filings; slag, dross" PSm. 370a; SL 989a. Syr., *swprh*, *swprt*ʾ (*suppārā*, *suppārtā*) n. f. "sweepings" CAL. JBA, JPA, Sam., Ma., Syr., *spr* v. "to shear; to cut (hair), clip; to shave" DJBA 828a; DJPA 387a; DSA 607a; MD 335a; Manna 509a; Audo 659b; SL 1034b.

The word *supīrātu* occurs as a *hapax legomenon* in an obscure NA context. It is attested in the lower part of a fragmentary administrative document (ND 3468),[1351] which probably represents a list of wood and linen objects. The text (ND 3468:1′–6′) reads as follows:[1352]

> GIŠ.⸢DA$^{?}$⸣–GU.ZA / *ša* É–*ra*$^{!}$-*ma-ki*$^{!}$ / GIŠ.*na-ra-ma-tú*$^{!}$ / *ša* KASKAL / *su-pi-ra-ti* *ša* GADA / É–*su-*⸢*x*⸣-*ti*

1345 See Parpola *apud* Nissinen, SAAS VII (1998), pp. 109–111, esp. n. 430. See also M. Nissinen, *Prophets and Prophecy in the Ancient Near East* (Atlanta 2003), p. 172, n. ad 115, b; PSm., (p. 598a s.v. ܫܪܚ).

1346 See CAD (S, p. 171b s.v. *sarāḫu*).

1347 See Wehr-Cowan, p. 463a; Elias & Elias, p. 338b.

1348 See Wehr-Cowan, ibid; Elias & Elias, p. 339a.

1349 See n. 71 above.

1350 For the representation of Aramaic *ḥ* by NA *ḫ*, see n. 313 above.

1351 See D.J. Wiseman, "The Nimrud Tablets, 1953," *Iraq* 15 (1953), p. 146.

1352 The transliteration of ND 3468:1′–6′given above is taken from the Corpus of Neo-Assyrian Texts (CNA). For a previous transliteration of the same text, see Wiseman, ibid.

> The … wood of the bathroom, the *naramatu* (mace)[1353] of the road, the *clippings* of linen, …

In CDA (p. 328b s.v. *supīrātu*), the word is tentatively considered to be a loan from Aramaic in the sense "trimmings (of linen)." AHw. (p. 1060a s.v. *supīrātu*) defines the word as (etwas aus Leinen), and tentatively refers to the Aramaic word *spr* "scheren." The editors of CAD (S, p. 392a s.v. *supīrātu*) define the word as (a linen object). AEAD (p. 101b s.v. *supīrtu*), lists a feminine singular form of the word and renders it tentatively as "clipping."

The fragmentary condition of the NA text and the obscurity of its context do not allow a firm conclusion about the meaning of *supīrāti*. However, the word is connected, in a genitive phrase, with the logogram GADA. The latter, as a textile, refers in Akkadian to the word *kitû* "flax, linen; linen garment."[1354]

Etymologically, the root SPR is very rare in Akkadian and does not provide any satisfactory meaning which would fit the context where the word under discussion occurs. In Aramaic, the root SPR means, among other things, "to shear; to cut, clip; to shave," of which a derivation with the sense "clippings" seems to fit the NA context. The Aramaic *spr* "to shear; to cut, clip; to shave" is cognate with Hebrew סָפַר "to cut, shear"[1355] and the Arabic word شَفْرَة "large knife, blade (of a sword, of a knife)."[1356] The West-Semitic evidence points to a derivation from a PS root *ŚPR in the sense "to cut."[1357] However, the nominative feminine singular of the NA *supīrāti* can be reconstructed as **supīrtu*.[1358] The latter is of the nominal pattern *PuRīStu*, which in Akkadian constitutes a semantic class with a diminutive and pejorative meanings.[1359] This, in turn, substantiates the renderings "clippings; trimmings" given above. However, in the case of a borrowing from Aramaic, the NA word *supīrāti* is expected to appear as *šupīrāti*; i.e., it is supposed to comply with the *š* $\gtrless$ *s* interchange between alphabetic and NA cuneiform renderings. The form of the NA word *supīrāti* with initial *s* instead of the expected *š* is probably due to the voiceless dental fricative *ś* of the root *ŚPR, which at the time of the borrowing was perhaps represented by *š* in Old Aramaic.[1360]

ṣaḫūrānūtu n. f. "puberty, teens, youth"

Loanword	Reference	Provenance	Origin	Genre	Date
ṣa-ḫu-ra-nu-tú	SAA X 290 s.1	Nineveh	Nineveh	L	Esh

Aram. =▷ NA [?]

1353 Cf. CAD (N/I, p. 342a s.v. *nar'amtu*).

1354 See Borger, ABZ, no. 90; W. Schramm, *Akkadische Logogramme* (Göttingen 2003), p. 52.

1355 See Dalman (p. 285b s.v. סָפַר II); Jastrow (p. 1017a s.v. סָפַר).

1356 See *Al-munǧidu* (p. 394c s.v. شفر no. 3); Wehr-Cowan, p. 478a.

1357 Cf. Fraenkel, p. 247.

1358 See AEAD (p. 101b s.v. *supīrtu*).

1359 See GAG § 55k.

1360 Cf. A.R. Millard, "^{f}*ša ekalli – šgl –* ^{d}*sagale*," *UF* 4 (1972), p. 162.

Sam., *z'wrnw*, *z'wrnwt'* (*z'ōrānū*, *z'ōrānūṯā*) n. f. "youth" DSA 237b; CAL. Com., *z'r* v. "to be(come) small" CAL; SL 391b; PSm. 119a; Manna 205b; Audo 285b. Syr. *zə'ōrūtā* n. f. "smallness, young age; childhood" SL 390a. Syr., *ṣ'r* v. "to be(come) small, little; to be disgraced; to insult" Audo 873b; Manna 644a; SL 391b; PSm. 482a.

The word *ṣaḫūrānūtu* occurs as a *hapax legomenon* in NA. It is attested in a letter concerning the performance of the rites of the month Abu (V). The letter was sent to king Esarhaddon by Urdu-Gula, the royal exorcist from Nineveh. Urdu-Gula is worried about the immaturity of his colleague Nabû-le'ûti's son and is anxious about leaving the pair to perform the rites unsupervised. In AHw. (p. 1075a s.v. *ṣaḫūrānūtu*), the word is glossed "Jungend." The editors of CAD (B, p. 107a s.v. *barāru* A, mng. no. 2) translate the word as "youth."[1361] CDA (p. 332a s.v. *ṣaḫurānūtu*) glosses the word as "(time of) youth," and considers its origin to be the Akkadian verb *ṣeḫēru(m)/ṣaḫāru(m)* "to be(come) small, young, little." AEAD (p. 102b s.v. *ṣaḫūrānūtu*) glosses the word as "puberty, teens, youth." The passage where the word occurs (SAA X 290:13e–s.3), reads as follows:

> ^mdPA–ZU-*tú* DUMU-*šú ú-de-šú-nu / šum-ma šá-al-me la šá-al-me* / ⌜*man*!⌝-*nu ú-ka-an-šú-nu u a-na-ku* / [0] *a-ta-mar* DUMU-*šú an-ni-i* / [*ina*] ŠÀ *ba-ra-ar ṣa-ḫu-ra-nu-tú šú-u* / [*is-s*]*i-šú-nu a-za-za dul-lu nu-šal-lam* / [0] *né-pa-áš ú*!*-ra-ma-šú-nu-u ú-de-šú-nu-ni*
>
> (When) Nabû-le'utu and his son are alone, who can vouch for them, whether it is safe or not? Even I have noticed that this son of his is (still) in the unsteadiness of youth. (While) I stay [wit]h them, we perform the ritual correctly – (but) can I leave them alone?

Based on the context, Deller translates *ṣaḫūrānūtu* as "Jugend," and indicates that the word has a nominal formation with double affixes.[1362] He points out however that NA uses the word *ṣaḫurtu/ṣuḫurtu*, which has the meanings "adolescent, juvenile; youth, teenager."[1363] Von Soden, on the other hand, tentatively attributes the nominal form of the NA *ṣaḫūrānūtu* to Aramaic, though he is of the opinion that such a derivation is not attested for the Aramaic *ṣ'r* or *z'r*.[1364] In contrast, Abraham and Sokoloff, state that the meaning of this word is derived from the Akkadian verb *ṣeḫēru* "to be young," and they dismiss a

[1361] Note that the word *ṣaḫūrānūtu* is not listed in the Ṣ volume of CAD.

[1362] See K. Deller, Review of "The Assyrian Dictionary of the Oriental Institute of the University of Chicago. Vol. 16: Ṣ" by A.L. Oppenheim et al., *Or* 33 (1964), p. 91. See also AHw. (p. 1075a s.v. *ṣaḫurānūtu*).

[1363] See Deller, ibid; CAD (Ṣ, p. 65b s.v. *ṣaḫurtu*, p. 237a s.v. *ṣuḫurtu* mng. no. 2). See also AEAD (p. 102b s.v. *ṣaḫurtu*, p. 105b s.v. *ṣuḫurtu*). For a cognate in OA, cf. the word *ṣú-ùḫ-ra-*⌜*am*⌝ "child" (kt 94/k 520:14) in G. Barjamovic & M.T. Larsen "An Old Assyrian Incantation against the Evil Eye," *AoF* 35/1 (2008), p. 145.

[1364] See von Soden, *Or* 46 (1977), p. 194:216; AHw. (p. 1588a s.v. *ṣaḫurānūtu*).

borrowing from Aramaic, saying that the latter employs the related root Zʿ R, and that the root *Ṣʿ R is completely absent from Aramaic.[1365]

Akkadian ṢḪR, Arabic ṢĠR, Hebrew Ṣʿ R, Phoenician and Punic Ṣʿ R[1366] and Syriac Ṣʿ R and Zʿ R, all with the sense "to be(come) small," are cognates. In Arabic صَغِرَ means "to be(come) small," but صَغُرَ means "to belittle, ridicule," and the expression صَغير السِّنّ means "young."[1367] In Hebrew the word צָעִיר means "young."[1368] As for Aramaic, both *zʿr* and *ṣʿr* are in fact attested in Syriac and are considered cognates.[1369] However, the Syriac ܙܥܪ means "to be(come) small," but in the Afʿel, i.e., ܐܙܥܪ, it means "to belittle, ridicule," and the expression ܙܥܘܪ ܫܢܝܢܐ means "young."[1370] The Syriac word ܨܥܪ, on the other hand, is primarily used in the sense "to belittle, ridicule."[1371] According to Audo, the Syriac words ܙܥܪ and ܨܥܪ are the same.[1372] Most likely the Syriac words ܙܥܪ and ܨܥܪ were originally a single word derived from the root Ṣʿ R < PS *ṢĠR,[1373] but later diverged in shape and specialized in meaning. Nevertheless, von Soden's attribution of the nominal form of the NA *ṣaḫūrānūtu* to Aramaic can now be corroborated by a corresponding Samaritan Aramaic nominal form זעורנותה meaning "youth."[1374]

ṣallu n. "tanned hide"

Loanword	Reference	Provenance	Origin	Genre	Date
KUŠ.*ṣal-li*	SAA XI 26:13′	Nineveh	Nineveh	AD	7th c.
ša LÚ.*ṣal-li-šú-nu*	SAA VII 115 r. i 5	Nineveh	Nineveh	AD	Sg

Aram. ⇒ NA; LB [?]

OffAr., JBA, Syr., LJLA *ṣl, ṣlʾ* (*ṣāl, ṣālā*) n. m. "hide, leather" DNWSI 967; DJBA 963b; Jastrow 1282a; SL 1285b; PSm. 478b; Manna 636a; CAL. JBA, Syr., *ṣlʾ* (*ṣūlā*) n. m. "hide, leather" DJBA 955a;[1375] SL 1287b.[1376] JBA *ṣlʾ*, *ṣlʿʾ* n. m. "tanner, worker or dealer in leather" DJBA 963b;[1377] Jastrow 1285b; Dalman 348a; CAL. JBA *ṣlʾlʾ* n. m. "small piece of leather" DJBA 965b; CAL.

1365 See Abraham & Sokoloff, *Reassessment*, p. 51:219.
1366 See DNWSI (p. 971f s.v. *ṣʿr_2*).
1367 See *Al-munǧidu*, p. 425; Elias & Elias, p. 373b.
1368 See Dalman, p. 350a.
1369 See SL (p. 1296a s.v. ܨܥܪ).
1370 See Manna, pp. 205f.
1371 Ibid., p. 644a.
1372 See Audo (p. 873b s.v. ܨܥܪ), where he also refers to the correspondence of *z* and *ṣ* in the Syriac word ܙܕܝܩܐ "righteous, just," and its Arabic cognate صِدِّيق "righteous; just."
1373 Cf. L. Kogan, "*ġ in Akkadian," *UF* 33 (2001), p. 264.
1374 See DSA (p. 237b s.v. זעורנו).
1375 Cf. Maclean (p. 263b s.v. ܨܘܠܐ "pair of shoes").
1376 See SL (p. 1285b s.v. ܨܠܐ).
1377 For the improper use of ע for א in JBA (צַלְעָא), see Th. Nöldeke, Review of "Opuscula Nestoriana," by G. Hoffmann, *ZDMG* 35 (1881), p. 497, n. 1.

This word occurs as a *dis legomenon* in NA. It is attested in an administrative document (SAA XI 26:13′) consisting of a record of merchants' transactions. The passage SAA XI 26:13′–15′, reads:

> 84 KUŠ.*ṣal-li ina* ŠÀ 2 MA.NA 53? GÍN KUG.UD / TA* KUR.*ku-mu-uḫ-ḫu la-qi-ú / šu-ma-nu ša* LÚ*.DAM.GÀR.MEŠ *la ú-d*[*a*]
>
> 84 *cured skins* purchased for 2 minas 53 shekels of silver from Kummuh – I don't know the names of the merchants.[1378]

The other instance is attested in a compound word, namely *ša-ṣallēšu*, in the sense "dealer in leather hides."[1379] It occurs in a passage in a NA administrative document (SAA VII 115 r. i 5–6), which reads as follows:

> 5 GÚ *ša* LÚ.*ṣal-li-šú-nu / ša né-ri-bi*
>
> 5 talents, the hide-dealers of the entrance.

In AHw. (p. 1077b s.v. *ṣallu* II), this word in the sense "(Tier-)Haut, ein Leder," is considered to be a loan from Aramaic, and the NA expression *ša-ṣallēšu* is rendered "ihres Lederhändlers."[1380] The editors of CAD (Ṣ, p. 74a s.v. *ṣallu*) define this word as (tanned hide, a type of leather), and tentatively consider it to be a loan from Aramaic. On the other hand, they render NA *ša-ṣallēšu* as "dealer in *ṣallu*-leather."[1381]

Salonen states that the raw and unworked hide is called *dušû*, but the processed hide is designated *ṣallu*, which he considers to be a borrowing from Aramaic *ṣallā*, in the sense "tanned hide."[1382] Abraham and Sokoloff point out that the usual Akkadian word for "leather" is *mašku*, which is a cognate with Official Aramaic משך.[1383] On the other hand, they deem it difficult to decide the ultimate source of the Akkadian word *ṣallu* and Aramaic צלא, both meaning "leather," because the word occurs only in the later dialects of Akkadian and in the Aramaic dialects of the first millennium A.D.[1384]

According to DNWSI (p. 967 s.v. *ṣl*$_1$), the word is attested in Official Aramaic as *ṣl* "leather." In Syriac the word ܨܰܠܳܐ means "hide (especially dry)."[1385] In Arabic lexica, the word صَلَّة is listed with the sense "dried hide before tanning,"

[1378] In SAA XI 26:13′, the word KUŠ.*ṣal-li* is tentatively translated as "cured skins," but in the Glossary of SAA XI (p. 167b s.v. *ṣallu*), the word is simply translated as "hide, leather."

[1379] See AEAD (p. 103a s.v. *ṣallu* B, p. 107a s.v. *ša-ṣallēšu* B).

[1380] See also von Soden, *Or* 37 (1968), p. 267:137; idem, *Or* 46 (1977), p. 194:137. Cf. CDA (p. 332b s.v. *ṣallu* II), where the NA expression *ša ṣallišunu* is rendered "leather-sellers."

[1381] See CAD (Ṣ, p. 74b s.v. *ṣallu* in *ša ṣallišu*).

[1382] A. Salonen, *Die Wasserfahrzeuge in Babylonien: nach šumerisch-akkadischen Quellen* (Helsinki 1939), p. 145; idem, *Die Fussbekleidung der alten Mesopotamier nach sumerisch-akkadischen Quellen: eine lexikalische und kulturgeschichtliche Untersuchung* (Helsinki 1969), pp. 77f.

[1383] See Abraham & Sokoloff, *Reassessment*, p. 51:220. See also DNWSI (p. 700 s.v. *mšk*$_1$).

[1384] See Abraham & Sokoloff, ibid.

[1385] See Manna (p. 636a s.v. ܨܰܠܳܐ).

and “putrefied hide in tanning,” as well as “sandal; shoe.”[1386] According to Fraenkel, Arabic صَلَّة, Syriac ܨܠܐ and JBA צלא, all in the sense “Leder,” are derived from the root צלצל “stinken.”[1387] In Arabic, for that matter, the root ṢLL means, among other things, “to become putrid, decay, rot (meat); brackish (water).”[1388] In our case, the meanings associated with the West-Semitic root ṢLṢL or ṢLL given above may be connected with the process of tanning, and ultimately with the word *ṣālā* “tanned hide.” Etymologically and semantically, the West-Semitic evidence speaks in favor of a borrowing into NA and LB. Most likely, the word was borrowed from Aramaic because the language contact between NA and Aramaic was more intensive.

ṣippirrāte n. f. pl. “early morning”

Loanword	Reference	Provenance	Origin	Genre	Date
ṣip-pir-ra-a-te	SAA X 274:9	Nineveh	Nineveh	L	670?

Aram. ⇒ NA

Com., *ṣpr*, *ṣpr*ʾ (*ṣpar*, *ṣaprā*) n. m. “morning, early morning, daybreak, dawn” DNWSI 973; DJBA 971a; DJPA 469a; Jastrow 1298b; SL 1299a; PSm. 483a; DSA 742a; LSp. 172a; DCPA 358a; CAL. Ma., *ṣipra* n. m. “dawn, early morning” MD 394b. Syr., *ṣaprāyāṯā* n. f. pl. “the times of (early) morning” Manna 645b. Syr., *ṣaprāwāṯā* n. m. pl. “early mornings” Audo 875b; SL 1299a.

This word occurs as a *hapax legomenon* in NA and is attested in a letter addressed to Esarhaddon by his exorcist Nabû-nādin-šumi concerning the performance of the anti-witchcraft ritual Maqlû. In AHw. (p. 1104a s.v. *ṣippa(r)rātu* I), the word is glossed “Morgen,” and is considered to be a borrowing into NA from Aramaic *ṣip(pā)rā*.[1389] The editors of CAD (Ṣ, p. 202a s.v. *ṣipparātu* A) list the word with the sense “morning,” and consider it to be a borrowing from West-Semitic into NA. In the Glossary of SAA X, the word is subsumed under *ṣiprāti* “early morning.”[1390] However, the passage where the word occurs (SAA X 274:7–r.1) reads as follows:

> *ša nu-bat-te ma*!*-aq-lu-u* / LUGAL *e-pa-áš* / *ina ṣip-pir-ra-a-te* / *re-eḫ-te* / [*dul*]-⸢*li*!⸣ // ⸢LUGAL⸣ *e-pa-áš*

[1386] Scc *Al-munǧidu* (p. 431a s.v. صَلَّ, no. 1); Ibn Manẓūr, *Lisān al-ʿarab* (Cairo [196-?]–1986), vol. 4, pp. 2487b, 2488a s.v. الصِّلَّةُ.

[1387] See Fraenkel, p. 167. Note that Fraenkel did not consider the Arabic word صلّة “Leder” to be a borrowing from Aramaic; rather he regarded the Arabic word مصَلّة, which designates a vessel for filtering or straining, to be a borrowing from Aramaic. Cf. LS (p. 628a s.v. ܨܠܐ); SL (p. 1285f, s.v. ܨܠܐ); DJBA (p. 963b s.v. צָלָא no. 1).

[1388] See *Al-munǧidu* (p. 431a s.v. صَلَّ, no. 2).

[1389] Cf. CDA (p. 339a s.v. *ṣippa*(*r*)*ātu* I); DNWSI (p. 973 s.v. *ṣprh*$_1$); Tadmor, *Aramaization*, p. 455.

[1390] See the Glossary of SAA X, p. 357b. Cf. AEAD (p. 105a s.v. *ṣippirrāti* “early morning”).

> At night the king will perform *Maqlû*; in the early morning the king will perform the balance of the ritual.

Von Soden associates *ṣippirrāte* with Aramaic *ṣip(pā)rā* "morning," from which he considers it to be a borrowing into NA.[1391] He regards the NA word to represent an older form of the Syriac and Jewish Aramaic *ṣaprā* and Mandaic *ṣiprā*.[1392] Abraham and Sokoloff consider the connection between NA *ṣippirrāte* and Aramaic צפר "morning" to be plausible.[1393] However, they state that a feminine nominal form of the word is nowhere to be found in Aramaic.

Etymologically, Brockelmann compares Syriac ܨܦܪܐ "morning," with Arabic أَصْفَرُ "yellow."[1394] However, the former is probably cognate with Syriac ܫܦܪܐ "dawn, morning light,"[1395] and Arabic سفر "dawn; to shine."[1396] Actually, Syriac has two nominal forms in the plural, namely f. pl. ܨܦܪ̈ܬܐ and m. pl. ܨܦܪ̈ܘܬܐ, both meaning "early mornings."[1397]

Streck rightly points out that the f. pl. *ṣippirrāte* has parallels in Akkadian expressions for evening and morning, such as *līlâtu* pl. tant. "evening," *tamḫâti* f. pl. "evening," *šērāti* f. pl. "in the morning hours," and *kaṣâtu* f. pl. "early morning."[1398] He suggests that the spelling *ṣippirrāte* can be interpreted as Akkadographic *ṢIP-PIR-ra-a-te* for *ṣiprāte*, which fits better the Aramaic etymon *ṣa/iprā*.[1399] The first syllable of the NA *ṣip-pir-ra-a-te* is written with the CVC-sign (zib), which when occurring in the first position of the word can be read as (ṣip).[1400] The second syllable is written with the CVC-sign (tam), which when occurring in the second position of the word can be read as (pir).[1401]

Semantically, the expression *ina ṣippirrāte*, constitutes a compound adverb in the sense "in the morning."[1402] Apparently, the word *ṣippirrāte* in the NA letter occurs in contrast to the preceding word *nubattu* "evening," where both signify a specific time of the day. The combination of the two contrasting words is used here to express entirety or completeness. According to Nili, the meaning of *ṣippirrāte* is clear due to a fixed arrangement – obviously an instance of merism – instead of the usual combination: *šēru/šērtu–nubattu*.[1403] The distribution of the word points to a borrowing from Aramaic into NA.

1391 See von Soden, *Or* 37 (1968), p. 267:138; idem, *Or* 46 (1977), p. 195:138.
1392 See von Soden, ibid.
1393 See Abraham & Sokoloff, *Reassessment*, p. 51:226.
1394 LS (p. 635a s.v. ܨܦܪܐ).
1395 SL (p. 1592b s.v. ܫܦܪܐ).
1396 See *Al-munǧidu* (p. 337a s.v. سفر no. 2); Wehr-Cowan (p. 412b s.v. سفر).
1397 See Manna, p. 645b. Cf. Audo, p. 875b; SL (p.1299a s.v. ܨܦܪܐ).
1398 M.P. Streck (personal communication).
1399 Ibid.
1400 See Luukko, SAAS XVI, § 3.14, especially p. 68 s.v. zib. See also Borger, ABZ, no. 395.
1401 See Luukko, ibid., p. 66 s.v. tam. See also Borger, ABZ, no. 381.
1402 Cf. Hämeen-Anttila, SAAS XIII, § 3.2.3.2.
1403 See Nili, p. 217:103. Cf. CAD (N/II, p. 307a s.v. *nubattu* A, d); idem (R, p. 338b s.v. *rīḫtu* 1, 6′).

ṣipputu n. f. "cover"

Loanword	Reference	Provenance	Origin	Genre	Date
ṣi-ip-pu-tu	SAA IX 2 iii 21′	Nineveh	*Arbela*	P	Esh

Aram. ⇒ NA

JBA, Syr., *ṣph*, *ṣpt'* (*ṣeppā*, *ṣepptā*, *ṣīptā*) n. f. "rush mat, matting" DJBA 962b; Jastrow 1279b; SL 1299b; PSm. 483b; Manna 644b; Audo 874b; CAL. JBA *ṣippətā* n. f. "ceiling, cover; mat" Dalman 351a.

This *hapax legomenon* is attested in a NA oracle of encouragement from Ištar of Arbail proclaimed to Esarhaddon by a prophetess, probably Sinqīša-āmur.[1404] In his edition of the NA oracle, Parpola tentatively translates *ṣi-ip-pu-tu* as "cover." The passage where the word occurs (SAA IX 2 iii 21′) reads as follows:

> *ṣi-ip-pu-tu ša* LÚ.˹KÚR.MEŠ˺-*ka a*!-*na*!-*sa-aḫ*
>
> I will pull away the *cover* of your enemies.

The editors of CAD (Ṣ, p. 203a s.v. *ṣippatu* A mng. b) render the word under discussion as "orchard," and the same NA passage where the word is attested is translated as follows: "I will tear out the orchard of your enemies."[1405] However, they comment that the entirety of the evidence suggests that *ṣippatu* is a poetic synonym of the Akkadian word *kirû*, "orchard." In AHw. (p. 1104a s.v. *ṣippatu(m)* I, 1)), the word is glossed "Obstgarten." On the other hand, AEAD (p. 105a s.v. *ṣipputu*) glossed the word as "cover."[1406]

Parpola states that none of the different meanings ascribed to Akkadian *ṣippatu* in CAD ("orchard," a vegetable, a metal or alloy, a reed), fit the present context.[1407] For his translation of *ṣi-ip-pu-tu* as "cover," he adduces the Syriac word ܨܶܦܬ݂ܳܐ "mat, matting," as well as JBA צִפְּתָא "Decke, Matte," and notes that "an Aramaic loanword is very likely to be in question."[1408]

From the West-Semitic evidence, Hebrew צפה means "to lay out, lay over, overlay (object, often with metal)."[1409] In addition, the word צָפִית, as a feminine noun, perhaps means "covering."[1410] In Ugaritic the root ṢPY has the meanings "to cover; to plate, coat (with precious metal)."[1411] In Arabic the word صُفَّة is

[1404] Cf. PNA 3/I (p. 1141b s.v. Sinqīša-āmur).
[1405] Cf. S. Langdon, *Tammuz and Ishtar* (Oxford 1914), p. 140 and pl. III.
[1406] Cf. AEAD (p. 105a s.v. *ṣippatu* "orchard").
[1407] See n. ad SAA XI 2 iii 21f.
[1408] Ibid. Cf. PSm. (p. 483b s.v. ܨܶܦܬ݂ܳܐ); Dalman (p. 351a s.v. צִפְּתָא); DJBA (p. 962b s.v. צִיפְּתָא).
[1409] See David J.A. Clines (ed.), *The Concise Dictionary of Classical Hebrew* (Sheffield 2009), p. 383a s.v. צפה II; E. Klein, *A Comprehensive Etymological Dictionary of the Hebrew Language for Readers of English* (New York 1987), p. 554a s.v. צפה^{II}.
[1410] See Klein, ibid., p. 554c s.v. צָפִית.
[1411] See J. Tropper, *Kleines Wörterbuch des Ugaritischen* (Wiesbaden 2008), p. 114 s.v. √*ṣpy*; J. Aistleitner, *Wörterbuch der Ugaritischen Sprache* (Berlin 1963), p. 269 s.v. *ṣpi*.

defined as (a summer house roofed with palm-leaf stalks and the like).[1412] Hence, the borrowing of the word under discussion from Aramaic into NA is quite likely based on the meaning of the Aramaic word, which is corroborated by possible West-Semitic cognates. Phonologically, this loanword is fully integrated into NA because it displays the Assyrian vowel harmony.

šaglû n. "deportee"; (see the discussion above s.v. *galû*)

Loanword	Reference	Provenance	Origin	Genre	Date
[L]Ú.*ga-li-te*	SAA XV 102 r.3	Nineveh	*Kār-Šarrukīn*	L	Sg
LÚ*.*šá-ga-l*[*u-te*]	SAA XV 41:14′	Nineveh	–	L	Sg
LÚ*.*šag-lu-te*	SAA I 219:6, 10 LÚ*.*šag-lu-*[*te*], 13, 16	Nineveh	*Middle Euphrates*	L	Sg
	SAA XIII 157:10′	Nineveh	*Nineveh*	L	7th c.
	ND 2386 r. i 15	Calah	*Calah*	AD	Sg
LÚ*.*šag-lu-u-te*	SAA I 257:5	Nineveh	–	L	Sg
	SAA XV 233:5′	Nineveh	*Babylonia*	L	Sg

Aram. ⇒ NA

šaglûtu n. f. "deportation, exile"; (see the discussion above s.v. *galû*)

Loanword	Reference	Provenance	Origin	Genre	Date
šá-ga-lu-ti	SAA XXI 50:4′ (RL)	Nineveh	*Nineveh*	L	Asb

Aram. ⇒ NA

šapīnutu n. f. "boat, ship"

Loanword	Reference	Provenance	Origin	Genre	Date
šá-ap[!]*-pi-na*[!!]*-te*	SAA VII 115 ii 14	Nineveh	Nineveh	AD	Sg

Aram. ⇒ NA; LB

OffAr., JBA, JPA, Syr., Sam., Ma., *spynh*, *spynt'* (*spīnā*, *spīntā*/ *spīttā*) n. f. "ship, boat" DNWSI 797; DJBA 825b; DJPA 385b; Jastrow 1013b; SL 1030b; LS 490b; PSm. 385b; Manna 507a; Audo 657b; DSA 604b; MD 334b; CAL.

[1412] See *Al-munğidu* (p. 425c s.v. صَفَّ no. 2). Cf. Wehr-Cowan (p. 516b s.v. صفة).

This word is a *hapax legomenon* in NA and is attested in its plural feminine form.[1413] In AHw. (p. 1027a s.v. *sapīn(a)tu*; p. 1175b s.v. *šappinātu*), the word is considered to be an Aramaic foreign word in NA and LB meaning "Schiff."[1414] The editors of CAD (S, p. 164b s.v. *sapīnatu* (*sapinnatu*, *šappinatu*)) gloss the word as "ship," and consider it to be a borrowing from Aramaic into NA and NB. In AEAD (112a s.v. *šapīnutu*), the word is listed with the sense "boat, ship." The NA passage where the word is attested (SAA VII 115 ii 13–14), reads as follows:

2 GÚ URU.*a-li-ḫu* / *a-na šá-ap*[!]*-pi-na*[!!]*-te*

2 talents, the city Aliḫu, for the boats.

Salonen states that the meaning of *sapīnatu* "ship," which is attested in LB, is evident from the context, where it alternates with the word *eleppu*.[1415] He adds that the former is perhaps a loanword from Aramaic סְפִינְתָּא "ship."[1416] He also suggests that the word is derived from the root SPN "to cover; to panel," and therefore originally meant a "ship with a deck."[1417] In his articles on Aramaic loanwords, von Soden lists the word as "Schiff," and also considers it to be a borrowing from Aramaic *spintā*.[1418] Kaufman notes that the general terms used to refer to "boat" were the words *spynh* and *ʾlp*, which probably had different complementary meanings in relation to each other at different periods.[1419] He points out that the common Aramaic *ʾ(y)lpʾ* "boat" lacks a clear Semitic etymology, and considers it most likely to be an old culture word for "boat" which is a cognate in Akkadian and Aramaic.[1420] Abraham and Sokoloff state that the usual word for boat in Akkadian is *eleppu* and that the appearance of *sapīnatu* in the late dialects of Akkadian definitely indicates a borrowing from the common Aramaic word.[1421]

It is known that Aramaic סְפִינְתָּא was borrowed into late Biblical Hebrew as סְפִינָה "ship."[1422] Fraenkel has shown that the Aramaic word was also borrowed into Arabic as سَفِينَة "ship, vessel, boat."[1423] In fact, it is also borrowed into Mehri

[1413] The other supposedly NA instance of this word was considered to be attested in ND 2656:6′, see H.W.F. Saggs, "The Nimrud Letters, 1952–Part IV: The Urarṭian Frontier," *Iraq* 20 (1958), p. 187, 40:6′. The word is listed as [giš]*sa*!?*-pi-nu-tú* in AHw. (p. 1027a s.v. *sapīn(a)tu*), and as GIŠ *sa*(or *ša*, text *i*)*-pi-nu-tú* in CAD (S, p. 164b s.v. *sapīnatu*), but the same word is now read differently as GIŠ.*i-pi-nu-tú* "carriage," and therefore is not taken into account here. Cf. the new edition of ND 2656 in, SAA XIX 54. Cf. also CTN V, p. 186; K. Radner, "Salmanassar V. in den *Nimrud Letters*," *AfO* 50 (2003/2004), pp. 103f. Cf. Nili, p. 291:162.

[1414] See also CDA (p. 317a s.v. *sapīnatu*). Cf. DNWSI (p. 797 s.v. *spynh*).

[1415] See A. Salonen, *Die Wasserfahrzeuge in Babylonien: nach šumerisch-akkadischen Quellen* (Helsinki 1939), p. 19.

[1416] Ibid.

[1417] Ibid.

[1418] See von Soden, *Or* 37 (1968), p. 265:130; idem, *Or* 46 (1977), p. 194:130.

[1419] See Kaufman, AIA, p. 48, n. 86.

[1420] Ibid., p. 48.

[1421] See Abraham & Sokoloff, *Reassessment*, p. 49:208.

[1422] See M. Wagner, *Die lexikalischen und grammatikalischen Aramaismen im alttestamentlichen Hebräisch* (Berlin 1966), p. 88 no. 204, with previous literature.

[1423] See Fraenkel, pp. 216f. Cf. Wehr-Cowan, p. 414a.

as *sfenēt*.[1424] Perhaps an etymology for the Aramaic word can be found in the archaic or obsolete Classical Syriac verb ܨܦܢ "to overlay or cover with wooden boards."[1425]

Postgate suggests that the NA *šá-ap-pi-na*?*-te* may be a syllabic writing of the word GIŠ.MÁ.MEŠ.[1426] The latter is a plural form of the word GIŠ.MÁ, which refers to Akkadian *eleppu* "ship, boat" and occurs in a preceding line in the same NA text (SAA VII 115 ii 3). A question that arises here is why did the scribe of this NA text write one word in two different ways, i.e., logographically as GIŠ.MÁ.MEŠ and syllabically as *šá-ap*!*-pi-na*!!*-te*, to refer to the same object, namely "boat"? Most probably, the scribe intended to indicate two different objects by differentiating between a "boat," and a "ship." Hence, he wrote GIŠ.MÁ.MEŠ to indicate *eleppāni/elippāti* "boats," but utilized the Aramaic loanword *šapīnātu* to mean "ships," or vice versa. While this Aramaic loanword is attested as *sa-pi-na-a-tú* in LB, i.e., with the initial radical *s*,[1427] it occurs in NA as *šá-ap*!*-pi-na*!!*-te*, i.e., with the initial radical *š*, which complies with the expected *š* ⋧ *s* interchange between alphabetic and NA cuneiform renderings.[1428]

ša-ṣallēšu n. "dealer in leather hides"; (see the discussion above s.v. *ṣallu*)

Aram. ⇒ NA [?]

šiāḫu n. "earnest talk(?)"

Loanword	Reference	Provenance	Origin	Genre	Date
ši-a-ḫu	SAA V 243 e.20	Nineveh	*Qunbuna*	L	Sg
	SAA V 126 r.14 *ši-a-*⌜*ḫ*⌝*u*!	Nineveh	Northern border	L	Sg

Aram. ⇒ NA [?]

JPA *śyḥ* n. m. "talk(?)" CAL; DNWSI 1126.[1429] QA, LJLA *swḥ* v. "to talk, tell, discuss" Jastrow 962b; CAL. Syr., *swḥ* v. "to go towards eagerly, long for, earnestly desire" SL 977a; PSm. 364a; Manna 481b; Audo 620b.

This word occurs as a *dis legomenon* in NA. It is attested as *ši-a-ḫu* in two different letters (SAA V 126 r.14) and (SAA V 243 e.20). The editors of CAD (Š/II, p. 371a s.v. *šiāru* A mng. no. 2) read the word in the NA letter ABL 243 r.14 (= SAA V 126 r.14) as ⌜*ši*⌝*-a-*⌜*ri*(?)⌝ and subsume it under the heading *šiāru*

1424 See Salonen, ibid.
1425 See Manna (p. 507a s.v. ܨܦܢ); Audo (p. 657b s.v. ܨܦܢ).
1426 See TCAE, p. 327, n. ad ADD 953 ii 14.
1427 See CAD (S, p. 164b s.v. *sapīnatu*).
1428 See n. 71 above.
1429 See DNWSI (p. 1126 s.v. *šyḥh*).

"the next following day."[1430] In AHw. (p. 1226a s.v. *šiāru*(*m*)), the word in the NA letter ABL 317:20 (= SAA V 243 e.20) is tentatively subsumed under *šiāru*(*m*) "Morgen." On the other hand, in CDA (p. 369b s.v. *šiāḫu* II) the meaning of the NA word is considered to be unclear. In AEAD (p. 115b s.v. *šiāḫu*), the word is tentatively glossed as "earnest talk." The contexts where the NA word occurs are provided below:

> SAA V 126 r.14–15, reads:[1431]
>
> *ši-a-˹ḫ˺u*! *šu-ú / a-˹na˺* MAN EN-*ia a-sa-˹par˺-ra*
>
> I did write to the king, my lord, *in full earnest.*
>
> SAA V 243 e.18–r.1, reads:[1432]
>
> *ina* ŠÀ-*bi an-ni-e / ina* É.˹GAL˺ *li-iḫ*!*-˹ḫi*!˺-[*kim*] */ ki-i ši-a-ḫu //* TA LUGAL *a-da-bu-bu-ni*
>
> From this act, it should be understood in the Palace that I speak *earnestly* with the king.

Lanfranchi and Parpola, the editors of SAA V, tentatively translate the word *ši-a-ḫu* as "earnestly, in full earnest," and suggest a connection with the Syriac word ܣܘܚܐ, in the sense "earnest desire, eagerness."[1433] They also compare the NA word with Hebrew *śīaḥ* "business, concern."[1434]

The known Akkadian word *šiāḫum* or *šâḫu* "to grow (in size or age)" does not provide a satisfactory meaning that would fit into the contexts of the two NA letters.[1435] Nevertheless, the NA *šiāḫu* points to a derivation from a middle weak root ŠĪḪ, i.e., with *ī* as the theme vowel, whereas the Syriac word ܣܘܚ is derived from a middle weak root SŪḤ, i.e., with *ū* as the theme vowel.[1436] The Syriac word is probably cognate with Arabic شَاحَ "to be earnest, serious."[1437] It is probably also cognate with the Hebrew words סוּחַ, שׂוּחַ "to talk, to tell,"[1438] and שִׂיחַ "to think, talk,"[1439] as well as סִיחָה, שִׂיחָה "talk, conversation."[1440]

1430 See also CAD (Š/II, p. 372b s.v. *šiāru* A mng. no. 3, d), for the NA letter ABL 317:20 (= SAA V 243:20).

1431 This text is cited as ABL 243 r.13 in CAD (Š/I, p. 331b s.v. *šamru*, c), but the word under discussion is read *ši-a-˹ri*(?)˺ and the rendering "tomorrow?" is suggested tentatively. Cf. CAD (Š/II, p. 371a s.v. *šiʾāru* A, 2), where the same word is read ˹*ši*˺*-a-˹ri*(?)˺.

1432 This text is cited as ABL 317:20 in CAD (Š/II, p. 372b s.v. *šiāru* A, d). See also AHw. (p. 1226a s.v. *šiāru*(*m*)).

1433 See n. ad SAA V 243:20. See also SAA V 126 r.14. Cf. the Glossary of SAA V (p. 238b s.v. *šiāḫu* "earnest talk(?)"). Cf. also PSm., (p. 364a s.v. ܣܘܚ).

1434 See n. ad SAA V 243:20.

1435 See CAD (Š/I, p. 106b s.v. *šâḫu* A); CDA (p. 369b s.v. *šiāḫum* I).

1436 Cf. the discussion on the word *miāru* above.

1437 See *Al-munǧidu* (p. 410c s.v. شَاحَ mng. no. 2).

1438 See Jastrow, p. 962a.

1439 Ibid., p. 1559a.

1440 Ibid., pp. 977b, 1559b.

Most important, however, is the fact that "the majority of the Akkadian loanwords in Aramaic have what must be considered the correct reflex of the posited Akkadian form, both as to vowel quality and quantity."[1441] Hence, a borrowing in this case from Akkadian into Aramaic is excluded. Given the difference in vowel quality between NA *šiāḫu* and Aramaic *swḥ*, the evidence indicates a borrowing from Aramaic into NA.

taḫtānu prep. "under, beneath"

Loanword	Reference	Provenance	Origin	Genre	Date
taḫ-ta-n[*u-ni*?]	SAA XV 116 r.14′	Nineveh	*Der*	L	Sg

Aram. ⇒ NA

OAram., *tḥtn* adj "lower" DNWSI 1211. OffAr., JPA, JBA, CPA, Sam., Syr., LJLA *tḥt*, *tḥwt*, *tḥyt* (*taḥt*, *tḥot*, *tḥet*)[1442] prep. "under, below, beneath" DNWSI 1209; DJPA 579b; DJBA 1201a; Jastrow 1661a; LSp. 219b; DCPA 452a; DSA 947a; SL 1637b; PSm. 610a; Manna 835b; Audo 1109b; CAL.

The word *taḫtānu* is a *hapax legomenon* attested in a broken context in a NA letter sent to king Sargon II, concerning pacifying a city and gathering troops. The term is not in AHw., CAD or CDA. In AEAD (p. 121a s.v. *taḫtānu*), it is listed as a preposition with the sense "under, beneath." The passage where the word occurs (SAA XV 116 r.13′–15′) reads as follows:

> LÚ*.*e-rib-tú i-si-ni nu-še-*[*x x*] / *ma-a* LÚ*.*e-rib-tú taḫ-ta-n*[*u-ni*? *x x*] / *ma a-ni-ni* :. *ni-ḫa-ṣi-in* [*x x*]
>
> We shall bri[ng in] the incomers with us; we shall take care of the incomers *under* [*us* …].

Fuchs and Parpola tentatively render *taḫtānu* as "under us," compare it with El-Amarna *taḫta* and West-Semitic/Arabic *taḥat*/*taḥta* "under," and suggest that it is probably an Aramaism which ought to be added to von Soden's list of Aramaic loanwords in NA.[1443]

A word probably comparable to NA *taḫtānu* is *taḫtamu*, which in AHw. (p. 1302b s.v. *taḫta*) is rendered "unter sie," and is considered to be a Canaanite foreign word in El-Amarna.[1444] According to DNWSI (p. 1211 s.v. *tḥtn*), an Old

[1441] See Kaufman, AIA, p. 146.

[1442] In Syriac the forms ܬܚܶܬ, ܬܚܽܘܬ and ܬܚܺܝܬ are all attested, but they are generally differentiated in usage; for instance, the form ܬܚܶܬ is used with pronominal suffixes. See CAL s.v. *tḥwt*.

[1443] See n. ad SAA XV 116 r.14. See also the Glossary of SAA XV (p. 250a s.v. *taḫtānu*). Cf. AHw. (p. 1302b s.v. *taḫta*).

[1444] See also CDA (p. 394a s.v. *taḫta*). Cf. CAD (T, p. 54b s.v. *taḫta*, p. 299a s.v. *ta'tamu* (*taḫtamu*) "assembly(?)"). Cf. also H. Tawil, *An Akkadian Lexical Companion for Biblical Hebrew* (Jersey City 2009), p. 431a s.v. תַּחַת.

Aramaic word *tḥtn* in the singular absolute is attested, written on an object which perhaps had to be placed under something else. However, in Aramaic a pronominal suffix can be added to prepositions to indicate possession. The potential Aramaic source word probably meant "under us," and was a combination of the preposition *taḥt* and the possessive pronominal suffix of the 1p. pl. *-ān*: **taḥtān* < *taḥt* + *ān*.

Most important, however, is that the root TḤT in the sense "under; bottom" is Common Semitic, except for Akkadian.[1445] The word is attested in Hebrew as תַּחַת prep. "under, beneath," and in Arabic as تَحْتَ prep. "under, below, underneath."[1446] In Targumic Aramaic and Syriac, *tḥt* is attested figuratively in combination with the word *yd* "hand," in the sense "under the command of."[1447] In Syriac a denominative verb, namely ܬܚܬܝ, is also attested with the meaning "to bring into subjection."[1448]

tuānu n. (a bathroom)

Loanword	Reference	Provenance	Origin	Genre	Date
tu-a-ni	StAT 2 53:4, 5	Assur	Gūzāna	LD	700

Aram. ⇒ NA

OffAr., JBA, Palm., Nab., Syr., *twn*, *twn'* (*tawwān*, *tawwānā*) n. m. "chamber, room" DNWSI 1206f; DJBA 1197a; Jastrow 1651b; SL 1631b; Manna 833a; Audo 1107a; CAL.

This word occurs as a *dis legomenon* in a NA legal document from Assur (StAT 2 53:4, 5). The document is a conveyance concerning the sale of a piece of real estate located in the city of Gūzāna. The object of the sale is specifically described as *tu-a-ni*, and is subsequently referred to by the complex É–TU$_5$. The latter, when occurring in connection with private houses, is read *bēt ramāki*, and is understood to be a "bathroom."[1449] The word *tuānu* as a designation for bathroom is not listed in CAD, AHw. or CDA. On the other hand, in AEAD (p. 125a s.v. *tuānu* B), the term is defined as (a bath). The context where the word occurs (StAT 2 53:2–10) reads as follows:

> [*ṣu-pur*] ^{m}*sa-ma-a'* LÚ*.*si-me-ri-šu-a-a* / [A ^{md}U]TU–EN–ZI *ša* URU.*gu-za-ni* / [E]N *tu-a-ni* SUM-*an* / *tu-a-ni a-di* GIŠ.ÙR.MEŠ-*šú a-di* GIŠ.IG.MEŠ-*šú* / *i-ga-a-ri bir*$^{!!}$-*te* ^{m}*ri-bi-ṣi-ṣi bir*$^{!!}$-*te* ^{m}*ḫa-na-bé-eš*$^{?}$ / *ša* ^{m}*sa-ma-a'* *ina* URU.*gu-za-ni* / *ú-piš-*

1445 See LS (p. 821a s.v. ܬܚܬܝܐ); Brauner (p. 627 s.v. *tḥt(yh)*).
1446 See Jastrow (p1662b s.v. תַּחַת); Dalman (p. 420a s.v. תַּחַת); Wehr-Cowan (p. 91b s.v. تحت).
1447 See CAL s.v. *tḥwt*.
1448 See PSm. (p. 610b s.v. ܬܚܬܝ).
1449 See LAS II ad no. 310:6′; K. Radner, *Die neuassyrischen Privatrechtsurkunden als Quelle für Mensch und Umwelt* (Helsinki 1997), p. 269; AEAD (p. 16b s.v. *bēt ramāki*, p. 92a s.v. *ramāku*).

ma [m]*qi-še-ra-a-a* LÚ*.GAL–*x x-a-a* / *ina* ŠÀ-*bi* 50 GÍN.MEŠ KÙ.BABBAR *il-qi* / *kas-pi ga-mur* SUM-*an* / É–TU$_5$ *šu-a-te za-rip la-qi.*

[Fingernail] of Sama', a Damascene, [son of Ša]maš-bēl-ketti from Gūzāna, owner of the *tuanu* (bath) being sold. A *tuanu* (bath) with its beams (and) doors, and a wall between Ribiṣiṣi and Ḫanabeš, (property) of Sama' in the city of Gūzāna – Qišeraya, chief [...]ean, has contracted and bought it for fifty shekels of silver. The money is paid completely. The bathroom in question is acquired and purchased.

Zimmern states that Akkadian *tu'u*, which he renders as "chamber," was borrowed into Late Hebrew as *tā*('), as well as into Aramaic as *tawwā*, *tawwānā* and *tauwānā*.[1450] Von Soden criticizes the etymology advanced by Zimmern as being inaccurate.[1451] He argues that Akkadian *tu'u* is a loanword from Sumerian DU$_6$ "hill," (Akkadian *tillu*), which refers to cultic posts of various kinds (therefore often in parallel with *parakku* "cult dais; sanctuary"), and is not associated with a space.[1452] Instead, he connects Hebrew תָּא "chamber" and Jewish Aramaic תָּוָא, תַּוְנָא, as well as Syriac ܬܘܢܐ, all in the sense "room," with Akkadian *ta'û* which he explains as referring to an inner space of a temple or a house, the function of which is not yet determined.[1453]

Donbaz and Parpola, the editors of the NA legal document (StAT 2 53), tentatively define the word under discussion as (*tuānu* (bath)).[1454] However, based on the form of the word *tuānu* and the subsequent reference to the term by the complex É–TU$_5$ which designates a bathroom, Fales states that *tuānu* is certainly a borrowing from Aramaic into NA in the sense "bathroom."[1455] He argues that the insertion of the -*w*- as well as the addition of an afformative -*ān* represent clear novelties in the Aramaic epigraphical record.[1456]

Nevertheless, the word under discussion here ought to be distinguished from another *tuānu*, a *hapax legomenon* attested in a NA letter (SAA V 171:10), which refers to a color or breed of horses.[1457] Etymologically, the OAkk. and OB word *tā'um*, and the Hebrew word תָּא, as well as the Aramaic תונא, are all cognates meaning "room, chamber."[1458] According to Fox, the reconstructed nominal form

[1450] See Zimmern, AF, p. 32.
[1451] See W. von Soden, "Akkadisch *ta'û* und hebräisch *tā'* als Raumbezeichungen," *WO* 1 (1950), p. 356. Cf. CDA (p. 61a s.v. *di'u*(*m*) II "(deity's) throne-platform", p. 411b s.v. *tu'u*).
[1452] See W. von Soden, ibid.
[1453] See W. von Soden, ibid., pp. 356–361.
[1454] See also the Glossary of StAT 2 (p. 238b s.v. *tuānu*).
[1455] See F.M. Fales, "*tuanu*: an Aramaic loanword in Neo-Assyrian," *NABU* 2003/103; L. Bachelot & F.M. Fales (eds.), *Tell Shiukh Fawqani 1994–1998*, II (Padova 2005), p. 603.
[1456] For a reference, see F.M. Fales, "*tuanu*: an Aramaic loanword in Neo-Assyrian," *NABU* 2003/117, comment no. 4.
[1457] See CAD (T, p. 444b s.v. *tuānu*); AHw. (p. 1364b s.v. *tuānu*); AEAD (p. 125a s.v. *tuānu*); CDA (p. 408b s.v. *tuānu*). See also the Glossary of SAA V (p. 240a s.v. *tuānu*).
[1458] Cf. AHw. (p. 1340b s.v. *tā'um*); CDA (p. 402b s.v. *tā'um* "inner room"); H. Tawil, *An Akkadian Lexical Companion for Biblical Hebrew* (Jersey City 2009), p. 427a s.v. תָּא. Note, however, that the editors of CAD (D, p. 27a s.v. *daiš*), do not list an entry as *ta'û* in the sense "room, chamber." Instead they read the word as *daiš* and take it to be a preposition meaning "toward, to the side of." Cf. CAD (T, p. 300b s.v. *ta'u*).

of all these words is: **tawa*' < **qatal*.[1459] Audo states that Syriac ܬܘܢܐ "room" ought to be written ܬܐܘܢܐ and ܐܘܢܐ, as derived from a reconstructed verb ܐܝܘܐ*/ܐܘܝ*, which he relates to Arabic آوى "to shelter, house, lodge, accommodate," and مَأوَى "place of refuge, retreat, shelter; abode; dwelling, habitation,"[1460] Semantically, the Aramaic word is only attested in the sense "room, chamber." That is to say, we do not have an explicit connection between the Aramaic word תונא and a building or part of a building reserved for bathing or washing. Nevertheless, based on the form of the NA word, the evidence points to a borrowing from Aramaic into NA.

tūbāqu, *dubāqu* n. "glue, elm glue, bird-lime"

Loanword	Reference	Provenance	Origin	Genre	Date
GIŠ?.*tu-ba*!-*qi*	SAA XI 36 ii 20	Nineveh	Nineveh	AD	–
tu-ba-qi	SAA II 6:582	Calah	Calah	T	672

Aram. ⇒ NA; SB[1461]

Syr., *dwbq*, *dwbq*' (*dubbāq*, *dubbāqā*) n. m. "glue, birdlime" SL 277a; PSm. 84b; Manna 134a; Audo 172a; CAL. JBA, Syr., *dbwq*, *dbwq*' (*dāḇōq*, *dāḇōqā*) n. m. "glue" DJBA 311a; SL 269a; CAL. OffAr., JPA, JBA, CPA, Syr., Ma., *dbq* v. "to stick to, adhere, cleave" DNWSI 238; DJPA 138b; DJBA 312b; Jastrow 278a; LSp. 41b; DCPA 79b; Manna 133b; Audo 171b; PSm. 82a; SL 271a; MD 101b. Syr., *dūbāqā* n. m. "elm" Manna 134b; PSm. 84b.

The word *tūbāqu* occurs as a *dis legomenon* in NA. A variant, *dubāqu*, is attested in the duplicates of Esarhaddon's succession treaty.[1462] In AHw. (p. 1364b s.v. *tubāqu*), the word is tentatively defined as (ein Gebüsch?). By contrast, CDA (p. 408b s.v. *tubāqu*) glosses the word as "trap, snare," but in the list of addenda and corrigenda of CDA the word is glossed as "mistletoe (as glue used to catch birds)."[1463] On the other hand, in CAD (T, p. 445a s.v. *tubāqu*, b and c), the word is defined as (a plant), and only one NA instance (Wiseman Treaties 582 = SAA II 6:582) is considered to mean "birdlime." In AEAD (p. 22a s.v. *dubāqu*, p. 125a s.v. *tūbāqu*), the word is glossed "glue, bird-lime." The following are the contexts where the two NA instances of *tūbāqu* occur:

[1459] See J. Fox, *Semitic Noun Patterns* (Winona Lake 2003), p. 83.
[1460] See Audo (p. 10f s.v. ܐܘܢܐ, p. 1107a s.v. ܬܘܢܐ). See also SL (p. 1631b s.v. ܬܘܢܐ); Wehr-Cowan (p. 36b s.v. اوى and ماوى).
[1461] See CDA, *Justifications, Addenda and Corrigenda*. Online 15/09/2022: https://www.soas.ac.uk/cda-archive/lemmata/
[1462] See n. ad SAA II 6:582. See also the Glossary of SAA II (p. 106a s.v. *tubāqu*).
[1463] See CDA, ibid.

SAA II 6:582–584, reads:

(KI.MIN KI.MIN) *ki-i šá* MUŠEN *ina tu-ba-qi iṣ-ṣab-bat-u-ni / a-na ka-šú-nu* ŠEŠ.MEŠ-*ku-nu* DUMU.MEŠ-*ku-nu ina* ŠU.2 EN–MÚD.MEŠ-*ku-nu / liš-ka-nu-ku-nu*

(Ditto, ditto;) just as one seizes a bird with bird-lime, so may they deliver you, your brothers and your sons into the hands of your mortal enemy. [1464]

SAA XI 36 ii 19–21, reads:

20 MA GIŠ.ḪÉ.MED / 2 BÁN GIŠ?.*tu-ba*!-*qi* / LÚ*.GAL–TÚG.UD

20 minas of *red dye*, 2 seahs of *glue*: chief fuller. [1465]

In discussing the designation used for mistletoe in Akkadian, Deller remarks that the word is not yet identified in the Assyriological literature, including AHw., CAD and Thompson's Dictionary of Assyrian Botany.[1466] Deller argues that *d/tubāqu* or (*dubbāqu*, *tubbāqu*) means "mistletoe."[1467] He compares *dubāqu* with the Syriac word *dubbāqā*, which he considers to denote "mistletoe" and its fruit, which is used to produce glue and is applied to a rod or a bar to catch birds.[1468] As a plant, however, the Syriac word ܕܘܒܩܐ refers to "elm."[1469] Deller also states that Salonen's rendering of *tubāqu* as "(vier)eckiges Fanggerät mit Lockvogel," is ultimately based on a false etymological connection between the word *tubāqu* and the word *tubqu* "corner."[1470] In addition, Deller considers the writing *tu-ba-qu*, with a single *b*, to be a defective form of the word in comparison with the SB equivalent Ú.*t/dúb-ba-qi*, as cited in KADP 33:15.[1471]

Unlike Akkadian, Aramaic utilizes the well-attested root DBQ in the sense "to stick to, adhere, cleave," of which the derivative noun *dubbāqā* "glue, bird-lime" is known. This fact, as well as the distribution of the word in the Aramaic dialects, points to a borrowing from Aramaic into NA. In Arabic we have the

[1464] Note that SAA II 6:582 translates *tu-ba-qi* as "a trap." In the Glossary of SAA II (p. 106a s.v. *tubāqu*), the word is defined as (a kind of trap). Cf. AEAD (p. 125a s.v. *tūbāqu* "glue, bird-lime"). Cf. also CAD (T, p. 445b s.v. *tubāqu*, c).

[1465] Note that SAA XI 36 ii 20, leaves the word GIŠ?.*tu-ba*!-*qi* partially translated as "of ...-wood." However, in the Glossary of SAA XI (p. 169b s.v. *tubāqu*), the word is defined as (a kind of trap). Cf. CAD (T, p. 445b s.v. *tubāqu*, b).

[1466] See K. Deller, "Die Bezeichnungen für die Mistel (mistletoe, gui, vischio, viscum)," *NABU* 1991/11. Cf. R.C. Thompson, *A Dictionary of Assyrian Botany* (London 1949), p. 25 and pp. 164–166.

[1467] Deller, ibid.

[1468] Deller, ibid.

[1469] See Manna, p. 134b; PSm., p. 84b.

[1470] See Deller, ibid. Cf. CAD (T, p. 447a s.v. *tubqu*, 1). Cf. also A. Salonen, *Vögel und Vogelfang im alten Mesopotamien* (Helsinki 1973), pp. 40, 47 s.v. *tubāqu*.

[1471] See Deller, ibid. See F. Köcher, *Keilschrifttexte zur assyrisch-babylonischen Drogen- und Pflanzenkunde* (Berlin 1955), 33:15. See also CAD (T, p. 445a s.v. *tubāqu*, a)); AHw. (p. 1364b s.v. *tubāqu*). Cf. AEAD, p. 125a, which transcribes the word as *tūbāqu*.

words دِبْق, دَابُوق and دَبُوقاء, all meaning "bird-lime; lime."[1472] There is also the expression دَبَقَ الطَيْرَ "to birdlime; catch (birds) with birdlime."[1473] Nevertheless, the Arabic word for "bird-lime; lime" given above is considered to be a borrowing from Aramaic.[1474]

However, in the first NA instance (SAA II 6:582–584), the meaning bird-lime fits perfectly well in the context. On the other hand, in the second NA instance (SAA XI 36 ii 19–21), the interpretation of the word GIŠ$^{?}$.*tu-ba*$^{!}$*-qi* is admittedly problematic, because the reading of the preceding determinative GIŠ is uncertain. Hence, the rendering "glue" suggested here is tentative. It remains to be pointed out that the two NA forms of the word attested as *dubāqu* and *tūbāqu* probably reflect NA's phonological variation between voiced and voiceless consonants, i.e., the alternation of <*d*> and <*t*>.[1475] If so, this Aramaic loanword is fully integrated into NA.

tukku, (pl. *tukkāni*) n. "oppression, persecution"

Loanword	Reference	Provenance	Origin	Genre	Date
tuk-ka-ni	SAA V 149 r.11	Nineveh	Eastern Province	L	Sg
	SAA XIII 25 r.16e	Nineveh	Assur	L	Asb

Aram. ⇒ NA; NB; SB [?]

Syr., Ma., *twk'* (*tukkā*) n. m. "oppression; damage; transgression" SL 1629b; PSm. 607b; Manna 837a; MD 483a; CAL. Syr., LJLA *tkk* (*tukkā*, *tūkā*) n. m. "oppression; transgression; damage" SL 1629b; PSm. 607b; Manna 837a; Audo 1111a; Dalman 418b; CAL. Syr., *tkk* v. "to suppress, overwhelm, subdue" SL 1644a; Manna 836b; Audo 1111a. Syr., LJLA *twk* v. "to oppress, suppress, hurt, subdue" SL 1629a; PSm. 611a; Manna 836b; Audo 1111a; Dalman 418b; CAL. Palm., *tkk* v. "to menace" DNWSI 1214.

This word is a *dis legomenon* in NA. However, it occurs more often in NB, where it is found in the singular as *tukku*, and in the plural as *tukkānu* or *tukkātu*.[1476] The editors of CAD (T, p. 458a s.v. *tukku* B) list this word in the sense "oppression, coercion." In AHw. (1367b s.v. *tukku* II), the word is tentatively considered to be a Canaanite foreign word with the meaning "Bedrückung(sakt)." In comparison, in CDA (p. 409a s.v. *tukku* II), the word is glossed "(act of) oppression," and is hesitatingly considered to be a borrowing

---

[1472] See *Al-munğidu* (p. 206a s.v. دبق); Elias & Elias (p 208a s.v. دِبق); Wehr-Cowan (p. 271b s.v. دبق). See also Deller, ibid.

[1473] See Elias & Elias, p. 208a.

[1474] See SL (p. 269a s.v. ܕܒܘܩܐ). See also Fraenkel, pp. 120f.

[1475] See Luukko, SAAS XVI, § 4.1.1, esp. p. 70 s.v. (*tubāqu*).

[1476] See, for instance, ABL 1136 r.6′, 7′; ABL 1274 r.5; SAA XIII 182 r.7; SAA XVII 135 r.9′; SAA XVIII 23 s.4; SAA XVIII 54 r.18; SAA XVIII 118 r.2; SAA XVIII 181 r.21. Cf. the comment on the NB plurals *tukkāta/i* in CAD (T, p. 458a s.v. *tukku* B).

from West-Semitic. In AEAD (p. 125b s.v. *tukku*), the term is rendered "oppression, persecution." The two NA occurrences are presented below:

SAA V 149 r.11–14, reads:

a-ta-a i-na tuk-ka-ni ma-a-t[*i*!] / *i-ga-mar bir-ti* IGI.2.MEŠ-*šú* [0] / *lu-ma-di-du* TA* *ša* ŠU.⸢2⸣-[*ia*] / ⸢*lu*!⸣ *la*! *i-da-bu*-⸢*ub*⸣ [0]

Why is he destroying [my] country by oppression? Let it be impressed upon him that he may not lay claims to people under [my] jurisdiction.

SAA XIII 25 r.16e–17e, reads:

URU! *ina tuk*!*-ka-ni lu la i-ḫa-pi-u* / ⸢LÚ*!⸣.*šá*–UGU–URU LUGAL *be-lí lip-qid*

But the city must not be wrecked on account of repressive measures. The king, my lord, should appoint a city overseer.

In Akkadian the word *tukku* is already found in OB and Mari in the sense "rumor, warning; noise, call."[1477] Nevertheless, none of these meanings fit the context for the term *tukku* in the two NA occurrences cited above. From the West-Semitic evidence, on the other hand, a comparative term is found in Aramaic, namely *tukkā* or *tūkā* n. m., "oppression; damage; transgression," and is derived from the root TKK or TWK "to oppress, subdue, to menace."[1478] This Aramaic word has a cognate in Biblical Hebrew, תּוֹךְ "to press, make to suffer, punish,"[1479] and probably also in Ugaritic as *tk*.[1480]

Semantically, the meanings associated with Aramaic *tukkā* "oppression; damage; transgression," fit well in the context of the two NA instances.[1481] Chronologically, the late occurrence of *tukku* in the sense "oppression" in NA, NB and SB points to a borrowing from West-Semitic, most likely from Aramaic. Hence, CAD and AHw. rightly enter two separate headings for the word because *tukku* "oppression; damage; transgression," which probably is a loanword from Aramaic, seems to be etymologically unrelated to Akkadian *tukku* "rumor, warning; noise, call."

ṭullumâ adj. "treacherous, deceitful"[1482]

Loanword	Reference	Provenance	Origin	Genre	Date
ṭùl-lu-ma-a	SAA IX 2 ii 17′	Nineveh	Arbela	P	Esh

[1477] See CAD (T, p. 457a s.v. *tukku* A); AHw. (p. 1367b s.v. *tukku*(*m*) I).
[1478] See SL (p. 1629b s.v. ܬܘܟܐ). Cf. CAL s.v. *twk*.
[1479] See Jastrow (p. 1652b s.v. תּוֹךְ).
[1480] See AHw. (p. 1367b s.v. *tukku* II).
[1481] See the Glossary of SAA V (p. 240a s.v. *tukku* "oppression") and SAA XIII (p. 198a s.v. *tukku* "oppression").
[1482] The rendering follows AEAD (p. 127b s.v. *tullumâ*), which seems to fit the NA context nicely.

Aram. ⇒ NA ⇒ NB

LJLA *ṭlwm* (*ṭallūm*) adj. "oppressed" CAL. CPA, Sam., Syr., Ma., LJLA *ṭlwm*, *ṭlwm'* (*ṭalōm*, *ṭalōmā*) n. m. "oppressor, tyrant; denier" LSp. 75b; DCPA 145b; DSA 313b; PSm. 174a; LS 530b; SL 530b; Manna 284b; Audo 403a; CAL. PTA, Sam., CPA, Ma., Syr., *ṭlm* v. "to oppress, treat with injustice; to assert a false statement, deceive, cheat; to deny" DJPA 225b; DSA 313a; LSp. 75a; DCPA 150a; MD 180b; SL 533a; PSm. 175a; Audo 402b; Manna 284b.

The word *ṭullumâ* occurs as a *hapax legomenon* in NA. It is attested in an oracle of Ištar of Arbail proclaimed by the prophet Lā-dāgil-ili to Esarhaddon, promising to bless and protect the king of Assyria and to get rid of his enemies. The word is listed in AHw. (p. 1394a s.v. *ṭullummā'u*), with the sense "Gewalttäter," and is considered to be a loanword in NA and NB, borrowed from Aramaic *ṭālōmā* "oppressor; denier."[1483] The editors of CAD (Ṭ, p. 125a s.v. *ṭullumā'u*) gloss the word as "liar, cheater," and also consider it to be an Aramaic loanword in NA and NB. AEAD (p. 127b s.v. *ṭullumâ*), on the other hand, classifies the word as an adjective meaning "treacherous, deceitful." The NA passage (SAA IX 2 ii 17′–18′) where the word occurs, reads as follows:

a-me-lu-tu ṭùl-lu-ma-a / a-na-ku ši-i qa-bi-tu e-pi-is-su

Mankind is deceitful; I am one who says and does.[1484]

In his articles on Aramaic loanwords, von Soden translates *ṭullu*(*m*)*mā'u* as "Übeltäter," and considers it to be a loanword from Aramaic *ṭālomā*, stating that in Jewish Aramaic it means "Bedrücker," but in Syriac "Leugner."[1485] Referring to an instance attested in NB as *ṭùl-lu-um-ma-a'-u* (ABL 281 r.4),[1486] von Soden states that one of the significant indicators that disclose an Aramaic foreign word here is the phonetic structure of the NB word, which does not exhibit the expected contraction.[1487] He also points out that the spelling of the NA and NB words is peculiar, and explains that the first *u* probably indicates a darkening of the long vowel *ā* caused by the *ṭ*, and the doubling of the *l* and the *m* in NB may point to a form of Aramaic *nomen actoris* that somewhat deviates from the pattern *QāṬōLā*.[1488] Referring to von Soden, Parpola also considers NA *ṭùl-lu-ma-a* to be an Aramaic loanword, but based on the context he translates the word as

---

1483 See also CDA (p. 415b s.v. *ṭullummā'u* "perpetrator of violence"). Cf. DNWSI (p. 423 s.v. *ṭlm*). For a comparative word in OB, see AHw. (p. 1394a s.v. *ṭullumum* "unrecht tun?"); CAD (Ṭ, p. 125a s.v. *ṭullumu* (mng. unkn.)).

1484 CAD (Ṭ, p. 125a s.v. *ṭullumā'u*), translates this passage as: "mankind is deceitful (I, Ištar, am she who does what she says)."

1485 See von Soden, *Or* 37 (1968), p. 268:153; idem, *Or* 46 (1977), p. 196:153.

1486 See J.M.C.T. de Vaan, *"Ich bin eine Schwertklinge des Königs": Die Sprache des Bēl-ibni* (Kevelaer 1995), pp. 244, 393. The other supposedly NB instance as *ṭùl-lum-ma-a'* (CT 54 276 r.2 = K 14657 r.2) is now read differently as *šulummû*, see CAD (Ṭ, p. 125a s.v. *ṭullumā'u*; Š/III, p. 262a s.v. *šulummû*). Cf. von Soden, *Or* 37 (1968), p. 268:153.

1487 See von Soden, *Or* 35 (1966), p. 4; idem, *Or* 37 (1968), p. 268:153.

1488 See von Soden, *Or* 37 (1968), p. 268:153.

"treacherous, deceitful," a meaning which he believes fits the NB instance as well.[1489] Abraham and Sokoloff concur with von Soden in connecting this word with Syriac ܛܠܘܡܐ "liar," and state that the morphological form of the word in Akkadian is ambiguous.[1490]

Etymologically, a West-Semitic cognate with Aramaic טלם "to oppress, treat with injustice; to assert a false statement, deceive, cheat; to deny," is the Arabic word ظَلَمَ "to do wrong or evil; to wrong, treat unjustly, oppress."[1491] On the other hand, Arabic ظَلِمَ "to darken, grow dark, darkle" is cognate with Akkadian *ṣalāmu* "to become dark, to turn black."[1492] Hence, we can reconstruct a PS root *ṮLM meaning "to oppress, treat unjustly; to darken, grow dark." Obviously, in our case, the initial radical *ṭ* of NA *ṭullumâ* and NB *ṭullummā'u* suggests a borrowing from Aramaic because the PS **ṯ̣* is expected to appear in Akkadian as *ṣ*.

Phonologically, the first vowel *u* instead of the expected *a* in *ṭullumâ* is probably the result of writing an Aramaic word using Akkadographic spelling. In our case, the first syllable *ṭùl* in *ṭùl-lu-ma-a* is written with the CVC-sign (dul$_6$),[1493] which when occurring in the first position in a NA word, has also the sound value (ṭùl).[1494]

Nevertheless, the form of this loanword still remains difficult to explain. However, it seems to represent a verbal adjective of the D-stem with intensified meaning, and having a nominal pattern with doubling of the second radical and probably a suffix. The NB form shows a doubling of the third radical *m* as well. It is currently believed that the change *ṯ̣* > *ṭ* took place in Aramaic in about the middle of the first millennium B.C.[1495] However, this loanword suggests that this change should be dated to ca. 669 B.C. or earlier, assuming that the NA oracle originated by the end of Esarhaddon's reign at the latest.

ummu n. f. "water channel"

Loanword	Reference	Provenance	Origin	Genre	Date
um-me	SAA VI 24:5	Nineveh	–	LD	723
	SAA VI 27 e.12′	Nineveh	*Ḫanūri*	LD	Sg
	SAA VI 211:2′	Nineveh	*Nineveh*	LD	676?
	SAA VI 271:8	Nineveh	*Nineveh*	LD	678
	SAA XIV 276:6′ *um*!-[*me*]	Nineveh	–	LD	–
um-mi	SAA VI 31 e.27, 28	Nineveh	Nineveh	LD	709

Aram. ⇒ NA; SB

1489 See n. ad SAA IX 2 ii 17. See also the Glossary of SAA IX (p. 52b s.v. *ṭullumâ*).
1490 See Abraham & Sokoloff, *Reassessment*, p. 56:265.
1491 See Wehr-Cowan, p. 582b; Elias & Elias, p. 419a.
1492 See Elias & Elias, ibid; CAD (Ṣ, p. 70a s.v. *ṣalāmu*).
1493 For the reading of the cuneiform sign, see SAA IX, pl. iv (K 12033 + 82–5–22,527).
1494 See Luukko, SAAS XVI, § 3.14, especially p. 53 s.v. dul$_6$. See also Borger, ABZ, no. 459a.
1495 See S. Moscati, *An Introduction to the Comparative Grammar of the Semitic Languages: Phonology and Morphology* (Wiesbaden 1964), § 8.18.

Syr., QA, JLA *ʾm, ʾmʾ* (*ʾam, ʾammā*) n. f. "canal, conduit, aqueduct" SL 52b; PSm. 19a; Manna 24a; CAL.

The term *ummu* in the NA texts referred to above occurs often in descriptions of borders of a property in legal transactions concerning the purchase of land or estates. The term is written syllabically, but sometimes also logographically as AMA.[1496] In one NA text (SAA VI 27:10′, e.12′), the word is first written logographically as AMA and then syllabically as *um-me*. A possibly related word also found in a SB lexical list is *am-mu*, used as a designation of the Tigris.[1497] The editors of CAD (U/W, p. 133a s.v. *ummu* E) define the word as (a topographical feature).[1498] AHw. (p. 1417a s.v. *ummu(m)* I, mng. no. 16) considers the meaning of the word to be unclear in connection with topographical descriptions.[1499] In AEAD (p. 129a s.v. *ummu*), the word is listed with the sense "side road."

Kwasman rendered the word under discussion as "road."[1500] Later, all the instances of *ummu* and its corresponding logogram AMA that are attested in SAA VI and SAA XIV were tentatively rendered as "side road."[1501] Fales, on the other hand, rejects the rendering "road" as being unfounded.[1502] Instead, he connects NA *ummu* with the Aramaic word אם, attested twice on a clay tablet recording a judicial settlement (AO 25.341), from 641* B.C., which he interprets as meaning a "boundary-stone."[1503] Fales states that this Aramaic אם might be the ultimate West-Semitic source of the NA word discussed here.[1504] Kaufman concurs with Fales' interpretation of אם and renders the Aramaic word as "boundary document."[1505]

However, the most recent discussion on the origin of the NA word treated here is put forward by Lipiński, who states that the word אם, attested in the judicial settlement mentioned above, appears at present to be the Aramaic noun *ʾamm* "water channel," which was borrowed into NA as *ummu* in a similar sense, but with the vowel change *a* > *u* in front of the labial *m*.[1506] The Aramaic word is

---

1496 The term is written logographically in the following NA texts: SAA VI 10:5, 10, 13; 11:4′, 6′, 13′; 12:8; 13:8; 27:10′; 226:6; SAA XIV 42:8, r.4, 10; 114:5; 118:5; 168:9′; 460 e.14′; 468 r.1. The word *ummu* and the logogram AMA are more often used in Akkadian to mean "mother."

1497 See Lipiński, ibid., p. 567 n. 63. See also AHw. (p. 44b s.v. *ammu* II).

1498 A similar definition is given by Postgate, FNALD, p. 210a s.v. *ummu*.

1499 See also CDA (p. 422b s.v. *ummu(m)* I, mng. no. 4). Cf. DNWSI (p. 68 s.v. *ʾm*$_2$).

1500 See the Glossary of NALDK (p. 491a s.v. AMA, mng. no. 2).

1501 See n. ad SAA VI 10:5, which compares the word with Hebrew *ʾemm hadderek*, "crossroads, parting road." See the Glossary of SAA VI (p. 316b s.v. *ummu*); the Glossary of SAA XIV (p. 335a s.v. *ummu*). See also the discussion by F.M. Fales, "The Rural Landscape of the Neo-Assyrian Empire: A Survey," *SAAB* 4 (1990), pp. 134f.

1502 See F.M. Fales, ibid., p. 135, n. 321.

1503 See F.M. Fales, AECT, pp. 253–258, no. 58, with reference to previous literature dealing with the same tablet. For the date of the Aramaic clay tablet, see E. Lipiński, *The Aramaeans: Their Ancient History, Culture, Religion* (Leuven 2000), p. 568, n. 66.

1504 See Fales, ibid., pp. 96, 254f. Cf. F.M. Fales, "Sulla tavoletta aramaica A.O. 25.341," *AION* 35 (1976), p. 544; DNWSI (p. 68 s.v. *ʾm*$_2$).

1505 See S.A. Kaufman, "Assyro-Aramaica," *JAOS* 109 (1989), p. 100, n. on l. 58, and p. 102 s.v. אם.

1506 See Lipiński, ibid., pp. 567f., n. 64; idem, *Semitic Languages: Outline of a Comparative Grammar* (Leuven 1997), § 27:10. For the NA change /a/ > /u/, in closed syllables ending in a labial, cf. Luukko, SAAS XVI, p. 85 § 4.3.1.

used in a Qumran text as אמה בריתא "the outer canal."[1507] According to Lipiński, the Aramaic term was also borrowed into Mishnaic Hebrew as a feminine word אַמָּה, which probably designates a river-arm, i.e., a canal, dyke or sewer.[1508] In Syriac, the term occurs as ܐܡܬܐ ܕܡܝܐ (or without the word ܡܝܐ "water") in the sense "pool; spring; canal, conduit; streamlet."[1509]

Phonologically, the glottal stop ʾ (hamza) is normally not represented in writing when it occurs in word-initial position in Akkadian and its dialects. However, it has been shown that when Akkadian words beginning with a vowel are borrowed into Aramaic, they usually have an initial <ʾ> in their Aramaic forms.[1510] This would suggest that the Aramaic loanword under discussion here, which in NA is traditionally transcribed as *ummu* "water channel," may stand for a word with initial ʾ (hamza).[1511] Nevertheless, it has been also argued that the initial <ʾ> of the Aramaic words borrowed from Akkadian words with initial vowel is merely an Aramaic phenomenon, not NA, as it was impossible in Aramaic to write a word-initial vowel without an aleph.[1512] On the other hand, many sandhi writings in NA give the impression that the word-initial glottal stop ʾ (hamza) was dropped altogether.[1513]

urbānu n. "papyrus"

Loanword	Reference	Provenance	Origin	Genre	Date
ur-ba-ni	Iraq 25, 56:43 (= ND 11000)[1514]	Calah	Calah	Inscr. (Shalm. III)	9th c.

Aram. ⇒ NA; NB; SB [?]

JBA *ʾwrbnʾ* (*ʾurbānā*) n. m. "papyrus reed" DJBA 93b; Jastrow 33a; CAL. Syr., LJLA *ʾrbn* (*ʾarbān*, *ʾarbānā*) n. m. "rush, reed; the papyrus reed" PSm. 27b; SL 94a; Manna 38a; Audo 47a; CAL.

This word occurs as a *hapax legomenon* in a SB/NA inscription written on a carved throne-base of Shalmaneser III.[1515] In AHw. (p. 1428a s.v. *urbānu*), the word is glossed "Papyrus(staude)" and is considered to be a loanword from Aramaic *a/urbānā*.[1516] In contrast, CDA (p. 425b s.v. *urbānu*) glosses the word as

---

1507 See CAL s.v. *ʾm*. Cf. E. Lipiński, *The Aramaeans: Their Ancient History, Culture, Religion* (Leuven 2000), p. 567, n. 63.

1508 See Lipiński, ibid., p. 568, n. 65. Cf. Jastrow (p. 75b s.v. אַמָּה mng. no. 4).

1509 See PSm. (p. 19a s.v. ܐܡܬܐ); Manna (p. 24a s.v. ܐܡ).

1510 See Kaufman, AIA, p. 142.

1511 Cf. ibid.

1512 See Hämeen-Anttila, SAAS XIII, § 2.1.4., n. 20. See also Luukko, SAAS XVI, § 3.11.

1513 Ibid. Cf. Lipiński, *Semitic Languages*, § 19.9.

1514 See P. Hulin, "The Inscriptions on the Carved Throne-Base of Shalmaneser III," *Iraq* 25 (1963), p. 56. Cf. A.K. Grayson, *Assyrian Rulers of the Early First Millennium BC II (858–745 B.C.)*, (Toronto 1996), p. 104.

1515 See von Soden, *Or* 46 (1977), p. 196:156.

1516 Cf. DNWSI (p. 101 s.v. *ʾrbn*).

"papyrus," but does not assume a borrowing here. The editors of CAD (U/W, p. 211a s.v. *urbānu*) list the word as "papyrus," but provide no etymology or loan hypothesis for it, referring instead to von Soden's etymological discussion. The passage where the word occurs (Iraq 25 56:43 = ND 11000) reads as follows:[1517]

> *si-ta-at* ERIM.ḪI.A-MEŠ-*šú-nu ina* GIŠ.MÁ-MEŠ *ur-ba-ni ir-ka-bu-ma a-na tam-ti ú-ri-du*
>
> The rest of their troops rode down to the sea on boats of papyrus.[1518]

Zimmern considered the Akkadian word *urbānu* "Schilf, Papyrus-urkunde," probably to be borrowed into Aramaic as *ʾurbānā* and *ʾarbānā* "Schilf, Papyrus."[1519] In contrast, von Soden suggests that *urbānu* in the sense "Papyrusstaude," in SB, NA and NB, is a loanword from Aramaic *u/arbānā*.[1520] He considers the latter to be etymologically connected with Akkadian *urbatu* "rush, reed," and points out that the SB comment to *Ludlul bēl nēmeqi* II 69 explains *ur-ba-tu* through GIŠ.*ur-ba-nu*.[1521] Abraham and Sokoloff state that, although this word is attested in JBA and Syriac, it has no clear etymology in Aramaic.[1522] They add that the hypothesis of a borrowing from Aramaic into Akkadian depends merely on the late and rare attestation of the word *urbānu* in Akkadian in lieu of the usual words *niāru* "papyrus," and *urbatu* "rush, reed."[1523]

Nevertheless, von Soden is right in pointing out the connection between Aramaic *u/arbānā* "papyrus reed, rush" and the Akkadian word *urbatu* "rush, reed." In fact, the Syriac word ܐܒܘܪܐ "a rush" is probably also cognate with Akkadian *urbatu*, taking into consideration the possibility of a metathesis of the second and third radicals, i.e., *b* and *r*, in the Syriac word.[1524] However, the most salient factor pointing to a borrowing from Aramaic is the form of the word in NA, SB, and NB.

ziblu n. "dung, manure"; (see also above s.v. *bēt zibli*)

Loanword	Reference	Provenance	Origin	Genre	Date
zi-ib-li	SAA VI 28:4	Nineveh	Nineveh	LD	710
	SAA VI 271:3	Nineveh	*Nineveh*	LD	678

Aram. ⇒ NA

[1517] The transliteration of the passage is taken from the Corpus of Neo-Assyrian Texts (CNA).
[1518] The translation is that of CAD (U/W, p. 211b s.v. *urbānu*).
[1519] See Zimmern, AF, pp. 19f, 56.
[1520] See von Soden, *Or* 37 (1968), p. 269:156; idem, *Or* 46 (1977), p. 196:156. Cf. I. Löw, *Aramäische Pflanzennamen* (Leipzig 1881), p. 54:30.
[1521] See von Soden, *Or* 37 (1968), p. 269:156, with reference to previous literature.
[1522] See Abraham & Sokoloff, *Reassessment*, p. 56:268.
[1523] Ibid.
[1524] Cf. Löw, ibid., p. 55; SL (p. 5b s.v. ܐܒܘܪܐ); Kaufman, AIA, p. 32 s.v. *aburru*.

JBA, Sam., JLA, Syr., LJLA *zbl*, *zbl'* (*zēḇal*, *ze/ēḇlā*) n. m. "dung, manure, dung heap; excrement" DNWSI 303; DJBA 406a; Jastrow 379a; DSA 219a; SL 363a; PSm. 109b; Manna 187a; Audo 250a; CAL. Syr., *bēṯ zeḇlā* "dump; lavatory" Manna 187a; Audo 250a. JBA, Syr., *zbl* v. Pa. "to dung, to manure, spread manure" DJBA 398a; Jastrow 379a; SL 362b; Psm. 109b; Manna 186b; Audo 250a; CAL.

The word *ziblu* is attested as a *dis legomenon* in NA. It occurs in a legal document from 710 B.C. (SAA VI 28:4) concerning a purchase of land. It also occurs in another legal document from 678 B.C. (SAA VI 271:3) regarding a pledge of more than 24 hectares of land. In AHw. (p. 1524b s.v. *ziblu*), the word is listed for M/LB as well as NA with the sense "Abfall, Schutt," and is tentatively considered to be derived from Akkadian *zabālu* "tragen, überbringen." The editors of CAD (Z, p. 103b s.v. *ziblu*) list this word for Nuzi and NA, but consider its meaning to be uncertain, commenting: "Probably referring to certain dues incumbent upon a field, and to be connected with *zabālu*." CDA (p. 447a s.v. *ziblu*) lists the word for M/NB and NA as meaning "waste matter, refuse, debris," and cautiously derives it from the Akkadian word *zabālu* "(G) to carry, deliver; (D) keep (s.o.) waiting." AEAD (p. 134a s.v. *ziblu*), glosses the word as "dross, litter, refuse, trash, waste matter, waste," and subsumes under it the expression *bēt zibli* in the sense "dung house." The following are the two NA instances in their contexts:

SAA VI 28:3–5, reads:

É 3 ANŠE A.ŠÀ SUḪUR LÚ.*sa*$^{!}$-⸢*ak*$^{?}$⸣-*lu*$^{!}$-*te* / [SUḪUR] ⸢É⸣ *zi-ib-li* SUḪUR ^{md}KU$^{!}$–KAM-*eš* / [*x x x x x x*] ^{m}*da-a-di-i*

An estate of 3 hectares of land adjoining the simpletons, the *dump*, and (the estates of) Marduk-ēreš, [NN and] Dādî.[1525]

SAA VI 271:3–5, reads:

⸢É⸣ 10 ANŠE É *zi-ib-li* SUḪUR / [*na-ḫal*$^{?}$ SUḪ]UR ^{md}PA-*u-a* SUḪUR KASKAL.2 *šá a-na* URU.*ib-li* DU-*u-ni* / [SUḪ]UR KASKAL *šá a-na* URU.*su-mur-u-nu* DU-*u-ni*

An estate of 10 hectares (with) a *lavatory*, adjoining [*the wadi*], (the estate of) Nabû'a, the road leading to Ibla, and the road leading to Sumurunu.[1526]

The Akkadian word *zabālu*(*m*), which is occasionally written *s/ṣabālu*(*m*), has in the G-stem the following meanings: when said of humans or animals "to carry, deliver" goods; when said of tools, earth-baskets; news; penalties or misfortune

[1525] Note that SAA VI 28:4 tentatively translates the phrase ⸢É⸣ *zi-ib-li* as "*manure* house." Cf. the Glossary of SAA VI (p. 318b s.v. *ziblu* "dung, manure").

[1526] Note that SAA VI 271:3, tentatively translates the phrase É *zi-ib-li* as "*manure* house."

"to bear." In the D-stem it means "to keep (s.o.) waiting"; of disease "linger."[1527] Most likely this Akkadian word is cognate with Official Aramaic *sbl* "to carry,"[1528] as well as with Syriac ܣܒܠ "to bear, carry; to endure; to suffer."[1529] It is probably also cognate with JBA סבל "to suffer; support,"[1530] and Mandaic *sbl* "to bear, carry; endure, sustain."[1531]

Semantically, however, none of the meanings given above, which are associated with Akkadian *zabālu(m)*, fits the context for the word *ziblu* in the two NA legal documents. Obviously, the NA word *ziblu* is etymologically unrelated to the Akkadian word *zabālu(m)*. In Aramaic, on the other hand, we have JBA זִיבְלָא n. m. "excrement, manure,"[1532] and Syriac ܙܶܒܠܳܐ n. m. "dung, excrement, manure."[1533] Of the latter we have the denominative verb ܙܰܒܶܠ v. Pa. "to manure, spread manure."[1534] Most interestingly, we have in Syriac the expression ܒܶܝܬ ܙܶܒܠܳܐ in the sense "dump (of garbage); lavatory."[1535] Semitic cognates with Aramaic *zbl'* are Arabic زِبْل "dung, manure; droppings"[1536] and Mishnaic Hebrew זָבַל "to deposit foliage in the field for manure, to manure," which is a denominative of זֶבֶל "manure, deposits."[1537]

Noticeably, in both NA instances, the word *zibli* is preceded by the logogram É, which in Assyrian stands for *bētu* "house." This explains the combinatory form, i.e., the construct before the dependent genitive *bēt zibli*. Syntactically, the NA *bēt zibli* seems to correspond to Syriac ܒܶܝܬ ܙܶܒܠܳܐ mentioned above, and most likely is a borrowing from Aramaic in the senses "dump" and "lavatory."

ziqqu, (pl. *ziqqāti*) n. "wineskin"

Loanword	Reference	Provenance	Origin	Genre	Date
KUŠ.*zi-*[*q*]*a-a-t*[*i*]	CTN III 89:21′	Calah	Calah	WL	PC?
KUŠ.*zi-qa-*˹*te*˺	CTN I 23 r.14′	Calah	Calah	WL	PC?
KUŠ.*zi-qu*	Iraq 14, 35, 116[1538] (= ND 1104)	Calah	Calah	Inscr. (Asn)	879

Aram. ⇒ MA; NA [?]

[1527] See CDA (p. 442a s.v. *zabālu(m)*). Cf. AHw. (p. 1500a s.v. *zabālu(m)*); CAD (Z, p. 1a s.v. *zabālu*).
[1528] Cf. DNWSI (p. 774 s.v. sbl_1).
[1529] Cf. SL (p. 962b s.v. ܣܒܠ mng. no. 1).
[1530] Cf. DJBA (p. 783b s.v. סבל mng. no. 1).
[1531] Cf. MD (p. 316b s.v. SBL).
[1532] See DJBA, p. 406a.
[1533] See SL, p. 363a; PSm., p. 109b.
[1534] See SL, p. 362b; PSm., ibid.
[1535] See Manna 187a; Audo 250a.
[1536] See Elias & Elias, p. 272b; Wehr-Cowan, p. 373a.
[1537] See Jastrow (p. 379a s.v. זָבַל and זֶבֶל).
[1538] See D.J. Wiseman, "A New Stela of Aššur-naṣir-pal II," *Iraq* 14 (1952), p. 35, l. 116.

OffAr., Palm., JPA, JBA, Sam., Syr., *zyq*, *zyq'* (*zīq/zeq*, *zīqā/zeqqā*) n. m. & f. "wineskin, water skin, leathern bottle" DNWSI 339; DJPA 176a; DJBA 411a; Jastrow 396a; DSA 238a; SL 393a; PSm. 119a; Manna 206b; Audo 288a; CAL.

Written syllabically, the word *ziqqu* occurs as a *tris legomenon* in NA. It is attested once in two different wine lists, and also once on a stele of Ashurnasirpal II (883–859 B.C.), as skins with wine for the royal banquet. In AHw. (p. 1531b s.v. *ziqqu* IV), the word is glossed as "Wein-Schlauch," and is considered to be a loanword from Aramaic.[1539] The editors of CAD (Z, p. 129a s.v. *ziqqu* B) define the word as (a wineskin) and comment that it is probably a borrowing from Aramaic.

Zimmern was of the opinion that *ziqqu* is an Akkadian loanword in Aramaic, and that from the latter it also entered Arabic and Ethiopic.[1540] In contrast, von Soden considers the word to be a borrowing into NA from Aramaic *zi/eqqā*.[1541] Abraham and Sokoloff state that since *ziqqu* is attested in different dialects of Aramaic, it is most likely a loanword in NA.[1542] Nevertheless, Millard argues that the word *ziqqu*, in the sense "wineskin," is already attested as KUŠ.*zi-qu*, KUŠ.*zi-qu*.MEŠ and KUŠ.*zi-qa-tu* in a fragmentarily preserved MA text (BM 122635+) found at Nineveh.[1543] This is an administrative text, from the mid-twelfth century B.C. or later, listing *nāmurtu*, "audience gifts" contributed to the king by various dignitaries.[1544] Millard notes that if the term *ziqqu* is a loanword from Aramaic, as suggested by CAD, it can be reckoned as one of the few early Aramaic loans that entered into Assyrian, most likely via wine trade.[1545]

According to CAL, the term *zyq* n. m. "water skin" is a Common Aramaic word attested also in Old Aramaic.[1546] The word is found in Syriac as ܙܩܐ̈ n. f. "water skin, wineskin, leathern bottle,"[1547] and in JBA as זִיקָּא n. f. "skin bottle."[1548] It is also attested in Arabic as زِقّ "water-skin,"[1549] and in Ethiopic as *zeqq* "water-skin."[1550]

Semantically, from OB on, the word *ziqqu* is attested in the sense "crest, edge, battlements," and it also designated (an ornament in the shape of a crest or battlement).[1551] On the other hand, in M/LB the word *ziqqu* refers to (a woven fabric).[1552] However, none of the meanings given above fits the context of the word *ziqqu* in the NA texts cited above, where it is obvious that the word designates "wineskin." In NA, the word is often written as a logogram, i.e.,

1539 See also CDA (p. 448b s.v. *ziqqu* III). Cf. DNWSI (p. 339 s.v. *zq*); AEAD (p. 134b s.v. *ziqqu*).
1540 See Zimmern, AF, p. 34.
1541 See von Soden, *Or* 37 (1968), p. 269:162; idem, *Or* 46 (1977), p. 197:162.
1542 See Abraham & Sokoloff, *Reassessment*, p. 57:279. Cf. Nili, p. 297:183.
1543 See A.R. Millard, "Fragments of Historical Texts from Nineveh: Middle Assyrian and Later Kings," *Iraq* 32 (1970), pp. 172f.
1544 Ibid., p. 173.
1545 Ibid., p. 173, n. 19.
1546 See CAL, s.v. *zyq*.
1547 See SL, p. 393a; PSm., p. 119a.
1548 See DJBA, p. 411a.
1549 See Elias & Elias (p 277a s.v. زِقّ الماء).
1550 Cf. Fraenkel, p. 171; LS (p. 203b s.v. ܙܩܐ).
1551 See CAD (Z, p. 128b s.v. *ziqqu* A). Cf. AHw. (p. 1531b s.v. *ziqqu*(*m*) I).
1552 See AHw. (p. 1531b s.v. *ziqqu* II); CDA (p. 448b s.v. *ziqqu* II).

KUŠ.SAL(.MEŠ),[1553] which perhaps was read *ziqqu* (pl. *ziqqāti*).[1554] As a matter of fact, on one NA wine list (CTN III 89:21′, 23′, 26′) the word occurs both syllabically and logographically. As an object, *ziqqu* was also used as a measure of wine, but its volume is undecided. However, the approximate size of the skins is clear from the frequent depiction in Assyrian art of tribute-bearers carrying wineskins.[1555] Nevertheless, the distribution of the word points to a borrowing from Aramaic into NA. Chronologically, however, the attestation of *zeqqu* in the sense "wineskin" in MA falls in a period prior to that of language contact between Aramaic and the various dialects of Akkadian.

2.2 Rejected proposals of Aramaic loanwords in Neo-Assyrian

This group of proposed Aramaic loanwords in Neo-Assyrian consists of those words that, after analyzing the evidence required to establish the borrowing, are rejected as Aramaic loanwords in Neo-Assyrian. An explanation of the scheme for presentation of data, including a clarification of a number of operators and abbreviations used here to facilitate the discussion, is given in section (1.10) above.

akku adj. "angry, furious"; (see the discussion in chapter 2.1 s.v. *ḫangaru*)

//Aram. ⇒ NA//

This word occurs only once in a NA oracle of encouragement of Ištar of Arbail (SAA IX 1 iv 7), promising to bless and protect Esarhaddon, king of Assyria, and get rid of his enemies. The editors of CAD (Ḫ, p. 79b s.v. *ḫangaruakku*) list the word *akku* and the word *ḫangaru*, which immediately precedes it, as one word, i.e., *ḫangaruakku*. They consider its meaning to be unknown and express uncertainty about its reading. They also suggest two other possible readings, *ḫanga ruʾakku* and *ḫangaru akku*. AHw. (p. 1542b s.v. *akku*)[1556] glosses this word as "grimmig," and considers it to be an Aramaic foreign word.[1557] The passage where the word is attested (SAA IX 1 iv 5–10) reads as follows:

> [m]*aš-šur*–PAB–AŠ *ap-lu* / *ke-e-nu* DUMU [d]NIN.LÍL / *ḫa-an-ga-ru ak-ku* / *ina* ŠU.2-*ia* / LÚ.KÚR.MEŠ-*ka* / *ú-qa-at-ta*

[1553] See for instance: SAA 7 179 i′ 8′ KUŠ.SAL, ii′ 1′ KUŠ.S[AL?]; CTN I 6 r.16 KUŠ.SAL.MEŠ; CTN III 88 r.7′ KUŠ.SAL.MEŠ; CTN III 89:26′ KUŠ.SAL.MEŠ; TH 14 r.2 KUŠ.SAL.MEŠ-*šú-nu*.

[1554] See Postgate, FNALD, § 6.4.4. Cf. n. ad CTN III 89:21′. Cf. also CTN I, p. 107.

[1555] Cf. Postgate, ibid; CTN I, p. 114.

[1556] Cf. AHw. (p. 1559a s.v. *ḫangaru*).

[1557] See also CDA (p. 10a s.v. *akku*), where the word is glossed "furious" and described as a borrowing from Aramaic.

> Esarhaddon, rightful heir, son of Mullissu! With an angry dagger in my hand I will finish off your enemies.

In his account of Aramaic loanwords in NA, NB and LB, von Soden states that *akku* is used instead of the Akkadian word *aggu* "grimmig, zornig," and connects it with Aramaic *ʾakkəṯā* "Zorn."[1558] Nissenen, on the other hand, interprets *akku* as "sharp" and takes it to be verbal adjective of *akāku/ekēku* "scratch."[1559] A different analysis is put forward by Parpola who, in his editing of the NA oracle, takes *ak-ku* as an unvoiced variant of the Akkadian adjective *aggu* "angry."[1560] For phonological comparison, he adduces *akappi* "wing" (SAA IX 2 ii 6′) as a variant of *agappi*, and for semantic comparison, he offers Ištar's anger (*uggugat*), attested in Streck (Asb., p. 118: 76).[1561] Luukko, referring to Parpola, also adduces *akku* as an example of the alternation between the stops the voiced velar plosive *g* and the voiceless velar plosive *k*, based on a strict rule of voicing in NA according to which "a voiceless stop may become voiced in a voiced environment."[1562] Abraham and Sokoloff consider the connection of *akku* with Aramaic to be doubtful because the reading of the NA text is uncertain and the Syriac word ܐܰܟ݁ܬ݂ܐ "anger" is only found in the feminine.[1563] However, the Aramaic word is only attested in Syriac as ܐܰܟ݁ܬ݂ܐ "anger," with its masculine adjective ܐܰܟ݁ܬ݂ܳܢܐ "angry," and as a denominative verb ܐܟܬ in the Etpaʿʿal mode in the sense "to become angry."[1564]

buḫḫušu v. (D) "to check"

Aram. ⇒ SB [?]

JBA, Syr., LJLA *bḥš* "to search, examine" DJBA 196a; Manna 60b; Jastrow 155b; Dalman 49b; CAL. Ma., *bhš* "to search, examine" MD 54a.

This word is attested as *ú-ba-aḫ-ḫi-iš-ma* and occurs in a colophon (BAK 299:6 = 3R 2 no. 22:58 = K 2670) from Nineveh in 684 B.C.[1565] The tablet, of which only the colophon is preserved, contains the third excerpt of the series

---

[1558] See von Soden, *Or* 46 (1977), p. 184:174.
[1559] See M. Nissinen, *Prophets and Prophecy in the Ancient Near East* (Atlanta 2003), p. 108, n. ad 73, d.
[1560] See n. ad SAA IX 1 iv 7.
[1561] Ibid. Cf. Nili, p. 241:6.
[1562] See Luukko, SAAS XVI, § 4.1.1., esp. p. 71 s.v. (*aggu*). See also S. Parpola, "The Neo-Assyrian word for 'Queen'," *SAAB* 2 (1988), p. 76, n. 13; Hämeen-Anttila, SAAS XIII, § 2.1.6.1; Kaufman, AIA, pp. 139f; W. von Soden, "Zur Laut- und Formenlehre des Neuassyrischen," *AfO* 18 (1957), p. 122.
[1563] See Abraham & Sokoloff, *Reassessment*, p. 25:6. Cf. preliminary Z. Cherry, *Aramaic Loanwords in NA: Rejecting some Proposals*, p. 20 s.v. *akku*.
[1564] See SL, p. 46a.
[1565] See H. Hunger, *Babylonische und assyrische Kolophone* (Kevelaer 1968), pp. 92f.

i.nam.giš.ḫur.an.ki.a, and was prepared by the illustrious Assyrian scholar Nabû-zuqup-kēnu, to be read by his son Issār-šumu-ēreš.[1566]

The editors of CAD (B, p. 186a s.v. *be'ēšu, b) mng. no. 2′) defined the meaning of this word as uncertain, but translated it in the sense "to check," and considered it possibly to be an Aramaism in a NA colophon, taken from Aramaic *bəḥaš* "to examine." AHw. (p. 1549a s.v. *buḫḫušu*) glossed this term in the D-stem as "prüfen," and considered it to be an Aramaic foreign word. CDA (p. 47b s.v. *buḫḫušu*) lists the word in the sense "to check," and considers it to be an Aramaic loanword in a SB text from Assyria. The passage where *buḫḫušu* occurs (BAK 299:6) reads as follows:

> *di-ig-la ú-kab-bir-ma za-mar ú-ba-aḫ-ḫi-iš-ma ab-r*[*i*?]
>
> I overtaxed my eyesight, quickly .... and checked (the tablet for my son's perusal).[1567]

Referring to CAD's interpretation, Hunger notes that *ú-ba-aḫ-ḫi-iš* is an Aramaic loanword used instead of the Akkadian *asniq*, and taken from *sanāqu* "to check," which is usually employed in a similar context.[1568] In agreement with Hunger, von Soden reads the word as *ú-ba-aḫ-ḫi-iš* with the meaning "prüfen," which he also considers to be a loanword from Jewish Aramaic *bḥaš* "to examine."[1569] Livingstone translates the same passage where the word *ú-ba-aḫ-ḫi-iš* occurs as follow: "I strained my eyesight, quickly studied and checked."[1570] In addition, he comments on the word as follows:

> *ubaḫḫiš* is apparently a 1st sing. IIɪ/pret. of *baḫāšu*, a root which provides no suitable meaning in Akkadian. It is understood as an intrusion of the vernacular, which was at the period that the manuscript was written strongly influenced by Aramaic and translated with CAD ad loc. by analogy with Aramaic *b^eḥaš*, 'to study' (this follows CAD B p. 186).[1571]

On the other hand, Nili is of the opinion that CAD incorrectly subsumes *ú-ba-aḫ-ḫi-iš* under a controversial heading, namely *be'ēšu*, *ba'āšu*, instead of listing the word under its own separate heading as in AHw.[1572] She rejects von Soden's suggested Aramaic origin of the word, arguing that Aramaic lacks a corresponding form with a similar sense.[1573] Abraham and Sokoloff point out that Aramaic בחש has not only the general meaning "to stir," but also the meaning "to search," which is semantically close to the sense "to check."[1574] In fact, the

1566 Cf. PNA 2/II (p. 913a s.v. Nabû-zuqup-kēnu).
1567 The translation is taken from CAD (B, p. 186a s.v. *be'ēšu*, b mng. no. 2′).
1568 See Hunger, ibid., p. 93, n. 4.
1569 See von Soden, *Or* 46 (1977), p. 185:179.
1570 See A. Livingstone, *Mystical and Mythological Explanatory Works of Assyrian and Babylonian Scholars* (Oxford 1986), p. 29.
1571 Ibid., p. 44 comment on l. 8.
1572 See Nili, p. 144:60.
1573 Ibid.
1574 See Abraham & Sokoloff, *Reassessment*, pp. 28:31 and 64.

Aramaic בחש and Syriac ܒܚܫ are etymologically cognate with the Arabic word بَحَثَ "to investigate, search, examine."[1575] Recently, Jiménez cautiously suggested rendering *buḫḫušu* as "to copy," and rejected Hunger's equating of *buḫḫušu* with *sanāqu* in the sense "to check," as well as his equating *ubaḫḫiš-ma abr*[*i*] with the expression *saniq-ma bari* which is frequently used in colophons.[1576] However, since the text where *buḫḫušu* occurs is not NA, but rather a SB text from Assyria, the word must be excluded from the inventory of the Aramaic loanwords in NA.[1577]

burbāni n. pl. "shackle?"; (see also the discussion above s.v. *gammuzu*)

//Aram. ⇒ NA//

Syr., *parbil* v. "to fetter, shackle; to hinder, detain" Manna 605b. Syr., *pūrbālā* n. "fetters, shackles; obstacle, hindrance" Manna 605b.

This word is not listed in CAD. However, according to AHw. (p.1549b s.v. *bur/bu-ur-ba*(*-a*)*-ni*), the word occurs in NA, but its meaning is considered unclear.[1578] In AEAD (p. 18b s.v. *burbāni*), the word is considered to be a substantive in the plural, and its meaning is defined as unknown. In fact, the word *burbāni* occurs as a *dis legomenon* in NA, and as such the plausibility of an etymology proposed for it is determined by the sentence context. The word is attested as *bur-ba-a-ni* in an undated letter (SAA V 64 r.6) sent by the chief cupbearer Na'id-ilu to the Assyrian king Sargon II, reporting on the reception of 120 horses. Here, *burbāni* is preceded by the word *ga-mu-zu*!, which is a *hapax legomenon* in NA. This fact complicates our efforts to deduce the meaning of *bur-ba-a-ni* from the context. The other attestation of the word occurs as *bu-ur-ba-ni* in a letter (SAA X 239 r.9′) which was probably addressed by Marduk-šākin-šumi, the chief exorcist, to the Assyrian king Esarhaddon.[1579] The context of this letter is damaged to such an extent that no plausible sense can be surmised for *burbāni*.

Nevertheless, an attempt to solve the etymology of this enigmatic NA word and to arrive to its meaning has been made by Parpola who tentatively renders *burbāni* as "foals," and notes: "Both *ga-mu-zu* and *bur-ba-a-ni* seem to be Aramaic loanwords; cf. Syr. *gmz* 'to mangle clothes, press heavily' (Payne Smith, pp. 71f) and *bar bānā* 'calf, bullock that has not yet been yoked' (ibid. 53b)."[1580] The following are the two NA contexts where the word *burbāni* is attested:

1575 Cf. Elias & Elias, p. 50b; Wehr-Cowan, p. 42a.
1576 See E. Jiménez, "Three colophons* – 1. *buḫḫušu*, 'to copy' (?)," *NABU* 2013/92.
1577 See CDA (p. 47b s.v. *buḫḫušu*). Cf. DNWSI (p. 150 s.v. *bḥš* "to examine").
1578 Cf. CDA (p. 49a s.v. *burbāni*), which considers the meaning of this word to be unknown.
1579 Cf. LAS II, ad no. 237.
1580 See n. ad SAA V 64 r.4, 6. See also the Glossary of SAA V (p. 221b s.v. *burbānu*); the Glossary of SAA X (p. 331a s.v. *burbānu*).

SAA V 64 r.4–6, reads:

i-se-niš ANŠE.KUR.RA.ME / *ga-mu-zu*! / *lip-šu-ḫu* / *bur-ba-a-ni*
All the same, the horses have been *heavily pressed*; the *foals* should rest.

SAA X 239 r.8′–13′, reads:

[LUGAL *be-lí ṭ*]*è-e-mu liš-ku-un* / [*x x x x x*]*-i-šú-nu bu-ur-ba-ni* / [*x x x x x*]*x* UZU.MEŠ-*šú-nu* / [*x x x x x*] *a-na-ku ša kal-bu* / [*x x x x x x x*]*-ri la ṭa-ban-ni* / [*x x x x x x x x š*]*u-u* (rest broken away)

[The king, my lord], should give an order […], […] …, [..] their flesh […] I, who [am] (but) a dog […] not good (Rest destroyed).

Nevertheless, a closer look at the proposed Syriac word reveals that the term *bar baqrā* (ܒܪ ܒܩܪܐ) "calf, bullock that has not yet been yoked" was erroneously read as *bar bānā*.[1581] In fact, the actual Syriac word ܒܪ ܒܩܪܐ exhibits no phonological resemblance to the problematic word *burbāni*. Consequently, Parpola's suggested etymology was abandoned.[1582] However, if the NA word *burbāni* is read differently as *purbāni*, which is possible, then it may be related to Syriac ܦܘܪܒܠܐ "shackle, hobble," which is derived from a quadrilateral root, i.e., PRBL "to fetter, shackle."[1583] The Syriac word ܦܘܪܒܠܐ is synonymous with Syriac ܦܘܪܟܠܐ "a bond, strap, shackle," from ܦܪܟܠ "to shackle, hobble" (a horse).[1584] Of course, it would be advantageous to read the last syllable of the NA word as *lí* instead of *ni*, hence *purbāli*, but that is an unusual use of the sound value *lí* for the cuneiform sign *ni*, which is exclusively restricted in NA to the word *be-lí* "my lord." As we lack solid and convincing evidence leading to a firm conclusion, the meaning and etymology of *burbāni* remain difficult to explain. We are probably dealing with a culture word with the meaning "shackle" which entered NA and Aramaic independently and in a slightly different form.

darāku v. (D) "to thresh"; (see also below s.v. *mudarriktu*)

//Aram. ⇒ NA//

Com., *drk* v. Af. "to tread, trample" DNWSI 261; DJPA 156a; DJBA 352b; MD 114b; DSA 194a; SL 322b; PSm. 97b; Manna 160b; Audo 213b; CAL. Syr., *drk* v. Af. "to thresh" SL 323a. JLA *drk* v. Pa. "to thresh" CAL.

[1581] Cf. PSm. (p. 53b s.v. ܒܪ ܒܩܪܐ). See the discussion in chapter 2.1 above s.v. *gammuzu*.
[1582] See AEAD (p. 18b s.v. *burbāni*), which considers the meaning of this word to be unknown. Cf. preliminary Z. Cherry, *Aramaic Loanwords in NA*: *Rejecting some Proposals*, p. 21 s.v. *burbānu*.
[1583] See Manna (p. 605b s.v. ܦܪܒܠ).
[1584] Cf. SL (p. 1170b s.v. ܦܘܪܟܠܐ). According to SL (p. 1241b s.v. ܦܪܟܠ), this Syriac verb in the sense "to bind, shackle, tether" is derived from the root PKR with added *-l*.

This word supposedly occurs in two NA letters from Calah/Nimrud. It is allegedly attested as *lu-du*[!]*-ri*!(Deller)-*ku* (ND 2460 r.9′ = NL 34 r.9′),[1585] and as *ú-du*[!]*-ru*!*-ku* (ND 2452:7 = NL 35:7).[1586] For these two NA instances, AHw. (p. 1550a s.v. *darāku* III) glosses the word in the D-stem as "dreschen," and considers it to be a borrowing into NA from Aramaic *darreḵ*, *adreḵ*.[1587]

Recently, however, the first alleged instance, i.e., *lu-du*[!]*-ri*!(Deller)-*ku*, is read and interpreted differently as *lu-du-ri-*[*su*] "they should thre[sh]" (SAA XIX 53 r.9′). The word is taken as probably coming from *darāsu*, a supposed *hapax legomenon* in NA in the D-stem with the meaning "to thresh."[1588] The other instance, *ú-du*[!]*-ru*!*-ku* (SAA XIX 109:7) is collated and interpreted differently, as *ú-du-*⸢*bi*⸣*-ku* "piled up." The word is here taken to be from *tabāku* "to pile up."[1589]

Another possibly related word is the term *mudarriktu*, which is a *hapax legomenon* in NA, attested as *mu-da-ri-ik-t*[*u*] in a letter from Nineveh (SAA XIII 135 r.7). AHw. (p. 1575b s.v. *mudarriktu*) lists this word as a feminine participle meaning "Drescherin," and considers its origin to be the supposedly Aramaic loanword *darāku* "to thresh."[1590] Parpola, on the other hand, interprets *mudarriktu* as "a cultic ceremony."[1591] In AEAD (p. 66a s.v. *mudarriktu*), the word is also defined as (a cultic ceremony).[1592]

Hence, according to the recent reading and interpretation of the NA instance in SAA XIX 109:7, the word *darāku* in the sense "to thresh," is a "ghost word." The other word, with the sequence *lu-du-ri-*[*x*] in SAA XIX 53 r.9′, is not sufficient to reliably establish a verb *darāku* in the D-stem. The interpretation of *mudarriktu*, on the other hand, is not entirely clear.[1593]

egertu n. f. "letter; document"

//Aram. ⇒ NA//

Com., *'grh*, *'grt*, *'grt'* (*'eggrā*, *'eggarṯā*) n. f. "letter" Brauner 19; DNWSI 12; DJPA 48a; DJBA 110b; Jastrow 45a; PSm. 3b; Manna 5a; DSA 7a; LSp. 3a;

1585 The reading *lu-du*[!]*-ri*!(Deller)-*ku* is quoted in AHw. (p. 1550a s.v. *darāku* III). Cf. H.W.F. Saggs, "The Nimrud Letters, 1952–Part III," *Iraq* 18 (1955–56), p. 49, no. 34:9′; idem, CTN V, p. 266.

1586 Cf. H.W.F. Saggs, "The Nimrud Letters, 1952–Part III," *Iraq* 18 (1955–56), p. 50, no. 35;7; idem, CTN V, p. 33. The reading *ú-du*[!]*-ru*!*-ku* is quoted in AHw. (p. 1550a s.v. *darāku* III).

1587 See also CDA (p. 57a s.v. *darāku* III D). Cf. DNWSI (p. 261 s.v. *drk*$_1$). Cf. also CAD (D, p. 108b s.v. *darāku*), which does not include the NA instances.

1588 See n. ad SAA XIX 53 r.9. See also the Glossary of SAA XIX (p. 232b s.v. *darāsu*). Cf. the discussion in Chapter 2.1, s.v. *darāsu*.

1589 See n. ad SAA XIX 109:7. See also the Glossary of SAA XIX (p. 232b s.v. *dabāku*, p. 252a s.v. *tabāku*).

1590 See also CDA (p. 214a s.v. *mudarriktu*).

1591 See S. Parpola, Review of "Akkadisches Handwörterbuch. Vols. II & III/1 (Lfg. 7–12)," by W. von Soden, *OLZ* 74 (1979), p. 26 ad 666a. See also AEAD (p. 66a s.v. *mudarriktu*). Cf. K. Deller & W. Mayer, "Akkadische Lexikographie: *CAD* M," *Or* 53 (1984), p. 87 ad [160b].

1592 Cf. the Glossary of SAA XIII (p. 188b s.v. *mudarriktu* (a ritual)).

1593 See Abraham & Sokoloff, *Reassessment*, p. 29:35; M. Kalinin & S. Loesov, "Lexical *Sondergut* of Neo-Assyrian," *SAAB* 23 (2017), p. 3, 1.3.

DCPA 4b; CAL. OAram, Gal., Syr., CPA, LJLA *'grt'* n. f. "contract, legal document" DNWSI 12; DJPA 48a; DJBA 110b; DCPA 4b; CAL. Ma., *'ngyrt'* (*'ngirta*) "letter" MD 353a.

The etymology and the direction of borrowing of this word have been widely debated.[1594] The editors of CAD (E, p. 45b s.v. *egirtu*) gloss this word as "letter; tablet," but provide no etymology for it other than referring to previous discussions of the topic. In AHw. (p. 190a s.v. *egertu*), the word is listed as meaning "Brief; eine Tafelart," and its origin is considered likely to be Aramaic *iggərā, iggartā*. In contrast, CDA (p. 67a s.v. *egertu*) glosses the word as "inscribed tablet," and considers its origin to be the Akkadian *egāru*, which is tentatively rendered as "to write down."[1595] In DNWSI (p. 12 s.v. *'grt*), the word is considered to be a borrowing from Akkadian into Aramaic.

Zimmern considered *egertu* to be an Akkadian loanword in Aramaic, but he did not elaborate on the subject.[1596] On the other hand, in his effort to analyze the etymology of Aramaic *eggar<u>t</u>ā*, Köbert argued that a derivation from Aramaic is not likely because the nominal pattern *QiTTiL, QiTTaL* in West-Semitic was restricted to mainly expressing physical defects.[1597] In contrast, von Soden, in his articles on Aramaic loanwords in NA and N/LB, regarded *egertu* as a loanword from Aramaic *iggərā, iggartā*.[1598] A Persian etymology was also proposed earlier, but Kaufman and later Mankowski ruled this possibility out on grounds of chronology and phonology.[1599] Kaufman regards a borrowing from Aramaic as highly improbable and concurs with Köbert that the nominal form *QiTTaL* is unusual in Aramaic.[1600] Later, Kaufman suggested considering *egertu* a feminine verbal adjective of the Akkadian verb *egēru* "to be crossed, twisted."[1601] In fact, *egāru* "to twist," is attested in the Ntn-stem in an Assyrian oracle (SAA III

1594 See Kaufman, AIA, p. 48, n. 81. For the references and discussion of a connection with Persian, see Mankowski, ALBH, pp. 23ff. See also P.E. Dion, "Aramaic Words for 'Letter,'" *Semeia* 22 (1981), pp. 77–88. On the term *egertu* in general, see S. Parpola, "Assyrian Library Records," *JNES* 42 (1983), p. 2, n. 5; idem, SAA I, p. xxiv, n. 10; K. Radner, *Die neuassyrischen Privatrechtsurkunden als Quelle für Mensch und Umwelt* (Helsinki 1997), pp. 60–62; A. Millard, "Words for Writing in Aramaic," in M.F.J. Baasten & W.Th. van Peursen (eds.), *Hamlet on a Hill: Semitic and Greek Studies Presented to Professor T. Muraoka on the Occasion of his Sixty-Fifth Birthday* (Leuven 2003), esp. p. 353.

1595 See CDA (p. 67a s.v. *egāru* "to write down"?).

1596 See Zimmern, AF, p. 19.

1597 See R. Köbert, "Gedanken zum semitischen Wort- und Satzbau. 1–7," *Or* 14 (1945), pp. 278f. Cf. J. Fox, *Semitic Noun Patterns* (Winona Lake 2003), p. 280, where he emphasizes that almost no native nouns in the **QiTTaL* pattern are extant in Syriac.

1598 See von Soden, *Or* 35 (1966), p. 8:18; idem, *Or* 46 (1977), p. 185:18. Cf. Abraham & Sokoloff, *Reassessment*, p. 30:42. Cf. also, E.Y. Kutscher, "Aramaic," in T.A. Sebeok (ed.), *Current Trends in Linguistics*, 6. *Linguistics in South West Asia and North Africa* (The Hague 1970), p. 357.

1599 See Kaufman, ibid; Mankowski, ibid.

1600 See Kaufman, ibid., p. 48.

1601 See S.A. Kaufman, "An Assyro-Aramaic *egirtu ša šulmu*," in M. De Jong Ellis (ed.), *Essays on the Ancient Near East in Memory of J.J. Finkelstein* (Hamden 1977), p. 124, n. 44. See also S.A. Kaufman, "Reflections on the Assyrian-Aramaic Bilingual from Tell Fakhariye," *Maarav* 3 (1982), p. 139, n. 4. Cf. LAS II, p. 197.

13:10): *lišānka la ta-at-ta-ni-gi-ir ina*(TA*[!]) *šaptēka* "your tongue shall not falter on your lips."[1602]

In favor of Kaufman's interpretation above, Postgate rejects an Aramaic origin for the word *egertu*, and argues that the MA legal phrase *ana la mašā'e e-gi-ir* employs the Akkadian verb *egāru* instead of the usual *šaṭāru*, and thus provides a native etymon for *egertu.*[1603] The legal phrase is to be rendered "written in order not to be forgotten," where *e-gi-ir* is taken as the stative of *egāru* in the G-stem. According to Zaccagnini, the phrase *a-na la ma-ša-e e-gi-ir*, mentioned above, "provides an isolated yet unquestionable piece of evidence for the verb *egāru* 'to write,' which must be considered the Akkadian antecedent of NA *egirtu* and Aramaic *'grt*."[1604] Nevertheless, the nominal pattern *QiTTaL* is extremely rare in Aramaic and exhibits the gemination of the second radical, in compliance with the Aramaic tendency to double the second root consonants of loanwords.[1605] Hence, the evidence points to a borrowing from Akkadian into Aramaic and not vice versa.[1606]

gašūru n. "log, timber, beam, roof beam"

//Aram. ⇒ NA//

The word *gašūru* is actually the NA form of the Akkadian word *gušūru*(*m*) "log, beam," which was borrowed from the Sumerian word GIŠ.ÙR, GIŠ.ÙR.RA, or GIŠ.ŠU.ÙR "beam."[1607] AHw. (p. 300a s.v. *gušūru*(*m*)), glosses this word as "gefälter Baumstamm; Balken," regards it as a borrowing from Sumerian, and also considers the word to be a borrowing into Aramaic, as *gəšūrā*. The editors of CAD (G, p. 144a s.v. *gušūru*) list the word as "log, beam," and consider it probably to be a Sumerian loanword. Kaufman regards the term *gšr*, *gšwr'* "log, beam" as a loanword in Aramaic, possibly of Sumerian etymology.[1608] In contrast, DNWSI (p. 236 s.v. *gšr*) glosses this word as "beam," but considers it an Aramaic loan in Akkadian.

Indeed, the word under discussion here has a good Sumerian etymology and is a loanword in Akkadian. The Sumerian term GIŠ.ÙR "beam" consists of two

---

[1602] See the Glossary of SAA III (p. 131a s.v. *egāru*). The Assyrian *egāru* "to twist" corresponds to Babylonian *egēru*. Cf. GAG § 10a.

[1603] See J.N. Postgate, Review of "Mittelassyrische Rechtsurkunden und Verwaltungstexte," by H. Freydank, *BiOr* 37 (1980), p. 68. See also N. Postgate & B.K. Ismail (eds.), *Texts from Niniveh* (Baghdad 1993), p. 18.

[1604] See C. Zaccagnini, "On the Juridical Terminology of Neo-Assyrian and Aramaic Contracts," in H. Waetzoldt & H. Hauptmann (eds.), *Assyrien im Wandel der Zeiten* (Heidelberg 1997), p. 204.

[1605] See Mankowski, ALBH, p. 25.

[1606] Cf. preliminary Z. Cherry, *Aramaic Loanwords in NA*: *Rejecting some Proposals*, p. 22. However, the notion that *egertu* is an Aramaic loanword in NA is still found in some recent scholarly literature. See, for instance, L. Bachelot & F.M. Fales (eds.), *Tell Shiukh Fawqani 1994–1998, II* (Padova 2005), p. 612.

[1607] See S.J. Lieberman, *The Sumerian Loanwords in Old-Babylonian Akkadian, Volume One: Prolegomena and Evidence* (Ann Arbor 1977), p. 298, no. 299.

[1608] See Kaufman, AIA, p. 53. See also Zimmern, AF, p. 31.

elements, namely GIŠ "wood; tree" and ÙR "roof (of house)."[1609] The latter ÙR, is even borrowed individually into Akkadian as *ūru* "roof."[1610] Hence, the term is analyzable in Sumerian, lost its internal structure after entering Akkadian as a single unit *gušūru*. The morphological criterion was decisive here in identifying this Sumerian loanword in Akkadian. It must be mentioned that any Sumerian loanword in Akkadian which is attested later in Aramaic is generally presumed to be a trans-Akkadian loan in Aramaic.[1611] Accordingly, the loan direction given in DNWSI is erroneous and ought to be corrected.

ḫanāpu v. (G) "to flatter, fawn"

//Aram. ⇒ NA//

JBA *ḥnp* v. Pa. "to favor; to flatter" DJBA 474a; Jastrow 485a; Dalman 146a; CAL. JPA *ḥnp* n. m. "flattery, hypocrisy" DJPA 209a.

This word is attested as *taḫ-ti-ni-ip*, and occurs in a NA poetical work (SAA III 14 r.9 = TIM 9 54 r.9) consisting of love lyrics of Nabû and Tašmētu. However, a difference in interpretation seems to prevail among scholars as to the meaning of *taḫ-ti-ni-ip*, mainly based on an observation of morphological nature.

As for the Akkadian lexica, the NA text is cited in AHw. (p. 1559a s.v. *ḫanāpu*), and the word is tentatively rendered "schmeicheln." In CAD (Ḫ, p. 76b s.v. *ḫanāpu* A, B), the NA text in question is not cited. CDA (p. 105b s.v. *ḫanāpu* II) lists a new heading for NA in the G-stem of the *i*-class and renders it approximately as "to flatter, fawn," in connection with a female divine name. In AEAD (p. 34b s.v. *ḫanāpu*), the word is considered to be SB.

In his article on Aramaic loanwords, however, von Soden renders NA *taḫ-ti-ni-ip* as "schmeicheln," and considers it to be a loanword from Jewish Aramaic חנף "to flatter."[1612] In his edition of the NA text in question, Matsushima leaves *taḫ-ti-ni-ip* untraslated, apparently because the verb *ḫanāpu* normally belongs to the *u*-class and means "to commit villainy, to act basely," which does not fit the NA context.[1613] On the other hand, Nissinen interprets *taḫ-ti-ni-ip* as meaning "to be exuberant," and connects it with the verb *ḫanābu* "to be luxuriant, flourish, thrive, to grow abundantly; to be radiant."[1614] He provides parallels to his interpretation and explains thus: "Cf. the use of the verb *ḫanāb/pu* 'to flourish' of a woman in an erotic sense in Lambert 1975, 120 B 17: *tuḫtannab tuḫta*[*ššaš*] 'You are

[1609] See Borger, ABZ, nos. 255 ÙR, 296 GIŠ, GIŠ.ÙR.
[1610] See CAD (U/W, p. 261a s.v. *ūru* A).
[1611] See Kaufman, AIA, p. 20, n. 48.
[1612] See von Soden, *Or* 46 (1977), p. 187:187.
[1613] See E. Matsushima, "Le Rituel Hiérogamique de Nabû," *Acta Sumerologica* 9 (1987): pp. 143ff. Cf. CAD (Ḫ, p. 76b s.v. *ḫanāpu* A); CDA (p. 105b s.v. *ḫanāpu* I).
[1614] See M. Nissinen, "Love Lyrics of Nabû and Tašmetu: An Assyrian Song of Songs?" in M. Dietrich & I. Kottsieper (eds.), *"Und Mose schrieb dieses Lied auf": Studien zum Alten Testament und zum Alten Orient: FS für Oswald Loretz zur Vollendung seines 70. Lebensjahres* (Münster 1998), p. 589, n. 23. Cf. CAD (Ḫ, p. 75b s.v. *ḫanābu*); AEAD (p. 34b s.v. *ḫanābu*).

exuberant, you are made [happy]' and KAR 158 vii 52: *ina lalīka ḫunbi* 'You are exuberant in your charm.'"[1615] In a re-edition of the same NA text, Livingstone (SAA III 14 r.9) also renders *taḫ-ti-ni-ip* as "to be luxuriant."[1616] The passage where the NA word occurs (SAA III 14 r.9) reads as follows:

> *taḫ-ti-ni-ip* ^{d}LÁL$^{!}$ *ina* É–GIŠ.NÁ-*e te-tar-ba*
>
> Tašmetu, looking luxuriant, entered the bedroom.

Admittedly, the form of *taḫtinip* in our passage reveals a derivation from the verb *ḫanāpu* of the semantic *i*-class and meaning "to commit villainy, to act basely," a meaning which does not fit the NA context.[1617] On the other hand, the verb *ḫanābu* "to be luxuriant" is of the *u*-class and would have yielded *taḫtunub*. Even the rendering "schmeicheln," suggested by von Soden for *taḫ-ti-ni-ip,* based on Aramaic *ḥnp* "to flatter," does not fit well in the context of the NA passage. Von Soden himself was hesitant about his rendering. Nevertheless, since it is possible for the verb *ḫanābu* in NA to have the variant *ḫanāpu*,[1618] it seems most likely that the scribe utilized a variant of *ḫanābu*, namely *ḫanāpu*, but mistakenly conjugated the latter according to the inflection of the other *ḫanāpu* of the semantic *i*-class with the meaning "to commit villainy, to act basely." However, according to the interpretation of *taḫ-ti-ni-ip* in the latest edition of the NA text (SAA III 14 r.9), and in light of the discussion above, the suggested borrowing from Aramaic ought to be rejected and the word should be subsumed under the heading *ḫanābu*.[1619]

ḫarurtu n. f. "throat"

//Aram. ⇒ NA//

This word is a *hapax legomenon* attested in NA as *ḫa-ru-ur-ti-šú*. It occurs in a letter (SAA I 205:10) from the time of Sargon II (721–705 B.C.). The letter was excavated at Nineveh, but was originally sent from Raṣappa. The rendering of *ḫarurtu* as "throat" is not in doubt because the context from which it is determined is fairly clear. The relevant passage in which *ḫarurtu* occurs (SAA I 205:4–11) reads as follows:

> *šu-uḫ* ^{m}AMAR.UTU–SU / *ša* LUGAL *be-lí-iá iš-pur-an-ni* / *šúm-ma* ^{md}AMAR.UTU–SU *si-par-ri* AN.BAR / *a-sa-kan si-par-ri* AN.BAR-*e-šú* / ⸢*li*⸣-*i*[*p*]$^{!}$-*ṭu-ru ina* GÌR.2-*e-a* / *liš-ku-nu ú-la-a* ⸢*ša*$^{!}$⸣ *a-na* LUGAL *be-lí-iá* / *is-lu-ni* EME-*šú* TA* *ḫa-ru-ur-ti-šú* / *li-iš-du-du-u-ni*

1615 See Nissinen, ibid.
1616 See also the Glossary of SAA III (p. 133a s.v. *ḫanāpu*).
1617 See CAD (Ḫ, p. 76b s.v. *ḫanāpu* A); CDA (p. 105b s.v. *ḫanāpu* I).
1618 For variation between the stops *b* and *p*, see Luukko, SAAS XVI, § 4.1.1; Hämeen-Anttila, SAAS XIII, § 2.1.6.1.
1619 Cf. Abraham & Sokoloff, *Reassessment*, p. 34:77.

> As to Marduk-erība, about whom the king, my lord, wrote to me, if I have put Marduk-erība in irons, let them release his shackles and put them on my own feet! If not, let them pull the tongue out of the throat of the man who lied to the king, my lord!

In his comprehensive lexical and etymological study of the names of parts of the body in Assyrian-Babylonian, Holma referred to the same NA text cited above and rendered *ḫarurtu* as "throat."[1620] He connected the word with Syriac ܚܪܫ, Hebrew חרש, and Arabic خرس, all in the sense "to be dumb, silent," and explained that etymologically *ḫarurtu* is undoubtedly associated with Syriac ܚܪܘܫܬܐ "throat."[1621] He also stated that *ḫarurtu* originally comes from *ḫaruštu* and based on Meissner's grammar presented the following phonological development: *š* > *r* before *t*.[1622] Albright accepts the rendering "throat" for *ḫarurtu*, but remarks that the root behind this word is not ḤRŠ, as suggested by Holma, rather ḪRR, which has the primary meaning "to dig, sink."[1623] Albright considers Syriac ܚܪܘܫܬܐ to be borrowed from Akkadian **ḫaruštu*.[1624] By contrast, von Soden, in his study of Aramaic loanwords, regards *ḫarurtu* as a borrowing from an unattested Aramaic form **ḥa(r)rortā*, and goes on to explain that in Syriac the latter became *ḥarroštā* in accordance with a known sound change *št* > *rt* in LB.[1625] Kutscher states that he is less convinced by von Soden's interpretation of the word *ḫarurtu*.[1626] Kaufman also considers von Soden's suggested borrowing direction to be very uncertain and thinks that "the Syriac word would have to have been borrowed from an unattested Babylonian form, while an etymology from *ḥrš* is not ruled out."[1627] Abraham and Sokoloff state that because the sound change *št* > *rt* occurs only in NB, the form of the Syriac word was most certainly borrowed into Aramaic from an unattested Akkadian **ḫaruštu* and not vice versa.[1628] The editors of CAD (Ḫ, p. 121a s.v. *ḫarurtu*) render the word as "throat," and consider the Syriac word *ḥərōštā* to be probably a loan from *ḫarurtu* in the pronunciation **ḫaruštu*. In AHw. (p. 329a s.v. *ḫarurtu*), von Soden glossed

---

[1620] See H. Holma, *Die Name der Körperteile im assyrisch-babylonischen: Eine lexikalisch-etymologische Studie* (Helsinki 1911), p. 42.

[1621] Ibid. Cf. T.G. Pinches, Review of "*Die Name der Körperteile im assyrisch-babylonischen: Eine lexikalisch-etymologische Studie*," by H. Holma, *JRAS* (1912), pp. 832f.

[1622] See Holma, ibid. Cf. B. Meissner, *Kurzgefaßte assyrische Grammatik* (Leipzig 1907), § 11e.

[1623] See W.F. Albright, "Notes on Egypto-Semitic Etymology, II," *AJSL* 34 (1918), p. 240. For the Akkadian word, see AHw. (p. 323b s.v. *ḫarāru(m)* I).

[1624] Ibid.

[1625] See von Soden, *Or* 35 (1966), p. 10:49; idem, *Or* 46 (1977), p. 187:49. See also GAG § 35c. Cf. DNWSI (p. 407 s.v. *ḥrrt*). Cf. also Tadmor, *Aramaization*, pp. 455, 467 n. 97.

[1626] See E.Y. Kutscher, "Aramaic," in T.A. Sebeok (ed.), *Current Trends in Linguistics*, 6. *Linguistics in South West Asia and North Africa* (The Hague 1970), p. 357.

[1627] See Kaufman, AIA, p. 54, n. 109.

[1628] See Abraham & Sokoloff, *Reassessment*, p. 35:87.

the word as "Gurgel," but reversed his previous interpretation and considered the word to be borrowed from Akkadian into Syriac.[1629]

Albright's interpretation that NA *ḫarurtu* is derived from the root ḪRR "to dig" merits consideration, and his reasoning, which is based on positing the semantic development "hole > throat," is persuasive.[1630] Such a relationship is found, for instance, between Syriac ܒܠܘܥܬܐ "deep pit"[1631] and ܒܠܥܘܡܐ "pharynx,"[1632] as well as between Arabic بَالُوعَة "sink" and بُلْعُوم "pharynx."[1633] In Syriac, ܚܪ means "to be hoarse; to dig, make a hole."[1634] In Sūret, on the other hand, the words ܚܪܚܪܐ and ܚܪܚܪܬܐ (pronounced respectively as *ḫirḫirā* and *ḫirḫirtā*), both meaning "throat," are probably onomatopoetic. However, some dialects of Sūret tend to derive a noun from a second geminated roots, i.e., $C_1C_2C_2$, according to the nominal pattern $C_1C_2C_1C_2$. Hence, from the root ḤRR we probably have the above ܚܪܚܪܐ n. m. "throat"[1635] and ܚܪܚܪܬܐ n. f. "throat."[1636] Probably the Sūret ܚܪܚܪܬܐ is somehow related to NA *ḫarurtu* "throat."

ḫašābu v. (G) "to count"

//Aram. ⇒ NA//

In AHw. (pp. 332b, 1560a s.v. *ḫašābu*), this entry is connected with the Semitic word *ḥš/sb* "to count," and for a NA instance a suggested reading as *iḫ-šub* (ABL 1245 r.19) is cited.[1637] However, in his article on Aramaic loanwords, von Soden translates the passage from the NA letter where the word is supposedly attested as follows: LUGAL *be-lí ki ma-ṣi iḫ-šub* "wieviel (d.h. wie viele Tage) hat mein Herr König gerechnet?"[1638] He takes the word *iḫ-šub* as a borrowing from Aramaic *ḥšb* "to count."[1639] Nevertheless, the NA letter is now edited as SAA XVI 65, where the word *iḫ-šub* is read and translated differently, as *aḫ-ru* "still," and is considered to be the NA adverb *aḫḫūr* "further, still, once more." The passage where the word occurs (SAA XVI 65 s. 2) reads as follows:[1640]

> LUGAL *be-lí ki ma-ṣi aḫ-ru* IGI.2.MEŠ [*x x x x*]
>
> O king, my lord! How long still [will *my*] eyes […]?

1629 Cf. CDA (p. 109a s.v. *ḫarurtu*). Cf. also Abraham & Sokoloff, *Reassessment*, p. 35, n. 251.
1630 See Albright, ibid.
1631 See Manna, p. 67b.
1632 Ibid., p. 68a.
1633 Cf. Albright, ibid.
1634 See Manna, p. 258b. Cf. SL (p. 495b s.v. ܚܪ no. 2).
1635 See Oraham, p. 179a.
1636 See Ashitha, p. 189b.
1637 See also CDA (p. 110b s.v. *ḫašābu*). Cf. DNWSI (pp. 409f s.v. *ḥšb₁*).
1638 See von Soden, *Or* 46 (1977), p. 187:189.
1639 Ibid.
1640 See the Glossary of SAA XVI (p. 177b s.v. *aḫḫūr*).

It seems that the reading *aḫ-ru* in the sense "still" fits the NA context better. Consequently, von Soden's suggested borrowing from Aramaic has been rejected.[1641] The NA entry *ḫašābu* "to count" is a "ghost word" and ought to be stricken from AHw.[1642]

izqātu n. f. pl. "fetters, handcuffs"

//Aram. ⇒ NA//

The two major dictionaries, CAD and AHw., differ as to the reading and etymology of this word. The editors of CAD (I/J, p. 205a s.v. *iṣ qātī* (*iš qātī*)) provide attestations for SB and NB and list the word with the sense "fetter, handcuffs," i.e., a compound in a genitive combination consisting of the words *iṣu* "wood" and *qātu* "hand." The reading *iṣ qātī* in CAD is based on the fact that the term *iṣ qātī* is replaced by *šāt qātī* in an inscription of Assurbanipal, as well as on the fact that the determinative GIŠ is usually utilized in Akkadian with words denoting fetters.[1643] In AHw. (p. 408b s.v. *izqātu* (*išqātu*)), the word is glossed "(Ring-)Fesseln," and is listed in SB, NA and LB and considered to be a borrowing from Aramaic *ḥizqā* and *ʿizqəṯā* with the meaning "ring."[1644] In contrast, the editors of CDA (p. 137b s.v. *izqātu* (*išqātu*)) gloss the word as "fetters, handcuffs," and tentatively consider it to be consisting of two Akkadian words (*iṣu* + *qātu*). AEAD (p. 88a s.v. *qātu*) lists the combination as *eṣ qāti* meaning "handcuffs."

Zimmern rendered Akkadian *išqātu*, *isqātu* or *izqātu* as "Fessel," and considered it probably to be derived from the root ḤZQ.[1645] He also considered the word probably to be borrowed into Aramaic as *ʿizqətā* or *ʿezqətā* in the sense "Ring; Fessel," despite the initial voiced pharyngeal fricative *ʿ*.[1646] In contrast, von Soden considers *iz/šqātu* n. pl. tant. "(Ring-)Fesseln" to be borrowed from Aramaic *ḥizqā* or *ʿizqəṯā* "ring," and regards the interpretation given in CAD to be incorrect.[1647] In a separate treatment of this word, von Soden gives two reasons why he rejects the interpretation given in CAD. First, according to the texts, the fetters are often made of iron, and the reading *iṣ qātī* in CAD literally means "wood of the hand," which does not make sense.[1648] Secondly, the word is attested in a synonym list as *iš-qa-tu*, and there is clearly no genitive relationship in the word.[1649] Von Soden remarks that Akkadian provides no convincing

[1641] Cf. preliminary Z. Cherry, *Aramaic Loanwords in NA*: *Rejecting some Proposals*, pp. 22f. Cf. Abraham & Sokoloff, *Reassessment*, p. 35:89.
[1642] This also applies to CDA, ibid., and DNWSI, ibid.
[1643] See CAD (I/J, pp. 205f s.v. *iṣ qātī*).
[1644] Cf. DNWSI (pp. 836f s.v. *ʿzqh*), where the word is considered to be a loan either into or from Akkadian.
[1645] See Zimmern, AF, p. 35.
[1646] Ibid.
[1647] See von Soden, *Or* 35 (1966), p. 12:57; idem, *Or* 46 (1977), p. 188:57.
[1648] See W. von Soden, "*izqātu, išqātu* 'Kettenringe', ein aramäisches Lehnwort," *AfO* 20 (1963), p. 155.
[1649] Ibid.

etymology, which is why he suggests the Jewish Aramaic *ḥizqā* "Ring" as a source word and explains that, probably due to the decline of the laryngeal in younger dialects of Aramaic, it produced the variant *ʿezqəṯā*.[1650] Nevertheless, Kaufman points out that *ʿzqth* "signet ring" is already attested in Imperial Aramaic and argues that von Soden's suggested development *ḥizqā* > *ʿezqəṯā* is impossible at an early stage of Aramaic.[1651]

It is not certain that the word under discussion appeared in NA texts. However, there is a word in an epic narrative relating to Assurbanipal's Elamite wars (SAA III 20 r.1) which is read *iṣ–qa-ti* and is rendered "hand-cuffs,"[1652] but this text appears to be neither a letter nor a royal inscription, and it is difficult to decide its literary genre.[1653]

kabsu n. "young sheep, young ram"

//Aram. ⇒ NA//

This term is found in NA letters, administrative documents, and the vassal treaties of Esarhaddon. It occurs in the masculine form as *kab-su*,[1654] UDU.*kab-si*,[1655] and UDU.*kab-su*.[1656] However, in the feminine it is attested as *kab-su-tú* "young ewe," and is a *hapax legomenon* in NA.[1657] The word is listed in AHw. (p. 418a s.v. *kabsu* II),[1658] for SB, NB and NA as meaning "Jungwidder." In CAD (K, p. 23b s.v. *kabsu*), the word is listed only for NA and is glossed "young (male) sheep."[1659]

Luukko and van Buylaere, however, translate the word *kabsu* as "old ram," based on the Syriac word ܟܒܫܐ "a wether sheep, old ram."[1660] The late attestation of the word in Akkadian as well as the *š* ⋛ *s* interchange between the alphabetic and NA cuneiform renderings may point to a borrowing from Aramaic. Nevertheless, Nöldeke has shown, based on phonological considerations, that the Syriac ܟܒܫܐ is a borrowing from Arabic.[1661] Even Mandaic *kabiš* "ram" is probably an Arabism.[1662] In Arabic, the word is known as كَبْش "ram, male sheep, bellwether."[1663] In Hebrew, a similar word occurs in the masculine as כֶּבֶשׂ

[1650] Ibid.

[1651] See Kaufman, AIA, p. 61, n. 142. Cf. Abraham & Sokoloff, *Reassessment*, p. 36:97.

[1652] Cf. the Glossary of SAA III (p. 135a s.v. *iṣ qāti*).

[1653] Cf. J. Hämeen-Anttila, "A New Text Relating to Ashurbanipal's Elamite Wars," *SAAB* 1 (1987), pp. 13ff.

[1654] See SAA II 6:551; SAA XVI 5 r.6.

[1655] See Billa 70:5.

[1656] See SAA XVI 22:8; SAA XVI 236:4′ [UDU.*k*]*ab*?-*su*; SAA VII 130 r.5′ UDU.⌜*kab*!⌝-*su*.

[1657] See SAA II 6:551.

[1658] Cf. CDA (p. 140b s.v. *kabsu* II).

[1659] See also CAD (K, p. 23a s.v. **kabsatu*).

[1660] See n. ad SAA XVI 5 r.6. See also the Glossary of SAA XVI (p. 184b s.v. *kabsu*). Cf. PSm., p. 204b; SL (p. 598b s.v. ܟܒܫܐ no. 2); AEAD (p. 44a s.v. *kabsu*).

[1661] See Th. Nöldeke, in S. Fraenkel, *Die Aramäischen Fremdwörter im Arabischen* (Hildesheim 1982), p. 109.

[1662] Cf. MD, p. 195a.

[1663] See Elias & Elias, p. 579b; Wehr-Cowan, p. 811b.

"sheep," and in the feminine as כִּבְשָׂה.[1664] In Amorite the word occurs as *kabśum*.[1665] According to the Hebrew, Arabic and Amorite instances, the expected PS root would be *KBŚ. Most importantly, however, is that the word *kabsu* has been found as UDU.*ka-ab-si* with the meaning "male lambs" in a late OB letter (YOS 13, 109, 12 = AbB 9 162:12).[1666] Hence, the NA *kabsu* has a forerunner in OB. Based on the information given above, a borrowing from Aramaic or West-Semitic is rejected.

kabsutu n. f. "young ewe"; (see the discussion above s.v. *kabsu*)

kuspu, (in *kusup libbi*) n. "broken heart"

//Aram. ⇒ NA//

JBA *ksp* v. "to embarrass, put to shame" DJBA 592b; Jastrow 655a; CAL. JBA *ksypw*, *ksypwt'* n. f. "shame" DJBA 591b; Jastrow 654a; CAL.

This word occurs as a *hapax legomenon* in NA. It is attested in the expression *kusup libbi* in a letter (ABL 525 r.10 = SAA X 334 r.10) sent to the Assyrian king (reign of Esarhaddon or Assurbanipal)[1667] by Nabû-tabni-uṣur, complaining that he has been treated less favorably than his associates. In AHw. (p. 515a s.v. *kuspu* II), this term is glossed "Scham," and is considered to be an Aramaic foreign word in NA. On the other hand, the editors of CAD (K, p. 587b s.v. *kuspu*) compare the word with Akkadian *kasāpu* "to break off a piece, to be broken,"[1668] and translate the expression *kusup libbi* as "heartbreak." They also compare *kusup libbi* with the expression *ḫīp libbi* "panic, anxiety," which occurs in the subsequent lines in the same NA text.[1669] In CDA (p. 170a s.v. *kuspu*), the word is also considered to be derived from Akkadian *kasāpu* "to break (into bits)," and the expression *kusup libbi* is tentatively rendered "heartbreak." The NA context where the word *kuspu* occurs (SAA X 334 r.9–12) reads as follow:

> *ša is-si-ia gab-bu ḫa-di-iu-u / a-na-ku i-na ku-su-up*–ŠÀ-*bi / a-mu-at ki-i ša ma-ṣar-tú / ša* LUGAL *be-lí-iá la a-na-ṣar-u-ni*
>
> (While) all my associates are happy, I am dying of a broken heart. I have been treated as if I did not keep the watch of the king, my lord.

1664 See G.J. Botterweck et al. (eds.), *Theological Dictionary of the Old Testament*, Vol. 7 (Michigan 1995), p. 43.
1665 Ibid.
1666 See J.J. Finkelstein, *Late Old Babylonian Documents and Letters* (New Haven 1972). Cf. AHw. (p. 1565a s.v. *kabsu*(*m*)).
1667 See PNA 2/II (p. 893a s.v. Nabû-tabni-uṣur, no. 2). Cf. n. ad SAA X 334.
1668 Cf. CAD (K, p. 241b s.v. *kasāpu* A); AHw. (p. 453a s.v. *kasāpu*(*m*) I); AEAD (p. 55b s.v. *libbu*).
1669 Cf. CAD (Ḫ, p. 196b s.v. *ḫīpu* mng. no. 4). Cf. also the Glossary of SAA X (p. 336a s.v. *ḫīp libbi*).

In his articles on Aramaic loanwords, von Soden renders NA *kuspu* as "Scham," and takes it to be derived from the Aramaic root KSP "sich schämen," as attested in Jewish Aramaic.[1670] In contrast, Parpola, in his re-edition of the NA letter, applies the interpretation given in CAD and translates *kusup libbi* as "heartbreak."[1671]

Nevertheless, there are two reasons to reject von Soden's proposed loan hypothesis. Semantically, the context supports the rendering "heartbreak," and, as pointed out in CAD, in the following lines the text provides a comparable expression, *ḫīp libbi*, meaning "panic, anxiety." In addition, the proposed Aramaic loanword כסף "to embarrass, shame" clashes with the well-known rule of the shift of sibilants between NA and Aramaic. The proposed Aramaic loanword is expected to appear in NA as *kšp*, in accordance with the *š* ⋛ *s* interchange between the alphabetic and NA cuneiform renderings.[1672] From the other Semitic languages, Syriac provides comparative expressions such as ܬܒܺܝܪ ܠܶܒܳܐ "heartbreak" and ܬܒܺܝܪܳܐ ܠܶܒܳܐ "sad, grieved, distressed."[1673] In Arabic, the word كَسَفَ means "to put to the blush; mortify; cause to feel humiliated,"[1674] and the expression كاسِفُ البالِ means "down-hearted, low-spirited, depressed."[1675]

la prep. "from";[1676] (see the discussion below s.v. *lapān*(*i*))

//Aram. ⇒ NA//

Com., *l*- prep. "(indicating direction) to, towards" DNWSI 549ff; DJBA 611a; DJPA 274a; MD 226a; DSA 419a; DCPA 190b; SL 665a; PSm. 232a; Manna 362ff; Audo 495a; CAL.

In AHw. (p. 520a s.v. *la*), this preposition is glossed for NA as "(örtl.) nach" and is considered to be an Aramaic loanword. On the other hand, in CAD (L, p. 5a s.v. *la*), the preposition is listed with the meaning "from, out of," and is regarded as a West-Semitic word in NA and NB. Spatially, CDA (p. 173a s.v. *la*) glosses this preposition as "from (a place)" and regards it as a West-Semitic loanword in NA and NB.

Oppenheim was able to show that a preposition *la* actually occurs in NB.[1677] However, he emphasized that the equivalence of this *la* with the Akkadian preposition *ina* in the sense "from" eliminates any connection between the NB preposition *la* and the well-known West-Semitic preposition *la*, which always

---

1670 See von Soden, *Or* 35 (1966), p. 13:72; idem, *Or* 46 (1977), p. 189:72. Cf. DNWSI (p. 524 s.v. *ksp*$_1$); D.O. Edzard, Review of "CAD 8 'K' and 9 'L'," *ZA* 64 (1975), p. 124, n. 8; Nili, p. 264:85; Abraham & Sokoloff, *Reassessment*, p. 38:113.
1671 See the Glossary of SAA X (p. 342a s.v. *kusup libbi*).
1672 Cf. above, n. 71.
1673 See Manna (p. 839a s.v. ܬܒܺܝܪ).
1674 See Elias & Elias, p. 592b.
1675 See ibid., p. 593a. Cf. *Al-munğidu* (p. 685c s.v. كسف).
1676 See AEAD (p. 53a s.v. *la*).
1677 See A.L. Oppenheim, "The Neo-Babylonian Preposition *la*," *JNES* 1 (1942), pp. 369–372.

means "to, in the direction of, belong to, referring to," and never means "out of."[1678] Nevertheless, in his articles on Aramaic loanwords, von Soden considered the NA, NB and LB *la* with the meaning "für, zu, nach" to be a borrowing from Aramaic.[1679] Abraham and Sokoloff, on the other hand, reject von Soden's loan hypothesis, arguing that the meaning of the preposition *la* in both Hebrew and Aramaic is never "from," but rather "to, towards."[1680] They note, as well, that the Semitic languages very seldom have prepositions with opposite meanings.[1681] Parpola too comments that there is no proof of an intrusion of Aramaic *la* into NA.[1682]

The instances quoted in CAD and AHw. for this supposedly West-Semitic or Aramaic loanword in NA are ABL 94:12 and ABL 421:13. However, the former is now re-edited as SAA I 91:12, and the previous reading of the concerned word, namely *la šipirtu* is now after collation read differently as *la-li*$^{!}$-*ka*$^{!}$. The other NA instance, i.e., ABL 421:13, is re-edited as SAA X 173:13, and *la* is now taken to be a scribal error for *ša* "of."[1683] Accordingly, both NA instances given in the two dictionaries ought to be stricken out.

However, an instance of *la* in the sense "from" is found in the phrase ⌈*la*⌉ *a-ra-an-tú* "from Orontes," occurring in a royal letter from the 8th century B.C., namely SAA XIX 3 s.4. Luukko considers this *la* to be an Aramaism in NA.[1684]

Nevertheless, the most telling factor speaking against the supposed borrowing of the NA preposition *la* in the sense "from" from Aramaic or West-Semitic is that the Aramaic or West-Semitic preposition *la* has never been attested with the meaning "from."[1685]

lapān(i) prep. "from"; (see the discussion above s.v. *la*)

//Aram. ⇒ NA//

AHw. (p. 534b s.v. *lapān*(*i*)) glosses this word for SB and LB as "vor (örtlich u übertragen)" and considers it to consist of the Aramaic preposition *la* and the Akkadian word *pānu* "face." In contrast, CDA (p. 177b s.v. *lapān*(*i*)) lists the word for SB and NB in the sense "in front of," but considers it to consist of the Akkadian words *la* and *pānu*. The editors of CAD (L, p. 81b s.v. *lapani* mng. c)) regard the word as a preposition in SB, NA, NB and LB meaning "from, before,

---

1678 Ibid., p. 372.

1679 See von Soden, *Or* 35 (1966), p. 13:73; idem, *Or* 46 (1977), p. 189:73. Cf. DNWSI (pp. 549ff s.v. l_5).

1680 See Abraham & Sokoloff, *Reassessment*, p. 38:114.

1681 Ibid., p. 38, n. 320.

1682 See LAS II ad no. 114:13.

1683 See n. ad SAA X 173:13. See also LAS II, ibid; Luukko, SAAS XVI, § 3.6 s.v. (*ša*).

1684 See n. ad SAA XIX 3 s.4.

1685 On the Old Aramaic preposition *la*, see R. Degen, *Altaramäische Grammatik der Inschriften des 10.–8. Jh. v.Chr.* (Wiesbaden 1969), § 45. Cf. V. Hug, *Altaramäische Grammatik der Texte des 7. und 6. Jh.s v.Chr.* (Heidelberg 1993), § 4.1.

on account of, by, in front of." AEAD (p. 79b s.v. *pān*) lists the combination *la–pān* as a preposition meaning "from," but only for NB.[1686]

In his articles on Aramaic loanwords, von Soden considers *lapān* to be a prepositional expression in SB, NB and LB, and rarely in NA, in the sense "vor," and takes it to be a combination of the Aramaic preposition *la–* "from" and the Akkadian word *pānu* "face."[1687] Abraham and Sokoloff reject von Soden's proposed loan hypothesis, stating that the Aramaic *la* is never attested in the meaning "from."[1688]

However, the NA instance *la-pa-ni*, which supposedly occurs in ABL 685:23, as quoted in CAD (L, p. 81b s.v. *lapani*, mng. c), ought to be stricken out for stemming from erroneous reading. In a later edition of the same NA text as SAA XV 136:23, the word is read differently as two separate words, i.e., *la pa-né-ša*, in the sense "not inclined towards."[1689] Still, the word *la–pa-ni* in the sense "from," does indeed occur in a NA letter addressed to Esarhaddon (SAA XVI 29:5),[1690] but as mentioned above, the Aramaic preposition *la* is never attested in the sense "from."[1691]

laqā'u v. (G) "to suffer"

//Aram. ⇒ NA//

JPA, Gal., *lqy* v. "to suffer" DJPA 286b; CAL. JPA, CPA, Sam., *lqy* v. "to be smitten" Jastrow 718b; CAL; LSp. 105a; DCPA 204a; DSA 445b. JPA, JLA, Gal., JBA, LJLA *lqy* v. "to receive lashes" DJPA 286b; DJBA 633a; CAL.

The word is attested as *la-qa-ni* in a NA letter concerning approaching the king (ABL 333 r.19 = SAA XVI 121 r.19e). The letter was sent by Bēl-nāṣir, a royal official, to the Assyrian king Esarhaddon, reminding him of their meeting in Arbela when the king became angry with his servant (i.e., with Bēl-nāṣir).

In AHw. (p. 1570b s.v. *laqā'u* II), the term is glossed "leiden," and is considered to be an Aramaic foreign word in NA. CDA (p. 178a s.v. *laqā'u*) also regards this word as a borrowing from Aramaic in NA, with the meaning "to suffer." In the latest edition of the NA letter, however, the word is left untranslated, but the passage where it occurs (SAA XVI 121 r.19e–20e) is read and rendered as follows:[1692]

1686 For *la–pān* "in front," as Aramaism in LB, see H. Schaudig, *Die Inschriften Nabonids von Babylon und Kyros' des Großen* (Münster 2001), § VII.2.5, d).

1687 See von Soden, *Or* 35 (1966), p. 14:77; idem, *Or* 46 (1977), p. 189:77. Cf. GAG § 114e and § 115l.

1688 See Abraham & Sokoloff, *Reassessment*, p. 39:118.

1689 Cf. preliminary Z. Cherry, *Aramaic Loanwords in NA: Rejecting some Proposals*, p. 23 s.v. *lapān(i)*.

1690 See also the Glossary of SAA XVI (p. 186a s.v. *la pān*).

1691 For NB, cf., S.W. Cole, *Nippur IV: The Early Neo-Babylonian Governor's Archive from Nippur* (Chicago 1996), p. 119, n. on l. 15, and p. 331 s.v. *la pān*.

1692 In the Glossary of SAA XVI (p. 186a s.v. *laqānu*), the meaning of the word is given as obscure.

TA* *pa-an la-qa-ni* [0] / *lu la ni-qar-ri-ib*

May we not arrive because of ...!

In his article on Aramaic loanwords, von Soden renders *la-qa-ni* as "leiden (von Schlägen usw.)" and considers it to be a borrowing from Aramaic into NA, citing Jewish Aramaic לקי "to suffer, to be struck."[1693] He reads the passage quoted above in a similar manner, but translates it differently, as "da wir nun leiden, wollen wir nicht (vor dem König) erscheinen."[1694] The editors of DNWSI (p. 584 s.v. *lqy*) consider von Soden's loan hypothesis to be uncertain.

It seems that von Soden analyzes the word *la-qa-ni* as m. pl. in the stative with the meaning "we are suffering," supposedly derived from the Aramaic root *LQʾ > LQY. But if the word *la-qa-ni* is indeed derived from *LQʾ or LQY, then the NA m. pl. in the stative is expected to appear as *laqʾāni* or *laqiāni*.

Nili rejects von Soden's interpretation on the basis of the content of the NA letter, which deals with performing a ritual.[1695] Instead, she cites a different interpretation offered by Cohen, whose rendering of the same passage runs approximately as follows:[1696]

TA* PA.AN (GARZA = *parṣu*) *la-qa-ni* / *lu la ni-qar-ri-ib*

Now when the ritual is performed, we did not come before the king.[1697]

Abraham and Sokoloff translate the same passage slightly different as follows: "Because the ritual is being performed; we should not approach the king."[1698] Hence, *la-qa-ni* is taken to be derived from the usual Akkadian verb *leqû/laqû* "to take," and the preceding word is read PA.AN, i.e., (GARZA = *parṣu*), which denotes "cult, rite, ritual, ceremony."[1699] The combination *parṣa/ī leqû* is an idiomatic expression in Akkadian and means "to perform a ritual, to be capable of performing rites."[1700] A comparable expression is found in another NA letter (SAA X 70:9): GARZA (*pa-ar-ṣi*) *il-qí* "(if) he wants to take the cult ceremonies."[1701]

Accordingly, the entry *laqāʾu* "to suffer," ought to be stricken out of AHw. and CDA, for stemming from erroneous interpretation and rendering. The word *la-qa-ni* in (ABL 333 r.19 = SAA XVI 121 r.19e), should be subsumed in AHw., and CDA under the heading *leqû*(*m*) II, with the meaning "to take."

1693 See von Soden, *Or* 46 (1977), p. 189:191.
1694 Ibid.
1695 See Nili, p. 264:87.
1696 Ibid.
1697 Translated tentatively from the Hebrew text in Nili, ibid.
1698 See Abraham & Sokoloff, *Reassessment*, p. 39:119.
1699 Cf. Borger, ABZ, no. 295b. Cf. also AEAD (p. 81a s.v. *parṣu*).
1700 See CAD (L, p. 145a s.v. *leqû* no. 5); CDA (p. 180b s.v. *leqû*(*m*) no. 6).
1701 For further examples, see CAD, ibid. Cf. the Glossary of SAA X (p. 352a s.v. *parāṣu*).

magādu v. (G) "to pick fruit; to pick a quarrel, pick on, nag at"[1702]

//Aram. ⇒ NA//

Palm., *mgd* v. "to bestow, give generously" DNWSI 592; CAL. JBA, JLA, PTA, Sam., *mgd* (*ma/egdā*) n. m. "choice fruit" DJBA 663b; Jastrow 726a; DJPA 289b; DSA 449b; CAL. Syr., *mgd* n. m. "fruit" Manna 385b; Audo 523b; SL 707a; PSm. 249b.

The word *magādu* is not listed in AHw., CAD or CDA. On the other hand, in AEAD (p. 57b s.v. *magādu*) it is listed as meaning "to pick fruit; to pick a quarrel, pick on, nag at." The word occurs as *ma-ga-di* in a NA letter (ABL 117:11) sent probably by the court exorcist Urdu-Gula to the Assyrian king Esarhaddon, and dealing with a complaint against an unnamed colleague. The letter is now re-edited by Parpola and the relevant passage where the word occurs (SAA X 289:7–12) reads as follows:

> *dul*[!]*-lu*[!] *an-ni-ú gab-bi-šú am–mar* LUGAL[!] / UD-22-KÁM *ù* UD*-mu an-ni-ú e-pu-šu-u-ni / a-ni-in-nu gab-bu nu-us-sa-aṣ-bit / ù ṭup-pa-a-ni is-se-niš ni-is-sa-ṭar / šu-ú*[!] TA* IGI *ma-ga-di ù ba-ṣa-a-ri / ina* UGU *mé-mé-e-ni la-a iq-ri-ib*
>
> We prepared all this work that the king performed on the 22nd day and today, and we also wrote the tablets, (while) *he* did not go near anything because of the picking (of fruit) and harvesting (of grapes).

Fales connected *ma-ga-di* with Hebrew מֶגֶד "choice fruits; choice gifts, rich presents" and Syriac ܡܓܕܐ "fruit," and took it as a verbal infinitive of Aramaic/Canaanite origin.[1703] He rendered *ma-ga-di* in the sense "to pick/choose fruit."[1704] However, Fales admitted that *mgd*, in the sense "to pick/choose fruit," is unattested in the contemporary West-Semitic languages.[1705] He also asked: "Could it then be possible to reconstruct the presence of a mid-first millennium Aramaic/Canaanite acceptation of the verbal root *mgd*, with the meaning 'to pick, to choose (fruit, etc.)'?"[1706]

In the re-edition of the NA letter, as quoted above, Parpola accepts Fales' interpretation.[1707] Furthermore, in a NA legal document from Assur (StAT 2 81 r.8) concerning the adoption of an infant daughter, Donbaz and Parpola tentatively render the term *i-ma-ga-sa* in the sense "to pick on," and also consider

[1702] See AEAD (p. 57b s.v. *magādu*).
[1703] See F.M. Fales, "Assyro-Aramaica: Three Notes," *Or* 53 (1984), pp. 70f.
[1704] Ibid., p. 71.
[1705] Ibid.
[1706] Ibid.
[1707] However, in the Glossary of SAA X (p. 345a s.v. *magādu*), the meaning of this word is considered uncertain. Cf. n. ad SAA X 289:11; LAS II ad no. 224:11. Cf. also S. Parpola, Review of "Akkadisches Handwörterbuch. Vols. II & III/1 (Lfg. 7–12)," by W. von Soden, *OLZ* 74 (1979), p. 24 ad 576b.

it to be a loanword from Aramaic **mgd* "to pick."[1708] However, Abraham and Sokoloff consider Fales' argument and interpretation to be unconvincing and reject his attempt to connect the NA *ma-ga-di* with a non-existent (Hebrew and) Aramaic root.[1709]

As a matter of fact, the root MGD is not productive in Akkadian. It is only attested NA. From the Aramaic sources, a denominative verb *mgd* in the sense "to give generously," is only attested in Palmyrene, and is considered to be derived from *mgd'* "liberality, generous gift, offering." However, the origin of Palmyrene *mgd'* is hesitatingly traced back to Arabic.[1710] As it stands, we have no other choice than to leave the etymology of the NA *magādu* unsettled, in anticipation of further and more decisive data.

***magattu** n. "scraper (for bricks)"; (see the discussion below s.v. *magazzutu*)

magazzutu n. f. "shears, clippers"

//Aram. ⇒ NA//

Syr., *magzānā* n. m. "shears; saw (for stone)" Manna 100b. Syr., *magzwn*, *mgzwn'* (*magzōn*, *magzōnā*) n. m. "sickle" SL 708a; PSm. 250a; Manna 100b; Audo 132b; CAL. Com., *gzz* v. "to shear" CAL. Sam., *gzz* v. "to hew (stone)" DSA 139b; CAL.

This word occurs as a *hapax legomnon* in NA. It is attested in a dowry list in a marriage conveyance (ND 2307 r.10 = Iraq 16, p. 38, 34 = FNALD 14 r.34). In AHw. (p. 576b s.v. *magattu*), the NA word is tentatively read as *ma-ga-a*[*t*?-]*tú*, is glossed "Kratzer (für Backsteine)," and is considered to be a foreign word from Aramaic *ghṭ* "schaben."[1711] On the other hand, in CAD (M/I, p. 44a s.v. **magattu*), the NA word is cautiously read *ma-ga-*⌜*da*(?)⌝*-tú*, defined as (a metal utensil), and considered to be a loanword from Aramaic. According to Postgate, the reading *magattu* for the NA word in AHw., is certainly incorrect.[1712] He tentatively transliterates the NA word in question as *ma-ga-zu*?*-tú* and renders it in the sense of "shears."[1713] Accordingly, in the addenda and corrigenda section of AHw. (p. 1572a s.v. *magattu*), the NA word is read as *ma-ga-zu*?*-tú*, is defined as (Schere), and is considered to be an Aramaic foreign word. On the other hand,

[1708] See n. ad StAT 2 81 r.8. See also the Glossary of StAT 2 (p. 230a s.v. *magādu*). Note that there are two other instances of *magādu* in NA: *i-ma-gi-du-u-ni* (StAT 2 164 s.1), and *ma-ag-da-at* (ND 2316 r.2 = Iraq 16, p. 40, 15). The transliteration *ma-ag-da-at* is taken from CNA, s.v. *magādu*. For a different earlier reading of *ma-ag-da-at*, see B. Parker, "The Nimrud Tablets, 1952–Business Documents," *Iraq* 16 (1954), p. 40, ND 2316.
[1709] See Abraham & Sokoloff, *Reassessment*, p. 24, n. 31:12.
[1710] See DNWSI (p. 592 s.v. mgd_1 and mgd_2). Cf. W. Gesenius, *Hebräisches und Aramäisches Handwörterbuch über das Alte Testament* (Berlin 2005), p. 625b s.v. *meged*.
[1711] Cf. DNWSI (p. 592 s.v *mghṭ*).
[1712] See Postgate, FNALD, pp. 103f, no. 14 r.34, p. 197b s.v. *magazzutu*.
[1713] Ibid. Note that also CNA reads the NA word as *ma-ga-zu*?*-tú*.

the NA word is not referred to in CDA. In AEAD (p. 58a s.v. *magazzutu*), the word is glossed "clippers, shears."

In his articles on Aramaic loanwords, von Soden considered the term to be a borrowing from Aramaic and referred to Jewish Babylonian Aramaic and Mandaic *ghṭ* "to erase, rub over."[1714] Abraham and Sokoloff consider von Soden's loan hypothesis to be highly unsubstantiated.[1715] They assert that the meaning given by von Soden for the Akkadian word is merely conjectural and is founded on the proposed etymology.[1716] They also argue that there are no nominal derivatives attested for the suggested Aramaic verbal root.[1717] In addition, they point out that the supposed Akkadian borrowing does not show any traces of the laryngeal and pharyngeal *h/ḥ* of the suggested Aramaic source word גהט and גחט.[1718] However, in view of the existence of a native Akkadian verb *gazāzu* meaning "to shear (sheep and goats)", Streck correctly finds no reason to consider the NA *magazzutu* to be an Aramaic foreign word.[1719]

Etymologically, the root GZZ with identical second and third radicals is found in the *doubled* verb *gazāzu* "to shear (sheep and goats)," which is attested from Old Akkadian onward.[1720] In Akkadian the verb is also attested as *g/kaṣāṣu*.[1721] However, the root GZZ in the sense "to shear (sheep and goats)" is Common Semitic except for Ethiopic.[1722] From the same root a substantive, *magzazu* "shears," is also attested in a SB lexical list.[1723] Other comparative words derived from GZZ are found in Syriac as well, such as ܡܓܙܙܐ "shears," and ܡܓܙܘܙܐ "shears; sickle."[1724] Arabic has the word مِجَزّ "shears, wool shears."[1725] The Syriac and Arabic substantives are only attested in the masculine form.

Since the NA *magazzutu* has an Akkadian etymology and is attested in the feminine, and also displays the Assyrian vowel harmony, the suggested borrowing from Aramaic into NA ought to be rejected. A feminine nominal form derived from a root with identical second and third radicals preceded by the preformative *ma-*, such as *magazzutu* < *magazzatu*, is not out of the question in Akkadian.[1726] However, NA *magazzutu* should be listed separately under its own heading, as in AEAD.

1714 See von Soden, *Or* 35 (1966), p. 16:84; idem, *Or* 46 (1977), p. 190:84. Cf. DJBA (p. 262b s.v. גהט, גחט); MD (p. 81a s.v. *ghṭ*).
1715 See Abraham & Sokoloff, *Reassessment*, p. 40:126.
1716 Ibid.
1717 Ibid.
1718 Ibid.
1719 See M.P. Streck, "Die Nominalformen *maPRaS*(*t*), *maPRāS* und *maPRiS*(*t*) im Akkadischen," in N. Nebes (ed.), *Neue Beiträge zur Semitistik* (Wiesbaden 2002), p. 239, n. 156. Cf. preliminary Z. Cherry, *Aramaic Loanwords in NA*: *Rejecting some Proposals*, p. 23.
1720 See AHw. (p. 284a s.v. *gazāzu*(*m*)); CAD (G, p. 59b s.v. *gazāzu*).
1721 See AHw., ibid.
1722 Ibid.
1723 See CAD (M/I, p. 49a s.v. *magzazu*); AHw. (p. 577b s.v. *magzāzu*).
1724 See Manna, p. 100b. Cf. Audo, p. 132b.
1725 See Elias & Elias, p. 113b; Wehr-Cowan, p. 122b.
1726 Cf. K. Deller & W.R. Mayer, "Akkadische Lexikographie: *CAD* M," *Or* 53 (1984), p. 76, ad [44a]. AEAD (p. 61b), for instance, lists the word *maṣallutu* "rest room, rest-house," derived from *ṣalālu* "to be at rest; to lie down, sleep."

maḫītu n. f. "whip" (also in *bēt maḫītāti* "whip case")

//Aram. ⇒ NA//

JLA *mḥt'* n. f. "whip?" Jastrow 756b; CAL. JPA, JBA, CPA, Sam., LJLA *mḥh*, *mḥt'* n. f. "stroke, blow; wound; plague" DJPA 299a; DJBA 658a; LSp. 108a; DCPA 215a; DSA 460b; Jastrow 756b; CAL. Ma., *mhita* n. f. "blow; wound; beating" MD 260a. Com., *mḥy* v. "to strike, beat, hit" CAL.

This word occurs in NA twice as GIŠ.*ma-ḫi-tú* (SAA III 37:24′, 25′), and once as GIŠ.*ma-ḫi-tu* (SAA XX 53 i 17′).[1727] Probably, it occurs as [GIŠ.*ma*]-*ḫi-tú* in SAA XX 52 r. i 35′. The word is also attested in the expression É *ma-ḫi-ta-te* "whip case" (StAT 3 8:11 = VAT 9777:11).[1728]

Von Soden states that *maḫītu* "Peitsche" seems to be a feminine participle in the G-stem of the Aramaic verb מחי "to hit," which corresponds to the Akkadian verb *maḫāṣu*.[1729] He remarks that one would take *maḫītu* to be an Aramaic loanword if it were not already attested in a set of Middle Assyrian horse training regulations.[1730] In contrast, Landsberger doubts von Soden's interpretation and suggests, instead, a derivation from a reconstructed Akkadian verb **maḫû* "to whip."[1731] In its etymological commentary, CAD (M/I, p. 103a s.v. *maḫītu*) considers Landsberger's interpretation to be supported by an OB reference attested as *mi-ḫi-tum* in a list of parts of a wagon.[1732] However, Abraham and Sokoloff state that the OB reference given in CAD is unlikely to be semantically related to the word under discussion.[1733] In addition, they dismiss von Soden's interpretation, arguing that although the verb מחא is attested in Aramaic, no such nominal form with the sense "whip" is attested in any of its dialects.[1734] Nevertheless, the most relevant reason to reject the borrowing of the word from Aramaic into NA is the chronological evidence, which proves that the word is already attested in MA, i.e., prior to the period of language contact between NA and Aramaic.

[1727] Cf. E. Ebeling, "Kultische Texte aus Assur," *Or* 22 (1953), p. 28 i 17, who reads the word erroneously as (*iṣ*)*ma-šár-tu* instead of GIŠ.*ma-ḫi-tu*. Cf. also von Soden, *Or* 35 (1966), p. 16:85b.

[1728] See also AEAD (p. 58b s.v. *maḫītu*), which lists *bēt maḫītāti* in the sense "whip case."

[1729] See von Soden, *Or* 35 (1966), p. 16:85b; idem, *Or* 46 (1977), p. 190:85b. For a possible cognate relationship between the Akkadian word *maḫāṣu*, Ugaritic *mḫṣ*, Hebrew *mḥṣ* and Aramaic *mḥ'*, and a possible origin of the latter as a PS **məḥa'*, see M. Held, "*mḫṣ*/**mḫš* in Ugaritic and Other Semitic Languages (A Study in Comparative Lexicography)" *JAOS* 79 (1959), p. 171.

[1730] See von Soden, ibid. Cf. AHw. (p. 584b s.v. *māḫītu*).

[1731] See B. Landsberger, *The Date Palm and its By-products According to the Cuneiform Sources* (Graz 1967), p. 31, n. 95.

[1732] Cf. DNWSI (p. 616 s.v. *mḥt*$_2$), which also considers von Soden's interpretation to be improbable.

[1733] See Abraham & Sokoloff, *Reassessment*, p. 40, n. 365. Note that CDA (p. 191a s.v. *māḫītu*) also lists the word for OB.

[1734] See Abraham & Sokoloff, ibid., p. 40:129.

***muāšu** v. (G) "to check, to look over"

//Aram. ⇒ NA//

Syr., *mwš* v. "to search, explore; to probe; to examine, test, scrutinize" SL 730b; PSm. 259b; Manna 419a; Audo 531a; CAL.

This alleged NA word was previously mistakenly considered to be occurring in the phrase *aš-ur mu-šu.*[1735] It supposedly occurs in a royal letter (*abat šarri*) from Calah (NL 23:5 = ND 2644:5), sent to Inūrta-bēlu-uṣur, concerning camels.[1736] It supposedly also occurs in another letter from Calah (NL 37 r.9′ = ND 2470 r.9′),[1737] which was sent by Inūrta-ilā'ī to the palace scribe and concerned the people of Puqudu.

In his article on Aramaic loanwords, von Soden argues that the form of *mu-šu* could be the imperative of a final weak verb with a *ū* as the third radical, similar to *munu* "count," but it could also come from a hollow root, in which case a so-called "overhanging" vowel would have to be present.[1738] He states that the Akkadian dictionary does not provide help and therefore suggests deriving the word from Aramaic *mūš*, attested in Syriac with the meaning "to search, examine."[1739]

Consequently, in AHw. (p. 665a s.v. *muāšu*), this word is glossed "berühren, prüfen," and is considered to be an Aramaic foreign word in NA. The editors of CAD (M/I, p. 403a s.v. **mâšu*) accept von Soden's loan hypothesis, render this term as meaning "to check, to look over," and consider it to be an Aramaic loanword in NA. In CDA (p. 213b s.v. *muāšu*), the word is tentatively rendered "to chick," and is considered to be a loan from Aramaic. The editors of DNWSI (p. 605 s.v. *mwš*) also accept von Soden's loan hypothesis. In contrast, Abraham and Sokoloff find von Soden's interpretation to be problematic and reject it on morphological grounds, arguing that the final "overhanging" vowel *u* is characteristic of NB and not of NA.[1740]

Most important, however, is that in the re-edition of the two NA letters, NL 23 as (CTN V 175ff) and NL 37 as (CTN V 84f), Saggs reads and interprets the word under discussion differently, as *mu-ḫur* "receive," and analyzes it as an imperative in the singular of the Akkadian verb *maḫāru* "to receive." This reading and interpretation was overlooked by Abraham and Sokoloff. On the other hand, Luukkoo, in the latest re-edition of the two NA letters, also adopts Saggs' reading and interpretation.[1741] In fact, in both NA instances the word *mu-ḫur* is preceded by the word *ašur*, which is the imperative singular of the Akkadian verb *ašāru* "to check, to review."[1742] Hence, the phrase *ašur muḫur* is rendered "check and

---

1735 See von Soden, *Or* 35 (1966), p. 20:97.
1736 See Saggs, *Iraq* 17 (1955), p. 142, no. 23:5.
1737 See Saggs, *Iraq* 18 (1956), pp. 52f., no. 37 r.9′.
1738 See von Soden, ibid.
1739 See von Soden, ibid; idem, *Or* 46 (1977), p. 191:97.
1740 See Abraham & Sokoloff, *Reassessment*, p. 42:144, n. 399, and p. 67 s.v. *mâšu*.
1741 See SAA XIX 3:5; SAA XIX 56 r.10′.
1742 See CAD (A/II, p. 420b s.v. *ašāru* A).

receive!" Accordingly, the entry *muāšu* or **māšu* for NA is a "ghost word" which originated as a result of erroneous reading and ought to be stricken out of the Akkadian lexica and DNWSI.

mudarriktu n. f. "woman thresher"; (see the discussion above s.v. *darāku*)

nakālu v. (G) "to outwit"; (see the discussion below s.v. *niklu*)

napāṣu v. (G) "to empty"

//Aram. ⇒ NA//

This NA word occurs in a cultic text from Assur (KAR 215 ii 15 = VAT 8882 (+) VAT 10464 (PKTA 16)). In AHw. (p. 736a s.v. *napāṣu* II), the word is read *i-na-piṣ* and tentatively glossed "ausleeren," and is considered to be an Aramaic foreign word in NA.[1743] In contrast, the editors of CAD (N/I, p. 288a s.v. **napāṣu* B) express doubt about the reading of this word, which they refer to as *i-ba*(or -*na*?)-PIŠ with uncertain meaning.

In his articles on Aramaic loanwords, von Soden took *i-na-piṣ* to be a loanword from Aramaic *npṣ*.[1744] The editors of DNWSI (p. 741 s.v. *npṣ*) regard von Soden's interpretation as highly uncertain. Abraham and Sokoloff, on the other hand, state that this word ought to be eliminated because both its reading and meaning are doubtful.[1745]

The word is now collated and read differently in SAA XX 15 ii 15′, as *i-ba*[!]-*kir*, and is tentatively translated as "he *sprinkles*." It is taken to be derived from the verb *bakāru* "to sprinkle?"[1746] AEAD (p. 12b s.v. *bakāru*) tentatively lists the word with the meaning "to sprinkle?"

> SAA XX 15 ii 15′ reads as follows:
>
> ZÍD.DA.MEŠ *i-ba*[!]-*kir*
>
> He *sprinkles* flour.

Hence, the word *napāṣu* II in AHw. and **napāṣu* B in CAD in the sense "to empty" is a "ghost word" and ought to be stricken out as stemming from erroneous reading.

[1743] Cf. the earlier reading of the word as *i-na-piš* in, E. Ebeling, "Kultische Texte aus Assur," *Or* 20 (1951), p. 402 ii 15.
[1744] See von Soden *Or* 37 (1968), p. 261:100; idem, *Or* 46 (1977), p. 191:100. Cf. Nili, p. 275:115.
[1745] See Abraham & Sokoloff, *Reassessment*, p. 43:150.
[1746] See the Glossary of SAA XX, p. 171a s.v. *bakāru*.

nasīku, *nasikku* (pl. m. & f. *nasīkāni*, *nasīkāti*) n. "sheikh, chieftain"

//Aram. ⇒ NA//

In AHw. (p. 754a s.v. *nasīku* II), this word is glossed "Aramäerscheich," and is tentatively considered to be a borrowing from Aramaic. The editors of CAD (N/II, p. 27a s.v. *nasīku*) render the word as "chieftain, sheikh," and consider it to be a foreign word without specifying its origin. According to CDA (p. 243b s.v. *nasīku* II), the word is also attested in MA in the sense "sheikh, tribal leader."[1747] In NA and NB textual sources, *nasīku* usually designates the head of an Aramean clan.[1748] In SB there is another word, namely *nasīkūtu* "rank or position of a sheikh."[1749]

In his articles on Aramaic loanwords, von Soden considers the origin of the word *nasīku* to be the Official Aramaic noun *nəsīḵā*.[1750] A similar noun is also attested in Biblical Hebrew as נָסִיךְ "prince."[1751] Nevertheless, Abraham and Sokoloff state that the Biblical Hebrew designation does not refer to Arameans, but to rulers of various nations.[1752] They also add that the term is definitely foreign in Akkadian, and is probably of West-Semitic origin, but certainly not from Aramaic.[1753]

According to Eph'al, the title [lú]*nasīku* means leaders of West-Semitic nomads in general.[1754] The supposedly Aramaic source word was thought to be occurring as *nsyky* in the Proverbs of Aḥīqar.[1755] However, according to Porten and Yardeni, *nsyky* is now read differently, as *ksyky* (*ksy* "covering" + *-ky* suffix 2p. f. sg., lapsus for suffix 2p. m. sg.).[1756] Lipiński also remarks that *nsyky* ought to be read *ksyky* in the Proverbs of Aḥīqar.[1757] He points out that the Biblical Hebrew *nāsīk* "prince," or "sheikh," is translated by the Targum into Aramaic *rabrəbē* "great men, princes," which leads to the understanding that *nasīku* is not an Aramaic word.[1758] Therefore, Lipiński rules out the hypothesis of an Aramaic origin of the

---

1747 Cf. M. Sigrist, "Miscellanea," *JCS* 34 (1982), p. 246:5; K. Deller, W.R. Mayer & W. Sommerfeld, "Akkadische Lexikographie: *CAD* N," *Or* 56 (1987), p. 215 ad [27]; E.J. Pentiuc, "West Semitic Terms in Akkadian Texts from Emar," *JNES* 58 (1999), p. 93.

1748 See P.-E. Dion, *Les Araméens à l'âge du fer: histoire politique et structures sociales* (Paris 1997), pp. 233–235; J.A. Brinkman, *A Political History of Post-Kassite Babylonia 1158–722 B.C.* (Rome 1968), p. 274.

1749 See CAD (N/II, p. 28a s.v. *nasīkūtu*). Cf. AHw. (p. 754a s.v. *nasīkūtu*).

1750 See von Soden *Or* 37 (1968), p. 261:101; idem, *Or* 46 (1977), p. 191:101.

1751 See Dalman, p. 260a. Cf. נְסַךְ in Jastrow (p. 917a s.v. נְסִיךְ).

1752 See Abraham & Sokoloff, *Reassessment*, p. 43:152.

1753 Ibid.

1754 See I. Eph'al, *The Ancient Arabs: Nomads on the Borders of the Fertile Crescent 9th–5th Centuries B.C.* (Leiden 1982), p. 93, n. 300.

1755 See E.Y. Kutscher, "Aramaic," in T.A. Sebeok (ed.), *Current Trends in Linguistics*, 6. *Linguistics in South West Asia and North Africa* (The Hague 1970), p. 357. See also DNWSI (p. 735 s.v. *nsyk*).

1756 See B. Porten & A. Yardeni, *Textbook of Aramaic Documents from Ancient Egypt, III Literature, Accounts, Lists* (Jerusalem 1993), p. 46, C1.1, 167.

1757 See E. Lipiński, *The Aramaeans: Their Ancient History, Culture, Religion* (Leuven 2000), p. 494.

1758 Ibid.

term *nasīku*.[1759] Instead, he suggests that the title *nasīku* ought to be interpreted in the light of the North-Arabian term *musuk*, which refers to the ceremonies of the spring pilgrimage and sacrifices and must be a borrowing from Babylonian *nisakku* "first offering; spring," as well as in the light of the Akkadian word *nešakku* "priest."[1760] In fact, the latter is a Sumerian loanword in Akkadian.[1761] On the other hand, Parpola finds a possible connection between *nasīku* and the noun *niššīku(m)* with a variant as *naššīku(m)*, meaning "prince," attested in OB and SB as a name and epithet of Ea.[1762] However, according to AHw. (p. 796b s.v. *niššīku(m)*), the origin of this word is unknown.

Hence, based on chronological evidence, as well as the fact that the word never occurs in Aramaic, the designation *nasīku* cannot be considered a loanword from Aramaic. As it stands, the origin of this noun is uncertain and we have to leave its etymology unsettled in anticipation of further and more decisive data.

niklu (in *niklu nakālu*) n. "ingenuity; trick, deception"

//Aram. ⇒ NA//

The root NKL is attested with various meanings in different Semitic languages.[1763] In Akkadian, *nakālu* has the meaning "to be clever, skilful; to trick, deceive, cheat."[1764] The substantive *niklu*, in NA, NB and SB, bears the meanings "ingenuity; trick, deception."[1765] In Aramaic, the word נכל means "to deceive, cheat, betray, beguile,"[1766] and the verbal noun נִיכְלָא means "deceit, cunning, guile."[1767] However, in AHw. (p. 717b s.v. *nakālu(m)*, mng. no. 3b; p. 789b s.v. *niklu*, mng. no. 2), the expression *niklu nakālu* is considered to be a borrowing from Aramaic meaning "arglistig sein, handeln." On the other hand, neither CAD nor CDA claim a borrowing from Aramaic in this regard.[1768]

In his articles on Aramaic loanwords, von Soden also considers the verbal noun *niklu* in the expression *niklu nakālu* with the meaning "arglistig sein" to be borrowed from Aramaic into NA, NB and LB.[1769] However, the authors of DNWSI (p. 731 s.v. *nkl*$_1$) believe that von Soden's interpretation is less probable. Abraham and Sokoloff state that the nominal form of *niklu* is regular in Akkadian

1759 Ibid., p. 495.
1760 See ibid., pp. 495f.
1761 See AHw. (p. 782b s.v. *nêšakku(m)*); CAD (N/II, p. 190b s.v. *nešakku*). See also S. Lieberman, *The Sumerian Loanwords in Old-Babylonian Akkadian* (Missoula 1977), p. 420 no. 524 B.
1762 S. Parpola (personal communication). Cf. CAD (N/II, p. 282b s.v. *niššīku*).
1763 See the etymological section in C. Brockelmann, *Lexicon Syriacum* (Hildesheim 1995), p. 428b. See also the etymological section in AHw. (p. 717b s.v. *nakālu(m)*).
1764 See CAD (N/I, p. 155a s.v. *nakālu*); AHw. (p. 717b s.v. *nakālu(m)*); AEAD (p. 71b s.v. *nakālu*).
1765 See CAD (N/II, p. 231a s.v. *niklu*); AEAD (p. 77a s.v. *niklu*).
1766 See DJBA (p. 754b s.v. נכל); SL (p. 918b s.v. ܢܟܠ); Audo (p. 588a s.v. ܢܟܠ); Manna, p. 447b; MD, p. 300b; LSp., p. 124a; DSA, p. 526a; CAL.
1767 See DJBA (p. 751a s.v. נִיכְלָא); SL (p. 919a s.v. ܢܟܠܐ); Audo (p. 588a s.v. ܢܟܠܐ); MD, p. 298a.
1768 See CAD, ibid; CDA (p. 233a s.v. *nakālu(m)*).
1769 See von Soden, *Or* 37 (1968), p. 261:99; idem, *Or* 46 (1977), p. 191:99. The expression in question occurs in NA in the following texts: SAA X 183 r.3 (*ni-ik-lu…nak-la*); ABL 523:3–4 (*nik*$^!$-[*lu*] *i-nak*$^!$-*kil*$^!$); SAA II 8 r.13–14 ([*nik-l*]*u* ...*i-nak-kil-an-ni*).

and reject von Soden's interpretation, arguing that there is no convincing reason to presume a borrowing from Aramaic.[1770]

palû v. (G) "to search through"

//Aram. ⇒ NA//

This word occurs in a NA document (ADD 826 r.2), which is a note concerning deported families. It is listed in AHw. (p. 817b s.v. *palû* III) as *pa-li-ʾa* and glossed as "durchsuchen." The word is considered to be an Aramaic foreign word in NA. In his articles on Aramaic loanwords, von Soden takes *pa-li-ʾa* to be borrowed from Aramaic *plʾ* "to scrutinize, to scan."[1771] However, the NA document is now re-edited as SAA XI 172 r.2, where the word under discussion is read differently, as GIŠ.*le-ʾi*, and rendered in the sense "writing-board."[1772] The passage where the word occurs (SAA XI 172 r.1–2), reads as follows:

> PAB 17 ZI.MEŠ / *ša la* GIŠ.*le-ʾi*
>
> In all 17 people, who are not on the writing-board.

Accordingly, the word *palû* in the sense "to search through" ought to be stricken from AHw. as stemming from erroneous reading.[1773] CDA correctly does not list the word *palû* in the sense "to search through." The editors of CAD (P, p. 76a s.v. ***palû*) refer to AHw., but enter the latest reading and interpretation of the word, i.e., GIŠ.*le-ʾi*.

palāḫu v. (G) "to serve"

//Aram. ⇒ NA//

In an article on the Aramaic of upper Mesopotamia in the 7th century B.C., Lemaire states that since in Akkadian, including NA, *palāḫu* usually indicates "to fear, to be terrifying," while in Aramaic the verb *plḥ* means "to serve," one is inclined to take NA *palāḫu* in the sense "to serve" as a borrowing from Aramaic."[1774] In fact, the word *palāḫu* in the sense "to serve, to perform service," is already attested in OA, OB and MA, i.e., before the period of language contact

---

[1770] See Abraham & Sokoloff, *Reassessment*, p. 43:156. Cf. GAG § 55c.

[1771] See von Soden, *Or* 37 (1968), p. 262:110; idem, *Or* 46 (1977), p. 191:110. Cf. DNWSI (p. 911 s.v. *plʾ*$_1$); Tadmor, *Aramaization*, pp. 455, 467 n. 103.

[1772] See also the Glossary of SAA XI (p. 163b s.v. *lēʾu*).

[1773] See preliminary Z. Cherry, *Aramaic Loanwords in NA*: *Rejecting some Proposals*, pp. 23f. See also Abraham & Sokoloff, *Reassessment*, p. 44:163.

[1774] See A. Lemaire, "Remarks on the Aramaic of Upper Mesopotamia in the Seventh Century B.C.," in H. Gzella & M.L. Folmer (eds.), *Aramaic in its Historical and Linguistic Setting* (Wiesbaden 2008), p. 82. Cf. F.M. Fales et al., "An Aramaic Tablet from Tell Shioukh Fawqani, Syria," *Semitica* 46 (1996), p. 97.

between NA and Aramaic.[1775] Therefore, the proposed borrowing from Aramaic into NA must be rejected, mainly based on chronological evidence.

qadduru adj. "blackened"

//Aram. ⇒ NA//

This word occurs in a NA document (ADD 964 r.9) recording copper items. In AHw. (p. 891b s.v. *qadduru*), the word is cited as *qa-dúr*(*u*) and is rendered as "geschwärzt." It is considered to be a loanword from Aramaic קְדַר "to become *or* be black," and is also connected with Arabic قذر "dirty, filthy."[1776] In contrast, the editors of CAD (Q, p. 47a s.v. **qadduru*) cite the NA document and suggest amending the reading of the word to *qa-lu*, i.e., *qallu* in the sense "small." They point to a parallel occurring in the preceding lines as *dannu*, which approximately means "large." At the same time, in CAD (Q, p. 63b s.v. *qallu* mng. no. 3a), the NA document is cited again and the word under discussion is read *qa-lu* meaning "small."

However, the NA document is now edited as (SAA VII 88 r.9), and after collation the word under discussion is read as *qa-lu*! meaning "small."[1777] Accordingly, the word *qadduru* ought to be stricken out of AHw. and CAD for stemming from erroneous reading.[1778] The word *qadduru* is correctly not listed in CDA and AEAD.

qarsu adj. "dry?"

//Aram. ⇒ NA//

In AHw. (p. 905b s.v. *qarsu*), this term is cautiously rendered "trocken," and is tentatively considered to be an Aramaic foreign word occurring in SB as *qar-su*.[1779] In his article on Aramaic loanwords, von Soden lists the word erroneously as NA.[1780] In fact, the word occurs in a Standard Babylonian text (KADP 21 a 12 = VIO 28).[1781]

1775 See CAD (P, p. 45b s.v. *palāḫu* no. 5); AHw. (p. 813a s.v. *palāḫu*(*m*) no. 4).

1776 See also von Soden, *Or* 46 (1977), p. 192:198. Cf. DNWSI (p. 993 s.v. *qdr*$_3$). Cf. also Tadmor, *Aramaization*, pp. 455, 467 no. 104.

1777 See also the Glossary of SAA VII (p. 220a s.v. *qallu*). Cf. the parallel (*dan-nu-te* … QÀL.MEŠ) in a NA text from Calah/Nimrud (CTN II 155 ii 13–15, 18–19).

1778 Cf. preliminary Z. Cherry, *Aramaic Loanwords in NA*: *Rejecting some Proposals*, p. 24. Cf. also Abraham & Sokoloff, *Reassessment*, p. 45:174.

1779 Cf. CAD (Q, p. 145 s.v. *qarrišu* and *qarsu*); CDA (p. 285b s.v. *qarrišu*); DNWSI (p. 1035 s.v. *qrs*$_2$).

1780 See von Soden, *Or* 46 (1977), p. 192:200.

1781 See F. Köcher, *Keilschrifttexte zur assyrisch-babylonischen Drogen- und Pflanzenkunde: Texte der Serien* uru.an.na: maltakal, HAR.ra: hubullu *und* Ú GAR-šú. (KADP = VIO 28). Berlin: Akademie-Verlag, 1955. For further discussion on this SB word, see Nili, p. 279:128; Abraham & Sokoloff, *Reassessment*, p. 46:180.

qi'ʾu, *qinʾu* n. "envy"

//Aram. ⇒ NA//

This NA word is attested in the expression EN–*qi-ʾi*, which occurs in Esarhaddon's succession treaty (VTE, p. 53:328 = Iraq 20, 53:328).[1782] The word is listed in AHw. (p. 924b s.v. *qiʾu*), but its meaning is given as unknown. In the addenda and corrigenda section of AHw. (p. 1584b s.v. *qinʾu*), the word is transcribed differently and rendered as "Neid."[1783] On the other hand, CAD (Q, p. 285a s.v. *qiʾu*) glosses the word as "envious, jealous person."[1784]

In his article on Aramaic loanwords, von Soden normalizes the term as **qinʾu* (or *qiʾʾu*?) in the sense "envy," and states that the word is a borrowing from Aramaic קְנָא "to be jealous," if it is not a loanword from Phoenician.[1785] Abraham and Sokoloff reject von Soden's interpretation, which they think is fraught with difficulties, and argue that the context of the phrase where the word occurs is uncertain.[1786]

However, the word *qiʾʾi* in the expression *bēl qiʾʾi* is expected to be derived from the Semitic root QNʾ, which means, among other things, "envy." The form of the NA word exhibits complete assimilation of the second radical *n* to the following glottal stop ʾ (hamza): *qiʾʾu* < *qinʾu*.[1787] Interestingly, the word is also attested as *qa-ʾi* "envy" in a NA letter from Calah/Nimrud (SAA XIX 91 r.22).[1788] Most importantly, however, a predecessor of NA *qiʾʾu* "envy" is now attested as *qinʾum* in an Old Assyrian text from Kārum Kaneš (Kültepe).[1789] Veenhof notes that "*qinʾum* must be the same word as Hebrew/Aramaic *qinʾā*, which is also once attested in Neo-Assyrian, in *bēl qí-ʾi*."[1790] This provides a precursor in Assyrian before the NA and Aramaic language contact. Accordingly, von Soden's suggested borrowing from Aramaic must be rejected based on the chronology evidence.

salāʾu v. (Š) "to insult"

//Aram. ⇒ NA//

[1782] See D.J. Wiseman, "The Vassal-Treaties of Esarhaddon," *Iraq* 20 (1958), p. 53:328. For the latest re-edition of the Vassal-Treaties, see SAA II 6:328. See also the Glossary of SAA II (p. 100a s.v. *qiʾʾu*).

[1783] Cf. CDA (p. 289b s.v. *qinû(m)*).

[1784] Cf. AEAD (p. 88b s.v. *qiʾʾu*), where the expression *bēl qiʾʾi* is rendered as "envier, jealous person."

[1785] See von Soden, *Or* 46 (1977), p. 193:204. Cf. AHw. (p. 897a s.v. *qannāʾu*). Cf. also DNWSI (p. 1014 s.v. *qnʾ*$_2$).

[1786] See Abraham & Sokoloff, *Reassessment*, p. 47:187.

[1787] Cf. K. Watanabe, *Die adê-Vereidigung anlässlich der Thronfolgeregelung Asarhaddons* (Berlin 1987), p. 186, § 28, n. 328.

[1788] See n. ad SAA XIX 91 r.22. See also the Glossary of SAA XIX (p. 245b s.v. *qaʾʾu, qiʾʾu*).

[1789] See K.R. Veenhof, *Kültepe tabletleri V: The Archive of Kuliya, son of Ali-abum (Kt. 92/k 188–263)*, (Ankara 2010), p. 112, n. on l. 12.

[1790] Ibid.

Aram. ⇒ SB [?]

This word is attested as *tu-šá-as-li* in a unique composition depicting an Assyrian prince's vision of the underworld (ZA 43, 17:58).[1791] In AHw. (p. 1015a s.v. *salā'u(m)* II, Š), the word is rendered "mißachten," and is tentatively considered to be an Aramaism in NA. In CDA (p. 314a s.v. *salā'u(m)* II, Š), the word is cautiously regarded as an Aramaic loanword in NA meaning "disdain, neglect." On the other hand, the editors of CAD (S, p. 98a s.v. *salā'u* B, b) iv) note that the word under discussion should probably be restored as *tušaṣli[m]*.

Nevertheless, the text where the word is attested is now re-edited as (SAA III 32 r.18), and *tu-šá-as-li* is translated as "you insult."[1792] Although the word *tušasli* might be a borrowing from Aramaic *sly* "to despise," as suggested by AHw., the text under discussion is not a NA text but rather a SB text from Assyria.[1793] Accordingly, corrections in AHw., CDA and CAD are required.

samādiru n. "flower; oil of blossom"

//Aram. ⇒ NA//

Syr., JLA *smdr, smdr'* (*smāḏar, smāḏrā*) n. m. "blossom, young shoots of the vine, vine-buds" SL 1016b; PSm. 380a; Manna 498b; Audo 645a; Jastrow 998b; CAL. JBA, Ma., *smdr'* (*sīmadrā*) n. m. "blossom" DJBA 805b; MD 327a; CAL.

The word *samādiru* occurs as a *dis legomenon* in NA. It is attested in a short label from Calah (ND 2303:1), from 724 B.C., in the reign of Shalmaneser V.[1794] In addition, it is attested in a miniature label also from Calah (ND 2304:2).[1795] The two NA texts read as follows:[1796]

ND 2303:1–r.2, reads:

Ì *sa-ma-di-ri* / MÍ.*mar-i-di* / ITI.GUD UD-21-KÁM / *lim-mu* ^{m}*aš-šur–*ḪAL-*a-ni*

Oil of Samadir (*issued to*) the woman Mārīddi, 21st of May, 724 B.C.

ND 2304:1–r.1, reads:[1797]

Ì.MEŠ / ŠEM.*sa-ma-di-ir* / *ša* MÍ.*a-ḫu-ú-a*

[1791] See von Soden, "Die Unterweltsvision eines assyrischen Kronprinzen: Nebst einigen Beobachtungen zur Vorgeschichte des Aḫiqar-Romans," *ZA* 43 (1936), p. 17:58.
[1792] See also the Glossary of SAA III (p. 146b s.v. *salû*, Š).
[1793] See a brief description of text no. 32 in SAA III, p. xxviii. Cf. AEAD (p. 97b s.v. *salā'u*). Cf. also the Syriac meanings in SL (p. 1013a s.v. ܣܠܐ).
[1794] See B. Parker, "Administrative Tablets from the North-West Palace, Nimrud," *Iraq* 23 (1961), p. 19, pl. ix.
[1795] Ibid.
[1796] The transliterations of the texts are taken from the Corpus of Neo-Assyrian Texts (CNA).
[1797] For a note on the meaning of *samādiru*, see Parker, ibid., p. 20.

Oil of Samadir belonging to the woman Aḫū'a.

In AHw. (p. 1016b s.v. *samādiru*), this word is glossed "Blüte," and is considered to be a loanword in NA from Aramaic סְמַדְרָא.[1798] In CDA (p. 314b s.v. *samādiru*), it is glossed "flower; oil of blossom," and is considered to be an Aramaic loanword in NA. The editors of CAD (S, p. 107a s.v. *samādiru*) define the word as (an oleiferous aromatic plant), and refer to von Soden for a possible connection with Aramaic סְמַדְרָא.

Abraham and Sokoloff reject an Aramaic origin of *samādiru*, arguing that the form of the word clearly indicates that it is not of Aramaic origin, but rather was borrowed into Semitic.[1799] Tawil, on the other hand, is of the opinion that one may better consider NA *samādiru* to be of West-Semitic origin in light of an ancient Hebrew inscription written on a wine jar from Hazor ca. 732–740 B.C., which reads: לפקח סמדר "to Peqah, savoring wine."[1800] Nili also considers the word to be a borrowing from West-Semitic, but not from Aramaic.[1801]

It has been suggested that *samādiru* is derived from the root MDR in the sense "to turn over, turn upside down," with an *s* as a prefix,[1802] but the word is probably derived from a quadrilateral root SMDR. In JBA the word is attested as סִימַדְרָא "blossom," and in Syriac as ܣܡܕܪ̈ܐ "blossom."[1803] On the other hand, Syriac ܣܰܡܕܰܪ "to blossom, put forth blossoms" is a denominative verb from ܣܡܕܪ̈ܐ.[1804] The word is also attested in Biblical Hebrew as סְמָדַר "berry (in the budding stage)."[1805] In one of the NA texts, namely ND 2304:2, the word is preceded by the determinative ŠEM, which signifies perfume or scent plants. This corroborates the semantic connection between the NA, Aramaic and Hebrew words.

Morphologically, the nominal form of the NA word seems to be non-Akkadian, and therefore suggests a borrowing.[1806] Phonologically, the loan hypothesis clashes with the well-known rule of the shift of sibilants between West-Semitic and NA. If the NA word is borrowed from West-Semitic or specifically from Aramaic, it is expected to appear as *šamādiru* due to the *š* ⋛ *s* interchange between alphabetic and NA cuneiform renderings.[1807] Perhaps *samādiru* was a foreign word which was independently borrowed into NA and West-Semitic.

1798 See also von Soden, *Or* 46 (1977), p. 193:212. Cf. DNWSI (p. 791 s.v. *smdr*).

1799 See Abraham & Sokoloff, *Reassessment*, p. 49:204.

1800 See H. Tawil, *An Akkadian Lexical Companion for Biblical Hebrew* (Jersey City 2009), p. 264a s.v. סְמָדַר. Cf. Jastrow (p. 998b s.v. סְמָדַר).

1801 See Nili, p. 214:98, with reference to literature on a Hebrew cognate.

1802 See M. Wagner, *Die lexikalischen und grammatikalischen Aramaismen im alttestamentlichen Hebräisch* (Berlin 1966), p. 88:203, with previous literature.

1803 See DJBA, p. 805b; SL, p. 1016b.

1804 See Manna (p. 498b s.v. ܣܡܕܪ̈ܐ). Cf. I. Löw, *Aramäische Pflanzennamen* (Leipzig 1881), p. 89.

1805 See Jastrow, p. 998b.

1806 Cf. GAG § 57c.

1807 Cf. above, n. 71.

samāku v. (D) “to support”

//Aram. ⇒ NA//

This verb is attested in the D-stem as *us-sa-am-mì-ik* in an unclear context in a NA letter (ABL 611 r.4). The editors of CAD (S, p. 110a s.v. *samāku*, mng. no. 3b) do not translate this word, and consider its meaning to be uncertain.[1808] In AHw. (p. 1017a s.v. *samāku(m)*, D mng. no. 2), the term is rendered “stützen,” and is considered to be a loanword in NA borrowed from Aramaic *smk*, which has the basic meaning “to support, sustain, uphold.”[1809]

In a slightly different approach, Fales takes *samāku* in the same NA text as a verbal loan with the meaning “to support,” and taking into consideration the regular NA phonological development *š* + *t* > *ss* argues in favor of reconciling it with West-Semitic root SMK “to support.”[1810] He then suggests to list the verbal form involved, i.e., *us-sa-am-mì-ik*, under an additional lexeme as **šamāku*, due to the *š* ⋛ *s* interchange between alphabetic and NA cuneiform renderings.[1811] ABL 611 is now edited as SAA XIII 44, but according to the context, *us-sa-am-mì-ik* is tentatively rendered “to damage,” and is taken to be derived from *samāku* “(D) to damage(?).”[1812] The passage where the word occurs (SAA XIII 44:9′–r.6) reads as follows:[1813]

> *a-na-ku* GIŠ.GIGIR *ra-qu-te-šá* / ˹*e*˺-*t*[*e*]-*l*[*i*$^{?}$ *x x x t*]*al-la-ka* // [*ma-a k*]*aq-qu-ru sa-ni-qi* / *ma-a* ˹*a*$^{?}$-*na*$^{?}$˺ GIŠ.*še-er-ni at-taḫ-rid*$^{!?}$ / *si-ip-pu ša* GIŠ.BANŠUR *ù pa*$^{!}$-*ni*$^{!}$ / *ša ṣa-al-*[*me*] *us-sa-am-mì-ik* / É$^{!}$ *ke-e-tú ina* UGU *kaq-qi-ri* / [*i*]*n-*[[*qu*]]*-tú-qu-tu*
>
> I myself *asce*[*nded*] the chariot when it was empty. It kept going [*all right*], but the ground was *narrow* and while I *paid attention* to the chariot’s ..., I *damaged* the rim of the table and the front side of the image. The house truly fell to the ground!

Nevertheless, the editors of DNWSI (p. 792 s.v. smk_1) consider the interpretation given in AHw. to be highly uncertain. Also Abraham and Sokoloff consider the context where the word under discussion occurs to be unclear. The verb *samāku* in the D-stem appears as *ú-sa-me-ka-ni* in a NA literary text (SAA III 16 r.12), and based on the context it is translated as “terrible.”[1814] It also occurs as *ú-sam-ma-ak-ak-ku-nu-ni*, in a NA letter (SAA XXI 65 r.20′ = BM 132980 r.20′ = JCS 54 82 r.20′).[1815] Additional attestations of *samāku* in the D-stem are

---

[1808] See also CAD (S, p. 303b s.v. *sippu* A, mng. no. 4a).

[1809] See also von Soden, *Or* 46 (1977), p. 194:213; CDA (p. 314b s.v. *samāku(m)*, D).

[1810] See F.M. Fales, “Assyro-Aramaica: Three Notes,” *Or* 53 (1984), p. 69, n. 14. See also Luukko, SAAS XVI, § 4.2.4. Cf. Hämeen-Anttila, SAAS XIII, § 2.2.3.1.

[1811] Fales, ibid., p. 69, n. 14. Cf. above, n. 71.

[1812] See n. ad SAA XIII 44 r.3–4. See also the Glossary of SAA XIII (p. 192b s.v. *samāku*). Cf. AEAD (p. 97b s.v. *samāku*).

[1813] Cf. the discussion below s.v. *šernu* “axle, axis.”

[1814] See the Glossary of SAA III (p. 146b s.v. *samāku*), where this word is glossed “to treat harshly.”

[1815] See M.W. Waters, “A Letter from Ashurbanipal to the Elders of Elam (BM 132980),” *JCS* 54 (2002): 79–86. See further the commentary on lines 19′–20′, ibid., p. 84. Cf. the translation of the

found in a NA letter (SAA XXI 121:5′, 10′, 11′ = ABL 1148:5′, 10′, 11′), and are respectively attested as *us-sa-me-ku*, *us-sa-am-me-ek*, and *lu-sa-am-me-ek*. However, SAA XXI renders the meaning of *samāku* in all these instances as "to treat harshly, to do terrible things."[1816] Since the context where our word occurs in the NA letter (SAA XIII 44:9′–r.6) is unclear, the meaning of the word cannot be decisively established.

saqālu v. (D) "to smooth, polish"

//Aram. ⇒ NA//

According to AHw. (p. 1027b s.v. *saqālu* II), this is an Aramaic foreign word which occurs in a NA text from Calah (ND 2759 = Iraq 20, 182, 30), as *lu-saq-qí-lu* with the meaning "glätten, polieren."[1817] The NA text concerned is a letter from the Assyrian king Sargon II referring to Midas of Phrygia. However, the same text is also quoted in CAD (Š/III, p. 219a s.v. *šukkulu*, c),[1818] where the word in question is transliterated differently, as *lu-šak-ki-lu*, and its origin is considered to be the Akkadian verb *šukkulu* "to wipe," which is attested from OB onward. Later, a correction was made in the addenda and corrigenda section of AHw. (p. 1590b s.v. *šukkulu(m)* D), where *saqālu* II is corrected and subsumed under the Akkadian heading *šukkulu(m)*, in the sense "aus-, abwischen." The NA letter is re-edited as SAA I 1:30, and also there the word is transliterated *lu-šak-ki-lu* meaning "to wipe."[1819] The passage where the word occurs (SAA I 1:28–30), reads as follows:

> *aš-šur* ^{d}UTU EN *u* ^{d}PA / *liq-bi-u* LUGAL.MEŠ-*ni ḫa-an-nu-ti gab-bi-šú-nu* TA* *ziq-ni-šú-nu* / KUŠ.DA.E.SIR-*ka lu-šak-ki-lu*
>
> Aššūr, Šamaš, Bēl and Nabû command that all these kings should wipe your sandals with their beards!

Accordingly, the suggested Aramaic foreign word ought to be stricken off the list of Aramaic loanwords in NA for stemming from erroneous reading.[1820]

---

same passage in CAD (S, p. 110a s.v. *samāku* 3 mng. a). See also Luukko, SAAS XVI, p. 65 s.v. šam 318 (Ú), p. 96 s.v. (klm D).

1816 See the Glossary section of SAA XXI (p. 155a s.v. *samāku*).

1817 See also von Soden, *Or* 37 (1968), p. 266:131; idem, *Or* 46 (1977), p. 194:131. Cf. H.W.F. Saggs, "The Nimrud Letters, 1952–Part IV: The Urarṭian Frontier," *Iraq* 20 (1958), p. 182, 39:30; idem, CTN V, pp. 188ff; J.N. Postgate, "Assyrian Texts and Fragments," *Iraq* 35 (1973), pp. 21f no. 5; Tadmor, *Aramaization*, pp. 455, 467 n. 107. Cf. DNWSI (p. 801 s.v. *sql*).

1818 Cf. CAD (S, p. 168a s.v. ***saqālu*).

1819 See the Glossary of SAA I (p. 227a s.v. *šakkulu*). See also AEAD (p. 109a s.v. *šakkulu*).

1820 See Abraham & Sokoloff, *Reassessment*, p. 49:209.

***suānu** v. (G) "to punish"

//Aram. ⇒ NA//

The enigmatic word *a-su-na*[!]*-ka*, which occurs in a NA letter (SAA V 31 r.21′), is a *hapax legomenon* and is difficult to explain. The editors of SAA V made a tentative attempt to interpret this word based on the context. They analyzed the word as a present tense derived from an otherwise unattested Akkadian verb **swn* "to punish," which in turn is taken from a supposedly Syriac word **šnw* "to punish, abuse; to inflict severe pain, punishment, torture."[1821] This implies a borrowing from a supposed Aramaic word **šnw*, which in NA underwent the phonological development *š* > *s*, to correspond to the *š* ⋛ *s* interchange between alphabetic and NA cuneiform renderings, and also underwent metathesis of the second and third radicals *n* and *w*. Hence: **šnw* > **snw* > **swn*.

However, closer examination of the suggested Syriac source word makes it obvious that the Syriac ܫܢܩ "to punish, abuse, to inflict severe pain" was erroneously read and transcribed as *šnw*, i.e., ܫܢܘ.[1822] Most importantly, however, no verb of type III*w* is extant in Syriac or Aramaic, because all verbs there of the types III*y*, III*w* and III' have merged into the verbal group III*y*.[1823] Accordingly, the interpretation that *a-su-na*[!]*-ka* is taken from Aramaic **šnw* is incorrect. For now, the origin and meaning of *a-su-na*[!]*-ka* remain unsettled.

sumāmītu n. f. "poisonous matter, poisonous substance"

Loanword	Reference	Provenance	Origin	Genre	Date
su-ma-me-tú	SAA XXI 104 r.2	Nineveh	Babylonia	L	Asb

//Aram. ⇒ NA//

Syr., JPA *smmy, smmyt'* (*smāmī, smāmīṯā*) n. f. "gecko, poisonous lizard" Manna 498a; Audo 644a; SL 1020b; DJPA 382b; CAL. Syr., JBA *sm, sm'* (*sam, sammā*) n. m "poison; medicine" Manna 497b; Audo 643b; SL 1016a; DJBA 817b; CAL.

This word occurs as a *hapax legomenon* in NA. It is attested in a letter (SAA XXI 104 r.2 = ABL 1385:13) sent to the Assyrian king Assurbanipal by his brother Šamaš-šumu-ukīn mentioning the Elamite crown prince Ummanigaš and concerning the passage of certain boats.

AEAD (p. 101a s.v. *sumāmītu*), lists a feminine singular form of the word in the sense "poisonous matter." As with other *hapax legomena*, the possibility of

---

[1821] See n. ad SAA V 31 r.21′. Cf. the words section of the Register Assyriologie: *AfO* (1993/1994), p. 482b s.v. **swn*.

[1822] See PSm., (p. 587b s.v. ܫܢܩ).

[1823] See Ch. Müller-Kessler, "Zu dem Hapax legonemon [*sic*] *a-su-na-ka* ABL 139+," *NABU* 1991/62. Cf. preliminary Z. Cherry, *Aramaic Loanwords in NA*: *Rejecting some Proposals*, p. 24.

establishing the meaning of *sumāmītu* is determined by the sentence context, here SAA XXI 104:13– r.2, which reads:

> ^{m}*um-man-ni-gaš / am-mì-i* DUMU–MAN LUGAL *ú-da / ra-as-mu šu-u mu-uk / pi-iq-ta-a-te ina* ŠÀ *it-tu-sa-te*$^{!}$ */ ša* ŠE$^{!}$ ⌜PAD$^{!}$⌝.MEŠ *an-ni-ti / me-me-ni e-pa-šá*$^{!}$ [0] */ su-ma-me-tú i-kar-ra-á*[*r*$^{!}$]
>
> The king knows that Ummanigaš, that crown prince, is *hot-headed.* I thought, "Perhaps he will put something in the *sacks* holding this grain and cause *poisoning.*"

Parpola rendered the word *su-ma-me-tú*, from the passage above, in the sense "poisonous matter" and explained that this *hapax legomenon* is probably an Aramaic loanword.[1824] He adduced the Syriac word ܣܰܡܶܡ "to poison," derived from the word ܣܡܐ "poison; drug" as a possible etymon for the NA word.

Phonologically, the proposed Aramaic etymon as found in the Syriac word *samem* "to poison," clashes with the rule of the shift of sibilants between NA and Aramaic. The proposed Aramaic loanword is expected to appear as *šumāmītu* or *šamāmītu* in NA in accordance with the *š* ⋛ *s* interchange between the alphabetic and NA cuneiform renderings.[1825] Semantically, the rendering of the NA word *sumāmītu* in the sense "poisonous matter/substance" is based only on a single context which is not entirely clear. According to the evidence available at hand, a borrowing from Aramaic into NA cannot be determined with certainty. As it stands, the origin of *sumāmītu* is unclear and we have to leave its etymology unsettled in anticipation of further and more decisive data.

sūsānu n. "horse trainer, groom"

//Aram. ⇒ NA//

This word is already attested in MA and also occurs frequently in NA as *sūsānu* with the meaning "horse trainer, groom."[1826] In NB and LB it is attested as *šušānu* and has the same meaning as the Assyrian word, but it also refers to (a class of state dependants). In AHw. (p. 1288b s.v. *šušānu*), the term is glossed "Diener, Betreuer," and is considered to be a loanword from Imperial Aramaic *šušānā* "Diener."[1827] In contrast, Mayrhofer has shown that the etymology of the Akkadian term is found in the Indo-Iranian term *aśva-śani* which includes the word *aśva-* "horse," and means "horse trainer."[1828] The editors of CAD (Š/III, p. 379b s.v. *šušānu*) note in the commentary section that this term is a loanword from Indo-Iranian *aśva-śani* "looking after horses," and was transmitted via MA

[1824] See n. ad SAA XXI 104 r.2. See also the Glossary section of SAA XXI (p. 155b s.v. *sumāmītu*).
[1825] Cf. above, n. 71.
[1826] See AEAD (p. 101b s.v. *sūsānu*).
[1827] See also von Soden, *Or* 46 (1977), p. 196:234. Cf. DNWSI (p. 1197 s.v. *ššn*$_2$).
[1828] See M. Mayrhofer, "Zu den arischen Sprachresten in Vorderasien," *Die Sprache* 5 (1959), p. 87.

and NA to NB.[1829] Abraham and Sokoloff state that the meaning of the suggested Imperial Aramaic word שושן is unclear, and that any connection between this word and the Akkadian *šušānu* is unsure.[1830] Hence, a borrowing from Aramaic ought to be rejected based on chronological grounds and a possible Indo-Iranian etymology.

ṣāpītu n. f. "tower"

//Aram. ⇒ NA//

PTA, LJLA *ṣpy*, *ṣpyt'* n. f. "watchtower" DJPA 468b; CAL. JPA, JBA, Sam., JLA *ṣpy* v. "to see at a distance, look out, observe" DJPA 468b; DJBA 970b; DSA 741a; Jastrow 1297a; CAL.

The rendering of the word *ṣāpītu* as "(wooden) tower" used for the siege of a walled town was proposed by Oppenheim.[1831] In AHw. (p. 1082a s.v. *ṣāp/bītu*), the word is considered to be an Aramaic foreign word in NA and LB in the sense "Wachtturm (bei Belagerungen)" and is taken to be from Aramaic *spā* "schauen."[1832] According to CAD (Ṣ, p. 97a s.v. *ṣāpītu*), the word is only attested in SB and NB. Abraham and Sokoloff point out that the root ṢPY is well attested in Biblical Hebrew, but consider its existence in Aramaic to be doubtful, making an Aramaic loanword unlikely.[1833] However, there is reference in JPA to the occurrence of the word צפיתה in the sense "watchtower," which is supposedly derived from צפי "to see at a distance, look out, watch."[1834] Nevertheless, the word *ṣāpītu* occurs only in SB and LB, but never in NA.[1835]

ṣappuḫu v. D "to squeeze out"

//Aram. ⇒ NA//

This word occurs as a *hapax legomenon* in NA and is attested in Esarhaddon's succession treaty (SAA II 6:653). In AHw. (p. 1082a s.v. *ṣappuḫu*), this word is hesitatingly glossed "hinausdrücken," and is considered to be an Aramaic foreign word in NA. In contrast, the editors of CAD (S, p. 154a s.v. *sapāḫu* mng. no. 5:a) read the word differently, with an initial *sà* instead of *ṣa*, i.e., *sà-ap-pa-ḫu-u-ni*,

---

[1829] Note that CDA (p. 389a s.v. *šušānu*) also considers the word to be a borrowing from Indo-Iranian.

[1830] See Abraham & Sokoloff, *Reassessment*, p. 54:250.

[1831] A.L. Oppenheim, "Babylonian and Assyrian Historical Texts," in J.B. Pritchard (ed.), *Ancient Near Eastern Texts Relating to the Old Testament* (Princeton 1955), p. 304, n. 8.

[1832] See also von Soden, *Or* 46 (1977), p. 194:217. Cf. CDA (p. 333b s.v. *ṣāpītu*); DNWSI (p. 972 s.v. *ṣpyt*); Tadmor, *Aramaization*, pp. 455, 467 n. 108.

[1833] See Abraham & Sokoloff, *Reassessment*, p. 51:221.

[1834] See DJPA (p. 468b s.v. צְפִי no. 2, and צפי); CAL s.v. *ṣpy*.

[1835] Cf. AEAD (p. 103b s.v. *ṣāpītu*).

render it as "(its water) is spilled," and take it to be derived from *suppuḫḫu* "to scatter, spill."[1836] The passage where the word occurs in the latest edition of the text (SAA II 6:652–655), reads as follows:[1837]

> *ki-i šá* KUŠ.*na-a-du šal-qa-tu-u-ni* A.MEŠ-*šá* / *ṣa-ap-pa-ḫu-u-ni*! *ina kaq-qar ṣu-ma-mit lap-lap-tu* / KUŠ.*na-da-ku-nu lu ta-ḫi-bi* / [*ina ṣ*]*u-um* A.MEŠ *mu-u-ta*
>
> Just as (this) waterskin is split and its water runs out, so may your waterskin break in a place of severe thirst; die [of th]irst!

Wiseman translates the word as "scattered."[1838] In his article on Aramaic loanwords, von Soden considers the meaning of the word perhaps to be "(Wasser) hinausdrücken," and connects it with Syriac ܨܦܚ "fallen."[1839] However, Watanabe notes that the reading *sà-ap-pa-ḫu-u-ni* given in CAD requires taking the first cuneiform sign of the word to be ZA = *sà*, which is foreign to both the NA syllabary and the Vassal-Treaties of Esarhaddon.[1840]

Nevertheless, the root ṢPḤ in Syriac means "to fall upon; to take by surprise, seize; to refute, contradict."[1841] Therefore, Abraham and Sokoloff are skeptical about the loan hypothesis and rightly point out that the semantic connection between NA *ṣappuḫu* and Syriac ܨܦܚ is unclear and that the alternative reading *sà-ap-pa-ḫu-u-ni* eliminates any etymological connection between the NA and Syriac words.[1842]

ṣibtātu n. "fetters?, chains?"

//Aram. ⇒ NA//

This word is attested in a NA administrative document (CTN II 155 iv 19), consisting of a lengthy inventory found in the Governor's Palace archive at Calah/Nimrud. The line where the word occurs reads:

> 2-*te ṣib-ta-*⸢*te*⸣ ⸤AN.BAR.KAL.ME⸥
>
> 2 sets of large iron chains(?)

1836 Note that CDA (p. 316b s.v. *sapāḫu(m)*) lists the NA word as stative of *sapāḫu(m)*, in the D-stem and translates it "(of water) is dissipated." However, following AHw. (p. 1082a s.v. *ṣappuḫu*), the editors of CDA (p. 333b s.v. *ṣappuḫu* D) also list *ṣappuḫu* as an Aramaic loanword in NA meaning "to squeeze out."

1837 The editors of SAA II:6 translate the word under discussion as "(its water) runs out." In the Glossary of SAA II (p. 102a s.v. *ṣapāḫu* D), the word is rendered "to scatter, spill." Cf. AEAD (p. 103b s.v. *ṣappuḫu*).

1838 See Wiseman, VTE, p. 80.

1839 See von Soden, *Or* 46 (1977), p. 194:218. Cf. DNWSI (p. 972 s.v. *ṣpḥ*₁).

1840 See K. Watanabe, *Die adê-Vereidigung anlässlich der Thronfolgeregelung Asarhaddons* (Berlin 1987), p. 208b, n. on l. 653. Cf. Borger, ABZ, no. 586.

1841 See SL (p. 1297a s.v. ܨܦܚ); PSm., (p. 482b s.v. ܨܦܚ).

1842 See Abraham & Sokoloff, *Reassessment*, p. 51:222.

Postgate tentatively translates the word *ṣibtāte* as "chains," and states that this word may be the NA equivalent of the known NB *ṣibtētu* "fetters."[1843] Von Soden, on the other hand, tentatively renders the NA and LB *ṣibtā/ētu* as "Fesseln," stating that it is hardly derived from Akkadian *ṣibtu* I or *ṣibittu*, but probably is a loanword from Aramaic *ṣiḇtā* "Zange."[1844] Contrary to von Soden's suggestion that *ṣibtētu* "fetters" is a borrowing from Aramaic *ṣiḇtā* "pincers, pair of tongs," Cole states that the NB *ṣibtētu* may just be a plural of the Akkadian terms *ṣibtu* or *ṣibittu*.[1845] Referring to Cole's statement, Abraham and Sokoloff also consider von Soden's interpretation to be unlikely.[1846]

Etymologically, the evidence points to an Akkadian origin of the word under discussion. In Akkadian, *ṣabātu* means, among other things, "to imprison, detain a person, to put a person in fetters; to catch, arrest, apprehend a person," and the word *ṣibtu* means, among other things, "imprisonment."[1847] The NB substantive *ṣibtētu*, on the other hand, represents a pl. tant. meaning "fetters, imprisonment."[1848]

ṣipirtu n. f. "(woven) girdle, sash, waist-belt, cummerbund"

//Aram. ⇒ NA//

This word occurs in NA and LB. Gaspa mentions that the word is also attested in NA in the form *ṣipittu* with the assimilation of *rt* > *tt*.[1849] The editors of CAD (Ṣ, p. 201b s.v. *ṣipirtu* A) define the word as (a sash woven or treated in a special technique), and compare it with the Akkadian word *ṣepēru* in the sense "to strand (hair and linen), to dress (hair), to trim, decorate."[1850] In AHw. (p. 1103b s.v. *ṣipirtu* III), the word is tentatively defined as (Band oder Schärpe aus Textilgeflecht), and is tentatively considered to be an Aramaic foreign word[1851] connected with the supposedly Jewish Aramaic צפר "to plait."[1852] The editors of CDA (p. 339a s.v. *ṣipirtu* III) define the word as (an item of clothing), and tentatively consider it to be an Aramaic loanword in NA and NB. In AEAD (p. 105a s.v. *ṣipirtu*) the word is glossed "(woven) girdle, sash, waist-belt, cummerbund." However, according to Abraham and Sokoloff, the supposedly

---

[1843] See n. ad CTN II 155 iv 19–20.

[1844] See von Soden, *Or* 46 (1977), p. 194:220. Cf. AHw. (p. 1097b s.v. *ṣibtā/ētu*). Cf. also CDA (p. 337b s.v. *ṣibtātu*); DNWSI (p. 959 s.v. *ṣbt*$_5$); DJBA (p. 959a s.v. צִיבְתָא no. 1 "tongs").

[1845] See S.W. Cole, *Nippur IV: The Early Neo-Babylonian Governor's Archive from Nippur* (Chicago 1996), p. 71, n. on l. 17.

[1846] See Abraham & Sokoloff, *Reassessment*, p. 51:224, n. 615.

[1847] See CAD (Ṣ, p. 5a s.v. *ṣabātu*, p.163a s.v. *ṣibtu* B). Cf. AEAD (p. 104b s.v. *ṣibtu*).

[1848] See CAD (Ṣ, p. 158a s.v. *ṣibtētu*).

[1849] See S. Gaspa, "Garments, Parts of Garments, and Textile Techniques in the Assyrian Terminology: The Neo-Assyrian Textile Lexicon in the 1st-Millennium BC Linguistic Context," in S. Gaspa et al. (eds.), *Textile Terminologies from the Orient to the Mediterranean and Europe, 1000 BC to 1000 AD* (Lincoln, 2017), p. 76b s.v. *ṣipirtu*. See also ZTT I 8:1 ˹TÚG˺.*ṣi-pi-tú*. Cf. Luukko, SAAS XVI, § 4.2.1, p. 78 s.v. *r* + *t* > [*tt*].

[1850] See CAD (Ṣ, p. 132b s.v. *ṣepēru*), and the concluding remarks in p. 133b.

[1851] Cf. DNWSI (p. 973 s.v. *ṣprh*$_2$).

[1852] See, for instance, Dalman (p. 351a s.v. צְפַר no. 2).

JPA צפר "to weave," has now been shown to be incorrect, and should almost certainly be read as צפד.[1853] Consequently, the loan hypothesis proposed by von Soden in AHw., and in his articles on Aramaic loanwords,[1854] is rejected because the suggested Aramaic source word does not exist.

That *ṣipirtu* refers to an item of clothing is obvious because in cuneiform texts the word is frequently preceded by the sign TÚG, which is a determinative referring to garments. We probably ought to seek the etymology for our word in the Akkadian verb *ṣepēru* "to strand (hair and linen)," which is cognate with the Arabic verb ضَفَرَ "to braid; plait (hair); interweave; interlace, intertwine, twine (a rope)."[1855] If so, the expected underlying root would be *ṢPR.

šapānu v. (G) "to level"

//Aram. ⇒ NA//

This headword in AHw. (1170a s.v. *šapānu*) is glossed "einebnen," and is considered to be an Aramaic foreign word in NA. It refers to a word that appears twice as *i-si-ib/p-nu* in a NA letter (ABL 503 r.5, 7 + CT 53 331 r.5, 7).[1856] Von Soden states that this word is probably not related to Akkadian *sapānu* "to flatten, lay flat," which he considers to have a different usage; instead he connects it with the Syriac verb ܣܦܢ "to smooth, harrow (terrain)."[1857] In contrast, the editors of CAD (Š/1, p. 427b s.v. ***šapānu* (*labānu*)), consider the meaning of this word to be uncertain and, based on the context, they read the word differently as *i-si-ib-nu* and take it most likely to be derived from *labānu* "to mold bricks." Furthermore, they consider the suggested borrowing from Aramaic, as indicated in AHw., to be unnecessary and point out that Aramaic *ś/spn* is cognate with Akkadian *sapānu*.[1858]

Nevertheless, the NA letter (ABL 503+) is now edited as SAA XV 156, and as in CAD, the word in question is read *i-si-ib-nu*. It is understood as a strong verb with *i* as the theme vowel in the G-stem, 3p. m. pl. perfect of *labānu* "to mold bricks," i.e., *issibnū* < **iltibnū* < **iltabnū*, with the Assyrian vowel harmony in analogy with the corresponding singular form **iltibin*.[1859] As is well known, in NA the *t* of the infix *-ta-* undergoes a reciprocal consonantal assimilation to the

---

1853 See Abraham & Sokoloff, *Reassessment*, p. 51:225. Cf. DJPA (p. 468b s.v. צפד).
1854 See von Soden, *Or* 46 (1977), p. 195:221.
1855 See CAD (Ṣ, p. 132b s.v. *ṣepēru*), and the concluding remarks in p. 133b. Cf. Elias & Elias, p. 393a; Wehr-Cowan, p. 543a.
1856 Note that CDA does not list this headword. Cf. DNWSI (p. 1183 s.v. *špn*$_1$).
1857 See von Soden, *Or* 46 (1977), p. 195:225. See also AHw. (p. 1025b s.v. *sapānu*(*m*)); SL (p. 1590a s.v. ܣܦܢ). Cf. preliminary Z. Cherry, *Aramaic Loanwords in NA*: *Rejecting some Proposals*, p. 25. Cf. also Nili, p. 290: 161; Abraham & Sokoloff, *Reassessment*, p. 52:237.
1858 See the concluding remarks in CAD (Š/I, p. 427b s.v. ***šapānu*).
1859 See n. ad SAA XV 156 r.5. For the so-called Assyrian vowel harmony and especially for the uniqueness of the form of the NA word *i-si-ib-nu*, see Hämeen-Anttila, SAAS XIII, § 2.4.5; K. Deller, *Lautlehre des Neuassyrischen* (Wien 1959), p. 154.

preceding dental lateral *l*: *l* + *t* > *ss*.[1860] Hence, according to the analysis given above, the attested NA word *i-si-ib-nu*, ought to be subsumed under *labānu*(*m*) II in AHw., and under *labānu* A in CAD.[1861]

šārītu n. (a metal beam or bar)

//Aram. ⇒ NA//

This NA word was previously read as *šá-a-ri-a-te*. It is mentioned after other bronze objects received as tribute in the annals of Ashurnaṣrpal II (883–859 B.C.).[1862] In AHw. (p. 1187a s.v. *šārītu*), the word is defined as (ein Balken od Barren) and is considered to be a loanword in NA from Aramaic *šārīṯā*.[1863] The editors of CAD (Š/II, p. 63b s.v. *šārītu*) define this word as (a metal beam or bar) and regard it as a foreign word in NA. They compare it with Aramaic *šārīṯā*, for which they refer to von Soden's suggested loan hypothesis,[1864] and they assume that the indicated object is made of metal because it is preceded by other bronze objects.

In contrast, Nili states that the proposed Aramaic origin of this word is questionable and points out that the Aramaic שָׁרִיתָא means "beam of wood," and therefore the Akkadian usage differs from that of its Aramaic counterpart.[1865] Abraham and Sokoloff also believe that the likelihood that this word is related to Aramaic שָׁרִיתָא "beam" is low, because beams were made of wood as is clearly indicated by the Aramaic texts.[1866]

However, Postgate states that the reading of the word as *šá-a-ri-a-te* is suppressed and suggests a different reading, as *ša ariāte*,[1867] consisting of the pron. *ša* "(s)he who, that which; of," and n. f. *arītu* "shield (of leather, wood or metal)."[1868] He also dismisses the pseudo-logographic writing ŠÁ.RI.A.MEŠ, which was suggested in an earlier edition of the text in question, as not firmly attested.[1869] In fact, the expression *ša-arīti* in NA designates "shield-man, (regular) spearman."[1870] Hence, based on the usage of the word as well as the suggested different reading, the proposed Aramaic origin of our word is doubtful.

1860 See Hämeen-Anttila, SAAS XIII, § 2.2.3.1; Luukko, SAAS XVI, § 4.2.4; Deller, ibid., § 43a–b; GAG § 34d.

1861 Cf. CDA (p. 173b s.v. *labānu*(*m*)).

1862 See A.K. Grayson, *Assyrian Rulers of the Early First Millennium BC I* (*1114–859 B.C.*), (Toronto 1991), pp. 207:75, 248:96. For a previous edition, see Budge & King, AKA 321 ii 75.

1863 See also von Soden, *Or* 46 (1977), p. 195:226. Cf. DNWSI (p. 1193 s.v. *šryt*).

1864 Note that the word *šārītu* is not listed in CDA and AEAD.

1865 See Nili, p. 291:164.

1866 See Abraham & Sokoloff, *Reassessment*, p. 52:238. Cf. DJPA (p. 566b s.v. שרי); DJBA (p. 1181a s.v. שָׁרִיתָא no. 1).

1867 The expression *ša ariāte* is probably related to the term *ša-arīti* "shield-man, (regular) spearman." Cf. AEAD (p. 9b s.v. *arītu*); CDA (p. 23b s.v. *arītu*(*m*) II).

1868 See Postgate's comment s.v. [*šārītu*], in the list of queries, additions and corrections made to CDA. Online 15/09/2022: https://www.soas.ac.uk/cda-archive/lemmata/

1869 See Postgate, ibid. Cf. AKA, p. 321.

1870 See AEAD (p. 9b s.v. *arītu*); CDA (p. 23b s.v. *arītu*(*m*) II).

šernu, *širnu* n. "axle; spoke"

//Aram. ⇒ NA//

JBA, Syr., JLA *srn*, *srn*ʾ (*sren*, *sarnā*) n. m. "axle, axis" DJBA 832b; PSm. 392a; SL 1048b; Manna 516a; Audo 672a; CAL. Syr., *srn*ʾ (*sarnā*) n. m. "spoke" SL 1048b; CAL.

In AHw. (p. 1217b s.v *še/irnu(m)*), this word is defined as (ein Holzggst.), and is listed for OB, MA and NA. In CAD (Š/II, p. 317a s.v. *šernu*), the word is defined as (part of a chariot), and is listed for Nuzi, MA and NA. CDA (p. 367b s.v. *šernu(m)*) also defines the word as (a wooden chariot part). In AEAD (p. 115a s.v. *šernu*), the word is glossed "axle, axis."

However, the word *še/irnu* appears twice in NA. It is attested as GIŠ.*ši-ir-nu* in the so-called Practical Vocabulary of Assur (PVA 598), and it also occurs in a letter (SAA XIII 44 r.2) from the 7th century B.C. found in Nineveh. The letter is about a runaway chariot and the word is attested as GIŠ.*še-er-ni* in a context concerning part of the chariot. Parpola suggests that *šernu* here is to be taken as a loanword from Aramaic סַרְנָא "axle, axis; pole," also attested in Syriac as ܣܪܢܐ "axle."[1871] Contextually, the NA word appears to be designating a part of a chariot. The passage where the word occurs, SAA XIII 44:9′–r.6, reads as follows:[1872]

> *a-na-ku* GIŠ.GIGIR *ra-qu-te-šá* / ⌜*e*⌝-*t*[*e*]-*l*[*i*? *x x x t*]*al-la-ka* // [*ma-a k*]*aq-qu-ru sa-ni-qi* / *ma-a* ⌜*a*?-*na*?⌝ GIŠ.*še-er-ni at-taḫ-rid*!? / *si-ip-pu ša* GIŠ.BANŠUR *ù pa*!-*ni*! / *ša ṣa-al-*[*me*] *us-sa-am-mì-ik* / É! *ke-e-tú ina* UGU *kaq-qi-ri* / [*i*]*n*-[[*qu*]]-*tú-qu-tu*
>
> I myself *asce*[*nded*] the chariot when it was empty. It kept going [*all right*], but the ground was *narrow* and while I *paid attention* to the chariot's *axle*, I *damaged* the rim of the table and the front side of the image. The house truly fell to the ground!

The Aramaic word, on the other hand, is found in JBA as סַרְנָא n. m. "axle, axis," such as in the expression סַרְנָא דְרֵיחְיָא "axle of the millstone."[1873] It is also found in Syriac as ܣܪܢܐ n. m. "axle, axis," such as in the expression ܣܪܢܐ ܕܓܝܓܠܬܐ ܕܡܪܟܒܬܗ "the axle of the wheels of his chariot."[1874] Moreover, the Syriac word also designates "spoke," as found in the following passage: ܓܝܓܠܐ ܕܠܝܬ ܠܗܘܢ ܣܪܢܐ ܠܐ ܡܥܕܪܢ ܠܡܕܡ "wheels without spokes are not useful for anything."[1875]

[1871] S. Parpola (personal communication).

[1872] Note that SAA XIII 44 r.2, leaves the word GIŠ.*še-er-ni* untranslated. However, in the Glossary of SAA XIII (p. 196b s.v. *šernu*), the word is defined as (a part of a chariot).

[1873] See DJBA (p. 832b s.v. סַרְנָא).

[1874] See SL (p. 1048b s.v. ܣܪܢܐ).

[1875] See ibid. See also CAL, s.v. *srn*.

However, the word is attested in a Nuzi text as GIŠ.*ši-ir-nu*, in connection with chariot.[1876] It is also attested as GIŠ.*ši-ir-nu* in a MA text, among other chariot parts.[1877] Accordingly, a forerunner for the NA word is already found in the Nuzi and MA dialects. Chronologically, the evidence points to a borrowing from NA into Aramaic, not the other way around. Based on the Aramaic evidence, on the other hand, it is now possible to retrieve, with certainty, the meaning of the Akkadian word *še/irnu* as "axle; spoke."

šubbuḫu v. (D) (mng. uncertain)

Aram. ⇒ NB?

The word under discussion occurs in a NB letter (ABL 968:6) concerning events in Babylonia. In AHw. (p. 1256b s.v. *šubbuḫu*), this word is glossed "(Gott) preisen," and is regarded as an Aramaic foreign word in NB.[1878] Von Soden considers it to be borrowed from the Aramaic word *šabbaḥ*.[1879] In CAD (Š/III, p. 171a s.v. *šubbuḫu*), the meaning of this NB word is given as uncertain, and a reference to von Soden's suggested borrowing from Aramaic is provided.

The letter is now re-edited as (SAA XIII 179:6′), and the word *ú-šab-ba-aḫ* is tentatively translated as "I will *disperse*," derived from the verb *sapāḫu* "to scatter." [1880] However, according to Abraham and Sokoloff, the word is erroneously considered to be NA.[1881] In fact ABL 968 is a NB letter, and as such the discussion of the word *ú-šab-ba-aḫ* is outside the scope of the present study.

šullāmu n. (designation of horses and mules)

//Aram. ⇒ NA//

This word occurs in different NA texts containing lists of horses.[1882] In AHw. (p. 1267a s.v. *šullāmu*), it is defined as (Bez. v Pferden), and is considered to be an Aramaic foreign word in NA, based on the Syriac word ܫܘܠܡܐ "completion."[1883] The editors of CAD (Š/III, p. 240b s.v. *šullāmu*), define this word as (a breed of or way of training horses). However, in AEAD (p. 118a s.v. *šullāmu*), the word is glossed "complement."[1884] Fales renders this word tentatively as meaning "in

[1876] See CAD (Š/II, p. 317a s.v. *šernu*).
[1877] Ibid.
[1878] See also CDA (p. 379b s.v. *šubbuḫu*). Cf. DNWSI (p. 1100 s.v. *šbḥ*$_1$).
[1879] See von Soden, *Or* 46 (1977), p. 195:230.
[1880] See the Glossary of SAA XIII (p. 192b s.v. *sapāḫu*).
[1881] See Abraham & Sokoloff, *Reassessment*, p. 53:246.
[1882] See SAA XIII 85 r.1; SAA XIII 88:8; SAA XIII 105:11; ND 2482:1, e.8, r.2; ND 2491:4′; ND 2768:7′, r.7. See also B. Parker, "Administrative Tablets from the North-West Palace, Nimrud," *Iraq* 23 (1961), pp. 15–67.
[1883] See also von Soden, *Or* 46 (1977), p. 195:232; CDA (p. 382b s.v. *šullāmu*).
[1884] Cf. the Glossary of SAA XIII (p. 197a s.v. *šullāmu*), where this word is defined as (a type of horse).

excellent condition."[1885] However, Abraham and Sokoloff note that the actual meaning of the Akkadian word is not certain and consider the semantic connection between NA *šullāmu* and Syriac ܫܘܠܡܐ "end, completion" to be unsubstantiated.[1886] Therefore, they reject von Soden's proposal of a borrowing from Aramaic into NA.[1887]

Etymologically, the root ŠLM in Akkadian is attested in OA and OB as *šalāmu(m)* in the sense "health, (physical) wellbeing,"[1888] and "to stay well; to be completed, to reach completion."[1889] Admittedly, the nominal form *PuRRāS* is very rare in Akkadian.[1890] In Syriac the nominal form *PuRRāS* forms a semantic group of colors.[1891] As far as we know, the Syriac word ܫܘܠܡܐ is not used in connection with horses. In other words, we do not have a usage in Syriac that corroborates von Soden's suggested loan hypothesis.

šūqāqu n. "narrow street"

//Aram. ⇒ NA//

This word is supposedly attested as *šu-qa-qi* in a NA legal document (ADD 519:5 = AR 369:4) concerning a purchase of real estate.[1892] Nevertheless, von Soden suggested that *šu-qa-qi* is a late secondary form of NA *sūqāqû* "alley, street," and should be considered an Aramaism attributable to Aramaic *(e)šqāqā*.[1893] Von Soden's suggestion implies a reborrowing into NA.[1894]

However, the NA legal document is now re-edited as SAA VI 99:5′, and after collation the NA word in question is read as ⸢*su*!⸣-*qa-qi* meaning "street." Hence, von Soden's suggested Aramaism must be rejected as being based on erroneous reading.[1895]

ṭaḫru n. "noon"

//Aram. ⇒ NA//

This word occurs on the left side of a NA envelope (ADD 74 s.1 = AR 138, 17) concerning a land lease and loan of silver. Postgate reads the clause where the

[1885] See Fales, CLNA, pp. 168f, 190.
[1886] See Abraham & Sokoloff, *Reassessment*, p. 53:248, n. 667. Cf. SL (p. 1528b s.v. ܫܘܠܡܐ).
[1887] Abraham & Sokoloff, ibid.
[1888] See CAD (Š/I, p. 206a s.v. *šalāmu* A).
[1889] Ibid., p. 208b s.v. *šalāmu*.
[1890] See GAG § 55o.
[1891] See J. Fox, *Semitic Noun Patterns* (Winona Lake 2003), p. 280.
[1892] See AHw. (p. 1061a s.v. *sūqāqû*); CDA (p. 328b s.v. *sūqāqû*). Cf. CAD (S, p. 398b s.v. *suqāqu* mng. a); DNWSI (p. 1189 s.v. *šqq*).
[1893] See von Soden, *Or* 46 (1977), p. 196:233.
[1894] Cf. Kaufman, AIA, p. 93f; Zimmern, AF, p. 43. Cf. also DNWSI (p. 1152 s.v. *šlm*$_5$).
[1895] See Abraham & Sokoloff, *Reassessment*, p. 54:249.

word occurs as EGIR (= *urki*) *ṭa-aḫ-ri* and renders it "after noon."[1896] Referring to Postgate's reading and interpretation, AHw. (p. 1379a s.v. *ṭaḫru*) lists this word with the meaning "Mittag," and considers it to be a borrowing from Aramaic *ṭahrā* "noon."[1897] The editors of CAD (Ṭ, p. 44b s.v. ***ṭaḫru*) do not attempt to render or define *ṭaḫru*, but provide references treating the word.

However, in the re-edition of the envelope (SAA VI 259 s.1), Kwasman and Parpola read the clause, after collation, differently as EGIR *da*!-⸢*ra*!-*ri*!⸣ and render it "after the remission of the debts."[1898] The word *da*!-⸢*ra*!-*ri*!⸣ is taken to be derived from *darāru* "remission of debts."[1899] This reading and interpretation is much more in line with similar legal documents.[1900] Accordingly, the entry *ṭaḫru* ought to be stricken out of AHw. and CAD, because it originated as a result of erroneous reading.[1901]

urû n. "team (of horses, mules)"

//Aram. ⇒ NA//

The word *urû* in the sense "team (of horses, mules)" is supposedly attested in a NA administrative text consisting of a list of flock (ADD 753:7). In AHw. (p. 1435b s.v. *urû* II, 2, b) the word is hesitantly entered as *ú-re-ia* and considered to be a loan from Aramaic. It is taken to be a plural in the sense "Gespann." However, the NA text is now reedited by Fales and Postgate as SAA XI 77 and the word is read differently as *ú-ri-ṣ*[*i*] and rendered as "billy-goats."[1902]

SAA XI 77 r.1–2, reads:

⸢2?⸣ ÙZ *ú-ri-ṣ*[*i*] / *ša* m⸢*sa*⸣-*gi-bi-i*

2 billy-goats, belonging to Sagibî.

In CDA (p. 427a s.v. *urû(m)* I, 3) the word under discussion is also glossed as "team (of horses)." The commentary section of CAD (U, p. 259a s.v. *urû* B, c), on the other hand, provides the new reading of the word as given in SAA XI 77 r.1. Hence, the word *urû* in (ADD 753:7) is a ghost word in NA.

[1896] See Postgate, FNALD, § 2.2.5.

[1897] Note that the word *ṭaḫru* is not listed in CDA or AEAD.

[1898] See also S. Parpola, "Collations to Neo-Assyrian Legal Texts from Nineveh," *Assur* 2 (1979), p. 12.

[1899] See the Glossary of SAA VI (p. 294b s.v. *darāru*). The word *darāru* in the sense "remission of debts" ought to be entered in AEAD and under a new headword. Cf. AHw. (p. 163a s.v. *darāru*(*m*) I, N, mng. no. 2); CDA (p. 57a s.v. *darāru*(*m*) I, N).

[1900] See Nili, p. 294:173.

[1901] See Abraham & Sokoloff, *Reassessment*, p. 55:259.

[1902] See the Glossary of SAA XI, p. 170a s.v. *urīṣu* "male of sheep and goats." See also T. Kwasman, "Notes and Communications: Two Aramaic Legal Documents," *BSOAS* 63/2 (2000), p. 278.

3. SUMMARY AND CONCLUSIONS

3.1 Summary

The core theme of this study was to identify Aramaic loanwords in Neo-Assyrian for the period 911–612 B.C. This is the time when these two Semitic languages came into contact and exerted influences on each other. Evidence was provided, both textual and visual, substantiating the contact between the two languages and clearly illustrated that Aramaic was current in Assyria proper during the period studied. The textual evidence consists of Neo-Assyrian documents written in cuneiform with brief Aramaic texts written in their margins, and Neo-Assyrian tablets bearing a bilingual text, the Assyrian written on one face of the tablet and the Aramaic on the other. The textual evidence also comes in the form of bronze lion-weights inscribed in Aramaic, ostraca bearing Aramaic text, and monolingual clay tablets written entirely in Aramaic. The visual evidence, on the other hand, consists of numerous depictions in the Assyrian palace reliefs of two scribes standing next to each other holding different type of writing equipment, in the act of writing. One scribe is writing with a stylus on a clay tablet or on a wax-coated, ivory or wooden, hinged writing board; the other scribe with a pen or brush on papyrus or a leather scroll.

The main previous study offering a presentation of Aramaic loanwords in Neo-Assyrian is von Soden's series of articles, *Aramäische Wörter in neuassyrischen und neu- und spätbabylonischen Texten. Ein Vorbericht*, I–III, the last of which was published in 1977. In his articles, he proposed 240 Aramaic loanwords, of which he considered 81 to be borrowed into Neo-Assyrian. Von Soden's study was meant to be a starting point for further research on the subject. Regrettably, no further extensive research on the subject has been carried out until now. However, von Soden's study on Aramaic loanwords has been criticized by scholars for often lacking critical examination of the evidence. Recently, Abraham and Sokoloff produced a review of von Soden's study where they reduced his proposed loanwords in Neo-Assyrian and Neo- and Late-Babylonian to slightly more than 40 certain, and about the same number of possible loans. Nevertheless, Abraham and Sokoloff's review has been described as being overly pessimistic.

Although important as a starting point for further research on Aramaic loanwords in Neo-Assyrian and Neo- and Late-Babylonian, von Soden's study is in dire need of revision and bringing up-to-date with existing Akkadian and Aramaic lexical tools which have increased in number and improved in quality. Moreover, a large number of cuneiform texts have been edited and published since the late 1970s, some of which include lexicographical analysis that needs to be incorporated into any up-to-date study of Aramaic loanwords in Neo-Assyrian and Neo- and Late-Babylonian. For the Neo-Assyrian texts, the situation has improved significantly through the series of new text editions issued by the *State*

Archives of Assyria project (SAA), which contain not only many new Neo-Assyrian texts and improved editions of many old ones, but also valuable Neo-Assyrian glossaries. Hence, the corpus of Neo-Assyrian texts available today not only is larger than before, but many of the previously edited texts have been re-edited more accurately and commented upon by various scholars. In addition, the study of Neo-Assyrian grammar has recently been advanced by the publication of two valuable works, namely *A Sketch of Neo-Assyrian Grammar* (SAAS XIII), and *Grammatical Variation in Neo-Assyrian* (SAAS XVI).

Thus, in our study, the textual citations and their renditions quoted in CAD and AHw., or by von Soden in his articles, are replaced, whenever possible, by the new editions of the same texts that appeared in SAA volumes I–XXI, or in other current Neo-Assyrian text editions appearing for instance in CTN, StAT, SAAB and BATSH. In addition, all Aramaic words from different Aramaic languages/dialects which may contribute to identifying a possible Aramaic loanword in Neo-Assyrian are quoted for the sake of discussion and analysis of the loan hypothesis. All previously proposed Aramaic loanwords in Neo-Assyrian that were accepted as such in recent dictionaries, glossaries, lexical studies and current Assyriological literature were collected and the evidence (whether phonological, morphological, semantic or cultural/historical) upon which the loanwords were identified was systematically scrutinized to make explicit whether the loan hypothesis for each proposed loanword should be accepted or rejected. Also, an effort was made to identify additional Aramaic loanwords in Neo-Assyrian that were not previously recognized, as well as to investigate another type of borrowing which involves semantic loan, i.e., a change in the meaning of an established Neo-Assyrian word to accommodate a new meaning acquired from Aramaic.

Thanks to the advancements in Akkadian and Aramaic lexicography and the increased Neo-Assyrian textual material at hand, it was possible, in the current study, to reinterpret and evaluate some of the previous contributions to the study of Aramaic loanwords in Neo-Assyrian. Consequently, some of the previously proposed Aramaic loanwords are now rejected and others are corroborated on a much broader basis. It was also possible to identify additional Aramaic loanwords in Neo-Assyrian that were not yet recognized.

For the purpose of identifying and studying Aramaic loanwords a total of 9057 unique Neo-Assyrian texts of different genre were utilized in this study. These texts are stored in the State Archives of Assyria Project's electronic database, Corpus of Neo-Assyrian Texts (CNA), which includes almost all published and unpublished Neo-Assyrian texts in its electronic database. Furthermore, a total of 169 proposed Aramaic loanwords in Neo-Assyrian are included and discussed in this study. However, after a systematic analysis of the proposed Aramaic loanwords, only 67 words (see Table 1) are considered to be certain loanwords, and 53 (see Table 3) are considered to be possible loanwords. Additionally, 49 words (see Table 4) are rejected for different reasons and are not considered Aramaic loanwords in Neo-Assyrian.

In contrast to Abraham and Sokoloff's conclusions concerning von Soden's research on Aramaic loanwords mentioned above, our study considers 35 of von Soden's 81 proposed Aramaic loanwords in Neo-Assyrian to be certain. The certain words are *anēnu, anīna, durā'u, Eber nāri, gadiu, galû, garīṣtu, gubbu, gumāru, ḫalābu, ḫālu, ḫannīu, ḫarurtu, ḫilpu, ḫulūṭu, ianūqu, im-magāni, kanāšu, katāru, kirku, madbar, marāsu, paḫāzu, pušku, qallīlu, qarābu, qarḫu, qarūḫu, radāpu, ra'su, šalṭu, sapāqu, šapīnutu, ṣippirrāte* and *ṭullumâ*. In addition, our study regards 14 of von Soden's 81 proposed Aramaic loanwords in Neo-Assyrian to be possible loanwords. These possible Aramaic loanwords are *aqqabu, aṣūdu, gazālu, ḫangaru, maqartu, nibzu, niqittu, qapīru, saḫaru, salītu, ṣaḫūrānūtu, ṣallu, urbānu* and *ziqqu*. On the other hand, our study rejects 32 of von Soden's 81 proposed Aramaic loanwords in Neo-Assyrian. The rejected words are *akku, buḫḫušu, egertu, ḫanāpu, ḫašābu, izqātu, kuspu, la, lapān(i), laqā'u, (magāṭātu) magazzutu, maḫītu, *muāšu, nakālu, napāṣu, nasīku, niklu, palû, qadduru, qarsu, qi''u, samādiru, samāku, šapānu, ṣāpītu, ṣappuḫu, saqālu, šārītu, ṣibtātu, ṣipirtu, šullāmu,* and *šūqāqu*.

As we known, the *Assyrian-English-Assyrian Dictionary* (AEAD), which focuses on the vocabulary of the Neo-Assyrian dialect, contains about 13,000 Assyrian entries, of which the Neo-Assyrian words and phrases constitute ca. 50%, i.e., approximately 6,500 words. This means that our 67 certain Aramaic loanwords make up ca. 1.0% of the entire Neo-Assyrian vocabulary. On the other hand, our 53 possible Aramaic loanwords make up ca. 0.8% of the entire Neo-Assyrian vocabulary. Together, our certain and possible Aramaic loanwords in Neo-Assyrian constitute ca. 1.8% of the existing repertoire of Neo-Assyrian words. This relatively small number of certain and possible Aramaic loanwords in Neo-Assyrian confirms, beyond a doubt, the contact between the two languages and is additional evidence for the use of Aramaic in Assyria proper. The same evidence, however, speaks against the impression that Aramaic was widely spread in Assyria proper as a vernacular language, especially towards the end of the period studied, i.e., 911–612 B.C. On the other hand, the evidence corroborates the conclusion based on the extant prosopographical data that the predominantly Assyrian character was maintained in Assyria proper until the very end of the Assyrian empire. However, these observations must be viewed with reservation since the prosopographical and linguistic data are obtained from textual material stemming mainly from urban areas. Indeed, the large majority of the texts belong to the Assyrian palace archives in Nineveh, Assur and Calah/Nimrud, and we hardly have textual material from rural areas.

To further illuminate the Aramaic loanwords in Neo-Assyrian, this study quotes all the forms attested for a given Aramaic loanword in Neo-Assyrian and, whenever possible, provides information on the provenance, origin, genre and date of the Neo-Assyrian texts containing the loanwords, as well as information on the frequency of these loanwords. A semantic classification and a classification according to parts of speech, as well as phonological analysis of the certain Aramaic loanwords in Neo-Assyrian, based on the results derived from the current study, are also provided below.

3.2 Conclusions

3.2.1 The proposed Aramaic loanwords in Neo-Assyrian

3.2.1.1 Certain Aramaic loanwords in Neo-Assyrian

Table 1 below consists of 67 words that are considered to be certain Aramaic loanwords in Neo-Assyrian. The evidence, whether phonological, morphological, semantic or cultural/historical, makes it clear that these words are certainly borrowings from Aramaic into Neo-Assyrian.

The investigation clearly showed that syllabic writing of the loanwords is predominant. Only some confirmed loanwords consist of a combination of syllabic and logographic writings. For instance: UZU.*du-ra-'u*, *e-bir*–ÍD, *ḫar-bat*.MEŠ, DUG.*kan-du*$^{!}$, ⸢LÚ.*ki*⸣-*na*-⸢*al*⸣-*ti*, É.*ku-ur-ḫu*, KUR.*mu-da-bi-ri*, DUMU-*ia*, LÚ.*pa-ḫi-zu*, LÚ.GAL *šag-lu-te*, LÚ*.*re-e'-sa-ni*, KUŠ.*sa-al-ṭa-ni*, LÚ*.*šag-lu-u-te* as well as GIŠ$^{?}$.*tu-ba*$^{!}$-*qi*. This combination of syllabic and logographic writings indicates that these loanwords are integrated into the Neo-Assyrian writing system.

A distinctive characteristic of the Assyrian dialect in all periods is the so-called Assyrian vowel harmony, whereby a short *a* in an open unstressed syllable is assimilated to the vowel of the following syllable. Some confirmed Aramaic loanwords that are substantives exhibit the Assyrian vowel harmony and are phonologically integrated into NA. For instance: TÚG.*ga-me-de-te* or TÚG.*ga-me-du-tú* n. f. "mangled garment," *ḫal-pe-te* n. f. "successor," *ki-qi-lu-tu* or *ki-qil-li-ti* n. f. "dung heap, dunghill, refuse dump," KUR.*mu-da-bi-ri* n. "desert, plateau, steppe," and *ṣi-ip-pu-tu* n. f. "cover."

Table 1: Certain Aramaic loanwords in Neo-Assyrian

Nos.	The loanword	page
1	*adê* n. pl. tant. "(vassal) treaty, covenant, pact"	61
2	*akê* adv. "so"	67
3	*anēnu, anīni, anīnu* personal pron. "we"	68
4	*anīna, anīnu* int. "hear me!"	72
5	**baru* n. "son"	79
6	*bēt zibli* n. "dump; lavatory"	85
7	*darāsu* v. (G) "to expound, interpret, debate"; (D) "to thresh"	90
8	*durā'u, adrā'u* n. "arm; foreleg"	92
9	*Eber nāri, Ebir nāri* n. cp. "Across the river, Transeuphratia"	93
10	*gabdi, gabdu* adj. "beside, next to, adjoining"	95
11	*gadiu* n. "male kid (1–2 years of age)"	101
12	*galītu* n. f. "deportation"	102
13	*galû* v. (G) "to go into exile"; (Š) "to carry away, deport, exile"	102
14	*gammīdutu* n. f., *gammīdu* n. m. "mangled garment"	105
15	*gammuzu* v. (D) "to jib, balk, move restively (of horse)"	107
16	**garīṣtu*, **girīṣtu* n. f. "round flat loaf of bread"	108
17	*gubbu*, (pl. *gubbāni*) n. "cistern, well; pit"	114
18	*gumāru* n. "live coal, coal"	118
19	*ḫalābu, ḫalāpu* v. (G) "to milk"	122

20	*ḫalputu*, (gen., *ḫalpete*) n. f. "successor"	126
21	*ḫālu* n. "vinegar"	128
22	*ḫannīu* dem. pron. "this"	132
23	*ḫarbutu*, *ḫarbūtu* n. f. "ruin"	134
24	*ḫilpu* n. "milk"	136
25	*ḫulūṭu* n. (a meal made of a mixture of different grains(?))	136
26	*ḫurbānu* n. pl. tant. "deserted places/regions"	138
27	*iābilu* n. "ram"	140
28	*ianūqu* n. "suckling animal, animal before being weaned"	141
29	*im-magāni* adv. "gratuitously, gratis, in vain"	143
30	*kandu* n. "pitcher; vessel, pot"	146
31	*kannušu* v. (D) "to assemble (people, harvest); "to die; to bury"	147
32	*katāru* v. (G) "to wait; hesitate"	150
33	*kināltu* n. f. "congregation, assembly"	151
34	*kiqillutu* n. f. "dung heap, dunghill, refuse dump"	153
35	*kirku* n. "scroll, roll"	156
36	*kurḫu* n. "a separate little dwelling; a hut, cabin"	157
37	*leḫmu* n. "bread; food, victuals"	160
38	*madbar*, *midbar*, *mudābur* n. "desert, plateau, steppe"	162
39	*magguru* v. (D) "to tear down"	164
40	*marāsu* v. (G) "to mash, squash, squeeze"	174
41	*mar'u*, *māru* n. "lord"	175
42	*miāru* v. (G) "to buy, deal in"	179
43	*miglu* n. "scroll"	180
44	*paḫāzu* v. (G) "to be insolent; to boast; (Š) "to leave loose"	186
45	*pusku*, *pušku* n. "palm (as a linear measure: $^1/_6$ cubit = ca. 8 cm.)"	194
46	*puṭuru* n. "mushroom, fungus"	195
47	**qallīlu*, (f. *qallīssu*) adj. "unimportant; little, small"	197
48	*qarābu* n. "battle, fight, combat"	203
49	*qarḫu*, (pl. *qarḫāte*) n. "ice, frost"	205
50	*qarūḫu* adj. "white-spotted (of animal)"	206
51	*rab šaglûti* n. "deportation officer"	211
52	*radāpu*, *radābu* v. (G) "to pursue, chase; to hurry, urge"	211
53	**ra'su*, **re'su*, (pl. *re'sāni*) n. "chieftain"	214
54	*ridpu* n. "pursuit, chase"	215
55	*salṭu*, (pl. *salṭāni*) n. "quiver, bow-and-arrow case"	221
56	*sapāqu* v. (G) "to suffice, be enough, be sufficient"	224
57	*ṣippirrāte* n. f. pl. "early morning"	234
58	*ṣipputu* n. f. "cover"	236
59	*šaglû* n. "deportee"	237
60	*šaglûtu* n. f. "deportation, exile"	237
61	*šapīnutu* n. f. "boat, ship"	237
62	*taḫtānu* prep. "under, beneath"	241
63	*tuānu* n. (a bathroom)	242
64	*tūbāqu*, *dubāqu* n. "glue, elm glue, bird-lime"	244
65	*ṭullumâ* adj. "treacherous, deceitful"	247
66	*ummu* n. f. "water channel"	249
67	*ziblu* n. "dung, manure"	252

3.2.1.2 Certain Aramaic loanwords in Neo-Assyrian that are considered to be semantic loans

Only two words (see Table 2), are considered to be confirmed semantic loans from Aramaic into Neo-Assyrian. The words consist of one noun and one adjective and together they make up ca. 3% of the total number of the certain Aramaic loanwords in Neo-Assyrian.

Table 2: Certain Aramaic loans in Neo-Assyrian that are considered to be semantic loans

Nos.	The loanword	page
1	*Eber nāri, Ebir nāri* n. cp. "Across the river, Transeuphratia"	93
2	**qallīlu*, (f. *qallīssu*) adj. "unimportant; little, small"	197

3.2.1.3 Possible Aramaic loanwords in Neo-Assyrian

Table 3 below lists the 53 possible Aramaic loanwords in Neo-Assyrian. Based on one or several factors, such as lacking an obvious or convincing Semitic etymology, the form of the word, chronology, distribution of the word or possibility of a cognate relationship, these words are judged to be only possible Aramaic loanwords in Neo-Assyrian.

Table 3: Possible Aramaic loanwords in Neo-Assyrian

Nos.	The loanword	page
1	*agappu, aqappu, akappu* n. "wing"	65
2	*aqqabu*, (pl. *aqqabāni*) n. "lower part, hind part"	74
3	*aṣūdu*, (pl. *aṣūdātu*) n. f. "kneading bowl, fruit bowl; fruit offering"	76
4	*badāqu* v. "to repair"	78
5	*basālu* v. "to melt"	82
6	*bašā'u* v. "to despise; to neglect"	84
7	*bunbullu* n. "cone?"	85
8	*būṣīnu* n. "lamp"	88
9	*gab'u* n. "lair(?), pit(?)"	98
10	*gaddāiu* n. "pruner(?); reed- or wood-cutter(?)"	99
11	*gazālu* v. "to steal, carry off"	111
12	*gazāru* v. "to cut"	112
13	*gidlu* n. "braid, plait, twining"	113
14	*gulēnu* n. "cloak, tunic"	116
15	*ḫalīdu* n. "cavity, burrow(?)"	125
16	*ḫangaru* n. "dagger"	130
17	*kadāru* v. "to toil, to be wearied, to be burdened"	145
18	*kuribtu* n. f. "a plowed field?"	159
19	*makaḫalūtu* n. f. "kohl pen, eyeliner"	166
20	*maqarrutu*, (pl. *maqarrātu*) n. f. "bale (a measure for straw of reeds)"	167
21	*maqartu* n. f. "cooling (vessel)?"	170
22	*maqaṭṭutu*, (pl. *maqaṭṭāte*) n. f. "(short) felt-gown"	172
23	*maṣû* v. (Š only) "to make overcome"	177
24	**mil'u*, (pl. *mil'āni*) n. "flood"	181

25	*natānu* v. "to give"	182
26	*nibzu*, (pl. *nibzāni*) n. "(clay) tablet, document"	183
27	*niqittu* n. f. "revenge"	185
28	*parāḫu* v. (D) "to squander"; (N) "to depart(?)"	188
29	*parāmu* v. (N) "to shred (of shoes)"	190
30	*pašāqu* v. (D) "to explain"	191
31	*pispisu* n. "bedbug, bug"	192
32	*purṣīnu*, (pl. *purṣīnāte*) n. "pomegranate seed; kernel of grapes"	193
33	*qamāru* v. "to strap; to tie; to swathe, bind tightly"	199
34	*qanū'āte* n. pl. "reeds"	201
35	*qapīru* n. (a container or measure for fish and dates)	202
36	*qarāḫu* v. (G) "to freeze"	204
37	*qūbāti* n. pl. "ague(?)"	207
38	*qumbutu* n. f. "vault, arch, dome"	209
39	*rad(d)īdu* n. (a textile or garment, perhaps "veil")	213
40	*sādiu*, (pl. *sādiāni*) n. "slinger"	216
41	*saḫaru* n. "tower(?)"	217
42	*salītu* n. f. "(fishing) net"	219
43	*sapāku*, **sabāku* v. (D) "to seize; to attack"; (N) "to ensnare, catch in"	222
44	*sarābu*, (pl. *sarabāte*) n. "heat; sultry wind, hot wind; drought"	225
45	*sarḫu* adj. "enraptured, ravished"	227
46	*supīrātu* n. f. pl. "clippings(?), trimmings(?)"	229
47	*ṣaḫūrānūtu* n. f. "youth"	230
48	*ṣallu* n. "tanned hide"	232
49	*ša-ṣallēšu* n. "dealer in leather hides"	239
50	*šiāḫu* n. "earnest talk(?)"	239
51	*tukku*, (pl. *tukkāni*) n. "oppression, persecution"	246
52	*urbānu* n. "papyrus"	251
53	*ziqqu*, (pl. *ziqqāti*) n. "wineskin"	254

3.2.1.4 Rejected Aramaic loanwords in Neo-Assyrian

Table 4 below contains 49 previously proposed Aramaic loanwords in Neo-Assyrian that, according to the analysis carried out in this study, no longer can be considered Aramaic loanwords in Neo-Assyrian. The reason for rejecting each of these proposed loanwords may be a single factor or a combination of different factors. One of these reasons is that the Neo-Assyrian word turns out to be a "ghost word," i.e., that it does not exist in the textual corpus of Neo-Assyrian, having instead originated as a result of modern error during the copying, analyzing or learning of the language, or, similarly, because the suggested Aramaic source word is a "ghost word." Another reason is the fact that there exists an Akkadian etymology, or that the direction of the borrowing is actually from Akkadian into Aramaic. Additional factors in rejecting some previously proposed Aramaic loanwords in Neo-Assyrian are specified below.

Table 4: Rejected Aramaic loanwords in Neo-Assyrian

(i) Word of Akk origin; (ii) NA ghost word; (iii) Aram ghost word; (iv) Not NA; (v) Akk loan in Aram; (vi) Incompatible Aram source word, either phonologically (p), morphologically (m), and/or semantically (s); (vii) Origin unknown or not Semitic; (viii) Attested in Akk before first mill. B.C.; (ix) Uncertain mng., broken or obscure context

Nos.	Rejected loanwords	i	ii	iii	iv	v	vi	vii	viii	ix
1	*akku*	*					*			*
2	*buḫḫušu*				*					
3	*burbāni*			*						*
4	*darāku*		*							*
5	*egertu*	*				*				
6	*gašūru*					*				
7	*ḫanāpu*	*					s			
8	*ḫarurtu*	*								
9	*ḫašābu*		*							
10	*izqātu*	*					*			
11	*kabsu*	*					*		*	
12	*kabsutu*	*					*		*	
13	*kuspu*	*					p, s			
14	*la*		*				s			
15	*lapān(i)*						s			
16	*laqā'u*	*	*				s			
17	*magādu*			*			*			
18	*magazzutu*	*								
19	*maḫītu*	*					m		*	
20	**muāšu*	*	*							
21	*mudarriktu*						*			*
22	*nakālu*	*								
23	*napāṣu*		*							
24	*nasīku*	*?		*					*?	
25	*niklu*	*								
26	*palû*	*	*							
27	*palāḫu*	*							*	26
28	*qadduru*		*							
29	*qarsu*				*					
30	*qi''u*	*							*	
31	*salā'u*				*					
32	*samādiru*						p			
33	*samāku*									*
34	*saqālu*	*	*							
35	**suānu*			*			m, p			
36	*sumāmītu*						p			
37	*sūsānu*						s	*	*	
38	*ṣāpītu*				*					
39	*ṣappuḫu*	*?					s			
40	*ṣibtātu*	*								
41	*ṣipirtu*	*?		*						
42	*šapānu*	*								
43	*šārītu*	*	*				s			

44	*šernu*					*?			*	
45	*šubbuḫu*				*					
46	*šullāmu*						s			*
47	*šūqāqu*	*	*							
48	*ṭaḫru*	*	*							
49	*urû*		*							

3.2.2 The provenance, origin, genre and date of the Neo-Assyrian texts with confirmed Aramaic loanwords

The present study also intended to further illuminate the Neo-Assyrian texts that include confirmed Aramaic loanwords by providing information on the provenance, origin, genre and dates of the texts. The results of the investigation show that only 377 Neo-Assyrian texts contain confirmed Aramaic loanwords. This means that ca. 4.2% of the 9057 known Neo-Assyrian texts contain confirmed Aramaic loanwords.

As for the provenance of these texts (see Table 5), a total of 250 texts were excavated at Nineveh. These texts constitute the largest group, making up ca. 66.3% of the total number of the texts. The second largest group consists of 59 texts that were excavated at Calah, and makes up ca. 15.6% of the total. The third largest group was excavated at Assur and consists of 52 texts making up ca. 13.8% of the total.

The survey of the provenance of the NA texts with confirmed Aramaic loanwords yields nothing remarkable. It merely reflects the fact that most of the NA texts stem from the major cities of Nineveh, Calah and Assur, where the main excavations were carried out.

Table 5: The provenance of the Neo-Assyrian texts with confirmed Aramaic loanwords

Provenance	Total	%
Assur	52	13.8
Balaṭ	1	0.3
Calah	59	15.6
Dūr-katlimmu	7	1.8
Girnavaz	1	0.3
Gūzāna	1	0.3
Ḫuzīrīna	2	0.5
Kullanīa	1	0.3
Nabula	1	0.3
Nineveh	250	66.3
Unknown Provenance	2	0.5
Total	377	100.00

The origin of the Neo-Assyrian texts with confirmed Aramaic loanwords was also investigated. The texts originate from 57 different places (see Table 6). However, the origin of 39 Neo-Assyrian texts is unknown. The results of the investigation also show that 122 texts originate from Nineveh. These constitute the majority of the texts, and make up ca. 32.3% of the total. The second largest group originates from Assur and consists of 62 texts, which comprise ca. 16.4% of the total. The third largest group consists of 39 texts which originate from Calah and make up ca. 10.3% of the total. This means that most of the NA texts come, as expected, from the major Assyrian metropolises, namely Nineveh, Assur and Calah.

Table 6: The origins of Neo-Assyrian texts with confirmed Neo-Assyrian loanwords

Origin	Total	%
Abi-ila'i	1	0.3
Amidi	3	0.7
Arbela	3	0.7
Arrapḫa	1	0.3
Arzūḫina	1	0.3
Assur	62	16.4
Assyria	1	0.3
Babylon	4	1.1
Babylonia	10	2.6
Balaṭ	1	0.3
Bit-abi-ila'i	1	0.3
Bit-Zamani	1	0.3
Calah	39	10.3
Carchemish	1	0.3
Damascus	1	0.3
Darati	1	0.3
Daria	1	0.3
Dayyan-Adad	1	0.3
Der	6	1.5
Dūr-katlimmu	7	1.8
Eastern Provinces	4	1.1
Girnavaz	1	0.3
Gūzāna	4	1.1
Ḫamāt	2	0.5
Hamrin area	1	0.3
Ḫanūri	1	0.3
Harran	7	1.8
Hulî	1	0.3
Ḫuzīrīna	2	0.5
Kār-Šarrukīn	8	2.1
Kumme	4	1.1
Kurba'il	1	0.3
Laḫīru	1	0.3
Lāqê	1	0.3
Māzamua	3	0.7
Middle Euphrates	1	0.3
Nabula	1	0.3
Naṣibina	2	0.5
Nineveh	122	32.3
Northeastern Frontier	1	0.3
Northern Babylonia	2	0.5
Northwest	1	0.3
North-Western Province	1	0.3
Parsua	2	0.5
Phoenicia	1	0.3
Province of the Treasurer	1	0.3
Qurubi	1	0.3
Rab Šaqê Porvince	2	0.5
Raṣappa	1	0.3
Ṣimirra?	2	0.5
Šingibūtu	1	0.3
Sumurzu	1	0.3
Ṣūpat	2	0.5
Tīdu	2	0.5
Urarṭian Frontier	1	0.3
Western Provinces	3	0.7
Unknown origin	39	10.2
Total texts	377	100.00

As for the genre of the Neo-Assyrian texts with confirmed Aramaic loanwords (see Table 7), a total of 210 texts are letters (L) and constitute ca. 55.7% of the total number of texts. 84 texts are legal documents (LD) and make up ca. 22.2% of the total texts. 43 texts are administrative documents (AD) which make up ca.

11.4% of the total. The rest of the texts which include confirmed Aramaic loanwords in Neo-Assyrian consist of Astrological reports (AR), Inscriptions (Inscr.), Lexical lists (LL), Literary texts (LT), Mystical & cultic texts (MC), Prophecies (P), Rituals (R), Treaties (T), Textile lists (TL) and a Wine list (WL).

Table 7: The genre of the Neo-Assyrian texts with confirmed Aramaic loanwords

Genre	Total	%
Administrative document (AD)	43	11.4
Astrological report (AR)	3	0.8
Inscription (Inscr.)	1	0.5
Letter (L)	210	55.7
Legal document (LD)	84	22.2
Lexical list (LL)	4	1.1
Literary text (LT)	6	1.6
Mystical & cultic (MC)	4	1.1
Prophecy (P)	4	1.1
Ritual (R)	4	1.1
Treaty (T)	9	2.3
Textile list (TL)	2	0.5
Wine list (WL)	1	0.3
Unspecified	1	0.3
Total texts	377	100.00

The results of investigating the date of the Neo-Assyrian texts with confirmed Aramaic loanwords (see Table 8), show that only six texts date to the 9th century B.C., and make up ca. 1.6% of the total number of texts. On the other hand, 145 texts date to the 8th century B.C., and make up ca. 38.5% of the total. But the largest group consists of 180 texts dated to the 7th century B.C., and make up ca. 47.7% of the total. The rest consist of five texts which belong to the post-canonical period (648*–609* B.C.), and 41 texts which either are not dated or their date is lost. The chronological distribution of the Neo-Assyrian texts with confirmed Aramaic loanwords suggests that language contact between Neo-Assyrian and Aramaic increased with time and reached its peak in the 7th century B.C.

Table 8: The chronological distribution of the Neo-Assyrian texts with confirmed Aramaic loanwords

Date (B.C.)	Total texts	%
9th c.	6	1.6
8th c.	145	38.5
7th c.	180	47.7
Post-canonical (PC)	5	1.3
Not dated *or* date lost	41	10.9
Total texts	377	100.00

3.2.3 Semantic distribution of the confirmed Aramaic loanwords in Neo-Assyrian

The Aramaic loanwords in Neo-Assyrian can be grouped under different semantic categories. The classification of the loanwords is approximate since some words might be arranged under more than one heading. Nevertheless, the semantic distribution of the confirmed Aramaic loanwords in NA (see Table 9) shows that 18 of the words belong to the general vocabulary. This group of words is the largest, and makes up ca. 26.1% of all the confirmed Aramaic loanwords. The next largest group consists of eight words pertaining to husbandry and making up ca. 11.6% of all the confirmed loanwords. The third largest group consists of seven words designating topographical features and making up ca. 10.1% of all the confirmed Aramaic loanwords in Neo-Assyrian.

A survey of the semantic fields shows that the terms from the field of husbandry and some of the terms from the field of foodstuffs can perhaps be associated with the Arameans' partial background as nomadic sheep herders. Loanwords in the field of material culture are only five, the most important of which are the words *kirku* "scroll, roll" and *miglu* "scroll." The political terminology contains the word *galû* "to go into exile; to deport," and its derivatives *galītu* "deportation," *rab šaglûti* "deportation officer," *šaglû* "deportee" and *šaglûtu* "deportation, exile," perhaps because deportations were very frequent among the Aramean population during the Neo-Assyrian period. Topographical features and terms such as *Eber nāri* "Across the river, Transeuphratia," *gubbu* "cistern, well; pit," *ḫarbutu* "ruin" and *madbar* "desert, plateau, steppe" can also be connected with the non-urban background of the Arameans.

Table 9: Semantic categories of the confirmed Aramaic loanwords in Neo-Assyrian

Semantic category	Total	%
Architecture	2	2.9
Foodstuffs	6	8.7
Husbandry	8	11.6
Items of Material Culture	5	7.2
Measurements	1	1.5
Military	2	2.9
Political terminology	6	8.7
Social rank & social organization	6	8.7
Tools and utensils	2	2.9
Topographical feature	7	10.1
Weather or natural condition	3	4.3
Words expressing location	2	2.9
Words expressing time	1	1.5
General vocabulary	18	26.1
Total certain loanwords	69	100.00

Architecture:
kurḫu "a separate little dwelling; a hut, cabin"; *tuānu* (a bathroom).

Foodstuffs:
**garīṣtu* "round flat loaf of bread"; *ḫālu* "vinegar"; *ḫilpu* "milk"; *ḫulūṭu* (a meal made of a mixture of different grains(?)); *leḫmu* "bread; food, victuals"; *puṭuru* "mushroom, fungus."

Husbandry:
gadiu "male kid"; *gammuzu* "to jib, balk, move restively (of horse)"; *ḫalābu*, *ḫalāpu* "to milk"; *iābilu* "ram"; *ianūqu* "suckling animal, animal before being weaned"; *kiqillutu* "dung heap, dunghill, refuse dump"; *qarūḫu* "white-spotted (of animal); bald (of an old animal)"; *ziblu* "dung, manure."

Items of material culture:
gammīdutu "mangled garment"; *gumāru* "live coal, coal"; *kirku* "scroll, roll"; *miglu* "scroll"; *tūbāqu*, *dubāqu* "glue, elm glue, bird-lime."

Measurements:
pusku "span, palm (as a linear measure: $^1/_6$ cubit = ca. 8 cm.)."

Military:
qarābu "battle, fight, combat"; *salṭu* "quiver, bow-and-arrow case."

Political terminology:
adê "(vassal) treaty; *galītu* "deportation"; *galû* "to go into exile; to deport"; *rab šaglûti* n. "deportation officer"; *šaglû* "deportee"; *šaglûtu* "deportation, exile."

Social rank & social organizations:
**baru* "son"; *ḫalputu* "successor"; *kannušu* "to assemble; "to die; to bury, inter"; *kināltu* "congregation, assembly"; *mar'u* "lord"; **ra'su* "chieftain."

Tools and utensils:
kandu "pitcher; vessel, pot"; *šapīnutu* "boat, ship."

Topographical features:
bēt zibli n. "dump; lavatory"; *Eber nāri* "Across the river, Transeuphratia"; *gubbu* "cistern, well; pit"; *ḫarbutu* "ruin"; *ḫurbānu* "deserted places/regions"; *madbar* "desert, plateau, steppe"; *ummu* "water channel."

Weather or natural conditions:
qarḫu "ice, frost"

Words expressing location:
gabdi "beside, next to, adjoining"; *taḫtānu* "under, beneath."

Words expressing time:

ṣippirrāte "early morning."

General vocabulary:

akê "so"; *anēnu* "we"; *anīna* "hear me!"; *darāsu* "to expound, interpret; to thresh"; *durā'u* "arm; foreleg"; *ḫannīu* "this"; *im-magāni* "gratis, in vain"; **qallīlu* "unimportant; little, small"; *katāru* "to wait; hesitate"; *magguru* "to tear down"; *marāsu* "to mash, squash, squeeze"; *miāru* "to buy, deal in"; *paḫāzu* "to be insolent, be loose, be reckless; to leave loose"; *radāpu* "to pursue, chase; to hurry, urge"; *ridpu* "pursuit, chase"; *sapāqu* "to suffice, be enough, be sufficient"; *ṣipputu* "cover"; *ṭullumâ* "treacherous, deceitful."

3.2.4 Distribution of the confirmed Aramaic loanwords in Neo-Assyrian according to part of speech

When the confirmed Aramaic loanwords in Neo-Assyrian are classified according to part of speech (see Table 10), the results show that they can be divided into eight different categories, namely adjective, adverb, demonstrative pronoun, interjection, noun, preposition, personal pronoun and verb. As expected, the largest group consists of nouns, which amount to a total of 46 in number and make up ca. 66.6% of the total number of words.

Not surprisingly, the second largest group consists of 13 verbs making up ca. 18.8% of the total. Inter-Semitic verbs can easily be borrowed because they share a similar morphological structure. This is also observed, for instance, in Amorite loanwords in OB, as well as in Aramaic loanwords in Arabic. In contrast, we do not find a single verb among the Sumerian loanwords in Akkadian.

The third largest group consists of four adjectives and makes up ca. 5.7% of the total words. Remarkably, one loanword is a personal pronoun, even though personal pronouns are generally considered to be the most "hard-to-borrow" lexical item because they are deeply rooted within the linguistic system of the language.

Table 10: Confirmed Aramaic loanwords in NA according to part of speech

Category	Total	%
Adjective	4	5.7
Adverb	2	2.9
Demonstrative pronoun	1	1.5
Interjection	1	1.5
Noun	46	66.6
Preposition	1	1.5
Personal pronoun	1	1.5
Verb	13	18.8
Total loanwords	69	100.00

Adjective:

gabdi adj. "beside, next to, adjoining"; **qallīlu* adj. "unimportant; little, small"; *qarūḫu* adj. "white-spotted (of animal); bald (of an old animal)"; *ṭullumâ* adj. "treacherous, deceitful."

Adverb:

akê adv. "so"; *im-magāni* adv. "gratuitously, gratis, in vain."

Demonstrative pronoun:

ḫannīu dem. pron. "this."

Interjection:

anīna int. "hear me!"

Noun:

adê n. "(vassal) treaty"; **baru* n. "son"; *bēt zibli* n. "dump; lavatory"; *durāʾu* n. "arm; foreleg"; *Eber nāri* n. cp. "Across the river, Transeuphratia"; *gadiu* n. "male kid (1–2 years of age)"; *galītu* n. f. "deportation"; *gammīdutu* n. f. "mangled garment"; **garīṣtu* n. f. "round flat loaf of bread"; *gubbu* n. "cistern, well; pit"; *gumāru* n. "live coal, coal"; *ḫalputu* n. f. "successor"; *ḫālu* n. "vinegar"; *ḫarbutu* n. f. "ruin"; *ḫilpu* n. "milk"; *ḫulūṭu* n. (a meal made of a mixture of different grains(?)); *ḫurbānu* n. "deserted places/regions"; *iābilu* n. "ram"; *ianūqu* n. "suckling animal, animal before being weaned"; *kandu* n. "pitcher; vessel, pot"; *kināltu* n. f. "congregation, assembly"; *kiqillutu* n. f. "dung heap, dunghill, refuse dump"; *kirku* n. "scroll, roll"; *kurḫu* n. "a separate little dwelling; a hut, cabin"; *leḫmu* n. "bread; food, victuals"; *madbar* n. "desert, plateau, steppe"; *marʾu* n. "lord"; *miglu* n. "scroll"; *pusku* n. "span, palm (as a linear measure: 1/6 cubit = ca. 8 cm.)"; *puṭuru* n. "mushroom, fungus"; *qarābu* n. "battle, fight, combat"; *qarḫu* n. "ice, frost"; **raʾsu* n. "chieftain"; *rab šaglûti* n. "deportation officer"; *ridpu* n. "pursuit, chase"; *salṭu* n. "quiver, bow-and-arrow case"; *sarābu* n. "heat; sultry wind, hot wind; drought"; *ṣippirrāte* n. f. pl. "early morning"; *ṣipputu* n. f. "cover"; *šaglû* n. "deportee"; *šaglûtu* n. f. "deportation, exile"; *šapīnutu* n. f. "boat, ship"; *tuānu* n. (a bathroom); *tūbāqu* n. "glue, elm glue, bird-lime"; *ummu* n. f. "water channel"; *ziblu* n. "dung, manure."

Preposition:

taḫtānu prep. "under, beneath."

Personal pronoun:

anēnu personal pron. "we."

Verb:

darāsu v. "to expound, interpret, debate; to thresh"; *galû* v. "to go into exile; to carry away, deport"; *gammuzu* v. "to jib, balk, move restively (of horse)"; *ḫalābu* v. "to milk"; *kannušu* v. "to assemble; "to die; to bury"; *katāru* v. "to wait; hesitate"; *magguru* v. "to tear down"; *marāsu* v. "to mash, squash, squeeze"; *miāru* v. "to buy, deal in"; *paḫāzu* v. "to be insolent, be loose, be reckless; to leave loose"; *radāpu* v. "to pursue, chase; to hurry, urge"; *sapāqu* v. "to suffice, be enough, be sufficient."

3.2.5 Phonological analysis of the certain Aramaic loanwords in Neo-Assyrian

From the words discussed and analyzed in Chapter 2.1 above, we are able to identify, as shown below, the phonological characteristics of the Neo-Assyrian words that are borrowed from Aramaic as well as shed some light on the phonetic correlations between the two languages. The loanwords included in the phonological analysis are those that are considered to be confirmed loanwords. The other loanwords that are deemed to be possible loans, whose loan hypothesis is followed by a question mark in square brackets, i.e., [?], are not included in this phonological analysis. For the most part, the phonological characteristics of the Neo-Assyrian words that are definitely borrowed from Aramaic correspond to the general phonological characteristics of the Neo-Assyrian words as described in two quite recent studies dedicated to Neo-Assyrian grammar, SAAS XVI and SAAS XIII.

Labial stops

The Aramaic labial stops *b* and *p* are continued by NA. However, the occurrence of *p* in the word *ḫilpu* as opposed to *b* in the Aramaic *ḥlb*, is due to the variation between the two stops in NA. NA *ḫilpu* provides evidence of the application of the NA variation between voiced and voiceless stops *b* and *p* to loanwords as well.

Dental stops

Aramaic *d*, *t* and *ṭ* are identically represented by *d*, *t* and *ṭ* in NA. The variant of *dubāqu*, *tūbāqu*, which was borrowed from Aramaic *dbq*, represents the NA phonological variation between voiced and voiceless consonants, i.e., the alternation of <*d*> and <*t*>. Apparently, this NA phonological variation applies to this Aramaic loanword as well.

Velar stops

The Aramaic *k*, *g* and *q* are also represented by *k*, *g* and *q* in NA. Furthermore, the Aramaic intervocalic *k* is not represented by *g* in NA, but rather continues as *k*. An example is the NA *akê* adv. "so," which is borrowed from Aramaic *hākē*. This is unlike Aramaic, which consistently has *g* for NA intervocalic *k*. The initial velar plosive *q* of the Aramaic word *qlqlt'* exhibits dissimilation to *k* in the NA *kiqillutu*. This dissimilation (*q*...*q* > *k*...*q*) is a regular feature of NA.

Sibilants

The expected *š* ⪆ *s* interchange between alphabetic Aramaic and NA cuneiform renderings is operative. Exceptions are the words *kannušu* "to assemble; to bury, entomb," *marāsu* "to mash, squash, squeeze," *pušku* "handbreadth, palm," and *sapāqu* "to suffice, be enough, be sufficient." In the case of *kannušu*, the expected *š* ⪆ *s* interchange is not observed, most likely because *kanāšu* is a native Akkadian word attested also in NA, and the borrowing from Aramaic *knš* only involves the semantic extension of the NA word. As for *marāsu*, the word is either a trans-SB borrowing from Aramaic, in which case no change of the sibilant is required, or, most likely, the new meaning "squash, squeeze," borrowed from Aramaic, was simply considered a semantic extension of the already existing SB *marāsu* "to stir into a liquid." On the other hand, it remains difficult to account for the form of the NA *pušku* which is borrowed from Aramaic *pšk'*. A trans-NB Aramaic loan in NA would not require the *š* ⪆ *s* shift, but *pušku* is, so far, only attested in LB. Concerning *sapāq*, it is likely that the Aramaic source word *spq* is derived from **śpq*. Consequently, the form of the NA word *sapāqu* did not require the otherwise expected *š* ⪆ *s* shift. The other Aramaic sibilants, i.e., *z* and *ṣ*, are continued in NA accordingly.

The glottal stop and pharyngeals

The glottal stop ʾ (hamza) is normally not represented in writing when it occurs in word-initial position in NA. However, it has been shown that when Akkadian words beginning with a vowel are borrowed into Aramaic, they usually have an initial <ʾ> in their Aramaic forms. This would suggest that the Aramaic loanword in NA, which is traditionally transcribed as *ummu* "water channel," perhaps stands for a word with initial ʾ (hamza). Nevertheless, it has been also argued that the initial <ʾ> of the Aramaic words, which are borrowed from Akkadian words with initial vowel, is merely an Aramaic phenomenon, not NA, as it was impossible in Aramaic to write a word-initial vowel without an aleph. On the other hand, many sandhi writings in NA give the impression that the word-initial glottal stop ʾ (hamza) was entirely dropped.

The glottal stop ʾ which is expected to result from the reduction of the initial voiced pharyngeal plosive /ʿ/ of a borrowed Aramaic word is dropped in NA as expected, but without causing the so-called *e*-coloring of the neighboring *a*, i.e., an umlaut of *a* > *e*. Such is the case in the NA word *adê* "treaty," which is borrowed from Aramaic *ʿdy*, as well as the NA interjection *anīna* "hear me!", which is borrowed from Aramaic *ʿny*.

The voiceless pharyngeal fricative *ḥ* is reduced to *Ø* in *anē/īu* "we," which is borrowed from Aramaic *anaḥnā* "we." The reason why there is no reflex of the Aramaic *ḥ* in the NA word is because it was borrowed into the latter via SB. Otherwise, the Aramaic voiceless pharyngeal fricative *ḥ* is always continued in NA by the voiceless velar fricative *ḫ*. Examples are the words *ḫalābu*, *ḫalputu*, *ḫālu*, *ḫarbutu*, *ḫilpu*, *ḫulūṭu*, *ḫurbānu*, *kurḫu*, *leḫmu*, *paḫāzu*, *qarḫu*, and *taḫtānu*. This corroborates the evidence from phonetic correlations surmised from the graphic renderings of non-Assyrian phonemes in Neo-Assyrian transcriptions of West-Semitic names.

The initial voiceless laryngeal fricative *h* is reinforced in NA by the voiceless velar fricative *ḫ*, such as in the case of the NA pronoun *ḫannīu* "this," which is borrowed from the Aramaic *hn'*. It has been suggested that the velar fricative *ḫ* in *ḫannīu* is not a pure *ḫ*, but probably only an attempt by the Neo-Assyrian scribes to reproduce a spoken voiceless laryngeal fricative *h*. However, in the NA adv. *akê* "so," which is borrowed from Aramaic *hky*, the initial *h* is entirely dropped.

Approximants

The etymological initial semivowel *y* is almost always dropped in Akkadian and is very rarely preserved in initial position, notably in the pronominal forms of the first person singular. However, in loanwords from Aramaic, the initial semivowel *y* is preserved and represented in the word-initial ligature I+A. Examples of this phenomenon are the words *iābilu* "ram," from Aramaic *ybl*, and *ianūqu* "suckling animal," from Aramaic *ynq'*. In one case, the semivowel *y*, as the third radical of the Aramaic word, is represented by the glottal stop ' (hamza) in the NA word, e.g., *bašā'u* v. "to despise; to neglect," from Aramaic *bsy*.

Vowels

Some of the Aramaic loanwords in NA have a different vowel reflex of the posited Aramaic form. For instance, the NA word *miāru* "to buy, deal in," which is borrowed from Aramaic *mūr*, exhibits a difference in vowel quality. In this case, the presence of the vowel *ī* of the NA word, instead of the vowel *ū* of the Aramaic source word, is difficult to explain. Probably, the voiced dental rolled *r* brings about the vowel change *ū* > *ī*.

The first vowel /i/ in the borrowed word *ḫilpu* "milk," instead of the expected /a/, is probably an allophone of the latter. The change /a/ > /i/ in NA occurs in a closed syllable before /l/. Otherwise, the first vowel /i/ in *ḫilpu* occurs by analogy with the vowel /i/ in the corresponding original Akkadian word for milk *šizbu*, which in NA has the form *zizibu*.

As for the NA word *puṭuru* "mushroom, fungus," it is difficult to explain the vowel *u* in the first syllable of the word in view of the corresponding vowel *i* of the suggested Aramaic etymon. Most likely, the change *i* > *u* in the NA word is a vowel assimilation triggered by the neighboring bilabial plosive *p*, as well as by the vowel *u* of the second syllable.

The vowel in the NA loanword is in certain cases different than its corresponding vowel in the Aramaic etymon. This happens as a result of using Akkadographic spellings in writing the Aramaic words. For example, the first vowel *i* instead of the expected *a* in *midbar* "desert," and the first vowel *u* instead of the expected *a* in *ṭullumâ* "treacherous, deceitful," as well as the addition of an extra vowel *i* in the second syllable of the word *ṣippirrāte* "early morning."

3.2.6 Morphological analysis of the certain Aramaic loanwords in Neo-Assyrian

The majority of the Aramaic loanwords in NA consist of substantives, and the next largest group is verbs. Normally the borrowed nouns and verbs are fully integrated into the NA inflectional system. Hence, Aramaic morphological features are rarely maintained in the Aramaic loanwords in NA.

In one case, the noun pattern *maPRaS* is preserved in the NA word *madbar* "desert," which is a loan from Aramaic, although the root contains a labial. According to the so-called "Barth's law," the initial *m* of the nominal preformative *m*^{a}*/e-* dissimilates to *n*, which then becomes *n*^{a}*/e-* when prefixed to roots containing a labial radical in Akkadian. Accordingly, the NA *madbar* was expected to undergo the change *maPRaS* > *naPRaS*, but it preserved the West-Semitic and Aramaic form.

As units, loanwords are usually not analyzable in the borrowing language, whereas their corresponding source words in the donor languages may sometimes be a complex or a phrase whose internal structure is lost after entering the recipient language. This is observable in the NA adv. *akê* "so," which is borrowed from Aramaic הכי "so." The latter is a compound consisting of the following: הכ < הכן < הא כן, i.e., the interjection הָא "behold!" and the adverb כֵּן "so, thus," with elision of the final *n*. Here, the most salient feature which points to a borrowing from Aramaic into NA is that the Aramaic source word is an analyzable complex, but its internal structure was lost after entering NA as a single unit. In other words, the Aramaic source word is a compound consisting of two morphemes, but its compound nature was no longer recognizable when the word entered NA as a monomorphemic word, i.e., *akê*.

In general, the Akkadian language, as opposed to the other Semitic languages, hardly tends to form denominative verbs. Hence, one of the reasons behind considering NA *ḫalābu* "to milk," to be a borrowing from Aramaic *ḥlb* "to milk," is that the latter is a denominative verb from West-Semitic *ḥala/īb* "milk." On the other hand, the NA word *qarāḫu* "to freeze" (see Table 11) is a denominative verb from NA *qarḫu* "ice, frost," which in turn is a borrowing from Aramaic *qrḥ*ʾ "ice, frost."

As two Semitic languages, Neo-Assyrian and Aramaic form a number of verbal stems from predominantly triconsonantal roots. The results obtained from this study show that nine out of thirteen NA verbs (see Table 11), which are certainly borrowed from Aramaic, maintain a corresponding verbal stem as that of their parallel in Aramaic. However, NA inflects the loanword *galû* "to go into exile" even in the Š-stem with the meaning "to carry away, deport, exile, lead into exile," for which no inflection in the Š-stem is found in Aramaic. The fact that this loanword occurs even in the causative Š-stem in NA as *šaglû* and *šaglûtu*, whereas the proposed Aramaic etymon גלי is never attested in the Šafʿel mode, is a clear indication that this loan is fully integrated into the NA morphological system. This also means that the Šafʿel conjugation was probably not yet functioning in Aramaic during the period of its contact with NA. In contrast, the causative conjugation in the West-Semitic languages, including Aramaic, was usually expressed by the -ה prefix.

Another instance is the NA loan *paḫāzu* "to be reckless; to boast." This loanword occurs even in the causative Š-stem in two different NA letters, as *ú-šap-ḫu-zu*, while its proposed Aramaic etymon פחז is never attested in the Šafʿel conjugation. This is also a clear indication that this loan is fully integrated into the NA morphological system. It is also an additional example which shows that the Šafʿel conjugation was probably not yet functioning in Aramaic during the period of its contact with NA. However, it seems that the meaning "to leave loose," associated with *paḫāzu* in the Š-stem is only a NA internal semantic development.

Only in one case the NA loanword is inflected in a verbal stem other than that of its etymon in Aramaic. This is found in the NA word *katāru* "to wait; hesitate," which is always conjugated in the G-stem, while the Aramaic source word *ktr* is conjugated in the Paʿʿel mode that corresponds to the NA intensive D-stem. In another case, the NA loan *mâru* "to buy" is a middle weak verb with *ī* as the theme vowel, but its Aramaic etymon *mūr* "to buy; to barter, exchange," is a middle weak verb with *ū* as the theme vowel.

Table 11: NA verbs that are certainly loans from Aramaic

Nos.	Neo-Assyrian loanword	Proposed Aramaic etymon
1	*darāsu* v. (G) "to expound, interpret" (D) "to thresh"	*drš* v. Pe. "to interpret, to expound" *drš* v. Pe. & Pa. "to thresh, tread"
2	*galû* v. (G) "to go into exile" (Š) "to carry away, deport, exile, lead into exile"	*gly* v. Pe. "to go into exile"
3	*gammuzu* v. (D only) "to jib, balk, move restively (of horse)"	*gmḏ* v. Pe. & Pa. "to jib, balk, move restively (of horse)"
4	*ḫalābu, ḫalāpu* v. (G) "to milk"	*ḥlb* Pe. v. "to milk"
5	*kannušu* v. (D only) "to assemble, collect, gather (people, harvest); "to die; to bury, inter"	*knš* v. Pe. & Pa. "to gather, collect, assemble; to bury, inter; to die"
6	*katāru* v. (G) "to wait; hesitate"	*ktr* v. Pa. "to remain; wait for; to hesitate"
7	*magguru* v. (D only) "to tear down"	*mgr* v. Pa. "to drag down; to destroy"
8	*marāsu* v. (*i/i*) (G) "to mash, squash, squeeze"	*mrs* v. Pe. "to crush, press" *mrs* v. Pe. & Pa. "to squash, squeeze"
9	*miāru* v. (G) "to buy, deal in"	*mwr* v. Pe. "to buy; to barter, exchange"
10	*paḫāzu* v. (G) "to be insolent, be loose, be reckless; to boast, brag" (Š) "to leave loose"	*pḥz* v. Pe. & Pa. "to be lewd, wanton, boisterous, reckless, heedless"
11	*radāpu* v. (G) "to pursue, chase; to hurry, urge"	*rdp* v. Pe. "to pursue, follow after; to urge, drive on"; Etpa. "to be hurried"
12	*sapāqu* v. (G) "to suffice, be enough"	*spq* v. Pe. "to suffice, be enough"

3.2.7 Frequency of the certain Aramaic loanwords in Neo-Assyrian texts

An investigation of the frequency of the confirmed Aramaic loanwords in Neo-Assyrian shows that 21 words are *hapax legomena* (see Table 12). The large majority of these are nouns. Since the confirmed Aramaic loanwords in Neo-Assyrian total 67 words, the *hapax legomena*, as a group, constitute ca. 31% of all the certain loanwords. In addition, 9 words, also mostly nouns, occur as *dis legomena* (see Table 13), and as such make up ca. 13.4% of all the certain loanwords. Also, 5 words are attested as *tris legomena* (see Table 14), and make up ca. 7.5% of all the certain loanwords.

The study also shows that 34 Neo-Assyrian texts include two certain but different Aramaic loanwords (see Table 15). Furthermore, 8 Neo-Assyrian texts have more than 2 certain but different Aramaic loanwords (see Table 16). Interestingly, the result of the study shows that even 16 Neo-Assyrian royal letters (*abat šarri*) include confirmed Aramaic loanwords (see Table 17).

Table 12: Confirmed Aramaic Loanwords in Neo-Assyrian that are *hapax legomena*

Nos.	Loanword	Reference	Provenance	Origin	Genre	Date
1	**baru* n. "son"	SAA VI 173:6 *bur*!	Nineveh	Nineveh	LD	685
2	*darāsu* v. "to expound, interpret, debate"	SAA X 235 r.15 *ad-di-ris*	Nineveh	Nineveh	L	673?
3	*gadiu* n. "male kid (1–2 years of age)"	SAA II 6:636c *ga-de-e*	Calah	Calah	T	672
4	*gammuzu* v. "to jib, balk, move restively (of horse)"	SAA V 64 r.4 *ga-mu-zu*!	Nineveh	*Rab Šaqê Porvince*	L	Sg
5	*gumāru* n. "live coal, coal"	SAA XX 33 ii 9 *gu-ma-ru*	Nineveh	Nineveh	R	–
6	*ḫalputu* n. f. "successor"	SAA IX 7:4 *ḫal-pe-te*	Nineveh	Nineveh	P	Esh
7	*ḫilpu* n. "milk"	SAA IX 7 r.9 *ḫi-il-pa-ka*	Nineveh	Nineveh	P	Esh
8	*iābilu* n. "ram"	PVA 331:306 *ia-bi-li*	Assur	Assur	LL	–
9	*im-magāni* adv. "gratuitously, gratis, in vain"	SAA XXI 63:5 *im-ma-ga-a-ni*	Nineveh	Nineveh	L	Asb
10	*kandu* n. "pitcher; vessel, pot"	SAA VII 130:9 DUG.*kan-du*!	Nineveh	Nineveh	AD	7th c.
11	*leḫmu* n. "bread; food, victuals"	SAA XIII 147 r.6 *liḫ-mu*	Nineveh	*Nineveh*	L	7th c.
12	*marāsu* v. "to mash, squash, squeeze"	SAA II 6:602 *li-im*(var. *lim*)-*ri-is- ku-nu*	Calah	Calah	T	672
13	*miglu* n. "scroll"	SAA XIII 28 r.4 *mi-ig-li*	Nineveh	Assur	L	Asb?

14	*puṭuru* n. "mushroom, fungus"	SAA VII 130:1 *pu-ṭu-ri*	Nineveh	Nineveh	AD	7th c.
15	*qarūḫu* adj. "white-spotted (of animal)"; hornless (ram)	SAA XI 106 r.1 *qa-ru-ḫi*	Nineveh	*Nineveh*	AD	–
16	**ra'su* n. "chieftain"	SAA XIX 87:5′ LÚ*.*re-e'-sa-ni*	Calah	Eastern Provinces	L	Tgl
17	*ṣippirrāte* n. f. pl. "early morning"	SAA X 274:9 *ṣip-pir-ra-a-te*	Nineveh	Nineveh	L	670?
18	*ṣipputu* n. f. "cover"	SAA IX 2 iii 21′ *ṣi-ip-pu-tu*	Nineveh	*Arbela*	P	Esh
19	*šapīnutu* n. f. "boat, ship"	SAA VII 115 ii 14 *šá-ap*$^{!}$*-pi-na*$^{!!}$*-te*	Nineveh	Nineveh	AD	Sg
20	*taḫtānu* prep. "under, beneath"	SAA XV 116 r.14′ *taḫ-ta-n*[*u-ni*$^{?}$]	Nineveh	*Der*	L	Sg
21	*ṭullumâ* adj. "treacherous, deceitful"	SAA IX 2 ii 17′ *ṭùl-lu-ma-a*	Nineveh	Arbela	P	Esh

Table 13: Confirmed Aramaic Loanwords in Neo-Assyrian that are *dis legomena*

Nos.	Loanword	Reference	Provenance	Origin	Genre	Date
1	*ḫalābu*, *ḫalāpu* v. "to milk"	SAA III 34:33 *i-ḫal-li-bu-ni*	Assur	Assur	LT	–
		SAA III 13 r.8 *ta-ḫal-líp*	Nineveh	Nineveh	LT	Asb
2	*ḫarbutu*, *ḫarbūtu* n. f. "ruin"	KAV 197:16 *ḫar-bat*.MEŠ	Assur	Assur	L	–
		SAAB 9 73:7 *ḫar-bu-u-tú*	Assur	Assur	LD	698
3	*ḫurbānu* n. "dserted places/regions"	SAA XX 40 r. iii 35′ *ḫur-ba-nu-šá*	Nineveh	Nineveh	R	7th c.
		SAA XX 42 r. iii 13′ *ḫur-ba-nu-šú*	Assur	Assur	R	PC
4	*ianūqu* n. "suckling animal, animal before being weaned"	SAA XI 106 r.2 *ia-nu-qi*	Nineveh	*Nineveh*	AD	–
		SAA XX 33 r. i 30′ [UZU].*ia-nu-qu*	Nineveh	Nineveh	R	–
5	**qallīlu*, (f. *qallīssu*) adj. "unimportant; little, small"	SAA X 194 r.11′ *qa-li-su*	Nineveh	Nineveh	L	670
		SAA XVI 62:4 *qàl-li-su*	Nineveh	–	L	671?
6	*sapāqu* v. "to suffice, be enough, be sufficient"	SAA XVI 5 r.4 *i-sa-ap*$^{?}$-[*pi*]*-qa*	Nineveh	Nineveh	L	Esh
		SAA XV 142 r.2 *i-sa-pi-qu*	Nineveh	*Der*	L	Sg

7	*tuānu* n. (a bathroom)	StAT 2 53:4, 5 *tu-a-ni*	Assur	Gūzāna	LD	700
8	*tūbāqu, dubāqu* n. "glue, elm glue, bird-lime"	SAA XI 36 ii 20 GIŠ?.*tu-ba*!-*qi*	Nineveh	Nineveh	AD	–
		SAA II 6:582 *tu-ba-qi*	Calah	Calah	T	672
9	*ziblu* n. "dung, manure"	SAA VI 28:4 *zi-ib-li*	Nineveh	Nineveh	LD	710
		SAA VI 271:3 *zi-ib-li*	Nineveh	*Nineveh*	LD	678

Table 14: Confirmed Aramaic Loanwords in NA that are *tris legomenon*

Nos.	Loanword	Reference	Provenance	Origin	Genre	Date
1	*ḫālu* n. "vinegar"	SAA VII 119 i 12′ ⸢*ḫa-li*⸣, ii 8′ *ḫa-li*	Nineveh	Nineveh	AD	–
		PVA 188 *ḫa-lu*	Assur	Assur	LL	–
2	*kināltu* n. f. "congregation, assembly"	SAA XI 155 e.7 LÚ.*ki-na-al*?-*ti*!	Nineveh	*Nineveh*	AD	7th c.
		SAA XVI 20:5 ⸢LÚ.*ki*⸣-*na*-⸢*al*⸣-*ti*	Nineveh	Nineveh	L	Esh
		SAA XIX 1:3 LÚ*.*ki-na-a*[*l-t*]*i*	Calah	Calah	L	729?
3	*kiqillutu* n. f. "dung heap, dunghill, refuse dump"	SAA VI 200:5 *ki-qí*!-*il-te*	Nineveh	Nineveh	LD	Sn?
		SAA X 294:15 *ki-qil-li-ti*	Nineveh	Nineveh	L	Esh
		SAA VI 31 r.3 *ki-qi-lu-tu*	Nineveh	Nineveh	LD	709
4	*magguru* v. "to tear down	SAA XIX 100 r.13′ *tu-un*-⸢*ta*⸣-*gi-ir*	Calah	Babylonia	L	Tgl
		SAA I 179:12 *un-ta-gír*	Nineveh	*Ṣūpat*	L	Sg
		SAA XIX 196:2′ *ú-ta-gi-i*[*r*]	Calah	–	L	8th c.
5	*mar'u, māru* n. "lord"	SAA XIX 13:3, 5 DUMU-*ia*	Calah	Calah	L	8th c.
		SAA I 220:3 ⸢DUMU⸣-*ia*	Nineveh	Lāqê	L	Sg

Table 15: Neo-Assyrian texts with two certain but different Aramaic loanwords

Nos.	Reference	Loanword	Provenance	Origin	Genre	Date
1	SAA XXI 50:4′	*šá-ga-lu-ti*	Nineveh	*Nineveh*	L	Asb
	SAA XXI 50 r.4	*ú-šá-ga-lu-ka-nu-ni*	Nineveh	*Nineveh*	L	Asb
2	CTN II 1:5′	*pu-uš-ka-a-a*	Calah	Calah	TL	–
	CTN II 1:12′	TÚG.*ga-me-da-te*	Calah	Calah	TL	–
3	KAV 197:15	*ip*!*-ḫi-zu*!	Assur	Assur	L	–
	KAV 197:16	*ḫar-bat*.MEŠ	Assur	Assur	L	–
4	Rfdn 17 10:8	É.*kur*!*-ḫu*	Assur	Assur	LD	612*
	Rfdn 17 10 r.12	*a-de-(e)*	Assur	Assur	LD	612*
5	SAA I 176 r.15	*mad*!*-bar*	Calah	Ḫamāt	L	Sg
	SAA I 176 r.16	*ḫa-nu-te*	Calah	Ḫamāt	L	Sg
6	SAA I 178:12	*i-me-ru*	Nineveh	*Ṣūpat*	L	Sg
	SAA I 178 r.4	*mad-bar*!	Nineveh	*Ṣūpat*	L	Sg
7	SAA I 179:7	*i-me-ru*	Nineveh	*Ṣūpat*	L	Sg
	SAA I 179:12	*un-ta-gír*	Nineveh	*Ṣūpat*	L	Sg
8	SAA I 204 r.10	KUR.*e-bir*–ÍD	Nineveh	Raṣappa	L	Sg
	SAA I 204 r.11	*ú-sa-ga-li-uš*	Nineveh	Raṣappa	L	Sg
9	SAA I 256:3′	[*ú-šag*]*-la-na-a-ši*	Nineveh	–	L	Sg
	SAA I 256:4′	*mad-bar*	Nineveh	–	L	Sg
10	SAA II 1:6′	*ul-te-eg-lu-ma*	Nineveh	*Nineveh*	T	825?
	SAA II 1 e.15′	*a-de-e*	Nineveh	*Nineveh*	T	825?
11	SAA II 2 i 13′	*a-de-e*	Nineveh	*Nineveh*	T	754?
	SAA II 2 iv 33′	*ta-ga-lu-ni*	Nineveh	*Nineveh*	T	754?
12	SAA V 3 r.4	*qa-ra-bi*	Nineveh	Amidi	L	Sg
	SAA V 3 r.20	*nu-ka-na-šú-ú-ni*	Nineveh	Amidi	L	Sg
13	SAA VI 31 e.27	*um-mi*	Nineveh	Nineveh	LD	709
	SAA VI 31 r.3	*ki-qi-lu-tu*	Nineveh	Nineveh	LD	709
14	SAA VI 271:3	*zi-ib-li*	Nineveh	*Nineveh*	LD	678
	SAA VI 271:8	*um-me*	Nineveh	*Nineveh*	LD	678
15	SAA VII 115 ii 14	*šá-ap*!*-pi-na*!!*-te*	Nineveh	Nineveh	AD	Sg
	SAA VII 115 r. ii 18	*ga-me-da*!*-te*	Nineveh	Nineveh	AD	Sg
16	SAA IX 7:4	*ḫal-pe-te*	Nineveh	Nineveh	P	Esh
	SAA IX 7 r.9	*ḫi-il-pa-ka*	Nineveh	Nineveh	P	Esh
17	SAA X 72 r.1	*a-ke-e*	Nineveh	Nineveh	L	670?
	SAA X 72 r.15	⸢*i*!⸣*-pa-aḫ-ḫi-iz*	Nineveh	Nineveh	L	670?
18	SAA X 227 e.29	*ḫa-an-ni-ma*	Nineveh	Nineveh	L	666?
	SAA X 227 r.12	*ú-kan*!*-ni-šú-u-ni*	Nineveh	Nineveh	L	666?
19	SAA X 273:12	*a-de-e*	Nineveh	Nineveh	L	672?
	SAA X 273:14	*ir*!*-di-pa*	Nineveh	Nineveh	L	672?
20	SAA X 294:15	*ki-qil-li-ti*	Nineveh	Nineveh	L	Esh
	SAA X 294 r.17	*mu-da-bi-ri*	Nineveh	Nineveh	L	Esh
21	SAA XI 106 r.1	*qa-ru-ḫi*	Nineveh	*Nineveh*	AD	–
	SAA XI 106 r.2	*ia-nu-qi*	Nineveh	*Nineveh*	AD	–
22	SAA XV 41:9′	*qar-ḫa-a-te*	Nineveh	–	L	Sg
	SAA XV 41:14′	LÚ*.*šá-ga-l*[*u-te*]	Nineveh	–	L	Sg

23	SAA XV 98:6	*a-né-e-nu*	Nineveh	*Kār-Šarrukīn*	L	Sg
	SAA XV 98 r.4′	*a-de-e*	Nineveh	*Kār-Šarrukīn*	L	Sg
24	SAA XV 116 r.5′	*a-ni-ni*	Nineveh	*Der*	L	Sg
	SAA XV 116 r.14′	*taḫ-ta-n*[*u-ni*$^{?}$]	Nineveh	*Der*	L	Sg
25	SAA XV 130:14	*qar-a-bi*	Nineveh	*Der*	L	Sg
	SAA XV 130:21	*a-ni-ni*	Nineveh	*Der*	L	Sg
26	SAA XVI 59:4	*a-de-e*	Nineveh	*Nineveh*	L	Esh
	SAA XVI 59:8	*a-ni-nu*	Nineveh	*Nineveh*	L	Esh
27	SAA XVI 60:5	*a-de-e*	Nineveh	*Nineveh*	L	Esh
	SAA XVI 60 r.18′	*a-ni-nu*	Nineveh	*Nineveh*	L	Esh
28	SAA XVI 126:13	*ḫa-nim-ma*	Nineveh	Phoenicia	L	Esh
	SAA XVI 126:19	*a-de-e*	Nineveh	Phoenicia	L	Esh
29	SAA XIX 3:15	KUR.⸢*mu-da*⸣*-bi-ri*	Calah	Calah	L	8th c.
	SAA XIX 3 s.2	*g*[*a-l*]*i-*⸢*ti*⸣	Calah	Calah	L	8th c.
30	SAA XIX 12 r.8′	*mu-da-*⸢*bir*⸣	Calah	Calah	L	8th c.
	SAA XIX 12 r.9′	*me-e-ru*	Calah	Calah	L	8th c.
31	SAA XIX 19:6	*ka-nu-šá*	Calah	*Calah*	L	Sg
	SAA XIX 19:13	KUR.*mu-da-bi-ri*	Calah	*Calah*	L	Sg
32	SAA XIX 87:5′	LÚ*.*re-e'-sa-ni*	Calah	Eastern Provinces	L	Tgl
	SAA XIX 87 r.9	*i-ga-li-ú*	Calah	Eastern provinces	L	Tgl
33	StAT 2 263:8	É.*kur*$^{?}$*-ḫi*	Assur	Assur	LD	622*
	StAT 2 263:13	*gab-du*	Assur	Assur	LD	622*
34	StAT 3 1:14	TÚG.*ga-me-da-te*	Assur	Assur	TL	–
	StAT 3 1 r.5	*pu-uš-ka-a-a*	Assur	Assur	TL	–

Table 16: Neo-Assyrian texts with more than two certain but different Aramaic loanwords

Nos.	Reference	Loanword	Provenance	Origin	Genre	Date
1	SAA I 1:8	*qa-ra-bi*$^{!}$	Calah	Calah	L	Sg
	SAA I 1 r.52	*ḫa-an-ni-tú*	Calah	Calah	L	Sg
	SAA I 1 r.59	*kan-nu-šú*	Calah	Calah	L	Sg
2	SAA II 6:1, 10, 12, 41, 64, 96, 104, 132, 153, 175, 283, 289, 291, 351, 358, 382, 387, 390, 398, 400, 513, 526, 573, 616, 666	*a-de-e*	Calah	Calah	T	672
	SAA II 6:311	*qa-ra-a-bu*	Calah	Calah	T	672
	SAA II 6:494, 507	*a-ni-nu*	Calah	Calah	T	672
	SAA II 6:531, 548,	*ḫa-an-ni-e*	Calah	Calah	T	672

	580, 623, 629, 638					
	SAA II 6:582	*tu-ba-qi*	Calah	Calah	T	672
	SAA II 6:602	*li-im*(var. *lim*)*-ri-is-ku-nu*	Calah	Calah	T	672
3	SAA III 35:25	*pa-ḫa-a-z*[*u*]	Nineveh	Nineveh	LT	–
	SAA III 35:25	[LÚ.*pa*]*-aḫ-ḫi-zu*	Nineveh	Nineveh	LT	–
	SAA III 35:41	*qa-ra-bu*	Nineveh	Nineveh	LT	–
4	SAA V 53:15	*ḫa-ni-u*	Nineveh	*Province of the Treasurer*	L	Sg
	SAA V 53:19	*ir-ti-di-bi*	Nineveh	*Province of the Treasurer*	L	Sg
	SAA V 53 r.7	*an-ni-nu*	Nineveh	*Province of the Treasurer*	L	Sg
	SAA V 53 r.7	*ri-id-pu*	Nineveh	*Province of the Treasurer*	L	Sg
5	SAA V 105:12	*a-ni-nu*	Nineveh	*Kumme*	L	
	SAA V 105:23	*ú-šá-ga-lu-šú-nu*	Nineveh	*Kumme*	L	
	SAA V 105 r.6	*qar-ḫu*	Nineveh	*Kumme*	L	
6	SAA VII 115 ii 9	*ma-qa-ṭí*	Nineveh	Nineveh	AD	Sg
	SAA VII 115 ii 14	*šá-ap!-pi-na!!-te*	Nineveh	Nineveh	AD	Sg
	SAA VII 115 r. i 5	*ša* LÚ.*ṣal-li-šú-nu*	Nineveh	Nineveh	AD	Sg
	SAA VII 115 r. ii 17	*aq-qa-ba-ni*	Nineveh	Nineveh	AD	Sg
	SAA VII 115 r. ii 18	*ga-me-da!-te*	Nineveh	Nineveh	AD	Sg
7	SAA X 221 r.1	*ḫa-an-nim-ma*	Nineveh	Nineveh	L	669?
	SAA X 221 r.4	*ni-kàt-tir*	Nineveh	Nineveh	L	669?
	SAA X 221 r.8	*a-ni-nu*	Nineveh	Nineveh	L	669?
8	SAA XVI 243 r.2′	*qa-ra-b*[*u*]	Nineveh	–	L	Esh
	SAA XVI 243 r.5′	*a-ni-nu*	Nineveh	–	L	Esh
	SAA XVI 243 r.6′	*a-de-e*	Nineveh	–	L	Esh

Table 17: Neo-Assyrian royal letters (*abat šarri*) with certain Aramaic loanwords

Nos.	Reference	Loanword	Provenance	Origin	Genre	Date
1	SAA XXI 50:4′	*šá-ga-lu-ti*	Nineveh	*Nineveh*	L	Asb
	SAA XXI 50 r.4	*ú-šá-ga-lu-ka-nu-ni*	Nineveh	*Nineveh*	L	Asb
2	SAA XXI 63:5	*im-ma-ga-a-ni*	Nineveh	Nineveh	L	Asb
3	SAA XXI 104 r.3	*a-ni-nu*	Nineveh	Babylon	L	7th c.
	SAA XXI 104 r.4	*a-ni-nu-ni*	Nineveh	Babylon	L	7th c.
4	SAA I 1:8	*qa-ra-bi!*	Calah	Calah	L	Sg
	SAA I 1 r.52	*ḫa-an-ni-tú*	Calah	Calah	L	Sg
	SAA I 1 r.59	*kan-nu-šú*	Calah	Calah	L	Sg
	SAA I 1:29	*ḫa-an-ni-ú*	Calah	Calah	L	Sg
	SAA I 1 r.52	*ḫa-an-ni-tú*	Calah	Calah	L	Sg

5	SAA I 5:4	*ḫa-an-ni-ú*	Nineveh	Nineveh	L	Sg
6	SAA I 7:10′	*ḫa-an-ni-i*	Nineveh	Nineveh	L	Sg
7	SAA I 10:5	*ḫa-an-ni-ú*	Nineveh	Nineveh	L	Sg
	SAA I 10:10	*ḫa-an-ni-i*	Nineveh	Nineveh	L	Sg
8	SAA I 13:15′	*mid-bar*	Nineveh	Nineveh	L	Sg
9	SAA I 15:7′	*ḫa-an-ni-e*	Nineveh	Nineveh	L	Sg
10	SAA I 18 r.9′	*ḫa-an-ni-ú*	Nineveh	Nineveh	L	Sg
11	SAA I 21 r.1	*ḫa-an-ni-u*	Nineveh	Nineveh	L	Sg
12	SAA X 289 r.14′	*a-né-en-nu-ni*	Nineveh	Nineveh	L	672?
	SAA X 289 r.13′	*a-ni-nu*	Nineveh	Nineveh	L	672?
13	SAA XVI 5 r.4	*i-sa-ap*$^{?}$*-[pi]-qa*	Nineveh	Nineveh	L	Esh
14	SAA XVI 20:5	⸢LÚ.*ki*⸣*-na-*⸢*al*⸣*-ti*	Nineveh	Nineveh	L	Esh
15	SAA XIX 1:3	LÚ*.*ki-na-a[l-t]i*	Calah	Calah	L	729?
16	SAA XIX 3:15	KUR.⸢*mu-da*⸣*-bi-ri*	Calah	Calah	L	8th c.
	SAA XIX 3 s.2	*g[a-l]i-*⸢*ti*⸣	Calah	Calah	L	8th c.
	SAA XIX 3:12	⸢KUR⸣.mu-⸢da-bir⸣	Calah	Calah	L	8th c.

Table 18: Loanword hypotheses according to different lexica (only the loanwords confirmed by our study are included)

KEY:

[?]	= a possible but questionable loan	Fw.	= foreign word
< , >	= loan direction	Lw.	= loanword
–	= no loan hypothesis forwarded	mng.	= meaning

Nos.	Neo-Assyrian	Current study	Aram.	AHw.	CAD	CDA	DNWSI
1	*adê*	< Aram.	*ʿdyʾ*	–	–	–	Akk. < or > Akk.
2	*akê*	< Aram.	*hky*	–	–	–	–
3	*anēnu, anīni, anīnu*	< Aram.	*ʾnḥn*	Aram. Lw.	–	< Aram.	Akk. <
4	*anīna, anīnu*	< Aram.	*ʿny*	–	–	–	–
5	**baru*	< Aram.	*br*	–	–	< Aram.	–
6	*bēt zibli*	< Aram.	*zblʾ*	–	–	–	–
7	*darāsu*	< Aram. or W.Sem.	*drš*	–	mng. obscure	–	–
8	*durāʿu, adrāʾu*	< Aram.	*drʿ*	Aram. Fw.	< W.Sem.	< Aram.	Akk. <
9	*Eber nāri*	< Aram.	*ʿbr nhrʾ*	–	–	< Akk.	Akk. <
10	*gabdi, gabdu*	< Aram.	*gbʾ*	–	–	–	–
11	*gadiu*	< Aram. or W.Sem.	*gdy*	Aram. Lw.	< W.Sem.	< Aram.	Akk. <
12	*galītu*	< Aram.	*gly*	Aram. Fw.	–	–	–
13	*galû*	< Aram.	*gly*	< Aram.	Aram. Lw.	< Aram.	Akk. <

14	*gammīdutu*	< Aram.	*gmydh*	< Akk.	< Aram.?	< Akk.	–
15	*gammuzu*	< Aram.	*gmd*	mng. unclear	–	mng. unkn.	–
16	**garīṣtu, *girīṣtu*	< Aram.	*grṣ*	Aram. Lw.	–	< Aram.	Akk. <
17	*gubbu*	< Aram.	*gbb*	prob. Aram. Lw.	< prob. W.Sem.	< Aram.?	Akk. <
18	*gumāru*	< Aram.	*gmr*	–	perhaps > Aram.	–	Akk. < or > Akk.
19	*ḫalābu*	< Aram.	*ḥlb*	–	–	< Sem.	Akk. <
20	*ḫalputu*	< Aram.	*ḥlp*	uncertain	mng. unkn.	mng. unkn.	Akk. <
21	*ḫālu*	< Aram.	*ḥll*	Aram. Lw.	< Aram. in NB	< Aram.	Akk. <
22	*ḫanniu*	< Aram.	*hn'*	–	–	–	–
23	*ḫarbutu, ḫarbūtu*	< Aram.	*ḥrbt'*	–	–	–	–
24	*ḫilpu*	< Aram.	*ḥlb*	–	–	< W.Sem.	Akk. <
25	*ḫulūṭu*	< Aram.	*ḥlṭ*	Aram. Fw.	–	< Aram.	Akk. < possibly
26	*ḫurbānu*	< Aram.	*ḥrbn'*	–	–	–	–
27	*iābilu*	< Aram.	*ybl*	< Canaanite	–	< W.Sem.	Akk. <
28	*ianūqu*	< Aram.	*ynq*	Aram. Fw.	Foreign word(?)	< Aram.	Akk. < unce. interpret.
29	*im–magāni*	< Aram.	Sanskrit *magha-* + *-nnu*	Aram. Fw.	< Indo-Iranian	< Aram.	Akk. <
30	*kandu*	< Aram.	*knd* < *kd'*	Aram. Lw.	–	< Aram.	Akk. <
31	*kannušu*	< Aram.	*knš*	Aram. Lw.	< Akk. *kummusu*	< Aram.	Akk. <
32	*katāru*	< Aram.	*ktr*	Aram. Lw.	–	< Aram.	Akk. <
33	*kināltu*	< Aram.	*knš*	Aram. Lw.	< Aram.	< kanāšu II = < Aram.	Akk. <
34	*kiqillutu*	< Aram.	*qlqlh*	orig. unkn.	mng. uncert.	< Aram.	–
35	*kirku*	< Aram.	*krk'*	Aram. Lw.	< Aram.?	< Aram.	Akk. <
36	*kurḫu*	< Aram.	*kwrḥ'*	–	–	–	–
37	*leḫmu*	< Aram.	*lḥm'*	–	–	–	–
38	*madbar, midbar, mudābur*	< Aram.	*mdbr'*	< W.Sem.	–	< W.Sem.?	Akk. <
39	*magguru*	< Aram.	*mgr*	–	–	< Aram.	–

40	*marāsu*	< Aram.	*mrs*	Aram. Fw.?	< Aram.	< Aram.	Akk. < poss. interpret
41	*mar'u, māru*	< Aram.	*mr'*	–	–	–	–
42	*miāru*	< Aram.	*mwr*	< Aram.	< Aram.	< Aram.?	Akk. <
43	*miglu*	< Aram.	*mglh, mglt'*	–	–	–	–
44	*paḫāzu*	< Aram.	*pḥz*	Aram. Fw.	< W.Sem.	–	Akk. <
45	*pusku, pušku*	< Aram.	*pšk'*	Aram. Fw.	< Aram.	< Aram.	Akk. <
46	*puṭuru*	< Aram.	*pṭwr'*	–	–	–	–
47	**qallīlu*	< Aram.	*qlyl*	–	possibly < Aram.	< Aram.	Akk. < poss. interpret
48	*qarābu*	< Aram.	*qrb'*	Aram. Lw.	< Aram.	< Aram.	Akk. < or > Akk.
49	*qarḫu*	< Aram.	*qrḥ, qwrḥ*	–	–	–	–
50	*qarūḫu*	< Aram.	*qrḥ*	Aram. Fw.	–	< Aram.	Akk. < less prob. interpret
51	*rab šaglûti*	< Aram.	*gly*	–	–	–	–
52	*radāpu, radābu*	< Aram.	*rdp*	< Aram.	–	< Aram.	Akk. <
53	**ra'su, *re'su*	< Aram.	*r'š*	Aram. Fw.	< Aram.	< Aram.	Akk. < unce. interpret.
54	*ridpu*	< Aram.	*rdp*	Aram. Fw.	–	–	Akk. <
55	*salṭu*	< Aram.	*šalṭā*	Aram. Fw.	–	< Aram.	Akk. <
56	*sapāqu*	< Aram.	*spq*	Aram. Fw.	–	< Aram.	Akk. <
57	*sarābu*	< Aram.	*šrb*	–	–	–	–
58	*ṣippirrāte*	< Aram.	*ṣpr'*	< Aram.	< W.Sem.	< Aram.	Akk. < poss. interpret
59	*ṣipputu*	< Aram.	*ṣpt'*	–	–	–	–
60	*šaglû*	< Aram.	*gly*	–	–	–	–
61	*šaglûtu*	< Aram.	*gly*	–	–	–	–
62	*šapīnutu*	< Aram.	*spynt'*	Aram. Fw.	< Aram.	< Aram.	Akk. <
63	*taḫtānu*	< Aram.	*tḥtyh*	–	–	–	–
64	*tuānu*	< Aram.	*twn'*	–	–	–	–
65	*tūbāqu, dubāqu*	< Aram.	*dwbq'*	–	–	–	–
66	*ṭullumâ*	< Aram.	*ṭlm*	< Aram.	< Aram.	< Aram.	Akk. <
67	*ummu*	< Aram.	*'m'*	–	–	–	–
68	*ziblu*	< Aram.	*zbl'*	–	–	–	–

3.3 Avenues for further research

Further research concerning Aramaic loanwords in Neo-Assyrian can investigate the possibility of finding Aramaic loanwords in Neo-Assyrian personal names and divine names. This is now feasible, especially because *The Prosopography of the Neo-Assyrian Empire* (PNA), has finally been completed. As for other Aramaic influences on Neo-Assyrian, a study could be devoted to examining if there are Aramaic loan-translations (calques) in Neo-Assyrian or to identifying Aramaic phraseology in Neo-Assyrian legal documents if possible. Also, a few features of Neo-Assyrian syntax may have been borrowed from Aramaic, or influenced by it, and this too needs to be amply investigated.

Of course, Aramaic loanwords also occur in Standard Babylonian and Neo- and Late-Babylonian dialects of Akkadian. Previous investigations in this regard also need to be updated and expanded if possible. In addition, Aramaic loanwords are also found in Standard Babylonian and Neo-Babylonian texts composed in Assyria. All these need to be examined as well.

It is hoped that the results of this study will provide sufficient research materials for linguists to undertake future studies of a sociolinguistic and historical linguistic nature within the framework of Neo-Assyrian and Aramaic language contact. The final synthesis will further illuminate the degree of language contact between the two Semitic languages as well as improve our understanding of the extent of the Aramaic influence that was exerted upon Neo-Assyrian.

BIBLIOGRAPHY

Abou-Assaf, A., P. Bordreuil and A.R. Millard, *La statue de Tell Fekherye et son inscription bilingue assyro-araméenne*. Etudes Assyriologiques, cahier 7. Paris: Editions Recherche sur les grandes civilisations, 1982.

Abraham, K. and M. Sokoloff, "Aramaic Loanwords in Akkadian – A Reassessment of the Proposals," *AfO* 52 (2011): 22–76.

Adams, J.N., M. Janse and S. Swain (eds.), *Bilingualism in Ancient Society: Language Contact and the Written Text*. Oxford: Oxford University Press, 2002.

Afram, G., *Svensk-assyrisk ordbok*. Syriac title: *Sfar mele swīdōyō-suryōyō*. Skärholmen: Gabriel Afram, 2005.

Aggoula, B., *Inscriptions et graffites araméens d'Assour*. Naples: Istituto Orientale di Napoli, 1985.

Ahmad, A.Y., "The Archive of Aššur-mātu-taqqin Found in the New Town of Aššur and Dated Mainly by Post-Canonical Eponyms," *Al-Rāfidān* 17 (1996): 207–288.

Ahmad, A.Y. and J.N. Postgate, *Archives from the Domestic Wing of the North-West Palace at Kalhu/Nimrud*. EDUBBA 10. [London]: NABU Publications, 2007.

Aistleitner, J., *Wörterbuch der Ugaritischen Sprache*. Berlin: Akademie-Verlag, 1963.

Albright, W.F., "Notes on Egypto-Semitic Etymology, II," *AJSL* 34 (1918): 215–255.

——. "An Ostracon from Calah and the North-Israelite Diaspora," *BASOR* 149 (1958): 33–36.

Al-munğidu fīl-luġati wal'e'lāmi. 27th edition. Beirut: Dar El-Mashreq, 1984. (Arabic-Arabic Dictionary).

Al-Qinai, J.B.S., *Morphophonemics of Loan-words in Translation*. Online 15/09/2022: http://img2.timg.co.il/forums/75882210.pdf

Aprim, F.A., *Assyrians: The Continuous Saga*. Xlibris Corporation, 2005.

Aro, J., *Studien zur mittelbabylonischen Grammatik*. StOr 20. Helsinki: Suomalaisen Kirjallisuuden Kirjapaino, 1955.

——. "Die semitischen Zischlaute (ṯ), *š*, *ś* und *s* und ihre Vertretung im Akkadischen," *Or* 28 (1959): 321–335.

Asbaghi, A., *Persische Lehnwörter im Arabischen*. Wiesbaden: Harrassowitz, 1988.

Ashitha, O.M.G., *Hilqa de Leshana: Assyrian-Arabic Dictionary*. Baghdad: Al-Maghreb Printing, 1997.

Audo, T., *Sīmṯā də-lišānā sūryāyā*, I–II. Mosul, 1897. Reprinted in one volume by Assyrian Language and Culture Classes Incorporated – Chicago, with the title: *Assyrian Dictionary*. Ann Arbor: Edwards Brothers, 1978. (Syriac-Syriac Dictionary).

Bachelot, L. and F.M. Fales (eds.), *Tell Shiukh Fawqani 1994–1998*, II. History of the Ancient Near East: Monographs VI/2. Padova: S.A.R.G.O.N. Editrice e libreria, 2005.

Baker, H.D. (ed.), *The Prosopography of the Neo-Assyrian Empire*, vols. 2/I–II, 3/I–II. [Helsinki]: The Neo-Assyrian text corpus project, 2000–2011. (see also Radner, K. [ed.]).

Barjamovic, G. and M.T. Larsen, "An Old Assyrian Incantation against the Evil Eye," *AoF* 35/1 (2008): 144–155.

Barth, J., "Das Nominalpräfix *na* im Assyrischen," *ZA* 2 (1887): 111–117.

——. "Assyrisches *iš*, hebr. -aram. *t* als Adverbialendung," *ZA* 28 (1914): 307–309.

Bartholomae, C., *Altiranisches Wörterbuch*. Strassburg: Karl J. Trübner, 1904.

Beaulieu, P.-A., "Official and Vernacular Languages: The Shifting Sands of Imperial and Cultural Identities in First-Millennium B.C. Mesopotamia," in S.L. Sanders (ed.), *Margins of Writing, Origins of Cultures*, pp. 187–216. Oriental Institute Seminars 2. Chicago: The Oriental Institute of the University of Chicago, 2006.

——. "Aspects of Aramaic and Babylonian Linguistic Interaction in First Millennium BC Iraq," *Journal of Language Contact* 6 (2013): 358–378.

Beckman, G., Review of "*Assur – Gott, Stadt und Land: 5. Internationales Colloquium der Deutschen Orient-Gesellschaft 18.–21. Februar 2004 in Berlin* (Wiesbaden, 2011), by J. Renger, *JAOS* 132 (2012): 167–168.

Beeston, A.F.L., "On the Correspondence of Hebrew *s* to ESA s^2," *JSS* 22 (1977): 50–57.

Bergsträsser, G., *Introduction to the Semitic Languages: Text Specimens and Grammatical Sketches*. Translated with Notes and Bibliography and an Appendix on the Scripts by Peter T. Daniels. Winona Lake: Eisenbrauns, 1983.

Beyer, K., *The Aramaic Language: Its Distribution and Subdivisions*. Translated from the German by John F. Healey. Göttingen: Vandenhoeck & Ruprecht, 1986.

——. "Akkadisches *līmu* und aramäisches *l'm* 'Eponymat'," *Or* 57 (1988): 82–83.

——. *Die aramäischen Inschriften aus Assur, Hatra und dem übrigen Ostmesopotamien: (datiert 44 v. Chr. Bis 238 n. Chr.)*. Göttingen: Vandenhoeck & Ruprecht, 1998.

Bezold, C., *Babylonisch-Assyrisches Glossar*. Heidelberg: Carl Winter's Universitätsbuchhandlung, 1926.

Black, J. and A. Green, *Gods, Demons and Symbols of Ancient Mesopotamia: An Illustrated Dictionary*. London: British Museum Press, 1992.

Black, J., A. George and N. Postgate (eds.), *A Concise Dictionary of Akkadian*. 2nd (corrected) printing. SANTAG 5. Wiesbaden: Harrassowitz Verlag, 2000.

——. *A Concise Dictionary of Akkadian: Addenda, Corrigenda, and Supporting Bibliography*.
Online 15/09/2022: https://www.soas.ac.uk/cda-archive/lemmata/

Blasberg, M., *Keilschrift in aramäischer Umwelt: Untersuchungen zur spätbabylonischen Orthographie*. Köln: Univ., Diss., 1997.

Bloch, Y., *Alpahbet Scribes in the Land of Cuneiform: Sēpiru Professionals in Mesopotamia in the Neo-Babylonian and Achaemenid Periods*. Piscataway: Gorgias Press, 2018.

Boiy, T., *Late Achaemenid and Hellenistic Babylon*. OLA 136. Leuven: Peeters, 2004..

Bonatz, D., "The Myth of Aramean Culture," in A. Berlejung & A.M. Maeir (eds.), *Research on Israel and Aram: Autonomy, Independence and Related Issues. Proceedings of the First Annual RIAB Center Conference, Leipzig, June 2016*, pp. 159–177. Research on Israel and Aram in Biblical Times I. Tübingen: Mohr Siebeck 2019.

Bongenaar, A.C.V.M., *The Neo-Babylonian Ebabbar Temple at Sippar: Its Administration and its Prosopography*. [Istanbul]: Nederlands historisch-archaeologisch instituut te Istanbul, 1997.

Bordreuil, P., "Les sceaux inscrits phéniciens et araméens de Khorsabad et leur signification historique," in A. Caubet (ed.), *Khorsabad, le palais de Sargon II, roi d'Assyrie*, pp. 253–282. Paris: La documentation française, 1995.

Borger, R., *Die Inschriften Asarhaddons, Königs von Assyrien*. AfO, Beiheft 9. Graz, 1956.

——. *Handbuch der Keilschriftliteratur*, 3 Vols. Berlin: Walter de Gruyter, 1967–1975.

——. "Die Waffenträger des Königs Darius: Ein Beitrag zur alttestamentlichen Exegese und zur semitischen Lexikographie," *VT* 22 (1972): 385–398.

——. with contributions by F. Ellermeier, *Assyrisch-babylonische Zeichenliste*. AOAT, 33. Kevelaer: Verlag Butzon & Bercker Kevelaer, 1978.

Borobio, E.M., "Tratados neoasirios y arameos," *Anuari de filologia* 20 (1997): 27–43.

Botterweck G.J. and H. Ringgren (eds.), *Theological Dictionary of the Old Testament*, Vol. 4, *z*^{e}*'ēbh–ḥmṣ*. Grand Rapids: Eerdmans, 1980.

Botterweck G.J., H. Ringgren and H.-J. Fabry (eds.), *Theological Dictionary of the Old Testament*, Vol. 7, *k*^{e}*–*lyṣ*. Translated from *Tehologisches Wörterbuch zum Alten Testament, Band* IV, *Lieferungen 1–5*. Grand Rapids: Eerdmans, 1995.

Bowman, R.A., "An Interpretation of Asshur Ostracon," in L. Waterman (ed.), *Royal Correspondence of the Assyrian Empire: Translated into English, with a Transliteration of the Text and a Commentary*, Part IV, pp. 275–282. Ann Arbor: University of Michigan Press, 1936.

——. "Arameans, Aramaic, and the Bible," *JNES* 7 (1948): 65–90.

Brauner, R.A., *A Comparative Lexicon of Old Aramaic*. Ann Arbor: University Microfilms, A XEROX Company, 1974.

Brinkman, J.A., *A Political History of Post-Kassite Babylonia 1158–722 B.C.* AnOr 43. Rome, Pontificium institutum biblicum, 1968.

——. "Babylonian Influence in the Šēḫ Ḥamad Texts Dated under Nebuchadnezzar II," *SAAB* 7 (1993): 133–138.

Brock, S., "Three Thousand Years of Aramaic Literature," *ARAM Periodical* 1 (1989): 11–23.

Brockelmann, C., *Grundriss der vergleichende Grammatik der semitischen Sprachen*, 2 Vols. Berlin: Reuther & Reichard, 1908–1913.

——. *Lexicon Syriacum*. Third unchanged graphic reproduction of the 2nd ed., Halle an der Saale 1928. Hildesheim: Georg Olms Verlag, 1995.

Brünnow, R.E., "Eine assyrisch-aramäische Bilinguis," *ZA* 3 (1888): 238–242.

Buccellati, G., *A Structural Grammar of Babylonian*. Wiesbaden: Harrassowitz Verlag, 1996.

——. "Akkadian," in R. Hetzron (ed.), *The Semitic Languages*, pp. 69–99. London: Routledge, 1997.

Budge, E.A.W. and L.W. King, *The Annals of the Kings of Assyria: The Cuneiform Texts with Translations, Transliterations, etc., from the Original Documents in the British Museum*, Vol. I. London: Printed by order of the Trustees, 1902.

Buβmann, H., *Lexikon der Sprachwissenschaft*, 3rd updated and extended edition. Stuttgart: Alfred Kröner Verlag, 2002.

Butts, A.M. (ed.), *Semitic Languages in Contact*. Leiden: Brill, 2015.

Cagni, L., *Altbabylonische Briefe in Umschrift und Übersetzung, 8: Briefe aus dem Iraq Museum* (TIM II). AbB 8. Leiden: Brill, 1980.

Campbell, L., *Historical Linguistics: An Introduction*. 2nd edition. Edinburgh: Edinburgh University Press, 2004.

Caplice, R.I., "Languages (Akkadian)," in D.N. Freedman et al. (eds.), *The Anchor Bible Dictionary*, Vol. 4, *K–N*, pp. 170–173. New York: Doubleday, 1992.

Caquot, A., "Une inscription araméenne d'époque assyrienne," in A. Caquot and M. Philonenko (eds.), *Hommages à André Dupont-Sommer*, pp. 9–16. Paris: Maisonneuve, 1971.

Cetrez, Ö.A., S. Donabed and A. Makko (eds.), *The Assyrian Heritage: Threads of Continuity and Influence*. Uppsala: Acta Universitatis Upsaliensis, 2012.

Cherry, Z., "Aramaic Loanwords in Neo-Assyrian: Rejecting Some Proposals," in M. Luukko, S. Svärd and R. Mattila (eds.), *Of God(s), Trees, Kings, and Scholars: Neo-Assyrian and Related Studies in Honour of Simo Parpola*, pp. 19–25. StOr 106. Helsinki: Societas Orientalis Fennica, 2009.

Ciancaglini, C.A., *Iranian Loanwords in Syriac*. Beiträge zur Iranistik 28. Wiesbaden: Reichert, 2008.

Civil, M., "Early Semitic Loanwords in Sumerian," in M.T. Roth, W. Farber, M.W. Stolper and P. von Bechtolsheim (eds.), *Studies Presented to Robert D. Biggs, June 4, 2004*, pp. 11–33. AS 27. Chicago: Oriental Institute of the University of Chicago, 2007.

Civil, M., R.D. Biggs, H.G. Güterbock, H.J. Nissen and E. Reiner (eds.), *The Series lú = ša and Related Texts*. Rome: Pontificium Institutum Biblicum, 1969.

Clines, David J.A. (ed.), *The Concise Dictionary of Classical Hebrew*. Sheffield: Sheffield Phoenix Press, 2009.

Clyne, M., *Dynamics of Language Contact*. Cambridge: Cambridge University Press, 2003.

Cohen, C., "The 'Held Method' for Comparative Semitic Philology," *JANES* 19 (1989): 9–23.

Cohen, M.E., *An English-to-Akkadian Companion to the Assyrian Dictionaries*. Bethesda: CDL Press, 2011.

Cole, S.W., *Nippur IV: The Early Neo-Babylonian Governor's Archive from Nippur*. OIP 114. Chicago: The Oriental Institute of the University of Chicago, 1996.

Cole, S.W. and P. Machinist (eds.), *Letters from Priests to the Kings Esarhaddon and Assurbanipal*. SAA XIII. Helsinki: Helsinki University Press, 1998.

Cooper, J.S., "Bilingual Babel: Cuneiform Texts in Two or More Languages from Ancient Mesopotamia and Beyond," *Visible Language* 27 (1993): 69–96.

Costaz, L., *Dictionnaire syriaque-français, Syriac-English Dictionary, Qāmūs siryānī ʿarabī*. Beirut: Imprimerie Catholique, 1963.

Couey, J.B., "Amos vii 10–17 and Royal Attitudes Toward Prophecy in the Ancient Near East," *VT* 58 (2008): 300–314.

Cowan, J.M. (ed.), *The Hans Wehr Dictionary of Modern Written Arabic (Arabic-English)*. 3rd edition. New York: Spoken Language Services, 1976.

Cowley, A., *Aramaic Papyri of the Fifth Century B.C.* Oxford: Clarendon Press, 1923.

Craig, J. (ed.), *Assyrian and Babylonian Religious Texts Being Prayers, Oracles, Hymns etc Copied from the Original Tablets Preserved in the British Museum and Autographed*, Vols. I–II. Bibliothek, Assyriologische 13. Leipzig, 1895–1897.

Creason, S., "Aramaic," in R.D. Woodard (ed.), *The Ancient Languages of Syria-Palestine and Arabia*, pp. 108–144. Cambridge: Cambridge University Press, 2008.

Crisostomo, C.J., "Language, Writing, and Ideologies in Contact: Sumerian and Akkadian in the Early Second Millennium BCE," in A.M. Butts (ed.), *Semitic Languages in Contact*, pp. 159–180. Studies in Semitic Languages and Linguistics 82. Leiden: Brill, 2015.

Crystal, D., *The Penguin Dictionary of Language*. 2nd edition. First published as *An Encyclopedic Dictionary of Language and Languages* by Blackwell, 1992. London: Penguin Books, 1999.

——. *A Dictionary of Linguistics and Phonetics*. 5th edition. Malden: Blackwell Publishing, 2003.

Curtis, J.E. and J.E. Reade (eds.), *Art and Empire: Treasures from Assyria in the British Museum*. London: British Museum Press for the Trustees of the British Museum, 1995.

D'Agostino, A. "The Assyrian–Aramaean Interaction in the Upper Khabur: The Archaeological Evidence from Tell Barri Iron Age Layers," *Syria* 86 (2009): 17–41.

Dalley, S.M., "Neo-Assyrian Tablets from Til Barsib," *Abr-Nahrain* 34 (1996–1997): 66–99.

——. "Shamshi-Ilu, Language and Power in the Western Assyrian Empire," in G. Bunnens (ed.), *Essays on Syria in the Iron Age*, pp. 79–88. Ancient Near Eastern Studies – Supplement 7. Louvain, Paris, Sterling & Virginia: Peeters Press, 2000.

Dalley, S. and J.N. Postgate, *The Tablets from Fort Shalmaneser*. CTN III. Oxford: The Alden Press, 1984.
Dalman, G.H. (ed.), *Aramäisch-neuhebräisches Wörterbuch zu Targum, Talmud und Midrasch: Mit Lexikon der Abbreviaturen von G.H. Händler*. Frankfurt a. M.: J. Kauffmann, 1901.
Dandamayev, M.A., "Eber-Nāri," in E. Yarshater (ed.), *Encyclopaedia Iranica*, Vol. 7, pp. 654–655. London: Routledge & Kegan, 1985–.
de Vaan, J.M.C.T., *"Ich bin eine Schwertklinge des Königs": Die Sprache des Bēl-ibni*. AOAT 242. Neukirchen-Vluyn: Neukirchener Verlag, 1995.
Degen, R., *Altaramäische Grammatik der Inschriften des 10. – 8. Jh. v.Chr.* Wiesbaden: Kommissionsverlag Franz Steiner GMBH, 1969.
Deimel, P.A., *Šumerisches Lexikon*. Rome: Verlag des päpstl. Bibelinstituts, 1925–1950.
Del Olmo Lete, G. and J. Sanmartín, *A Dictionary of the Ugaritic Language in the Alphabetic Tradition*, 2 vols. 2nd revised edition. English version edited and translated by Wilfred G.E. Watson. Handbuch der Orientalistik 67. Leiden & Boston: Brill, 2004.
Delaporte, L., *Épigraphes Araméens: étude des textes Araméens gravés ou écrits sur des tablettes cunéiformes*. Paris: Geuthner, 1912.
Delitzsch, F., *Assyrisches Handwörterbuch*. Leipzig: J.C. Hinrichs'sche Buchhandlung, 1896.
Deller, K., "Zur sprachlichen Einordnung der Inschriften Aššurnaṣirpals II. (883–859)," *Or* 26 (1957): 144–156.
——. *Lautlehre des Neuassyrischen*. Unpublished Ph.D. thesis, Vienna, 1959.
——. "Zur Terminologie neuassyrischer Urkunden," *WZKM* 57 (1961): 29–42.
——. "Getreidekursangaben in neuassyrischen Rechtsurkunden," *Or* 33 (1964): 257–261.
——. Review of "The Assyrian Dictionary of the Oriental Institute of the University of Chicago. Vol. 16: Ṣ," by A.L. Oppenheim et al., *Or* 33 (1964): 89–96.
——. "Marginalien zu den Rechtsurkunden aus Balawat," *Or* 34 (1965): 169.
——. "Neuassyrisches aus Sultantepe," *Or* 34 (1965): 457–477.
——. "The Neo-Assyrian Epigraphical Remains of Nimrud," *Or* 35 (1966): 179–194.
——. "Die Briefe des Adad-šumu-uṣur," in W. Röllig and M. Dietrich (eds.), *Lišān mitḫurti: Festschrift Wolfram Freiherr von Soden zum 19.4.1968 gewidmet von Schülern und Mitarbeitern*, pp. 45–64. Neukirchen-Vluyn: Verlag Butzon & Bercker Kevelaer, 1969.
——. "Old Assyrian *Kanwarta*, Middle Assyrian *Kalmarte*, and Neo-Assyrian *Garmarte*," *JEOL* 29 (1985–1986, Leiden 1987): 43–49.
——. "Assurbanipal in der Gartenlaube," *BaM* 18 (1987): 229–238.
——. "Bibliography of Neo-Assyrian – 1988 and Updates," *SAAB* 2 (1988): 129–135.
——. "Bēt-Adad-erība, Provinz Tamnūnu," *NABU* 1990/66.
——. "Die Bezeichnungen für die Mistel (mistletoe, gui, vischio, viscum)," *NABU* 1991/11.
Deller, K. and S. Parpola, "Progressive Vokalassimilation im Neuassyrischen," *Or* 36 (1967): 337–338.
Deller, K. and W.R. Mayer, "Akkadische Lexikographie: *CAD* M," *Or* 53 (1984): 72–124.
Deller, K. and I.L. Finkel, "A Neo-Assyrian Inventory Tablet of Unknown Provenance," *ZA* 74 (1984): 76-91.
Deller, K. and A.R. Millard, "Zwei Rechtsurkunden aus Aššur im British Museum," *AfO* 32 (1985): 38–52.
Deller, K., W.R. Mayer and W. Sommerfeld, "Akkadische Lexikographie: *CAD* N," *Or* 56 (1987): 176–218.

Deller, K., W.R. Mayer and J. Oelsner, "Akkadische Lexikographie: *CAD* Q," *Or* 58 (1989): 255–282.

Deller, K. and A.R. Millard, "Die Bestallungsurkunde des Nergal-āpil-kūmūja von Kalḫu," *BaM* 24 (1993): 217–242.

Deller, K. and A. Fadhil, "Neue Nimrud – Urkunden des 8. Jahrhunderts v. Chr.: (Taf. 55 – 114)," *BaM* 24 (1993): 243–270.

Deller, K., F.M. Fales and L. Jakob-Rost, with contributions by V. Donbaz, "Neo-Assyrian Texts from Assur: Private Archives in the Vorderasiatisches Museum of Berlin, Part II," *SAAB* 9 (1995, printed 1997): 3–137.

Delsman, W.C., "Das Barth'sche Gesetz und Lehnwörter," *UF* 11 (1979): 187–188.

Dercksen, J.G., "On Anatolian Loanwords in Akkadian Texts from Kültepe," *ZA* 97 (2007): 26–46.

Desmond, D.-M., *Dictionary of Manichaean Middle Persian and Parthian. Dictionary of Manichaean Texts*, Vol. III: *Texts from Central Asia and China*, Part 1. Turnhout: Brepols, 2004.

Dietrich, M., "Untersuchungen zur Grammatik des Neubabylonischen," in W. Röllig and M. Dietrich (eds.), *lišān mitḫurti: Festschrift Wolfram Freiherr von Soden zum 19.VI.1968 gewidmet von Schülern und Mitarbeitern*, pp. 65–99. AOAT 1. Neukirchen-Vluyn: Verlag Butzon & Bercker Kevelaer, 1969.

——. (ed.), *The Babylonian Correspondence of Sargon and Sennacherib*. SAA XVII. Helsinki: Helsinki University Press, 2003.

Dietrich, M. and O. Loretz, "*GZR* 'Abschneiden, Abkneifen' im Ugar. und Hebr.," *UF* 9 (1977): 51–56.

Dion, P.E., "Aramaic Words for 'Letter'," *Semeia* 22 (1981): 77–88.

——. *Les Araméens à l'âge du fer: histoire politique et structures sociales*. Paris: Gabalda, 1997.

Donbaz, V., "Some Neo-Assyrian Contracts from Girnavaz and Vicinity," *SAAB* 2 (1988): 3–30.

——. "Some Selected Neo-Assyrian Texts from Istanbul and Elsewhere," *SAAB* 12 (1998): 57–82.

——. *Cuneiform Texts in the Sadberk Hanim Museum*. Istanbul: Sadberk Hanim Müzesi, 1999.

——. "A Neo-Assyrian Text of Unknown Provenance," *NABU* 2002/90.

Donbaz, V. and S. Parpola, *Neo-Assyrian Legal Texts in Istanbul*. StAT 2. Saarbrücken: Saarbrücker Druckerei und Verlag, 2001.

Donef, R., *Assyrians Post-Nineveh: Identity, Fragmentation, Conflict and Survival (672 BC – 1920): A Study of Assyrogenous Communities*. Racho Donef, 2012.

Donner H. and W. Röllig, *Kanaanäische und aramäische Inschriften*, *Band* I, *Texte*. 5th extended and revised edition. Wiesbaden: Harrassowitz, 2002.

Dornauer, A., *Das Archiv des assyrischen Statthalters Mannu-kī-Aššūr von Gūzāna/Tall Ḥalaf*. Vorderasiatische Forschungen der Max Freiherr von Oppenheim-Stiftung 3, III. Wiesbaden: Harrassowitz, 2014.

Dougherty, R.P., "Writing upon Parchment and Papyrus among the Babylonians and the Assyrians," *JAOS* 48 (1928): 109–135.

Driver, G.R., "An Aramaic Inscription in the Cuneiform Script," *AoF* 3 (1926): 47–53.

——. "Aramaic Names in Accadian Texts," *RSO* 32 (1957): 41–57.

Drolet, J., "Akkadian Loans in Arabic? The Linguistic and Historical Evidence," in M. St-Amour and M. Fowlie (eds.), *Proceedings of McCCLU: 23rd–25th March 2007, McGill University, Montreal, Quebec*, pp. 9–23. McGill's Canadian Conference for Linguistics Undergraduates. Montreal: McGill University, 2007.

Drower, E.S. and R. Macuch, *A Mandaic Dictionary*. Oxford: Clarendon Press, 1963.

Dupont-Sommer, A., "L'ostracon araméen d'Assour," *Syria* 24 (1944): 24–61.
Durand, J.-M., *Archives épistolaires de Mari* I/1. ARM 26. Paris: Editions Recherche sur les Civilisations, 1988.
——. "Précurseurs syriens aux protocoles néo-assyriens – Considérations sur la vie politique aux Bords-de-l'Euphrate," in D. Charpin and F. Joannès (eds.), *Marchands, diplomates et empereurs: études sur la civilisation mésopotamienne offertes à Paul Garelli*, pp. 13–71. Paris: Éditions Recherche sur les Civilisations, 1991.
Durkin, P., *The Oxford Guide to Etymology*. Oxford: Oxford University Press, 2009.
Ebeling, E., *Keilschrifttexte aus Assur religiösen Inhalts*. WVDOG 35. Leipzig, Hinrichs, 1920.
——. *Keilschrifttexte aus Assur juristischen Inhalts*. WVDOG 50, MA texts. Leipzig: Hinrichs, 1927.
——. *Tod und Leben nach den Vorstellungen der Babylonier*. Berlin & Leipzig: Walter de Gruyter, 1931.
——. "Eine Weihinschrift Aššureṭililânis für Marduk," *AnOr* 12 (1935): 71–73.
——. "Mittelassyrische Rezepte zur Herstellung von wohlriechenden Salben," *Or* 19 (1950): 265–278.
——. *Parfümrezepte und kultische Texte aus Assur*. Sonderdruck aus Orientalia 17–19. Rome: Pontificium Institutum Biblicum, 1950.
——. "Kultische Texte aus Assur," *Or* 20 (1951): 399–405.
——. "Kultische Texte aus Assur," *Or* 21 (1952): 129–148.
——. "Kultische Texte aus Assur," *Or* 22 (1953): 25–46.
——. *Glossar zu den neubabylonischen Briefen*. München: Verlag der Bayerischen Akademie der Wissenschaften, 1953.
——. *Stiftungen und Vorschriften für assyrische Tempel*. VIO 23. Berlin: Akademie-Verlag, 1954.
Edzard, D.O., Review of "CAD 5 'G'," *ZA* 53 (1959): 292–300.
——. Review of "CAD 8 'K' and 9 'L'," *ZA* 64 (1975): 123–126.
Edzard, L., "Inner-Semitic Loans and Lexical Doublets v. Genetically Related Cognates," in A.M. Butts (ed.), *Semitic Languages in Contact*, pp. 181–197. Studies in Semitic Languages and Linguistics 82. Leiden: Brill, 2015.
Elias, A.E. and Ed.E. Elias (eds.), *Elias' Modern Dictionary: Arabic-English*. Cairo: Elias' Modern Publishing House, 1982. Arabic title: *Qāmūs elias al-ʿaṣrī*.
Emerton, J.A., "New Evidence for the Use of *Waw* Consecutive in Aramaic," *VT* 44 (1994): 255–258.
Encyclopaedia Judaica,Vol. 3, ANH–AZ. Jerusalem: Keter Publishing House, 1971.
Ephʿal, I., *The Ancient Arabs: Nomads on the Borders of the Fertile Crescent 9th–5th Centuries B.C.* Jerusalem: Magnes Press, 1982.
Epstein, J.N., "Gloses babylo-araméennes," *REJ* 73 (1921): 27-58.
Eskhult, M., "The Importance of Loanwords for Dating Biblical Hebrew Texts," in I. Young (ed.), *Biblical Hebrew: Studies in Chronology and Typology*, pp. 8–23. Journal for the Study of the Old Testament Supplement Series 369. Sheffield: Sheffield Academic Press, 2003.
Faist, B., "Sprachen und Schriften in Assur," in J. Marzahn and B. Salje (eds.), *Wiedererstehendes Assur: 100 Jahre deutsche Ausgrabungen in Assyrien*, pp. 149–156. Mainz am Rhein: Philipp von Zabern, 2003.
——. *Alltagstexte aus neuassyrischen Archiven und Bibliotheken der Stadt Assur*. StAT 3. Wiesbaden: Harrassowitz Verlag, 2007.
——. with a contribution by E. Klengel-Brandt, *Keilschrifttexte aus neuassyrischer Zeit 3: Neuassyrische Rechtsurkunden III*. WVDOG 110. Saarwellingen: Saarländische Druckerei & Verlag, 2005.

——. with a contribution by E. Klengel-Brandt, *Keilschrifttexte aus neuassyrischer Zeit 4: Neuassyrische Rechtsurkunden IV.* WVDOG 132. Wiesbaden: Harrassowitz Verlag, 2010.

Fales, F.M., *Censimenti e catasti di epoca neo-assira.* Studi economici e tecnologici 2. Rome, Istituto per l'Oriente, 1973.

——. "Sulla tavoletta aramaica A.O. 25.341," *AION* 35 (1976): 541–548.

——. "On Aramaic Onomastics in the Neo-Assyrian Period," *OrAnt* 16 (1977): 41–68.

——. "A Cuneiform Correspondence to Alphabetic ש in West Semitic Names of the I Millennium B.C.," *Or* 47 (1978): 91–98.

——. "L'onomastica aramaica in età neo-assira: raffronti tra il corpus alfabetico e il materiale cuneiforme," in *Atti del I° Convegno Italiano sul Vicino Oriente Antico: (Roma, 22–24 aprile 1976)*, pp. 199–229. Orientis Antiqvi Collectio 13. Rome: Centro per le antichità e la storia dell'arte del vicino oriente, 1978.

——. "Studies on Neo-Assyrian Texts I: Joins and Collations to the Tell Halaf Documents," *ZA* 69 (1979): 192–216.

——. "A List of Assyrian and West Semitic Women's Names," *Iraq* 41 (1979): 55–73.

——. "New Assyrian Letters from the Kuyunjik Collection," *AfO* 27 (1980): 136–153.

——. "Accadico e aramaico: livelli dell'interferenza linguistica," *Vicino Oriente* 3 (1980): 243–267.

——. "Two Neo-Assyrian Notes," *RA* 75 (1981): 67–69.

——. *Cento lettere neo-assire: traslitterazione e traduzione, commento e note,* I: *nn. 1–45.* Venezia: [Seminario di iranistica, uralo-altaistica e caucasologia dell'Università degli studi di Venezia], 1983.

——. "Studies on Neo-Assyrian Texts II: 'Deeds and documents' from the British Museum," *ZA* 73 (1983): 232–255.

——. "Le double bilinguisme de la statue de Tell Fakheriye," *Syria* 60 (1983): 233–250.

——. "Assyro-Aramaica: Three Notes," *Or* 53 (1984): 66–71.

——. "Assiro e aramaico: filologia e interferenza linguistica," *Atti del Sodalizio Glottologico Milanese* 25 (1985): 21–30.

——. *Aramaic Epigraphs on Clay Tablets of the Neo-Assyrian Period.* AECT. Studi Semitici N.S. 2. Rome: Università degli studi "la Sapienza", 1986.

——. "Aramaic Letters and Neo-Assyrian Letters: Philological and Methodological Notes," *JAOS* 107 (1987): 451–469.

——. "Formations with *m*-Prefix in the Bilingual Vocabularies," in H. Waetzoldt and H. Hauptmann (eds.), *Wirtschaft und Gesellschaft von Ebla: Akten der Internationalen Tagung Heidelberg 4.–7. November 1986*, pp. 205–209. HSAO 2. Heidelberg: Heidelberger Orientverlag, 1988.

——. "Nuovi dati sull'onomastica aramaica in cuneiforme neo-assiro," *Atti del Sodalizio Glottologico Milanese* 27 (1988): 75–84.

——. "Istituzioni a confronto tra mondo semitico occidentale e Assiria nel I millennio a.C.: il trattato di Sefire," in L. Canfora, M. Liverani and C. Zaccagnini (eds.), *I trattati nel mondo antico: forma ideologia funzione*, pp. 149–173. Saggi di storia antica 2. Rome: "L'Ema" di Bretschneider, 1990.

——. "The Rural Landscape of the Neo-Assyrian Empire: A Survey," *SAAB* 4 (1990): 81–142.

——. "West Semitic Names in the Assyrian Empire: Diffusion and Social Relevance," *StEL* 8 (1991): 99–117.

——. "West Semitic Names in the Šēḫ Ḥamad Texts," *SAAB* 7 (1993): 139–150.

——. "Assyro-Aramaica: The Assyrian Lion-Weights," in K. van Lerberghe and A. Schoors (eds.), *Immigration and Emigration within the Ancient Near East. Festschrift E. Lipiński*, pp. 33–55. OLA 65. Leuven: Peeters Publishers, 1995.

——. "Most Ancient Aramaic Texts and Linguistics: A Review of Recent Studies," *Incontri Linguistici* 19 (1996): 33–57.
——. "People and Professions in Neo-Assyrian Assur," in H. Waetzoldt and H. Hauptmann (eds.), *Assyrien im Wandel der Zeiten*, pp. 33–40. HSAO 6. Heidelberg: Heidelberger Orientverlag, 1997.
——. "The Tablets From Tell Shioukh Fawqani/Burmarina in the Context of Assyro-Aramaic Studies," in G. del Olmo Lete and J.-L. Montero Fenollós (eds.), *Archaeology of the Upper Syrian Euphrates, the Tishrin Dam Area: Proceedings of the International Symposium Held at Barcelona, January 28th – 30th 1998*, pp. 625–636. AuOr - Supplement 15. Barcelona: Editorial Ausa, 1999.
——. "The Use and Function of Aramaic Tablets," in G. Bunnens (ed.), *Essays on Syria in the Iron Age*, pp. 89–124. Ancient Near Eastern Studies - Supplement 7. Louvain, Paris, Sterling & Virginia: Peeters Press, 2000.
——. "*tuanu*: an Aramaic loanword in Neo-Assyrian," *NABU* 2003/103.
——. "Assyrian-Aramaic Cultural Interrelation: Older and Newer Results," in L. Bachelot and F.M. Fales (eds.), *Tell Shiukh Fawqani 1994–1998*, pp. 596–616. Padova: S.A.R.G.O.N. Editrice e libreria, 2005.
——. "Multilingualism on Multiple Media in the Neo-Assyrian Period: A Review of the Evidence," *SAAB* 16 (2007): 95–122.
——. "New Light on Assyro-Aramaic Interference: The Assur Ostracon," in F.M. Fales and G.F. Grassi (eds.), *CAMSEMUD 2007: Proceedings of the 13th Italian Meeting of Afro-Asiatic Linguistics Held in Udine, May 21th –24th, 2007*, pp. 189–204. History of the Ancient Near East: Monographs VI/2. Padova: S.A.R.G.O.N. Editrice e Libreria, 2010.
——. "Old Aramaic," in S. Weninger (ed.), in collaboration with G. Khan, M.P. Streck and J.C.E. Watson, *The Semitic Languages: An International Handbook*, pp. 555–573. Handbücher zur Sprach- und Kommunikationswissenschaft 36. Berlin: De Gruyter Mouton, 2011.
——. "Ethnicity in the Assyrian Empire: A View from the Nisbe, (I): Foreigners and 'Special' Inner Communities," in D.S. Vanderhooft and A. Winitzer (eds.), *Literature as Politics, Politics as Literature: Essays on the Ancient Near East in Honor of Peter Machinist*, pp. 47–74. Winona Lake: Eisenbrauns, 2013.
——. "Ethnicity in the Neo-Assyrian Empire: A View from the Nisbe, (II): 'Assyrians'," in M.G. Biga, J. Cordoba et al. (eds.), Homenaje a Mario Liverani, *Isimu* 11-12 (2009-2010, but 2015): 183-204.
——. "Ethnicity in the Assyrian Empire: A View from the Nisbe, (III) 'Arameans' and Related Tribalists," in Y. Heffron, A. Stone and M. Worthington (eds.), *At the Dawn of History: Ancient Near Eastern Studies in Honour of J.N. Postgate*, Vol. 1, pp. 133–177. Winona Lake: Eisenbrauns, 2017.
——. "Neo-Assyrian," in J.-P. Vita (ed.), *History of the Akkadian Language, Vol. 2, The Second and First Millennia BCE Afterlife*, pp. 1347–1395. Leiden-Boston: Brill, 2021.
——. "Aramaic Epigraphy from Assyria: New Data and Old Issues," in A.M. Maeir, A. Berlejung, E. Eshel and T. Oshima (eds.), *Neo Perspectives on Aramaic Epigraphy in Mesopotamia, Qumran, Egypt and Idumea*, pp. 5–16. Tübingen: Mohr Siebeck, 2021.
Fales, F.M. and L. Jakob-Rost, "Neo-Assyrian Texts from Assur: Private Archives in the Vorderasiatisches Museum of Berlin, Part 1," *SAAB* 5 (1991): 3–157.
Fales, F.M. and J.N. Postgate (eds.), *Imperial Administrative Records, Part* I: *Palace and Temple Administration*. SAA VII. Helsinki: Helsinki University Press, 1992.
——. *Imperial Administrative Records, Part* II: *Provincial and Military Administration*. SAA XI. Helsinki: Helsinki University Press, 1995.

Fales, F.M., (Introduction by L. Bachelot; Appendix by E. Attardo), "An Aramaic Tablet From Tell Shioukh Fawqani, Syria," *Semitica* 46 (1996): 81–121.

Fassberg, S.E., "The Forms of 'Son' and 'Daughter' in Aramaic," in H. Gzella and M.L. Folmer (eds.), *Aramaic in its Historical and Linguistic Setting*, pp. 41–53. Wiesbaden: Harrassowitz Verlag, 2008.

Field, F.W., *Linguistic Borrowing in Bilingual Contexts*. Amsterdam & Philadelphia: John Benjamins Publishing Company, 2002.

Finegan, E., *Language: Its Structure and Use*. Fort Worth: Harcourt Brace College Publishers, 1999.

Finkel, I.L., "On Late Babylonian Medical Training" in A.R. George and I.L. Finkel (eds.), *Wisdom, Gods and Literature: Studies in Assyriology in Honour of W.G. Lambert*, pp. 137–223. Winona Lake: Eisenbrauns, 2000.

Finkelstein, J.J., "Cuneiform Texts from Tell Billa," *JCS* 7 (1953): 109–176.

——. "Assyrian Contracts from Sultantepe," *AnSt* 7 (1957): 137–145.

——. *Late Old Babylonian Documents and Letters*. YOS 13. New Haven: Yale University Press, 1972.

Fitzmyer, J.A., "The Phases of the Aramaic Language," in J.A. Fitzmyer, *A Wandering Aramean: Collected Aramaic Essays*, pp. 57–84. Society of Biblical Literature, Monograph Series 25. Chico: Scholars Press, 1979.

——. *The Aramaic Inscriptions of Sefire*. Revised edition. Biblica et orientalia 19. Rome: Editrice Pontificio Istituto Biblico, 1995.

Fitzmyer, J.A. and S.A. Kaufman, *An Aramaic Bibliography, Part* 1: *Old, Official, and Biblical Aramaic*. Baltimore: The Johns Hopkins University Press, 1992.

Folmer, M.L., *The Aramaic Language in the Achaemenid Period: A Study in Linguistic Variation*. OLA 68. Leuven: Peeters, 1995.

——. "Imperial Aramaic as an Administrative Language of the Achaemenid Period," in S. Weninger (ed.), in collaboration with G. Khan, M.P. Streck and J.C.E. Watson, *The Semitic Languages: An International Handbook*, pp. 587–598. Handbücher zur Sprach- und Kommunikationswissenschaft 36. Berlin: De Gruyter Mouton, 2011.

——. "Old and Imperial Aramaic," in H. Gzella (ed.), *Languages from the World of the Bible*, pp. 128–159. Original edition "*Sprachen aus der Welt des Alten Testaments*" 2009 by WBG (Wissenschaftliche Buchgesellschaft), Darmstadt. Boston: De Gruyter, 2011.

Fox, J., *Semitic Noun Patterns*. Harvard Semitic Studies 52. Winona Lake: Eisenbrauns, 2003.

Fraenkel, S., *Die Aramäischen Fremdwörter im Arabischen*. 2nd reprint of the edition published in Leiden, 1886. Hildesheim & New York: Georg Olms Verlag, 1982.

Friedrich, J., G.R. Meyer, A. Ungnad and E.F. Weidner (eds.), *Die Inschriften vom Tell Halaf: Keilschrifttexte und aramäische Urkunden aus einer assyrischen Provinzhauptstadt*, reprint of the edition published in 1940. AfO, Beiheft 6. Osnabrük: Biblio-Verlag, 1967.

Frye, R.N., "Assyria and Syria: Synonyms," *JNES* 51 (1992): 281–285.

Fuchs, A., "Kapitel VII: Die Inschrift vom Ištar-Tempel," in R. Borger, *Beiträge zum Inschriftenwerk Assurbanipals. Die Prismenklassen A, B, C = K, D, E, F, G, H, J und T sowie andere Inschriften*, pp. 259–296. Wiesbaden: Harrassowitz, 1996.

Fuchs, A. and S. Parpola (eds.), *The Correspondence of Sargon II, Part* III: *Letters from Babylonia and the Eastern Provinces*. SAA XV. Helsinki: Helsinki University Press, 2001.

Galter, H.D., "Cuneiform Bilingual Royal Inscriptions," in S. Izre'el and R. Drory (eds.), *Language and Culture in the Near East*, pp. 25–50. IOS 15. Leiden: Brill, 1995.

Garelli, P., "Importance et rôle des araméens dans l'administration de l'empire assyrien," in H.-J. Nissen and J. Renger (eds.), *Mesopotamien und seine Nachbarn: Politische und kulturelle Wechselbeziehungen im Alten Vorderasien vom 4. bis 1. Jahrtausend v. Chr*, pp. 437–447. CRRA 25. Berlin: Dietrich Reimer Verlag, 1982.

Garr, W.R., "The Comparative Method in Semitic Linguistics," *AuOr* 25 (2005): 17–21.

Gaspa, S., "A Bibliography of Neo-Assyrian Studies (2007–2012)," *SAAB* 19 (2011-2012): 279–328.

——. "Textile Production and Consumption in the Neo-Assyrian Empire," in M.-L. Nosch and H. Koefoed (eds.), *Textile Production and Consumption in the Ancient Near East: Archaeology, Epigraphy, Iconography*, pp. 224–247. Ancient Textiles Series 12. Oxford: Oxbow Books, 2013.

——. "Garments, Parts of Garments, and Textile Techniques in the Assyrian Terminology: The Neo-Assyrian Textile Lexicon in the 1st-Millennium BC Linguistic Context," in S. Gaspa, C. Michel and M.-L. Nosch (eds.), *Textile Terminologies from the Orient to the Mediterranean and Europe, 1000 BC to 1000 AD*, pp. 47–90. Lincoln: Zea Books, 2017.

Geers, F.W., "The Treatment of Emphatics in Akkadian," *JNES* 4 (1945): 65–67.

Gelb, I.J., "Notes on von Soden's Grammar of Akkadian," *BiOr* 12 (1955): 93–111.

——. *Old Akkadian Writing and Grammar.* 2nd edition revised and enlarged. MAD 2. Chicago: Chicago University Press, 1961.

——. "The Early History of the West Semitic Peoples," *JCS* 15 (1961): 27–47.

——. "Comments on the Akkadian Syllabary," *Or* 39 (1970): 516–546.

Geller, M.J., "The Last Wedge," *ZA* 87 (1997): 43–95.

——. Review of "A Sketch of Neo-Assyrian Grammar," by J. Hämeen-Anttila, *BSOAS* 65/3 (2002): 562–564.

Gensler, O.D., "Why Semitic Adverbializers (Akkadian *-iš*, Syriac *-ā'īṯ*) Should not be Derived from Existential *'īṯ*," *JSS* 45 (2000): 233–265.

George, A.R., *The Babylonian Gilgamesh Epic: Introduction, Critical Edition and Cuneiform Texts*, 2 Vols. Oxford: Oxford University Press, 2003.

——. "Babylonian and Assyrian: A History of Akkadian," in N.J. Postgate (ed.), *Languages of Iraq, Ancient and Modern*, pp. 31–71. London: British School of Archaeology in Iraq, 2007.

Gesenius, W., *Wilhelm Gesenius' Hebräisches und Aramäisches Handwörterbuch über das Alte Testament.* In Verbindung mit H. Zimmern, W. Max Müller u. O. Weber, bearbeitet von Frants Buhl. Leipzig: F. C. W. Vogel, 1915.

——. *Hebräisches und Aramäisches Handwörterbuch über das Alte Testament.* Wilhelm Gesenius; begonnen von Rudolf Meyer; unter verantwortlicher Mitarbeit von Johannes Renz; bearbeitet und herausgegeben von Herbert Donner. 18. Auflage, 3. Lieferung כ–מ. Berlin, Heidelberg & New York: Springer, 2005.

Goetze, A., "Cuneiform Inscriptions from Tarsus," *JAOS* 59 (1939): 1–16.

Görke, S., "Aramäischer Einfluss in Assyrien," in M. Novák, F. Prayon and A-M. Wittke (eds.), *Die Außenwirkung des späthethitischen Kulturraumes: Güteraustausch – Kulturkontakt – Kulturtransfer, Akten der zweiten Forschungstagung des Graduiertenkollegs "Anatolien und seine Nachbarn" der Eberhard-Karls-Universität Tübingen (20. bis 22. November 2003)*, pp. 325–333. Münster: Ugarit-Verlag, 2004.

Grayson, A.K., *Assyrian Rulers of the Early First Millennium BC I (1114–859 B.C.)*. RIMA 2. Toronto: University of Toronto Press, 1991.

——. "Three Neo-Assyrian Documents," in D. Charpin and F. Joannès (eds.), *Marchands, diplomates et empereurs: études sur la civilisation mésopotamienne offertes à Paul Garelli*, pp. 357–362. Paris: Éditions Recherche sur les Civilisations, 1991.

——. *Assyrian Rulers of the Early First Millennium BC II (858–745 B.C.)*. RIMA 3. Toronto: University of Toronto Press, 1996.

Greenberg, J.H., "The Patterning of Root Morphemes in Semitic," *Word* 6 (1950): 162–181.

Greenfield, J.C., "Some Reflections on the Vocabulary of Aramaic in Relationship to the Other Semitic Languages," in P. Fronzaroli (ed.), *Atti del Secondo Congresso Internazionale di Linguistica Camito-Semitica: Firenze, 16–19 Aprile 1974*, pp. 151–156. QuadSem 5. Florence: Istituto di Linguistica e di Lingue Orientali, Università di Firenze, 1978.

——. "the Meaning of פחז," in Y. Avishur and J. Blau (eds.), *Studies in the Bible and the Ancient Near East Presented to Samuel E. Loewenstamm, on His Seventieth Birthday*, pp. 35–40. Jerusalem: E. Rubinstein, 1978.

——. "The Dialects of Early Aramaic," *JNES* 37 (1978): 93–99.

——. "Aramaic and Its Dialects," in H.H. Paper (ed.), *Jewish Languages: Theme and Variations. Proceedings of Regional Conferences of the Association for Jewish Studies Held at the University of Michigan and New York University in March—April 1975*, pp. 29–43. Cambridge: Association for Jewish Studies, 1978.

——. "Babylonian-Aramaic Relationship," in H.-J. Nissen and J. Renger (eds.), *Mesopotamien und Seine Nachbarn: Politische und kulturelle Wechselbeziehungen im Alten Vorderasien vom 4. bis 1. Jahrtausend v. Chr., Teil* 2. XXV. Rencontre Assyriologique Internationale Berlin, 3. bis 7. Juli 1978, pp. 471–482. CRRA 25. Berlin: Dietrich Reimer Verlag, 1982.

——. "*ana urdūti kabāsu* = כבש לעבד," *StOr* 55:11 (1984): 259–263.

——. "The Aramaic Legal Texts of the Achaemenian Period," *Transeuphratène* 3 (1990): 85–92.

——. "Some Glosses on the Safire Inscriptions," *Maarav* 7 (1991): 141–147.

——. "Three Related Roots: *KMS*, *KNS* and *KNŠ*," in Sh.M. Paul, M.E. Stone and A. Pinnick (eds.), *ʿAl Kanfei Yonah: Collected Studies of Jonas C. Greenfield on Semitic Philology*, Vol. 2, pp. 840–846. Leiden: Brill, 2001.

Greenfield, J.C. and A. Shaffer "Notes on the Akkadian-Aramaic Bilingual Statue from Tell Fekherye," *Iraq* 45 (1983): 109–116.

——. "*qlqlt'*, *tubkinnu*, Refuse Tips and Treasure Trove," *AnSt* 33 (1983): 123–129.

Groneberg, B.R.M., *Untersuchungen zum hymnisch-epischen Dialekt der altbabylonischen literarischen Texte*. Münster: University of Münster, 1971.

Gzella, H., "Aramaic in the Parthian Period: The Arsacid Inscriptions," in H. Gzella and M.L. Folmer (eds.), *Aramaic in its Historical and Linguistic Setting*, pp. 107–130. Wiesbaden: Harrassowitz Verlag, 2008.

——. "Imperial Aramaic," in S. Weninger (ed.), in collaboration with G. Khan, M.P. Streck and J.C.E. Watson, *The Semitic Languages: An International Handbook*, pp. 574–586. Handbücher zur Sprach- und Kommunikationswissenschaft 36. Berlin: De Gruyter Mouton, 2011.

——. "Late Imperial Aramaic," in S. Weninger (ed.), in collaboration with G. Khan, M.P. Streck and J.C.E. Watson, *The Semitic Languages: An International Handbook*, pp. 598–609. Handbücher zur Sprach- und Kommunikationswissenschaft 36. Berlin: De Gruyter Mouton, 2011.

——. *A Cultural History of Aramaic: From the Beginnings to the Advent of Islam*. Handbuch der Orientalistik. Abt. 1, Der Nahe und Mittlere Osten 111. Leiden: Brill, 2015.

——. "New Light on Linguistic Diversity in Pre-Achaemenid Aramaic: Wandering Arameans or Language Spread?" in A. Berlejung, A.M. Maeir and A. Schüle (eds.),

Wandering Arameans: Arameans Outside Syria: Textual and Archaeological Perspectives, pp. 19–37. Wiesbaden: Harrassowitz Verlag, 2017.
Hackl, J., "Language Death and Dying Reconsidered: The Rôle of Late Babylonian as a Vernacular Language," to be published in Wunsch, C. (ed.), *The Neo-Babylonian Workshop of the 53rd Rencontre Assyriologique Internationale. City Administration in Neo-Babylonian Times*. Winona Lake: Eisenbrauns. Available as a pre-paper (Version 01, July 2011), online:
https://www.academia.edu
Hämeen-Anttila, J., "A New Text Relating to Ashurbanipal's Elamite Wars," *SAAB* 1 (1987): 13–16.
——. "Bibliography of Neo-Assyrian (Post-War Period)," *SAAB* 1 (1987): 73–92.
——. *A Sketch of Neo-Assyrian Grammar*. SAAS XIII. Helsinki: The Neo-Assyrian Text Corpus Project, 2000.
Harper, R.F., *Assyrian and Babylonian Letters Belonging to the K̲. Collection of the British Museum*. Parts I–XIV, reprinted in 5 vols., by N. & N. Press, 1977. Chicago: The University of Chicago Press, 1892.
Haspelmath, M., "Lexical Borrowing: Concepts and Issues," in M. Haspelmath and U. Tadmor (eds.), *Loanwords in the World's Languages: A Comparative Handbook*, pp. 35–54. Berlin: De Gruyter Mouton, 2009.
Hasselbach, R., *Sargonic Akkadian: A Historical and Comparative Study of the Syllabic Texts*. Wiesbaden: Otto Harrassowitz Verlag, 2005.
——. "The Affiliation of Sargonic Akkadian with Babylonian and Assyrian: New Insights Concerning the Internal Sub-Grouping of Akkadian," *JSS* 52 (2007): 21–43.
Haugen, E., "The Analysis of Linguistic Borrowing," *Language* 26 (1950): 210–231.
Haupt, P., "Some Assyrian Etymologies," *AJSL* 26 (1909): 1–26.
Healey, J.F., "Lexical Loans in Early Syriac: A Comparison with Nabataean Aramaic," *Studi Epigrafici e Linguistici* 12 (1995): 75–84.
Hecker, K., *Grammatik der Kültepe-Texte*. AnOr. 44. Rome: Pontificio Istituto Biblico, 1968.
Held, M., "*mḫṣ/*mḫš* in Ugaritic and Other Semitic Languages (A Study in Comparative Lexicography)" *JAOS* 79 (1959): 169–176.
——. "On Terms for Deportation in the OB Royal Inscriptions with Special Reference to Yaḫdunlim," *JANES* 11 (1979): 53–62.
Herbordt, S., *Neuassyrische Glyptik des 8.–7. Jh. v. Chr.* Helsinki: The Neo-Assyrian Text Corpus Project, 1992.
Hetzron, R., "Two Principles of Genetic Reconstruction," *Lingua* 38 (1976): 89–108.
Hickey, R. (ed.), *The Handbook of Language Contact*. Chichester: Wiley-Blackwell, 2010.
Hilgert, M., *Akkadisch in der Ur III–Zeit*. Münster: Rhema-Verlag, 2002.
——. "New Perspectives in the Study of Third Millennium Akkadian," *Cuneiform Digital Library Journal* 4 (2003). Online 15/09/2022:
https://cdli.ucla.edu/file/publications/cdlj2003_004.pdf
Hoftijzer, J. and K. Jongeling, *Dictionary of the North-West Semitic Inscriptions*, 2 vols. Leiden: Brill, 1995.
Holma, H., *Die Namen der Körperteile im assyrisch-babylonischen: Eine lexikalisch-etymologische Studie*. Annales Academiae scientiarum Fennicae. Ser. B, 7:1. Helsinki; Suomalaisen Tiedeakatemian Kustantama, 1911.
Hope, T.E., "Loan-words as Cultural and Lexical Symbols," *Archivum Linguisticum* 15 (1963): 29–42.
Hübschmann, H., *Armenische Grammatik*, I Teil, *Armenische Etymologie*. Indogermanischer Grammatiken, Vol. 6. Leipzig: Breitkopf & Härtel, 1897.

Huehnergard, J., Review of "Grammatical Analysis and Glossary of the Northwest Semitic Vocables in Akkadian Texts of the 15th–13th C.B.C. from Canaan and Syria," by D. Sivan, *JAOS* 107 (1987): 713–725.
——. "Northwest Semitic Vocabulary in Akkadian Texts," *JAOS* 107 (1987): 713–725.
——. "What is Aramaic," *ARAM* 7 (1995): 261–282.
——. *A Grammar of Akkadian*. Atlanta: Scholars Press, 1997.
——. "Comparative Semitic Linguistics," *IOS* 20 (2002): 119–150.
——. "Akkadian *ḫ* and West Semitic **ḥ*," in L. Kogan (ed.), *Studia Semitica* (Fs. Alexander Militarev, pp. 102–119. Orientalia: Papers of the Oriental Institute 3. Moscow: Russian State University for the Humanities, 2003.
——. "Features of Central Semitic," in A. Gianto (ed.), *Biblical and Oriental Essays in Memory of William L. Moran*, pp. 155–203. Biblica et orientalia 48. Rome: Editrice Pontificio Istituto Biblico, 2005.
——. "Semitic Languages," in J.M. Sasson et al. (eds.), *Civilizations of the Ancient Near East*, reprint of the 1st edition published by Charles Scribner's Sons 1995, pp. 2117–2134. Massachusetts: Hendrickson Publishers, 2006.
Huehnergard, J. and C. Woods, "Akkadian and Eblaite," in R.D. Woodard (ed.), *The Ancient Languages of Mesopotamia, Egypt, and Aksum*, pp. 83–152. Cambridge: Cambridge University Press, 2008.
Hug, V., *Altaramäische Grammatik der Texte des 7. und 6. Jh.s v.Chr.* HSAO 4. Heidelberg: Heidelberger Orientverlag, 1993.
Hulin, P., "The Inscriptions on the Carved Throne-Base of Shalmaneser III," *Iraq* 25 (1963): 48–69.
Hunger, H., *Babylonische und assyrische Kolophone*. AOAT 2. Kevelaer: Verlag Butzon & Bercker Kevelaer, 1968.
——. *Spätbabylonische Texte aus Uruk*, I. Ausgrabungen der Deutschen Forschungsgemeinschaft in Uruk-Warka, 9. Berlin: Gebr. Mann, 1976.
——. *Astrological Reports to Assyrian Kings*. SAA VIII. Helsinki: Helsinki University Press, 1992.
Ibn Manẓūr, Muḥammad ibn Mukarram, *Lisān al-ʿarab / li-Ibn Manẓūr*; [*taḥqīq ʿAbd Allāh ʿAlī al-Kabīr, Muḥammad Aḥmad Ḥasab Allāh, Hāshim Muḥammad al-Shadhilī*]. *Ṭabʿah jadīdah, muḥaqqaqah wa-mashkūlatah shaklan kāmilan wa-muḏayyalah bi-fahāris mufaṣṣalah.* Cairo: Dār al-Maʿārif, [196-?]–1986.
Ismail, B.Kh., "Two Neo-Assyrian Tablets," *SAAB* 3 (1989): 61–64.
Jakob-Rost, L., F.M. Fales, with a contribution by E. Klengel-Brandt, *Keilschrifttexte aus neuassyrischer Zeit 1: Neuassyrische Rechtsurkunden I.* WVDOG 94. Berlin: Gebr. Mann Verlag, 1996.
Jakob-Rost, L., K. Radner and V. Donbaz, with contributions by E. Klengel-Brandt, *Keilschrifttexte aus neuassyrischer Zeit 2: Neuassyrische Rechtsurkunden II* WVDOG 98. Saarbrücken: Saarbrücker Druckerei und Verlag, 2000.
Jastrow, M. (ed.), *A Dictionary of the Targumim, the Talmud Babli and Yerushalmi, and the Midraschic Literature.* A Copy of 1971, first published in 4 vols., 1886–1890. New York: The Judaica Press, 1989.
Jastrow, O., "The Neo-Aramaic Languages," in R. Hetzron (ed.), *The Semitic Languages*, pp. 334–377. London: Routledge, 1997.
——. "Neo-Aramaic Dialectology: The State of the Art," in S. Izre'el (ed.), *Semitic Linguistics: The State of the Art at the Turn of the Twenty-First Century*, pp. 365–377. IOS 20. Winona Lake: Eisenbrauns, 2002.
——. "Old Aramaic and Neo-Aramaic: Some Reflections on Language History," in H. Gzella and M.L. Folmer (eds.), *Aramaic in its Historical and Linguistic Setting*, pp. 1–10. Wiesbaden: Harrassowitz Verlag, 2008.

Jean, Ch.-F. and J. Hoftijzer, *Dictionnaire des inscriptions sémitiques de l'Ouest*. Leiden: Brill, [1960]-1965.
Jespersen, O., *Growth and Structure of the English Language*. 9th edition. Oxford: Basil Blackwell, 1948.
Jiménez, E., "Three colophons* – 1. *buḫḫušu*, 'to copy' (?)," *NABU* 2013/92.
Johns, C.H.W., *Assyrian Deeds and Documents*, Vols., I (1898), II–III (1901) and IV (1923). Cambridge: Deighton Bell, 1898–1923.
——. "Assyrian Deeds and Documents," *AJSL* 42 (1926): 170–204 and 228–275.
Jursa, M., Review of "Legal Transactions of the Royal Court of Niniveh [*sic*], Part I. Tiglath-Pileser III through Esarhaddon," by K. Theodore and S. Parpola, *WZKM* 84 (1994): 204–209.
——. "Ein Beamter flucht auf Aramäisch: Alphabetschreiber in der spätbabylonischen Epistolographie und die Rolle des Aramäischen in der babylonischen Verwaltung des sechsten Jahrhunderts v. Chr.," in G.B. Lanfranchi, D.M. Bonacossi, C. Pappi and S. Ponchia (eds.), *Leggo! Studies Presented to Frederick Mario Fales on the Occasion of His 65th Birthday*, pp. 379–397. Wiesbaden: Harrassowitz Verlag, 2012.
Jursa, M. and K. Radner, "Keilschrifttexte aus Jerusalem," *AfO* 42/43 (1995/96): 89–108.
Kalinin, M. and S. Loesov, "Lexical *Sondergut* of Neo-Assyrian," *SAAB* 23 (2017): 1–45.
Kämmerer, T.R. and D. Schwiderski, *Deutsch-Akkadisches Wörterbuch*. AOAT 255. Münster: Ugarit-Verl., 1998.
Kataja, L., *On the Rection of Verbs Motion and Communication in Neo-Assyrian and Aramaic*. [in Finnish; Unpubl. M.A. Thesis, University of Helsinki, 1986].
Kataja, L. and R. Whiting (eds.), *Grants, Decrees and Gifts of the Neo-Assyrian Period*. SAA XII. Helsinki: Helsinki University Press, 1995.
Kaufman, S.A., "Akkadian and Babylonian Aramaic–New Examples of Mutual Elucidation," *Leš* 36 (1972): 28–33.
——. *The Akkadian Influences on Aramaic*. AS 19. Chicago & London: The University of Chicago Press, 1974.
——. "An Assyro-Aramaic *egirtu ša šulmu*," in M. de Jong Ellis (ed.), *Essays on the Ancient Near East in Memory of Jacob Joel Finkelstein*, pp. 119–127. Memoirs of the Connecticut Academy of Arts and Sciences 19. Hamden: Archon Books, 1977.
——. "Reflections on the Assyrian-Aramaic Bilingual from Tell Fakhariyeh," *Maarav* 3 (1982): 137–175.
——. "The History of Aramaic Vowel Reduction," in M. Sokoloff (ed.), *Arameans, Aramaic and the Aramaic Literary Tradition*, pp. 47–55. Ramat-Gan: Bar Ilan University Press, 1983.
——. "The Classification of the North West Semitic Dialects of the Biblical Period and Some Implications Thereof," in M. Bar-Asher (ed.), *Proceedings of the Ninth World Congress of Jewish Studies, Jerusalem, August 4–12, 1985 (Panel Sessions: Hebrew and Aramaic)*, pp. 41–57. Proceedings of the World Congress of Jewish Studies 9. Jerusalem: World Union of Jewish Studies, 1988.
——. "Assyro-Aramaica," *JAOS* 109 (1989): 97–102.
——. "Aramaic," in D.N. Freedman et al. (eds.), *The Anchor Bible Dictionary*, Vol. 4, K-N, pp. 173–178. New York: Doubleday, 1992.
——. "Aramaic," in R. Hetzron (ed.), *The Semitic Languages*, pp. 114–130. London: Routledge, 1997.
——. "Languages in Contact: The Ancient Near East," *IOS* 20 (2002): 297–306.
——. "The Comprehensive Aramaic Lexicon Project and Twenty-First Century Aramaic Lexicography: Status and Prospects," in H. Holger and M.L. Folmer (eds.), *Aramaic in its Historical and Linguistic Setting*, pp. 353–371. Wiesbaden: Harrassowitz Verlag, 2008.

Kaufman, S.A. et al. (eds.), *The Comprehensive Aramaic Lexicon.* Online 15/09/2022: https://cal.huc.edu/

Kessler, K., "Assyria until 800 B.C.," *TAVO* B IV 10 (1987). [a map]

——. "The Neoassyrian Empire (720–612 B.C.) and the Neobabylonian Empire (612–539 B.C.)" *TAVO* B IV 13 (1991). [a map]

Khan, G., "Aramaic and the Impact of Languages in Contact with It through the Ages," in P.B. de la Peña et al. (eds.), *Lenguas en contacto: el testimonio escrito*, pp. 87–108. Madrid: Consejo superior de investigaciones científicas, 2004.

——. "Aramaic in the Medieval and Modern Periods," in J.N. Postgate (ed.), *Languages of Iraq, Ancient and Modern*, pp. 95–113. [London]: British School of Archaeology in Iraq, 2007.

——. "Remarks on the Historical Background of the Modern Assyrian Language," *The Journal of Assyrian Academic Studies* 21/2 (2007): 4–11.

——. "The Language of the Modern Assyrians: The North-Eastern Neo-Aramaic Dialect Group," in Ö.A. Cetrez, S. Donabed and A. Makko (eds.), *The Assyrian Heritage: Threads of Continuity and Influence*, pp. 173–199. Uppsala: Acta Universitatis Upsaliensis, 2012.

Kienast, B., *Historische Semitische Sprachwissenschaft.* Wiesbaden: Harrassowitz Verlag, 2001.

Kinnier-Wilson, J.V., *The Nimrud Wine Lists: A Study of Men and Administration in the Eighth Century, B.C.* CTN I. London: British School of Archaeology in Iraq, 1972.

Klauber, E.G., *Politisch-religiöse Texte aus der Sargonidenzeit.* Leipzig: Eduard Pfeiffer, 1913.

Klein, E., *A Comprehensive Etymological Dictionary of the Hebrew Language for Readers of English.* New York: Macmillan, 1987.

Klengel, H., "Fernbeziehungen und Kulturkontakte in den westlichen Randgebieten des Assyrerreiches," *Jahrbuch des Römisch-Germanischen Zentralmuseums Mainz* 37 (1990): 405–414.

Knudsen, E.E., "Cases of Free Variants in the Akkadian *q* Phoneme," *JCS* 15 (1961): 84–90.

——. "Spirantization of Velars in Akkadian," in M. Dietrich and W. Röllig (eds.), *lišān mitḫurti: Festschrift Wolfram Freiherr von Soden zum 19. VI. 1968 gewidmet von Schülern und Mitarbeitern*, pp. 147–155. Neukirchen-Vluyn: Verlag Butzon & Bercker Kevelaer, 1969.

Köbert, R., "Gedanken zum semitischen Wort- und Satzbau. 1–7," *Or* 14 (1945): 273–283.

Köcher, F., *Keilschrifttexte zur assyrisch-babylonischen Drogen- und Pflanzenkunde*: *Texte der Serien* uru.an.na: maltakal, ḪAR.ra: ḫubullu und Ú GAR-šú. VIO 28. Berlin: Akademie-Verlag, 1955.

Koehler, L. and W. Baumgartner, *The Hebrew and Aramaic Lexicon of the Old Testament*, 5 vols., translated and edited under the supervision of M.E.J. Richardson. Leiden, New York & Köln: Brill, 1994–2000.

Kogan, L., "ġ in Akkadian," *UF* 33 (2001): 263–298.

——. "Old Assyrian vs. Old Babylonian: The Lexical Dimension," in G. Deutscher, and N.J.C. Kouwenberg (eds.), *The Akkadian Language in its Semitic Context: Studies in the Akkadain of the Third and Second Millennium BC*, pp. 177–214. Leiden: Nederlands Instituut voor het Nabije Oosten, 2006.

——. *Genealogical Classification of Semitic: The Lexical Isoglosses*. Berlin: De Gruyter, 2015.

Kohler, J. and A. Ungnad, *Assyrische Rechtsurkunden in Umschrift und Ubersetzung nebst einem Index der Personen-Namen und Rechtserläuterungen.* Leipzig: Eduard Pfeiffer, 1913.
Kouwenberg, B., "The Reflexes of the Proto-Semitic Gutturals in Assyrian," in G. Deutscher and N.J.C. Kouwenberg (eds.), *The Akkadian Language in its Semitic Context: Studies in the Akkadian of the Third and Second Millennium BC*, pp. 150–176. Leiden: Nederlands Instituut voor het Nabije Oosten, 2006.
——. "Akkadian in General," in S. Weninger (ed.), in collaboration with G. Khan, M.P. Streck and J.C.E. Watson, *The Semitic Languages: An International Handbook*, pp. 330–340. Handbücher zur Sprach- und Kommunikationswissenschaft 36. Berlin & Boston: Walter de Gruyter, 2011.
Krebernik, M., "The Linguistic Classification of Eblaite: Methods, Problems, and Results," in J.S. Cooper and G.M. Schwartz (eds.), *The Study of the Ancient Near East in the Twenty-First Century: The William Foxwell Albright Centennial Conference*, pp. 233–249. Winona Lake: Eisenbrauns, 1996.
Kühne, H., "Vier spätbabylonische Tontafeln aus Tall Šēḫ Ḥamad, Ost-Syrien," *SAAB* 7 (1993): 75–107.
Kuhrt, A., *The Ancient Near East: c. 3000–330 BC,* I–II. London: Routledge, 1995.
Kutscher, E.Y., "Aramaic," in T.A., Sebeok, (ed.), *Current Trends in Linguistics vol. 6. Linguistics in South West Asia and North Africa*, pp. 347–412. The Hague: Mouton, 1970.
——. *Hebrew and Aramaic Studies*. Jerusalem; Magnes Press, 1977.
Kwasman, T., *Neo-Assyrian Legal Documents in the Kouyunjik Collection of the British Museum*. Studia Pohl: Series Maior 14. Rome: Editrice Pontificio Istituto Biblico, 1988.
——. "*bunbullu*," *NABU* 1999/60.
——. "Notes and Communications: Two Aramaic Legal Documents," *BSOAS* 63.2 (2000): 274–283.
——. "'Look it up in…'? Aramaic Lexicography: Some General Observations," *Aramaic Studies* 1 (2003): 191–209.
Kwasman, T. and S. Parpola (eds.), *Legal Transactions of the Royal Court of Nineveh, Part* I: *Tiglath-Pileser III through Esarhaddon*. SAA VI. Helsinki: Helsinki University Press, 1991.
Landsberger, B., "Lexikalisches Archiv," *ZA* 42 (1934): 152–169.
——. *Materialien zum sumerischen Lexikon*. Rome: Pontificio istituto biblico, 1937.
——. "Jahreszeiten im Sumerisch-Akkadischen," *JNES* 8 (1949): 248–272.
——. *The Date Palm and its By-products According to the Cuneiform Sources*. AfO, Beiheft 17. Graz: (Weidner), 1967.
Landsberger, B. and O.R. Gurney, "Practical Vocabulary of Assur," *AfO* 18 (1957–58): 328–341.
Lanfranchi, G.B. and S. Parpola (eds.), *The Correspondence of Sargon II, Part* II: *Letters from the Northern and Northeastern Provinces*. SAA V. Helsinki: Helsinki University Press, 1990.
Langdon, S., *Tammuz and Ishtar: A Monograph upon Babylonian Religion and Theology Containing Extensive Extracts from the Tammuz Liturgies and All of the Arbela Oracles*. Oxford: Clarendon Press, 1914.
——. "Philological Notes," *RA* 28 (1931): 13–22.
Lauinger, J., "Esarhaddon's Succession Treaty at Tell Tayinat: Text and Commentary," *JCS* 64 (2012): 87–123.
——. "The Neo-Assyrian *adê*: Treaty, Oath, or Something Else?" *ZAR* 19 (2013): 99–115.

Lehmann, W.P., *Historical Linguistics: An Introduction*, reprint of the 3rd edition published 1992. London & New York: Routledge, 1994.
Lemaire, A., *Nouvelles tablettes araméennes*. Geneva: Librairie Droz, 2001.
——. "Remarks on the Aramaic of Upper Mesopotamia in the Seventh Century B.C.," in H. Gzella and M.L. Folmer (eds.), *Aramaic in its Historical and Linguistic Setting*, pp. 77–92. Wiesbaden: Harrassowitz Verlag, 2008.
Levine, B.A., "On the Role of Aramaic in Transmitting Syro-Mesopotamian Legal Institutions," in A. Panaino and G. Pettinato (eds.), *Ideologies as Intercultural Phenomena: Proceedings of the Third Annual Symposium of the Assyrian and Babylonian Intellectual Heritage Project Held in Chicago, USA, October 27–31, 2000*, pp. 157–166. Melammu Symposia 3. Milano: Università di Bologna, 2002.
Lidzbarski, M., "Ein aramäischer Brief aus der Zeit Ašurbanipals," *ZA* 31 (1917/1918): 193–202.
——. *Altaramäische Urkunden aus Assur*. Leipzig: J.C. Hinrichs'sche Buchhandlung, 1921.
Lieberman, S.J., "The Aramaic Argillary Script in the Seventh Century," *BASOR* 192 (1968): 25–31.
——. *The Sumerian Loanwords in Old-Babylonian Akkadian, vol. I: Prolegomena and Evidence*. Missoula: Scholars Press, 1977.
Lipiński, E., "Textes juridiques et économiques araméens de l'époque sargonide," *AcAn* 22 (1974): 373–384.
——. *Studies in Aramaic Inscriptions and Onomastics*, I. OLA 1. Leuven: Leuven University Press, 1975.
——. "La correspondance des sibilantes dans les textes araméens et les textes cunéiformes néo-assyriens," in P. Fronzaroli (ed.), *Atti del secondo congresso internazionale di linguistica camito-semitica, Firenze, 16—19 aprile 1974*, pp. 201–210. QuadSem 5. Firenze: Università di Firenze, 1978.
——. "Aramaic-Akkadian Archives from the Gozan-Ḫarran Area," in J. Amitai (ed.), *Biblical Archaeology Today: Proceedings of the International Congress on Biblical Archaeology, (Jerusalem, April 1984)*, pp. 340–348. Jerusalem: Israel Exploration Society, 1985.
——. "In Search of the Etymology of Some Semitic Loan-Words," in Y.L. Arbeitman (ed.), *Fucus: A Semitic/Afrasian Gathering in Remembrance of Albert Ehrman*, pp. 325–333. Amsterdam: J. Benjamins, 1988.
——. *Studies in Aramaic Inscriptions and Onomastics*, II. OLA 57. Leuven: Peeters Publishers & Department of Oriental Studies, 1994.
——. "Aramaic Clay Tablets from the Gozan-Harran Area," *JEOL* 33 (1993–94, published 1995): 143–150.
——. "Straw in the Neo-Assyrian Period," in E. Wardini (ed.), *Built on Solid Rock: Studies in Honor of Professor Ebbe Egede Knudsen on the Occasion of His 65th Birthday April 11th 1997*, pp. 187–195. Oslo: Novus, 1997.
——. *Semitic Languages: Outline of a Comparative Grammar*. OLA 80. Leuven: Peeters Publishers & Department of Oriental Studies, 1997.
——. "Aramaean Economic Thought," *AoF* 25 (1998): 289–302.
——. "'Leadership' The Roots *DBR* and *NGD* in Aramaic," in M. Dietrich and I. Kottsieper (eds.), *"Und Mose schrieb dieses Lied auf": Studien zum Alten Testament und zum Alten Orient: Festschrift für Oswald Loretz zur Vollendung seines 70. Lebensjahres mit Beiträgen von Freunden, Schülern und Kollegen*, pp. 501–514. AOAT 250. Münster: Ugarit-Verlag, 1998.

——. "The Linguistic Geography of Syria in Iron Age II (*c.* 1000–600 B.C.)," in G. Bunnens (ed.), *Essays on Syria in the Iron Age*, pp. 125–142. Ancient Near Eastern Studies – Supplement 7. Louvain, Paris, Sterling & Virginia: Peeters Press, 2000.
——. *The Aramaeans: Their Ancient History, Culture, Religion.* OLA 100. Leuven & Paris: Peeters Publishers, 2000.
——. "New Aramaic Clay Tablets," *BiOr* 59 (2002): 245–259.
——. *Studies in Aramaic Inscriptions and Onomastics*, III, *Maʿālānā.* OLA 200. Leuven: Peeters, 2010.
Liverani, M., *Assyria: The Imperial Mission.* Winona Lake: Eisenbrauns, 2017.
Livingstone, A., *Mystical and Mythological Explanatory Works of Assyrian and Babylonian Scholars.* Oxford: Clarendon Press, 1986.
——. *Court Poetry and Literary Miscellanea.* SAA III. Helsinki: Helsinki University Press, 1989.
Loud, G. and C.B. Altman (eds.), *Khorsabad II: The Citadel and the Town.* OIP 40. Chicago: The University of Chicago Press, 1938
Löw, I., *Aramäische Pfalnzennamen.* Leipzig: Wilhelm Engelmann, 1881.
Luukko, M., *Grammatical Variation in Neo-Assyrian.* SAAS XVI. [Helsinki]: The Neo-Assyrian text corpus project, 2004.
——. "The Administrative Roles of the 'Chief Scribe' and the 'Palace Scribe' in the Neo-Assyrian Period," *SAAB* 16 (2007): 227–256.
——. *The Correspondence of Tiglath-pileser III and Sargon II from Calah/Nimrud.* SAA XIX. Winona Lake: Eisenbrauns, 2012.
Luukko, M. and G. Van Buylaere (eds.), *The Political Correspondence of Esarhaddon.* SAA XVI. Helsinki: Helsinki University Press, 2002.
Luukko, M. and S. Gaspa, "A Bibliography of Neo-Assyrian Studies (1998–2006)," *SAAB* 17 (2008): 189–257.
MacGinnis, J., "Tablets from Nebi Yunus," *SAAB* 6 (1992): 3–19.
——. "Middle and Neo-Assyrian Cunriform Texts from Anatolia," in K. Köroğlu, and S.F. Adali (eds.) *The Assyrians Kingdom of the God Aššur from Tigris to Taurus*, pp. 208–229. Istanbul: Yapi Kredi Yayinlari, 2018.
Maclean, A.J., *A Dictionary of the Dialects of Vernacular Syriac: As Spoken by the Eastern Syrians of Kurdistan, Northwest Persia and the Plain of Mosul.* Oxford: Clarendon Press, 1901.
Macuch, R. and E. Panoussi (eds.), *Neusyrische Chrestomathie.* Wiesbaden: Otto Harrassowitz, 1974.
Madhloom, T.A., *The Chronology of Neo-Assyrian Art.* London: The Athlone Press, 1970.
——. "The Influence of Foreign Societies as Shown in Assyrian Art," in J. Harmatta and G. Komoróczy (eds.), *Wirtschaft und Gesellschaft im Alten Vorderasien*, pp. 385–387. Budapest: Akadémiai Kiadó, 1976.
——. "al-fannān al-ʾāšūrī yurāfiq al-ḥamalāt al-ʿaskarīyah," in *Researches on the Antiquities of Saddam Dam Basin Salvage and Other Researches*, pp. 245–248. [Baghdad]: State Organization of Antiquities & Heritage, 1987.
Maeir, A.M. et al. (eds.), *New Perspectives on Aramaic Epigraphy in Mesopotamia, Qumran, Egypt and Idumea: Proceedings of the Joint RIAB Minerva Center and the Jeselsohn Epigraphic Center of Jewish History Conference. Research on Israel and Aram in Biblical Times II.* Orientalische Religionen in der Antike 40. Tübingen: Mohr Siebeck, 2021.
Mankowski, P.V., *Akkadian Loanwords in Biblical Hebrew.* Winona Lake: Eisenbrauns, 2000.

Manna, J.E., *Leksīqōn kaldāyā-'arbāyā* – Arabic title: *Qāmūs kaldānī-'arabī* – English title: *Chaldean-Arabic Dictionary*. Reprint of the Mosul 1900 edition with a new appendix by R.J. Bidawid. Beirut: Babel Center Publications, 1975.

Margoliouth, J.P., *Supplement to the Thesaurus Syriacus of R. Payne Smith*, collected and arranged by J.P. Margoliouth; reprint of the edition published in Oxford 1927. Hildesheim: Georg Olms Verlag, 1981.

Matras, Y. and J. Sakel, *Grammatical Borrowing in Cross-Linguistic Perspective*. Berlin: Mouton de Gruyter, 2007.

Matsushima, E., "Le Rituel Hiérogamique de Nabû," *Acta Sumerologica* 9 (1987): 131–175.

Matthews, P.H., *The Concise Oxford Dictionary of Linguistics*. Oxford: Oxford University Press, 1997.

Mattila, R., (ed.), *Legal Transactions of the Royal Court of Nineveh, Part* II: *Assurbanipal through Sin-šarru-iškun*. SAA XIV. Helsinki: Helsinki University Press, 2002.

Mattila, R. and K. Radner, "A Bibliography of Neo-Assyrian Studies (1988–1997)," *SAAB* 11 (1997): 115–137.

Maul, S.M. and N.P. Heeβel (eds.), *Assur-Forschungen: Arbeiten aus der Forschungsstelle "Edition literarischer Keilschrifttexte aus Assur" der Heidelberger Akademie der Wissenschaften*. Wiesbaden: Harrassowitz Verlag, 2010.

Mayer, W., *Untersuchungen zur Grammatik des Mittelassyrischen*. AOAT, Sonderreihe 2. Neukirchen-Vluyn: Verlag Butzon & Bercker Kevelaer, 1971.

Mayrhofer, M., "Zu den arischen Sprachresten in Vorderasien," *Die Sprache* 5 (1959): 77–95.

Meissner, B., *Supplement zu den assyrischen Wörterbüchern*. Leiden: E.J. Brill, 1898.

——. *Kurzgefaßte assyrische Grammatik*. Hilfsbücher zur Kunde des alten Orients 3. Leipzig: J.C. Hinrichs'sche Buchhandlung, 1907.

Messerschmidt, L., *Zur Technik des Tontafel-Schreibens*. (Erweiterter Sonderabdruck aus der Orientalistischen Literaturzeitung 1906). Berlin: Wolf Peiser Verlag, 1907.

Militarev, A., L. Kogan and A. Belova (eds.), *Semitic Etymological Dictionary*, Vol. I, *Anatomy of Man and Animals*. AOAT 278:1. Münster: Ugarit-Verlag, 2000.

Militarev, A. and L. Kogan (eds.), *Semitic Etymological Dictionary*, Vol. II, *Animal Names*. Münster: Ugarit-Verlag, 2005.

Millard, A.R., "Alphabetic Inscriptions on Ivories from Nimrud," *Iraq* 24 (1962): 41–51.

——. "Fragments of Historical Texts from Nineveh," *Iraq* 32 (1970): 167–176.

——. "Some Aramaic Epigraphs," *Iraq* 34 (1972): 131–137.

——. "^{F}*ŠA EKALLI – ŠGL – ^{D}SAGALE*," *UF* 4 (1972): 161–162.

——. "Assyrian Royal Names in Biblical Hebrew," *JSS* 21 (1976): 1–14.

——. "Assyrians and Arameans," *Iraq* 45 (1983): 101–108.

——. "The Graffiti on the Glazed Bricks from Nimrud," appendix in J. Curtis, D. Collon and A. Green, "British Museum Excavations at Nimrud and Balawat in 1989," *Iraq* 55 (1993): 1–37.

——. "Cognates Can Be Deceptive: Some Aramaic Distinctives," in M.J. Geller, J.C. Greenfield and M.P. Weitzman (eds.), *Studia Aramaica: New Sources and New Approaches*, pp. 145–149. Journal of Semitic Studies Supplement 4. Oxford: Oxford University Press, 1995.

——. "Words for Writing in Aramaic," in M.F.J. Baasten and W.Th. van Peursen (eds.), *Hamlet on a Hill: Semitic and Greek Studies Presented to Professor T. Muraoka on the Occasion of his Sixty-Fifth Birthday*, pp. 349–355. Leuven: Peeters, 2003.

——. "Aramaic Documents of the Assyrian and Achaemenid Periods," in M. Brosius (ed.), *Ancient Archives and Archival Traditions: Concepts of Record-Keeping in the Ancient World*, pp. 230–240. Oxford: Oxford University Press, 2003.

——. "Early Aramaic," in J.N. Postgate (ed.), *Languages of Iraq, Ancient and Modern*, pp. 85–94. [London]: British School of Archaeology in Iraq, 2007.

——. "Assyria, Aramaeans and Aramaic," in G. Galil, M. Geller and A. Millard (eds.), *Homeland and Exile: Biblical and Ancient Near Eastern Studies in Honour of Bustenay Oded*, pp. 203–214. Leiden: Brill, 2009.

Millard, A.R. and P. Bordreuil, "A Statue from Syria with Assyrian and Aramaic Inscription," *BiAr* 45 (1982): 135–141.

Millard, A., with a Contribution by R. Whiting, *The Eponyms of the Assyrian Empire 910–612 BC.* SAAS II. [Helsinki]: The Neo-Assyrian text corpus project, 1994.

Moscati, S. (ed.), *An Introduction to the Comparative Grammar of the Semitic Languages: Phonology and Morphology*. Wiesbaden: Harrassowitz, 1964.

Müller, K.F., *Das assyrische Ritual*, Teil I: *Texte zum assyrischen Königsritual.* MVAeG 41/3, 60ff. Leipzig: J.C. Hinrichs Verlag, 1937.

Müller-Kessler, Ch., "Zu dem Hapax legonemon [*sic*] *a-su-na-ka* ABL 139+," *NABU* 1991/62.

Muffs, Y., *Studies in the Aramaic Legal Papyri from Elephantine.* Leiden: E.J. Brill, 1969.

Muraoka, T. and B. Porten, *A Grammar of Egyptian Aramaic.* Leiden, New York & Köln: Brill, 1998.

Muss-Arnolt, W., *Assyrisch-Englisch-Deutsches Handwörterbuch*, I–II. Berlin: Verlag von Reuther & Reichard, 1905.

Myers-Scotton, C., *Contact Linguistics: Bilingual Encounters and Grammatical Outcomes.* New York: Oxford University Press, 2002.

Na'aman, N. and R. Zadok, "Assyrian deportation to the province of Samerina in the light of two cuneiform tablets from Tel Hadid," *Tel Aviv* 27 (2000): 159–88.

Nili, I., *Hapax Legomena in the Akkadian Language.* (Unpublished Ph.D. thesis) Ramat-Gan: Bar Ilan University, 2004. [in Hebrew].

Nissinen, M., *References to Prophecy in Neo-Assyrian Sources.* SAAS VII. [Helsinki]: The Neo-Assyrian text corpus project, 1998.

——. "Love Lyrics of Nabû and Tašmetu: An Assyrian Song of Songs?" in M. Dietrich and I. Kottsieper (eds.), *"Und Mose schrieb dieses Lied auf": Studien zum Alten Testament und zum Alten Orient: Festschrift für Oswald Loretz zur Vollendung seines 70. Lebensjahres mit Beiträgen von Freunden, Schülern und Kollegen*, pp. 585–634. AOAT 250. Münster: Ugarit-Verlag, 1998.

Nissinen, M., with contributions by C.L. Seow and R.K. Ritner; edited by P. Machinist, *Prophets and Prophecy in the Ancient Near East.* Atlanta: Society of Biblical Literature, 2003.

Nöldeke, Th., *Mandäische Grammatik: Mit einer lithographirten Tafel der Mandäischen Schriftzeichen.* Halle: Verlag der Buchhandlung des Waisenhauses, 1875.

——. Review of "Opuscula Nestoriana," by G. Hoffmann, *ZDMG* 35 (1881): 491–501.

——. *Persische Studien.* Wien: Adolf Holzhausen, 1888.

Novák, M., "Assyrians and Aramaeans: Modes of Cohabitation and Acculturation at Guzana (Tell Halaf)," in J. Aruz and M. Seymour (eds.), *Assyria to Iberia: Art and Culture in the Iron Age*, pp. 123–135. New York: The Metropolitan Museum of Art, 2016.

Nyberg, H.S. et al. (eds.), *Frahang i Pahlavik.* Edited with transliteration, transcription and commentary from the posthumous papers of H.S. Nyberg by B. Utas; with the collaboration of C. Toll. Wiesbaden: Harrassowitz, 1988.

O'Connor, M.P., "The Arabic Loanwords in Nabatean Aramaic," *JNES* 45 (1986): 213–229.

——. "Semitic **mgn* and its Supposed Sanskrit Origin," *JAOS* 109 (1989): 25-32.

Oded, B., *Mass Deportations and Deportees in the Neo-Assyrian Empire*. Wiesbaden: Dr. Ludwig Reichert Verlag, 1979.

Odisho, E.Y., *The Sound System of Modern Assyrian: (Neo-Aramaic)*. Semitica Viva 2. Wiesbaden: Otto Harrassowitz, 1988.

——. "The Ethnic, Linguistic and Cultural Identity of Modern Assyrians," in R.M. Whiting (ed.), *Mythology and Mythologies. Methodological Approaches to Intercultural Influences. Proceedings of the Second Annual Symposium of the Assyrian and Babylonian Intellectual Heritage Project. Held in Paris, France, October 4–7, 1999*, pp. 137–148. Helsinki: The Neo-Assyrian Text Corpus Project, 2001.

——. "Bilingualism: A Salient and Dynamic Feature of Ancient Civilizations," *Mediterranean Language Review* 14 (2002): 71–97.

Oelsner, J., Review of "The Akkadian Influences on Aramaic," by S.A. Kaufman, *OLZ* 75 (1980): 535–537.

Olmstead, A.T., "Tattenai, Governor of 'Across the River'," *JNES* 3 (1944): 46.

Oppenheim, A.L., "The Neo-Babylonian Preposition *la*," *JNES* 1 (1942): 369–372.

——. "Babylonian and Assyrian Historical Texts," in J.B. Pritchard (ed.), *Ancient Near Eastern Texts Relating to the Old Testament*, 2nd edition, corrected and enlarged, pp. 265–317. Princeton: Princeton University Press, 1955.

Oraham, A.J., *Oraham's Dictionary of the Stabilized and Enriched Assyrian Language and English*. Chicago: Consolidated Press (Assyrian Press of America), 1943.

Pardee, D., Review of "The Akkadian Influences on Aramaic," by S.A. Kaufman, *JNES* 36 (1977): 318–319.

——. Review of "Textbook of Syrian Semitic Inscriptions, vol. 2. Aramaic Inscriptions, Including Inscriptions in the Dialect of Zenjirli," by John C.L. Gibson, *JNES* 37 (1978): 195–197.

Parker, B., "The Nimrud Tablets, 1952—Business Documents," *Iraq* 16 (1954): 29–58.

——. "Excavation at Nimrud, 1949–1953, Seals and Seal Impressions," *Iraq* 17 (1955): 93–125.

——. "Nimrud Tablets, 1956—Economic and Legal Texts from the Nabu Temple," *Iraq* 19 (1957): 125–138.

——. "Administrative Tablets from the North-West Palace, Nimrud," *Iraq* 23 (1961): 15–67.

——. "Economic Tablets from the Temple of Mamu at Balawat," *Iraq* 25 (1963): 86–103.

Parpola, S., *Neo-Assyrian Toponyms*. Programming and computer printing by Kinmo Koskenniemi. AOAT 6. Neukirchen-Vluyn: Kevelaer, 1970.

——. "The Alleged Middle/Neo-Assyrian Irregular Verb **naṣṣ* and the Assyrian Sound Change *š* > *s*," *Assur* 1 (1974): 1–10.

——. Review of "Akkadisches Handwörterbuch. Unter Benutzung des lexikalischen Nachlasses von Bruno Meissner (1868–1947) bearbeitet. Vols. II & III/1 (Lfg. 7–12). Wiesbaden: Harrassowitz 1972 und 1974," by W. von Soden, *OLZ* 74 (1979): 23–35.

——. *Cuneiform Texts from Babylonian Tablets in the British Museum, Part* 53: *Neo-Assyrian Letters from the Kuyunjik Collection*. London: British Museum publications, 1979.

——. "Collations to Neo-Assyrian Legal Texts from Nineveh," *Assur* 2 (1979): 109–197.

——. "Assyrian Royal Inscriptions and Neo-Assyrian Letters," in F.M. Fales (ed.), *Assyrian Royal Inscriptions: New Horizons, in Literary, Ideological, and Historical Analysis: Papers of a Symposium Held in Cetona (Siena) June 26–28, 1980*, pp. 117–134. Rome: Istituto per l'oriente, 1981.

——. "Assyrian Library Records," *JNES* 42 (1983): 1–29.

——. "The Royal Archives of Nineveh," in K.R. Veenhof (ed.), *Cuneiform Archives and Libraries: Papers Read at the 30ᵉ Rencontre Assyriologique Internationale Leiden, 4–8 July 1983*, pp. 223–236. Istanbul: Nederlands Historisch-Archaeologisch Instituut, 1986.

——. "Neo-Assyrian Treaties from the Royal Archives of Nineveh," *JCS* 39 (1987): 161–189.

——. "The Forlorn Scholar," in F. Rochberg-Halton (ed.), *Language, Literature, and History: Philological and Historical Studies Presented to Erica Reiner*, pp. 257–278. New Haven: American Oriental Society, 1987.

——. *The Correspondence of Sargon II*, Part I: *Letters from Assyria and the West.* SAA I. Helsinki: Helsinki University Press, 1987.

——. "Neo-Assyrian Treaties from the Royal Archives of Nineveh," *JCS* 39 (1987): 161–189.

——. "The Neo-Assyrian Word for 'Queen'," *SAAB* 2 (1988): 73–76.

——. "The Reading of the Neo-Assyrian Logogram ᴸᵁ́SIMUG.KUG.GI 'goldsmith'," *SAAB* 2 (1988): 77–80.

——. *Letters from Assyrian and Babylonian Scholars.* SAA X. Helsinki: Helsinki University Press, 1993.

——. *Assyrian Prophecies.* SAA IX. Helsinki: Helsinki University Press, 1997.

——. *The Standard Babylonian Epic of Gilgamesh.* Helsinki: Helsinki University Press, 1997.

——. "Guidelines of the Transcription System," in K. Radner, *The Prosopography of the Neo-Assyrian Empire*, Vol. 1/I, pp. xxii–xxvii. Helsinki: The Neo-Assyrian Text Corpus Project, 1998.

——. "Assyrians after Assyria," *JAAS* 12 (2000): 1–16.

——. "A Letter to Sennacherib referring to the Conquest of Bit-Ha'iri and Other Events of the Year 693," in O. Loretz et al. (eds.), *Ex Mesopotamia et Syria Lux: Festschrift für Manfried Dietrich zu seinem 65. Geburtstag*, pp. 560–580. Münster: Ugarit-Verlag, 2002.

——. "Assyria's Expansion in the 8th and 7th Centuries and its Long-Term Repercussions in the West," in W.G. Dever and S. Gitin (eds.), *Symbiosis, Symbolism, and the Power of the Past: Canaan, Ancient Israel, and Their Neighbors from the Late Bronze Age through Roman Palaestina; Proceedings of the Centennial Symposium W.F. Albright Institute of Archaeological Research and American Schools of Oriental Research, Jerusalem, May 29–31, 2000*, pp. 99–111. Winona Lake: Eisenbrauns, 2003.

——. "Assyrian Identity in Ancient Times and Today," (Paper Presented at the Convention of the Assyrian Youth Federation in Sweden, Held in Göteborg in March 28, 2004).
Online 15/09/2022: http://www.nineveh.com/parpola_eng.pdf

——. "National and Ethnic Identity in the Neo-Assyrian Empire and Assyrian Identity in Post-Empire Times," *Journal of Assyrian Academic Studies* 18/2 (2004): 5–22.

——. *Letters from Assyrian Scholars to the Kings Esarhaddon and Assurbanipal*, Part I, Texts & Part II, Commentary and Appendices; reprint of the 1st edition 1970 and 1983. Winona Lake: Eisenbrauns, 2007.

——. "The Neo-Assyrian Ruling Class," in T.R. Kämmerer (ed.), *Studien zu Ritual und Sozialgeschichte im Alten Orient / Studies on Ritual and Society in the Ancient Near East: Tartuer Symposien 1998–2004*, pp. 257–274. Berlin: Walter de Gruyter, 2007.

——. "Cuneiform Texts from Ziyaret Tepe (Tušḫan), 2002–2003 (Plates I–XXV)," *SAAB* 17 (2008): 1–113.

——. *The Correspondence of Assurbanipal, Part I: Letters from Assyria, Babylonia, and Vassal States.* SAA XXI. Pennsylvania: Penn State University Press, 2018.

Parpola, S. and K. Watanabe (eds.), *Neo-Assyrian Treaties and Loyalty Oaths*. SAA II. Helsinki: Helsinki University Press, 1988.

Parpola, S. and M. Porter (eds.), *The Helsinki Atlas of the Near East in the Neo-Assyrian Period.* Helsinki: The Neo-Assyrian Text Corpus Project, 2001.

Parpola, S. et al. (eds.), *Assyrian-English-Assyrian Dictionary.* Helsinki: The Neo-Assyrian Text Corpus Project/Eisenbrauns, 2007.

Parpola, S. (ed.), with Contributions by K. Deller (†), B. Pongratz-Leisten and S. Ermidoro, *Assyrian Royal Rituals and Cultic Texts*. SAA XX. Winona Lake: Eisenbrauns, 2017.

Parrot, A. and J. Nougayrol, "Asarhaddon et Naqi'a sur un bronze du Louvre (AO 20, 185)," *Syria* 33 (1956): 147–160.

Payne Smith, J. (ed.), *A Compendious Syriac Dictionary. Founded upon the Thesaurus Syriacus of R. Payne Smith, D.D.* Oxford: Clarendon Press, 1903.

Payne Smith, R. et al. (eds.), *Thesaurus Syriacus*, 2 vols; reprint of the edition published in Oxford 1879–1901. Hildesheim: Georg Olms Verlag, 1981.

Pearce, L.E., "*sepīru* and ^{lú}A.BA: Scribes of the Late First Millennium," in K. Van Lerberghe and G. Voet (eds.), *Languages and Cultures in Contact: At the Crossroads of Civilizations in the Syro-Mesopotamian Realm; Proceedings of the 42th RAI*, pp. 355–368. OLA 96. Leuven: Peeters, 1999.

Pedersén, O., *Archives and Libraries in the City of Assur: A Survey of the Material from the German Excavations, I.* Acta Universitatis Upsaliensis: Studia Semitica Upsaliensia 6. Uppsala; Almqvist & Wiksell, 1985.

——. *Archives and Libraries in the City of Assur: A Survey of the Material from the German Excavations, II.* Acta Universitatis Upsaliensis: Studia Semitica Upsaliensia 8. Uppsala; Almqvist & Wiksell, 1986.

——. "Use of Writing among the Assyrians," in H. Waetzoldt and H. Hauptmann (eds.), *Assyrien im Wandel der Zeiten*, pp. 139–152. HSAO 6. Heidelberg: Heidelberger Orientverlag, 1997.

——. *Archives and Libraries in the Ancient Near East 1500–300 B.C.* Bethesda: CDL Press, 1998.

——. "Neo-Assyrian Texts from Nebuchadnezzar's Babylon: A Preliminary Report," in M. Luukko, S. Svärd and R. Mattila (eds.), *Of God(s), Trees, Kings, and Scholars: Neo-Assyrian and Related Studies in Honour of Simo Parpola*, pp. 193–199. StOr 106. Helsinki: Societas Orientalis Fennica, 2009.

Pei, M.A. & F. Gaynor (eds.), *A Dictionary of Linguistics*. London: Peter Owen, 1960.

Pentiuc, E.J., "West Semitic Terms in Akkadian Texts from Emar," *JNES* 58 (1999): 81–96.

Pfeiffer, R.H., *State Letters of Assyria: A Transliteration and Translation of 355 Official Assyrian Letters Dating from the Sargonid Period (722–625 B.C.).* New Haven: American Oriental Society, 1935.

Pinches, T.G., Review of "Die Name der Körperteile im assyrisch-babylonischen: Eine lexikalisch-etymologische Studie," by H. Holma, *JRAS* (1912): 831–834.

Podolsky, B., "A Selected List of Dictionaries of Semitic Languages," in S. Izre'el (ed.), *Semitic Linguistics: The State of the Art at the Turn of the Twenty-First Century*, pp. 213–221. IOS 20. Winona Lake: Eisenbrauns, 2002.

Ponchia, S., "The Neo-Assyrian *Adê* Protocol and the Administration of the Empire," in S. Gaspa, A. Greco, D.M. Bonacossi, S. Ponchia and R. Rollinger (eds.), *From Source to History: Studies on Ancient Near Eastern Worlds and Beyond Dedicated to Giovanni*

Battista Lanfranchi on the Occasion of His 65th Birthday on June 23, 2014, pp. 501–525. AOAT 412. Münster: Ugarit-Verlag, 2014.
Poole, S.C., *An Introduction to Linguistics*. Hong Kong: Macmillan Press, 1999.
Porten, B. and A. Yardeni, *Textbook of Aramaic Documents from Ancient Egypt. III, Literature, Accounts, Lists*. Jerusalem & Winona Lake: Eisenbrauns, 1993.
Porter, B.N., "Language, Audience and Impact in Imperial Assyria," in S. Izre'el and R. Drory (eds.), *Language and Culture in the Near East*, pp. 51–72. IOS 15. Leiden: Brill, 1995.
Postgate, J.N., *Neo-Assyrian Royal Grants and Decrees*. Studia Pohl: Series Maior 1. Rome: Pontifical Biblical Institute, 1969.
——. "A Neo-Assyrian Tablet from Tell al Rimah," *Iraq* 32 (1970): 31–35.
——. "More 'Assyrian Deeds and Documents'," *Iraq* 32 (1970): 129–164.
——. *The Governor's Palace Archive*. CTN II. London: British School of Archaeology in Iraq, 1973.
——. "Assyrian Texts and Fragments," *Iraq* 35 (1973): 13–36.
——. *Taxation and Conscription in the Assyrian Empire*. Studia Pohl: Series Maior 3. Rome: Biblical Institute Press, 1974.
——. *Fifty Neo-Assyrian Legal Documents*. Warminster: Aris & Phillips Ltd, 1976.
——. Review of "Mittelassyrische Rechtsurkunden und Verwaltungstexte," by H. Freydank, *BiOr* 37 (1980): 67–70.
——. "The Ownership and Exploitation of Land in Assyria in the 1st Millennium B.C.," in M. Lebeau and Ph. Talon (eds.), *Reflets des deux fleuves: Volume de mélanges offerts à André Finet*, pp. 141–152. Akkadica, Supplementum 6. Leuven: Peeters, 1989.
——. "Ancient Assyria – A Multi-Racial State," *Aram* 1 (1989): 1–10.
——. "The Four 'Neo-Assyrian' Tablets from Šēḫ Ḥamad," *SAAB* 7 (1993):109–124.
——. "Middle Assyrian to Neo-Assyrian: the Nature of the Shift," in H. Waetzoldt and H. Hauptmann (eds.), *Assyrien im Wandel der Zeiten*, pp. 159–168. HSAO 6. Heidelberg: Heidelberger Orientverlag, 1997.
——. "Assyrian Uniforms," in W.H. van Soldt (ed.), *Veenhof Anniversary Volume: Studies Presented to Klaas R. Veenhof on the Occasion of his Sixty-Fifth Birthday*, pp. 373–388. Leiden: Nederlands Instituut voor het Nabije Oosten, 2001.
——. *Languages of Iraq: Ancient and Modern*. [London]: British School of Archaeology in Iraq, 2007.
Postgate, N. and B.Kh. Ismail (eds.), *Texts from Niniveh*. Baghdad: Dar al-Ḥurrīyah liṭṭibaʿah, (no publication date given in the book but ca. 1993).
Powell, M.A., "Masse und Gewichte," in E. Ebeling et al. (eds.), *Reallexikon der Assyriologie und Vorderasiatischen Archäologie, vol. 7 (Libanukšabaš – Medizin)*, pp. 457–517. Berlin: Walter de Gruyter, 1987–1990.
Radner, K., "Samaria 1825 = Fi. 16. Zum Verbleib einer nA Urkunde aus Sāmirīna (Samaria)," *NABU* 1995/100.
——. *Die neuassyrischen Privatrechtsurkunden als Quelle für Mensch und Umwelt*. SAAS VI. Helsinki: Neo-Assyrian Text Corpus Project, 1997.
——. *The Prosopography of the Neo-Assyrian Empire*. [Helsinki]: The Neo-Assyrian text corpus project, 1998–99. Vols. 1/I–II. (see also Baker, H.D. [ed.]).
——. *Ein neuassyrisches Privatarchiv der Tempelgoldschmiede von Assur*. StAT 1. Saarbrücken: Saarbrücker Druckerei und Verlag, 1999.
——. *Die Neuassyrischen Texte aus Tall Šēḫ Ḥamad. (Mit Beiträgen von Wolfgang Röllig zu den aramäischen Beischriften)*. BATSH 6/2. Berlin: Dietrich Reimer Verlag, 2002.

——. "An Assyrian View on the Medes," in G.B. Lanfranchi, M. Roaf and R. Rollinger (eds.), *Continuity of Empire (?): Assyria, Media, Persia*, pp. 37–64. History of the Ancient Near East / Monographs – V. Padova: S.a.r.g.o.n. Editrice e Libreria, 2003.
——. "Salmanassar V. in den *Nimrud Letters*," *AfO* 50 (2003/2004): 95–104.
——. *Das mittelassyrische Tontafelarchiv von Giricano Dunnu-ša-Uzibi*. Subartu 14. Turnhout: Brepols, 2004.
——. "Neue neuassyrische Texte aus Dūr-Katlimmu: Eine Schülertafel mit einer sumerisch-akkadische Königshymne und andere Keilschriftfunde aus den Jahren 2003–2009," in H. Kühne (ed.), *Dūr-Katlimmu 2008 and Beyond*, pp. 175–186. Wiesbaden: Harrassowitz Verlag, 2010.
——. "Schreiberkonventionen im assyrischen Reich: Sprachen und Schriftsysteme," in J. Renger (ed.), *Assur – Gott, Stadt und Land: 5. Internationales Colloquium der Deutschen Orient-Gesellschaft 18.–21. Februar 2004 in Berlin*, pp. 385–403. Wiesbaden: Harrassowitz Verlag, 2011.
——. "The Assur-Nineveh-Arbela Triangle: Central Assyria in the Neo-Assyrian Period," in P.A. Miglus and S. Mühl (eds.), *Between the Cultures: The Central Tigris Region from the 3rd to the 1st Millennium BC; Conference at Heidelberg, January 22nd–24th, 2009*, pp. 321–329. HSAO 14. Heidelberg: Heidelberger Orientverlag, 2011.
——. "Neo-Assyrian Tablets," in A.R. George et al. (eds.), *Assyrian Archival Texts in the Schøyen Collection and Other Documents from North Mesopotamia and Syria*, pp. 77–93. Bethesd: CDL Press, 2017.
——. "Diglossia and the Neo-Assyrian Empire's Akkadian and Aramaic Text Production," in L.C. Jonker, A. Berlejung and I. Cornelius (eds.), *Multilingualism in Ancient Contexts: Perspectives from Ancient Near Eastern and Early Christian Contexts*, pp. 147–181. Stellenbosch: African Sun Media, 2021.
Rawlinson H.C., *The Cuneiform Inscriptions of Western Asia*, Vol. III*: A Selection from the Miscellaneous Inscriptions of Assyria*, edited by George Smith. London: R. E. Bowler, 1870.
Reade, J., "Neo-Assyrian Monuments in Their Historical Context," in F.M. Fales (ed.), *Assyrian Royal Inscriptions: New Horizons, in Literary, Ideological, and Historical Analysis: Papers of a Symposium Held in Cetona (Siena) June 26–28, 1980*. Rome: Istituto per l'oriente, 1981.
——. *Assyrian Sculpture*. London: British Museum Publications, 1983.
——. "Visual Evidence for the Status and Activities of Assyrian Scribes," in G.B. Lanfranchi, D.M. Bonacossi, C. Pappi and S. Ponchia (eds.), *Leggo! Studies Presented to Frederick Mario Fales on the Occasion of His 65th Birthday*, pp. 699–717. Wiesbaden: Harrassowitz Verlag, 2012.
Reallexikon der Assyriologie und Vorderasiatischen Archäologie. Berlin & New York: Walter de Gruyter, 1928–.
Reiner, E., "The Phonological Interpretation of a Subsystem in the Akkadian Syllabary," in R.D. Biggs and J.A. Brinkman (eds.), *Studies Presented to A. Leo Oppenheim, June 7, 1964*. Chicago: The Oriental Institute of the University of Chicago, 1964.
——. *A Linguistic Analysis of Akkadian*. Janua Linguarum 21. The Hague: Mouton & Co., 1966.
——. "The Vassal-Treaties of Esarhaddon," in J.B. Pritchard (ed.), *Ancient Near Eastern Texts Relating to the Old Testament*, 3rd edition with supplement, pp. 534–541. Princeton: Princeton University Press, 1969.
Reiner, E. and M. Civil, *A Reconstruction of Sumerian and Akkadian Lexical Lists*. Rome: Pontificium Institutum Biblicum, 1969.
Rendsburg, G.A., "On the Writing ביתדוד in the Aramaic Inscription from Tel Dan," *IEJ* 45 (1995): 22–25.

Reynolds, F. (ed.), *The Babylonian Correspondence of Esarhaddon.* SAA XVIII. Helsinki: Helsinki University Press, 2003.
Richardson, M.E.J., Review of "Akkadian Loanwords in Biblical Hebrew," by P.V. Mankowski, *BSOAS* 65 (2002): 567–569.
Rimalt, E.S., "Wechselbeziehungen zwischen dem Aramäischen und dem Neubabylonischen," *WZKM* 39 (1932): 99–122.
Ritner, R.K., "The Earliest Attestation of the *kpḏ*-Measure," in P.D. Manuelian (ed.), *Studies in Honor of William Kelly Simpson*, pp. 683–688. Boston: Museum of Fine Arts, 1996.
Robinson, T.H., *Paradigms and Exercises in Syriac Grammar.* 4th edition revised by L.H. Brockington. Oxford: Clarendon Press, 1962.
Röllig, W., Review of "The Akkadian Influences on Aramaic," by S.A. Kaufman, *ZDMG* 127 (1977): 453.
——. "Die Aramäischen Beischriften auf den Texten 1 und 3," *SAAB* 7 (1993): 125–128.
——. "Zur Historischen Einordnung der Texte," *SAAB* 7 (1993): 129–132.
——. "Aramaica Haburensia II: Zwei datierte aramäische Urkunden aus Tall Šēẖ Ḥamad," *AoF* 24/2 (1997): 366–374.
——. "Aramaica Haburensia I: Eine ostaramäische Inschrift parthischer Zeit aus Tall Šēẖ Ḥamad," in J. Marzahn and H. Neumann (eds.), *Assyriologica et Semitica*, pp. 377–386. AOAT 252. Münster: Ugarit-Verlag, 2000.
——. "Aramäer und Assyrer: die Schriftzeugnisse bis zum Ende des Assyrerreiches," in G. Bunnens (ed.), *Essays on Syria in the Iron Age*, pp. 177–186. Ancient Near Eastern Studies - Supplement 7. Louvain, Paris, Sterling & Virginia: Peeters Press, 2000.
——. "Aramaica Haburensia V: Limu-Datierungen in Aramäischen Urkunden des 7. Jh. v. Chr," in P.M. Michèle Daviau, J.W. Wevers and M. Weigl (eds.), *The World of the Aramaeans* II, pp. 45–56. JSOTS 325. Sheffield: Sheffield Academic Press, 2001.
——. "Keilschrift versus Alphabetschrift: Überlegungen zu den *Epigraphs* auf Keilschrifttafeln," in P. Bienkowski, C. Mee and E. Slater (eds.), *Writing and Ancient Near Eastern Society: Papers in Honour of Alan R. Millard*, pp. 119–126. New York and London: T&T Clark International, 2005.
Rollinger, R., "The Terms 'Assyria' and 'Syria' Again," *JNES* 65 (2006): 283–287.
Rosenthal, F., *Die aramaistische Forschung seit Th. Nöldeke's Veröffentlichungen.* Leiden: E.J. Brill, 1939.
——. *A Grammar of Biblical Aramaic.* Wiesbaden: Harrassowitz Verlag, 1995.
Rössler, O., "Zur Frage der Vertretung der gemeinsemitischen Laryngale im Akkadischen ($`_5$ = ġ)," in H. Franke (ed.), *Akten des vierundzwanzigsten internationalen Orientalisten-Kongresses München, 28. August bis 4. September 1957.* Wiesbaden: Franz Steiner Verlag, 1959.
Rost, P., *Die Keilschrifttexte Tiglat-Pilesers III., nach den Papierabklatschen und Originalen des Britischen Museums, Band II: Autographierte Texte.* Leipzig: Eduard Pfeiffer, 1893.
Rubio, G., "Falling Trees and Forking Tongues: On the place of Akkadian and Eblaite within Semitic," in L. Kogan (ed.), *Orientalia: Papers of the Oriental Institute, 3*, pp. 152–189. Moscow: Russian State University for the Humanities, 2003.
——. "The Languages of the Ancient Near East," in D.C. Snell (ed.), *A Companion to the Ancient Near East*, pp. 79–94. Blackwell companions to the ancient world. Ancient history. Malden: Blackwell Publishing, 2005.
——. "Writing in Another Tongue: Alloglottography in the Ancient Near East," in S.L. Sanders (ed.), *Margins of Writing, Origins of Cultures*, pp. 33–66. University of

Chicago Oriental Institute seminars 2. Chicago: Oriental Institute of the University of Chicago, 2006.
Russell, J.M., *Sennacherib's Palace without Rival at Nineveh.* Chicago: University of Chicago Press, 1991.
Sabar, Y., *A Jewish Neo-Aramaic Dictionary: Dialects of Amidya, Dihok, Nerwa and Zakho, northwestern Iraq.* Semitica Viva 28. Wiesbaden: Harrassowitz Verlag, 2002.
Saggs, H.W.F., "The Nimrud Letters, 1952 – Part I: The Ukin-zer Rebellion and Related Texts," *Iraq* 17 (1955): 21–50, pls. IV–IX.
——. "The Nimrud Letters, 1952 – Part II: Relations with the West," *Iraq* 17 (1955): 126–154, pls. XXX–XXXV.
——. "The Nimrud Letters, 1952 – Part III: Miscellaneous Letters," *Iraq* 18 (1956): 40–56, pls. IX–XII.
——. "The Nimrud Letters, 1952 – Part IV: The Urarṭian Frontier," *Iraq* 20 (1958): 182–212, pls. XXXVII–XLI.
——. "The Nimrud Letters, 1952 – Part V: Administration," *Iraq* 21 (1959): 158–179, pls. XLIII–XLIX.
——. "The Nimrud Letters, 1952 – Part VI: The Death of Ukin-zer; and Other Letters," *Iraq* 25 (1963): 70–80, pls. XI–XIV.
——. "The Nimrud Letters, 1952 – Part VII: Apologies; A Theft; and Other Matters," *Iraq* 27 (1965): 17–32, pls. II–VII.
——. "The Nimrud Letters, 1952 – Part VIII: Imperial Administration," *Iraq* 28 (1966): 177–191, pls. LIII–LVI.
——. "The Nimrud Letters, 1952 – Part IX," *Iraq* 36 (1974): 199–221, pls. XXXIV–XXXVII.
——. *The Nimrud Letters, 1952.* CTN V. London: The British School of Archaeology in Iraq, 2001.
Salonen, A., *Die Wasserfahrzeuge in Babylonien nach šumerisch-akkadischen Quellen (mit besonderer Berücksichtigung der 4. Tafel der Serie* ḪAR-*ra =ḫubullu): Eine lexikalische und kulturgeschichtliche Untersuchung.* StOr 8:4. Helsinki: Societas Orientalis Fennica, 1939.
——. *Die Hausgeräte der alten Mesopotamier nach sumerisch-akkadischen Quellen: eine lexikalische und kulturgeschichtliche Untersuchung. Teil II; Gefässe.* Annales Academiae Scientiarum Fennicae, Ser. B, 144. Helsinki: [Academia Scientiarum Fennica], 1966.
——. Review of "Akkadisches Handwörterbuch. Lieferungen 3—5," by W. von Soden, *AfO* 21 (1966): 96–98.
——. *Die Fussbekleidung der alten Mesopotamier nach sumerisch-akkadischen Quellen: eine Lexikalische und kulturgeschichtliche Untersuchung.* Helsinki: Suomalaisen Kirjallisuuden Kirjapaino Oy, 1969.
——. *Vögel und Vogelfang im alten Mesopotamien.* Annales Academiae Scientiarum Fennicae 180. Helsinki: [Academia Scientiarum Fennica], 1973.
Salonen, E., *Die Waffen der alten Mesopotamier: eine lexikalische und kulturgeschichtliche Untersuchung.* StOr. 33. Helsinki: [Academia Scientiarum Fennica], 1965.
——. "Über den Laut H im Akkadischen," *StOr* 46 (1975): 291–299.
Sanders, S.L. (ed.), *Margins of Writing, Origins of Cultures.* Oriental Institute Seminars 2. Chicago: The Oriental Institute of the University of Chicago, 2006.
Saporetti, C., "Intorno a *VDI* 80 (2/1962) 71," *Or* 35 (1966): 275–278.

Schaudig, H., *Die Inschriften Nabonids von Babylon und Kyros' des Grossen samt den in ihrem Umfeld entstandenen Tendenzschriften: Textausgabe und Grammatik.* AOAT 256. Münster: Ugarit-Verlag, 2001.
Schlözer, A.L., "von den Chaldäern," in J.G. Eichhorn (ed.), *Repertorium für biblische und morgenländische Literatur*, vol. VIII, pp. 113–176. Leipzig: Weidmanns Erben & Reich, 1781.
Schmitt, R., "Assyria grammata und ähnliche: Was wuβte die Griechen von Keilschrift und Keilschriften?" in C.W. Müller, K. Sier and J. Werner (eds.), *Zum Umgang mit fremden Sprachen in der griechisch-römischen Antike: Kolloquium der Fachrichtungen Klassische Philologie der Universitäten Leipzig und Saarbrücken am 21. und 22. November 1989 in Saarbrücken*, pp. 21–35. Palingenesia 36. Stuttgart: Steiner, 1992.
Schramm, W., *Akkadische Logogramme.* Göttingen: Universität Göttingen, Seminar für Keilschriftforschung, 2003.
Schroeder, O., *Keilschrifttexte aus Assur verschiedenen Inhalts.* WVDOG 35. Leipzig: J.C. Hinrichs'sche Buchhandlung, 1920.
Schulthess, F., *Lexicon Syropalaestinum.* Berlin: G. Reimer, 1903.
Schwemer, D., "Lehnbeziehungen zwischen dem Hethitischen und dem Akkadischen," *AfO* 51 (2005–2006): 220–234.
Sebba, M., S. Mahootian and C. Jonsson (eds.), *Language Mixing and Code-Switching in Writing: Approaches to Mixed-Language Written Discourse.* Routledge critical studies in multilingualism. London: Routledge, 2012.
Segal, J.B., "An Aramaic Ostracon from Nimrud," *Iraq* 19 (1957): 139–145.
Segert, S., Review of "La statue de Tell Fekherye et son inscription bilingue assyro-araméenne," by A. Abou-Assaf, P. Bordreuil and A.R. Millard, *AfO* 31 (1984): 90–94.
——. *Altaramäische Grammatik mit Bibliographie, Chrestomathie und Glossar.* 4th edition. Leipzig: VEB Verlag Enzyklopädie Leipzig, 1990.
Seidl, U., "Assurbanipals Griffel," *ZA* 97 (2007): 119–124.
Shaked, S., "Iranian Loanwords in Middle Aramaic," *Encyclopaedia Iranica, 2* (1986): 258–261.
——. "Iranian Words Retrieved from Aramaic," in D. Weber (ed.), *Languages of Iran: Past and Present: Iranian Studies in Memoriam David Neil MacKenzie*, pp. 167–176. Wiesbaden: Harrassowitz, 2005.
——. "Aramaic Loan-words in Middle Persian," *Bulletin of the Asia Institute*, N.S., 19, Iranian and Zoroastrian Studies in Honor of Prods Oktor Skjærvø (2005): 159–168.
Sigrist, M., "Miscellanea," *JCS* 34 (1982): 242–252.
Sivan, D., *Grammatical Analysis and Glossary of the Northwest Semitic Vocables in Akkadian Texts of the 15th–13th C.B.C. from Canaan and Syria.* AOAT 214. Kevelaer: Butzon & Bercker, 1984.
Skaist, A., "The *Clasula Salvatoria* in the Elephantine and Neo-Assyrian Conveyance Documents," in M. Sokoloff (ed.), *Arameans, Aramaic and the Aramaic Literary Tradition*, pp. 31–41. Ramat-Gan: Bar Ilan University Press, 1983.
Sokoloff, M., *The Targum to Job from Qumran Cave XI.* Ramat-Gan: Bar Ilan University, 1974.
——. *A Dictionary of Jewish Palestinian Aramaic of the Byzantine Period.* 2nd edition. Ramat-Gan: Bar Ilan University Press, 2002.
——. *A Dictionary of Jewish Babylonian Aramaic of the Talmudic and Geonic Periods.* Ramat-Gan: Bar Ilan University Press, 2002.
——. *A Dictionary of Judean Aramaic.* Ramat-Gan: Bar Ilan University Press, 2003.

——. "New Akkadian Loanwords in Jewish Babylonian Aramaic," in Y. Sefati et al. (eds.), *"An Experienced Scribe Who Neglects Nothing": Ancient Near Eastern Studies in Honor of Jacob Klein*, pp. 575–586. Bethesda: CDL Press, 2005.

——. *A Syriac Lexicon: A Translation from the Latin, Correction, Expansion, and Update of C. Brockelmann's Lexicon Syriacum.* Winona Lake & Piscataway: Eisenbrauns & Gorgias Press, 2009.

——. *A Dictionary of Christian Palestinian Aramaic.* OLA 234. Leuven: Peeters, 2014.

Soldi, S., "Aramaeans and Assyrians in North-Western Syria: Material Evidence from Tell Afis," *Syria* 86 (2009): 97–118.

Sommerfeld, W., *Untersuchungen zum Altakkadischen.* Münster: Unpublished Habilitation, 1987.

——. "Bemerkungen zur Dialektgliederung Altakkadisch, Assyrisch und Babylonisch," in G.J. Selz (ed.), *Festschrift für Burkhart Kienast: zu seinem 70. Geburtstage dargebracht von Freunden, Schülern und Kollegen*, pp. 569–586. Münster, Ugarit-Verlag, 2003.

Sprengling, M., "An Aramaic Seal Impression from Khorsabad," *AJSL* 49 (1932/33): 53–55.

Starr, I., *Queries to the Sungod: Divination and Politics in Sargonid Assyria.* SAA IV. Helsinki: Helsinki University Press, 1990.

Steiner, R.C., "Why the Aramaic Script Was Called 'Assyrian' in Hebrew, Greek, and Demotic," *Or* 62 (1993): 80–82.

——. "Papyrus Amherst 63: A New Source for the Language, Literature, Religion, and History of the Aramaeans," in M.J. Geller, J.C. Greenfield and M.P. Weitzman (eds.), *Studia Aramaica: New Sources and New Approaches: Papers Delivered at the London Conference of the Institute of Jewish Studies, University College London, 26th–28th June 1991*, pp. 199–207. Journal of Semitic Studies Supplement 4. Oxford: Oxford University Press, 1995.

Steingass, F., *A Comprehensive Persian–English Dictionary: Including the Arabic Words and Phrases to be Met with in Persian Literature.* 5th impression. London: Routledge & Kegan Paul, 1963.

Stevenson, J.H., *Assyrian and Babylonian Contracts with Aramaic Reference Notes.* New York, Cincinnati & Chicago: American Book Company, 1902.

Stol, M., Review of "A Concise Dictionary of Akkadian," by J.A. Black, A.R. George and N. Postgate (eds.), *BiOr* 57 (2000): 625–630.

——. Review of "Assyrian-English-Assyrian Dictionary," by S. Parpola and R.M. Whiting et al. (eds), *BiOr* 69 (2012): 561–563.

Stolper, M.W., "Three Iranian loanwords in Late Babylonian texts," in L.D. Levine and T.C. Young (eds.), *Mountains and Lowlands: Essays in the Archaeology of Greater Mesopotamia*, pp. 251–266. Bibliotheca Mesopotamiaca 7. Malibu: Undena, 1977.

——. Review of "Fifty Neo-Assyrian Legal Documents," by J.N. Postgate, *BASOR* 239 (1980): 78–80.

——. "The Governor of Babylon and Across-the-River in 486 B.C.," *JNES* 48 (1989): 283–305.

Strassmaier, J.N., *Inschriften von Cyrus, König von Babylon (538–529 v. Chr.): von den Thontafeln des Britischen Museums copirt und autographirt von J.N. Strassmaier.* Babylonische Texte 7. Leipzig: E. Pfeiffer, 1890.

——. *Inschriften von Darius, König von Babylon (521–485 v. Chr.): von den Thontafeln des Britischen Museums copirt und autographirt von J.N. Strassmaier.* Babylonische Texte 10–12. Leipzig: E. Pfeiffer, 1892–1897.

Streck, M., *Assurbanipal und die letzten assyrischen Könige bis zum Untergange Nineveh's.* Leipzig: J.C. Hinrichs'sche Buchhandlung, 1916.

Streck, M.P., *Zahl und Zeit. Grammatik der Numeralia und des Verbalsystems im Spätbabylonischen.* Cuneiform Monographs 5. Groningen: STYX Publication, 1995.

——. *Das amurritische Onomastikon der altbabylonischen Zeit*: Vol I. AOAT 271/1. Münster: Ugarit-Verlag, 2000.

——. "Keilschrift und Alphabet," in D. Borchers, F. Kammerzell and S. Weninger (eds.), *Hieroglyphen – Alphabete – Schriftreformen: Studien zu Multiliteralismus, Schriftwechsel und Orthographieneuregelungen*, pp. 77–97. Lingua Aegyptia – Studia monographica 3. Göttingen: Seminar für Ägyptologie und Koptologie, 2001.

——. "Die Nominalformen *maPRaS*(*t*), *maPRāS* und *maPRiS*(*t*) im Akkadischen," in N. Nebes (ed.), *Neue Beiträge zur Semitistik: Erstes Arbeitstreffen der Arbeitsgemeinschaft Semitistik in der Deutschen Morgenländischen Gesellschaft vom 11. bis 13. September 2000 an der Friedrich-Schiller-Universität Jena.* Jenaer Beiträge zum Vorderen Orient 5. Wiesbaden: Harrassowitz, 2002.

——. Review of "A Sketch of Neo-Assyrian Grammar," by J. Hämeen-Anttila, *ZA* 93 (2003): 126–128.

——. "Schnee," in M.P. Streck et al. (eds.), *Reallexikon der Assyriologie und Vorderasiatischen Archäologie, vol., 12: Šamuḫa – Spinne* pp. 241–242. Berlin: De Gruyter, 2009/2011.

——. "Innovations in the Neo-Babylonian Lexicon," in L. Kogan, N. Koslova, S. Loesov and S. Tishchenko (eds.), *Language in the Ancient Near East: Proceedings of the 53e Rencontre Assyriologique Internationale, Vol.* 1, pp. 647–660. Winona Lake: Eisenbrauns, 2010.

——. "Akkadian and Aramaic Language Contact," in S. Weninger (ed.), in collaboration with G. Khan, M.P. Streck and J.C.E. Watson, *The Semitic Languages: An International Handbook*, pp. 416–424. Handbücher zur Sprach- und Kommunikationswissenschaft 36. Berlin: De Gruyter Mouton, 2011.

——. "Eblaite and Old Akkadian," in S. Weninger (ed.), in collaboration with G. Khan, M.P. Streck and J.C.E. Watson, *The Semitic Languages: An International Handbook*, pp. 340–359. Handbücher zur Sprach- und Kommunikationswissenschaft 36. Berlin: De Gruyter Mouton, 2011.

——. "Babylonian and Assyrian," in S. Weninger (ed.), in collaboration with G. Khan, M.P. Streck and J.C.E. Watson, *The Semitic Languages: An International Handbook*, pp. 359–396. Handbücher zur Sprach- und Kommunikationswissenschaft 36. Berlin: De Gruyter Mouton, 2011.

——. "Akkadisch," in M.P. Streck (ed.), *Sprachen des Alten Orients*, pp. 65–102. 4., überarbeitete und aktualisierte Auflage by wbg. Darmstadt: Wissenschaftliche Buchgesellschaft, 2021.

Tadmor, H., "Assyria and the West: The Ninth Century and its Aftermath," in H. Goedicke and J.J.M. Roberts (eds.), *Unity and Diversity: Essays in the History, Literature, and Religion of the Ancient Near East*, pp. 36–48. Baltimore & London: The Johns Hopkins University Press, 1975.

——. "The Aramaization of Assyria: Aspects of Western Impact," in H.-J. Nissen and J. Renger (eds.), *Mesopotamien und Seine Nachbarn: Politische und kulturelle Wechselbeziehungen im Alten Vorderasien vom 4. bis 1. Jahrtausend v. Chr, 2*, pp. 449–470. CRRA 25. Berlin: Dietrich Reimer Verlag, 1982.

——. "Towards the Early History of *qatālu*," *JQR* 76 (1985): 51–54.

——. "על מקומה של הארמית בממלכת אשור: שלוש הערות על תבליט של סרגון" Hebrew title: *ʿl mqomt šl harmet bmmlkt ašur: šaloš hʿrot ʿl tbleṭ šl srgon.* *EI* 20 (1989): 249–252.

——. "On the Role of Aramaic in the Assyrian Empire," in M. Mori (ed.), *Near Eastern Studies: Dedicated to H.I.H. Prince Takahito Mikasa on the Occasion of His Seventy-*

Fifth Birthday, pp. 419–426. Bulletin of the Middle Eastern Culture Center in Japan 5. Wiesbaden: Otto Harrassowitz, 1991.

Tal, A., *A Dictionary of Samaritan Aramaic*, 2 vols. Handbuch der Orientalistik I/50. Leiden: Brill, 2000.

Tallqvist, K.L., *Die Sprache der Contracte Nabû-nâ'ids (555–538 v. Chr.) mit Berücksichtigung der Contracte Nebukadrezars und Cyrus'*. Helsinki: J.C. Frenckell & Sohn, 1890.

——. *Assyrian Personal Names*. ASSF 43/1. Helsinki: Druckerei der Finnischen Litteraturgesellschaft, 1914.

Tavernier, J., *Iranica in the Achaemenid Period (ca. 550–330 B.C.): Lexicon of Old Iranian Proper Names and Loanwords, Attested in Non-Iranian Texts*. OLA 158. Leuven: Peeters, 2007.

Tawil, H., *An Akkadian Lexical Companion for Biblical Hebrew: Etymological-Semantic and Idiomatic Equivalents with Supplement on Biblical Aramaic*. Jersey City: Ktav, 2009.

Testen, D., "The Significance of Aramaic *r* < **n*," *JNES* 44 (1985): 143–146.

——. "An Akkadian-Arabic Cognate-Pair and the Formation of Stem-Based Diminutives in Early Semitic," in G. Deutscher and N.J.C. Kouwenberg (eds.), *The Akkadian Language in Its Semitic Contexts: Studies in the Akkadian of the Third and Second Millennium BC*, pp. 140–149. Leiden: Nederlands Instituut voor het Nabije Oosten, 2006.

The Assyrian Dictionary of the Oriental Institute of the University of Chicago. CAD. Chicago & Glückstadt: The Oriental Institute & J.J. Augustin, 1956–2011.

Thomason, S.G., *Language Contact: An Introduction*. Edinburgh: Edinburgh University Press, 2001.

Thomason, S.G. and T. Kaufman, *Language Contact, Creolization, and Genetic Linguistics*. Berkeley: University of California Press, 1988.

Thomason, S.G. and D.L. Everett, "Pronoun Borrowing," *Proceedings of the Annual Meeting of the Berkeley Linguistics Society* 27 (2001): 301–315.

Thompson, R.C., "The Cuneiform Tablet from House D," in C.L. Wooley (ed.), *Carchemish*, II, pp. 136–142. London: British Museum, 1921.

——. *Assyrian Medical Texts from the Originals in the British Museum*. London: Humphrey Milford, 1923.

——. *Dictionary of Assyrian Chemistry and Geology*. Oxford: Clarendon Press, 1936.

——. *A Dictionary of Assyrian Botany*. London: The British Academy, 1949.

Thompson, R.C. and R.W. Hamilton, "An Aramaic Inscription on a Piece of Black Painted Ware form Nineveh," *JRAS* 1 (1932): 29-31.

Thureau-Dangin, F., *Une relation de la huitième Campagne de Sargon*. TCL III. Paris: Librairie Paul Geuthenr, 1912.

Thureau-Dangin, F. and M. Dunand, *Til-Barsib: Par F. Thureau-Dangin et Maurice Dunand avec le concours de Lucien Cavro et Georges Dossin*. Bibliothèque archéologique et historique 23. Paris: Librairie Orientaliste Paul Geuthner, 1936.

Trask, R.L., *A Dictionary of Phonetics and Phonology*. 1th edition. London: Routledge, 1996.

Tremayne, A., *Records from Erech: Time of Cyrus and Cambyses (538–521 B.C.)*. YOS VII. New Haven: Yale University Press, 1925.

Tropper, J., "Akkadisch *nuḫḫutu* und die Repräsentation des Phonems /*ḥ*/ im Akkadischen," *ZA* 85 (1995): 58–66.

——. "Dialektvielfalt und Sprachwandel im frühen Aramäischen, Soziolinguistische Überlegungen," in P.M. Michèle Daviau, J.W. Wevers and M. Weigl (eds.), *The*

World of the Aramaeans III: Studies in Language and Literature in Honour of Paul-Eugène Dion, pp. 213–222. Sheffield: Sheffield Academic Press, 2001.

——. "Eblaitisch und die Klassifikation der semitischen Sprachen," in G.J. Selz (ed.), *Festschrift für Burkhart Kienast zu seinem 70. Geburtstage dargebracht von Freunden, Schülern und Kollegen*, pp. 647–657. Münster: Ugarit-Verlag, 2003.

——. *Kleines Wörterbuch des Ugaritischen*. Wiesbaden: Harrassowitz Verlag, 2008.

Tsereteli, K. (ed.), *Grammatik der modernen assyrischen Sprache (Neuostaramäisch)*. Leipzig: VEB Verlag Enzyklopädie, 1978.

Tuell, S.S., "The Southern and Eastern Borders of Abar-Nahara," *BASOR* 284 (1991): 51–57.

Ullendorff, E., "What is a Semitic Language?" *Or* 27 (1958): 66–75.

Ungnad, A., "Aus den neubabylonischen Privaturkunden," *Beiheft 2* zum *OLZ* (1908): 19–28.

——. *Akkadian Grammar*, fifth, corrected edition (1969), revised by L. Matouš and translated by H.A. Hoffner. Atlanta: Scholars Press, 1992.

Vaan, J.C.T. de, *"Ich bin eine Schwertklinge des Königs": Die Sprache des Bēl-ibni*. AOAT 242. Kevelaer: Butzon und Bercker, 1995.

van Dijk, J., *Texts in the Iraq Museum* II, *Cuneiform Texts: Old Babylonian Letters and Related Material*. Wiesbaden: Harrassowitz, 1965.

van Driel, G., *The Cult of Aššur*. Studia Semitica Neerlandica 13. Assen: Van Gorcum, 1969.

van Soldt, W.H., "Akkadian as a Diplomatic Language," in S. Weninger (ed.), in collaboration with G. Khan, M.P. Streck and J.C.E. Watson, *The Semitic Languages: An International Handbook*, pp. 405–415. Handbücher zur Sprach- und Kommunikationswissenschaft 36. Berlin: De Gruyter Mouton, 2011.

Vanstiphout, H., "The Twin Tongues: Theory, Technique, and Practice of Bilingualism in Ancient Mesopotamia," in H.L.J. Vanstiphout (ed.), *All Those Nations ... Cultural Encounters within and with the Near East. Studies Presented to Han Drijvers at the Occasion of his Sixty-Fifth Birthday by Colleagues and Students*, pp. 141–159. Groningen: Styx-Publications, 1999.

Veenhof, K.R., *Kültepe tabletleri V: The Archive of Kuliya, son of Ali-abum (Kt. 92/k 188–263)*. Ankara: Türk Tarih Kurumu, 2010.

Vita, J.-P., "Language Contact between Akkadian and Northwest Semitic Languages in Syria-Palestine in the Late Bronze Age," in A.M. Butts (ed.), *Semitic Languages in Contact*, pp. 375–404. Studies in Semitic Languages and Linguistics 82. Leiden: Brill, 2015.

——. (ed.), *History of the Akkadian Language. Vol. 1: Linguistic Background and Early Periods. Vol 2: The Second and First Millennia BCE. Afterlife*. Handbook of Oriental Studies, Vol. 152/2. Leiden-Boston: Brill, 2021.

Volkwein, B., "Masoreitisches *'ēdūt, 'ēdwōt, 'ēdōt* – 'Zeugnis' oder 'Bundesbestimmungen'?" *BZ* 13 (1969): 18–40.

von Soden, W., "Der hymnisch-epische Dialekt des Akkadischen," *ZA* 40 and 41 (1931–1933): 163–227 and 90–183.

——. *Die lexikalischen Tafelserien der Babylonier und Assyrer in den Berliner Museen*, vol. 2, *Die akkadischen Synonymenlisten*. Berlin: Staatl. Museen, Vorderasiat. Abt., 1933.

——. "Die Unterweltsvision eines assyrischen Kronprinzen: Nebst einigen Beobachtungen zur Vorgeschichte des Aḫiqar-Romans," *ZA* 43 (1936): 1–31.

——. "Akkadisch *ta'û* und hebräisch *tā'* als Raumbezeichnungen," *WO* 1 (1950): 356–361.

——. "Gibt es ein Zeugnis dafür, dass die Babylonier an die Wideraufserstehung Marduks geglaubt haben?," *ZA* 51 (1955): 130–166.

——. "Zum akkadischen Wörterbuch. 61–66," *Or* 24 (1955): 136–145.
——. "Zur Laut- und Formenlehre des Neuassyrischen," *AfO* 18 (1957): 121–122.
——. "*izqātu, išqātu* "Kettenringe", ein aramäisches Lehnwort," *AfO* 20 (1963): 155.
——. "Vedisch *magham*, 'Geschenk' – neuarabisch *maǧǧānīja*, 'Gebührenfreiheit'. Der Weg einer Wortsippe," *JEOL* 18 (1964): 339–344.
——. *Ergänzungsheft zum Grundriss der akkadischen Grammatik* (AnOr 33), AnOr 47. Rome: Pontificium institutum biblicum, 1969.
——. "Aramäische Wörter in neuassyrischen und neu- und spätbabylonischen Texten. Ein Vorbericht I–III," *Or* 35 (1966): 1–20; *Or* 37 (1968): 261–271; *Or* 46 (1977): 183–197.
——. Review of "The Akkadian Influences on Aramaic," by S.A. Kaufman, *JSS* 22 (1977): 81–86.
——. *Akkadisches Handwörterbuch.* 3 vols. Wiesbaden: Otto Harrassowitz, 1965–1981.
——. Review of "Legal Transactions of the Royal Court of Nineveh, Part I: Tiglath-Pileser III through Esarhaddon," by T. Kwasman and S. Parpola (= SAA VI); "Imperial Administrative Records. Part I: Palace and Temple Administration," by F.M. Fales and J.N. Postgate (= SAA VII), *WO* 25 (1994): 136–138.
——. Review of "Queries to the Sungod: Divination and Politics in Sargonid Assyria," by I. Starr, *WO* 25 (1994): 132–134.
——. Review of "The Correspondence of Sargon II, Part II: Letters from the Northern and Northeastern Provinces," (= SAA V) by G.B Lanfranchi and S. Parpola, *WO* 25 (1994): 134–135.
——. *Grundriss der akkadischen Grammatik.* 3., ergänzte Auflage, unter Mitarbeit von Werner R. Mayer. Rome: Editrice Pontificio Istituto Biblico, 1995.
von Soden, W. and W. Röllig, *Das Akkadische Syllabar,* 2., völlig neubearbeitete Auflage. Rome; Pontificio Istituto Biblico, 1967.
Wagner, M., *Die lexikalischen und grammatikalischen Aramaismen im alttestamentlichen Hebräisch.* Berlin: Alfred Töpelmann, 1966.
Warda, W.M., *Assyrians Beyond the Fall of Nineveh: A 2,624 Years Journey.* William M. Warda, 2013.
Watanabe, K., "Neuassyrische Siegellegenden," *Orient* 29 (1993): 109–138.
——. *Die adê-Vereidigung anlässlich der Thronfolgeregelung Asarhaddons.* BaM, Beiheft 3. Berlin: Gebr. Mann, 1987.
Waterman, L., *Royal Correspondence of the Assyrian Empire: Translated into English, with a Transliteration of the Texts and a Commentary, Parts* I, II and III, 1st reprint in three volumes of the 1st edition published 1930–1936. New York & London: Johnson Reprint Corporation, 1972.
Waters, M.W., "A Letter from Ashurbanipal to the Elders of Elam (BM 132980)," *JCS* 54 (2002): 79–86.
Watson, Wilfred G.E., Review of "A Sketch of Neo-Assyrian Grammar," by J. Hämeen-Anttila, *JSS* 48 (2003): 134–135.
——. "Akkadian Loanwords in Ugaritic: The Hippiatric Texts," in C. McCarthy and J.F. Healey (eds.), *Biblical and Near Eastern Essays: Studies in Honour of Kevin J. Cathcart*, pp. 240–257. New York & London: T&T Clark International, 2004.
——. "Loanwords in Semitic," *AuOr* 23 (2005): 191–198.
Weinreich, U., *Languages in Contact: Findings and Problems.* 7th printing. The Hague: Mouton, 1970.
Weninger, S. (ed.), in collaboration with G. Khan, M.P. Streck and J.C.E. Watson, *The Semitic Languages: An International Handbook.* Handbücher zur Sprach- und Kommunikationswissenschaft 36. Berlin: Walter de Gruyter, 2011.

Winford, D., *An Introduction to Contact Linguistics.* Malden: Blackwell Publishing, 2003.
Wiseman, D.J., "A New Stela of Aššur-naṣir-pal II," *Iraq* 14 (1952): 24–44.
——. "The Nimrud Tablets," *Iraq* 15 (1953): 135–160.
——. "Assyrian Writing-Boards," *Iraq* 17 (1955): 3–13.
——. "The Vassal-Treaties of Esarhaddon," *Iraq* 20 (1958): 1–99.
——. Review of "The Akkadian Influences on Aramaic," by S.A. Kaufman, *BSOAS* 40 (1977): 144.
Woodington, N.R., *A Grammar of the Neo-Babylonian Letters of the Kuyunjik Collection.* Ann Arbor: University Microfilms International, 1985.
Worthington, M., "Some New Patterns in Neo-Assyrian Orthography and Phonology Discernible in Nouns with Monosyllabic Stems," *JNES* 69 (2010): 179–194.
Wright, W., *A Grammar of the Arabic Language*, I–II. Translated from the German of Caspari and edited with numerous additions and corrections by W. Wright; 3rd edition revised by W. Robertson Smith and M.J. de Goeje. Cambridge: Cambridge University Press, 1967.
Yana, G.V., *Ancient and Modern Assyrians: A Scientific Analysis.* Xlibris, 2008.
Ylvisaker, S., *Zur babylonischen und assyrischen Grammatik: Eine Untersuchung auf Grund der Briefe aus der Sargonidenzeit.* LSS V/6. Leipzig: J.C. Hinrichs'sche Buchhandlung, 1912.
Zaccagnini, C., "On the Juridical Terminology of Neo-Assyrian and Aramaic Contracts," in H. Waetzoldt and H. Hauptmann (eds.), *Assyrien im Wandel der Zeiten. XXXIXe Rencontre Assyriologique Internationale: Heidelberg 6. — 10. Juli 1992*, pp. 203–208. CRRA 39. Heidelberg: Heidelberger Orientverlag, 1997.
——. "The Assyrian Lion Weights from Nimrud and the 'mina of the land'," in Y. Avishur and R. Deutsch (eds.), *Michael: Historical, Epigraphical and Biblical Studies in Honor of Prof. Michael Heltzer*, pp. 259–265. Tel Aviv: Archaeological Center Publications, 1999.
Zadok, R., "Addenda to 'Historical and Onomastic Notes'," *WO* 9 (1977): 240–241.
——. "Historical and Onomastic Notes," [I. The Date of the Document ADD 1110; II. Evidence for the Shift *ā* > *ō* in Neo-Assyrian, Neo-Babylonian and Late-Babylonian Onomastic Material; III. On the Element *'ayya* in Neo-Assyrian, Neo-Babylonian and Late-Babylonian Transcriptions; IV. On Some Syro-Palestinian Names in Neo-Assyrian Transcription], *WO* 9 (1977–1978): 35–56.
——. Review of "The Chicago Colloquium on Aramaic Studies, Journal of Near Eastern Studies Vol. 37, No. 2, April 1978," *WO* 12 (1981): 196–200.
——. "Assyro-Babylonian Lexical and Onomastic Notes," *BiOr* 41 (1984): 33–46.
——. "Notes on the Historical Geography of Mesopotamia and Northern Syria," *Abr-Nahrain* 27 (1989): 154–169.
——. "NA *ga-ba-'* = West Semitic *gb'*," *NABU* 1989/47.
——. "On the Onomasticon of the Old Aramaic Sources," *BiOr* 48 (1991): 25–40.
——. "Onomastic, Prosopographic and Lexical Notes," *BN* 65 (1992): 47–54.
——. "Foreigners and Foreign Linguistic Material in Mesopotamia and Egypt," in K. van Lerberghe and A. Schoors (eds.), *Immigration and Emigration within the Ancient Near East. Festschrift E. Lipiński*, pp. 431–447. OLA 65. Leuven: Peeters Publishers, 1995.
——. "The Ethno-Linguistic Character of the Jezireh and Adjacent Regions in the 9th–7th Centuries (Assyria Proper vs. Periphery)," in M. Liverani (ed.), *Neo-Assyrian Geography*, pp. 217–282. QGS 5. Rome: HERDER, 1995.
——. "On the Late-Assyrian Texts from Dūr-Katlimmu and the Significance of the NA Documentation for Ethno-linguistic Classification," *NABU* 1995/3.

——. "The Ethnolinguistic Composition of Assyria Proper in the 9th–7th Centuries BC," in H. Waetzoldt and H. Hauptmann (eds.), *Assyrien im Wandel der Zeiten*, pp. 209–216. HSAO 6. Heidelberg: Heidelberger Orientverlag, 1997.

——. "On aromatics and reeds," *NABU* 1997/55.

Zewi, T. and M. Oren, "Semitic Languages in Contact–Syntactic Changes in the Verbal System and in Verbal Complementation," in A.M. Butts (ed.), *Semitic Languages in Contact*, pp. 405–421. Studies in Semitic Languages and Linguistics 82. Leiden: Brill, 2015.

Zimmern, H., "Gilgameš-Omina und Gilgameš-Orakel," *ZA* 24 (1910): 166–171.

——. *Akkadische Fremdwörter als Beweis für babylonischen Kultureinfluß*. 2nd edition. Leipzig: J.C. Hinrichs'sche Buchhandlung, 1917.

——. "Babylonische Mysterien und kein Ende," *ZA* 36 (1925): 83–85.

INDICES

Grammatical Index

ablaut class: 174
absolute: 63, 154, 218, 219, 242
abstract: 139
ad hoc: 100, 167
adaptation: 2, 11
adjective: 75, 83, 93, 96, 130, 139, 187, 196, 198, 199, 228, 248, 249, 257, 262,
adverb: 16, 67, 70, 73, 235, 267
affix: 144, 231
Akkadian: 1, 4, 5, 6, 8, 9, 10, 12, 14, 15, 16, 17, 18, 19, 20, 21, 22, 23, 24, 25, 28, 31, 32, 44, 46, 49, 50, 51, 54, 55, 57, 63, 64, 65, 66, 67, 70, 71, 73, 77, 79, 80, 82, 83, 84, 88, 89, 90, 91, 93, 94, 95, 96, 97, 101, 102, 103, 106, 107, 109, 110, 111, 112, 113, 116, 118, 120, 121, 122, 123, 124, 125, 126, 127, 129, 130, 134, 137, 138, 139, 142, 143, 144, 146, 148, 149, 150, 151, 154, 155, 157, 158, 159, 157, 158, 159, 160, 161, 163, 164, 165, 166, 167, 169, 171, 173, 174, 175, 176, 178, 179, 181, 184, 190, 191, 192, 194, 195, 196, 197, 198, 199, 200, 201, 202, 203, 204, 205, 207, 210, 211, 212, 213, 214, 215, 217, 218, 219, 220, 221, 222, 225, 228, 229, 230, 231, 232, 233, 235, 236, 238, 239, 240, 241, 243, 245, 247, 249, 251, 252, 253, 255, 257, 258, 262, 263, 266, 267, 268, 269, 270, 271, 272, 273, 274, 276, 277, 278, 279, 280, 281, 282, 283, 287, 289, 290, 291, 292, 294, 295, 296, 598, 299
Akkadographic: 164, 235, 249
alloform: 66
alphabetic script: 35, 40, 45, 54
amending: 284
analogy: 106, 124, 134, 139, 140, 143, 193, 258, 295
analyzable: 15, 16, 67, 97, 264
anaptyctic vowel: 104
aphesis: 70, 71
Aramaism: 97, 204, 241, 258, 272, 286, 299
archaic: 24,70, 151, 239
Assyrian vowel harmony: 24, 25, 76, 107, 128, 131, 155, 210, 219, 237, 277, 295
Assyrianization: 55
Assyrianized: 26, 57
back-formation: 215
Barth's law: 16, 164
bilingualism: 1, 81
borrowing: 1, 2, 3, 4, 7, 10, 11, 12, 14, 15, 16, 18, 19, 61, 63, 65, 67, 70, 71, 72, 75, 94, 120, 126, 133, 134, 234, 256, 292
by-form: 66, 107
calque: 3, 7, 94, 148
case-marking: 3
causative: 58, 105, 188
Central Semitic: 10, 22, 31
chronology: 17, 31, 67, 70, 93, 262, 285
clash of homonyms: 11, 73, 112
clash: 11, 73, 99, 111, 112, 219, 271, 287, 291
closed syllable: 82, 113, 124, 130, 171, 250
cluster: 66, 93
cognate: 1, 3, 4, 7, 10, 11, 16, 18, 20, 31, 71, 75, 77, 78, 80, 81, 85, 90, 91, 92, 93, 97, 101, 102, 104, 107, 110, 113, 114, 115, 117, 118, 120, 121, 126, 127, 134, 139, 140, 146, 147, 149, 166, 167, 169, 175, 176, 181, 185, 188, 192, 201, 202, 203, 204, 210, 212, 213, 218, 221, 223, 225, 227, 229, 230, 231, 232, 233, 235, 237, 238, 240, 247, 249, 252, 254, 259, 278, 287, 295
collation: 8, 80, 200, 272, 284, 299, 300
colloquial: 51, 111, 137, 155

colophon: 38, 257, 258, 259
common ancestor: 3
Common Semitic: 66, 75, 135, 171, 204, 210, 214, 215, 242, 277
comparative and historical linguistics: 2
comparative method: 11, 12, 93
comparative process: 10
comparative Semitic: 22, 23
complex: 15, 16, 67, 90, 97, 242, 243
compound: 15, 16, 67, 68, 77, 94, 99, 104, 144, 216, 233, 235, 268
consonant doubling: 23
consonantal shift: 24, 25
construct: 50, 63, 94, 95, 96, 185, 202, 254
contact: 1, 2, 5, 10, 11, 17, 18, 19, 33, 36, 51, 57, 64, 72, 83, 97, 102, 105, 112, 125, 141, 164, 188, 206, 234, 256, 278, 283, 285
contemporaneous: 19, 65
context: 21, 47, 50, 56, 67, 72, 73, 74, 75, 78, 79, 80, 82, 84, 85, 86, 87, 89, 90, 91, 98, 99, 100, 111, 112, 119, 120, 123, 124, 125, 126, 127, 128, 129, 130, 135, 137, 139, 141, 142, 144, 145, 146, 147, 149, 150, 151, 154, 157, 159, 160, 161, 165, 166, 169, 171, 174, 175, 178, 180, 184, 185, 186, 187, 189, 190, 191, 192, 194, 195, 196, 199, 200, 206, 207, 208, 209, 210, 217, 218, 219, 225, 226, 227, 229, 230, 247, 294
contract: 23, 25, 27, 28, 83, 128
contraction: 23, 128, 248
copied: 2, 3
copying: 2, 4, 19
correlation: 14
cross-cultural: 3
cultural-historical claim: 11
culture word: 3, 118, 131, 213, 238, 260
cuneiform writing system: 21
darkening: 248
defective form: 245
definite state: 50
demonstrative pronoun: 133
demotic: 34, 57
denomination: 43
dental: 24, 25, 28, 77, 79, 91, 97, 112, 118, 144, 153, 166, 186, 210, 225, 230, 296
derivative: 78, 104, 105, 129, 164, 186, 205, 245, 277
determinative: 77, 82, 89, 106, 117, 146, 158, 169, 171, 187, 194, 210, 217, 246, 268, 287, 295
devoicing: 223
dialect: 1, 2, 3, 4, 5, 8, 9, 14, 17, 18, 19, 20, 21, 22, 23, 24, 25, 26, 28, 29, 31, 32, 34, 35, 51, 59, 64, 70, 71, 73, 75, 100, 102, 111, 112, 118, 120, 123, 129, 144, 146, 147, 148, 152, 154, 155, 175, 178, 191, 201, 205, 206, 210, 211, 215, 220, 222, 224, 225, 233, 238, 245, 251, 255, 256, 267, 269, 278, 298
diminutive: 80, 93, 118, 120, 139, 160, 230
diphthong: 23, 24
direction of borrowing: 2, 10, 11, 18, 63, 262
dis legomenon: 7, 85, 107, 122, 135, 138, 141, 182, 188, 197, 209, 222, 224, 233, 239, 242, 244, 246, 253, 286
dissimilate: 14, 164, 210
dissimilation: 14, 16, 80, 87, 100, 104, 109, 147, 155, 156, 173, 210
distribution: 18, 27, 45, 56, 67, 88, 90, 91, 93, 102, 114, 121, 140, 144, 155, 189, 191, 192, 204, 225, 235, 245, 256
diverge: 11, 232
donor language: 2, 3, 10, 11, 15, 16
durative: 151
East Semitic languages: 10
Eblaite: 10, 22
e-coloring: 12, 65, 70, 72, 75, 101, 162
elision: 16, 67, 128
emendation: 64
emphatic quality: 14
emphatic radical: 14
emphatic: 14, 63, 100, 109, 110, 173, 200
enigmatic: 85, 142, 206, 259, 290
epenthetic vowel: 95

epigraphic: 34, 80, 150, 243
epistolary: 44
erroneous reading: 64, 273, 280, 283, 284, 289, 299, 300
etymological commentaries: 8
etymological inquiries: 17
etymon: 16, 18, 67, 103, 105, 107, 118, 131, 188, 211, 217, 220, 224, 225, 235, 263, 291
extension: 3, 4, 7, 16, 90, 175, 178, 192, 204
figuratively: 242
foreign language: 1, 4
foreign word: 4, 74, 75, 77, 88, 92, 99, 117, 130, 137, 142, 143, 144, 174, 187, 195, 202, 207, 212, 214, 218, 220, 221, 224, 238, 241, 246, 248, 256, 258, 270, 273, 276, 277, 279, 280, 281, 283, 284, 287, 289, 292, 294, 295, 296, 298
forerunner: 73, 100, 108, 270, 298
Fremdwort: 4, 215
fricative: 12, 65, 68, 70, 71, 73, 76, 97, 124, 127, 129, 134, 161, 225, 230, 268
Geers' law: 14, 109, 110, 111, 156, 173
geminate: 267
gemination: 130, 263
genetically related languages: 3, 21
genitive: 95, 96, 97, 128, 144, 163, 195, 230, 254, 268
genre: 7, 25, 50, 58
geometric: 87, 88
ghost word: 4, 19, 261, 268, 280
glottal stop: 12, 23, 65, 70, 72, 73, 92, 93, 99, 124, 134, 161, 162, 215, 251, 285
gradation: 14
graffiti: 37
graphic rendering: 14, 15, 319
hamza: 12, 65, 70, 72, 73, 93, 99, 134, 161, 162, 182, 213, 215, 251, 285
hapax legomenon: 7, 74, 75, 78, 80, 82, 84, 85, 91, 98, 101, 102, 107, 111, 112, 119, 122, 125, 126, 128, 130, 140, 143, 144, 145, 146, 159, 161, 166, 174, 175, 178, 180, 186, 190, 191, 192, 196, 199, 200, 201, 206, 208, 214, 216, 217, 219, 226, 229, 231, 234, 236, 238, 241, 243, 248, 251, 259, 261, 265, 269, 270, 290, 291, 292
heading: 66, 78, 121, 138, 148, 170, 174, 186, 206, 207, 239, 247, 258, 264, 265, 274, 277, 289
hendiadys: 90, 178, 212, 227
historical contact: 2
historical linguistics: 2, 23
historical records: 17
hollow root: 99, 115, 279
homiletical: 91
homonym: 11, 73, 99, 112
homophone: 66
homophonic: 50, 176, 177
homorganic dissimilation: 210
homorganic: 23, 24, 210
hymn-epic dialect: 24
hypercorrection: 99
idiomatic expression: 274
incompatibility: 14
incompatible: 11, 226
indicator: 17, 18, 248
inflection: 4, 124, 165, 166, 265, 320
inscription: 21, 23, 24, 26, 28, 31, 32, 34, 36, 43, 48, 49, 51, 56, 58, 65, 131, 154, 155, 204, 251, 268, 269, 287
integrate: 14, 72, 105, 131, 153, 166, 188, 212, 237, 246
interchangeable: 110
interjection: 16, 67, 73
internal structure: 15, 16, 67, 97, 264
interrogative: 67
inter-Semitic: 10, 192, 315
intransitive: 151, 178
intra-Semitic: 11
Kassite: 24, 28
Kulturwort: 3
labial: 16, 79, 82, 118, 163, 164, 166, 186, 210, 250
language contact: 1, 2, 5, 11, 17, 18, 19, 36, 57, 83, 97, 112, 125, 164, 206, 234, 256, 278, 283, 285
lapse: 50, 177
laryngeal: 68, 134, 269, 277
lectio difficilior: 66, 70, 134, 155, 213
Lehnbildung: 72, 95, 202
levelling: 71
lexeme: 2, 5, 94, 164, 288
lexical data: 10, 19, 20, 31
lexical inventory: 2, 19, 20, 167
lexical item: 2, 17, 19, 72

lexical list: 21, 59, 129, 140, 156, 250, 277
lexical material: 2, 8, 20
lexicon: 2, 9, 10, 19, 20, 31, 77, 80, 116, 121, 131
ligature: 141, 143
lingua franca: 24, 34, 55, 56
linguistic provenance: 4
loan meaning extension: 3
loan shifts: 3
loan translations: 3
logogram: 21, 38, 58, 89, 116, 129, 171, 176, 177, 210, 230, 250, 254, 256
logographic writing: 24, 296
material borrowing: 3
meaning extension: 3, 4
mediae geminatae: 99, 115
merism: 235
metathesis: 112, 138, 147, 201, 218, 252, 290
mimation: 23, 24, 25, 28
mobility: 3
monomorphemic: 15, 16, 68
monophthongized: 23, 24
morpheme chronology: 17, 70
morpheme: 17, 70, 139
morphographemic: 182
morphological criterion: 15, 264
morphological patterns: 3
morphological structure: 2, 11
morphological: 10, 11, 15, 23, 97, 105, 188, 249, 264, 279
morphology: 10
native word: 7, 11, 17, 163, 192
near deixis: 133, 134
nominal form: 75, 93, 115, 120, 123, 128, 141, 158, 160, 167, 181, 191, 197, 207, 210, 212, 231, 232, 235, 243, 262, 277, 278, 282, 287, 299
nominal pattern: 16, 56, 93, 101, 120, 124, 128, 138, 139, 160, 181, 193, 197, 215, 230, 249, 262, 263, 267
nominal performative: 169
non-emphatic: 14
Northwest Semitic languages: 10, 31
nota accusativi: 7, 27
novelties: 243
onomatopoetic: 267
open syllable: 109, 130, 164
orthographically: 104, 107, 155
orthography: 33, 100
paleographic: 47
paranomastic: 205
partial assimilation: 104, 112, 166
passive participle: 106, 126
passive: 58, 84, 106, 124, 126
pejorative: 160, 230
penultimate syllable: 71, 79
penultimate: 71, 79
personal name: 7, 8, 23, 55, 81, 130, 156, 163, 177, 214
pharyngeal: 12, 65, 70, 71, 73, 76, 124, 128, 129, 134, 159, 161, 162, 167, 229, 268, 277
philology: 2, 25
phonetic shape: 11, 12
phonological pattern: 11, 14
phonological rules: 2
phonological system: 2, 71
phonological: 2, 3, 7, 10, 11, 14, 15, 23, 65, 66, 67, 71, 72, 75, 77, 75, 77, 79, 81, 87, 91, 93, 91, 93, 99, 101, 108, 109, 110, 112, 124, 129, 131, 137, 141, 150, 153, 161, 162, 166, 173, 175, 192, 193, 200, 201, 210, 211, 212, 215, 217, 219, 220, 222, 227, 229, 237, 246, 249, 251, 257, 260, 266, 269, 287, 288, 290, 291
phonology: 10, 81, 262
phraseology: 7
pictograph: 21
plurale tantum: 57, 61, 129
precative: 91, 182, 183, 190,
precedent: 17, 18
precursor: 285
preposition: 7, 27, 144, 241, 242, 271, 272, 273
productive: 23, 83, 124, 126, 137, 200, 210, 276
progressive partial assimilation: 112
progressive vowel assimilation: 71, 79, 83
prohibitive: 190
proper name: 47
prosopographical: 55
prosthetic vowel: 80, 93
Proto-Semitic: 3, 12, 20
pseudo-logogram: 96, 117
psycholinguistic factor: 105
quadrilateral root: 260, 287

quadrilateral verb: 155
radical: 14, 16, 22, 75, 79, 80, 87, 93, 93, 99, 101, 107, 116, 127, 131, 164, 166, 167, 197, 210, 212, 217, 222, 223, 229, 239, 249, 252, 263, 277, 279, 285, 290
recipient language: 2, 3, 10, 11, 14, 15, 17, 51
reconstructed: 58, 59, 75, 87, 124, 127, 198, 230, 243, 244, 278
reconstruction of historical grammar: 17, 70, 182
reconstruction: 17, 18, 20, 64, 70, 87, 181, 182
reduction: 12
regressive assimilation: 66, 166, 186
retrieve: 201, 217, 298
root consonant: 14, 104, 107, 112, 263
Šafʿel: 105, 188
sandhi: 144, 251
scribal error: 176, 272
secondary form: 124, 215, 299
semantic associations: 2
semantic borrowing: 178
semantic categories: 7
semantic change: 4, 7
semantic class: 124, 230, 304
semantic extension: 90, 175, 178, 192, 204
semantic loan: 3, 4, 7, 16, 59, 303
semantic: 2, 3, 4, 7, 10, 15, 16, 20, 50, 59, 66, 75, 77, 79, 80, 82, 84, 85, 87, 90, 91, 92, 97, 99, 110, 112, 120, 121, 124, 125, 131, 140, 149, 157, 160, 165, 166, 169, 174, 175, 178, 187, 190, 192, 196, 197, 199, 204, 218, 220, 223, 224, 227, 229, 230, 234, 235, 244, 247, 254, 255, 257, 258, 265, 267, 271, 278, 287, 291, 293, 299
Semitic languages: 3, 12, 14, 17, 18, 19, 20, 21, 22, 31, 36, 66, 70, 80, 93, 97, 102, 110, 112, 121, 124, 125, 127, 139, 144, 146, 147, 161, 164, 166, 167, 187, 188, 191, 196, 197, 200, 201, 206, 271, 272, 275, 282
semivowel: 128, 141, 143
sibling: 3
slip: 50, 124, 127, 177
sound value: 21, 81, 100, 117, 125, 158, 164, 249, 260
source language: 2, 51
source word: 15, 16, 17, 18, 59, 67, 68, 82, 83, 87, 91, 104, 108, 115, 138, 158, 171, 179, 181, 197, 200, 210, 217, 219, 220, 225, 242, 269, 277, 281, 290, 295
stative: 78, 84, 108, 121, 189, 228, 263, 274, 293
structural borrowing: 3
stylistic variation: 71
sub-branch: 22
substantivized: 83, 93, 204
substratum: 22
Sumerian: 15, 21, 22, 23, 243, 263, 264, 282
syllabic sign: 21
syllabic writing: 24, 239
syllabically: 77, 116, 118, 129, 140, 164, 176, 239, 250, 255, 256
syllable: 12, 23, 24, 38, 70, 71, 72, 79, 82, 100, 109, 113, 121, 124, 130, 138, 141, 164, 171, 181, 197, 235, 249, 260
synonym list: 21, 130, 203, 205, 268
synonym: 11, 121, 236, 260
syntactic patterns: 2
syntax: 7
tolerate: 14, 79
toponym: 94, 162
topos: 98
trans-: 153, 175, 185, 195, 201, 211, 264
transcription: 14, 15, 71, 155, 168, 197
transferred: 2
triconsonantal root: 14, 320
tris legomenon: 7, 129, 152, 154, 166, 176, 202, 255
Ugaritic: 10, 22, 31, 38, 80, 102, 104, 113, 124, 143, 144, 147, 163, 183, 236, 247
umlaut: 12, 65, 70, 72, 75, 162
uncontracted vowel: 23
usage: 58, 73, 83, 94, 121, 136, 145, 149, 150, 151, 157, 165, 175, 178, 189, 191, 212, 223, 225, 227, 295, 296, 299
variant: 66, 77, 78, 79, 89, 97, 104, 109, 110, 125, 133, 134, 148, 152, 163, 173, 175, 183, 205, 244, 257, 265, 269, 282
variation: 50, 71, 73, 109, 125, 130, 148, 171, 246
velar: 68, 79, 107, 110, 112, 124, 127, 129, 134, 155, 167, 200, 257

verbal adjective: 83, 249, 257, 262
vernacular: 25, 51, 155, 201, 258
vocabulary: 2, 8, 9, 10, 20, 107, 140, 173, 297
voiced: 12, 19, 23, 24, 65, 73, 75, 77, 78, 97, 110, 112, 118, 125, 167, 210, 212, 246, 257, 268
voiceless stop: 23, 24, 78, 257
voiceless: 14, 23, 24, 68, 70, 71, 77, 78, 107, 110, 112, 124, 125, 127, 129, 134, 161, 134, 161, 166, 167, 200, 212, 225, 230, 246, 257
voiceless: 14, 23, 24, 68, 70, 71, 77, 78, 107, 110, 112, 124, 125, 127, 129, 134, 161, 134, 161, 166, 167, 200, 212, 225, 230, 246, 257
voicing: 77, 257
vowel assimilation: 71, 79, 83, 197
vowel harmony: 24, 25, 76, 107, 109, 128, 131, 155, 163, 210, 219, 237, 277, 295
vowel length: 23
West-Semitic languages: 10, 17, 18, 102, 112, 124, 146, 147, 161, 164, 188, 191, 275

Subject Index

administrative document: 21, 33, 58, 74, 89, 92, 109, 128, 146, 216, 219, 229, 233, 269, 293
Assyria proper: 10, 35, 37, 41, 48, 51, 55
astrologer: 26, 133, 139
astronomical almanac: 22
audience gift: 45, 156, 255
bullae: 48
chancery: 23, 33
clay: 22, 28, 31, 32, 37, 48, 250
cohort commander: 47
conveyance: 41, 81, 242, 276
coronation ritual: 25
court: 25, 26, 38, 39, 42, 48, 49, 53, 133, 139, 217, 275
dedicatory inscription: 21, 31
deed: 26, 33, 36, 40, 54, 80, 81
divine name: 7, 264
diviner: 26, 49
docket: 40, 41, 42, 169, 184
edict: 21, 25, 26, 100
exorcistic text: 28
extispicy: 49
fresco: 52, 53
harem decree: 25
homer: 42
hymn: 21
incantation: 21
kudurru: 24, 145, 146
lament: 21
law code: 25
lion-weight: 43, 44
love poetry: 21
loyalty oath: 26, 64
magic spells: 21
marriage contract: 33, 166
materia medica: 85, 86
memoranda: 21, 40
memorandum: 39
monumental text: 21
mythological poetry: 21
officials' reports: 26
omen: 21, 28
oracle: 49, 130, 178, 222, 226, 228, 236, 248, 249, 256, 257, 262
oracular queries: 26, 49
ostracon: 31, 32, 46, 47, 48, 164
papyrus: 22, 31, 33, 34, 41, 45, 46, 48, 49, 51
parchment: 22, 56, 180
petitioner: 49, 98
poetic prayer: 28
prayer: 21, 28, 73, 120, 139, 185
private letter: 21
proverb: 21, 281
public archives: 26
query: 49, 50
relief: 51, 52, 54, 221
scribe: 17, 25, 28, 39, 40, 41, 43, 44, 45,

49, 50, 51, 52, 53, 54, 74, 81, 105, 133, 134, 139, 154, 155, 176, 177, 194, 239, 265, 279
scroll: 41, 45, 46, 51, 52, 53, 54, 156, 157, 180, 181
seal: 31, 41, 45, 48, 49, 125, 180
shred: 190
social status: 2
stylus: 51
treaties: 63, 64, 193, 269, 293
treaty: 12, 59, 61, 63, 64, 77, 94, 101, 174, 190, 192, 193, 222, 223, 244, 285, 292
visual: 37, 51, 52, 54, 221
votive inscription: 21
weight: 19, 31, 43, 44
wisdom literature: 21, 28

Personal Names

[B]arīku: 216
[Ṭ]āb-la-kunu: 216
Abā-gû: 39
Abdâ: 209
Adad-nērārī III: 59
Adda-bi'd[ī]: 216
Aḫū'a: 287
Alexander the Great: 29
Amiri: 165
Amur-Aššūr: 135
Aqar-Aia: 49
Arbail-šarrat: 40
Arīḫu: 50, 176, 177
Ashur-ketti-leshir: 26
Ashurnasirpal II: 26, 59, 255
Ašīru: 216
Assurbanipal: 1, 29, 34, 39, 40, 46, 50, 54, 59, 81, 86, 90
Aššūr-bēlu-taqqin: 39, 125
Aššūr-da''in-aplu: 45
Aššūr-nādin: 135
Aššūr-nērāri V: 63, 65
Aššūr-šallim-aḫḫē: 41, 42
Atueḫu: 39
Bābilāiu: 209
Bāia: 188, 189
Balassu: 83
Bar-Rakkāb: 32
Bēl-aḫu-uṣur: 228
Bēl-ēṭir: 47
Bēl-nāṣir: 142, 191, 207, 219, 273
Bēl-šallim: 153
Bēl-šarru-uṣur: 41, 42
Bir Hadad: 32
Bur-Aia: 81
Bur-Anate: 81
Bur-Zināni: 81
Dadâ: 149
Dād-aḫḫē: 200
Dannu-Nergal: 142, 219
Dunnaša-āmur: 226
Eriānu: 135
Esarhaddon: 46, 49, 56, 59, 77, 78, 81, 85, 90, 94, 101, 130, 133, 145, 152, 154, 161, 174, 178, 190, 191, 192, 222, 223, 228, 231, 234, 263, 244, 248, 249, 256, 257, 259, 269, 270, 273, 275, 285, 292, 293
Ḫamaṭuṭu: 42
Ḫanabeš: 243
Illil-bāni: 1
Ilu-iqbi: 40
Inūrta-bēlu-uṣur: 279
Inūrta-ilā'ī: 279
Issār-šumu-ēreš: 133, 258
Itti-Šamaš-balāṭu: 78
Kabtî: 45
Kanūnāyu: 40
Kiqillāni/u: 156
Lā-dāgil-ili: 178, 248
Lā-qēpu: 41, 42
Mannu-kī-māt-Aššūr: 216
Mār-bi'dī: 177
Marduk-erība: 266
Marduk-šākin-šumi: 90, 259
Mārīddi: 286
Mār-larīm: 177
Mār-nūrī: 177
Mār-sūrī: 177
Matī'-Adda: 40, 41

Matī'-ilu: 63
Mudabirāiu: 164
Nabû-duru-uṣur: 50
Nabû-ḫussanni: 222
Nabû-kabti-aḫḫēšu: 154
Nabû-le'ûtī: 231
Nabû-nādin-aḫḫē: 176
Nabû-nādin-šumi: 234
Nabû-reḫtu-uṣur: 228
Nabû-šallim: 49, 142, 207, 219
Nabû-šāpik-zēri: 39
Nabû-šarru-uṣur: 42
Nabû-šēzib: 44
Nabû-šulmu-ēreš: 188
Nabû-tabni-uṣur: 270
Nabû-zēru-ibni: 142, 507, 219
Nabû-zuqup-kēnu: 258
Na'id-ilu: 259
Nebuchadnezzar II: 27, 171
Nergal-āpil-kūmū'a: 26
Nūr-Aia: 39
Nūrāia: 39
Pān-Aššūr-lāmur: 48, 49
Pir'-Amurru: 47
Qibīt-Is(sār): 41, 42
Qiqillāni: 156
Qišeraya: 243
Qurdi-Aššūr-lāmur: 44
Ra'sūnu: 214
Ribiṣiṣi: 243
Ṣabu: 135
Sama': 243
Šamaš-šumu-ukīn: 34, 47, 290
Šamši-Adad V: 45
Sargon II: 45, 46, 48, 49, 50, 55, 59, 154, 177, 181, 206, 208, 241, 259, 265, 289
Šarru-dūrī: 176
Šarru-ēmuranni: 142, 207
Sāsî: 228
Śehr-nūrī: 169
Sennacherib: 25, 56, 59, 181, 228
Šēp-Aššūr: 41, 42
Shalmaneser III: 37, 45, 51, 59, 251
Shalmaneser V: 43, 51, 53, 286
Shamashshumukin: 34
Sîn-iddina: 45, 46
Sîn-na'di: 180
Sinqīša-āmur: 236
Ṣuḫru: 197, 199
Šumaya: 212
Tabālāyu: 142, 207, 219
Tadin-Ištar: 135
Taquni: 42
Tettenai: 94
Tiglath-pileser I: 26, 36
Tiglath-pileser III: 44, 51, 54, 59, 91, 153, 214
Urbî: 39
Urbu-Nabû: 209
Urdu-Gula: 145, 154, 231, 275
Zabinu: 40
Zakkūr: 32, 73, 202

Geographical Names

Abi-ila'i: 95
Aliḫu: 238
Amidi: 69, 114, 147, 182, 203
Arbela: 69, 132, 161, 225, 226, 236, 247
Arrapḫa: 69
Arzūḫina: 69
Assur: 25, 26, 32, 34, 40, 41, 42, 45, 46, 47, 61, 63, 65, 67, 68, 69, 76, 88, 92, 96, 63, 105, 106, 112, 114, 117, 122, 123, 126, 128, 132, 134, 135, 138, 140 147, 148, 156, 157, 158, 162, 164, 167, 168
Aššūr: 27, 36, 77, 137, 139, 289
Assyria: 1, 8, 33, 35, 37
Assyrian heartland: 27, 35, 51, 55
Assyria proper: 35, 37, 41, 48, 51, 55
Babylon: 31, 46, 62, 68, 69, 83, 94, 138, 153, 178
Balaṭ: 96
Bēt-Adad-erība (Tell Baqāq 2): 27
Bit-abi-ila'i: 95

Bit-Zamani: 211
Burmar'īna (Tell Shiukh Fawqāni): 27
Calah/Nimrud: 26, 27, 37, 39, 44, 47, 48, 50, 54, 89, 91, 100, 214, 261, 285, 293
Carchemish: 27, 132
Damascus: 69
Darati: 68
Daria: 61
Dayyan-Adad: 95
Deir ʿAlla: 32
Der: 68, 183, 203, 224, 241
Dunnu-ša-Uzibi: 26
Dūr-Bēl-ila'ī: 40
Dūr-Katlimmu (Tall Šēḫ Ḥamad): 27, 96
Dūr-Šarrukēn (Khorsabad): 27, 36, 48, 206
Eber nāri: 5, 93, 94, 95
Eğriköy: 27
El-Amarna: 25, 64, 241, 186
Erzen: 27
Gargamīs (Carchemish): 27
Gaziantep: 27
Gazru (Gezer, Gazara): 27
Giricano: 26
Girnavaz: 27, 96
Gūzāna (Tell Ḥalaf): 27, 46, 68, 85, 103, 114, 117, 167, 168, 216, 242, 243
Ḫamāt: 133, 162, 211
Ḫamê: 218
Hamrin area: 103, 182
Ḫanduate: 42
Ḫanūri: 249
Harran: 27, 55, 82, 83, 95, 102, 103, 114, 162, 189, 228
Hatra: 34, 67, 157
Hulî: 95
Ḫuzīrīna (Sultantepe): 27, 69, 72, 203
Ibla: 253
Imgur-Ellil (Balawat): 27
Jezireh: 56
Kalḫu: 27, 214
Kār-Aššūrnāṣirapli (Tell Masaikh): 27
Kār-Šarrukīn: 62, 68, 69, 102, 203, 237
Kārum Kaneš: 285
Kazane Höyük: 27
Kullanīa (Tell Tayinat): 27, 63
Kültepe: 24, 285
Kumme: 69, 103, 205
Kurba'il: 132, 133
Kuyunjik: 3, 27
Laḫīru: 68
Lāqê: 50, 175, 177
Lullumê: 102
Ma'allanāte: 27, 169, 183
Mardin: 27
Mari: 163, 228, 247
Māzamua: 102, 132
Middle Euphrates: 50, 177
Nabi Yunus: 27
Nabula (modern Girnavaz): 27, 62
Naṣibina: 90, 168
Nimrud (Calah): 91, 100, 214, 261, 285, 293
Nineveh (Nīnua): 26, 29, 35, 39, 41, 42, 49, 50, 51, 62, 63, 65, 67, 68, 69, 72, 74, 76, 78, 79, 81, 82, 84, 85, 86, 88, 90, 92, 93, 95, 98, 102, 103, 105, 107, 108, 109, 113, 114
Nīnua: 27, 36
Nippur: 1
Northeastern frontier: 132
Northern Babylonia: 62, 102
Northern border: 239
Northwest: 132
North-Western Province: 69
Nuzi: 25, 88, 144, 158, 253, 297, 298
Parsua: 102, 162
Phoenicia: 62, 78, 132
Province of the Treasurer: 69, 132, 211, 215
Puqudu: 279
Qalʿat Sherqat: 27
Qunbuna: 239
Quri': 168
Qurubi: 95
Rab Šaqê Province: 103
Raṣappa: 93, 103, 265
Rasm et-Tanjara: 27
Sam'al (Zinçirli): 27
Sāmirīna (Samaria): 27
Ṣariza: 27
Ša-Ṣillaia: 39
Sefire: 65
Šibanība (Tell Billa): 27, 116
Šiddi-asika: 168
Ṣimirra: 62, 203
Šingibūtu: 203
Sultantepe (Ḫuzīrīna): 27
Sumurunu: 253

Akkadian Words Discussed

adê: 12, 61, 63, 64, 65
adrā'u: 65, 92, 93
akê: 7, 16, 67, 68
akku: 5, 130, 256, 257
anēnu: 5, 18, 68, 71
anīna: 5, 72, 73, 74
anīnu: 18, 68, 70, 72, 73
aqqabāni: 74, 75
aqqabu: 5, 74, 75, 106
aṣūdātu: 76, 77
aṣūdu: 5, 76, 77
badāqu: 78, 79
**baru*: 79
basālu: 82
bašā'u: 7, 84
bēt zibli: 85, 252, 253, 254
buḫḫušu: 5, 257, 258, 259
bunbullu: 85, 86, 87
burbāni: 107, 108, 259, 260
būṣinnu: 88
būṣīnu: 7, 88, 89
darāku: 260, 261, 280
darāsu: 90, 91, 261
dubāqu: 244, 245, 246
durā'u: 5, 58, 65, 92, 93, 97
Eber nāri: 5, 93, 94, 95
Ebir nāri: 93
egertu: 5, 261, 262, 263
gabdi: 95, 96, 97
gabdu: 95, 97
gab'u: 98, 99, 114
gaddāi: 99
gadiu: 5, 101
galītu: 104, 102
galû: 5, 102, 103, 104, 105, 188, 211, 237
gamāru: 121
gammīdu: 74, 105, 106, 107
gammīdutu: 74, 105, 106, 107
gammuzu: 107, 108, 259, 260
garīṣtu: 5, 14, 108, 109, 110
gašūru: 263
gaṭṭa'a: 100, 111
gazālu: 5, 111
gazāru: 7, 112
gidlu: 7, 113, 114
**girīṣtu*: 14, 108, 109
gubbāni: 114
gubbu: 5, 98, 114, 115, 116
gulēnu: 116, 117, 118
gumāru: 5, 118, 119, 120, 121
ḫalābu: 5, 122, 124, 136
ḫalāpu: 122, 123, 124, 127
ḫalīdu: 7, 125
ḫalpete: 126, 128
ḫalputu: 126, 128
ḫālu: 5, 128, 129
ḫanāpu: 5, 264, 265
ḫangaru: 5, 130, 131, 256
ḫannīu: 5, 19, 20, 132, 133, 134
ḫarbutu: 7, 134
ḫarbūtu: 7, 134, 135, 136
ḫarurtu: 5, 265, 266, 267
ḫašābu: 5, 267, 268
ḫilpu: 5, 122, 123, 124, 125, 136
ḫulūṭu: 5, 136, 137, 138
ḫurbānu: 138, 139, 140
iābilu: 140, 141
ianūqu: 5, 141, 142, 143, 221
im–magāni: 143, 144
izqātu: 268
kabsu: 269, 270
kabsutu: 270
kadāru: 145, 146
kandu: 7, 146, 147
kannušu: 147, 148, 149, 150, 151, 153
katāru: 5, 150, 151
kinā1tu: 147, 149, 152
kiqillutu: 51, 153, 154, 155, 156
kirku: 5, 45, 156, 157
kurḫu: 7, 157, 158, 159
kuribtu: 159, 160
kuspu: 5, 270, 271
kusup libbi: 270, 271
lapān(i): 5, 271, 272, 273
laqā'u: 5, 273, 274
leḫmu: 7, 160, 161
madbar: 5, 16, 162, 163
magādu: 575, 276
**magattu*: 276
magazzutu: 5, 276, 277
magguru: 164, 165
maḫītu: 5, 278
makaḫalūtu: 166, 167
maqarrātu: 167
maqarrutu: 167, 168, 169, 170
maqartu: 5, 170, 17
maqaṭṭāte: 172

maqaṭṭu: 7, 76, 172, 173
maqaṭṭutu: 172, 173
marāsu: 5, 174, 175
mar'u: 50, 81, 175, 176, 177
maṣû: 177, 178
miāru: 179, 240
midbar: 162, 163
miglu: 54, 180, 181
mil'āni: 181, 182
**mil'u*: 181
**muāšu*: 279
mudābur: 162, 163
mudarriktu: 260, 261, 280
nakālu: 280, 282
napāṣu: 5, 280
nasīkāni: 281
nasīkāti: 281
nasikku: 281
nasīku: 5, 214, 281, 282
natānu: 182, 183
nibzāni: 183
nibzu: 5, 183, 184, 185
niklu: 5, 280, 282
niqittu: 5, 185
paḫāzu: 5, 105, 186, 187, 188
palāḫu: 283, 284
palû: 5, 283
parāḫu: 7, 188, 189, 190
parāmu: 190, 191
pašāqu: 191, 192
pispisu: 192, 193
purṣīnāte: 193, 194
purṣīnu: 7, 193, 194
pusku: 194, 195
pušku: 5, 194, 195
puṭuru: 7, 195, 196, 197
qadduru: 5, 284
**qallīlu*: 197, 198
qallīssu: 197, 198
qamāru: 7, 199, 201
qanū'āte: 201, 202
qapīru: 5, 202, 203
qarābu: 5, 203, 204
qarāḫu: 158, 204, 205, 206, 207
qarḫāte: 205
qarḫu: 205, 206
qarsu: 5, 284
qarūḫu: 5, 142, 143, 206, 207, 221
qin'u: 285
qi''u: 5, 285
qūbāti: 207, 208
qumbutu: 7, 209, 210, 211
rab šaglûti: 104, 211
rad(d)īdu: 213
radābu: 211
radāpu: 5, 211, 212, 215
**ra'su*: 214, 215
re'sāni: 214, 215
**re'su*: 214
ridpu: 211, 212, 213
**sabāku*: 222, 224
sādiāti: 216, 217
sādiu: 7, 216
saḫaru: 5, 217, 218, 219
salā'u: 285, 286
salītu: 5, 142, 206, 219, 220
salṭāni: 221
salṭu: 221, 222
samādiru: 5, 286, 287
samāku: 5, 288, 289
sapāku: 222, 223, 224
sapāqu: 5, 224, 225
saqālu: 5, 289
sarabāte: 225, 226, 227
sarābu: 7, 225, 226, 227
sarḫu: 7, 227, 228
**suānu*: 290
sūsānu: 291
ṣaḫūrānūtu: 5, 230, 231, 232
ṣallu: 5, 232, 233, 239
ṣāpītu: 5, 292
ṣappuḫu: 5, 292, 293
ṣibtātu: 5, 293, 294
ṣipirtu: 5, 294, 295
ṣippirrāte: 5, 234, 235
ṣipputu: 236
šaglû: 104, 105, 237
šaglûtu: 104, 105, 237
šapānu: 5, 295
šapīnutu: 5, 237, 238
šārītu: 5, 296
ša-ṣallēšu: 233, 239
šernu: 7, 288, 297, 298
šiāḫu: 197, 239, 240, 241
širnu: 297
šubbuḫu: 298
šullāmu: 5, 298, 299
supīrātu: 229, 230
šūqāqu: 5, 299
taḫtānu: 241
tuānu: 242, 243
tūbāqu: 7, 244, 245, 246

tukkāni: 246
tukku: 7, 246, 247
ṭaḫru: 299, 300
ṭullumâ: 5, 247, 248, 249
ummu: 249, 250, 251
urbānu: 5, 49, 251, 252
urû: 300
ziblu: 7, 58, 252, 253, 254
ziqqāti: 254, 256
ziqqu: 5, 254, 255, 256

Aramaic Words Discussed

arḏīḏā: 213
'aḥnan: 70
'aḥnū: 70
'am: 250
'ammā: 250
'anaḥnā: 70, 71
'anaḥnan: 70
'anḥnan: 70
'arbān: 251
'arbānā: 251, 252
'āṣū: 76, 77
'āṣūṯā: 76, 77
'dr': 92
'dr'': 92
'eḏrā': 92, 93
'eḏrā'ā: 92, 93
'eggarṯā: 261
'eggrā: 261
'gp: 66, 67
'gp': 66
'grh: 261
'grt: 261, 262, 263
'grt': 261, 262
'm: 250, 251
'm': 250
'nḥn: 18, 70, 71
'nḥnn: 70
'rbn: 251
'šrḥw: 227
'ṣw: 76, 77
'ṣwt': 76, 77
'urbānā: 251, 252
'wrbn': 251

balbulka: 85, 87
balbūltā: 85, 87
bambūlā: 85, 87
banbūltā: 85, 87
bar: 80, 81
bašlā: 82
bdq: 78, 79
bədāqā: 78
ber: 80
bešālānā: 82
bēṯ zeḇlā: 253
bḥš: 257, 259
bō/ūṣīn: 88
bō/ūṣīnā: 88
br: 81, 94
br': 80
brā: 80
brōnā: 80
bšl: 82, 83
bšln: 82
bšln': 82
bsy: 84, 85
būṣīn: 88
būṣīnā: 88
bwṣyn: 88
bwṣyn': 88

gaḇ: 96
gabbā: 96
gabbē: 96
gadia: 101
gadyā: 101
gaḏyā: 101
gālū: 103
gālūtā: 103
gāmūdūtā: 106
gārṣā: 109
gb: 86, 97, 98, 99
gb': 96, 97, 115
gb': 98, 99
gb'': 98
gb'h: 98
gb't': 98
gby: 96
gd': 99, 101
gḏālā: 113
gḏāltā: 113
gḏē: 101
gdl: 113
gdlh: 113

gdlt': 113
gdy: 101, 102
geḇ'əṯā: 98
gərīṣā: 109
gərīṣātā: 109
gərīṣē: 109
gərīṣətā: 109
gərīṣtā: 14, 109, 110
gerṣā: 109
giḏlā: 113
glw: 103
glwt': 103
gly: 103, 104
glym: 117
glym': 117
glz: 111
gmd: 106, 107, 108
gmr: 119, 120, 121
gmurtā: 119
gmwrt': 119
gmydh: 106
goḇ: 98, 99, 114, 115
gp: 66, 67
gp': 66
griṣh: 109
grṣ: 14, 109, 110, 111
grṣ': 109
gūbā: 114
gubbā: 98, 99, 114, 115
gumra: 119, 120
gumrā: 119
gūmrā: 119
gwb: 98, 99, 114, 115
gwb': 98, 114
gwmrh: 119
gwmrt': 119
gzl: 111, 112
gzr: 112, 113

dāḇōq: 244
dāḇōqā: 244
dbq: 244, 245
dbwq: 244
dbwq': 244
dr': 92
dr'': 92
dra: 92
drā': 92
drā'ā: 92
drk: 260
drs: 90
drš: 90, 91
dūbāqā: 244
dubbāq: 244
dubbāqā: 244, 245
dwbq: 244
dwbq': 244
dy: 12, 63, 65, 96, 97
hākan: 67
hākē: 67
hākēn: 67
hala: 128
hānā: 19, 133
hky: 67
hkyn: 67
hn': 133

zbl: 253, 254
zbl': 253, 254
ze/ēḇlā: 253
zēḇal: 253
zə'ōrūtā: 231
zīq/zeq: 255
zīqā/zeqqā: 255
z'ōrānū: 231
z'ōrānūṯā: 231
zr': 92
z'r: 231, 232
z'wrnw: 231
z'wrnwt': 231
zy: 40, 42, 43, 96, 97
zyq: 255
zyq': 255

ḥal: 128
ḥalḇ: 122
ḥalḇā: 122
ḥallā: 128
ḥalūṭā: 136, 138
ḥangrā: 130, 131
ḥarbā: 135
ḥarbānā: 138, 140
ḥarbəṯā: 135, 136
ḥarbṯā: 135
ḥarbū: 135
ḥarbūṯā: 135, 136
ḥəlapṯā: 126, 128
ḥəlīṭtā: 136
ḥelpā: 126
ḥilṭā: 136
ḥl: 128

ḥl': 128
ḥlb: 122, 123, 124
ḥlb': 122
ḥld: 125, 126
ḥlīpā: 126
ḥlīptā: 126
ḥlīṭā: 136
ḥlīṭṭā: 136
ḥlp: 126, 127
ḥlṭ: 136, 137
ḥlyph: 126
ḥlypt': 126
ḥlyṭh: 136
ḥngr: 130, 131
ḥngr': 130
ḥnp: 264, 265

ḥrbh: 135
ḥrbn: 138
ḥrbn': 138
ḥrbt': 135
ḥrbw: 135
ḥrbwt': 135
ḥurbān: 138
hurbana: 138
ḥurbānā: 138, 140
ḥurbānāyā: 138

ḫanǧār: 130

ṭallūm: 248
ṭalōm: 248
ṭalōmā: 248
ṭlwm: 248
ṭlwm': 248

yāneq: 141
yānōqā: 141, 207
yānqā : 141
yānūqā: 141
ybl: 140
ynq: 141, 143
ynq': 141, 143
ywbyl': 140

kaḏ: 146
kaddā: 146, 147
kaddān: 146
kaddānā: 146, 147
kandā: 146, 147
kd: 146, 147
kd': 146
kdn: 146
kdn': 146
kdr: 145, 146
kəḏānā: 146
kerkā: 156
kḥl: 166
knš: 148, 149, 150
knšh: 152
knšt': 152
knuštā: 152
knwšt': 152
knyšh: 152
knyšt': 152
krāb: 159
krābā: 159
krb: 159, 160
krb': 159
krḥ: 157
krk: 156, 157
krk': 156
ksp: 40, 270, 271
ksypw: 270
ksypwt': 270
ktr: 150, 151
kūraḥ: 157
kūrḥā: 157
kurḥāyā: 157
kūrḥōnā: 157
kwrḥ': 157

lahma: 160
laḥmā: 160
lḥem: 160
lḥm: 160, 161
lḥm': 160
lqy: 273, 274

ma/egdā: 275
maḏbar: 163
maḏbrā: 163
maggān: 143, 144
makəḥalətā: 166
maḵḥāl: 166
maḵḥālā: 166
maqqartā: 170
maqqərā: 170
maqrānā: 170
mārā: 176
māryā: 176
mašdē: 11

mdbr: 163
mdbr': 163
məgallā: 180
mel'ā: 181
məqaṭṭa'tā: 172
mga/illā: 180
mgd: 275, 276
mglh: 180
mglt': 180
mgn: 143
mgr: 165, 166
mḥh: 278
mhita: 278
mḥt': 278
mḥy: 278
mkḥl: 166
mkḥl': 166
mkḥlt': 166
ml': 181
mqrh: 168, 169, 170, 171
mqrt': 170
mr': 176, 177
mrs: 174, 175
mry': 176
mšdy: 216
mṣy: 178
mwr: 179
mwš: 279

nbz: 183, 184, 185
neqmā: 185
neqmətā: 185
nqamtā: 158
nqm: 185
nqmh: 185
nqmn: 185
nqmt': 185
ntn: 182, 183, 262
sāḥartā: 217
sahra: 217, 218
sāḥrā: 217
sarnā: 296
sḇak: 222
sḇāḵ: 222
sḇāḵā: 222
sbk: 222, 223, 224
sbk': 222
seḇḵā: 222
səḥartā: 217, 218
sḥrh: 217
sḥrt': 217, 218

silita: 219, 220
sīlītā: 219
spīnā: 237
spīntā: 237
spīttā: 237
spq: 223, 224, 225
spynh: 237, 238
spynt': 237
sren: 297
srn: 296, 297
srn': 296
sūpārtā: 229
sūpārūṯā: 229
suppārā: 229
suppārtā: 229
swḥ: 239, 241
swprh: 229
swprt': 229
śyḥ: 239
sylyh: 219
sylyt': 219

'āṣūtā: 76, 77
'bar nahrā: 94
'br nhr: 94
'br nhr': 94
'dy': 12, 63
'eqḇ: 74
'eqbā: 74
'eqḇā: 74
'na: 73
'ngirta: 262
'ngyrt': 262
'ny: 73
'qb: 74, 75
'qb': 74
'qeḇ: 74

parbil: 259
parṣānā: 194
parṣentā: 194
pašpəšā: 192
pašpūšā: 192
pe/ukšā: 195
peḥzā: 187
peṭōrtā: 196
pḥz: 186, 187
pḥz': 187
prḥ: 188, 189
prm: 190, 191
prm': 190

prmyn: 190, 191
prmyt': 190, 191
prṣnt': 194
pšak: 195
pšk: 195
pšk': 195
pšpš': 192
pšq: 191, 192
pṭwrt': 196
pūrbālā: 259
pūšpāšā: 192
pwrṣn: 194
pwrṣn': 194
pwrṣnt': 194
pyṭwr': 196

ṣāl: 232
ṣālā: 232, 234
ṣālīṯā: 219
ṣaprā: 234, 235
ṣaprāwāṯā: 234
ṣaprāyāṯā: 234
ṣəlīṯā: 219, 220
ṣeppā: 236
ṣeppṯā: 236
ṣippətā: 236
ṣipra: 234
ṣīptā: 236
ṣl: 232, 233
ṣl': 232
ṣl'': 232
ṣl'l': 232
ṣly: 219, 220
ṣlyt': 219
ṣpar: 234
ṣph: 236
ṣpr: 234
ṣpr': 234
ṣpt': 236
ṣpy: 236, 292
ṣpyt': 291
ṣ'r: 231, 232
ṣūlā: 232

qabbāḇī: 232
qabbāḇīṯā: 208
qaina: 201
qamrā: 199
qany': 201
qanyā: 201
qanyē: 201
qārəḥā: 205
qarḥā: 205, 206
qariḥā: 205
qbbh: 208
qbby: 208
qbbyt': 208
qənāwāṯā: 201, 202
qənayyā: 201
qərāḥā: 206
qərāḥā: 206
qīqalṯā: 154
qiqilta: 154
qiqla: 154
qīqlā: 154
qll: 197, 198
qlqlh: 154
qlqlt': 51, 154, 155, 156
qlyl: 197, 198, 199
qmar: 199
qmr: 199, 200
qmr': 199, 200
qnh: 201
qpīrā: 202
qpyr: 202, 203
qpyr': 202, 203
qrāḇ: 203
qrāḇā: 203
qrb: 203, 204
qrb': 203
qrḥ: 205, 206
qrḥ': 205
qrwḥ: 206
qṭ': 100, 101, 173, 176
qubbā: 209
qubbā: 209
qūbbāḇ: 208
qūbbāḇā: 208
qubbəṯā: 209, 210
qumba: 209, 211
qumbta: 209, 211
qūrḥā: 206
qwbb: 208
qwbb': 208
qwbh: 209
qwbt': 209
qyqlh: 154
qyqlt': 154

radpa: 211, 213
rdd: 21
rdp: 211, 212

rdyd: 213
rdyd': 213
rəḏāpā: 212
rəḏīḏ: 213
rəḏīḏā: 213
rəḏīdtā: 213
rēšā: 214, 215
rēšānā: 214, 215
rēšānē: 214
ridpa: 212
r'š: 214
ršn: 214
ryš': 215
ryšn: 214, 215

ša/urbā: 225
šāḏītā: 216
šāḏōy: 216
šāḏōyā: 216
šalṭā: 221
šalṭē: 221
šarābā: 225, 227
šddāy: 216
šddāyā: 216
šdwy: 216
šdwy': 216
šdy: 216, 217
šdy': 216
šdyt': 216
šərābā: 225, 226, 227
šərāḇā: 226

šilṭā: 221
širba: 226, 227
šlāṭ: 221
šlāṭā: 221
šlṭ: 221
šlṭ': 221
šnṣy: 178
šrb: 225, 226, 227
šrbrwby: 226
šrbrwbyt': 226
šreḇ: 225
šrḥ: 227, 228, 229
šrīḥā: 228
šwrb': 225

taḥt: 241, 242
tawwān: 242
tawwānā: 242, 243
tḥeṯ: 241
tḥoṯ: 241
tḥt: 241, 242
tḥtn: 241, 242
tḥwt: 241, 242
tḥyt: 241
tkk: 246, 247
tūkā: 246, 247
tukkā: 246, 247
twk: 246, 247
twk': 246
twn: 242
twn': 242

Textual References

ABL
94:12: 272
117:11: 275
243 r.14: 239
281 r.4: 248
317:20: 240
333 r.19: 273, 274
421:13: 272
455:13: 185
503 r.5, 7: 295
525 r.10: 270
541:4′, r.4: 105
611 r.4: 288
633:22: 85, 86
685:23: 273
791: 167
868 r.2: 225
968:6: 298
1148:5′, 10′, 11′: 289
1217: 8, 12:
1245 r.19: 267
1285:29: 145
1285:38: 98

ADD
964 r.15: 89

ALA
N9(13): 199

Ass
1384ae: 172, 173
14232t: 76
3070: 172

BATSH 6/2
8 r.12: 76
48:7: 96
113:6, 7, 8: 96

Billa
89:2′: 116

BM
132980 r.20′: 288

CT 53
46:21–6: 86
331 r.5, 7: 295
336:5′: 93
816:8′: 132

CTN I
9 r.18–20: 38
21 r.8′: 38
35 r.1 18′: 76

CTN II
1:5′: 195
1:11′: 117
1:12′: 105
119 r.18–19: 111

141:6–7: 89
141:7: 88, 89
144:4: 156
145:1–4: 157
145:3: 156
154 r.2′: 116
155 iv 19: 293, 294
188:5: 162
188:9: 162
207:3′: 211
207:6′: 211
212:9′: 194

CTN III
2:3: 157, 158, 159
2:4: 167
14 r.2: 76
15:1–3: 169
15 e.1: 168
16:1: 168
43:3: 168
55:5, 6, 7, 8, 9: 95
89:21′, 23′, 26′: 256
95 r.7, 21: 194
95 r.27: 194
102 iii 23′: 104, 111

CTN V
84f: 279
175ff: 279

FNALD
14:23: 156
14:25: 105, 116
14 r.1: 116
14 r.34: 276
32:9: 168

HAF
91: 68

Iraq 15
p. 138: 172
p. 142: 95

Iraq 16
p. 34: 167
p. 38, 34: 276

Iraq 19
1957, pl. 29: 76

Iraq 20
53:328: 285
182, 30: 289

Iraq 23
33: 88, 89
p. 20: 172
p. 43: 105
p. 44: 116
pp. 18f.: 116

Iraq 25
56:43: 252

KADP
21 a 12: 284

KAR
33:25: 92
215 ii 15: 280

KAV
197:15: 186, 187
214:27: 148
215:10: 188
215 r.19: 68

LAS
no. 171: 98

MVAeG
41/3 pl. 2:8–10: 119

NABU
02/90 r.9: 68

ND
10054 r.8′: 38
11000: 251, 252
11048 r.18–20: 38
2088:8: 167
2097:8: 116
2307 r.10: 276
2311:5: 172
2386 r. i 15: 237
2490+ r.1: 88, 89
2644:5: 279
2672:9: 170
2687:1, 7: 105
2687:3: 172
2691:9: 116
2759: 289
3407:5′: 172
3430:7, r.2: 95
3467:5, 12: 168
5461:2: 76

NL
23:5: 279

O
3698:1: 183

PVA
188: 128
246: 117
248: 105, 106
249: 172
269: 156

Rfdn 17
3 r.1: 62
10 r.12: 62
15:5: 201
30:11: 63

SAA I
1:8: 203
1:28–30: 289
1:29: 132
1:30: 289
1 r.52: 132
1 r.59: 147
5:4: 132
7:10′: 132
8 r.20: 62
10:5: 132
10:10: 132
13:15′: 162
15:7′: 132
18 r.9′: 132
21 r.1: 132
26:2: 168
27:5′: 167
34 r.19′: 45, 156
34:9, r.3′, 6′: 170
36 r.7′: 181
51:5: 65
54 r.14: 68
63 r.4: 68
71:9: 68
72:6′: 132
76:6: 62
91:12: 272
99:6: 132
105:4′: 168
105 r.1: 162
172 r.32, 36e: 69
175 r.12: 211
176 r.9: 162
176 r.16: 133
178:12: 179
178 r.4: 162
179:7: 179
179:8–12: 165
179:12: 164, 165
183:18′: 132
190 r.6′: 103
193: r.6: 116
194:18e: 102
204 r.10: 93
204 r.11: 103
205:4–11: 265
205:10:
219:6, 10, 13, 16: 237
220:1–3: 50, 176
220:3: 50, 175, 177
234:12: 103
236 r.2: 168
244:16: 211
256:3′: 103
256:4′: 162
257:5: 237
261:4′: 103

SAA II
1:6′: 103
1 e.15′: 62
2 i 13′, 15′, 24′, r. iv 17, 29′, r. v 8, 14, 16, 24′: 62
2 iv 33′: 103
5 iv 9′: 93, 94
6:1, 10, 12, 41, 64, 96, 104, 132, 153, 175, 283, 289, 291, 351, 358, 382, 387, 390, 398, 400, 513, 526, 573, 616, 666: 62
6:60: 132, 174, 192
6:292: 63
6:311: 203
6:447: 76, 77
6:494, 507: 68
6:531, 548, 580, 623, 629, 638: 132
6:582: 132
6:582–584: 245, 246
6:588–590: 222
6:589: 222
6:601–602: 174
6:602: 174
6:603: 192
6:604: 132
6:636A–636C: 101
6:636c: 101
6:652–655: 293
6:653: 292
6:656–658: 190
6:658: 190
8:9: 62
9:15′, r.3′: 68
12:1: 62

SAA III
7:2–3: 86
7:3: 85
13 r.6–8: 123
13 r.8: 122, 124
13:10: 262
14:2: 69
14 r.9: 264, 265
16 r.3: 72
16 r.12: 288
16:22: 69
17:14: 203
20 r.1: 269
32 r.18: 286
34:23, 69: 203
34:33: 122, 123
35:25: 187
35:29, 41: 203
36 r.1: 221
36 r.2: 221
37:24′, 25′: 278
38:4: 175
39:32: 88, 89

SAA IV
58 r.8–11: 49
108:3: 49
144:9: 50
156:2: 49
162:7′: 49
290 r.6: 183, 184
305:9′: 183, 184
311 r.2: 183

SAA V
2:12: 69
3 r.4: 203
3 r.20: 147
15:12: 114, 115
17 r.1: 182
21:14: 69
25:10: 132
31 r.21: 290
46:12′–e.19′: 84
46:16′: 84
47:13: 211
53 r.7: 69, 215
53:15: 132
53:18: 212, 215
53:19: 211
54:4′: 103
64 r.4: 107, 108, 260
64 r.4–6: 108, 260
64 r.6: 259
95:13: 69
105 r.6: 205
105:12: 69
105:23: 103
108 r.28: 69
112 r.2: 103
121:8: 133
121 r.10: 132
121 r.19: 133
126 r.14: 239, 240
126 r.14–15: 240
139:6: 240
139:9: 162
149 r.11: 246, 247
149 r.11–14: 247
149 r.21: 69
154 r.6′: 132
156 r.1–7: 208
156 r.6: 207, 208
160:12′: 69
171:10: 243
182 r.5′: 69
199:13: 132
203 s.1: 102
204:10: 132
243 e.18–r.1: 240
243 e.20: 239, 240
249:5′: 150
256 r.5′: 162
272 r.2: 205
272 r.2–3: 205
272 r.3: 204
293:7: 65
295 e.26: 194

SAA VI
22:4, 5, 6, 7: 95
24:5: 249
27:10′, e.12′: 250
27 e.12′: 249
28:3–5: 253
28:4: 252, 253
31 r.3: 51, 154
31 e.27, 28: 249
33:1′: 95
95 r.5: 62
99:5′: 299
127 r.3′–4′: 39
133 e.10: 69
137:2–4: 159
137:4: 159, 160
154:6, 7, e.8: 95
173:4–7: 80
173:6: 80
200:5: 51, 153, 154
211:2′: 249
217:4–10: 218
217:10: 217
259 s.1: 300
271:3: 252, 253
271:3–5: 253
271:8: 249
284 e.16: 81

SAA VII
62 iv 2′: 113
63 i 1, 9: 113
64 i 1: 221
72 r.15′: 113
73: 92
73:3, 6, 11: 92
88 r.9: 284
88 r.15: 88, 89
93:1: 172
94:2: 116
94:4: 172
95:1, 2: 172
96:5′: 116
96:6′: 213
97 r.1, 3, 5: 172
97 r.8: 105
98:8′: 116

98:11′: 213
98:12′: 116
99:2: 172
103 r.2′: 172
104:1′: 172
104:6′: 105
105:2′: 116
105:3′: 213
107 r.8′: 116
108 r. ii′ 3′: 172
109 iii 2′, r. ii 2′: 172
111:1: 172
112:10′: 172
113:1: 116
113:4: 116
115: 74, 75, 105, 172, 232
115 ii 3: 239
115 ii 9: 172
115 ii 13–14: 238
115 ii 14: 237
115 r. i 5: 232, 233
115 r. i 5–6: 233
115 r. ii 17: 74, 75
115 r. ii 18: 105
117 r.4: 116
118 i 9, 12, 13, 16: 113
119 i 12′: 128
119 r. ii′ 4′: 172
125:3: 76
130:1: 195, 196
130:5–9: 147
130:9: 146
136 ii′ 3′: 202
159 i 7, 8, r. i 2′: 109
161 i 1, 12, ii 1, r. i 1, 11, r. ii 1, 10: 108
207 r.3′: 136
208 r.4′: 136
208 r.5′: 76, 77
209 r.3: 136
209 r.4: 76
210 r.6: 136
215 r.2: 136
215 r.4: 76
216 r.6: 136
216 r.7: 76
217 r.4: 136
217 r.5: 76
218 e.5′: 136, 137
218 e.5′–6′: 137
218 e.7′: 76

SAA VIII
3 r.4: 69
55 r.7: 132
60:4: 69
163:6: 68

SAA IX
1 i 7: 65, 66
1 i 7′: 65
1 iv 5–10: 130, 256
1 iv 7: 130, 131, 256, 257
2 i 8′: 69
2 i 10′–12′: 222
2 i 11′: 222
2 ii 6′: 65, 257
2 ii 11′–12′: 178
2 ii 12′: 177, 178, 185
2 ii 17′: 247, 248, 249
2 ii 17′–18′: 248
2 iii 21′: 236
2 iii 27′: 65
3 ii 13: 72, 73
3 ii 27, 36; iii 11, 14: 62
3 iii 32: 76
7:4: 126, 127
7 r.7–11: 123
7 r.9: 136
9:10–14: 226
9:13: 225, 226

SAA X
3:8: 68
5 r.1: 62
6:9, 19, r.10, 17: 62
7:13, r.3: 62
8:23, r.14: 133
8 r.14: 132, 133
45 r.9: 132
50 r.7: 69
51 r.15: 69
56:15: 132
70:9: 274
72 r.1: 67, 186, 187
72 r.15: 186, 187
95 r.15′: 186, 187
173:13: 272
185:13: 69
194 r.10′–11′: 197
194 r.11′: 197
199 r.19′: 62
202 r.10′: 132
214:9: 69
221 r.1: 132
221 r.4: 150, 151
221 r.8: 69
226 r.11: 69
227 r.10–13: 149
227 r.12: 149
227 r.12, 13: 149
227 r.13: 147
227 e.29, r.17: 132
228 r.2: 69
235 r.10–15: 90
235 r.15: 90
236:9: 69
239 r.7′: 150
239 r.8′–13′: 260
239 r.9′: 259
241:9: 68
241 r.12: 132
242 r.8: 150
259 r.8: 68
273:12: 62
273:13–15: 212
273:14: 211, 212
274:7–r.1: 234
274:9: 234
289:7–12: 275
289:9, 14: 68
289 r.9′: 68
289 r.13′: 69
289 r.14′: 68
290 s.1: 230
290:13e–s.3: 231
294:15: 51, 153, 154
294:26–30: 154
294:29: 145, 146, 148
294 r.17: 162
316:22, e.25: 62
319:10: 132
322:13: 67
334 r.9–12: 270
334 r.10: 270
353 r.5: 186, 187
354:21: 62
365:8′: 183
365:10′, 12′: 183
368:9: 69

SAA XI
21 r.7′: 93
24 r.5, 7, 9, 11e: 167
25:2′: 168
26 r.1–4: 82
26 r.2: 82
26:13′: 232, 233
26:13′–15′: 233
27:7: 221
28:11: 116
36 ii 13: 117

36 ii 19–21: 245, 246
36 ii 20: 244, 245
37:2: 202
77 r.1–2: 300
106:1–r.3: 142, 207, 219
106:9: 219, 220
106 r.1: 206
106 r.2: 141, 207
155 e.7: 151
172 r.2: 283
202 i 7′: 114
206 i 12′: 162
209 r. i 3′: 114
210 r. iv 7′: 114
219 r. iv 7: 95
227:2, 5: 162

SAA XII
3:4′, 5′: 114
50 r.33′: 162
68:36: 65
69 r.20: 99
83 r.9: 99
86 r.31: 99

SAA XIII
19 r.5: 67
25 r.16e: 246, 247
25 r.16e–17e: 247
28 r.3–5: 180
28 r.4: 180
29:4: 132
32:10: 62
44:9′–r.6: 289, 297
102 r.6: 93
127 r.17: 204, 205
135 r.7: 261
138 r.10: 132
146:10: 69
147 r.2–8: 161
147 r.6: 160, 161
155 r.2: 132
157:10′: 237
157 r.4: 202
172 r.8′: 69
179:6′: 298

SAA XIV
29 s.1: 40
32:5: 168
32 e.8: 168
35:8, 10, 11: 95
41:7, 8, 9, 11, r.1′, 3′, 4′, 6′, 7′: 95
42:4, 5, 6, 7, 8, 9, 10, 11, 12, 13, 14, 15, 16, 17, 18, 19, 20, 21, 22, 24, 25, 28, r.2, 3, 4, 5, 6, 7, 8, 9, 10, 11: 95
43:10: 95
44:4, 6: 211
44:5, 7, 8: 95
63:1′: 209
63:1′–11′: 209
75:3: 39
94 r.9–10: 40
96 r.2: 62
98:1–9: 42
98 r.1–7: 42
109:7, 8, 9: 95
111:10, e.11, 12: 95
117:6, 7, 8, 9: 95
131:6′: 95
168:9′: 95
205 r.13: 39
248:8: 95
257:5′, 7′: 95
276:6′: 249
392:5′: 95
398 s.2–3: 40, 41
459 r.4′: 62
468:5, 7, 8, 9, 12, 13, 14, 17, e.19, 20, 21, 22, r.1: 96, 96
477:1–6: 95
477:4: 125

SAA XV
3:6, 7: 69
30:13: 185
40 r.2′: 103
40 r.3′: 103
40 r.6′: 103
40 r.7′: 103
41:14′: 237
41:9′: 205
50:6′: 182, 183
50:6′–8′: 183
53 e.12: 162
55:10, 12: 102
69:14: 203
76 r.9: 68
78:3′: 69
90:8, r.19: 62
91 r.8: 69
92 r.3′: 68
98:6: 68
98 r.4′: 62
100:6: 68
101:13: 203
102 r.3: 237
104 r.12′: 69
106 r.3′: 102
113:18: 203
116 r.5′, 9′, 15′: 68
116 r.13′–15′: 241
116 r.14′: 241
122:4: 183
129 e.40: 132
130:14, 22: 203
130:20: 203
131:18: 68
136:12: 68
136:23: 273
136 e.27: 68
142:5′–r.2: 225
142 r.2: 224, 225
150 r.2: 69
156: 295
169:10: 102
196:4′: 62
199:3, r.5: 68
221:3′, r.8: 103
233:5′: 237
247:7′: 183
286:13′: 148
306:6′: 132
314 r.3′: 103

SAA XVI
4:3: 132
5: 188, 189, 224
5 r.4: 224
5 r.10–11: 189
5 r.11: 188, 189
5 e.26–r.4: 224
20:1–7: 153
20:5: 151, 152
21:9, r.5: 62
29:5: 273
32 r.7: 72
37 r.8′: 132
41 r.14: 76
42 r.7: 69
59 r.2′–5′: 228
59 r.3′: 227
59:4: 62
59:5: 63
59:8, 12: 72
60:5: 62, 63
60 r.18′: 72
61:5: 62
62 r.1′: 185, 186
62:4: 197, 198
62:4–5: 198
63:13–14: 46
63:21–23: 85
63:22: 85, 86
63 r.5: 68
63:13, 14: 183
65: 267

65: 267
65 s. 2: 267
70:5: 72
71 r.3: 62
77 r.5: 203
79:9: 69
92:8: 76
95 r.6′, 13′: 69
99:6′: 132
99:10′: 44
121 r.19e: 273, 274
121 r.19e–20e: 273
121:11–13: 191
121:12: 191, 192
126:13: 132
126:19, 25: 62
126 r.21′–24′: 78
126 r.22′: 78
140 r.5: 68
150:8′: 62
171:11′: 62
197:4′: 194
212 r.3: 76
243 r.2′: 203
243 r.5′: 69
243 r.6′: 62

SAA XVII
2: 45, 46, 66
2:15–22: 46
39:8: 187
140 r.7′: 161

SAA XVIII
102:9′: 187
121:4: 75
192 r.5′–8′: 1

SAA XIX
1:1–8: 153
1:3: 152
3:12: 162
3:15: 162
3 s.2: 102, 105
3 s.4: 272
9:8: 167, 168
10:11, r.3: 168
10 r.3–4: 168
12 r.8′: 162
12 r.9′: 179
13:1–7: 176
13:3, 5: 50, 175, 176
19:13: 162
19:6: 147
23: 44, 103
23:13: 103
25:4: 203
26:11′: 211
28:4: 62
33 r.15: 69
35:9: 132
37 r.13′: 162
48:15, 20: 179
53 r.5′–11′: 91
53 r.9′: 90, 91, 261
71 r.1: 203
87 e.12′: 103
87 r.9: 102
87:5′: 214
87:5′–6′: 214
88:4, 6: 92
90:5′: 69
91 r.2: 285
98:11, 22, r.5, 10, 17: 68
100 r.12′–13′: 165
100 r.13′: 164
109:7: 261
125:27′: 203
127 r.3′: 103
127 r.7′: 103
127 r.8′: 102, 104
127:11′: 103
130:12′: 161
154:1–r.3: 39
156:22: 132
164 r.11′: 148
196:2′: 164, 165
196:2′–4′: 165

SAA XX
15 ii 15′: 280
19 r. ii 21′: 92
30 r.13′–15: 112
30 r.15′: 112
33 ii 4–6: 120
33 ii 6–10: 119
33 ii 9: 118
33 r. i 29′–31: 142
33 r. i 30′: 141
33 r. i 37′–40′: 120
33 r. i 39′: 121
40 32′–36′: 139
42 r. iii 11′–13′: 139
42 r. iii 13′: 138, 139
40 r. iii 35′: 138
52 r. i 35′: 278
53 i 17′: 278

SAA XXI
50:4′: 105, 237
50:4′, r.4: 105
50 r.4: 103
63:4–5: 144
63:5: 143
65 r.20′: 288
104 r.3: 68
104 r.4: 69
117 r.3′: 68
121:5′, 10′, 11′: 289
155:10: 150

SAAB
1 2 ii 13′: 105
1 3 ii′ 14′: 221
17 8:2 172
2 7:10, 11: 96
2 9 r.5′: 62
3 66:6, 7: 96
5 9:2: 167
5 12: 199, 200
5 12:1–e.7: 199
5 12:4: 199, 200
5 33:8, 11: 96
5 59 r.10: 62
7 1:4, 5, 6, 8: 96
7 2:6, 7, 10, 11, 13: 96
7 3:6, 7, 8: 96
7 4:8, 10: 96
9 71 r.13: 62
9 73:2–8: 135
9 77:11: 76
9 82:2′: 76
9 94:4: 76

StAT 1
39:3: 105
39 r.10: 105
49:1: 168
53 e.7: 183

StAT 2
33 e.6′: 63
53:2–10: 242
53:4, 5: 242
81 r.8: 275, 276
141 r.13: 99
133 e.6: 168
145 r.10: 63
146:13: 63
163 r.10: 69
163 r.11: 148
164:12: 173, 174
164:9: 83
164 r.7, 13: 63
207:7, 8, 9, 10, 11: 96
242 r.4: 63
255:6′: 173
263:13, 14, 15, 16, 17: 96
266 r.3′: 63
272 r.2: 63
315 r.3: 133

StAT 3
1:14: 106
1 r.5: 195
2:15: 63
8:11: 278
38:1: 168
39:2: 168
59 r.7: 63

60 r.6: 63
76 r.5′: 63
88 r.12′: 63
103 r.3: 63

Streck Asb.
72 viii 102:

T i 1, 13, 19, 46′, v 7, 15, 22, 46, 53, 56, 62, 64, 69, viii 66: 63

TCAE
387f: 170
399ff: 168

TCL III 365: 89

TH
17 r.5: 216
48:10: 117, 118
52 r.5: 117
54 r.2: 117
57:6: 114, 115
63 e.7: 117
108:1′: 168

TIM 9 54 r.9: 264

TuL 75, 25: 92

VAT
10464: 280
14453: 199
8659:2: 173, 174
8667: 76
8882: 280
9770:4: 69
9777:11: 278
9849:15: 173
9874: 188

VIO 28: 284

VTE, p. 53:328: 285

ZA
73 13:8: 67
74 80 r.16: 168
74 80 e.18: 168

ZTT I 8:2: 173